R.C.M.P. SECURITY BULLETINS

THE EARLY YEARS, 1919-1929

Previous volumes in this series:

The Depression Years, Part I, 1933-1934. ISBN 0-9695835-1-6
The War Series, 1939-1941. ISBN 0-9692060-5-4
The War Series, Part II, 1942-1945. ISBN 0-9695835-0-8

Forthcoming:

The Depression Years, Part II, 1935.
The Depression Years, Part III, 1936.
The Depression Years, Part IV, 1937.
The Depression Years, Part V, 1938-1939.

R.C.M.P. SECURITY BULLETINS

THE EARLY YEARS, 1919-1929

Edited by Gregory S. Kealey and Reg Whitaker

St. John's: Canadian Committee on Labour History

Canadian Committee on Labour History
Department of History
Memorial University of Newfoundland
St. John's, Newfoundland
A1C 5S7

Typography by Canadian Committee on Labour History

Printed and Bound in Canada

Canadian Cataloguing in Publication Data
Main entry under title:
Royal Canadian Mounted Police security bulletins

Partial contents: The early years, 1919-1929.
ISBN 0-9692060-9-7

1. Subversive activities — Canada.
2. Communism — Canada. 3. World War, 1939-1945.
4. Internal security — Canada. 5. Royal Canadian Mounted Police. I. Kealey, Gregory S., 1948- II. Whitaker, Reginald, 1943- III. Committee on Canadian Labour History.

HV7641.A6 1989 322.4'2'0971 C88-090461-5

TABLE OF CONTENTS

ACKNOWLEDGEMENTS

As was the case with previous volumes in this series, we would like to extend our thanks to the Canadian Security and Intelligence Service (CSIS) for their permission to reprint these documents. In addition, we would like to acknowledge the legal work of William Kaplan of the University of Ottawa who has aided us immensely with both his legal and historical knowledge.

In addition, we owe a debt of gratitude to a number of archivists at the National Archives of Canada (NAC) who have provided expert advice over the years; our thanks to Danny Moore, Peter DeLottinville, Judith Roberts Moore, and Gerry O'Brien. Thanks also to Glenn Wright of the RCMP Historical Section for help with photographs.

On the production side we would like to thank Margaret Gulliver, Sheila Silver, and Joan Butler for their keyboarding talents and above all for their patience. Proofreaders and indexers have included Christina Burr, Michael Butt, Sean Cadigan, John Hample, Robert Hong, Mark Leier, Martin Lobigs, and Bonnie Morgan. As always Irene Whitfield has overseen the project with enthusiasm and diligence. Russell Hann also worked on this project in a production capacity for a number of years. Our thanks to all those who worked on this project.

For details on the nature of CSIS deletions and the editorial apparatus used to indicate them, please see the "Preface" to Kealey and Whitaker, *R.C.M.P. Security Bulletins: The War Series, 1939-1941* (St. John's, 1989), 7-8. Please keep in mind that the Bulletins are rendered here as we found them. Spelling and other errors are the responsibility of the RCMP.

Our apologies to patient readers who had a lengthy wait for this volume to appear. Various production problems delayed its printing. These delays unfortunately have also meant that much of the material which was held by the CSIS when this volume was compiled has now been passed on to the NAC where it now resides in RG146. Most of this material, however, has not been cleared through the Access to Information procedures and it awaits the requests of intrepid researchers to get it opened up to public scrutiny. Indeed, only a series of access requests by myself, Reg Whitaker, and Bill Kaplan have led to the partial divulgence of the Finding Aids for RG146.

G.S.K. and R.W.
St. John's, NF, 12/04/94

ONE BIG UNION No. 11526

DUPLICATE ~~REPLACING~~ FOLDER OF SAME NO.

Official Membership Folder

Name J.W. Esselwein

Address 1949 Montreal st

City Regina Sask.

Joined

To maintain good standing, members dues must be paid up to date.

ONE BIG UNION ORIGINAL

Official Membership Receipt August 31st 1921

RECEIVED from J.W. Esselwein

Address 1949 Montreal st. O.B.U. No. 11526

Occupation Ledger No.

the sum of $3.00 Dollars

For June July August

Regina J.W. Esselwein

Name of Local Unit Secretary

RCMP Undercover Agent Constable John Leopold's 1921 OBU Membership Card in the name of J.W. "Jack" Esselwein. (Courtesy of RCMP Photo Archives)

INTRODUCTION

This volume contains a series of documents intended to augment the few remaining Security Bulletins from the period 1919 to 1929. Thus, this volume, unlike its predecessors, contains additional archival material from the collections of the National Archives of Canada (NAC) and from the Canadian Security Intelligence Service (CSIS).[1] The material in the NAC has had an intriguing history while the material still held by CSIS has not been previously available to researchers. All this material has been acquired through Access to Information requests.

The bulk of the material from the NAC is contained in Record Group (RG) 18, the papers of the Royal Canadian Mounted Police. This material was originally deposited in the then Public Archives of Canada (PAC) in the early 1960s. Since then, it has had a most interesting history.[2] In 1971 the RCMP Security Service decided that a grave error had been made in the early 1960s and removed from the Archives a considerable amount of the material that had been there for almost a decade and in which numerous historians had conducted research. To their great discredit officials of the PAC not only allowed this seizure of material to occur but they did not even keep a record of what materials were withdrawn. In a series of interviews conducted in 1988 concerning this affair, we were told by Assistant National Archivist Michael Swift that this removal was unprecedented and we were assured that it could never happen again.[3]

In 1982 much, but not all, of the material was returned to the NAC. Precisely what was not returned remains unclear because of the carelessness of not listing what was originally withdrawn. The major RCMP and CSIS sensitivity appears to surround the identification of secret agents in the employ of the security service. According to CSIS, these informants, a combination of hired civilians and undercover Mounties, merit perpetual

1 Gregory S. Kealey and Reg Whitaker, eds., *R.C.M.P. Security Bulletins: The War Series, 1939-1941*, St. John's, 1989; *R.C.M.P. Security Bulletins: The War Series, Part II, 1942-1945*, St. John's, 1993; *R.C.M.P. Security Bulletins: The Depression Years, Part I, 1935*, St. John's, 1993.

2 For a discussion of this affair see Gregory S. Kealey, "The Royal Canadian Mounted Police, the Canadian Security Intelligence Service, the Public Archives of Canada, and Access to Information: A Curious Tale," *Labour/Le Travail*, 21 (1988),199-226.

3 For a lengthier discussion of the issues implicit in this history, see Gregory S. Kealey, "National Security vs. the Public's Right to Know," *CBC Ideas*, 18 February 1989.

protection from public scrutiny in order to protect them and their families and to insure the ongoing source programme of CSIS. In other words, if 1919 agents' identities were revealed, it might discourage contemporary informants. We shall not pursue the logic of this argument, the desirability of the recruitment of such sources, nor the necessity for historical and public scrutiny of security forces in a democratic society in these pages. It should be obvious from the revelations in the following pages that we feel that CSIS is wrong in its contentions.

A series of Access to Information requests and subsequent complaints to the Information Commissioner of Canada, which commenced in 1985 and are still ongoing, has failed to turn up Bulletins prior to 1934. The Bulletins from 1919-1920 and from 1926 that are presented here are drawn from the collections of the NAC. In effect, three politicians, who received these Bulletins as part of the RCMP's attempt to keep their political masters aware of their concerns about national security, failed to return them to the force as was requested. Thus, in the papers of Prime Minster Robert Borden, his Minister responsible for the RCMP, A.L. Sifton, and Prime Minister Arthur Meighen, there are three sets of extant Bulletins. While there is some small chance that the ongoing investigation by the Information Commissioner's office may discover additional materials, we are no longer optimistic. It is also possible that some additional Bulletins are lodged in other politicians' papers of this period. If any reader knows of such material, please contact us.

The Bulletins themselves constitute Part I of what follows. It is extremely unfortunate that the Security Service in either its RCMP or CSIS guise have lost or destroyed the rest of these documents. As the reader can see, we are fortunate to have these early examples from 1919 to 1920 because, in combination with the various registers that constitute the rest of this volume, they allow for a relatively complete reconstruction of the activities of the RCMP Security Service at its birth, or, perhaps more accurately at its conception, because the earliest of these documents predate the RCMP and were compiled by the Criminal Investigation Branch (CIB) of the Royal North-West Mounted Police in 1919 while it still shared the security and intelligence mandate with the Dominion Police. Indeed Part II is a 1919 "List of chief agitators in Canada" compiled by the Dominion Police during the short, four-month reign of C.H. Cahan as Director of the Public Safety Branch of the Department of Justice.[4]

The Bulletins, or "Notes of the Work of the C.I.B. Division" as they were then termed, provide a useful weekly summary of the extensive surveillance work of the new secret service in its formative stages. The

4 For the list see NAC, RG 13, Vol. 231, File 132/1919, Cahan to Doherty, 17/1/19. For a detailed study of this early history, see my "The Surveillance State: The Origins of Domestic Intelligence and Counter-Subversion in Canada, 1914-1920," *Intelligence and National Security*, 7, 3 (1992), 179-210.

renamed "Weekly Summary" from 1926 is unfortunately not the entire document from the CIB. Instead it consists of the general notes, the table of contents, and the general information. While the contents list is present for the District Reports, they unfortunately were apparently not kept by Prime Minister Meighen, whose papers provided this material.

It should be noted as well that these Bulletins have not been subjected to deletions by CSIS. The material already present in the NAC collections before the passage of the Access and Privacy legislation is generally treated as open and not subject to access restrictions. (There are exceptions, however, but this material fortunately was not treated as such.)

Part II is the "List of chief agitators" compiled by the Public Safety Branch of the Department of Justice. This list appears to be a hasty compilation of names generated from the Dominion Police investigation of the Industrial Workers of the World (IWW) in February 1918. This investigation was prompted by warnings to Newton Rowell from Senator, and soon to be Labour Minister, Gideon Robertson and to Prime Minister Robert Borden from Imperial Munitions Board Chief Sir Joseph Flavelle.[5] The investigation conducted by the Acting Chief Commissioner of the Dominion Police, Albert Cawdron, initially reported in March 1918 that "the sum total of the reports is that we have nothing to fear from them at the present time."[6]

Indeed, in June a final report was issued by Chief Commissioner Sherwood that again tried to alleviate fears of the IWW, of which "no trace can be found in this country ... after a thorough and exhaustive investigation."[7]

These reports, however, did nothing to quiet the growing fears of industrial sabotage, trade union militancy, and Bolshevik subversion. Thus, Borden commissioned C.H. Cahan, a Montreal lawyer with British Secret Service ties, to survey the state of national security with special emphasis on "propaganda" and with the possible intention of establishing "some effective organization to investigate the whole subject."[8] Cahan used this mandate to commence a Canadian version of the American "Red Scare," one result of which was the passage of repressive legislation that allowed the use of the War Measures Act to prosecute socialist and labour leaders. Those charged or successfully prosecuted under the WMA for political "crimes" constituted the second major element of Cahan's list of chief agitators contained in Part II.

5 NAC, Borden Papers, Vol. 104, File Oc519, Robertson to Rowell, *et al.*, 20/2/18, and Flavelle to Borden, 22/2/18. See Kealey, "Surveillance State," for more details.
6 *Ibid.*, Cawdron to Minister of Justice, 5/3/18.
7 *Ibid.*, Sherwood to Minister of Justice, 16/6/18.
8 *Ibid.*, Cahan to Borden, 11/5/18 and Borden to Cahan, 19/5/18.

The list allows a sketchy geographic analysis as well as some sense of how individuals merited inclusion. First, of the 337 individuals designated, 178 or 54.3 per cent had been charged under the WMA provisions. The second major grouping was the 138 (42.1 per cent) listed as members of the IWW. Twelve individuals or 3.7 per cent were included because of membership in the United Mine Workers of America or the Social Democratic Party.

Geographically, the list contained 156 (49.5 per cent) individuals from Ontario, 138 (43.8 per cent) British Columbia, 13 (4.1) Alberta, and four each from Saskatchewan and Manitoba. By city Vancouver led with 36, followed by Toronto with 30, Ford City 25, Timmins 16, Cobalt and London 12, Sault Ste Marie and Windsor 11, and Sudbury 10. These figures reflect the sources of their compilation. The BC individuals were almost all involved with the IWW and many of the names stemmed from lists compiled as early as 1912. The Ontario figures were prominent ethnic and socialist radicals active in various organizations banned in fall 1918.[9] The list also reflects the rather different repressive strategies followed by the Dominion Police, especially in Cahan's short period of influence, and those developed by the RNWMP and continued by the RCMP under Commissioner A.B. Perry.

Cahan, with the active support of various Ontario Police Chiefs, pursued an active strategy of prosecution in fall 1918 after the passage of the anti-socialist Orders in Council PC2381 and 2384.[10] Arguably his high profile legal assault on the left cost him his job because it put him in direct conflict with a number of the former Liberal members of the Union Government, especially Newton Rowell and Thomas Crerar. The RNWMP, perhaps learning some lessons from the Cahan's short-lived experience, pursued a different strategy. While Cahan sought to prosecute and convict, Perry played a more calculated waiting game. As RNWMP Comptroller McLean explained to Rowell, "The policy carried out by the Commissioner is not to prosecute isolated cases wherefrom little benefit is derived, but to gather all possible data which will prove of the utmost value in the event of a general outbreak in any particular district."[11] A few months later Perry himself explained his rationale at greater length: "No isolated prosecutions" "eliminated the danger of uncovering our agents ...

9 For details on the prosecutions see Kealey, "Surveillance State." On the IWW in BC, see Mark Leier, *Where the Fraser River Flows: The Industrial Workers of the World in British Columbia*, Vancouver, 1990. Numbers in the text reflect incomplete data in all categories. A detailed comparison with the distribution of prosecutions under the anti-socialist Orders-in-Council makes clear the overlapping lists. For the list of those prosecuted under the WMA, see RG 18, Vol. 2380, Routledge to OCs, CIB#104, 16/8/19.

10 A convenient location of the text of these Orders-in-Council is Frances Swyripa and John Thompson, eds., *Loyalties in Conflict: Ukrainians in Canada During the Great War*, Edmonton, 1983, 190-6.

11 NAC, RG 18, Vol. 847, Comptroller to Rowell, 25/2/19.

and our channels of information were kept open at a very critical time." Moreover, he argued, "The movement must be viewed from a national standpoint, and that when action is taken it should be carried out simultaneously throughout the country." !12

Part III contains the Personal Files Registers of the RCMP from their inception in winter 1919 until the end of 1929. The genesis of the files lies in the expanded mandate given to the RNWMP as of January 1919. Basically the country was split in two at the Lakehead and the RNWMP became the only federal police force with full responsibility for all federal law enforcement from the twin cities of Port Arthur and Fort William west. The Dominion Police maintained their mandate east of the imaginary line. To execute this mandate, the largest in the history of the RNWMP, the authorized size of the force was increased to 1200 (Perry had sought 2000) and a commitment was given to speed the return of former RNWMP officers and men who were overseas with the Canadian Expeditionary Force.

Included in the RNWMP mandate was enforcement of the Orders-in-Council under the WMA and, more ominously, aiding and assisting the civil powers to preserve law and order. Thus, the question of the secret service dimensions of the task rose immediately. The first action taken was the incorporation of the Dominion Police apparatus into the RNWMP, although this gained the Force few secret agents. Therefore serious recruitment of agents began in January 1919.

Perry circularized all his Officers Commanding with two key memos. The first discussed the Bolshevik threat in general and the second issued more specific guidelines to detectives and secret agents. Proceeding from the premise that "the pernicious doctrines of Bolshevism" were spreading rapidly throughout the world and in Canada, he drew his officers attention particularly to Winnipeg, Edmonton, and Vancouver, and to the foreign settlements scattered through the Prairies, which he noted were especially "susceptible to Bolshevik teaching and propaganda." Officers Commanding were "to take steps to see that careful and constant supervision is maintained over these foreign settlements with a view to detecting the least indication of Bolshevik tendencies and doctrines." Socialists all over the west, he continued, regarded the Bolsheviks "as champions of workers everywhere" and that "serious unrest" was an obvious possibility. Therefore, "our duty is to prevent the efforts of misguided persons to subvert and undermine the settled Government of Canada." OCs were to keep informed and "energetically deal with all unlawful and pernicious propaganda." To do so they should "take steps to select some good, trustworthy men ... as secret agents and submit their names, records, and qualifications for my approval." He also urged them to survey all radical pamphlets and publications and, if appropriate, to

12 Borden Papers, Vol. 96, Pt. 1, File Oc485, Perry to McLean, 30/6/19.

prosecute under Section 174 of the Criminal Code. Similarly, they were to record all questionable public speeches if they expected any seditious or treasonable content and particularly to watch street meetings. All this, of course, was to be done in such a way as "not to arouse suspicion or cause antagonism." In conclusion, he reiterated, "The Government relies upon the RNWMP to keep it early advised of any development toward social unrest. It is extremely important that such unrest should not be permitted to develop into a menace to good order and public safety." !13

A second memo of the same date outlines the job expected of the undercover detectives and secret agents. They were to become "fully acquainted with all labour and other organizations in their respective districts." Each organization "should be carefully investigated with a view to determining" its purpose and object, its proclivity to Bolshevik influence, any current Bolshevik tendencies, or its Bolshevik nature. Not surprisingly, organizations in the last three categories "must receive careful and constant attention." Particular attention was to be addressed to "the officials and leaders of these organizations" who "must be carefully investigated and studied regarding their ways, habits, and antecedents." All such information was to be scrupulously recorded and the subsequent files would provide "a complete history of these men and their doings to date." Lest anyone had missed his point, Perry reiterated that "particular attention must be paid to the different labour unions in their district" because "this class of organization is particularly susceptible to Bolshevik teaching." He concluded by cautioning that great care needed to be taken to insure the reliability of such sources. !14

Thus from its origins the RNWMP targeted labour as its primary focus. As the Perry memo cited above suggests, the Commissioner attached considerable importance to the development of Personal History Files (PHF). Part III contains the register of these files which consists of a file number, an individual's name, place of residence, and an occasional additional comment. The files themselves are filled with all information gathered by the Force by any means concerning the individual. Many of these files recently have been transferred to the NAC by CSIS and are present in RG 146. The first Register, covering the years 1919-1924, can be found in the Archives and subsequent partial lists have been acquired by Access requests to CSIS.

Assistant Commissioner W.H. Routledge, the first head of the new

13 RG 18, Vol. 599, file 1328, Perry to OCs, 6/1/19, Circular Memo. #807. See also RG 13, Vol. 231, file 113/1919, Perry to DMJ, 14/1/19, with the enclosure of Memos 807 and 807A. Given the general lack of co-ordination of security matters and the fact that the RNWMP reported to Rowell not Doherty, the forwarding of these memos is of some interest, especially because it only went to Rowell at the same time. For evidence of this see RG 18, Vol. 2441, Register Entry 58/1919, date 14/1/19.

14 *Ibid.*, Perry to OCs, 6/1/19, Circular Memo. #807A.

Criminal Investigation Branch, followed up on Perry's initial memo to set up the PHF system in late February 1919. Routledge wrote the Officers Commanding instructing them personally to supervise the preparation of these files. Such files were to include the following information: "Names and usual descriptive particulars. A photograph if it is at all possible to obtain one without arousing suspicion. Date of arrival in Canada; if naturalized or not; married or single; family; home address; present occupation; particular associations affiliated with and standing in same; present locality of activities; points where he is known to have been in any way active; details of any police records which he may have had; degree of intelligence and education and all other possible information which would assist in compiling a complete record of the man."[15] Initially, these files were to be commenced only upon request of the CIB office, but two weeks later the instructions were modified to demand that the local OC should compile a PHF on "any prominent agitator coming under your notice ... but great care must be taken not to arouse the suspicions of the party being thus reported on."[16]

The Register available in the Archives covers the period from its conception in 1919 to the end of 1924. In those six years 2590 files were opened. These files concerned 2525 individuals once duplicates were removed. A subsequent access request to CSIS for the later registers to the end of 1929 succeeded in gaining a massively exempted list which indicated that in the following five years another 2216 individual files were opened. In other words, on average 437 Canadians had files opened on them annually from 1919 to 1929.[17]

The lists lend themselves to relatively limited analysis, but Table 1 shows the geographic breakdown for the first 2590 files. (The CSIS list had no geographical information for the 54 individuals whose names had not been deleted or could be identified by cross-referencing with subject files.) As can be seen, British Columbia and Alberta are significantly over-represented, Saskatchewan and Manitoba somewhat, and the rest of the country is badly under-represented. To some degree at least, this is partially a statistical artifact of the initial western-only jurisdiction of the RNWMP. For example, the first Toronto file is 1225 and the first Montreal file is 1254, which suggests that almost half of the total files were generated before 1 February 1920 when the new RCMP took over national jurisdiction. Other scattered information which can be gleaned from the list is the presence of 68

15 *Ibid.*, Vol. 2380, Memorandum CIB #10, Routledge to Officers Commanding, 28/2/19.

16 *Ibid.*, Circular Memorandum CIB #10A, Routledge to OCs, 14/3/19.

17 RG 18, Vol. 2448, Register of Bolsheviks, 1919-1924. My access request to CSIS was 87-A-41. The rate in the two periods was almost identical 432 versus 443, although given that the opening of files should be heavier initially this suggests some intensification over the period.

women, one of whom, Alli Koivisto is quaintly described as "an agitatress." In addition, the list includes 23 clergy (Ivens, Irvine, Smith, Woodsworth, and Bland are the most prominent), 14 doctors, six military, and five elected officials (John Queen of Winnipeg and Mayor Joseph Clarke of Edmonton, for example). The unfortunately rather random marginalia also identifies nine IWW and six OBU members, as well as an array of less predictable entries such as English harvester, Jewish lecturer, Esperanto teacher, Hindu wrestler, and perhaps most intriguing, "ex-RCMP."

TABLE 1

"Agitators" by Location, 1919-1924

Number on List	2590
Number Names (after adjustments)	2525
Number Places Listed	2287

A. Geographic Breakdown of Provinces

	# agitators	% agitators	% Canadian Population 1921
British Columbia	775	33.9	6.0
Alberta	477	20.9	6.7
Saskatchewan	286	12.5	8.6
Ontario	276	12.1	33.4
Manitoba	253	11.1	6.9
Quebec	158	6.9	26.9
Nova Scotia	15	1.0	6.0
Prince Edward Island	1	---	1.0
Yukon	1	___	
New Brunswick	0		4.4
USA	24	1.0	
Other Foreign	5	.2	
Unknown	16	.7	
	2287	100.3	

B. Geographic Breakdown by City 50+ Agitators

	# agitators	% agitators
Vancouver	427	34.4
Winnipeg	194	15.7
Montreal	156	12.6
Edmonton	118	10.0
Toronto	80	6.5
Calgary	74	6.0
Regina	73	5.9
Ft. William	65	5.2
Saskatoon	53	4.3
	1240	100.6

Source: RG 18, vol. 2448, Register of Bolsheviks.

Part IV are the registers of a second data series compiled by the new security section of the Force, namely subject files on radicalism. The register of these files was obtained from CSIS by means of three access requests.[18] The rate at which these files were compiled seems quite uneven. As Table 2 illustrates the Force opened the first 3459 subject files in 1919 or slightly over half of the total for the 11-year period. In the first four years fully 80 per cent of the total for the entire period were opened. This is primarily dictated simply by the cumulative nature of the development of a filing system, although it may also indicate a slowing of radical activities late in the decade and a consequent decline in RCMP activity. A comprehensive analysis of this data and a careful cross-tabulation of the data in each set is yet to be completed. Nevertheless, it should be readily apparent that the surveillance entered into by the RNWMP commencing in January 1919 was of a different order than what had gone before.

18 CSIS, 86-A-10 (1920); 87-A-125 (1921-1929); 88-A-91 (1919).

TABLE 2

Number Subject Files Opened by Year, 1919-1929	Number	% of Total
1919	3429	51.1
1920	299	4.4
1921	689	10.2
1922	789	11.7
1923	435	6.4
1924	344	5.1
1925	268	4.0
1926	178	2.6
1927	89	1.3
1928	126	1.9
1929	81	1.2
TOTAL	6767	99.9

Source: CSIS, Register of Bolsheviks Subject Files, Access Request.

Part V contains yet another set of Registers which contain files opened by the Force on "Prohibited or Objectionable Literature." This list also originated in 1919 when press censorship was still in force under the WMA but the list continued throughout the decade. The list for the first three years was obtained from the holdings of the NAC and thus is not exempted but the subsequent list for the rest of the decade was obtained from CSIS and has been subjected to many exemptions under the Access legislation. Table 3 shows the annual rate of file opening which suggests a slowing in the mid and late 1920s with a significant increase in activity in 1929.

An analysis of the first three years of activity, where the data remains unexempted, shows that of the 281 files opened 46.3 per cent concerned individuals in possession of such literature or geographic locations where such literature had been discovered. The next largest category of files was the 31 per cent concerning individual newspapers or magazines. Another 14.2 per cent concerned individual pamphlets or books and 2.1 per cent related to bookshops, publishers, or libraries. A surprising 8.2 per cent of the files covered the publications and activities of the International Bible Students Association, an early version of the Jehovah's Witnesses.[19]

The final section of this volume, Part VI, is another RCMP register from 1919-20. In this register a more detailed account of various incidents such as speeches and meetings were tracked. The precise relationship of

19 For the subsequent story, see William Kaplan, *State and Salvation: The Jehovah's Witnesses and Their Fight for Civil Rights*, Toronto, 1989.

this volume to the other registers is not known, but it was felt that it conveyed in slightly more detail the actions and attitudes of the secret service.

TABLE 3

RCMP Prohibited/Objectionable Literature Files, 1919-1929

Year	Number of Files	File Numbers	Per Cent of Total
1919-20	194	1-194	31.8
1921	87	194-281	14.3
1922	56	282-337	9.2
1923	31	338-368	5.1
1924	33	369-401	5.4
1925	35	402-436	5.7
1926	48	437-484	7.9
1927	25	485-509	4.1
1928	35	510-544	5.7
1929	66	545-610	10.9
Total	610		100.1

Source: NAC, RG18, vol. 2433 and CSIS, Access Request.

The materials contained in this volume provide our best and most detailed look at the early operations of the RCMP secret service. While they cover only the first decade of the Force's operations in this realm, the work we have done on subsequent periods makes clear that these initial years were the crucial ones in shaping the ideology and operations of the secret service. While technological innovation might change certain surveillance techniques, the targets of RCMP attention which were first identified in 1919 were to remain the same for the next seventy years.

A.B. Perry, Commissioner of the RNWMP and RCMP, 1900-22. (Courtesy of RCMP Photo Archives)

PART 1:

INTELLIGENCE BULLETINS

Cortlandt Starnes, Commissioner of the RCMP, 1923-31. (Courtesy of RCMP Photo Archives)

SECRET No. 5

NOTES ON THE WORK OF THE C.I.B. DIVISION FOR THE TWO WEEKS ENDING 31st DECEMBER, 1919.

N.B. - Owing to the interruptions of the holiday season, no Summary was issued for the week ending 26th December.

1. FEATURES OF THE PERIOD.

The features of the period have been the conviction of R. B. Russell at Winnipeg, and his sentence to two years' imprisonment; and the continued growth of the O.B.U. in the coal miners of Alberta.

Russell's appeal has not yet been heard.

The effect of the conviction will be most salutary. The important thing probably is the bare fact of conviction, apart from the nature of the sentence. One most useful circumstance is the conviction on the court of being a common nuisance; this is a verdict that a general strike by inflicting loss, etc., upon the general public comes under this category of the Criminal Code.

2. THE O. B. U.

Information concerning this body continues to be contradictory. Its fortunes vary widely in different localities. In Winnipeg up to the end of the trial it had been gaining strength and probably half the workmen of the city sympathized with it. In Southern Saskatchewan it is at a low ebb and the Winnipeg verdict may stun it; in Northern Saskatchewan the attempt to capture the loggers near Prince Albert for the L.W.I.A. is meeting with indifferent success. In the coal mining regions of Alberta, on the other hand it has made rapid strides, and a general coal strike seems quite possible. In Southern British Columbia the L.W.I.U. is gaining in the logging camps and the [2] O.B.U. seems to be making headway in the metalliferous mining districts. Northern British Columbia seems quiet. There have been no special developments in Vancouver. In Victoria the troublesome feature is the widespread unemployment.

At a meeting in Calgary on 5th December, P.F. Lawson asserted that V.R. Midgley had told him that at that that 36000 persons were carrying O.B.U. cards, "and thousands of orders in for more".

At this meeting Lawson said that within three days the miners could tie up all production; he advised workers to get in their supply of coal.

The finances of the Transport Workers' Unit of the O.B.U., Vancouver are at a low ebb.

There have been several short strikes in the Crow's Nest Pass. One at

Blairmore ended on 31st December.

At Taber, in the Crow's Nest Pass, the miners have returned their charter to the U.M.W.A. and have joined the O.B.U. At the Canada West Mine 240 out of 255 employes belong to the latter body.

3. THE TRIALS AT WINNIPEG.

Up to 7th December $7000 had been raised in British Columbia for the trial at Winnipeg. The quota assigned to the province is $20,000.

Great excitement has been occasioned among the revolutionaries in Calgary by the uncovering at Winnipeg of Corporal Zaneth, who as "Harry Black" was deep in their secrets. The Searchlight, the new paper just established by P. F. Lawson, tries to hide its consternation (he collected subscriptions for it) by declaring that the revolutionists were aware that he was a "stool-pigeon", but its assertions are incorrect. The incident should increase their mutual distrust.[3]

4. AGITATION IN VANCOUVER.

The Federated Labour Party has come to the front again in Vancouver and Victoria as a steady means of propaganda. Meetings are held constantly, usually moderately attended.

5. CLERICAL AGITATORS.

One of the features of the situation is the presence in the West of a number of ministers who preach revolutionary doctrine. Rev. Mr. Ivens, Rev. Mr. Woodsworth, Rev. A. E. Smith, are examples. The following are recent reports:-

The Revd. Wm. Irvine of Calgary, who is mentioned as likely to be appointed editor of the Farmers' Sun, on 7th December delivered a revolutionary speech at Calgary.

The Revd. George L. Ritchie of Edmonton on 14th December at the "Labour Church" there advocated revolution. His speech included an attack on the Board of Commerce, accusing it of investigating the small concerns and leaving the big profiteers alone. He also complained of the export of foodstuffs to Europe.

6. MISCELLANEOUS

During the past two weeks notice has been received of the prosecution of 76 aliens for breaches of the regulations. 160 applications for naturalization have been forwarded to Regina, and 290 investigations have been returned to the Secretary of State.

....

OTTAWA, 2nd January, 1920.

SECRET

No. 9

Notes on the work of the C.I.B. for the week ending 29th January.

N. B. These notes unless otherwise stated, are founded upon reports received by mail. The dates of incidents and reports consequently are stated.

1. Special Features of the Week.

During the week word has come of the possibility of a strike of longshoremen in Vancouver; so far particulars are meager. The dispute which may cause it has occurred in Seattle and the strike if it occurs will be a sympathetic one; it is remarked that it would be intended in part as a protest against the Winnipeg trials. There is much unemployment on the Pacific Coast, which in Victoria is beginning to be acute.

An O.B.U. convention for the whole of Western Canada was summoned at Winnipeg for 26th January. No word has been received about it as yet.

The L.W.I.U. (loggers' union) has unexpectedly appeared in a role of comparative moderation. The convention at Vancouver issued in Winch maintaining and strengthening his position; his conflict with the I.W.W. element which attempted to oust him has caused him to appear conservative in comparison. Word also comes from Southern British Columbia that the union is adopting a less extreme attitude.

The situation in the Alberta coal mines has improved, an arrangement having been reached between the coal operators and the U.M.W. of A.

2. Possible Strike of Longshoremen in British Columbia.[2]

On 12th January an American official wrote to the O.C. Vancouver that a strike of the longshoremen of the Pacific Coast was imminent, beginning with Seattle, and extending to Vancouver. Negotiations were on foot in December between the Northwest Waterfront Employers' Union in Seattle and the Pacific Coast District T.L.A.; early in January these broke down. Our own information confirmed this. The Seattle men are likely to strike, and have asked the Vancouver men to strike in sympathy. The Vancouver men at that date were regarded as likely to comply, partly out of sympathy with Seattle, partly in protest against the Winnipeg Trials.

The 15th and 21st January were mentioned as dates.

3. Convention of The Loggers' Union.

The Convention of the L. W. I. U. took place at Vancouver on 8th and 9th January. Winch was re-elected Secretary, defeating the extremist wing. The I.W.W. element were outnumbered and defeated; they hope that when the general convention is called the eastern delegates (i.e. from Northern Ontario) will be so strongly I.W.W. as to enable them to take charge. It was remarked that while outnumbered the I.W.W. men were "the smarter talkers".

One move made by Winch was to cut the number of delegates sent by the unit to the O.B.U. convention to three; the effect was to leave Allman and Hatherley, the principal I.W.W.'s. out of the delegation. Another extremist who has been ousted is McKenzie, until the Convention the Secretary-Treasurer of the Kamloops Branch. Pritchard and Johns will be delegates to the Winnipeg Convention.

The demands which the L.W.I.U. convention decided to make are:-

(1) A minimum wage of $6.00 a day for loggers and $5.00 a day for mill-men.

(2) Double time for overtime, Sundays and legal holidays.

(3) An 8 hour day, "Camp to camp".

(4) Certain improvements in living conditions.[3]

The convention was disposed to be cautious in calling strikes but favoured slowing down of production.

Extensive organization work throughout the east is planned.

The name of the organization may be changed to "The Lumber and Camp Workers' Union".

At the Convention a quarrel took place owing to Hatherley being attacked on the charge of enlisting men in the I.W.W. while an officer of the O.B.U.. Winch expressed regret at an effort being made to cause a split between the I.W.W. and the L.W.I.U..

4. The Loggers' Union in Southern British Columbia.

A report on the lumber camps in the Cranbrook district (East Kootenay) dated 10th January states that the L.W.I.U. in that district now number over 2000. The organization as a whole has over 12,000 members and a monthly income of more than $12,000. No other organization is in the field, and the L.W.I.U. is getting a strong position. This report says that this union has caused improvement in camp conditions, and that it is less radical than other portions of the O.B.U.. A bad feature in its circulation of radical reading matter. I.W.W.'s, coming in join this organization but so far have kept quiet. General conditions are described as good, labour plentiful, business prospects good, and no indications of strikes.

An investigation of certain logging camps near Prince Albert shows that the O.B.U. has made little headway in them.

5. Developments in Winnipeg.

On Sunday 18th January a meeting was held in the Strand Theatre, Winnipeg, to consider the legal effect of the Russell verdict. Admission was confined to delegates of the Central Labour Party, the Dominion Labour Party, Socialist Party of Canada, Ex-Soldiers' and [4] Sailors' Labour Party, the Labour Church, the Womens' Labour Church and the Trades and Labour Council. The attendance is variously estimated at 500 and 1000. Mr. W. H. Trueman of the legal firm of Bonnar, Trueman,

Hollands and Robinson attended and delivered an address in which he stated: (1) that general and sympathetic strikes are legal, despite the inconvenience to the public, provided they are not started with the intention of causing disorders, etc. (2) that Judge Metcalfe had misdirected the jury. (3) that they should appeal to the Privy Council and petition for Judge Metcalfe's impeachment. (4) that Mr. Andrews' connection with the Citizens' Committee unfitted him for the post of Crown prosecutor.

There was much talk, some of the accused men showing a desire to stir up demonstrations. A resolution pledging support of the accused was passed. There was wrangling between the O.B.U. and other elements.

The Defence have printed as a pamphlet what purports to be the official report of Judge Metcalfe's charge (it is badly reported and printed) and Judge Cave's charge in the case of Rex vs Burns in 1885. The point of the contrast is that in Burn's case the Crown apparently abstained from charging intent to create a disturbance, and argued that the accused must be deemed responsible for the consequences which followed the reckless and violent language they used; whereas in Winnipeg the charge was one of conspiracy, i.e. of intention and agreement. Justice Cave was rather favourable to the defence on the question whether subsequent violence should be regarded as proving seditious intent on the part of the accused. Judge Metcalfe dealt at length with the question of conspiracy.

Labour Church Services were held in Winnipeg on 18th January as follows:-

Park Theatre, Port Rouge A. Henry.
G.W.V.A. Hall, St. James Rev. Wm. Ivens "The World's Unrest".
Columbia Theatre, Winnipeg F.G. Tipping.
Centennial School, West - Rev. J.S. Woodsworth -
Kildenan. "Freedom".
S.O.E. Hall, Weston R.H. Gray "The Right of Self-Determination".[5]

Among the interesting observations made were:-

A. Henry:- "What the world wants today is autocracy, meaning independent power. Let every man have the same amount of power and make his own laws. Government of today was unreasonable, and only carried out their powers for democratic purposes, and the labouring class was never thought of".

Rev. W. Ivens:- "He knew that the road from the Law courts to the jail was greased, and that he would be serving two years, but they were going to try to tip the slide".

Rev. J. S. Woodsworth:- "They would never be free, as long as they had to go across the water for all their orders. There was a likelihood of their trials being taken across the water to the Privy Council, was that freedom?"

The regular weekly Socialist gathering was held at the Labour Temple, Winnipeg, on 11th January. Armstrong, one of the accused now under trial, made a violent speech, in which he attacked Judge Metcalfe, personally and by name.

We have additional report from Winnipeg to the effect that the O.B.U. is gaining at the expense of the International. This report puts the proportion of the labour unions who are O.B.U. at three fourths.

At Regina the O.B.U. recently asserted they had a membership of 40000.

6. The Alberta Coal Fields.

On 26th January the coal operators and the U.M.W. of A. concluded an agreement to the effect that the 14 p.c. advance is to be paid to all employes until the mines are organized by the U.M.W. of A.; when that condition is realized the increase will be restricted to members of this union, i.e. the "closed shop" will be instituted. The [6] Drumheller operators, who have formed an association of their own, have agreed to conform to this arrangement.

Information dated 26th January is that in the Drumheller area the U.M.W. of A. is in a satisfactory condition, 17 out of 20 mines being fully organized, and the organization of the rest being expected soon.

The O.C. Calgary under date of 19th January writes that Mr. Whiteside, President of the Western Coal Operators' Association seems most determined to oppose compliance by the operators with the Closed Shop order; and that he is supported by Mr. W.F. McNeil the secretary. The O.C.'s. inferences are:-

(1). That the operators are as hostile to the U.M.W. of A. as to the O.B.U..

(2). That they wish to discredit the local officials of the Labour Department, and the Minister of Labour.

On 7th January a strike took place at the Rosedeer Mine, Wayne (near Drumheller), the immediate cause being the action of the management in dismissing a check-weighman who had deserted the U.M.W. of A. and seceded to the O.B.U. About 80 men went out. It is a fight between the two unions, with the management availing itself of a falling off in orders to reduce operations and get rid of the turbulent element.

At Michell on 7th January the miners decided to accept the 14 p.c. increase, but to object to the "check-off" to the U.M.W. of A.

Mr. H. Ostlund, a barrister of Lethbridge, who for years has been the legal adviser of individual miners and the U.M.W. of A. now appears to be acting for the O.B.U..

7. The O.B.U. in Alberta.

At a meeting of the Miscellaneous Section, O.B.U., in Calgary on 15th January a man named Hoey of the Central Labour Council, O.B.U. reported that it had been proposed to divide the O.B.U. into five sections, each of which would finance itself, and the five to cover every industry in the country:-

1. Miners' Unit.[7]
2. Transportation Unit.
3. Industrial Unit. (Manufactures).
4. Agricultural Unit (including loggers and bushmen).
5. Educational and Hospital Section (Doctors, teachers, etc.)

Ill-temper was shown in the discussion, and there is a prospect of dissension.

The O.B.U. in Calgary have rented the Nolan Hall, 127a 8th Avenue West, for the purpose of holding their meetings. They also have rented offices in the same building. The hall is one used by various local labour unions.

8. The O.B.U. in British Columbia.

The amalgamation of the weaker O.B.U. units in Vancouver was advanced a step on 9th January. The units concerned were:-

1. Transport Workers; $30 in debt.
2. Construction Workers; a membership of over 300; over due debts of $280.
3. General Workers; no debts.
4. Engineers; a surplus of $100.

At a meeting of the General Workers' Unit of the O.B.U. in Vancouver on 12th January the President (James O. Smith) expressed a hope that the efforts of the employers in the United States to oust the Internationals and establish "open shop" conditions would succeed, and would reach Canada soon. Under open shop rules the O.B.U. could get into the shops, and once in would grow.

At a meeting in Vancouver on 9th January, V. R. Midgley stated that the O.B.U. started with $500 and at the first of the year had spent $17000; he added that the financial statement for the end of the year would show the organization in pretty good standing. He hoped that after the loggers' convention they would pay per capita on the full membership; this would give the O.B.U. another $1000 per month.

Midgley's explanation of the omission of the L.W.I.U. to pay per capita dues on its full membership was (1) that to do so would give the unit too many delegates; (2) Winch desired to keep certain men out of places of influence. The amount had been made up, he said, by the [8] Loggers defraying organization expenses which the O.B.U. would have had to meet.

9. Individual Agitators.

On 11th January, at a meeting of the Socialist Party, Vancouver, Charles Lester gave another of his violent speeches. One utterance was that when the working class came into its own and the capitalist class was overthrown there ought to be judges, and he hoped to be one. Should that happen, he would not be like the judge in Winnipeg and give a sentence of two years. If a capitalistic lawyer came before him he would give him twenty years.

Asked by a member of the audience what he worked at, Lester accused the questioner of being a stool-pigeon, and evaded answering.

Jack Kavanagh spoke at Merritt, B.C., on 11th January, in advocacy of the O.B.U.. He used some violent language.

10. Conditions in Victoria.

Under date of 14th January, the N.C.O. in charge, Victoria, reports the unemployment situation as showing no improvement. "The patience of the unemployed seems to be wearing out, and the idea of out-of-work parades in gaining in favour".

The only hope of early employment is the Cholberg Shipbuilding Company; it is not certain when it will begin operations. This company has a co-operative plan which involved deducting from 10 p.c. to 20 p.c. of the men's wages to pay for stock; this is much disliked as a device to reduce wages.

11. The Radical Press.

Addressing the new General Workers' Unit of the O.B.U. in Vancouver on 12th January, A. S. Wells, the editor of the "B.C. Federationist" stated that the paper had suffered much from the strike of last summer, its advertising having fallen off, partly through the [9] diminished purchasing power of its readers being known to merchants, partly because of the antagonism of the International unions, which it had opposed.

The "Worker", the very radical organ of the L.W.I.U. has ceased publication.

The "B.C. Federationist" will devote a certain amount of space in each issue to this union.

12. Ukrainian Propaganda.

On 10th January in the Greek Catholic Home, Edmonton, the "Samo-Obrazowania Society", formerly the Ukrainian Socialist Party, performed a play, "The Thorny Wreath" (? The Crown of Thorns) of a revolutionary tendency. This is the fourth drama of this sort performed since November. Our informant (who is of Central European Nationality) described it as effective propaganda against religion and government.

At a meeting of the "Shewchenko" meetings of the Ukrainian Greek Catholic Association at Edmonton 11th January a resolution was passed protesting against the assignment of Galicia to Poland. One speaker advocated raising troops in Canada to send to the Ukraine to fight Poland. The general trend of the meeting was described as adverse to the Canadianization of Ukrainian immigrants.

A secret society has been formed in Saskatoon in association with an institution styled "The Ukrainian National Home". The new body has a revolutionary tinge, but may be principally a benefit society.

13. Finnish Propaganda.

The Finnish Colony in Manyberries (southern Alberta) has an organization of a socialistic nature which has had three names within the last year or two:-

1. Finnish Social Democratic Organization.
2. Finnish Organization in Canada.
3. Finnish Socialist Organization of Canada.[10] Sanna Kannasto, a Finnish woman who has a reputation as an organizer is planning to visit this community, which as a whole has been quiet, though it has a small knot of agitators.

14. The International Bible Students.

The International Bible Students, whose meetings and reading matter were prohibited until the end of 1919, held a public meeting in Edmonton on 11th January. A man named Williams, who seems to be a travelling missionary of the body, delivered an address in which, in addition to attacking the various churches, attacked the present system of personal ownership of property. Our informant, who was present at the meeting, regarded the address as having a revolutionary tendency.

15. Miscellaneous.

Twenty-three applications of aliens for naturalization were sent to Regina. One hundred and thirty-two reports on aliens so applying were sent to the Under-Secretary of State for Canada.

....

OTTAWA, 30th January, 1920.

ROYAL CANADIAN MOUNTED POLICE HEADQUARTERS

Ottawa, 12th August, 1920.

SECRET

NO. 36

NOTES OF THE WORK OF THE C. I. B. DIVISION FOR THE WEEK ENDING 12TH AUGUST

N.B. In most cases these notes are founded upon reports received by mail. The dates of incidents and reports consequently are stated when this is necessary.

1. General Characteristics of the Period

Confidential reports of the convention of the loggers' union held in Vancouver in the middle of July exhibit this unit of the O.B.U. as expanding in a way which is beginning to be inconvenient to the general body of the O. B. U. An attempt is being made to take in agricultural workers, and there are symptoms of an alliance between this unit and the Alberta coalminers, the other large mass of labour which favours the O. B. U. principles. Midgley, who manages the head office of the O. B. U. manifested vexation over this tendency. An interesting feature was the strength and effectiveness of Carl Berg; in low water in Edmonton, he exercises much influence in Vancouver and is said to have been the principal agent in defeating the attack made on Winch by the I.W.W. element.

The financial statements showed that missionary effort in the East so far has had discouraging results. Ten organizers in three months spent $8,000, and brought only $1,100 in dues into the treasury. There is no further word, it may be added, of the rumoured deposition of J. R. Knight. Several of these organizers have been dropped because of the discrepancy between their expense account and their achievements, and one of them is a man named McKnight, who spent $1,300 and brought in $3; Joe Knight perhaps was confused with him. Graft charges may be [2] brought against W. Cowan, lately organizer in Sudbury.

Some interesting utterances have come from Winnipeg. On Friday 6th August a public debate took place there on the subject of the O. B. U. versus the International principle, Joe Knight and John Houston (editor of the O. B. U. Bulletin) taking the one side and W. H. Hoop (of the Western Labour News) and R. J. McCutcheon the other; about 3,000 were present. The Internationals won easily on merit, Knight making very poor speeches and Houston not taking his full time; the O. B. U. partisans interrupted Hoops and McCutcheon, and at the end of the meeting a band of them assaulted Hoop. In his speech Hoop declared that the O. B. U. principles meant revolution, and said that the general strike which was planned to begin in Winnipeg on 1st June 1919 was definitely intended to lead to a revolution. As Hoop is an extremist himself, and was deep in the Winnipeg strike this testimony is very valuable. McCutcheon, who avowed himself a former I.W.W. charged that the O. B. U. in effect is identical with that body. The Manitoba Free Press published a verbatim report of the speeches.

Kavanagh and Gage have been making statements to the Winnipeg Defence Committee on their visit to England. Both regarded England as very near a revolution, and Kavanaugh gave utterance to a remark about the general strike being a step in the raising of a revolution which it will be useful to remember.

The future of the Winnipeg prisoners is causing searchings of heart. On the one hand, the extremists are angry at Farnell being released, as the Internationals are claiming the credit for having procured clemency, and none of the noisy demands has been made on his behalf. The course to be pursued by Russell is causing much perplexity;[3] they evidently need him badly and he seems to be pretty sick of his imprisonment; all hands are much tempted to advise him to apply personally and in reasonably respectful terms for release, but are afraid that such a course would injure him with his following. Kavanaugh contributed to the discussion a characteristic remark that "honour and law could not be considered in this fight", on which ground he recommended the taking of any steps that were available to procure Russell's enlargement.

Yet another piece of frankness comes from Edmonton. Fresh from the O. B. U. convention at Vancouver, Carl Berg proclaimed the O. B. U. to represent the lower classes of labour, whom he described as more important than the skilled trades.

Signs continue to be reported of a struggle in the Alberta Coal fields next autumn or winter.

1. BRITISH COLUMBIA

2. The High Cost of Organizing

More intimate reports of the loggers' convention in Vancouver are beginning to come in. One feature was the cost of organizing work in Eastern Canada, and the meagre returns. A compilation of organizers' reports shows the following results:

P. G. Anderson, Winnipeg: expenses $860.00; fees earned $6.00, dues turned in $5.00.

Baird, Sudbury and Cobalt; expenses $495.95; fees $3.00; dues, $3.00.

Hanson, Fort Frances; expenses $673.00; fees $41.00; dues $205.00

M.J. Keane, expenses $573.00; fees $3.00; dues $7.00.

Lamont, expenses (1st April to 20th May) $768.53; fees $39.00, dues $150.00.

Labelle, Montreal; expenses, $1,065.65; fees $193.00; dues $429.00

Mawhinney, Sudbury and Port Arthur; expenses $938.00; fees $156.00; dues $259.00

A. W. McKnight, Northern Ontario (19th January to 7th April)

expenses $1,315.11; fees $1.00; dues $3.00
Clarke, Edmonton (January to April); expenses $856.25; fees $18.00, dues $5,306.[4]
Cowan, Sudbury, expenses $540; no returns.
The fees mentioned go into the pockets of the organizers.

Summarized, these men's expense accounts amounted to $8,085.49; they earned in fees $469.00, and they brought into the coffers of the unit $1,114.00.

This elicited a good deal of criticism. Several of these organizers have been dropped and are looking for employment; a charge of graft may be preferred against Cowan.

3. Berg's Influence in the Convention

The attempt to abolish Winch's office was persistent and strong the debate lasting for a day and a half; the attempt was defeated by Carl E. Berg, who led the defence in the general convention. The movement against the office came from the Coastal delegates, and the "eastern delegates" protected Winch. Our informant observes:-

> "Carl Berg, of Edmonton, was the strong man in this argument to stay with headquarters and carried the convention with him. He is an industrial unionist from start to finish and is the most logical man for Winch's job if he wants it. Berg floored his opponents in this argument with ease. He is not grafty, but appeals to the common-sense of his listeners and his report will make interesting reading when it is put in print".

It will be remembered that when the O. B. U. constitution was framed Berg exerted a decisive influence upon the precedings.

4. The Expanding L.W.I.U.

The loggers' union at its convention changed its name once again. It now is the "Lumber Camp and Agricultural Workers' Department of the One Big Union". The official explanation is:-

> "As it was realized that owing to a considerable inter-relationship of these occupations due mainly to the seasonal or casual nature of the work and the consequent passing from one to the other by the workers, it was the most logical thing for the organization of all workers so employed to be concentrated and socialized in one department, at least until such time as growth "and developments [5] called for some other arrangement".

Our confidential reports state that during the convention Midgley showed jealously of the L.W.I.U. saying that it was taking in members of the O.B.U. proper, and monopolising the general membership.

This seems a natural outcome of the move of the loggers to take in agricultural labourers. From the outside it looks as if Winch nourishes a purpose of expanding his organization within the O. B. U. until it absorbs it all. It may be noted that his allay Berg is strong among the foreigners in Northern Alberta, and specifically represents the coal-miners there.

In this connection the following extract from our confidential report may be noted:-

"McKnight has resigned as a member of the general executive board and Carl Berg, of Edmonton, was elected in his place. Berg has proven himself to be the strongest man in the convention and is an out and out O.B.U. advocate. He claims that in the near future the miners in district 18 will be lined up in this organization.

5. L.W.I.U. Policy

In connection with this convention, an extract from the reports of the Coast Secretary, CLARK, may be quoted as showing the present outlook of this body:-

"Nothing of a very serious nature has transpired during the time I have been in office, except it be the various methods to lead the members of this organization into a general strike. Last February, the Masters declared for an Open shop, when we as an organization, never tried for a closed one. Why this move? Like every effect, it must have its cause. It is obvious to any reasoning person that they thought it a transgression on "our rights and privileges", and that we would strike as a body to enforce a closed shop. In fact, the thing appeared to be an open challenge for a trial of strength, where we would be pitted against all the machinery of the Capitalist state. However, it did not work. In the months of May, April too, various newspapers carried an item in which they stated that the officials of the O. B. U. were going to call a general strike on June 1st. In my opinion, this was a move on their part to work up a feeling among the members of the organization to that point, where [6] they "would expect a general strike again. Their efforts prove futile and will prove futile while we remember that a 'constant dropping of water will wear away a stone'. By individual strikes, we keep them divided because some outfits want to settle terms that others will not stand for. As they tried to divide us, so we should concentrate every effort to divide them. Our strength lies in knowing how strong we are, and not overstepping that boundary. Knowing what concessions we have been able to wring from the boss by means of our industrial strength during the last eighteen months we have no cause for pessimism. In spite of what may be said to the contrary, this organization has left its mark in the concrete realities of improved living and working conditions; and it has also left a mark that cannot be seen, nor its magnitude measured. That is the class conscious knowledge which it has helped to plant in the brains of our members. The value of this knowledge cannot be measured at present, but in the future we will probably realize this fact better than we do at present".

6. L.W.I.U. Finance

Following are the financial statements of sundry L.W.I.U. districts:-

Cranbrook: June, receipts, $966.97; expenditures, $1,325.34; on hand 30th June, $1,602.11

Edmonton: May and June; receipts, $290.50; expenditures, $415.00, on hand 30th June $226.91.

Prince Labert: June Receipts, $210.20; expenditures, $156.62; on hand 30th June, $75.64.

Kamloops:- June, receipts $1,012,35; expenditures, $638.05; on hand 30th June, $973.19.

Nelson:- June: receipts, $259.00; expenditures, $173.30; on hand 30th June $173.72.

Fort Frances:- June; receipts $316.15; expenditures, $485.73; on hand 30th June, $313.97.

Sudbury:- June; receipts, $708.94; expenditures, $861.63; on hand 30th June, $428.98.

In four out of the seven expenditure considerably outran income.

7. Convention Notes

It is understood that a resolution was passed pledging support to the Sinn Fein movement.

P. F. Lawson addressed the Convention on behalf of the Searchlight, but seems to have received little encouragement.[7] H. Puro, editor of Vapaus, and M. Popovich of the Ukrainian Labour News, also attended the convention.

The two conventions, that of the loggers and that of the O. B. U. proper, cost rather more than $5,000. This has left the treasury much depleted.

The Miners of Copper Mountain have broken away from local headquarters, O. B. U. owing some $600. Their per capita tax has not amounted to enough to defray the cost of organizing them.

8. The Russian Deportees

Information received shows that the counsel for the Russian deportees at Vancouver (Mr. Rubinowitz) states that the perjury charges against our agents which he unsuccessfully pressed cost $2,000. He only paid $150, and while there is some talk of payment by degrees, he has no hope of this coming to anything. The report, which is dated 30th July, adds:-

> "The deportations, which the Russians and those sympathizing with them had hoped the Government would not dare to carry out, have produced a depressing effect amongst foreign and Canadian radicals".

The persons and organizations, other than Russian, who have shown deep interest in defending these men, and in convicting our agents, are:-

The Socialist Party of Canada, Vancouver Branch

The Defence Committee, Vancouver Branch.

A. S. Wells, Editor of the B. C. Federationist.

J. G. Smith, Secretary, General Workers' Unit, O. B. U.

9. British Columbia Detachment Reports

Alert Bay, 24th July:-

The management of all logging camps visited report work progressing satisfactorily, with no trouble through the interference of agitators. The camps are all in good condition and the food excellent. Practically all varieties of salmon are running now in this district and large catches are reported from all points.

Hazelton, 24th July:-

Things are quiet.[8]

Ocean Falls, 31st July:-

"There appears to be a slight improvement here with regard to the labour element of late. Very little agitation heard of and not much radical literature noticed anywhere in the district.

Port Alberni, 24th July:-

"District quiet and orderly. Camps and mills working steadily except Alberni Pacific which is still closed down............ No unemployment in the district. Construction camps are quiet and have not yet shown any signs of industrial trouble".

"Chakawana Detachment (Coastal Patrol) 23rd July:-

Conditions at Alice Arm satisfactory. The Dolly Varden mine has 150 men at work; no agitation and the men satisfied. No shortage of labour, and no labour trouble expected this summer. Things very quiet at Anyox, where some 1,300 men are employed.

10. Miscellaneous Notes

An attempt was made to cause a strike in a C. P. R. logging camp near Yahk. It only lasted a day, the cause being trivial, the local manager behaving in a conciliatory way, and the men not being unreasonable. The local O. B. U. delegate, a man named O. Dandineau, made every effort to stir up strife.

Dandineau, left the camp hurriedly on 23rd July, being frightened when the R. C. M. P. interviewed him. A correspondent says of him:-

> "My personal opinion of this man is that he is out to make trouble at every opportunity. He is a very intelligent man, but not very well educated. He can make a pretty good speech and sounds convincing when he talks. He speaks French fluently".

J. Harrington was the speaker at the Socialist meeting held in Vancouver on Sunday 1st August. His speech was a running commentary on recent events, and included remarks on the possibility of a closing-down of industries and a period of unemployment. The meeting was well-attended; the collection was $50.40.

Renewed reports come of intimidation in the Kootenay country, this time in connection with the obstinate strike at Meadows Lumber Camp, Erie, B.C. The men's demands were for higher pay, lower charge for food, shorter hours.[9]

II. ALBERTA

11. Unskilled versus Skilled Labour

The "Park Committee" (who are identical with the inner circle of the Labour Church) in Edmonton held an open-air meeting on Sunday 1st August, at which Carl Berg and P. M. Christophers spoke.

Berg said that he had just returned from the O. B. U. convention in Vancouver and that the O. B. U. was stronger than ever, especially in British Columbia. Our report continues:-

> "The O. B. U. was most bitterly attacked, said the speaker because they passed a resolution of greetings for the Russian Bolsheviks and the German Sparticans, and we (the O. B. U.) don't deny this because we support any labour class and in any country that does anything good for the labouring classes any where. The O. B. U. stand for equal rights of all classes and nationalities, and we believe the lower classes of labour such as section men are a greater power than the higher class of labour because if it were not for them doing the rough work the higher class would not be enabled to ride in luxury over the roads. Some people say, said the speaker, that the O.B.U. and the I.W.W. are one and the same organization. but I say that they are not, at the same time the O. B. U. support every case which is performed by the I.W.W."

P. M. CHRISTOPHERS described the O. B. U. as the largest labour organization in Canada at the present time. His speech was an argument for the O. B. U.

Berg's statement that the O. B. U. represents rough and unskilled labour as against skilled labour merits notice.

12. The Fernie Situation

Reports from two sources represent the situation in Fernie as interesting and perhaps dangerous.

One report, is that on 29th July a meeting of "Employes of the Crow's Nest Pass Co" was held; the term in this case meant the O. B. U. About 150 were present, and it was proposed that they sign up with the U. M. W. of A. This was hotly debated; the meeting dwindled to 65 and then a vote was taken which resulted 45 against and 20 for joining the U. M. W. of A. Our informant adds:-[10]

> "I would like to point out the significance of this vote, for this is the first time since the O. B. U. has started in this camp that an actual open vote has been cast in favour of signing up with the U. M. W. of A.; on the other hand, the attitude of the O. B. U. members that are signing up with the U. M. W. of A. is clearly shown by such statements as made by Jas. Clarke last night when he said 'Let us sign up with them and then we have a chance to work from the inside'.

> "During the last four days 83 additional members have signed up with the U. M. W. of A. and their total membership today is in the neighbourhood of 500 out of 800 members".

An attempt was made by the O. B. U. leaders to make a flank attack on the agreement, by instigating some returned soldiers to protest against being called upon to join the U. M. W. of A. This request was refused.

Another informant states, under date of 1st August, that a dispute over the timbering of the mines is in sight. This in itself is insignificant, but may be used by the O. B. U. as a grievance wherewith to stir up fresh discontent. This informant says:-

> "I had a long talk with Dick Beard this morning and he told me that inside of two months the miners will ditch the new agreement. All the men are signing the checkoff this week but are looking to this timbering agreement as a loop-hole".

13. A Coal Strike Prophesied

F. Bidder, an O. B. U. organizer in the East Kootenay sub-district when attending the District Convention of the O. B. U. at Cranbrook made a statement which is wholly in accord with the information which we have been receiving for months.- Our report is:-

> "Bidder announced at the L.W.I.U. District Convention today, that while mining department of the O.B.U. was not very strong right now he predicted that by mid winter, they would be the strongest department of the O.B.U.
>
> "When asked what he meant he replied that right now, while there is not much demand for coal the men are working because they need the money, but when winter starts they would have the upper hand and be in a position to force the recognition of the O.B.U. This particularly applies to District 18.[11]
>
> "He said he felt safe in saying that District 18 would start a bunch of trouble for the Operators when winter set in".

14. Agitators' Lies

In connection with the dispute at Coalhurst, a speech delivered at an O. B. U. meeting there by a man named Clarke may be noticed. Clarke is a returned soldier who "lets everyone know about it". He was chairman of the meeting. Our report is:-

> "He said this was started by the Capitalists of all the countries involved and that the 'Kaiser' and 'King George' were working hand in hand all through this war.
>
> "He told of the 'planes bombing London, stating that they never bombed the west end of this city because it belonged to the Capitalists, but that they always bombed the East-end because that was where the working people lived. He also said that when the Allied 'planes bombed German cities they never bombed any place where it would harm the Capitalists and he proceeded to give them

an instance of this by stating that one time an English plane bombed a Red Cross train that the 'Kaiser' was riding on and the Pilot of the plane was court-martialled for doing this. The inference he desired to draw was that the pilot of the plane was only court martialled on account of dropping the bombs on the train because the 'Kaiser' was abroad the train and not because it was a Red Cross train.

"He said that the capitalists were beginning to fear the working classes with their unions and socialism so they started a big War to break them up.

"Clark then said that no C.P.R. steamships were sunk by the enemy because German capital was in it, and he then denounced the Government as being wholly consistent of the capitalist class".

15. Strike Notes

The strike at Coalhurst continues. On 6th August 60 or 70 men were doing surface work, with no interference from the strikers.

A one-day strike took place, over a local matter about ventilation, in the Atlas mine, one of the best managed and steadiest mines in Drumheller. It is organized under the International, and it is unlikely that the O. B. U. had any hand in the affair.

16. O.B.U. Activity in Calgary

Transportation Unit No. 1. O.B.U. Calgary, is making progress in the Ogden Shops, C.P.R. Fourteen shop stewards have been appointed [12] and there is active canvassing for members, a number of recruits being secured. An agent says:-

"I think their aim is finally to try for closed shops at Ogden, and may succeed, as they are slowly but surely getting men from the International, Stewart is after men a great deal of the time while at work. He has good chances as the machinists are working on engines in the boiler shops, that is, a great many of them. The machinists are the International's strong hold at Ogden".

Concerning this the Officer Commanding Calgary, while admitting the energy shown by the O. B. U., expects the International to institute a counter-campaign, and adds:-

"The O. B. U., however, are out in the open, so far as meetings are concerned, and may succeed in becoming fairly strong in members, but it will be some time before they can talk closed shop".

At the "O. B. U. Class Meeting" held by Lewin at Calgary on 22nd July the leader gave definition of "Anarchism" which is somewhat interesting. It is thus reported:-

"Lewin said that this very day we were living under anarchism; that the Government and all concerned therein were nothing but a bunch of anarchists; that there was lawlessness from every portion of the Government and disorder in the worst possible form that must collapse. Every man serving the Government today, he said, was an anarchist. He brought up Russia as an illustration for the class and, I think, succeeded in showing them or teaching them what was the real meaning of anarchism".

The O. B. U. in Calgary has taken to holding open-air meetings in the parks on Sundays. It is thought by a competent observer that these will benefit the O. B. U., by interesting persons who before were indifferent to it. The first meeting was addressed by George Palmer and P. M. Christophers.

Christophers has been trying to organize the stockyard and floor mill workers in Calgary.

17. The East Kootenay Loggers

The District Convention of the Fernie District of the L.W.I.U. was held on 1st August in Cranbrook. Only 12 persons attended and the proceedings lasted 3 hours, little business being transacted. It principally related to the salary of the organizer (one Thompson) hospital matters, etc. Nothing was said about future wages. [13] A passage from our report is:-

"It was announced that two districts namely Prince Rupert and Fort George had definitely broken with the O.B.U. and the L.W.I.U. are just running a little union independently".

18. The Labour Press

The attempt to publish the Labour News in Cranbrook seems to have come to nothing. The Cranbrook Courier refuses to publish any further issues, and Kingsland seems to have left the district. The first issue comprised 1,000 copies; only 250 copies were sold; the rest are at the Courier office; the cost of printing has not been defrayed; and the paper was much disliked locally. The L.W.I.U. disclaim connection with it.

P. F. Lawson's visit to the Vancouver convention brought him no money for the Searchlight.

Lawson has returned to Calgary from Vancouver.

19. The Foreign Element

Dr. O. Sushko of Winnipeg on Sunday 25th July addressed the Ukrainians of Edmonton in the Samo-Obrazowania society. His speech began as a eulogy of Bolshevism as "the sunlight for all labourers", but become an electioneering address. It appeared that he and Popovich are rivals for the control of the Ukrainian Labour Temple, and that the latter has succeeded in carrying the Board of Directors. The meeting promised to support Susko, who is described as very eloquent in the Ukrainian language.

It may be worth noting that Popovich is in Vancouver at the moment that Sushko is in Edmonton. Popovich also seems to intend to tour the Crow's Nest Pass.

The Russian Ukrainian Drama Company on 28th and 29th July played at Coalhurst. It seems to be visiting all the coal mining towns.

III. SASKATCHEWAN

20. A Sidelight on O.B.U. Methods

Inquiry at Kamsack throws doubt upon the existence of a branch [14] of the O. B. U. there. A few employes in the C.N.R. shops have O. B. U. sympathies but they are in the minority, and the older men are adverse.

The interesting thing about this is that lists of O.B.U. locals include the following entry; "Transportation Unit, Kamsack Sask; C. Hannan, Kamsack (Secretary)". Investigation in this small place fails to discover either an organized unit, or any person named Hannan. It is recalled that in June a man visited Kamsack, made unsuccessful efforts to organize an O.B.U. local and left for Winnipeg; presumably this was Hannan. It has been suspected that many of the locals of the O. B. U. which appear in their lists are non-existent, or consist of the secretary alone, and this incident goes to confirm the suspicion. The Montreal unit and secretary, it will be recalled, are almost wholly supported by the head office in Vancouver.

21. A Foreign Would-be Revolutionist

A report on John Onishenko, the Bolshevist at Hafford, presents some interesting features. He is agent for a lumber company, and he and one or two men of the shop-keeper class lead the local Russians and Galicians; Onishenko speaks both languages and is on good terms with both races. He is exceedingly ignorant of Bolsheviki or Socialist doctrine, and yet is strongly revolutionary in disposition. Paraphrased, this probably means that he is in a very bad temper with the country in which he lives, is anxious to stir up trouble, and, owing to his ignorance, is at a loss how to go about it. He does not even know the names of any leaders to whom to write to help. Onishenko (whose name properly is Onishchenkoff) thinks that if he could import a good organizer he could get up a revolutionary society of 150 to 200 members in Hafford and two or three adjoining districts.

A feature of the situation here is that the local Greek Catholic priest is strongly opposed to Bolshevism, and that the branch [15] of the Ukrainian Nationalist Home Association, the only organization of foreigners in existence in Hafford, has no revolutionary purpose there, whatever it may have elsewhere. Any organization formed would be comprised of the most ignorant people of these nationalities. Another feature is that they all are much in fear of police supervision.

A circumstance which merits attention is that the leaders of this particular set of obscure discontented foreigners are shop-keepers, i.e., men, who are relatively advanced and well-to-do. Among English and French speaking Canadians such men usually are supporters of public order. Here is a case where the isolation of the foreigners tends to make their ablest and most energetic men leaders in disorders.

22. The Bienfait Affair.

From a confidential source it is learned that statements are being laid before the persons appointed by the Saskatchewan Government to investigate the Bienfait affair which reflect seriously upon the operators. These are in brief that the mine-owners were paying the men low wages and holding them in a species of "helotage"; that a quarrel arose between these operators and a lignite plant which desired to give higher wages; that in the course of this dispute some men were dismissed for belonging to the O. B. U. who had joined it months ago as an incident of subscribing to the Winnipeg Defence Fund, and then forgotten it; that Christophers' visit came after these events, and that the men who kidnapped him formed part of a whiskey-running enterprise.

Some of the details given almost certainly are incorrect.

23. The L.W.I.U. in the NORTH

George Tether, the O. B. U. organizer among the lumbermen of Northern Saskatchewan has moved his office from Prince Albert to the Pas. He does not intend to stay there long. The L.W.I.U. have been very quiet for the last two months.

A report from Prince Albert describes Tether's intention in [16] moving to the Pas to be to make his last stand there. The report continues:-

> "The delegates that Tether has had working for him, during the past 9 months, have been a crooked bunch and have done more harm than good to the Union, by absconding with O.B.U. membership funds. The latest delegate to do this was one of the best delegates that Tether has ever had, as far as getting members goes. This was Fred Wright, who skipped out of the Pas recently and must have taken about $200,00 O.B.U. money with him. This kind of thing has been going on, more or less, right along, until the public look upon the O. B. U. as a shady organization and its delegates a bunch of crooks".

24. Miscellaneous Notes

A meeting of the Self Determination for Ireland League was held on 29th July in the City Hall, Regina; J.K. McInnis presided and Miss Katherine Hughes spoke. About 100 joined the league. The meeting, at the suggestion of the Chairman, sang "God save the King".

George Babych, president of the Hotel and Restaurant Employes Unit, O. B. U. Moose Jaw, a very enthusiastic O. B. U, man, visited Regina at the end of July and tried to form a similar union there, but without success.

The danger of a strike of civic employees in Moose Jaw has been averted.

The membership in the Grand Army of United Veterans in Regina is asserted to be about 500.

At a meeting of the Zapomhe Towarsto. the Ukrainian Bolshevistic Society of Saskatoon, only about 40 persons were present, to the disappointment of the local leaders.

IV. MANITOBA

25. Gage on Conditions in England

Gage, the emissary sent by the Winnipeg Defence Committee to England, and Ald. A.A. Heaps reported at a meeting of the Committee held on Sunday 1st August.

Gage, while impressed by the status of labour in England,

"Said the different labour organization leaders who he had [17] interviewed from time to time gave him very little encouragement, as to the possibilities of the Russell appeal being heard by the Privy Council, as they said it was like everything else, and under control of the master class.

"The general feeling, he stated, of the workers themselves a was, that they would support any direct action to their fullest extent, and he had been informed to the effect that the rank and file of labour was really behind the cause, although the Labour leaders were very slow in taking interest in the situation.

"He mentioned having addressed meetings of the South Wales' Miners' Federation, all of whom he found in sympathy with the Russell appeal case, more so than any body of labour he ran across in England. In fact, he stated, this organization of miners was the only one which had donated any money to the Defence Committee outside of the regular collection which was always taken up at all meetings. He stated that this was practically the largest organized labour body in the Old Country and had up to millions of dollars in the Treasury for reserve purposes, and could easily afford to give some donation, but the smaller labour organizations were like their own here in Canada barely enough in the treasuries to keep them floating, and the labour leaders of these parties had expressed their opinions that the Defence Committee of Canada should be well able to finance their own appeal case when he had asked for financial assistance. Nevertheless, he said, the collections were very good and defrayed expenses considerably".

Gage said that a considerable number of the books and pamphlets issued by the Committee had been circulated.

Ald. Heaps gave a report of his journey through Eastern Canada, speaking in glowing terms of the attendance at his meetings and making the usual complaint of the "spy system".

It also came out that the English labour men had not been satisfied with Gage's credentials. Ernest Robinson, the secretary of the Winnipeg Trades and Labour Council, had avoided giving him credentials.

26. Kavanaugh's Speech

J. Kavanaugh spoke at a meeting of the Central Labour Council O.B.U. in Winnipeg on 3rd August, describing his experience in England. He passed lightly over the reception given him, saying that:-

> "Nobody thought anything at all of Russell being in jail, that was one of the most common things to them, as there were men amongst the leaders all over England who had done two and three years in jail, and when their time was up, had come out and renewed the [18] fight".

He described England as on the verge of revolution. Our report is as follows:-

> "Red propaganda was a very common thing over there, he said, but none of the authorities seemed to take any particular notice of it, red flags always being worn and carried on all labour parades and celebrations.
>
> "He also declared that as far as could be made out from the stand the Labour situation was taking in the old country, it predicted revolution. This was on the tongue of every working man, who was class conscious, and there were very few who were not.
>
> "He said a general strike to obtain any rights of the working class was practically of no use, unless the strike was a well organized one, and had the full power of the working class behind it, and in this case, to obtain the overthrow of the present Capitalist system, it would be necessary for a revolution to arise out of the general strike before their object could be obtained.
>
> "That was what the worker was being faced with all over England, Ireland and particularly in Russia, not in any way leaving out our own country, he declared".

A question about the treatment of souvenir guns in some parts of England having come up, Kavanaugh

> "declared that it was a fact that the large bodies of labour organizations, such as the Miners' Federation and the Dockers' Union had plenty of guns and ammunition actually stored away in case of a revolution coming, which was so greatly predicted in the old country".

27. The Release of Prisoners

The release of Farnell at Winnipeg has caused much anger among the Winnipeg Defence Committee. It was felt that the Internationals i.e. the Trade Congress, would claim credit for compassing it, whereas the Defence Committee had been paying his wife $55.00 a week during his sojourn in jail. This ill-feeling may have accounted for some of the disorder at the public debate on 6th August.

At the meeting of the Winnipeg Defence Committee held on 1st August a report was heard from the Committee which had seen R. B. Russell in the penitentiary. As a result of the interview, and in accordance with a hint from the Warden, it was decided that Russell should send to Ottawa a personal letter asking for clemency or for a parole.[19]

At the meeting of the Central Labour Council, O.B.U. on 3rd August, the question of Russell's release was sharply debated, the point at issue being whether Russell should appeal for clemency. The Lumber and Building Trades Unit dissented vigorously from the resolution of the Defence Committee that he should do so. P. G. Anderson, who represented this unit, predicted that the Internationals "would soon have a fine opportunity to come back with a yarn that Russell had to beg and crawl to get out of jail". Kaiser of the Metal Trades Unit also opposed Russell applying for clemency "if it was going to endanger his reputation after he had been set free". On the other side Kavanaugh remarked that it was Russell who was in jail, and not the various units of the O.B.U. who really put him there. Russell, he said, was doing no good in jail", and

> "if he could get out by making a plea of his own, why all well and good, as honour and law could not be considered in this fight between Capital and Labour, and therefore, he thought that nay means should be adopted if it were to gain them a point".

28. O.B.U. NOTES

There are three O.B.U. units among the building trades in Winnipeg. Recently a paragraph in the press stated that they planning to form one single unit without craft divisions. A well-informed correspondent contradicts this. According to him, there have been defections from the O.B.U. in these trades, and the executive have been sitting to consider measures to hold together the three units (which are small). The paragraph, he says, was cut out to cover these defensive measures.

It is noted that the O.B.U. in Winnipeg show themselves sympathetic with the Sinn Fein cause, regarding it as a capital and labour conflict. They also evince dislike for Orangemen.

An O.B.U. meeting in Portage la Prairie on Sunday 1st August was slimly attended. Few members joined. The speakers were P. G. Anderson and Jack Clancy.[20]

The dismissal of A. Emery from the Transcona shops, and the failure of the attempt to strike over it, have resulted in the men there being very quiet and obedient. Emery has opened a revolutionary news agency.

Mr. J. S. Woodsworth reported to the Defence Committee on 1st August that the Attorney General of Saskatchewan had promised to make a confidential inquiry into the abduction of Christophers at Bienfait.

The open air meeting of the Socialist party on 1st August in the Market Square in Winnipeg was addressed by C. Stewart. His speech needs no notice. The attendance was 200. Little interest was shown.

About 400 persons attended the Ukrainian Labour Temple picnic near Winnipeg on Sunday 1st August. The red flag was displayed but nothing else of a seditious nature occurred. The purpose was to collect money to pay the Temple's debts.

V. ONTARIO

29. Revolutionists in Hamilton

A Detroit I.W.W. named William Wilson has appeared in Hamilton and has been busy among the local O.B.U. members and revolutionary foreigners. In conversation this man said that "there was but little hostility between the I.W.W. and the O.B.U., and that they had decided to pull together in the States". He talked of bringing to Hamilton to speak a man named John Pancler, who served 18 months imprisonment at Fort Leavenworth, Kansas, and now is out on bail. The local revolutionaries are debating whether either of these men would not make a good local leader; since Flatman's departure from Hamilton they have lacked a man with the qualities of leadership, and Wilson has made a good impression on them, alike by his ability and by his acquaintance with revolutionary organizations in the United States.[21]

Wilson lately was going under the alias of William Edwards.

The Hamilton revolutionists have begun to arrange for halls, etc. for the coming winter. Our report says:-

> "Last year the speakers were secured by the Independent Labour Party and there was a great deal of dissatisfaction among the Radicals because they claimed the speakers were too moderate. This year the committee put in charge of securing speakers will be all Radicals". One of these is to be Joe Knight.

30. Events in Toronto

A report on the Jewish Socialist Party of Toronto is that on 22nd July a break-up occurred, some forming the "Jewish Socialist Democratic Party of Canada" (which seems identical with the "Anarchist Communist Party") and others joining the "Third International". Both are canvassing hard for recruits, and both meet in the same house in Beverly Street, one society on Wednesdays and the other on Fridays.

One of the Third International members is collecting for the fund for medical aid to Russia which has been noticed already.

On Sunday 8th August the O.B.U. tried to hold an open air meeting in Toronto, in Yonge Street. Mrs. J.R. Knight and Max Armstrong were to be the speakers, but the city police broke up the meeting, as they were blocking traffic and had no permit. A Socialist meeting shared the same fate on the same evening.

The O.B.U. local in Toronto on 29th July elected new officers, the President and secretary-treasurer being Arnold and Hunt. The attendance was 55. The funds on hand were $54.30. Few members are joining. The meeting decided on a policy of open-air meetings on Saturday and Sunday meetings; the untimely end of the first of these is noticed in the preceding paragraph.

VI. QUEBEC

31. Miscellaneous Montreal Notes

Another report has been received on "The Society for Technical Aid to Soviet Russia of the Russian Socialist Federal Soviet Republic", as its full name seems to be. The registration which was noticed before as conducted under orders from the Soviet Bureau at New York is to be completed, and new members must register. This organization is growing and expects to have a busy winter.

The Worker, the O.B.U. paper issued in Montreal, has reached its seventh number, which came out on 1st August. Attempts to induce the Montreal news dealers to handle it have been rebuffed and few copies are sold. The edition issued is very large.

A positive assertion comes from Hamilton that Ben Legere is in Montreal helping to issue this paper.

VII. THE MARITIME PROVINCES

32. General Conditions

The Officer Commanding Maritime Provinces in his confidential monthly report for June and July says:-

> "There has been a considerable amount of labour unrest in the Maritime Provinces during the period in question, the chief feature being a strike at the Halifax Shipyards, which commenced on June 1st, and is still unterminated, however 850 men are now back at work, and the plant is apparently in full swing. Other strikes of minor importance are dealt with. The great Cape Breton coal fields have been operating practically without any trouble, pending the finding of the Royal Commission now sitting in Glace Bay"

Other remarks are:-

> "Possibility of a general strike over the Shipyard strike is now almost out of the question. The management is to be complimented on their speedy action in compelling the city to give the men, who were anxious to return to work, ample protection. The prosecution of some militant pickets has had a good effect.
>
> "The merger of the Dominion and Scotia interests will no doubt have a good effect. A special department is being formed to look after complaints of miners, housing conditions etc.
>
> "Fresh developments are taking place in Cape Breton, and several old dis-used shafts are being reopened.
>
> "So far the O.B.U. has not obtained any footing in this district, nor is it anticipated that it ever will".[23]

Dealing with the visit of the Winnipeg Strike leaders to the Maritime Provinces, he says:-

> "In the early part of May, Heaps and Dunn of Winnipeg visited the provinces, with the object of raising funds for the defence of the

Winnipeg strike leaders. They were tendered a civic welcome by the council of Sydney C.B., which failed to materialize, and they were received with open arms by J.B. McLachlan and J.C. Watters. Their tour of the Province opened the eyes of the saner-minded people, and they were condemned by the Press and pulpit of the provinces. I was informed that the money collected by them barely paid their expenses in the Maritime Provinces.

"They were more or less disgusted with their trip to this part of the country. In Halifax only 200 attended their meeting and some $38.00 was collected.

"Owing to the opposition of organized labour in St. John N.B. they were unable to obtain a Hall to hold a meeting in that city.

"In Moncton N.B. they addressed practically an empty hall, and they collected $12.00 for their cause. This amount being practically all they collected in New Brunswick.

"A Prominent labour man in Halifax informed me that if the O.B.U. exponents did not know before, that Nova Scotia was not in sympathy with their cause, they are absolutely certain since they toured the Province, that the O.B.U. has few sympathizers here".

33. Miscellaneous Notes

On 6th August about 1,100 men were working at the Halifax shipyard, and picketting had been discontinued as a consequence of the injunction obtained by the company from the Supreme Court. On 5th August the Boiler Makers' Union decided to return to work on the company's terms; this is the first union to give up in a body.

A troublesome difference between the management and the men of the Inverness Railway had been settled. The men demanded the same pay as that received by those on the Canadian National; this was refused and negotiations were in progress, with some ill-feeling shown, when the railway came under new ownership, and the men's demands was promptly conceded. The men are reported to be much pleased.[24]

A convention of the U. M. W. of A. was called in Halifax for 7th August in connection with the expected report of the Royal Commission on Coal Mining. There was no particular intention of calling a strike unless certain demands for pay, such as an additional dollar a day for some men and 24 per cent increase for others, should be refused.

The strike at Minto is reported to be collapsing.

ROYAL CANADIAN MOUNTED POLICE HEADQUARTERS

Ottawa, 19th August, 1920.

SECRET

NO. 37

NOTES OF THE WORK OF THE C. I. B. DIVISION FOR THE WEEK ENDING 19TH AUGUST

N.B.In most cases these notes are founded upon reports received by mail. The dates of incidents and reports consequently are stated when this is necessary.

1. General Characteristics of the Period

During the week we have had reported a considerable number of "Hands off Russia" meetings, resolutions, etc. In Eastern Canada these have been trivial affairs, an open-air meeting in Toronto on Saturday afternoon, 14th August, being a mere fizzle when the size of the city is considered. In Western Canada they have been more considerable, a meeting in Winnipeg having been attended by 1,500 persons.

Indications exist that co-operation between the extremists in Western Canada and those in Great Britain. This may prove the real consequence of the visit of Messrs. Kavanaugh and Gage. Robertson, the Glasgow agitator who is sojourning rather quietly in Eastern Canada, may attempt some liaison work.

The issues of the rival Labour papers in Winnipeg, The Western Labour News and the O. B. U. Bulletin suggest that both sides thought that the O. B. U. champions had won the victory. The former paper makes no editorial comment whatever, and confines itself to a long report of the speeches; the O. B. U. Bulletin not only prints a report, but triumphs noisily through a couple of columns.

Side by side with proofs of the weakness of the appeal of the O. B. U. to the general public of Montreal there multiply indications of [2] Bolshevist attempts to prosecute missionary work there. We now hear that the rather bare-brained labour college is financed by the Soviet Bureau in New York. It may be conjectured that a Labour College under such auspices is much less to be dreaded than one inspired from the one in Glasgow, in which Robertson was "a student", and of which he may be an emissary.

The likelihood of a strike in the autumn or winter in Fernie if not elsewhere in the Alberta Coal fields is increasing.

I. BRITISH COLUMBIA

2. Strength of the O. B. U.

The Officer Commanding Vancouver in his confidential monthly report for July says of the O. B. U.:-

"According to O. B. U. officials, the total membership within this Police Division has reached to over 22,000, whilst the number of units is 29.

"From investigations by Staff Sergeant Mundy now ensuing, it would seem that both the total membership as well as the number of units is much inflated. As has already been pointed out by S/Sgt. Mundy in his reports on the O. B. U., the stronghold of the O.B.U.-- the L. W. I. U. is the largest unit by far, and the workers now in this organization previously were not organized at all. Take away the L. W. I. U. unit from the total membership of the O. B. U., and the balance of the O. B. U. membership would not exceed 2,000, if that. The A. F. of L. would be in the lead by many thousands of members.

"There have been 19 strikes called by the O. B. U. during the month. Few have been settled".

3. Conditions in Southern British Columbia

The Officer Commanding Vancouver in the same report quotes an appreciation of the O. B. U. situation in Southern inland British Columbia by the Officer Commanding Grand Forks, as follows:-

"Labour conditions at Trail and Rossland, where 1,700 men are employed, are quiet. The O. B. U. does not appear to be successful there.

"The strike in the Slocan district (Sandon an d Silverton," B. C. and [3] locality) is in about the same condition; that is to say that all the mines in that district are on strike, except the 'Silversmith', which is run by an American firm, which recognizes the O. B. U. and grants their demands. The other mines are some of them employing a few men, but seem to be having difficulty in getting the number of men they want, in spite of an agreement with the International Union to supply men on terms agreed upon. This strike has spread eastward to the mines on the extent that the men at one mine, the 'Blue Bell' at Riondel. The mine operators seem to be determined to fight the O. B. U. and the strike may be a prolonged one. The O. B. U. are very efficiently and effectively picketting the district; one method being to get employment on the Provincial Government road gangs in the district. The area affected by the strike is between the Arrow and Kootenay Lakes and nearer to the Arrow Lake; there is no complete railroad communication with the district; the district can only be got at by Lake steamboat; so with the Government Road gangs picketting for the O. B. U. and with pickets on the boat landings, any men seeking employment at the mines cannot get through without passing many very effective pickets.

"The strike at the Meadows Lumber Camp is still on, except that they are employing a few men; the firm seems determined to fight the O. B. U. to a finish and may gradually succeed in getting enough men to operate with.

"On the whole the O. B. U. seems to be rather in the ascendancy in the Slocan District; there are no reports of sabotage or violence of any kind; the strikes there are much in the nature of a "show down" between the O. B. U. and mine owners, and it is difficult to prophesy the result. Besides the picketing situation described above another thing which affects the situation is the fact that a lot of the firms are American firms and much of the labour employed is from the U. S. A. A very strong policy should be adopted in regard to the immigration into this district over the American railroad the Great Northern Railway, from the U. S. A. into Canada in this district (the G.N.R. from Spokane, Wash. via Marcus and Northport, Wash. to Nelson, B.C.)".

4. O. B. U. Claims Analized

The allegation by Winch that the L.W.I.U. in British Columbia number 20,000 is energetically disputed by the N. C. O. in charge of C. I. B. in Vancouver, who sticks to the view that their figure of about 13,350 is a liberal estimate. It is pointed out that Winch's report is couched in vague and misleading terms, and in particular that, whereas a firm of chartered accountants is retained by the Unit, no report from it was submitted. The memorandum by S. Sgt. Mundy says:-[4]

"The Committee, or Winch (whichever it is) first says the membership cannot be arrived at; then gives a reason which is inadequate; and then submits statistical figures as to membership in which there are unexplained blanks, but total of which works out to a little over 16,000 and that for the whole Dominion, not for the Province of British Columbia only, wherein he told me he had a membership of 20,000".

The memorandum remarks that "it is an organization of 'rough-necks' and 'grafters' who either do not know how to keep records, or don't want to, for purposes of their own".

The memorandum analyzes the O. B. U. in British Columbia outside of the L. W. I. U., and arrives at the following estimate, which is based on separate reports from the localities mentioned:-

Unit	Locality	Membership
General Workers' Unit	Prince George	Practically extinct
Metal Miners' Unit	Sandon	175
Metal Miners' Unit	Silverton	50
General Workers' Unit	Kamloops	75
General Workers' Unit	Princeton	50
Hedley Workers' Unit	Hedley	120
		470

5. The O. B. U. Convention Called

Midgley has issued a call for the second annual convention of the O. B. U. on 20th September at Port Arthur. In his call he declares that despite "the tactics used by some International fakirs, the incarceration of three O. B. U. leaders and the kidnapping of its organizers" the organization has doubled its numbers since the last convention.

6. British Columbia Detachment Reports

Prince George, 31st July:-

"The labour situation is very quiet. All labour required is available. No agitation in the district".

Nanaimo, 31st July:-

"Everything is quiet and orderly in this district, as far as the O. B. U. is concerned and the strike at Granby Mine is settled and the men now employed at that mine have a committee of their own, to settle their own disputes and troubles with the mine management and have deserted Andrew Dean and Albert Lane, O. B. U. organizers and agitators for that organization.

Port Alberni, 31st July:-

"The district is quiet and orderly, with mills and camps working steadily, with the exception of the Alberni Pacific, which is "still [5] closed down".

"Work on the E. and N. extension continue satisfactorily and their camps have been free from labour re oubles so far".

7th August:-

"District quiet generally, camps and mills working steadily, with no signs of trouble."

Nelson, 31st July:-

"The mining industry shows signs of improvement at Ymir, which at one time was a flourishing camp. The demand for men to work in mines is very strong, but very few offering".

7. Conditions at Allenby

An investigation of Allenby, near Merritt, shows that the International is uppermost there. The industry there is a mining plant. In April 1919 an attempt to establish the O. B. U. was defeated by a vote of 110 to 16; and in June 1919 a local of the International Mining, Mill and Smelter men was established; it now has a membership of 45 and seems to be composed of men of moderate views. While the plant is "openshop" the relations between the company and the local are good, and the latter is growing in strength.

At Copper Mountain, near Allenby, there exists another local of the same union, with 30 members, and with the same good relations between company and union. The men employed at the mine are expected to increase to 300. Those at Allenby number from 130 to 150. It is believed that there are few O. B. U. men in either place.

It will be recalled that the recent report of the O. B. U. admitted a failure at Copper Mountain.

8. O. B. U. Notes

There still is talk of agitation against Winch, on the ground that his post should be filled by a practical logger.

Joseph Naylor of Cumberland recently concluded his two months' organizing tour among the fishermen. In conversation he said that he had been successful, and had got 30 per cent of the fishermen of the [6] Fraser River District into the O. B. U.

The Sandon strike continues, with perhaps some sign of weakening among the men. Fresh evidence has been obtained of picketing by a gang of men employed by the Provincial Government on a road leading to one of the mines concerned.

9. Miscellaneous Notes

Unrest is reported as once more rife among the Vancouver longshoremen. Talk is heard of a general strike of longshoremen along the whole Pacific coast, to begin on 1st October.

The "Waterfront Freight Handlers' Association" at Vancouver are negotiating for increased wages. The C.P.R. offered to pay men of 3 years' service at the rate of $115.00 a month. The Association refused this and demanded a "flat salary" of $150 a month.

The indications are that the champions of the Russian deportees in Vancouver, encouraged by the recent postponement, will resort to every possible means to prevent their ejection from the country.

Frank Cassidy spoke at the meeting of the S. P. of C., Vancouver Local No. 1., on 8th August. The meeting was fairly well attended. Cassidy remarked that these Sunday meetings had been going on for ten years, and exulted in the change from conditions during the war, when they were mobbed. He boasted of the successes of the Bolsheviks, and concluded with an attack upon religion.

Tom Richardson, formerly a Labour M. P. in England, addressed a meeting in Prince Rupert on 30th July. The attendance was 40 or 50. Richardson's speech, which dealt largely with Prohibition, was moderate.[7]

II. ALBERTA

10. The Temper at Fernie

On 6th August a stoppage of work took place in Fernie. The members of the O. B. U. had yielded, and were signing the "check off" which makes them compulsory members of the U. M. W. of A. William Sherman, the local president of the O. B. U., was refused employment, and the men stopped work and showed great anger. Our correspondent says, under date of 6th August:-

> "The men are in ugly frame of mind and are looking for the most trivial thing to make it an excuse of starting a strike. It is true that with the possible exception of three or four the whole of the 800 employes have signed up with the U. M. W. of A., but there are scarcely 50 men who are really U. M. W. of A. at heart and in the

event of a strike I do not think sufficient men would stay at work to keep the mines running. The men have openly stated that they will have a strike this winter and they believe that the Coal company is trying to force their hand at the present time so that they will cease work now and therefore not be in a position to strike this winter. However, a large number have stated that if this is the case then they will leave Fernie altogether but it will not prevent them from striking if they take it in their heads to do so. The various leaders are taking good care that the men are kept in this frame of mind and they will utilize them whenever they are ready.

"Owing to existing conditions it is impossible, it seems to me, to avert trouble much longer".

The trouble at Fernie was settled on 9th August by the O. B. U. leader (Sherman) being taken on and given another trial by the management. Our informant adds:-

"However, it is common talk among the miners that they are going to call a strike and the time given is from the middle to the end of October. From little things gathered here and there, I feel certain that they will go on strike this fall or winter".

He goes to give an estimate of Sherman's character, the gist of which is that he possesses great influence with one particular set of rather young men, that he is a young man who cherishes the ambition of becoming an O. B. U. organizer; and that he consequently is doing his utmost to commend himself to that body.[8] The Officer Commanding East Kootenay (in which Fernie is situated) and the Officer Commanding Southern Alberta agree that the miners fully intend to strike in the autumn or winter.

11. Situation Elsewhere in the Coalfields

Trouble is threatened in Drumheller. The management of the N. A. C. mine does not belong to the western Coal Operators' Association, and has not enforced the "check-off"; as a result, the mine is an O. B. U. stronghold, and now the O. B. U. threaten a strike to get the same pay etc. as the U. M. W. of A. do. Christophers and Henry Beard were reported to be repairing to the scene, about 7th August.

The O. B. U. in Calgary early in August were expecting (i.e. hoping for) trouble at the mines at Kipp, Drumheller, Natal, Michel and Coalhurst.

The president of an U. M. W. of A. local at Lethbridge made an interesting statement in conversation on 10th August. All the miners, he said, are O. B. U. at heart; but for two months none have paid dues to the O. B. U., as they had to become members of the U. M. W. of A. to get work, and as no organizer of the O. B. U. was in town to urge them to pay to it as well.

Reports from Coalhurst dated 12th and 13th August are to the effect that the men still were out. Half the strikers were harvesting and the town was denuded of men.

Following is a report from Michel:-

"On August the 10th the United Mine Workers called a meeting to be held in the Michel Hall at 6.30 p.m. At the time the meeting should have been held about three hundred men gathered outside the Hall but none of them went, and the meeting and the result was that only the President and Secretary of the Local and two organizers from Calgary were present so that the meeting had to be called off.

"I mingled amongst the men when they were standing around the street and the common conversation was that if they forced them to sign the check-off they could not force them to attend or recognize the U. M. W. of A.[9]

"I also heard Joe Mangles say that the O. B. U. was not dead yet and that he was prepared to do all he could to knock the U. M. W. of A. and that he would show them what was later in the Fall".

12. The Russo-Polish War

Agitators throughout Canada are canvassing the possibility of a renewal of war over Poland and are opposing Canadian participation. An example is afforded by a report describing an incident in the Ogden shops in Calgary. The date is 9th August:-

"During the meal hour today, Stewart (an O.B.U. man) took advantage of half-an-hour to determine the feeling of the men with regard to the trouble with Russia and Poland. He asked the men what they would do if England were to declare war on Russia. Some of the men said they would not fight again, while others kept silent. Stewart was asked what he would so. 'Well', he said, 'I consider the ultimatum, if there was one sent, a huge joke. Surely England has more sense then to send an ultimatum to Russia, organized as they are, with practically all the working class in the whole country in sympathy with the Soviet Government.

"Stewart said he would go to prison first, but, in the meantime, will do all in his power to make the men see the right and best way for the workers".

13. International Bible Students

The International Bible Students held a convention in Edmonton on 30th July and 1st and 2nd August. The attendance was 150. J. B. Williams presided. It was claimed that the organization had increased rapidly in spite of government opposition. They were the usual confident predictions of the destruction of organized Government and society. Our report says:-

"J. B. Williams in all his speeches referred to Bolshevism, and said, it was only natural that it should come about out of the present existing conditions. The speakers spoke strongly against war, saying that neither them nor their children would ever fight, or take part in any war, no matter what the circumstance might be, they would refuse to fight, or take part in war. The national life of the State meant nothing to them, there is no such thing as patriotism or loyalty to the State in their religion. It would matter nothing to them who ruled this country Internationalism is to them as it is to the Socialist".[10]

14. Miscellaneous Notes

Transportation Unit No. 1. O. B. U. Calgary otherwise the O. B. U. of the Ogden shops have elected shop stewards, and are preparing to fight for recognition.

Christophers spoke at the C. N. R. shops in Edmonton on 2nd August. Some Internationals tried unsuccessfully to break up the meeting, the leader being one Findley. Christophers also held an open air meeting on Tuesday evening 3rd August. He laid stress on the non-Canadian character of the U. M. W. of A.

The "Park Committee" at Edmonton held an open-air meeting on Sunday 8th August, W. R. Ball of the United Farmers of Alberta speaking on the "High Cost of Living".

Joseph R. Knight addressed open-air meetings in Edmonton on 8th and 10th August. His speeches were of the usual sort. The second one was a failure, the attendance not exceeding 100, and few outside of the regular set of Socialists showing and interest.

A meeting of the S. P. of C. in Edmonton on 1st August heard some violent pro-Bolshevist and anti-governmental speeches by Maguire and a man named Findlay.

The Postal officials in July informed P. F. Lawson that if the Searchlight was not issued with greater regularity its mailing privileges would be withdrawn. This would extinguish the paper.

During his stay in the Edmonton district Dr. Sushko, the Ukrainian Bolshevist of Winnipeg, collected about $1,000, and borrowed $2,000 more from two men in Vegreville.

III. SASKATCHEWAN

15. The Bienfait Incident

A correspondent in the Bienfait district reports some circumstances which have a bearing upon recent events there. An [11] O. B. U. movement had been stirring before Christophers went there. Last autumn a man named Dan Diaczun, who had been active in the Winnipeg strike, obtained work at Taylorton, the chief seat of trouble in the Bienfait region, and set up as leader among the foreigners, an agitator for the O. B. U., and a troublemaker. Their intention had been to get organized and to strike and cripple the mines in the autumn; part of their anger is at having been anticipated.

Organization of the O. B. U. is proceeding actively, and an ugly temper prevails. Some at least of the foreigners, including some who do not belong to the O. B. U., except an O. B. U. transportation strike in the autumn which will tie up the country.

The company at Taylorton seems about to proceed with its plan of evicting the miners from houses which they built on its land.

16. An Excited Rhetorician

A new Ukrainian agitator has appeared in Saskatoon, named Peter Nestor, alias Nestoriuk; he is a student of the Peter Mehyla Institute. On 8th August he spoke at the Ukrainian National Home under the auspices of the Zapomhe Towarstwo, his address being a wild anti-Christian revolutionary harangue. Sample sentences are:-

> "The capitalists have forbidden us to read or educate ourselves, as by keeping us in darkness, they make it possible for themselves to own the luxuries, which we produce with our hands".
>
> "But who is this God they teach in the Churches, on which they have wasted millions of dollars? They tell you it is for your souls but what should you care for your souls, you have got to feed your bodies before you have a soul. But now the time has come when we know their tricks and we have men of ideals to tell us of scientific system in which we can all live in peace and plenty".

17. O. B. U. Notes

An L. W. I. U. delegate named Austin Stanley appeared in Regina on 5th August and stayed for a few days. He enrolled a few members in the O. B. U. Incidentally he is the possessor of a Ford car,[12] in which he tours the country.

At a meeting of the O. B. U. held in Regina on 6th August a resolution was submitted "denouncing the fetching of harvesters from Eastern Canada on the ground that "there is nearly sufficient farm help right at the present time here in this Province". It was modified to a protest that too many harvesters had been sent to Saskatchewan in the past.

A report has been received that the O. B. U. has been making headway at the Pas (whither Tether has recently moved) and now claims a membership of 250.

IV. MANITOBA

18. "Hands off Russia" Meeting

Organized by the Dominion Labour Party, a meeting was held in Winnipeg on Sunday 18th August to protest against any interference with the Soviet conquest of Poland. It was attended by about 1,500 people. It was entirely in the hands of the extremists, the Trades and Labour Council (i.e. Internationals) declining to take part. The speakers were:- Ald. A. A. Heaps, S. J. Farmer, Thomas Dunn, John Houston, Charles Stuart and C. A. Tanner, all active revolutionists. Four resolutions were passed:- (1) Protesting against any intervention by the Imperial or Canadian Government in Russia; (2) Congratulating British labour "on their deliberate opposition to attempted intervention in Russia", and endorsing the means employed to prevent it, (3) Assuring the people of Russia of the entire opposition of "the Winnipeg Workers" to "intervention of the Imperialist power"; (4) Congratulating Soviet Russia on its success" in meeting the aggression of the Poles and the intrigues of the Allies".

Some violent language was used. S. J. Farmer called Mr. Lloyd George "the most artistic liar Great Britain has ever had". Thomas Dunn exulted in the decay of patriotism; "we see aloofness written on the faces of the men in Winnipeg who once were patriotic".[13]

19. Sympathy with Soviet Russia

A report from Winnipeg states that there is great sympathy with Soviet Russia in all the labour parties and organizations outside the A. F. of L. Those include the O. B. U. the Dominion Labour Party, the Socialist Party, the Ex-Soldiers' and Sailors' Labour Party and the Social Democratic Party; the feeling is said to be strongest among the O. B. U. and the S. P. of C. and the feeling has grown with the difficulties between Great Britain and Russia. Kavanaugh has been active since his return to Winnipeg in stirring up feeling and in assuring his hearers that Labour in England will prevent any hostilities.

About 300 people attended an open-air meeting in Victoria Park, Winnipeg, held on Sunday 8th August, to hear Messrs. Kavanaugh, Gage and Heaps on their visit to England. The speeches did not differ from those already noted. It may be that their exposition of the revolutionary sentiment prevailing in Great Britain will have an effect.

20. The O. B. U. International Debate

Confidential reports upon the debate in Winnipeg on 6th August between the Internationals and the O. B. U. show that it was a even more tumultuous affair than was indicated by the press reports, and that the impression of most of our observers was that the O. B. U. champions had won. The O. B. U. had packed the meeting and in particular occupied the front of the hall and the galleries; Hoop, who read his speech from a typed MSS, could not be heard 20 or 30 feet away, so loud and constant were the interruptions; McCutcheon has a powerful voice, but only a few of his phrases could be heard. Yet a reading of the full reports of the several speeches conveys the impression that Hoop and McCutcheon had much the best of the argument, and one of our correspondents (who is well acquainted with labour conditions) expresses the opinion that a reading of the text of the speeches will cause a change of feeling.[14]

21. Clemency asked for Sava Zura

An attempt is being made to secure the release of Sava Zura, the Fort William revolutionist who in October 1919 was sentenced to two years' imprisonment for being in possession of prohibited literature. A copy of "The Workers' Defence Bulletin" has been issued, from which it appears that the defence of this man, of Ollikkala and of some other Finns has cost $5,542.28. The Fort William City Council has asked for clemency. The "Bulletin" described Mrs. Zura as being in very straitened circumstances; our private information contradicts this.

22. Miscellaneous Notes

The Winnipeg Defence Committee on 9th August once more discussed whether it should demobilize, or constitute itself a standing body. Gage and Kavanaugh, who were present, advocated the latter course.

Farnell, the recently paroled strike leader, is understood to have made the remark "I am through with the O. B. U. bunch for life".

It is reported that J. S. Woodsworth is about to quit Winnipeg for Vancouver.

A man signing himself "W. Gordon" recently addressed from Winnipeg a pro-Bolshevik letter to the Toronto Saturday Night. According to a report from Winnipeg, he is "a traveller from Washington" who at once has been commissioned by the Polish authorities to sell Polish bonds and to act as Polish agent, and works for the Russian Soviets. This seems an impossible combination; in addition, his letter to the paper is couched in such good, and almost scholarly English, as to make it unlikely that he has had any but an English education, and a good one at that.

V. ONTARIO

23. Quiet in Eastern Ontario

The confidential monthly report of the Officer Commanding [15] Eastern Ontario for July reveals a satisfactory state of affairs. No unusual activities by radical associations have been observed, and the labour situation in Ottawa is good.

24. J. R. Knight and Robertson on Future Policy

J. R. Knight's fortnightly report for the period ending 13th July deals largely with his conversations with Robertson, the Glasgow radical who has been active in Eastern Canada. An extract from this part of his report is:-

> "I had a few conversations with Robertson with respect to the Shop Stewards' movement, and learned much from him about the reactionary officialdom of the large organizations commonly referred to as the Triple Alliance. These three amalgamations approach as near the ideal Industrial Union as is possible, yet they exhibit precisely the same reactionary tendencies as the craft organizations. That is their form of organization has tended to develop what might be termed 'an industrial union patriotism' at the expense of the 'working class' organization........ Comrade Robertson was much interested in the constitution and structure of the O. B. U. and stated that it was the form of organization the shop stewards movement of Great Britain was trying to achieve. He thought that

> in this country with such an organization as the A. F. of L. it was foolish to attempt boring from within and more would be accomplished by definitely organizing in opposition to it. He considered too that, the workers of the American Continent had a great advantage over the workers of Great Britain in that their organizations could profit from the experience of the British. In Great Britain today it was a tremendous task to penetrate the habits of thought resulting from long association with organizations so deeply entrenched as those of the Triple Alliance, and it was not possible for the Shop Stewards' movement to launch a new organization, they must do all their work within the old. There is much that has been said re the affiliation of the Shop Stewards' movement with the I. W. W. but Robertson says it is all nonsense. I will deal with this whole matter in a separate report, but I hope before Robertson leaves that a corresponding arrangement between the two movements can be established.

It is not clear from the text whether the Shop Stewards are to be brought into touch with the I. W. W. or the O. B. U.; it may be conjectured that Knight means the latter.

Knight alludes very summarily to his operations during the fortnight in question.

25. Miscellaneous Notes

A "Hands off Russia" meeting was held in High Park, Toronto,[16] on 14th August; about 300 persons attended. The speakers were "Jimmy" Simpson, Max Armstrong, Berg and McDonald. Simpson predicted a Soviet Government in North America. All the speakers urged activity to elect M. P's.

Information continues to be received as to the movements of Wilson, the newcomer and possible revolutionary leader in Hamilton. Apparently he is not a salaried agitator, as he intends to obtain employment and to do his agitating in his spare time. He has in Detroit a supply of I. W. W. pamphlets, perhaps in foreign languages, though this point is not clear, which he wishes to fetch to and distribute in Hamilton.

It is understood that an O. B. U. local exists in Buffalo, Flatman being one of the active members. Flatman is an elusive person, difficult to meet; he moves about a good deal in the district between Buffalo and Hamilton, having visited the latter city lately. He is believed now to be employed in one of the plants in Buffalo, and so can hardly be a salaried agitator.

The O. B. U. lodge at Windsor now numbers 129 members.

K. K. Kakola, the organizer and speaker of the Finnish Socialist organization has been acting for some months as an O. B. U. delegate in the Sault Ste Marie district. He now has been appointed O. B. U. organizer, and apparently will begin work in British Columbia.

A Russian Jew named Morris Specktor has attracted attention as a

Communist in Toronto. He is a student at the University.

The Jewish Socialist Revolutionist Party in Toronto calls itself Polian Sion in Hebrew (or Yiddish). They are affiliated with the Third International. They propose to issue a paper to be called The [17] Sailt, or Times; it is to be printed in New York, and to be edited by New York Radicals.

VI. QUEBEC

26. A Soviet College in Montreal

At the O. B. U. meeting in Montreal on 12th August Miss Buller reported that the Labour College was "progressing splendidly". Its finances "were coming fast enough", and all it lacked was "the workers to take an interest in this institution". Concerning this organization our informant, who is an exceptionally competent observer, gives it as his opinion that this Labour College is supported by the Soviet Bureau of New York. "I am positive", he says "that the O. B. U. has nothing to do with it". He continues:-

> "The object in view, in establishing this College, is to get a group of workers, who already are in possession of a certain amount of knowledge along economic lines to get themselves posted in economics, so that some day, they will be able to take in their hands the distribution of food and clothing, take care of all industries under the Soviet form of Government, which in the mind of most of these radicals, it seems that a revolution is now inevitable and a Soviet Government will be established in Canada. If a revolution ever happens, these men or women, who are educated in this school will be in a position to enter any Manufacturers' offices and run that industry, whereas, if they lack that education, they will find themselves handicapped.
>
> "According to local radicals, it is evident that the world over is looking forward to a revolution and that they are preparing themselves".

27. A Protest Meeting

On 11th August a meeting was held in the Labour Temple, Montreal, under the auspices of the "Quebec Independent Socialist Party", to protest against any war with Russia. Several hundreds attended. F. W. Garrish presided, and speeches were delivered by L. J. N. Page, Miss B. Hall, U. Binette, Hyman Edelstein and Revd. J. B. Pike. Page sneered at the idea of aiding the Poles, Miss Hall attacked the [18] Poles and said that Capitalist Nations did not wish a Socialist nation to succeed, and Binette called Canada "the nation of sheep par excellence". The chairman read a telegram from the Russian Soviet Bureau in New York, regretting that one Ohsol, a "Soviet delegate who recently visited Canada" could not attend. A resolution of protest was passed.

28. A Seditious Parson

A person described as the "Revd. J. B. Pike" spoke at this meeting. Our informant thus reports his speech:-

"Pike stated 'There was no such thing in existence as a British Empire; an emperor is a Kaiser. That's what Emperor means in German and as King George is the Emperor of India, he is therefore a Kaiser'. Remember' Pike continued 'There will be wars as long as we let a 'Kaiser' remain in existence. An Emperor always wants to rule the world. I also want to point out to you that the King of England keeps a "Spy" in Canada at Ottawa in the person of the Governor General, we Canadians pay this "Spy" $50,000 a year plus $20,000 for his expenses. If the king wants to keep a spy in this country, let him pay him and his expenses out of his own pocket.

"I spoke here three years ago, against "Conscription" and it gives me great pleasure to speak to you tonight in support of the resolution which is now before you for consideration.

"We Canadians have not as yet a flag. The Union Jack is not a Canadian flag; personally I would like to see an "Internationale" flag' (at this remark H. Edelstein suggested a "red" flag, which remark was received with prolonged applause from the balance of the audience).

"There should be no King of the British Empire because it is made up of different nationalities and religions and the Canadian "Oath of Allegiance" is not to protect Canada but to protect King George of England".

"In Pronouncing the words 'King George' Pike's voice possessed a sneering manner, which he evidently used to emphasize his point of view.

29. Miscellaneous Notes

The General Workers' Unit O. B. U. Montreal on 12th August had $21.45 in the treasury, and owed more than $40.00. Only seven members attended the meeting on that date.

A lecturer on the staff of the Soviet Bureau of New York named Issac (?Isaac) McBride is touring the United States, and may be sent to Montreal to speak. The letter from New York in which this is mentioned [19] states that a number of lecturers are going about, preparing the populace for the revolution which it is hoped soon will come.

VII. THE MARITIME PROVINCES

30. Miscellaneous Notes

A report dated 11th August states that the Halifax Shipyard strike is "officially settled" on the company's terms. The Plumbers, pipe-fitters and coppersmiths on 9th August voted to abandon the strike, and returned to work on the 11th. There is some reason to believe that the Labourers' Unit is about broken up, and that the Marine Trades Federation is likely to dissolve. The unions concerned in the shipyards lost two fifths of their strength, and the cause of unionism in Halifax seems to have suffered a severe reverse.

J. B. McLachlan seems to have dropped his inclination to join the O. B. U. He is however, endeavouring to stir up a general strike of miners in Nova Scotia. The Royal Commission still is sitting; he has stated that if it grants the miners all they have been asking new demands will be made, to bring the wages up to the level which prevails in the United States and in Western Canada.

ROYAL CANADIAN MOUNTED POLICE HEADQUARTERS

Ottawa, 26th August, 1920.

SECRET

NO. 38

NOTES OF THE WORK OF THE C. I. B. DIVISION FOR THE WEEK ENDING 26TH AUGUST

Contents

End of the Shipyard strike in Halifax.
Supposed O. B. U. Defence Circulars.

1. CHARACTERISTICS OF THE PERIOD

The principal thing to note this week is the steady recurrence of warnings of a coal strike in Alberta in the autumn. We have had many predictions of trouble, and nothing has occurred to discredit these [2] predictions.

The O. B. U. have won their most noteworthy success for some time in the decision of the Winnipeg Street Railway union to turn over to them. This will give them a numerical superiority in Winnipeg. The Internationals will form a Street Railway Union of their own, but the event remains a gain for the union.

Preparations are beginning to be made for the O. B. U. convention at Port Arthur in September.

Montreal continues to be the part of the Dominion upon which the Soviet organization in New York exercises direct influence. One of its organizers, a man named McBride, is to come to Montreal to speak, and the man who is organizing the affair, and arranging for co-operation among the radical bodies, is the O. B. U. organizer, Binette, who draws his salary from Vancouver and so is under Winch's control.

I. BRITISH COLUMBIA

2. Loggers inclining to sabotage

An informant reports a change of policy among the L. W. I. U. to (1) more sabotage; (2) fewer strikes; (3) more energetic support of such strikes as are called. After describing a bad case of wilful damage to machinery done by an I. W. W. in a logging establishment known as the Dempsey Camp, he continues:-

> "The idea of sabotage is gaining favour among the loggers. Strikes have been proven almost useless and their system of dealing with men who refuse to join the union, or with employers who refuse to meet their demands, seems to lean strongly with the curtailment of production and sabotage. Operative believes that in future there will be less strikes than there have been in the past, and that where it is absolutely necessary to pull a strike, more support will be given to see it through."

3. O. B. U. Notes

The L. W. I. U. headquarters financial statement for July shows that the receipts were $5,667.94 and the expenditures $5,559.95. The cash on hand on 31st July was $435.18. Among the interesting outlays were the sum of $700 given to the British Columbia Federationist and $300 for organization in the East.

The O. B. U. strike at the Blue Bell Mine, Riondel, continues but the company has about 20 men working and is actually producing more than when the O. B. U. were installed.

At a convention held in San Francisco some time ago a proposal to change the name of the O. B. U. to "Progressive Workers of the Pacific" was vetoed.

4. British Columbia Reports

Ocean Falls, 7th August:-

"Although one can hear considerable radical talk in the labour circles of this district, there is also outspoken optimistic opposition to this".

Alert Bay, 14th August:-

"Logging is proceeding very satisfactorily and all camp superintendents spoken to report improving labour conditions; agitators are becoming less and less and their influence is fast decreasing, no trouble reported. "Shortage of labour reported at the canneries".

Chakawana (Coastal Patrol) Detachment, 6th August:-

"Labour conditions along the Coast patrolled by the Chakawana are very quiet at present, no trouble being reported. The supply of labour is good".

Hazelton, 7th August:-

"No trouble or complaints have been heard of or reported during the past week. Work still continues in the railroad construction.

Grand Forks, 7th August:-

"The majority of the mills and mines in this district have been visited during the two weeks under report and everything is reported quiet. Labour conditions are good at present and from appearances there is no unrest".

Nelson, 7th August:-

"There is no change in the Slocan strike situation during the week. Labour conditions remain quiet, very few men applying for work. Some have been taken to fight forest fires".

Merritt, 14th August:-

"There is little change in the labour situation locally. The mill continues to work full shifts; the mines are working a little more steadily and work has not been resumed at full strength as yet, in the woods".[4]

5. Miscellaneous Notes

Tomashewshy's paper "Pravda i Wola" (Truth and Freedom) after a lapse of several weeks has revived sufficiently to issue two numbers, No. 10 on 5th August and No. 11 on 19th August. John Boychuk, who with Popowich urged the Vancouver Ukrainians to abandon the local paper in favour of the Ukrainian Labour News, has left for Edmonton (whether permanently or not we do not know yet) and the Ukrainians are returning to Tomashewsky's leadership.

J. Smith addressed the Sunday Socialist meeting in Vancouver on 15th August; the attendance was small, Smith's speech was poor, and little interest was shown. The collection was $47.20.

The Socialist Party of Canada are holding open air meetings in Vancouver on four evenings in the week. They now have two "pitches".

II. ALBERTA

6. The Coal Mines

A report dated Blairmore, 14th August, after noting that the situation in the Crow's Nest Pass for the moment is quiet and orderly, adds:-

> "From conversations gathered on the street and other places, there is considerable indication of a big strike this fall, and October is the month spoken of when this proposed strike will occur".

At the same place the recording secretary of the local lodge of the U. M. W. of A. informed us, on 12th August, that out of the 370 men working at the Greenhill mine nine tenths were O. B. U.; and that although they had signed the U. M. W. of A. check-off, and so were contributing to that body, they still were paying their O. B. U. dues to the local secretary, Rod. McDonald.

The principal agitators in the Pass on that date were:-

P. M. Christophers, General Organizer, O. B. U. [5] Wm. Patterson, District Organizer, O. B. U.

Rod. McDonald, Secretary, Blairmore Local O. B. U.

Isaac Ray, not known to hold office.

Joe Legacy, not known to hold office.

Legacy is a leader among the Belgians in the district and is said to have full control over them. A Frenchman married to a Belgian woman, he is said to speak Belgian, which presumably means Flemish.

The new U. M. W. A. lodge at Fernie held a meeting on 15th August to elect officers. All chosen are O. B. U. sympathizers; they are not the most rabid ones, but none the less are on that side. The meeting was turbulent. The result of the compulsory joining of the U. M. W. of A. has been to put the O. B. U. in control of that lodge.

The dispute over timbering (noticed in an earlier Summary) continues to cause apprehension of a strike. This is due to the temper of the men, not to the intrinsic importance of the issue.

The Coalhurst strike has ended, a compromise having been effected, and the mines are in full swing again. About 70 per cent of the miners have returned to work; the rest are working at the harvest and are expected to return by 1st September.

The coal miners at Commerce, which is near Coalhurst and in the Lethbridge region, signed the U. M. W. A. check-off on 14th August. On 18th August Henry Beard, the O. B. U. organizer, appeared at the camp and induced the men to demand the revocation of the check-off, coupled with the retention of the additional pay which goes with it. On 19th the men struck, as the mine management refused to agree. About 70 per cent of the men were reluctant to strike.

Beard has considerable powers as a trouble-maker.

A report on the activities at Drumheller of George Palmer who is living there as an O. B. U. organizer, represents him as quiet and [6] exerting little influence.

7. O. B. U. Sympathy with Train Murderers

In connection with the shooting of Corporal Usher and Constable Bailey which followed the train robbery in the Crow's Nest Pass, an agent who is in a particularly good position to learn the real opinions of the O. B. U. was instructed to report their comments on the crimes. Following is his report:-

"From conversations I have had with the members of the O. B. U. I find that their sympathy without an exception lies with the men who held up the train in the Crow's Nest Pass. When the news came through with regards to the shooting and killing of Cpl. Usher and Const. Bailey I was in Dworkin's store on 8th Ave., there being present, Ben Dworkin, Wm. Lewin and another man by the name of Dworkin. Ben Dworkin passed the remark, that it was one less for us to get, (meaning the O. B. U.). The other man Dworkin, was ridiculing the fact that there was 104 Mounted Police trying to get two men and they could not do it, and was hoping that the men got away.

"When Christophers, Beard and Lawson got back from Drumheller Christophers was expressing his opinion of the Mounted Police in not too weak language and was wanting to bet that the bandits would make a clear getaway, and he made the boast that 10,000 Mounted Police could not catch him if he was in the position the bandits were in.

"Lawson did not have very much to say, only that he hoped the men would get clear".

"While out with Beard he expressed the fear that O. B. U. cards would be found on these men, and that the Government would use that to fight the O. B. U. with".

8. Miscellaneous Notes

Another issue of the Searchlight has been published, under date of 6th August.

Ald. East spoke at the open air meeting in the East End Park in Edmonton on Sunday 15th August, his subject being "Reconstruction", and the principal point of his address being the need for immediate nationalization of the banking system. W. Coombs, one of Mr. Ritchie's strong supporters, presided.

III. SASKATCHEWAN

9. The L.W.I.U. in Northern Saskatchewan

A report dated Prince Albert, 16th August, is to the effect that the L. W. I. U. intend to make a last effort to organize Northern [7] Saskatchewan. George Tether, who now is at The Pas, is to be replaced before long; he is an inefficient man, and a good organizer is to succeed him. Talking to the person furnishing the report, Tether said that since moving from Prince Albert to The Pas he had been much encouraged. The interview with Tether proceeds thus:-

> "The organization has spent, over and above all receipts some $5,000.00 in their attempts to organize the Prince Albert District, and the Central Executive Committee had contemplated giving it up, but had finally decided to make one more attempt and to employ every means within their power to make it a success. Their present plans call for an expenditure fully as large as the total amount already spent in the District, or more if necessary. One part of this plan, which is now in operation, is to enroll as many members as possible in the camps adjacent to The Pas and to meet all new men coming into the District and enroll them before they leave for whatever camp they may be going to. They figure that the majority of the men now employed in the mining camps are only waiting for the logging camps to open when they will change over. The members now being enrolled in the smaller lumber mills in the District will, when the camps open, be instructed to secure work in the camps of the Pas Lumber Company; as they already have over three hundred active members in the Pas District, exclusive of some seventy members now working in the Pas Lumber Company's Mill, they will have a rather large number of members to start with in the camps when they open. If the number of members obtained between now and the time the camps open is not considered sufficient for their purpose, their present plans call for the importation of a large number of selected L.W.I.U. members from British Columbia at the expense of the organization they are prepared to bring in 500 of more if necessary.
>
> "They will also have delegates at Regina, Saskatoon and Hudson Bay Junction to meet all trains when the loggers start travelling for the various camps; to head all members of the L.W.I.U. into the Pas District. Tether figures that this plan can not be beaten and that the tying up of the camps is an assured fact he has no hopes of being able to tie up the planing mill this winter but states that in the spring the 'home guards' now employed in this mill will either have to join the L.W.I.U. or be discharged by the company as the hours, wages, rules, etc. of the L.W.I.U. will by that time be in full effect and the alternative will be a general strike".

The Officer Commanding Northern Saskatchewan in commenting upon this report takes a cool view of these hopes of organizing the district. If the Pas Lumber Company continues its policy of fighting the O. B. U., it will be difficult for that organization to get a [8] foothold in its works.

As for importance of L.W.I.U.'s from British Columbia, the local supply of labour is sufficient and these missionaries of mischief would find it difficult to get employment.

10. Loss of Interest in the Christophers Case

Following are extracts from weekly surveys by an agent of the situation in Regina:-

"Nothing doing locally but the Christophers case has caused some talk, though not the stir that might be looked for in O. B. U. circles. Work has been plentiful lately meetings are poorly attended and the O. B. U. seems generally disorganized for the present".

Week ending 14th August:-

"Little interest is taken by O. B. U. men in the Christopher kidnapping case. Men with radical leanings seem more interested in knowing if the R.C.M.P. is involved than any other phase. What little interest may have been roused subsided when it became more apparent that they were not. I understand that all attempts to connect the Force with the case have fallen down. I talked to Rev. Ranns, he told me that he was convinced that no polic officer R. C. M. P. was mixed up in it. He promised to bring me a letter from Rev. Woodsworth, carrying an extract from Christophers' letter to Woodsworth. He has failed to produce it".

In forwarding these the Officer Commanding Southern Saskatchewan observes:-

"Labour men have lost all interest in the disappearance of Christopher, now that they know the Mounted Police were not implicated. The Rev. Ranns has also lost interest in the matter. The main object of the investigation was to implicate the Mounted Police and this has failed, they have only implicated the Provincial Police instead".

At Bienfait according to a report dated 14th August the mines were all working except the Western Dominion Mine at Taylorton; preparations were on foot for the engagement of new men and for production on a large scale. The foreigners who had joined the O. B. U. were negotiating to come back, but had not acceded to the company's condition, that they abandon the O. B. U. The company was understood to be preparing to evict them from the houses they had built on its land.[9] On 13th August the Sheriff served notice on the O. B. U. miners at Bienfait, preparatory to eviction. Some of the foreign-born O. B. U. men, notably one Diaczun, are disposed to be violent.

11. Miscellaneous Notes

About 16 shop labourers of the C. P. R. at Moose Jaw struck on 12th August for increased pay, and the 8-hour day. They have been getting 40 cents a hour. The men are foreigners. The strike was promoted by William McAllister, the local O. B. U. leader, who is himself a C. P. R. employe.

The men have been discharged and the company probably will have no difficulty in replacing them. McAllister probably will be dismissed.

The Regina Unit of the O. B. U. is too hard up to send a delegate to the O. B. U. convention at Port Arthur.

According to an I. W. W. named John Neddlec, at present in Regina, a number of French Radicals live at or near Gravelbourg. Some of them worked in lumber camps in British Columbia last winter and imbibed Socialistic opinions there.

The local body of the Grand Army of United Veterans in Moose Jaw is very weak; it numbers only about 15 and is embarrassed to meet debts of about $20.00.

The Regina branch of the Grand Army of United Veterans met on 11th August. Only 22 members attended, and proceedings showed that the treasury is low.

IV. MANITOBA

12. The O. B. U. and the I. W. W.

The meeting of the Central Labour Council, O.B.U. in Winnipeg on 17th August was attended by about 100 delegates.[10] An interesting discussion took place about the relations between the O. B. U. and the I. W. W. It arose over a complaint from Edmonton that an O. B. U. member there named "Berge" (? Carl Berg) had been attacking Joe Knight, saying that Knight was preaching the I. W. W. form of organization under cover of the letters "O. B. U."; "Berge" apparently himself was an I. W. W. This caused a discussion as to whether the organization should approve or hold aloof from the I. W. W., a faction favouring the former course. Some speeches are thus reported, the subject before the meeting being a resolution to have no relations with the I. W. W. and to accept no I. W. W. members in the O. B. U.:-

> "W. Hammond pointed out that no matter who they were, the O. B. U. organization needed them and needed them bad. He claimed they could be educated after having been signed up regarding the O. B. U. constitutions; and it was not yet decided nor would it be, until after the coming convention of the O. B. U. in Port Arthur in September, whether or not the I. W. W. was going to be a part of the O. B. U. constitution. This subject, he declared, would be thrashed out at the convention.
>
> "P. Anderson of the Lumber Workers' Unit, O. B. U. said although he was not an I. W. W. yet, he was not altogether opposed to the organization, as there were some good points in it, and he thought that the motion was very foolish and should not be put through, because if it were passed, they would very likely have to withdraw their motion entirely after the O. B. U. convention at Port Arthur, as he understood that this subject regarding I. W. W. ism in the O. B. U. was going to be the centre of debate.

"J. Houston said, as for himself, he thought a great number of the working class had been wrongly persuaded against the I. W. W. He stated there was only one thing wrong with that organization, and that was, it had thrown away one of its arms of gaining power, and was only using the other as its methods, and that was why it had not met with the favour which the O. B. U. had both arms in its constitutions, but he could see no reason why a man who had been or was an I. W. W. could not belong or be recognized by the O. B. U. as they were only the common labourers when those fearful letters, I. W. W. were taken away, and it should be possible to remove the words after they had got him schooled a little in the O. B. U.

"C. W. Foster of the Transcona Unit also was of the opinion that it did not matter who or what the men were they were all workers, as far as he was concerned, he said.[11] "Comrade Clancey, although against any I. W. W. methods being adopted in the O. B. U. was not against the O. B. U. taking them into the organization, as he stated he thought it would be a very foolish move to keep out any member of the working class regardless of what he was.

The resolution ultimately was dropped.

Another important matter was the receipt from the "Confederated Press" of a request for pecuniary assistance "to handle certain Soviet Russian news correspondence". J. Houston, editor of the O. B. U. Bulletin is thus reported:-

"He said, it was only one chance they had in a lifetime to support this cause, and it meant that steady news of some ten or eleven pages would be furnished direct from Russia, on the Soviet conditions. This would be called out and printed in the Bulletin and as much as possible in the Presses of the city. It was news which the Labour movement in general needed, he said, and he felt it was the duty of this delegation to donate as much as possible".

A grant of $100 was made.

13. Street Railwaymen go O. B. U.

The Street Railway Union in Winnipeg has decided to turn over to the O. B. U., the vote standing 850 to 120. Our information is that this is due to dissatisfaction with the award of the Provincial Board of Arbitration in the recent arbitration as to wages.

This will give the O. B. U. a majority of about 2,000 over the International in the city of Winnipeg.

The O. B. U. in Winnipeg are much pleased at this accession, no attempt will be made to amalgamate this unit with the Running Trades unit. Our report adds:-

"The Street Railway Unit, O. B. U. will be one of the strongest and most important units in the organization as far as the city is concerned, and is the starting point from which other cities will find their Street Railways also going O. B. U. in the near future".

A later report states that, while the Street Railwaymen's union voted by a large majority to turn O. B. U. only about half the men voted. An International organizer will soon be on the ground organizing an International local. This will be vigorously prosecuted.[12]

14. Other O. B. U. Notes

The Running Trades Unit O. B. U. Winnipeg, which has been dormant since June 1919, has been reorganized with a membership of about 150. The moving spirit is a man named Graham, who is secretary. He is displaying a good deal of organizing ability.

Two men named Elliott and Vancluk who belong to the Running Trades Unit O. B. U. in Winnipeg are members of the International body, the latter being an organizer. They intend to remain in the International in order to betray it.

15. The Imprisoned Strike Leaders

At a meeting of the Winnipeg Trades and Labour Council held on 16th August the Secretary, Ald. E. Robinson, reported on conferences which had been had with the convicts on the subject of clemency.

1. Russell was prepared to ask the government for his release on parole, ready to sign the usual requirements of such a parole, and had no objection to his fellow-convicts being told of his attitude.

2. Pritchard and Johns refused to discuss the subject at all with the representatives of the Internationals, saying that they would leave it to the Defence Committee.

3. Bray refused to talk with them at all. He will get his release in September.

4. Ivens and Queen decided to wait till they heard what were the terms of the parole enacted from Russell.

Ivens is ill, is trouble being described as an "internal rupture".

V. ONTARIO

16. Dworkin's Return

Early in the year a Polish Jew named Henry Dworkin who is in business in Toronto went to Poland on a mission more or less connected with Jewish relief. He has returned, and on 15th August he spoke at Welland, giving an account of his experiences. He had been in Poland, [13] Russia, the Ukraine, Lithuania, and Germany, as well as in England. His speech was strongly anti-Polish, his line being to represent the Poles as victimized by capitalists at the bidding of France and England. He said that soon Poland "will face the truth of the Russian Soviet Government", that Germany might go Bolshevik, and that "the Soviet Government would have control of all Europe soon and then make a true Government the best one in Europe". He said that he himself was not a Bolshevist.

17. O. B. U. Notes

The O. B. U. propaganda meeting on Yonge Street, Toronto, on Saturday evening, 14th August, was attended by 150 people.

The O. B. U. in Toronto have gained only 8 new members in some weeks. Many of their members are going over to the I. L. P. and the Communist Party.

A returned soldier named Rice, a man of little ability either as speaker or organizer, is trying to form in Toronto a soldier organization with radical tendencies. While the regular radicals O. B. U. and Socialists helped and a meeting was held on 15th August, the prospects are poor.

An O. B. U. organizer at Toronto signed up a number of foreigners in the harvester excursions.

A survey of the Gowganda district shows that it is pretty solidly organized by the O. B. U., but contains no dangerously clever agitators at present. The organization does not seem to feel itself very strong as yet, but probably is growing.

VI. QUEBEC

18. O. B. U. and Soviet Russia

Binette, the O. B. U. organizer in Montreal is organizing a committee of five to make arrangements for the visit of Issac McBride to [14] Montreal in October. McBride is representative of the Soviet organization in New York and his purpose is to advocate the establishment of the Soviet system in Canada, and to collect money for medical relief for Russia. The committee is to comprise one member each of the following bodies:-

Metal Trades O. B. U. Unit.
Labour College of Quebec.
Independent Socialist Party.
French Socialist Communist Party.
General Workers O. B. U. Unit of Montreal,
represented by U. Binette.

This is interesting as a case of direct and formal co-operation with the Soviet organization. Binette is a salaried organizer, paid by the head office at Vancouver.

VII. Maritime Provinces

19. Miscellaneous Notes

An informant who is well acquainted with conditions in the coal mining district of Cape Breton furnishes a rather pessimistic forecast of events there. he apprehends trouble soon, but remarks that the men are divided; for instance, the union officials have authority to call a strike without consulting the rank and file, but there is a possibility that the men may rebel and demand a referendum. If a strike comes, he thinks that it will mean the breaking up of the United Mine Workers of America, and that that will be followed by a slow growth of the One Big Union. "The men are desperate and easily led", he says.

One remark is that the Dominion Coal Company have brought in a number of experienced English and Belgian miners, and that these men are very discontented with conditions in Nova Scotia.

The strike at No. 24 Colliery Glace Bay, which began on 14th August, ended on 16th August. It was over working conditions.

Internationals officials are understood to be taking notice of [15] McLachlan's activities on behalf of the O. B. U.

The Shipyards strike in Halifax lasted for 71 days before ending in defeat. The labour leaders now are unpopular with the rank and file, and there may be defections.

Circulars have been sent to the several railway organizations east of Montreal soliciting contributions to a defence fund. This was suspected to be an O. B. U. affair, and in every case aid was refused.

APPENDIX

The weekly Secret Reports issued by the Directorate of Intelligence, Home Office, (London) for some time have been very gloomy. That for 12th August, which came to hand this week, is of an especially anxious nature. Following are extracts from or condensations of certain portions of it.

War with Russia

1. "The possibility of a war with Russia caused an amazing outburst of feeling. The propaganda was skillfully engineered by the Daily Herald, and the great mass of the people had all sorts of fantastic beliefs: they thought that men would be recalled to the Colours and that one or two weal Divisions would be sent out to be annihilated by the Red Army and so forth. The result has been to rehabilitate the moderate Labour leaders with their extreme supporters and to weld the whole temporarily into one body. The Daily Herald has achieved an importance which it has never had since the Railway Strike".

"Having the advantage of close association with Krassin's mission and the opportunity of increasing its funds from Russia by faithful service to the Soviet Government, the Daily Herald has been able by skilful perversion and suppression of the truth to work even the moderate Trade Union people into a surprising state of excitement".

"It is a new departure for the Labour Party to force the hand of the Government in a matter of foreign policy, and it is a precedent which will not easily be forgotten".

"There were remarkable demonstrations against war in practically every part of the country".

"Some fifty reports received on this subject may be summarized in the words of my Lancashire correspondents, who write: 'Never have we known such excitement and antagonism to be aroused against any project as had been aroused amongst the workers by the possibility of war with

Russia'."[2] "Most unfortunately in this instance the Right and Left Wings of Labour have joined forces".

COAL

2. Concerning the threatened coal strike, the Report says that at the date of compilation the two third majority necessary for a strike seemed likely to be obtained; but that a strike could scarcely materialize in less than four weeks.

The Miners were conducting an agitation against the accumulation of stocks of coal.

Miners in Fife have decided to issue promissory notes in small denominations, as a sort of strike currency. Local shopkeepers are said to have agreed to accept them.

The Engineering Industry

3. A strike in the near future is considered a certainty in Lancashire.

The engineering, foundry and shipbuilding trades have decided to recommend the termination of the agreement of 1917, whereby wages were reviewed every four months by the Industrial Court. This is regarded as a preliminary to more active measures.

The men are becoming very difficult to restrain.

In Coventry unemployment is growing and the engineers are much perturbed. One firm is rumoured to be on the verge of bankruptcy.

Labour and the Co-Operative Movement

4. Negotiations are on foot between the Co-operative societies and the trade unions with a view to the former providing food supplies for trade unionists in the event of a revolution.

The Co-Operative Societies are averse from paying income tax, and a refusal to pay is not impossible.[3] The Financial Propaganda Department of the Co-Operative Wholesale Society is trying to get more capital. Its spokesman says:- "Our object is to obtain capital, and use it in the movement as a means of destroying capitalism".

The Housing Question

5. Agitation on this subject is active. In Scotland a 24 hours strike on 23rd August was mooted by two large unions, miners and iron and steel workers. In Wales miners and co-operatives opposed the payment of increased rent. These are but examples.

Meanwhile the Building Trades object to "dilution". The Walthamstow branch of the Operatice Bricklayers Society has passed a strong resolution against the training of ex-Service men.

The Communists

6. Nine British delegates are believed to have been present at the recent meeting in Moscow. "It was there assumed that civil war for revolutionary ends is inevitable and the principle laid down that the Communist Party

(in England or elsewhere) 'must be built on the principle of strict centralization, and, in the event of civil war, must introduce iron military discipline into its ranks'".

"The danger of the British Communist Party, in the present time of grave unrest, lies not in the numerical strength which is small, but in its avowed intention 'to fan the already existing flames of discontent, to foment revolt and finally to bring about revolutionary action. To every struggle of the masses it will seek to give a revolutionary purpose and meaning'. The members of the party are, for the most part, shop stewards and are already alive to the possibilities of causing trouble in the Navy and the Army".[4] "A disquieting feature of the present state of unrest is the fact that the call for troops in Ireland has left England and Scotland bare of serviceable troops in the event of large disturbances, for it may be a little doubtful whether the ordinary Irish battalions are to be depended on for aid to the civil power. This, however, does not yet appear to be known to the extremists, and it is pretty certain that entire reliance can be placed upon the Brigade of Guards, and, it is believed, upon the Police Force".

Irish Affiars

7. The Mannix excitement was described as subsiding.

Sinn Feiners at a meeting in England assaulted a man who displayed the Union Jack. In the subsequent disturbance colliers who were present aided the police.

A branch of the Irish Self-Determination League has been formed in Rochdale.

A conference of all the Sinn Fein branches in England and Scotland was called for 23rd August at Tyneside. The call said that the step had been taken in view of the rapidly approaching Irish crisis.

Sinn Fein and the Communists are understood to be acting together.

"There is abundant evidence that the Sinn Fein leaders are very uneasy. In the various outrages their losses appear to have been heavier than we know; the quarrel between de Valera and the Clan-na-Gael has been disturbing and the Bolshevik tinge which is growing among their followers has alarmed them; and now comes the publication of the minutes of the Sinn Fein Cabinet, showing that money was to be spent by de Valera in corruption during the Presidential election".

"The number of putrages reported (in Ireland) is approximately 243 as against 287 last week. Of these only 7 were due to agrarian motives. 30 were serious offences attributable to the disordered state [5] of the country, and 206 were directy due to Sinn Fein".

"The railway trouble is causing Sinn Fein some anxiety. The number of men dismissed is very considerable and they are grumbling.

"Elements of disruption are said to be at work among Sinn Feiners; there is discontent with de Valera, and Arthur Griffiths is believed to be under suspicion."

ROYAL CANADIAN MOUNTED POLICE HEADQUARTERS

Ottawa, 2nd September, 1920.

SECRET

NO. 39

NOTES OF THE WORK OF THE C. I. B. DIVISION FOR THE WEEK ENDING 2ND SEPTEMBER

Table of Contents

The Educational Press Association.
"W. Gordon" denounced.
" 32. The Coal Fields.
Quiet in Nova Scotia.
J. J. McNeil's views.[3]

1. Characteristics of the Period

Three developments claim attention.

First, the plot to call a strike in the coal-mines of the Crow's Nest Pass seems to be thickening. A secret meeting was held at Hillcrest on 22nd August, and we understand that it was resolved to strike on a big scale on 7th October, or as soon as severe weather sets in. A district convention of the O. B. U. is to meet in Calgary on 10th September, and Edward Browne, the secretary of the district, has hinted that it would take steps to bring on a trial of strength.

Secondly, the O. B. U. convention at Port Arthur promises to be the scene of a fight which conceivably may split the organization. Caused partly by personal rivalries, three parties have appeared, championing a "Geographical", an "Industrial" and a "Class" type of organization. As information concerning this situation comes from several Provinces, it is epitomized in the second paragraph.

Thirdly, a survey of the foreign-born population in Toronto, Hamilton and the Niagara Peninsula confirms all we have heard as to its strongly revolutionary tendencies, and adds two disturbing facts. One is that the riot at Thorold has had a bad moral effect upon the foreigners, who have concluded, first, that it would be easy to upset the Government by mob action, and secondly, that the English-speaking working people are ready to revolt. The other is that the recent events in Great Britain, such as the "Hands off Russia" agitation and the threat of a general strike by the Triple Alliance, are encouraging the seditious-minded.

In this connection it may be noted that in Montreal two agitators, Michael Buhay and F. W. Gerrish have called for the formation of a "Committee of Action" or "Vigilance Committee" in emulation of the Committee of Action formed in England.[4]

The promptitude with which revolutionary actions in England provoke imitation here is becoming noticeable. For some time it has been observed that the revolutionary oress in Canada is coming to depend more and more upon the English, and less upon the American revolutionary press. This week a new development has been noted: a disposition to import revolutionary papers, pamphlets, etc. from Paris to circulate in Montreal. French Canadians are remarkably fond of reading good French, the principal qualification for a journalist in Quebec being the possession of a pure and elegant French style rather than activity in the collection of news; it may be surmised that the local radicals have felt their inferiority in this and have had recourse to France with this in mind.

2. The Internal Troubles of the O. B. U.

Most of our information on this point comes from Eastern Canada, where there have been some interesting avowals.

The O. B. U. convention is to take place on 20th September, and apparently at Port Arthur; Winch, as part of the game which he is playing, is agitating to have the place changed to Vancouver, on the plea of economy, but the reception of this proposal so far has been adverse. The gathering is to be small, comprising only 35 delegates and at Montreal at all events it has been resolved to give the delegate a free hand; these facts accord ill with the claim that the body is ruled entirely from below.

Personal quarrels seem to have arisen. Midgley and Winch are at daggers drawn; Joe Naylor, a member of the Executive, is siding with Midgley; Carl Berg has laid formal charges against J. R. Knight. The situation is mixed, for Berg recently gave great help to Winch at the loggers' convention and Knight and Winch to some extent seem allies.[5]

However, Knight is promoting a proposal to move the headquarters from Vancouver to Winnipeg, to secure more attention to the East, which will be distasteful to Winch. The dispute between Winch and Midgley is due to the former trying to extend the scope of his unit so as to edge the Central office out of important financial resources. Of the several parties to these rivalries, Knight seems the weakest and he apprehended that he might be ejected from office.

Somewhat masking these personal difficulties is a discussion which hitherto has seemed rather academic as to the form of the organization. Midgley champions the Geographical type, which would help him by cutting Winch from the outlying branches of the L. W. I. U. Winch is for the industrial system, and the coal miners are said, to favour it. Knight believes in the Class idea, the point of which is not so clear as that of the others. Winnipeg seems to be the centre of this theory.

It is to be noted that the O. B. U. cause is said to be looking up somewhat in Toronto.

I. BRITISH COLUMBIA

3. Friction among the Leaders

The L. W. I. U. are circularizing O. B. U. branches urging the holding of the approaching convention in Vancouver. The Regina unit voted in favour of Port Arthur.

Renewed reports reach us of the jealousy between Winch and Midgley. At present Winch is agitating to have the place of the approaching convention changed to Vancouver; as the loggers will have the majority of the delegates this would save expenses. The proposal is opposed by Midgley and Naylor and some others. A correspondent writes:-

"Naylor is a Midgley man and neither he nor Midgley have any time just now for Winch, whom they are apparently trying to get out of office.

Carl Berg has made formal charges against J. R. Knight, and [6]

Midgley has been asked to investigate. The charges are

(1)That 3,000 members of the loggers in the East had broken from the O. B. U.

(2)That J. R. Knight refused to speak for the O. B. U. at Cobalt, and, spoke in preference for the Socialist Party of Canada.

A reference to this, quarrel appeared in last week's issue of this summary, Berg's name, however, was not spelled correctly, and this somewhat obscured the fact.

4. Policy of the L. W. I. U.

Alexander, the L. W. I. U. organizer among the mill-workers, has been having a discouraging time. In conversation he recently said he was going to cease his activity in the Westminster district to give the impression that the local is a dead issue. He thought that when the millowners were convinced there was nothing doing over there they would cut wages, which would be certain to arouse the workers and revive interest in the union. He said that it would only be cut in wages that the workers in the sawmills could be made to realize that the O. B. U. was of any benefit to them.

More is being heard of the sabotage policy of the L. W. I. U. J. M. Clarke and Richard Higgins recently have been active in urging "job action" in preferred to strikes, and a specific case occurred recently in which some strikers accepted the company's offer and returned to work, imbubed with a spirit of revenge and bent upon following this policy.

On 18th August a strike occurred at Camp No. 17 of the Pacific Mills Company, near Ocean Falls. It was called by the O. B. U. because a delegate named Webster had been dismissed. The men were not unanimous, and it ended in about a day.

At the first meeting the men voted for the strike by a small majority soon after they held a second meeting at which they decided that the company was in the right, and ordered five trouble-makers,[7] including two O. B. U. delegates, out of camp. Some tore up their O. B. U. cards. Although the camp as a whole returned to work, 40 men left.

5. British Columbia Detachment Reports

Prince Rupert, 24th July:-

"District quiet and orderly".

Stewart, 7th August:-

"There has been no labour trouble reported during the week, in fact labour has been very quiet for the past two months. Up to date the only labour unions represented in this district is the O. B. U. and its affiliations".

Esquimalt, 14th August:-

"Labour conditions favourable".

Nanaimo, 14th August:-

"Everything is quiet and orderly in this district. All mines lumber and logging camps are working to full capacity and there is plenty of work to be had in the district".

Port Alberni, 14th August:-

"Mills and camps are working steadily with no signs of trouble"

Kamloops, 21st August:-

"Labour situation quiet".

Trail, 14th August:-

"Both mines at Trail and Rossland are working full time and thin and things moving smoothly. Strike still on at Lindsay Bros. Lumber Camp Meadows, otherwise things in general quiet.

Grand Forks, 14th August:-

"The farmers in the district report rain is needed very badly. The majority of the mines and mills in the district were visited by the men while on patrol, the managers of same reporting everything quiet. Labour conditions are good in the district and at present there are no indications of unrest".

In a number of these reports bad bush fires are mentioned. Near Nanaimo a sawmill and its logs etc. had been destroyed; near Kamloops a sawmill and some homesteaders' cabins had been burned, and one man burned to death and several injured.

The Chakawana in a recent patrol visited Stewart, Anyox and Alice Arm. Following are the observations made:-

Stewart:Labour conditions quiet. Labour supply good.

Anyox:Labour conditions quiet. About 1,200 men employed at the mine and smelter. No known agitator in the camp.[8]

Alice Arm:Labour Conditions quiet. About 150 men employed.

6. Miscellaneous Notes

T. Connors addressed the Socialist meeting in Vancouver on Sunday 22nd August. His address was an attack on H. G. Wells' book on "Socialism". In conclusion he expressed his hope that the Bolsheviki would defeat the Poles.

The chairman announced that the hire of the hall was $60, that this sum had not been realized for several Sundays, and that if there was no improvement they might have to cease holding the meetings. Despite this the collection was only $49.80. The audience was not large and not interested. It showed sympathy when Connors applauded the Bolshevists.

E. M. Mutch, who formerly was an agitator in Regina, now is living in Nakusp, and is working instead of agitating.

Clifford Roberts of Victoria on 15th August addressed a meeting of the International Bible Students Association at Prince Rupert. Among other predictions of a new order of things he declared that in the future the Jews would rule the world.

II. ALBERTA

7. The Proposed Coal Strike

The N. C. O. in charge at Blairmore in reporting on 21st August, after noting that the situation has been quiet throughout the week, that the men were working steadily, and that the output of coal was good, continues:-

"P. M. Christophers O. B. U. organizer, was in town latter end of the week, and he, and R. McDonald, O. B. U. Secretary, Blairmore, are very active amongst the miners at the present time, and by the talk amongst several of the miners in town, there is an indication of strike coming off this fall".

Two days later, on 23rd August, he reported further:-

"The One Big Union held a secret meeting at Hillcreat in the afternoon of the 22nd instant, and one at Blairmore the same evening of the same date, and I have obtained reliable information that they [9] propose "strike throughout the Crow's Nest Pass on a big scale, and I believe the date set for this strike /cold is October 7th 1920, or as soon as the severe/weather sets in, and the reason for such a strike, is that they consider the cold weather will effect a quicker settlement in their favour and are striking to have the One Big Union recognized.

"Four fifths of the miners at Hillcrest, Bellevue and Coleman, are paying dues into the O. B. U. Blairmore is not so strong, on account of their being so many returned soldiers working at this point. I may say that this information is reliable and I understand that they will not stop at bloodshed to carry their point. Any further information I can obtain will be submitted immediately".

Edward Browne, secretary of O. B. U. District No. 1. (i.e. U. M. W. of A. District No. 18) on 24th August notified the Canada West Local (an O. B. U. concern) that an O. B. U. convention will be held in Calgary on 10th September, and that one of the chief items of business would be "The elimination of the U. M. W. of A. check-off in District 18".

P. M. Christophers, P. F. Lawson and H. P. Hanson visited Blairmore recently, leaving on 24th August for Lethbridge. In view of prevailing conditions this is thought ominous. Lawson is known to have been soliciting assistance for the Searchlight.

8. O. B. U. Notes

A report made on 26th August showed that the Cinook Mine at Commerce, near Lethbridge had been idle for a week. About 100 men were effected by the strike. No disorders had occurred.

Some men at this mine signed the U. M. W. of A. check-off to get the retroactive pay due them under the agreement and then quit to go to Colahurst, that being an O. B. U. camp.

The Lethbridge Local of the U. M. W. of A. on 24th August resolved to endeavour to procure the discharge of 15 Japanese who were working in the mines.

Complaints were made that the local was not "recognized" by the head office at Indianapolis.[10]

A report upon conditions at Nordegg describes them as quiet. The Brazeau Collieries are having no trouble with their men, and intend to try to double their output in the coming winter.

A report upon the Crow's Nest Pass by a trustworthy agent states that there is much lawlessness and general disregard of authority, more especially with regard to the consumption of liquor. A general impression prevails that an appreciable number of the foreigners possess automatic pistols.

Some interest was aroused recently by a report that Christophers had been concerned in an attempt to buy arms. The incident seems to have been cleared up, and to be unimportant. What happened was that not long ago at Drumheller Christophers and a man named William Beard entered a hardware store and Beard asked what kind of rifles they had. The reply was "Only .22's". Beard said, "Well, that wouldn't knock a bull over", and the two men walked out. Christophers said nothing and as far as can be learned inquiries were made at no other store.

9. The Searchlight

No. 31 os the Searchlight was issued on 13th August. This issue contains an article strongly approving the "Self Determination for Ireland League", and stating that "The secret service of Canada is already shadowing all those who taking an active part in the formation of the league". It also says that the members of the League "have nothing to fear. For the most part the secret service men are pretty good scouts and some of them have more than a drop of Irish blood running through their veins".

A new labour paper, the Alberta Labour News, is to be established in Calgary. H. J. Roche will be manager and E. E. Roper is to be the editor. This should be a blow to Lawson.[11]

10. Miscellaneous Notes

The Socialists of Edmonton cancelled their usual propaganda meeting on Sunday 22nd August in order not to conflict with a meeting of the Self Determination for Ireland League.

The Park Committee of the Labour Church, Edmonton, held the usual open air meeting on Sunday 22nd August. It was devoted to the approaching referendum on prohibition, speeches being made by Mrs. Nellie McClung, Revd. Mr. Lloyd and Mr. Bishop. There was no socialistic propaganda, but copies of the O. B. U. Bulletin and the Searchlight were sold in the crowd.

A visit to the Eckville District, near Nordegg, shows conditions to be quiet. It is noted that the settlement by the Soldier Settlement Board of about 200 returned men in the district has steadied the foreign farmers, who have dropped any agitation in which they may have been indulging.

Some Finns of the district who are reputed to have socialistic views are talking of forming a society of some sort.

III. SASKATCHEWAN

11. No L. W. I. U. at Big River

An investigation into conditions at Big River, north west of Prince Albert, where there is a large lumbermill, shows that the L. W. I. U. is dead there. The situation there is governed by the fact the mill soon will be closed, owing to the exhaustion of its supplies. Our investigator says:-

"At one time the O. B. U. were making considerable progress in this district, having some 200 members, but when the time for action came they refused to act and allowed their leaders to be run out of camp without protest. Since that time to acknowledge membership in the L. W. I. U. is equivalent to asking for a discharge; this has caused all the old members to either turn in their cards or else pay their dues secretly of the latter, so far as I could ascertain, there do not appear to be more than 15 or 20, entirely Russians and Galicians.[12]

"There can be no doubt but that the L. W. I. U. is at an end in Big River, for the time being at least, and there are no delegates or agitators in the camp my opinion is that the L. W. I. U. being aware that this camp will close in the near future have decided that it would not be worth while to make any further attempts to organize it".

In commenting upon this the Officer Commanding Northern Saskatchewan says:-

"There is no doubt that the failure of the attempted strike last spring at Big River was the downfall of the O. B. U. in that district. I am sure that there will be no further trouble there".

12. O. B. U. Growing at Bienfait

Under the leadership of Dan Diaczun and the stimulus of the kidnapping of Christophers and the attempt to evict some the miners, the O. B. U. is making rapid progress at Bienfait. Our investigator says:-

"From my own point of view I think this district will be solid O. B. U. by fall. Mr. Miller, the manager, told me he thought the company would give in to the O. B. U. If they do the whole mining district around here will be solid. The company sent up 30 men from Toronto and they have nearly all quit work.

Wild statements have been made by Diaczun in his canvass. He told one man whom he was pressing to join that the O. B. U. had 300,000 members in the West and 58,000 in Winnipeg District; also that they were getting the farmers to join. Two quotations may be made from him:-

"We are getting lots of men to join us and we will be solid by the fall and when we go back to work here we will be boss. We don't want anyone to boss us we will be boss".

"We are not doing this for ourselves, because soon as things quiet down in our own country we are going back. It's to help the working man who are left in this country".

The O. B. U. have threatened violence in some cases in urging the men to join.

13. Miscellaneous Notes

Further information concerning the O. B. U. unit at Kamsack is to the effect that it is nearly negligible. It has only 15 or 18 [13] members and most of the railway men employed there are contented.

The strike of C. P. R. shop labourers at Moose Jaw seems to have reached rather an odd ending. The men have dispersed to work in the harvest fields, apparently content to quit the C. P. R. service permanently; they do not wish to return, and all sides are satisfied. It was promoted by the O. B. U.

The Regina Branch of the G. A. U. V. had only 14 members present at its on 18th August. The meeting voted against vocational training and settlement on land and demanded the $2,000 bonus.

The International Bible Students Association are active in circulating their periodical "The Golden Age".

A man named Crawford, a member of this Association, has written to the Prince Albert Herald to controvert the recent pamphlet of the Labour Department.

IV. MANITOBA

14. L.W.I.U. Unit in Winnipeg

Attention has been drawn to the existence of a unit of the L. W. I. U. at Winnipeg; it gave to one Austin Stanley a roving commission as organizer, which seemed likely to bring him into conflict with other organizers upon whose territories he might poach.

Investigation shows that P. G. Anderson is Secretary and Organizer of this Unit in the city of Winnipeg District. Our report says:-

> "The Unit consists of farm labour, lumber workers, bushmen miners and workers of all trades in the country. Practically no members belong to this Unit work in the city, therefore, the Unit has a great fluctuation in its strength, one day there may be forty of its members in the City, and the next eighty or ninety.
>
> "It is safe to say the full strength of the Unit throughout the [14] Western Provinces is not more than seven to eight hundred members, as in most mining localities the miners have a Unit of their own, thereby taking considerable members away from this Unit.
>
> "The membership is comprised principally of Russians and foreigners of different countries, there being scarcely any British subjects amongst their numbers.
>
> "The general feelings of this Unit lie with the I. W. W. of the United States, and on this account, they had considerable trouble getting their affiliation with the Central Labour Council of the O. B. U.
>
> "Although this Unit is not very strong in any particular part of the country, it is a very active unit, owing to the large scope of country

it covers, and the class of labourers it meets with, and can be called practically harmless as yet, but owing to its spreading propaganda through the country and every member being a practical organizer, the Unit is making very good headway.

"The Unit has not as yet extended any of its activities farther East than Sudbury, Ontario, its locality running West from this point to the Coast.

"The Unit takes in all miners who have not established themselves strong enough to support a unit of their own in their locality.

"Practically nothing has been heard regarding any farm labourers being members of this Unit. If any, they are Russians or Galicians, as no English speaking people are ever seen around the Unit's headquarters on Henry Ave.".

15. O. B. U. Building Trades Unit Possible

The Carpenters' Unit O. B. U. met in Winnipeg on 23rd August with an attendance of 60. Following was the business transacted:-

1.Arrangements were made for the O. B. U. convention at Port Arthur in September.

2.Hammond the organizer, said that the formation of a building Trades Unit, by amalgamation of the Carpenters with the painters, was expected.

3.Hammond claimed a paid-up membership of 400, said that the Internationals were showing signs of weakening and that the employers were slowly yielding and declared that the bricklayers showed signs of changing over.

4.One odd episode is thus reported:-

"It was then brought to the notice of the meeting under the heading of new business, that the Government was trying to issue new laws declaring the O. B. U. Ex-Soldiers' and Sailors' Labour Party and Dominion Labour Party illegal.[15]

"This was considered of very little importance as the Government had been trying to do that for some time, it was stated".

A recent incident in Winnipeg shows how keen is the quarrel in the building trades. The Eaton firm is erecting a new building. On 19th August the men working on it voted by a large majority not to discriminate against either O. B. U. or Internationals. Forthwith the officers of the Building Trades Federation had all the O. B. U. men employed on the job dismissed; they also showed a disposition to discipline all Internationals who voted for the resolution. Of those in danger of being dealt with one is James Winning, who was chairman of the strike committee in 1919.

Attention has been drawn to the fact that the O. B. U. Bulletin must be issued at a loss. The question arose as to how the deficit is met.

16. The Labour Church

The Winnipeg Labour Church celebrated its second anniversary on

22nd August by an open air meeting in Victoria Park. The attendance was 2,000. The speakers were W. D. Bailey, M.L.A., and Ald. A. A. Heaps. The speech of the latter was a review of the trial of the strike leaders, with the usual abuse of the R. C. M. P. Mr. Bailey's topic was "Industrial Peace". It was an attack on Capitalism and a Socialistic speech throughout.

V. ONTARIO

17. Knight on the O. B. U. Situation

J. R. Knight was in Hamilton on 25th August. In private conversation he made the following statements:-

1. He had just come from Montreal, where he had been helping W.E. Long to organize the men in the Angus shops to form two locals of the O. B. U.; he expected within the next two weeks to have 100 men organized.[16]
2. As a result of his two month's work in Northern Ontario he had established a Central Executive to oversee matters from Cochrane to North Bay; it would be self-supporting.
3. The situation in the East was picking up, and soon things would be better in Montreal, Toronto, Hamilton, Niagara Falls, etc.
4. He volunteered to represent the Hamilton local at the approaching O. B. U. convention at Port Arthur.
5. The O. B. U. now had the West pretty solidly organized and should devote more time to the East, it now being the more important of the two. For this reason he proposed to insist upon having the Central Executive Board moved from Vancouver to Winnipeg.
6. Several speakers are developing in the Labour College at Toronto. He also could draw men from Edmonton. Armstrong of Toronto also would be available.
7. He might be displaced at the convention, as there was strong criticism of him for neglecting the East in favour of the mining section of Northern Ontario.

Several of the foregoing remarks are explained by the attack made upon him by Carl Berg at Vancouver, and the rumours which have been mentioned as circulating about him.

18. O. B. U. Notes

A well informed correspondent in Toronto regards the O. B. U. cause as looking up. The District Trades Council recently passed resolutions of a sympathetic nature, as a result of which the International organizers there have redoubled their efforts.

"Jimmy" Simpson is expected to be a candidate at the approaching Dominion Trades Congress, perhaps for Secretary, possibly for President.

Additional cases have come to our attention of men proceeding to the West as harvesters being signed up by the O. B. U. at Toronto. It appears that the organizer spoke to them at the station and told them that it would be hard to find a job out West without an O. B. U. card.

A report on Iroquois Falls says:-

"About all the local O. B. U. succeeds in doing at Iroquois Falls is to prevent men forgetting petty grievances and in spite of all the [17] company is doing in the way of,well fare schemes there is a steady resentment against the company which shows itself in childish criticism of any scheme which has not been tried elsewhere."

Examples are given of the disposition to find fault, and it is added:-

"Meanwhile the efforts made to keep the men undoubtedly make for better conditions for the labouring men, and make it more difficult for small mines and such like to compete for men in the labour market with the big manufacturing plants".

A short strike of carpenters, in which they behaved rather unreasonably, is declared not to be due to the O. B. U.

A Toronto man named Jim Brereton has turned up in Hamilton. He is a brick-layer, carries an International Card, and is given to holding open-air meetings at which he denounces the Internationals. He ran away to the United States to escape conscription, and when away worked with the I. W. W. He may be employed by the local revolutionaries to join the Hamilton local of the Building Trades Union and "Work from the inside", in order to swing it to the O. B. U.

It is interesting to note that this man, who is 27 or 28 years of age, stated that he had enough money to keep him until next spring without doing a day's work.

We have received somewhat doubtful information to the effect:-

1. That a branch of the Ex-soldiers' and Sailors' Labour Union has been founded in Toronto, Farnell, the man recently released at Winnipeg, and J. Flinn (? J. H. Flynn) being concerned in it.
2. That an arrangement has been made whereby members of the "G.U.M.W." (?G.A.U.V.) will ipso facto be members of the Ex-Soldiers' and Sailors' Union.
3. That a project is entertained of carrying the "G.U.M.W." (? G.A.U.V.) over to the O. B. U.

19. The Thorold Riot and the Foreign-born Population

A particularly capable and trustworthy investigator informs us that the attempted lynching of McNeal at Thorold had a marked effort [18] upon the foreign-born population who were out in full force as spectators. Their conclusion was that the power of the people was mighty", and that the crowd which defied the authorities and the police could easily overthrow the Government.

This correspondent found established in a foreign colony just outside of Welland, called "Ontario", a secret Communist Anarchist organization led by a very extreme man named Teschkevich, who was taking the Thorold riot as a text to prove that labour was ready to overthrow the present capitalistic government "everywhere". This society maintained relations with one in St. Catharines. Our investigator regards it as ready to resort to violence if opportunity offers, and remarks that the colony is not far from the stores of explosives used in the work on the new canal. The people are Ukrainians, Russians and Poles.

20. The Foreign Colony in Hamilton.

The same correspondent furnishes us with an account of conditions in the foreign colony in Hamilton, which he describes as principally Ukrainian. There is in existence there, with what he calls a "charter" from the civic authorities, an organization called Ridna Schold (Ukrainian Native School); it has premises, and apparently so far has been well-behaved. There also is a branch of the Russian Communist Anarchist Party, it formerly was the Union of Russian Workmen, and had an office etc. but was broken up when the ban was issued. This new society is in difficulties as to a place of meeting; it used the I. O. O. F. Temple for a while, but the Oddfellows lately have refused the further use of their premises, and the city has refused to "grant a charter", moreover, the local police are suspicious of their open-air meetings.

In these circumstances the Communist Anarchists have conceived [19] the plan of uniting with the Ukrainian Native School and using its privileges to get in revolutionary books and papers. As part of this scheme they on 10th August put on a revolutionary play entitled "Strike".

They have a sort of reading room and centre for revolutionary reading matter in the office of "Rotenburgs Ltd.", afirm which does business among the foreigners as agents and bankers.

21. Foreign-Born Revolutionists at St. Catharines

The same agent has reported upon St. Catharines. The city authorities there recognize a society known as the Polish Co-operative Society; this contains only two Poles, the bulk of the members being russian, Ukrainian and Austrian; the younger members are very radical.

Our agents attended a wedding here which was entirely Communist, with no religious ceremony. One remark made was that when the first child of this wedding arrived the world would be free from capitalists and kings. A man named Afanasy made a speech in which he deplored the attention given by local Russians, Ukrainians and Poles to Church, drunkenness and card-games.

22. The Welland Communists

Later our agent visited Welland, where he confirmed our earlier reports, which came from an entirely different source, of Henry Dworkin's visit to Welland. Dworkin addresses a Ukrainian Socialist Democratic Party meeting; the Party meets every Sunday in Welland.

The two leaders in this set are Peter Najkalick and Karp Vakaluck. They get in much revolutionary reading matter. Najkalick on the occasion of our informant's visit made a good deal of his belief that "all English-speaking labourers" sympathized with the Bolsheviki. He also thought that they wanted a Bolshevist Government in Canada, and [20] would support a revolution in Canada.

Our correspondent describes the forcing element in this part of Ontario as very radical, ready for trouble and in high hopes of a revolution here. There will be more activity, he says, when the harvesters return from the West.

23. Zluka at Work in Toronto

Our correspondent on 22nd August attended a meeting of Zluka in Toronto. One Mike Malarchuck spoke on "The cause of Labour Weakness". The speech contained an attack on the Church, and a eulogy of the Bolshevists and Lenin.

Our correspondent was told by English-speaking revolutionists in Toronto that in England six million trade unionists were ready for revolution. This evidently is a reverberation of the agitation in England against a Russian War.

In addition to Zluka there are two other Russian organizations in Toronto, one called "The Russian Progressive Library", which seems a continuation of the "Union of Russian Workmen" and the other (which has just been started) called the Technical Motor School.

V. Dodokin, who seems the leader among the revolutionary Russians in Toronto, presided over a meeting held on Sunday 29th August to organize a "school". Some 18 men have joined and about $100 has been subscribed.

VI. QUEBEC

24. Conflicting Theories of O. B. U. Organization

A report from Montreal dated 20th August confirms Knight's statement that he had been in Montreal conferring with Long and Binette. Apparently his visit was designed to strengthen his party in the fight which is pretty sure to happen in the Port Arthur Convention. Our informant says that Knight "conveyed to Binette and Long the possibility [21] of a split amongst the O. B. U. delegates when they convene at Port Arthur".

The result of Knight's visit was seen at the joint meeting of the two Montreal Units, Metal Trades and General Workers, which was held on 26th August, to elect a delegate to Port Arthur. Although an urgent whip had been sent out, only 35 persons attended.

Rebecca Buhay moved that the delegate elected should be uninstructed but should be free to "support the best form of organization for the workers". Behind this was the issue of Industrial versus Geographical organization which has been mentioned several times in this summary, and which is agitating the O. B. U. Behind that, again, lie the personal interests of two groups of organizers. And a third idea, that of "Class" organization has champions.

There was a heated debate on this motion. Binette held that the delegates should represent, not his personal opinions, but those of the membership. He personally

> "Was in favour of an 'Industrial' form of organization, so that in case of a strike the O. B. U. would be able to paralyze the industries from Coast to Coast and if the O. B. U. ever gets away from that form of organization, it will be a failure like the Knights of Labour proved to be".

W. E. Long favoured the "Geographical" form; the L. W. I. U., he said, were the only organization who desired the "Industrial" form, whereas the miners and the transportation workers wanted the other. He supported the Buhay motion.

Binette in rejoinder angrily

> "Pointed out that the West is not in accordance with the middle West and the East some of the delegates from the Pacific Coast have already received instructions to support the Industrial platform, while others have instructions to support the Geographical form of organization. In Winnipeg they have decided to support a Class form of organization, and if we do leave it to our delegates to use his or her good judgment, I feel confident that this convention will cause a split in the O. B. U. movement and, instead of having 'One [22] Big Union' we will have "Three Small Unions".

There was a grand squabble over this and in the end Miss Buhay's motion was carried by 10 majority. The following is the report of her final utterance:-

> "During her long speech she said that, personally she would be for a Class form of organization, where all workers could be untied, irrespective of race, creed, or colour, with power to act, when the opportune time arrives. 'I believe in Mass Action, force is what we want' she stated. She went on to say that all the strikes taking place these days have not the same meaning as they had years ago, when they used to strike for better wages and shorter hours; the strikes today are direct between labour and the state and we must continue with those principles until we have become the owners of all industries and the dictation of the world.

The upshot is that the delegate, who is W. E. Long, with Rebecca Buhay as substitute, goes to the convention with a free hand. Long favour the Geographical, Miss Buhay the Class idea.

25. Personal Rivalries

Our correspondent, who is an exceptionally competent authority, gives the following elucidation of the inner significance of the quarrel:-

> "E. Winch, secretary-treasurer of the Lumber Workers O. B. U. unit, favours the Industrial form of organization. By so doing, he will be able to establish a large fund in his own Unit and instead of paying the dues into the O. B. U. Central Executive, he would only be

paying the 10 cents per capita tax, which action would make the Central O. B. U. Executive do some tall thinking.

"V. R. Midgley, secretary-treasurer, of the Executive of the O. B. U. is in favour of a Geographical form of organization, where he will be able to collect a dollar for every member affiliated with the O. B. U. each month and the ten per cent capita tax would go to the Central Labour Council O. B. U. which is in reality a strike fund, but, if a form of Industrial Organization is adopted, at the Fort Arthur Convention, Midgley will not be able to collect any more dues.

"There are also the Miners of District 18 who are in favour of an industrial organization and according to Joe Knight, E. Winch and Naylor, Miners, have already told V. R. Midgley that, if it were not for the miners and Lumber workers, there would be no O. B. U. and they intend to get the rest of the delegates to recognize their power of the Lumber Workers and the Mines. Long and Binette, [23] further informed me that Joe Knight and a few others especially from Winnipeg are in favour of a Class form of organization because Mass Action is the best policy and they will use all their power to convince the Conference to adopt that platform, but Long stated that the three different parties seem to have made up their minds to stick to their respective platforms, if none of these factions gives into the other, there will be a split which will destroy the O. B. U. for ever.

"Most of the members present at this meeting expressed dissatisfaction with the manner in which the meetings are being carried on lately.

"In my opinion, by adopting that resolution giving the delegate a free hand at the Convention, the members of the O. B. U. at Montreal have overlooked the fact that they are getting away from the O. B. U. constitution and, instead of the rank and file having the power to act, they look for leaders to carry out their work and wishes".

The N. C. O. in charge of C. I. B. work at Montreal suggests that there is a chance of a split which would be the beginning of the end of the O. B. U.

It will be noticed that Knight seemed to think that Winch and Naylor were allied against Midgley; whereas we have recent information to the effect that Naylor sides with Midgley. Knight has not been in Vancouver recently, and probably is wrong in his idea.

Later information from Montreal is that the O. B. U. convention at Port Arthur will comprise only 35 delegates. It also is that the adherents of the three parties, "Class", "Geographical" and "Industrial", are determined, so that a split is possible. If it is averted, there will be trouble for those delegates who give way when they face their locals.

26. The O. B. U. Policy

Interesting speeches were made at a meeting of the Metal Workers Unit, O. B. U. in Montreal on 19th August. W. E. Long, the secretary-treasurer, reported having asked leave of the civic authorities to hold an open air meeting on Sunday 22nd August. The granting of permission he regarded as gratifying proof that the O. B. U. had made its mark even in Montreal.[24] Thereupon, O. Charette, secretary-treasurer of the General Workers' Unit, O. B. U. objected that to ask permission was to make too great a concession, and wanted to put a motion that a letter be written to the city authorities informing them that the O. B. U. would hold open air meetings wherever and when ever they wished, and that as long as they were orderly the city was bound to protect them. Our report continues:-

> "W. Long, in replying to Charette's remarks, stated that he regretted more than any one present that the O. B. U. was not sufficiently strong enough to be able to do what Charette had in mind, and also regretted to say, that for the present, that's the only way the O. B. U. will be able to spread its propaganda. The O. B. U., Long continued, is not strong enough to carry out such action, the rank and file is not with the O. B. U. yet, and, until the workers get to understand their position in society, and fully realize that their interests are not identical as the master class, we will not be able to accomplish very much.
>
> "I was distinctly told, Long stated, that the workers in Montreal must not be worked up in such a state to create what the workers of Winnipeg have created during the sympathetic strike, and if that state of affairs is brought about, some of us might go to jail as they did in Winnipeg. If we had a strong organization like they have in England, Long said, we might be able to defy the Capitalistic Government and hold meetings at any place, but, under the circumstances, we must, act according to our strength".

Some references to Poland, Russia and the attitude of labour in England followed. Then:-

> "Long went on to say that he was also very pleased to see that the psychology of the rank and file has changed since 1914, the same spirit of patriotism does not exist as it did in 1914, the Capitalistic Government might have that flag before the rank and file, they might call for volunteers to defend their capital invested in Poland against Soviet Russia, but I am positive that none will respond to such a call".

In concluding Long referred in friendly terms to the Labour College which is being established.

The open air meeting on Sunday (which was reported in the press) was attended by 500 or 600 persons, 95 per cent of whom were Russian Jews. In his speech Long made the remarkably untruthful statement that the O. B. U. has no officials under salary.[25] One or two of the other speeches merit a word. Auna Buller described the O. B. U. organization and urged that it be converted into an organization like the Triple Alliance in England. Michael Buhay:-

"Stated that the workers of England are so well organized, that in a minute's notice they can paralyze the wheels of industry in the country and stated that the workers of Canada must, do likewise and put their industrial power into the hands of one man as they have done in England and when the opportune time arrives, take over the industries of production and run them for use instead of for profit. With that, Buhay asked the audience to get busy and form a committee of action".

27. O. B. U. Working with the Communists

Binette, the O. B. U., organizer in Montreal, on 15th August took the chair at a meeting of the French Socialist Communist Party, at which the cause of the Bolshevists was championed. Concerning this a well-informed agent says:-

> "I was very much surprised to notice that Binette accepted the offer to act as Chairman at the above mentioned meeting after he has been fighting the Communist Party since he, Binette, became an official of the O. B. U. because he claims that they are too far advanced in their ideas and that the O. B. U. should be the only organization that the workers should support.
>
> "It appears to me that since Russia has attacked Poland most of these radicals, who were rather quiet previous to this incident, now they seem revived against and support the most radical movement in existence, none of them were as bold as they are now".

Subsequently this agent asked Binette why he did this, and Binette's reply was:-

> "Oh, I'm just doing it to keep in the movement, my principal object to attend these meetings is to offset any attacks which may be made against the interests of the O. B. U."

28. "Forget the Church"

The same society held a meeting on 22nd August, at which Gottsall spoke. Our report is:-

> "He stated that the workers especially those belonging to the Province of Quebec are in need of an education very badly, they must [26] forget the Church and become members of the F.S.C.P. where they will achieve the proper education. Gottsell stated that, although the Province of Quebec is very backward in the movement, yet it does not hinder the Bolshevists of Russia from progressing and the day is coming when Quebec must follow and if the people are not ready to accept such conditions, there will be a wholesale of murders".

29. Gerrish; his Party and His Outlook

F. W. Gerrish, self-appointed Secretary-Treasurer of the proposed

Quebec Independent Socialist Party, has conceived the plan of throwing his organization into the Sinn Fein agitation, with the idea of attracting Irish members. His next mass-meeting will be devoted to the Irish question. He is looking hopefully for MacSwiney's death as a fillip to his meeting.

Gerrish admits that the other radicals of Montreal view him coldly. They all know, he said in conversation, that he aspires to political office in the Province. The following is his statement in private conversation, of his political outlook:-

> "If a revolutionary Government was established in this Province, it, would enable such a Government to get all the Radicals from the United States to come to Canada and carry on their propaganda; but under the present Conservative Provincial Government this Province is way far behind of all countries and we will never be able to accomplish our object until we use some of our power in the political fields; that the British Empire is about to crumble to ashes. If England is made a Republic, even a Capitalist Republic, Canada must also go Republic; the Western Parts of Canada are ready for it, but this province is very backward yet; that's why I would like to put some Socialist M.P.'s in the Quebec Provincial House who would be able to deal with the situation".

Our informant remarks that "there is much petty jealousy and hatred between these would-be labour leaders and would-be politicians".

Gerrish's self-seeking seems so artlessly open that it is impossible that he and his society will come to anything. It has not yet been really organized.

30. A Committee of Vigilance

However, he managed to hold a meeting of it on 20th August,[27] about 90 people attending, who presided, said that the object of the meeting was to get the opinion of the member present as to the formation in Canada of a "Committee of Vigilance" which would have the same power in this country as the Council of Action of the Allied Trades Unions in England. Our informant says:-

> "No one complied with the chairman's request, as to what action the meetings should follow with the view to elect a committee of vigilance, but I feel confident that another effort will be used endeavouring to form such committee".

Hyman Edelstein who has been mentioned before, moved a resolution protesting against Canadian action against Russia and made a violent speech. After attacking the press and the Government he is thus reported:

> "In his closing remarks Edelstein said that he was aware of the fact that by advocating the overthrow of the present form of Government by any methods, other than by political action was seditious, but stated that the time had arrived when they must come out openly,

that they intend to overthrow the present system of Government by industrial action. If something should happen they will do to us like they have done to the strike leaders in Winnipeg, throw us in jail for working in the best interest of our fellow workers.

"Edelstein recommended the O. B. U. for being the sole organization in Canada with that psychology that if a flag would replace the Union Jack in Canada, it would be the Red Flag. The Red Flag does not mean victory or aggression, but universal brotherhood, Edelstein said".

"Edelstein further stated that there are men giving financial support to this party, who do not wish their names to be mentioned for the present, but it will be a shock to the Government when the truth is revealed, because these men are holding a responsible position as officers of this Government.

"F. W. Gerrish informed me that what Edelstein has said about high officers giving official support to this party is true, but I have not been able to learn anymore.

Our correspondent's opinion of Gerrish and Edelstein is that they are merely political adventurers who are trying to obtain some personal advantage, such as being elected to Parliament.[28]

31. Miscellaneous Notes

At the meeting just mentioned those present were asked to sign a letter to the Minister of Justice asking him to release Sava Zura, who is serving a term of imprisonment for being in possession of prohibited literature. The letter is not couched in particularly respectful terms, and the terms in which Edelstein asked for signatures were contemptuous and sarcastic. He spoke, for example, of "The Dishonourable Minister of Justice".

The organization styled the "Educational Press Association" of Montreal is active in circulating revolutionary reading matter in French, brought from France. One Parisian paper which is imported is "Le Soviet".

Inquiry shows that "W. Gordon", mentioned in an earlier summary as at once a Pole and a Bolshevist has no official Polish standing.

VII. THE MARITIME PROVINCES

32. The Coal Fields

Reports from the Nova Scotia Coal Fields are to the effect that all is quiet at present.

However, we have a report of a conversation with J. J. McNeil, U. M. W. of A. Board member for Inverness and Port Hood. The following points appear in it:-

1. McNeil, who is a strong Socialist, favoured the O.B.U. and said that though it is practically dead in Nova Scotia at present, he expected it to be a live issue in the future. He deemed it the only solution of the labour problem.
2. He put the strength of the U. M. W. of A. in Nova Scotia at 14,000.

3. The miners were bent on having their wages raised to the same level as those of the United States miners.

Our informant says:

"I would take from McNeil's conversation that the miners in the ranks of the U. M. W. are prepared for a strike, and that these petty strikes, that have been taking place at various times in Cape Breton, are for the express purpose of showing their industrial strength, and influencing the Royal Commission to grant the miners their demands".

APPENDIX

The Weekly Report upon revolutionary organizations in England for 19th August is very grave.

The summary in part is as follows:-

"The event of the week has been the establishment of the "Council of Action", which tried to regularise its position in the Labour world by obtaining authority from the Conference held on August 13th. It is being borne in upon moderate men throughout the country that the "Council of Action" and its subsidiary Committees are Soviets and that the establishment of such bodies is in conflict not only with the constitution of the country but with the constitution of Trade Unions themselves. The revolutionaries alone have no misgivings. It has been a gala week for them and some of their speakers have shown symptoms of intoxication.

"The publication of the wireless messages indicating that the "Daily Herald" is subsidised from Russia has, to judge from the apologetic tone of the "Herald's" disclaimer, shaken the position of the paper. The publicity happens to have struck the exact psychological moment.

"Though the industrial situation is grave there are encouraging symptoms. The miners are determined to strike unless their demands are granted and the gas workers are nearly out of hand but there is a strong body among responsible labour which would be glad to defer the struggle. Moreover, the output in engineering centres has improved during the last three months an encouraging symptom.

"The tension over the Polish question is largely artificial and is really due only to the fear of conscription, but there are genuine grievances in the increase in rents, railway fares, bread and coal, and behind all hangs the dark shadow of unemployment.

Concerning the "Council of Action" the report says:-

"In form, the body is a Central Soviet and is in conflict with not only the Constitution of the country but the laws governing Trades Unionism.

"The Council is entrusted definitely with the executive power to call out at a moment's notice and without question this or that section of the Labour Movement. It can organize, and is prepared to organize, complete control of foreign policy, and of that domestic production and distribution of commodities which, in the last resort, determines policy".

"The arrogation of power to call a general strike cuts at the roots of trade union policy as, in the great majority of cases, a ballot of members is essential before even the properly election Union officials can call their men out."

Following are utterances by Labour speakers:-

Ebury at Leeds:- "Announced, in a very jubilant manner, that the British Central Soviet is now firmly established. They could call it 'Council of Action' or any other name they like. It [2] did not matter, revolution is imminent".

Bromley at Sheffield:- "Fifteen of his colleagues in London had practically taken over the Government of the Country for the purpose of peace or war".

A. Ponsonby, at the same meeting said he was proud to be on the same platform with a 'member of the present Government'.

N. Ablett at Swansea:- "He was formly convinced that the "Council of Action' would eventually become the real Government'.

A report by a correspondent in Yorkshire contains the following paragraph:-

"Great uncertainty also prevails amongst the more advanced section of the Independent Labour Party and the Communists as to the motives behind Thomas Clynes and their change of tone at the Congress on the 13th. They suspect some treacherous move by these men by which a sort of Kerensky or Noske regime may be finally set up if the present Government cannot carry on against the organized labour agitation".

There has letterly been a marked increase in the hostility shown to speakers from patriotic platforms.

There are disquieting reports that the loyalty of the Navy is being sapped.

ROYAL CANADIAN MOUNTED POLICE HEADQUARTERS

Ottawa, 9th September, 1920.

SECRET

NO. 40

NOTES OF THE WORK OF THE C. I. B. DIVISION FOR THE WEEK ENDING 9TH SEPTEMBER

Table of Contents

1. General Characteristics of the Period.

Little additional information has been received as to the projected strike in the Crow's Nest Pass. Christophers and the other agitators have been exceedingly active. Despite their plans, the leaders feel their position weak, probably because of the lack of money, and they are said to be trying to induce the railwaymen to join in the strike. The idea conceivably is to make it a species of general strike, to force surrender by the creation of impossible conditions. There is word of money being sent to Blairmore.

For some reason three of the O.B.U. leaders have reason to feel anxiety as to the outcome of the approaching O.B.U. Convention at Port Arthur. Knight's apprehensions were noted last week, as were Winch's difficulties; now it appears that Midgley expects to be overthrown. In this connection it may be noted that he I.W.W. are reappearing in Vancouver and British Columbia.

Revolutionary activities in Toronto are shifting from the O.B.U. (which so far has been a complete failure there) to the Communist Party. The Ontario Labour College seems to be the present centre of mischief there.

I. BRITISH COLUMBIA

2. V.R. Midgley's View of the Labour Situation

175*2409. V.R. Midgley recently was in close touch with one of our agents, and talked to him freely. His utterances were so interesting that very full excerpts may be given. It will be seen that he expects the coming Convention to throw both himself and Winch out of office;-

> "In various conversations with V.R. Midgley recently, he told me he expected to have to go to work again, "but", he said, "It will be a rest. I have had four years of strain now. Labor is ungrateful, and it is a 24- hour a day fight. One is fighting the employers, and fighting the opposition element in his own organization. One has to fight the extremists and the conservatives, and is always being charged with double-crossing and underhand dealings. WHEN one gets an ordinary job, he is through in eight hours. Also I have to fight men whom I like personally, like BLAKE WILSON and George Kidd. They are very fair and reasonable men to deal with and it goes against the grain sometimes to stand out against them."
>
> "Midgley expects to be sent out of active participation in labor and socialistic matters by the I.W.W. element at the coming O.B.U. convention. He has opposed their policy of national organization, he says, and has upheld the policy of local industrial organization. That is, the Province of B.C. should attend to its own affairs, and every other section should do the same. There should be no national general movement whenever one locality wants to gain something.
>
> "Speaking of conditions in Canada, he said that they would never be serious because the food question was settled, on account of the big surplus production. There was no real misery in Canada and the people could never be prevailed upon to make a general movement. There was also the fact that labor men in large majority respected their employers who were kindly, humane men. The most extreme labor element that Canada had to contend with was the common lumbering and laborer classes from the United States. In that

country common laborers were considered and treated as no better than animals. This had resulted in the I.W.W., formed of men who for ten, twenty, thirty years have been driven from pillar to post, from job to job, their own feelings never considered, their liberties abused by the authorities. This condition, having existed many years, had created the possibility of I.W.W. organization, and the bitterness of the I.W.W. against capitalistic methods was engendered not by Canadian treatment, but by the actions of the capital-controlled authorities of the United States. He expected there would be very wide and serious troubles in the U.S. and he thought it would be good business if the Canadians took care to watch the international border line very sharply.[5]

"Jack Kavanagh, who recently returned from England, informed him that civil war might break out in England at any time. It would not be directly from labor troubles, but would be through some extraneous dispute like the Irish question or the Polish trouble, which would line up definitely and solidly the opposing parties. The condition in England was to some extent due to the high cost of living and the rationing system which still was being carried on, according to Kavanagh's latest information. Kavanagh himself did not look for trouble in Canada.

"On the subject of the Third International, Midgley said it was, in the last analysis, nothing but the socialism preached by the socialists of Canada."

"Midgley also told me that Ernest Winch, of the loggers, would be down and out soon, probably at the next O.B.U. convention.

"He is opposed to the I.W.W.", he said, "But as the strength of that following has increased in his organization, he has deemed it wise to accept their policies, intending to block them in the execution. In words he is with them, but will not be in action. He is a man whose one desire is to gain power, and he thinks it is to be obtained by the route he has taken. He is not susceptible to money, excepting as a means to gain power. But no man can accept policies and then not carry them out. He must act or repudiate. This will be what will kill him. He will be forced to take a definite stand, and if he goes with the Wobblies he will be eventually ditched, and if he goes against them after what he has accepted of their principles, he will be a dead one too. He is more sure to be put out of an influential position in the O.B.U. organization than I am."

" 'That convention will please the Internationals', I said.

" 'Oh, I don't know', he replied. 'Although the O.B.U. and the I.W.W. elements are opposed in policies they are not personally opposed to each other, and they understand.'

" 'Will not a number of the moderates go back to International organizations?'

" 'Some, but not many. They all understand pretty well.'

" 'But, if the I.W.W.'s get control, what will happen?'

" 'They won't keep control long'.

"Midgley told me that about 71,000 membership cards in the O.B.U. had been issued. In January there has been some 42,000. I asked him if a large number had not lapsed and he said some had, but the per capita payments showed that the membership was strong. He estimated from this tax payment that there were about 50,000 or a little more in Canada. These figures included about 20,000 of whom 16,000 were in British Columbia."

---

3. Quarrel Between Midgley and Winch.[6]

175*237An Agent reports under date of 15th August;-

"There is a big fight on between Winch and Midgley. Winch wants to keep the Headquarters office open and Midgley is trying to have all dues paid direct to the O.B.U. headquarters. I look for Winch to send all the men he can get (who are blacklisted) East, to organize them Farm hands in the loggers' Union."

4. Per Capita Tax versus General Fund.

The General Workers Unit O.B.U. of Vancouver on 23rd August discussed the constitution in view of the approaching convention. They were specially interested in the per capita tax system of finance; a committee was appointed to draw up tentative proposals for the establishment of a General Fund scheme.

J.S. Smith published in the B.C. Federationist of 27th August an article denouncing the per capita tax system as a pernicious characteristic of craft unionism, and advocating of ownership of all union funds by the union as a whole. Thus weak units which do not pay their own way could use the money contributed by strong units. He depicts a number of benefits which would ensue from this "General Fund System", the most noteworthy being the ability to establish a daily paper.

5. The L.W.I.U. Short of Funds.

175*237.The L.W.I.U. in Vancouver are in an odd predicament. they have not enough money on hand to pay the $650. which the printer is charging for issuing the proceedings of the recent convention. A referendum is pending on sumdry proposals to change the constitution; the ballots have been printed, but are unintelligible until the proceedings can be consulted. The members are demanding the booklets impatiently. Further, so late as the end of August, Winch was unable to see how they could finance the approaching convention at Port Arthur.[7]

6. The I.W.W. once more Establishing itself.

175*237.According to reports, the I.W.W. once more is being established in Vancouver, and one observer believes that after a while it will be more dangerous to the operators than the O.B.U.

At present a knot of men, Magness, Boyd, Allman and possibly Hatherley, are at work on the project. Stack, who was reported to have succeeded Allman as chief of the I.W.W.'s in British Columbia, and who also is Chairman of the Resolutions Committee of the L.W.I.U. probably is helping. They have taken an office, and Boyd seems to be Secretary, with Allman managing from the back ground. During July Boyd took in $148.00 in dues. Allman is busy about the employment offices, expounding the I.W.W. doctrine and criticizing Winch and the O.B.U.

A somewhat earlier report from a different source stated that Allman now is charged with being in the secret service of the R.C.M.P. He and an agitator named Higgins were living together; Higgins was arrested during Allman's absence, and Higgins concluded that he had been betrayed. He now is making charges against Allman.

It was noticed in the report about the setting up of Boyd's office and that he and Allman were keeping somewhat aloof from the majority of the members of the loggers' union.

7. One Big Union Notes.

175*237.A somewhat amusing bit of news is that Lamont, who was active as an organizer, after a brief speel of manual work in a logging camp returned to Vancouver. He said that "he could not make good on this [8] work on account of having to pack the saw around the bush".

175*237.

Another bit of mild scandal about the L.W.I.U. is contributed by a letter from a Frenchwoman in Victoria who wished to join the O.B.U. there. With this in view she visited the O.B.U. Hall there and found it so filthy, so carelessly managed, and the Secretary-Caretaker so indifferent, that she changed her mind, and wrote to J.M. Clark in Vancouver for a card.

The comment made by our informant is;- "It is evident from the tone of the letter that the O.B.U. is a dead issue in Victoria. This opinion is shared by Clark also".

175*2142.The Secretary of the Merritt Unit of the O.B.U., a man named Fod Killer, has left, and interest in the unit is decreasing.

Labour Notes.

175*402.The following report upon labour conditions in Victoria has been received;-

> "Labour Unions and O.B.U. losing control. Situation in labour circles, quiet. No mass meetings. Ordinary meetings poorly attended. Active members decreasing, unemployment increasing. Approximately 2500 labour men left town since 1st October last; of whom 1000 at least will return between September 1st and 30th November."

175*3238.Messrs. T.E. Naylor and G.A. Isaacs, Labour members of the Imperial Press Party, have given several addresses during their tour. At Vancouver their statements that English labour is not revolutionary [9] were received with a surprise that bordered on incredulity. The N.C.O. in charge of C.I.B. work in Vancouver remarks;-

> "It is a pity that more speakers of the calibre of Naylor and Isaacs cannot be sent through Canada. I am sure they would establish a different feeling among the working class. Their words would go a long way to offset the rotten revolutionary speeches of men like Kavanagh, recently back from England, to misrepresent the real conditions existing there, and to reflect only the sentiments of men of his own stamp."

It is to be noted that Messrs. Naylor and Isaacs were far from "reactionary". They were, for example, strongly opposed to war in general and in particular the giving of aid to Poland.

175*2726A patrol from Prince George to Quesnel results in a report that labour conditions on the construction work of the Pacific Great Eastern Railway are good. About 800 men are employed on the grade at present; when the snow comes this force will be reduced to 300. The supply of labour is good, there are no agitators, officials and men alike are pleased with each other, and the men are making high wages.

175*622.The Labour Temple in Vancouver has been bought by the Provincial Government and all the tenants are under notice to quit. These include the printing office of the British Columbia Federationist, as well as the offices of numerous unions. The Company which held the Temple had become insolvent, and it is a question whether anything will be left of the purchase price, $165,000, when all obligations have been met.[10]

9. Kavanagh on Conditions in Great Britain

175*1523.J. Kavanagh addressed a meeting in Vancouver, about 600 persons being present, on his experiences in Great Britain. He attacked Tom Moore for hampering Gage and him, criticised the Trade Union officials of Great Britain, praised Smillie, and was greatly impressed with the strength of the revolutionary labour movement, particularly in Scotland and Wales.

10. The International Bible Students' Position.

175*1724.The International Bible Student's Association are busy contradicting the statement that they are a revolutionary society. A sample meeting was held at Vancouver on 29th August, when S.A. Cater repudiated the charge. He said in part;-

> "During the war they accused us of being Pacifists; now they call us revolutionists, but we know we take the only stand that any true christian can take at all times that is to be Neutral. A true Christian

can take no part in political affairs. We are in sympathy with Radicals (with which we are classed), as far as they are struggling for better conditions and righteousness; and on the other hand, we are in sympathy with the governing officials in so far as they are interested in the welfare and safeguarding of the people; but we are not allied to either parties."

He went on to make the usual prophecies (which must be very unsettling to persons tinged with their beliefs) of the certainty of the revolution which emanates from RUSSIA spreading here and upsetting the Government.

11. British Columbia Detachment Reports:-

175*2736 Prince George, 14th August:-

"Labour situation is very quiet, all labour required is available. No agitation in the district.

175*2734 Hazelton, 14th August:-

No trouble or complaints have been heard of or reported during the past week and the district is quiet".[11]

175/1595 Ocean Falls, 21st August:-

Situation rapidly becoming normal.

175/2831 Chakawana Detachment (Coastal Patrol) 14th August:

"Labour conditions along the coast patrolled by the Chakawana are very quiet at present, no trouble being reported".

175/2501 Nanaimo, 21st August:-

"Everything is quiet and orderly in this district. All mines and logging and lumbering operations are working to full capacity and there is plenty or work throughout the entire district. It is reported that there has been a complete lay off of No. 5 camp, of the Victoria Lumber Co. but have not as yet been able to confirm this report."

175/2531 Alert Bay, 14th August:-

"Labour conditions are quiet in this district. There is a great shortage of labour in the canneries, which, now that the big run of salmon is on, is causing great inconvenience. Logging camps are working smoothly without any noticeable labour trouble."

175/2500 Port Alberni, 21st August:-

"District quiet and orderly. Mills and camps are working steadily. Construction work proceeding smoothly on E. and N."

175/2743 Esquimalt, 21st August:-

"Sawmills and shipyard in full swing. Labour conditions favourable. All routine work and station orders carried out as per Naval Yard regulations.

175/2742 Cumberland, 21st August:-

No labour troubles mentioned.

175/2735 Merritt, 21st August:-

No labour troubles mentioned. Industry active.

175/2740Nelson, 14th August:-
"There are no new developments in labour conditions".
175/2778Midway, 14th August:-
"No labour troubles mentioned.

II. ALBERTA

12. Developments in the Crow's Nest Pass.

175/1965.A report dated 28th August, from the N.C.O. in charge at Blairmore, after noting Christophers' activity in the district, says;-[12]

"There is no doubt but what the miners will strike this Fall, and I have received reliable information that the O.B.U. are working hard and will endeavour to get the railway employees to go out on strike with the miners, and it is the opinion of some that unless the O.B.U. can get the railway men to go out, the strike will not amount to much."

175/420.

P.M. Christophers returned to Blairmore on 31st August and worked very actively among the miners. R. McDonald, the local O.B.U. Secretary on 1st September was reported to have received a good deal of registered mail, during the two previous days. This contained money, apparently a considerable sum.

175/420.P.M. Christophers visited Fernie on 25th and 26th August, apparently to confer with Thomas Uphill, a local agitator and the brains of the Fernie, O.B.U. and Sawyer, the local O.B.U. SECRETARY.

On 1st September, it is reported, the situation was quiet, the miners were more satisfied than they had been for some time, and the O.B.U. seemed at a standstill. In AUGUST barely 100 men paid dues to the O.B.U. and Sawyer was looking for a job".

---

13. One Big Union Notes.

175/4 P.M. Christophers' fortnightly report of 14th AUGUST claims considerable gains for the O.B.U. in Drumheller, where he spent some days. He was endeavouring to arrange an O.B.U. convention for "District No. 1", (i.e. Alberta in Calgary.)

175/3 .An investigation on 1st September showed that the strike at the Chinook Mines, Commerce. near Lethbridge, was continuing with no sign of a settlement. It had been in effect for two weeks. The manager [13] had about 20 men at work underground and 30 on the surface; the mines were working but at a loss.

---

14. Miscellaneous Notes.

175/451.A notice of Reverend Wm. Irvine of Calgary states that the recent attempt to found a Labour Church in Calgary, with him as "pastor" failed. At present he is editing the Western Independent, formerly the Alberta Non-Partisan, the organ of the U.F.A. He also is organizer for that body. Not long ago he presided at a meeting of the Self Determination for Ireland League; otherwise he has been quiet of late.

175/67.At the Socialist meeting in Edmonton on 29th August J.F. Maguire attacked the I.W.W. The attendance was only 40, and the collection only $2.36.

175/140.J.B. Williams of the I.B.S.A. was the speaker at the open-air meeting at Edmonton on Sunday 29th August. His discourse contained the usual predictions of the subversion of Government, Society etc.

175/200The Edmonton Statesman has suspended publication temporarily and perhaps permanently. It was in effect the organ of Mayor Joseph Clarke.

III. SASKATCHEWAN

15. End of the Bienfait Strike.

175/3183.There has been an exodus of foreign-born O.B.U. and from the Bienfait Mines. About 30 have gone to Kipp Mines, Alberta. The two [14] leaders, Diaczun and Michalowski, have gone to Winnipeg. About 10 have left the O.B.U. and returned to work.

Negotiations took place on 24th and 25th August between two part owners of the Taylorton Mine and two representatives of the O.B.U., E.J. McMurray the lawyer and H. Cottrel the organizer. The Company was disposed to re-employ the O.B.U. men, under agreement to cause no more trouble before May next; it would not, however employ Diaczun, who had made threats of violence. The O.B.U. resented this discrimination. At this stage, the Company consulted the men who had remained at work and refused to strike; most if not all of these were English-speaking. These men objected strongly to men who remained O.B.U. members being taken back. Our report is;-

> "Several of them told Mr. Sutherland that the O.B.U. was the first footing of Bolshevism and it would be a good thing for Taylorton and all Canada to get rid of them and that every white man refused to go to work if they were allowed back. They told Mr. Sutherland that the O.B.U. was agitating a rebellion and they were not going to work with a O.B.U. man".

This decided the management, and the men who persisted in remaining with the O.B.U. were ordered off, with the result already stated. Their families were allowed to remain in their houses on the Company's land for a month.

This has been a reaction in Winnipeg. On returning to Winnipeg Cottrell published in the O.B.U. Bulletin of 4th September an account of the transaction in which he displays great bitterness against the Anti-

O.B.U. miners. This is given the most conspicuous place in the paper and is headed "The English-speaking Workers Disloyal as Usual." This is likely to accentuate racial bitterness.[15]

---

16. Dissatisfaction with International Headquarters.

175/2587The Regina local of the Brotherhood of Electrical Workers on 25th August cut loose from their International Union headquarters at Springfield, Illinois. The local propose to continue as an independent union; whether they join the O.B.U. probably depends on whether it gains ground or not.

The principal reason for the defection, according to our informant, is the dissatisfaction over the "per capita tax" question, the men feeling that they sent away half their dues and got no service in return. On this subject our informant says;-

> "Speaking from an organized Workers' point of view, the O.B.U. is far superior to the International Union in-so-far as this per capita question is concerned. O.B.U. Organizers and agitators use this per capita question as one of their main weapons to fight International Unionism and I am of the opinion that this will be the main cause for many other Unions affiliated with the A.F. of L. breaking away from it. Another point which must be considered and which causes much criticism among the Labourers is the initiation fee paid by the different Tradesmen. For instance bricklayers pay the sum of $25.00 as initiation fee and $2.25 monthly dues".

After giving an instance of the lack of interest in the craft unionism by non-unionists in Regina, he adds:-

> "Apparently International Unionism is losing ground in this city, caused chiefly the fact that non-Union men receive just as much pay and just as much work as Union men are getting".

---

17. Miscellaneous Notes.

175/586.The O.B.U. Units at Moose Jaw are inactive and the members dissatisfied.[16]

175/2932.Investigation into reports of revolutionary activity at Gravelbourg show these to be unfounded.

175/3234The International Bible Students Association is very active now in Northern Saskatchewan. At Yorkton their membership number 100.

175/3231Attention has been drawn to a boat-captain named Hicks, who is employed about the Pas, who is active in this sect. He is given to defending Lenin and Trotsky and arguing that the Bolsheviki are carrying on God's work on earth in accordance with the prophecies of the Scriptures.

175/2989The meeting of the Regina branch of the G.A.U.V. held on 25th August was attended by 16 persons.

1V. MANITOBA

18. O.B.U. Notes.

175/3201The Winnipeg Running Trades Unit O.B.U. at a thinly attended meeting on 27th August decided to conduct the unit as a secret organization, so as to be able secretly to enroll men who were members of the International and as such forbidden to join any other labour organization.

The chairman of the meeting, a C.P.R. engineer named Stephenson, said he had to keep his connection with the O. B. U. secret until 1st December. He had gone on strike in 1919, and had been taken back into the Internationals on a friend's vouching for his good [17] behaviour until that date; to protect his friend he wished his violation of the conditions concealed.

175/424A strange incident occurred at a Socialist open-air meeting at Winnipeg on Sunday 29th August. The attendance was 200-250, and most of the O.B.U. leaders were present. The speaker, Charles Stewart, made a Socialistic address of the usual sort, including in his remarks a denunciation of W.H. Hoop as a traitor. He went on to say that recently a stranger who claimed to belong to the Socialist Party of Australia had come without credentials, had desired to speak, and had not been trusted. Thereupon a man in the audience avowed himself to be the person in question and took the platform. His speech was a series of taunts to Stewart for avoiding the point as to whether he believed in direct action. Stewart in his rejoinder suggested that the interloper was "one of the tools in the hands of the Capitalist Class", and challenged him to tell whence he came and who he was. On search being made the interrupter could not be found. Our informant inclines to the belief that he was a detective of some agency.

177/8The Winnipeg Typographical Union is said to be considering the advisability of refusing to set up the One Big Union Bulletin on the ground that it exists to destroy craft unionism.

---

19. The Federated Press.

175/3250The following curious report is furnished by an agent in Winnipeg;[18]

"It is thought by some members of the O.B.U. that the new wireless being erected by the Federated Press will be at Charleston, U.S.A.

"This new wireless is to be direct with Russia in order that the Federated Press, which is an organized radical Press system may get the direct news from Russia, concerning the Labour movement there, so that the same tactics may be used in this country, and the correct news procured for the numerous papers and Bulletins which make up the Federation.

"The head department of this Press Federation is in the U.S.A., I understand, but such a direct connection with Russia could be used for many purposes."

---

20. Miscellaneous Notes.

175/87The meeting of the Labour Church of Winnipeg on 29th August was attended by about 800 persons, which is much below the seating capacity of the theatre which was used. D.B. Harkness of the Social Council spoke on liquor control.

175/2620.A report from Winnipeg states that the Jews there have sent over $20000 "for the Jewish leaders in Soviet Russia"; and that about twice as much has been sent from the United States.

V. ONTARIO.

21. Revolutionary Activities in Toronto.

175/3253.A review of the revolutionary activities now being prosecuted in Toronto by a person acquainted with the foreign element shows the following organizations to be at work;-[19]

1. One Big Union.Speakers are Mr. and Mrs. J.R. Knight, J. Blodley and Max Armstrong.
2. Ontario Labour College.Speakers are George Wilshow, Curley Hodgins, "Lou the Greek" and some others from Continental Europe.
3. Workers' Educational League, Speakers are- Roberts and Mrs. Florence Constance (or Custance.)
4. Independent Labour Party. Speakers are O'Connor McDonald.

All of the foregoing are described as incessantly praising the Soviet Government of Russia and urging the overthrow of the Government of Canada. Our informant is of opinion that the audiences addressed are little impressed.

He states that the extremists are spreading the idea that there will be trouble in Canada this Winter.

There is a secession in progress from the O.B.U. to the Communist Party. This meets in the Ontario Labour College. Some of the extremists are assailing "Jammie" Simpson and the Independent Labour Party.

175/3252.The Workers' Educational League has made its appearance in Toronto in connection with the Ontario Labour College. On 29th

August the League held an open-air meeting, the speakers being Corley (or Curley) Hodgins and George Wilshow, (?Wiltshire) of the Labour College, Wilshow's speech was extremely revolutionary.

It may be noted that there has been working for some time in Toronto an excellent institution, the Workers' Educational Association; it is designed, to enable workingmen to undertake serious study, under the guidance of university men, of a number of subjects.[20]

175/2724.

175/3237.Our attention is being drawn to the Ontario Labour College, 28 Wellington Street, Toronto. It is described as the meeting place of the I.W.W. Communists and other Radicals of the city. These men are of different nationalities, Russians, Russian Jews, Bulgarians, Greeks, etc. It is a depositary for revolutionary literature, revolutionary conversation is constantly proceeding there, and it is an organizing point. The open-air meetings which the One Big Union now are holding always are attended by a know of these men; they form the nucleus of an audience, sell O.B.U. reading matter, and handle interrupters roughly. An account of the School supplied to the Star is described as untrue.

175/3237.The Labour College according to announcements at open air meetings, is starting a new course which will run from October till March or April. The teaching given would be far superior to that given at the university, and the library was far better than the selection of books at the Public Library. Our report adds:-

> "They stated that these Labour Colleges had originally sprung from the Ruskin College in London, but that the more progressive element had broken away from the Ruskin College and started Labour Colleges, and they had met with great success in several of the big industrial centres in Great Britain, notably in Glasgow, Birmingham and Wales".

175/2724.At an open-air meeting in Toronto on 21st August J.R. Knight was jubilant over the threat of hard times. "More men out of work is the best propaganda we can have. When the workers will get hungry, they will wake up and see what the labour conditions are in Canada. He said that something is going to happen here next Winter."[21]

175/2475Anna Buller of Montreal may go to Windsor for a while to superintend the distribution of revolutionary reading matter there.

175/2475J.R. Knight is arranging a circuitous route for the mailing of the O. B. U. Bulletin from Winnipeg to Toronto, as he thinks that when sent direct the bundles are "conveniently lost".

175/539.J.R. Knight's fortnightly report for 27th July, 27th to 10th

August described visits to Iroquois, Timmins, Kirkland Lake in New Ontario; his journey to Winnipeg to take part in the debate of 6th August; and his visit to Edmonton. On 10th August he was on his way to Toronto.

175/2830.Internationals in London are said to have bestirred themselves against the O.B.U. more particularly on the railway unions.

---

22. Foreign Revolutionists.

175/2638.We have heard additional particulars about the Russian Socialistic School in Toronto. The address is 111 Dundas Street. The teachers are Vasili Dedokin, Nestor and Mrs. Coldberg, the last named a Russian Jewess, Dedokin has stated that he obtained the money from Detroit.

175/325?.A notice of the "Society of Technical Help to the Soviet of Russia" of Detroit in the Russky Goles (Voice of Russia) shows that in that School the curriculum is Arithmetic, Algebra, Geometry, "technic", and the Russian language.[22]

175/3256.Mrs. Sonia Goldberg, the Russian Jewess who has appeared as a teacher in the Russian School at Toronto has stated in conversation that she arrived in Canada 3 months ago from Russia (Province of "Bocroisk"). She was a teacher for the Soviet for two years. She is well educated. She knows little English.

175/3255.The World Conference of Polia Sien (Jewish Anarchist Communist Party) held last August in Vienna by a small majority decided to join the Third International, and to abstain from the Zionist Conference. The American, English and Palestinian delegates left the conference in protest.

II. MARITIME PROVINCES.

23. General View of the Coal Situation.

The Officer Commanding Maritime Provinces in a careful review of the labour situation in the coal mines of Cape Breton comes to the conclusion that it requires careful observation and is difficult to judge; but he inclines to the belief that a strike this Winter is unlikely.

The general situation is much influenced by the character of the miners. They are insular, high spirited, impatient and very ignorant; they have little idea of the difference between Provincial and Federal spheres of action; and they hear nothing upon public affairs, except from their own leaders. On the other side, is lack of understanding between the mine management and the men, and the latter complain of red tape in management. It is noted that there has been a gratifying decrease in accidents since the readjustment of hours.[23]

These being the general conditions, particular aspects of the situation are;-

1. The pronouncement of the Royal Commission is impending. The Labour leaders are trying to discount it by threatening to strike if it does not hurry. "This talk is not taken seriously by well-informed men".
2. Sooner or later the Merger and the Miners will have a trial of strength; the exact date cannot be predicted. The financing of the Merger has not been completed; until it is complete the operators will not provoke a conflict. Once it is accomplished they may force a fight, but this seems remote at the moment.
3. The U.M.W. of A. while well organized, find the rank and file hard to handle and impatient. The steadier miners are being driven out of control of the locals by the more radical men and there are many unnecessary stoppages of work over trivial matters. While McLachlan and Barrett are regarded by the steadier men as too extreme; they in turn are troubled by these one-day strikes; and have threatened to revoke the charters of some locals.
4. The frequency of miner local strikes is promoting dissension between the miners who wish to work, and those who do not.
5. The miners are most suspicious of and hostile to all police forces, chiefly because of their dislike of the Dominion Coal Company's Police.
6. The production of coal has decreased since 1914, and the men are not disposed to increase it. Over 5000 men went overseas voluntarily and there has been no great importation of labour to replace them. The opening of additional mines should help to effect an increase.

as. <u>Miscellaneous Notes.</u>

175/3240. Following is a report from an agent in the Nova Scotia mines:-

"Some time ago 25 Germans made their way to No. 4 Mine Caladonia. They started in to work and appeared in their army uniform. For some time on account of so many returned men working in this mine, a serious riot was expected at any time, however, matters have been adjusted and now the Teutons appear at work in ordinary civilian clothes.[24]

"Some fear is felt among the people that trouble may yet arise among the returned men who don't seem at any way pleased at such men coming into our Country".

175/3241. The Royal Commission on the Coal Industry in Nova Scotia has removed a grievance suffered by the men at Nos. 10 and 11 Collieries,

Dominion Coal Company. The conditions have prevented the use of the horses ordinarily employed, and the men have had to push the coal boxes themselves, sometimes for 300 yards; the box when loaded weighs 1 ton 7 ewt. The Commission having inspected the mine have agreed with the men, and the company now are training ponies to do the work.

ROYAL CANADIAN MOUNTED POLICE HEADQUARTERS

Ottawa, 16th September, 1920.

SECRET

NO. 41

NOTES OF THE WORK OF THE C. I. B. DIVISION FOR THE WEEK ENDING 16TH SEPTEMBER

Table of Contents

" 13. The Plans of the Leaders.
Bringing out the railway men.
" 14. Later Reports.
Situation in Fernie.
Christopher in Coleman.
Christopher at Blairmore.
Attempt to cause a sympathetic strike of railway men.
The Michel Local, U.M.W. of A.
Strike at Wayne.
Lawson and the railway men.
Chinook strike over.
" 15. Then General Situation.
" 16. Events in Calgary.
The Shop Stewards.
Proposal to organize Russians and Germans.
Ald. Broatch a delegate to Port Arthur.
Marlow as an agitator.
The O.B.U. Class-meeting.
Affairs of the Searchlight.
" 17. Dissensions in Edmonton.
J.F. Maguire as an organizer.
Berg quarrelling with the Building Trades Unit.
Attempt to capture the Stationary Engineers.
" 18. Saskatchewan; Miscellaneous Notes.
Affairs of the Regina O.B.U.
" 19. Manitoba; General Notes.
Ex-soldiers and Sailors Labour Party Meeting.
The Ukrainians.
Jewish Contributions to Soviet Funds.
The Shop Stewards.
Bitterness towards Hoop.
The O.B.U. Bulletin.
Labour Day at Fort William.
" 20. Ontario; Labour Day events.
The Parade at Toronto.
The Extremists in the Niagara District.
" 21. O.B.U. Notes.
Open-air meetings in Toronto.
Agitation in Hamilton.
Knight's activities.
" 22. Foreign Revolutionaries.
Just-off at Niagara Falls.
Winding's movements.
Fugitive Russian Jews at Toronto.

Henry Dworkin's utterances.
The Bulgarian Socialist Party.
Incendiary reading matter in Toronto.
New Anarchist Communist Party and its Cover.

" 23. The Federated Order of Railway Employees.

" 24. Quebec: The Friction in the O.B.U.
Binette's Account of Knight's tactics.
The O.B.U. and the A.S.E.

" 25. A Thrifty Revolutionist.
Report on A. ST. Martin.
St. Martin's anti-religious language.[3]

" 26. Miscellaneous Notes.
The "Society for Technical Aid to Soviet Russia".
Report on Reverend J.B. Pike.

" 27. Conditions in the Cape Breton Coal Fields.[4]

1. Characteristics of the Period.

The approach of the dates set for the O.B.U. Convention and for the Alberta Coal Strike are the principal events of the week; the actual happenings include nothing very noticeable. As regards the Port Arthur Convention; we still hear of the rather mysterious ground-swell which is threatening the tenure of office of several of the O.B.U. leaders; our information this week is more in the nature of confirmations of last week's news than of fresh occurrences, though from one quarter comes the statement that one cause of the disturbance is J.R. Knight's attempt to utilize the absence of Russell and Johns from the counsils of the O.B.U. to give the organization an Anarchistic twist. It is noticeable in this connection that Knight's associates in Eastern Canada tend to come from the Communistic foreign elements.

As regards the Western Coal fields, evidence accumulates both that the leaders intend to provoke a strike, and that they feel too weak for a long struggle, and so desire to organize a sympathetic strike of railwaymen. The "Labour College" project is making an appearance in British Columbia.

I. BRITISH COLUMBIA

2. Cross Currents in the O.B.U.

The Officer Commanding British Columbia in his confidential monthly report for August makes some interesting observations of a general nature;-[5]

"A large number of loggers have been out of employment during the month owing to camps closing down because of fire risks. Forest fires have been prevalent. Altogether to date this season there have been 754 fires costing the Government $71,458.00, according to figures compiled by the Chief Forester.

"Not so much trouble has been experienced on account of strikes as heretofore. The I.W.W. element is gaining in power and indications are that E. Winch, the present general secretary-treasurer will have a hard fight to retain his position. This he realizes, and in order to hold on as long as possible he has ceased to oppose the I.W.W. openly, and is playing his cards in such a manner as to lead them to believe that he has come to their way of thinking, while in reality he will continue to oppose them. How long this will last is problematical. The result of the voting on Clause 5 on the Coast Referendum Ballot, which was put through by the I.W.W. element and reads as follows;-

> "Are you in favour That the Coast District withdraw from the Central Executive Board of the Lumber & Camp Workers' Industrial Union; and affiliate direct with the General Executive Board of the O.B.U.?"

will have a direct bearing on the term of his office, and no doubt this was the cause of Winch's change of tactics.

"Investigations have been carried on as usual during the month. Indications are that there has been no great activity towards advancement in membership, and the standards of its moral seems to be steadily, although perhaps slowly, weakening. One of its present main leaders is sick of the thanklessness of the work which he has been performing for the past four years; and confidently expects that the rank and file of the organization will leave him stranded high and dry without an executive position just as soon as the opportunity offers. This same leader expects also that another of the organization's officials will find himself in a similar position, mainly through the action of the I.W.W. element in the L.W.I.U. gaining strength. These leaders recognise that Canada is a 'land of plenty', that the employer is humane; that there is little room in the minds of the great mass of the Canadian public for 'Bolshevistic' thought, but they still hope that trouble may follow in the wake of labor trouble in Europe (Great Britain especially) and in the United States, and no doubt much will depend on that.[6]

"From time to time it is apparent that the conscientious workers, members of the O.B.U. having joined that organization in the full belief that it would be an act to their individual betterment, and having stayed with it long enough to find out its weak point, now repudiate it entirely and sever their connection. A notable instance of this may be found in the folios of a file 're O.B.U. Strike at Camp 17. Pacific Mills Ltd., Ocean Falls'. In this case an O.B.U. strike was called, which was at first supported by a majority. In its finality, however, the O.B.U. delegate and four others were ordered out of Camp by the men. These four men were able to control 40 others who took their time and left also. The rest went back to work, and many of these tore up their O.B.U. membership cards and declared they were through with the organization for ever.

"There have been no new strikes during the month, except that at Camp 17 aforesaid".

Dealing with unemployment he says;-

"Gratifying figures are shown in the Provincial Employment returns for the month of August and the results obtained were greater than in any previous month since the employment service was instituted. The main factor in bringing about this increase was the sending of men to the prairie provinces for harvest work. These still out of employment- Victoria having the usual high proportion- could obtain work if they interested themselves in jobs outside their own locality".

The interview with Winch was incorporated in the last issue of the Summary. The comments of the Officer Commanding show the importance which he attaches to it.

3. More about the O.B.U. Dissensions.

In a report dated 3rd September, the N.C.O. in charge of C.I.B. work at Vancouver says;-

"Recent reports indicate that the One Big Union organization is being gradually undermined, partly through mismanagement of its affairs; partly by apathy on the part of its officials; partly by the disgust which individual members have openly expressed from time to time; partly by the rebuffs of employers, and lastly but not least by any means, the growing activities of the I.W.W.

"It is too early to say that the O.B.U. is disintegrating, but it will be very interesting to see what will happen to it after the next convention".[7]

After recalling the interview with Midgley which has been quoted in these notes, he says;-

"Midgley and Winch have been hard workers for their organization. If these two men go out of its active service, it may be that it will be the commencement of 'Disintegration'.

After mentioning the present activities of Boyd and CAllman, he says;-

"There seems to be a general belief that an I.W.W. local will be launched here in the near future.

"In Victoria, the O.B.U. appears to be a dead issue. Half the time the Hall is deserted and unopened mail is lying around for anyone to do much as they like with".

Under date of 4th September he notes that,-

"Both Winch and Midgley of the O.B.U. fully expect to be ousted from office by the I.W.W. element in their ranks at the next Convention". He recalls in this connection Allman's enterprise at Vancouver, which has been noted already.

4. The O.B.U. in the Metalliferous Mines.

Further information has come to hand as to the standing of the O.B.U. in the Metalliferous Mines.

The N.C.O. in charge at Trail reports that at the Rossland works of the Consolidated Mining and Smelting Company about 150 persons are employed, of whom 100 are members of the O.B.U. At the Trail works 1600 men are employed, of whom 300 are, if not actual members, at all events sympathizers. Upon this the O.C. West Kootenay observes;-

> "There has been a good deal of investigation in regard to the actual membership of the O.B.U. at Trail and Rossland. On the one hand the O.B.U. was boasting of a membership of 700 to 800 or more and on the other hand the management of the C.S. & M. Co. claimed that there were not more than 50 actual members. Two S.A.'s at [8] different times were sent down to Trail in an effort to see whether the O.B.U. was actually strong there, as it was indicated that the employees of the Trail smelter were secretly members of the O.B.U. and that there was danger of labor troubles developing there. However, last Spring the O.B.U. attempted to call a strike at Trail; there was no response, none of the men leaving their work and only small numbers attending the meetings of the O.B.U. agitators who were in Trail attempting to call a strike. The mines at Rossland did go on strike at this time, but only stayed out a couple of days and the objects of the strike were not gained. The management of the C.S. & M. Co. are strongly opposed to the O.B.U. they do detective work on their own initiative and discharge any O.B.U. agitators immediately they discover them. Because of this there is an obvious tendency on the part of O.B.U. members and sympathizers to hide the fact and it is difficult to ascertain just what the actual paying membership of the O.B.U. is, I have heard of actual cases, of O.B.U. members putting their buttons in their pocket when they went to ask for a job at the smelter. However, there is so much to discourage membership of the O.B.U. at Trail that I think, that while Cpl. Withers may be correct in regard to the number of actual sympathizers, the number of paying members to the O.B.U. at Trail is much smaller".

The N.C.O. in charge at Nelson is of opinion that the O.B.U. members there is confined to the general workers' unit and is of a fluctuating nature, owing to the nomadic character of the labour concerned.

The strike in the Metalliferous mines of the Slocan district now has lasted for four months.

---

5. General O.B.U. Notes.

The O.B.U. are trying to organize the Chinese at Cumberland. Many of whom are coalminers. Pamphlets in Chinese are being distributed among them. The attempt is not viewed seriously. The N.C.O. in charge of the detachment in reporting this says;-

"The Chinese are split up into Tongs and factions each having a leader who practically owns the remainder of the Chinese in his faction. The result is that these men cannot do anything against the wishes of the few leaders and unless the O.B.U. can get these [9] few to join them any other attempts at organization are bound to prove a failure. There are about 500 Chinese working in the mines here, and should these men organize and go on strike it would seriously handicap the working of the mines although it would not necessarily cause them to close down. At present there is no prospect of anything like this happening".

In commenting on this the Officer Commanding British Columbia says;-

"The different elements of Chinese in Vancouver are controlled by about seven "Tongs", the leaders of which are fast becoming wealthy through their commercial enterprises".

The Finnish Unit, O.B.U. in Vancouver is in somewhat depressed circumstances. The Finnish Society about 7 years ago numbered about 350 members, and erected a hall at a cost of $15000. The membership now is only about 150, many having left Vancouver, some to return to Finland; and some of the younger men have learned trades, joined Canadian organizations, and drifted away. The Society consequently is hard put to it to keep up the hall, is offering it for sale at $13000. The O.B.U. Unit is a general workers one, and has only about a dozen members. It meets at the aforesaid hall.

A report from Yahk dated 29th August says that at the moment there was very little O.B.U. talk in the lumber camps of the district.

The O.B.U. has a paid organizer named Michael Casey living in Penticton. He is working in the camps from Penticton to Fairview; the men in these are employed upon an irrigation system which the Provincial Government is erecting. Most of these men are returned soldiers, and Casey's prospects are not considered good.

J.H. Thompson has been elected District Secretary L.W.I.U., for the Cranbrook District. The five members of the District Board are; Lee Rader; F. Bidder; W.L. Allen; G. Jorgenson; O.J. Dandineau. Of [10] these Bidder and Dandineau have attracted our notice before.

6. Other Labour Notes.

Following is a report from Vancouver dated 7th September;-

"The longshoremen are very quiet, now, and seem to wish to remain so. They recently reached an agreement with the coastwise lines for a new agreement, 90 cents an hour straight time and $1.15 for overtime, with special rates for hazardous or disagreeable jobs. The deep-sea workers are considering demands for some increases, but have not made them. They will ask $1, an hour, I am told.

"Some trouble was recently averted. The steamer 'Eastern Victor', a U.S. shipping board boat, came up to load steel rails for the Black Sea. It is understood that they are going to the Black Sea, for General Wrangel. The ship came in and loading had been going on for three days before a story appeared in the paper telling where the rails were going.

"I saw the Secretary George Thomas on the Street the following day and asked him how the boys felt about sending rails to General Wrangel. He replied that it was lucky the ship had been 'worked' for three days before the men knew where they were loading for. Had they known it when the ship arrived there would have been no rails loaded. As it was the 'reds' in the union tried very hard to persuade the men to quit, as soon as they found they were loading for an enemy to the Bolsheviki. But the majority of the men held that the job had proceeded so far it might as well be finished. The ship was not going to the Black Sea direct, any way, but was going to Seattle to pick up more rails. They would complete loading the 2600 tons that were in Vancouver, and meantime would notify the longshoremen of Seattle. If the latter thought it advisable to refuse to load the ship they could do so.

"The Eastern Victor" reached Seattle Tuesday night, August 31st, No word has yet reached here of any difficulties there".

A report from a well-informed source dated Vancouver 7th September, deals with the Street Railway situation, to the effect, that a strike is probable and that it will not be unwelcome to the Company, as a means of obtaining an increase in fares. The average pay of the [11] men is $125.00 a month, and they will ask for an increase of at least 10 cents an hour.

The Gas Workers of Vancouver, an O.B.U. organization struck on 8th September. A Conciliation Board made an award which the men rejected. V.R. Midgley represented the men on the Board and he made a minority report. The men, whose wages are high, put up rather a poor case. The COMPANY is maintaining the supply of gas, and seems determined. Midgley's personal belief, however, is that the Company is using the dispute to obtain an increase in the price of gas.

7. A "Labour College" Project in Vancouver.

The "Labour College" idea is spreading to the West. A circular letter dated 26th August 1920 has been sent out, signed by J.M. Clarke, Coast District Secretary of the L.W.I.U. It is as follows;-

"As the equilibrium of Capitalist Society gets more and more upset, and as the financial super-structure of Capitalism becomes more and more complicated and unworkable we realize as never before the vital necessity of as many members of our class understanding the social forces at work, and the vital problems that confront us. In the British Isles they have established labor colleges in which members of the various organizations receive an education in working class questions. Although the O.B.U. is not in a condition financially to maintain a college where members of the O.B.U. could go and receive an education; yet nevertheless, personally I cannot see why a correspondence school could not be started at some central point, which correspondence school could work in conjunction with an educational committee appointed in the various districts. Personally I cannot see why a scheme of that nature could not be worked out and put into operation. It would mean that the O.B.U. would this be in a position to disseminate working class propaganda; educate its members as to their class position in society; and thus make a good live membership, who would not think, or believe that a certain act on the part of the Master Class might mean a certain thing, but it would tend to give us a membership which would know [12] exactly what it did mean. A blind man can see that Capitalism is nearing its end, and it is up to us as members of the working class, the class that will have to carry on and administer industry, that we fully understand the problem we will be confronted with and thus be in a position to successfully carry on production after Capitalism has fallen. The O.B.U. Convention will be held at Port Arthur on September 20th, if you desire, or think that any action should be taken in this matter please notify us if there is any other matter which you would like to have taken up at that convention".

The fact that this move is made by a union which contains one of the roughest, most illiterate and most nomadic and unstable classes of labour should not blind us to the effect that such schools might have. They would be training places for soap-box orators.- promoters of half-knowledge and glibness.

In this connection it may be noted that the Citizens League of Winnipeg is moving on two lines. (1) To promote increased study of civics in the University. (2) TO EStablish a Public Service Committee of men trained to fight the Marxian School. These men will be trained to argue and to speak.

8. Kavanagh's Violent Utterances.

J. Kavanagh, spoke at the usual Sunday Socialist meeting in Vancouver on 5th September. There was a large audience, which included many foreigners. The collection was $98.00

Extracts from his speech are:-

After referring to the bringing of Austrian children to England for feeding he said;-

"I heard from good authority that they were children of the better class of Austrian people- the children of the other class were, of course, left to their fate. The reason for this was that the Master class of Britain preferred a more intelligent and healthy lot of children, so that when they grew up, they would be of a superior class. But Hungary made a big mistake when the Proletariat overthrew the Capitalist, and that was to have let any of them get away alive; they let them go in peace, which gave the Masters a chance to come back and cause greater bloodshed than would have been had the Proletariat murdered the whole of the Master class when they overthrew them".

Concerning the Irish question he said.-

"We knew that the pure Sinn Fein movement aims at establishing a strong capitalist system in Ireland. What we can't understand is why England is opposed to it, but the trouble in Ireland is not all Sinn Fein. England didn't send 80,000 soldiers into Ireland because of a little religious difference; they are simply trying to use religion to camouflage the situation; it's the old game of the Master class. While I was over there, the Railway men went on strike throughout the country, demanding that certain Political prisoners would be released, and they tied up things in such a way that they were soon granted their demands -so that's something for us to take notice of".

After saying that "The European question depends on the working class of Great Britain," and boasting of the freedom with which the red flag is flown in England, he said,-

"What we want to do in this country is just what our fellow workers of other countries are doing- refuse to load supplies for the enemies of our fellow-workers; refuse to make ammunition for the enemies of the working man. This is our one and only way to show our comrades in other countries that we are with them, heart and soul, and we can show the Masters that we are something of importance, because when we stop, everything stops".

9. Mrs. Rose Henderson at Vancouver.

Mrs. Rose Henderson spoke at a poorly attended meeting of the Federated Labour Party at Vancouver on 7th September. She urged political action, one passage in her speech is thus reported;-[14]

"The coming Coal strike in England will be unsuccessful on account of Lloyd George being unable (?able) to use all available power of the State to counteract the actions of the strikers. If we wish to be successful in the coming elections, we must remember that Machine guns are in the hands of our enemies and that they will use them against us. One machine gun will put to rent five thousand persons, so we must act accordingly, and educate ourselves to a political standpoint that will be superior to that of our enemies".

The Federated Labour Party has taken a lease of rooms in Vancouver for two years.

10. Miscellaneous Notes.

The Federated Labour Party held a convention at Summerland on 19th August and decided to contest the bye-election which is to be held in Yale in consequence of the resignation of the Hon. Martin Burrell. Mr. Tom Richardson, formerly a member of the British House, was invited to be the candidate.

Up to 4th September no reply had been received from Mr. Richardson. He is unknown in the constituency and is not likely to obtain more than seven or eight hundred votes at most.

The "Labour Temple" Ukrainian organization in Vancouver seems to be falling to pieces with the departure of John Boychuk. It has only 22 members. It managed to raise $158.00 for the Ukrainian Labour News, and has about $80.00 on hand.

Charles Lestor is leaving for England in a few weeks. He has no official backing, and is paying his own way.

The British Columbia Federationist of 3rd September, in its L.W.I.U. page contains an appeal to farm labourers to join the O.B.U. It is signed by J. McIntyre.[15]

At a propaganda meeting of the L.W.I.U. held on 22nd August the British Columbia Federationist was criticised as being inefficient, and a committee was appointed to go into the matter.

In this connection, a report comes from Lawson in Calgary that since the Federationist took up the O.B.U. cause its advertising patronage has fallen off by one quarter.

11. British Columbia Detachment Reports;-

Prince George, 22nd August:-

"The labor situation is quiet. There is a noticeable shortage of labor available in the lumbering industry. At Hutton, B.C. where some 300 men are employed they are at present doing what they can with 100 men. Men working in the saw-mills left in large numbers for the prairies for the harvesting in the district".

Alert Bay, 21st August:-

"Labor conditions are steadily becoming more satisfactory in this district. No reports of any labor trouble have been received during the week".

Port Alberni, 28th August.

"District quiet and orderly. Labor conditions quiet. Mills and camps working steadily".

II. ALBERTA

12. The Alberta Coalfields.

The N.C.O. in charge of C.I.B. work in Southern Alberta in a survey of the situation dated 30th August makes the following observations:-

(1) A convention of the "Mining Department, No. 1. O.B.U." was to be held in Calgary on 10th September. Notices calling it were out.

(2) The Convention was to decide whether to call a strike at the end of September or the end of October. This strike was not to be about wages, working conditions, etc., but to be a fight between the O.B.U. and the U.M.W. of A.[16]

"This is more or less the last stand of the O.B.U. in the mining field", and it all depends upon the backbone of the respective operators." "If the Operators will stand pat and abide by their agreement, it is believed that the strike will only last the matter of a few days. However, in the event of certain of the operators weakening and recognizing the O.B.U. it will mean a continued source of trouble and strikes throughout the mining district for sometime to come".

(4) "Rod McDonald, O.B.U. Secretary at Blairmore, stated in conversation,- "They were about to hold a meeting, the subject being "direct action, and that the O.B.U. element expected to call the strike the latter part of September or the beginning of October this year, the trouble to commence in the lignite fields of Drumheller and Lethbridge".

(5) Many miners, in view of the imminence of a strike, have gone to the harvest fields. THUS THE STRIKE will not affect them, and thee is some shortage of labour. This shortage is particularly noticeable in Blairmore.

(6) The U.M.W. of A. are getting impatient, and if the operators recognize the O.B.U. probably will abandon the district.

(7) He reiterates the view that everything depends upon the firmness of the operators, "If they show any signs of weakness, the miners are pretty sure to come out in strength".

A report dated 31st August confirms the fact that the convention was to be held on 10th September, Ten or fifteen mines would be represented. The Convention probably would be secret.

13. The Plans of the Leaders.

The plans entertained on 1st September were,- "Not to call a strike or set any date for a strike to be called, but to make arrangements throughout the district for the various mines to lay off work one at a time, till all the mines are out".

Our report continues,-

"Lawson is of the opinion that if the O.B.U. call a strike, there will be trouble for them, but states that no one can make a man work under a check-off of he doesn't want to, and that it is not illegal for a miner to "take a holiday" for a couple of weeks or so if the [17] miner wants to do so. "Lawson is further of the opinion that the O.B.U. will be so strong this Fall that there will be no need for more than a 24 hour strike, and stated that in the O.B.U. now there are enough trainmen, yardmen and switchmen to tie up the whole country as far as transportation is concerned".

Lawson (of the Searchlight) is one of the junta who are planning the strike.

14. Later Reports.

A report from Fernie dated 1st September says,-

"At present the majority of the men are all satisfied, and no talk of any kind among them. If there is going to be any trouble it would not start before November or December".

"Beard and Christopher will do all in their power to start trouble if they see men not paying O.B.U. dues, and men will not pay, as $1.50 is taken off the U.M.W. of A".

Christophers visited Coleman- on 2nd September arranging for an "Organization meeting" there on 5th September. The Unit there subsequently was resusciated on that date, about 80 men, mostly foreigners, attending. The feeling of the miners was described as aversion from the check-off but reluctance to strike.

P.M. Christophers returned to Blairmore on 31st August and worked very actively among the miners. R. McDonald, the local O.B.U. Secretary on 1st September was reported to have received a good deal of registered mail during the two previous days. This contained money, apparently a considerable sum.

A slightly earlier report, dated 28th August, from the N.C.O. in charge at Blairmore, after noting Christophers' activity in the district, says;-[18]

"There is no doubt but what the miners will strike this Fall, and I have received reliable information that the O.B.U. are working hard and will endeavour to get the railway employees to go out on strike with the miners, and it is the opinion of some that unless the O.B.U. can get the railway men to go out, the strike will not amount to much".

The Michel local of the U.M.W. of A. has been seized by the O.B.U. The President, Secretary and Treasurer were ejected from office and three Italians of O.B.U. sympathies replaced them; the meeting also voted to meet in the hall frequented by the O.B.U.

The N.C.O. in charge of the detachment say; under date of 3rd September;-

"From the way everything looks at present and the general conversation I am of the opinion that there will be another strike about November as at the present the U.M.W. of A. meetings are undoubtedly O.B.U.".

ANOTHER informant, who is well acquainted with the local situation, after reporting the same incident, says;-

"As a result of all this I find that while the miners at Michel are running normally at present the miners are divided and it would take but very little to precipitate matter and cause trouble".

On 2nd September a strike occurred at the Western Commercial Colleries at Wayne, in the Drumheller field. It affects about 10 men. It arose through a personal squabble, but feeling was shown against the U.M.W. of A. and the O.B.U. made the most of it.

P.F. Lawson attended a meeting of the Transportion Unit No. 1, O.B.U. held in Calgary on 3rd September. His speech is reported thus;-

"Lawson was present and spoke of the Searchlight and the miners. It seems that the leaders of the Union look for trouble this coming Winter. Lawson advised the meeting to attend the convention, as it would enable them to line up stronger and to discuss their lot and troubles together; also, that the Railway [19] Units would get a great deal of help from the miners of Alberta".

The strikers at the Chinook mines at Commerce, near Lethbridge, returned to work on 7th September. They had been out since 18th August. They failed to obtain exemption from the U.M.W. of A. check-off.

15. The General Situation.

Assembling the various reports, it is fair to conclude,-

(1) That the O.B.U. leaders are desperately anxious to call a strike.

(2) That there is perceptible some weakening among the rank and file.

(3) That because of this and perhaps because of shortage of funds, the leaders do not feel able to face a long strike, and on the whole feel rather weak.

(4) That for this reason every effort will be made to cause a railway strike and in general to make the attack on the community so violent as to force a quick decision.

16. Events in Calgary.

The Shop Steward's Committee at Calgary held their second meeting on 27th August. Not much had been done up to that time, though about 16 recruits have been secured for the O.B.U. It is held that the success of the O.B.U. movement among the C.P.R. employees there depends greatly upon this movement. It is too new to estimate what success it is likely to have.

In this connection the Officer Commanding Calgary remarks;-[20]

"This shop steward movement means that representatives, who have O.B.U. tendencies, are drawn from the various labor organizations and in effect appointed organizers for the O.B.U. in their respective industries. If the O.B.U. leaders are able to instruct and enthuse these men, they will, no doubt be able to do a good deal, individually towards spreading the O.B.U. doctrine".

A later report stated that the O.B.U. Shop Stewards in the Ogden Shops at Calgary had taken in 26 new members in the fortnight ending 3rd

September. They seem to have been aided by the bad impression made by McCutcheon, the International organizer who has appeared in Calgary. It is also reported that 24 freight handlers have joined the Transportation Unit.

The O.B.U. now propose to organize the Russians and Germans in Bridgeland, near Calgary.

Ald. Broatch is a delegate to the O.B.U. Port Arthur Convention from Calgary.

R.H. Morlow, an O.B.U. advocate of Calgary, who hitherto has confined himself to selling incendiary reading matter in the "Labour News Stand" has become active as an organizer. He has worked in the freight sheds, and early in September was contemplating a visit to Drumheller to peddle revolutionary books, etc.

The O.B.U. "Class Meeting" at Calgary is growing slightly in numbers. The present lot seem a muddle-headed crew, little likely to get anywhere. They are, however, being trained in argument, and it may turn out some capable agitators.[21]

James Bewsher, who is Secretary of the U.M.W. of A. local at Nordegg, has sent to P.F. Lawson a grant of $50.00 from the local and some money for subscriptions for the Searchlight. Bewsher apparently is acting treacherously.

P.F. Lawson lately has received rather more financial aid, having got $2251. in two gifts. He does a good deal of downright begging among the miners, more particularly among the foreigners. He is trying to organize a boycott for the new labour paper which is to be started by the Internationals. His debt to the printers now amounts to $700.

17. Dissension in Edmonton O.B.U.

The Edmonton O.B.U. have appointed an organizing committee of four, half from the Transportation Workers and half from the Building Trades Unit. J.F. Maguire was appointed organizer, his salary to be $25.00 for the first week.

Dissension has appeared. Carl E. Berg and Coombs appear to have fallen out. Berg and Maguire also appear to be at loggerheads. The Building Trades Unit seems to have turned against him.

The representatives of this unit on the Central Labour Council of Edmonton were instructed on 1st September to oppose sending a delegate to the Convention.

J.F. Maguire is trying to induce the Canadian Brotherhood of Stationary Engineers and Firemen and Helpers to turn O.B.U. This is a Provincial body without International affiliations. According to Maguire the men are conservative but the president is of O.B.U. sympathies. The Internationals also are courting them.[22]

III. SASKATCHEWAN

18. Miscellaneous Notes.

The O.B.U. in Regina has enrolled no new members recently. At least one foreign-born agitator under the influence of the Ukrainian Labour News is canvassing against the Western Labour News on the ground that it has ceased to be a Workingman's paper.

The Regina O.B.U. decided not to send a delegate to the Convention at Port Arthur. The deterrent was the expense, which would be from $130.00 to $140.00.

IV. MANITOBA.

19. General Notes.

The Ex-soldiers and Sailors Labour Party and the G.A.U.V. in Winnipeg held a meeting on 5th September to denounce participation in any way with Russia. It was attended by about 1300 men, principally ex-Servicemen, with a sprinkling of O.B.U.'s. The speeches were of a revolutionary nature.

One amusing incident occurred. S. Cartwright spoke and tired the audience by reading long extracts from newspapers, so that many of them left. This annoyed him and he "declared it would only be a short time until conditions would force the workers to attend these meetings whether they liked it or not".

The Ukrainians at the Ukrainian National Home in Winnipeg declared against Mr. Swystun's proposed Ukrainian National Church.

A report from Winnipeg states that the Jews there have sent over $20000 "for the Jewish leaders in Soviet Russia"; and that about twice as much has been sent from the United States.[23]

In an interview early in September one of the Shop Stewards in the C.N.R. Roundhouse at WINNIPEG said that he had enlisted eight new members. He was confident that in another year practically all switchmen, yardmen and firemen of the C.N.R. there would be O.B.U. But he had little hope of getting many conductors, engineers or brakemen for some time.

The move to expel W.H. Hoop from the Dominion Labour Party is being pressed with determination. The proceedings at the meeting at Winnipeg on 8th September have been published. Despite the passing of the four months hoist at that meeting the matter will be pursued. As the Internationals are behind Hoop, a split may follow.

The Manager of the O.B.U. Bulletin in a letter to the Regina O.B.U. stated that it now was on a paying basis.

At Fort William the Labour Day celebration passed off quietly and successfully; matters were taken out of the hands of the extremists and good feeling between the several classes was noticeable.

V. ONTARIO

20. Labour Day Events.

The Labour Day parade in Toronto was practically worked by the extremists; but they in turn seem to be disappointed at their showing. As reported in the public press, the speeches made at the Exhibition Grounds were of a most wholesome nature. An incident of the day is thus reported by the N.C.O. in charge of C.I.B. work in Toronto;-[24]

> "After the speaking was over several of the radical element tried to make speeches in the crowd. One little Englishman especially, who stated that he was born in the slums of London, said the economic conditions in this country would never let him have the same chance as any one else to make a living. Three or four old fellows then took part in the discussion. One said, "you have as much chance as I have, I have worked for $10. a month and now have enough to live on". Another said he had worked for $5.00 a month. ANOTHER old fellow said he had worked for $1.00 per month. By that time the little Cockney was mad and told the old fellows to go to h--l," and said they were nothing but a bunch of Capitalists, at which the old fellows had a real laugh and this ended the discussion?"

Reports dated 4th September stated that the foreign radicals were trying to break up the plans of the Labour leaders for parades on Labour Day, in the Niagara District.

O. B. U. Notes.

The O.B.U. open-air meetings on Yonge Street, Toronto, continue, with very moderate success. Our report of one of them notes that it began at 8;25 p.m. and ended at 9;40 p.m. "Because there was nobody to listen to them". The attendance had totalled 60. But the sale of seditious reading matter is considerable, at the same meeting 75 copies of the B.C. Federationist were sold, and a few O.B.U. Bulletins.

An impudent trick was played at Hamilton by the O.B.U. Roberts, one of their men, there asked permission to hold an open-air meeting, and on the Chief of Police showing reluctance declared that they would hold the meeting whether permission was granted or not, and that if they were interfered with the A.F. of L. and G.W.V.A. would help them to fight for free speech. The chief yielded, the meeting was held and J.R. Knight, who was the speaker, delivered a particularly violent attack on the A.F. of L.[25]

The O.B.U. in Hamilton has arranged for a policy of meetings, open-air and otherwise, through the Autumn and Winter.

Knight is busy denying the report that Hoop was assaulted at the Winnipeg debate.

A man named George Murch, Secretary of the Metal Trades Alliance in Hamilton, is secretly in negotiation with J.R. Knight.

22. Foreign Revolutionaries.

Word has been received of the presence in Niagara Falls of a local revolutionary leader named Justoff, who is described as "an old time red from Russian Siberia". This worthy "said the workers were in a pretty bad fix since the last general strike in Winnipeg and that if the Government could break a strike like that it seems that the only remedy for the workers was in mass action, altho it would take some time under the present conditions to stir the workers up to this state".

Winding, who was appointed organizer for the London District at the Communist Labour Party Convention at Detroit, turned up at Niagara Falls on 5th September. He had been roaming about the Niagara District. Apparently he has not been very successful.

A Russian and a Russian Jewess who are understood to be fugitives from Chicago have appeared at the Russian School in Toronto. They are trying to get from Canada to Russia.

An additional report on Henry Dworkin, 525 Dundas Street, West, Toronto, shows him to be pro-Bolshevist and Anti-Polish. In an [26] interview he stated that Polish radicals are being subsidized from the Russian Red Cross or Embassy at Berne to effect a revolution.

This man sailed for England, on his way to Poland again, on 15th September.

The Bulgarian Socialist Party at Toronto numbers 28. On 7th September it affiliated with a new Anarchist Communist Party which is being formed at the Ontario Labour College. These men get copies of an I.W.W. paper called "The Workers Thought" which is published in Chicago, in Bulgarian. These papers are enclosed in ordinary U.S. papers and sent through the mails.

It also is reported that Mestor, or Nestor, a man who keeps a Russian bookstore on Dundas Street, sold in one week 250 copies of "Soviet Russia". He is planning to get the agency for it, and to smuggle additional seditious reading matter across the border.

On 5th September a meeting was held under the presidency of George Wilshow at the Ontario Labour College to form a new Anarchist Communist Party. Opposition was offered, apparently principally to Wilshow's leadership and the meeting was adjourned for a week. It is proposed to call it the "Workers' Party" to allay suspicions.

23. The Federated Order of Railway Employees.

Evidence has been secured tending to show that the Federated Order of Railway Employees is obtaining money from merchants by a method not very remote from blackmail. A man calling himself W.J. Robinson has called on a considerable number of Toronto firms and has asked for orders for advertisements in the "Railroads men's Annual Year Book", to [27] be issued by this body, each to cost $50.00. As an inducement he said that their freight would move quickly, and when refused he threatened that it would be held up. He seems to have collected a good deal of money.

VI. QUEBEC.

The Friction in the O.B.U.

Further information as to the trouble in the O.B.U. ranks comes from

Montreal. A report dated 8th September says;-

"On the evening of the 2nd instant, while in conversation with U. Binette, I learned that Joe Knight is taking advantage of the fact that R.B. Russell and R. Johns are in Jail in imposing a certain form of organization of the O.B.U.

U. Binette stated that Russell and Johns wish for a form of Industrial organization, because they are old I.W.W. members and realize that is the only form of organization which will ever be able to function, whereas Joe Knight, being an ANARCHIST? wants the 'Class' form of organization. U. Binette stated that Joe Knight is impossible and no one can agree with him, he seems to think that he was the wisest of the O.B.U. leaders because he was not indicted along with the rest of the strike leaders in Winnipeg and, owing to the fact that he was his liberty, he wants to run the O.B.U. movement to suit himself, but you wait, Binette stated, as soon as the strike leaders are released they will put Joe Knight where he belongs".

At a meeting of the O.B.U. General Workers held in Montreal in 2nd September, W.E. Long stated that he had arranged for a couple of joint meetings on 11th September of the O.B.U. and the Amalgamated Society of Engineers; J.R. Knight was to address them.

25. A Thrifty Revolutionist.[28]

A curious report has been received upon A. St. Martin, a revolutionary agitator in Montreal. In Winter he lives in the City, having employment as an official stenographer in the law-courts; in Summer he conducts a large farm, whose situation as yet is uncertain. Nominally this farm is owned by St. Martin and about 40 other socialists in partnership; in reality the others get very small wages and St. Martin pockets the profits. He enjoys great prestige with the other revolutionists in Montreal, as they think he has great influence in civic affairs.

St. Martin spoke at a meeting held by the French Socialist Communist Party on Sunday, 5th September, his speech being violently anti-religious. He described Capitalists as "Blue-men," the clergy as "Black-men" and workers as "Red-men", and attacked the workers of Canada for their contentment with present conditions of living.

"As long as they can eat three meals a day, sleep and have a job, they are satisfied, while the Bluemen" and "Blackmen" have all the luxury and do not work and yet the "REDMEN" do not dare to revolt, because the "Blackmen" have told them that if they do revolt they must pay for their sin when they die.

"He went on to say that the 'Blackmen' are the tools of the Capitalists and pointed out to the audience that the workers of Russia have revolted. They have triumphed because they were not afraid to pay for their sins when they die. Saint-Martin continued by stating that the powerful 'Redmen' all over the world are making themselves felt by virtue of their industrial strength and the Capitalistic system is crumbling but Canada will not act until the workers are obliged to walk the streets with an empty stomach and stated that the time is very near now.

"He concluded by stating that there is a great number of workers unemployed in the City of Montreal, and if these workers were only class conscious they would be all present at these meetings."[29]

26. Miscellaneous Notes.

The Montreal "Society for Technical Aid to Soviet Russia" continued to work. Lately it has been busy with a celebration which was to take place on 11th September. The programme included music, and revolutionary songs, and a speech by Revenko, the organizer.

A report on the Reverend J.B. Pike, who made a seditious speech in Montreal, recently, shows that he is an Anglican clergyman, who for years has been a sort of clerical outcast. He is regarded as ill balanced. It is years since he had a charge.

VII. THE MARITIME PROVINCES.

27. Conditions in the Cape Breton Coal Fields.

The Special Agent employed by the Dominion Coal Company writes in confirmation of the views upon the labour situation in Cape Breton quoted in earlier issues. He says in part;-

"Since the coming in of the United Mine Workers organization and the recognition of same by the Dominion Coal Company two or three years ago by our late President Mark Workman through the advice of the then General Superintendent of Mines Mr. Tonge, conditions have been going from bad to worse. The radical element led by such men as McLaughlin, Barrett and Baxter, and who we had been fighting for years, were given every consideration, during this regime. This disheartened the better class of men and officials, who said it was no use for to fight this element any longer, as they did not have the backing of the management, consequently those who did not throw their lot in with this radical bunch simply remained neutral, with the result that this radical element got complete control of the mines as well as control of Municipal affairs. At their request the Dominion Coal Company's Police force, who were a strong factor in maintaining discipline and law and order around the whole industrial district, were practically done away with, hence the conditions as found today. The Police administration of these Towns is something disgraceful".[30]

As regarding the possibility of a strike. I think there is every chance of their being one. These Bolshevik leaders before mentioned, run for election to office this Fall, and while a lot of this stuff they are preaching is intended for election purposes, yet it is having a very bad effect with the workmen.

"I feel, however, that a strike may be the best thing that could happen, in order to clear the air".

"Owing to the lawless element that is in control around the mining districts, it is pretty hard to say just what might happen should a strike occur, I think we might expect the worst. I don't think our present police force could handle the situation should they start on a policy of destruction of property".

Inquiry is being made into the constitution and legal footing of the Dominion Coal Company's Police Force.

ROYAL CANADIAN MOUNTED POLICE HEADQUARTERS

Ottawa, 23rd September, 1920.

SECRET

NO. 42

NOTES OF THE WORK OF THE C. I. B. DIVISION

FOR THE WEEK ENDING 23RD SEPTEMBER

Table of Contents

" 34. The arrest of two I.W.W.'s John Currie and John Webber.
" 35. O.B.U. Meeting addressed by P. Leckie.
" 36. Russian Workers' School, Toronto.
" 37. Shapiro and the Jewish Socialist Revolutionary League.
" 38. Educational Press Association,
at 182 St. Catherine Street East, Montreal.
" 39. O.B.U. Quebec District.
" 40. Society for Technical Aid to Soviet Russia.
" 41. Halifax Stevedores and Longshoremen.[3]

Characteristics of the Period

The outstanding event of the week has been the Annual Convention of the Dominion Trades and Labour Congress held at Windsor, Ontario.

Prior to the convention rumours were rife regarding the Radical resolutions to be presented and supported by the Radical element; also the efforts to be made to control the Trades and Labour Congress by replacing the President and Secretary with men from the radical faction.

Whatever plans the Radicals may have had in view, they apparently resulted in complete failure.

The Prime Minister addressed the Convention, and our information, from a very reliable source is, that the Premier's speech had the effect of creating a good deal of thoughtfulness on the part of the milder type of Radicals.

The outcome of the Convention was a decided victory for the conservative element. All officers were re-elected and our informant says "there was less Socialistic and Revolutionary discussion than there has been at the Convention for a number of years".

The "Red" element were active amongst the delegates outside the convention. I.W.W. literature was distributed by two individuals named Currie and Webber, who crossed over from Detroit, U.S.A. for that purpose. They were both placed under arrest by the local Immigration Inspector and turned over to the City Police.

Full reports of the O.B.U. Miners' Convention held at Calgary on the 10th and 11th instant are now to hand. On the whole the proceedings appear to have been rather tame. Its chief result is embodied in a circular issued by the district Secretary and which is quoted in full elsewhere in this report.[4]

I. BRITISH COLUMBIA

2. Strike of Firemen and Deckhands Employed in North Vancouver Ferries

A report to hand from Vancouver advises that:-

"The Firemen and Deckhands employed on the North Vancouver Ferries went out on strike on the 4th September, demanding an increase of wages from $110 to $130 per month.

"A special meeting of the City Council was called on the afternoon of the same date, and after debating the question, they agreed to grant an increase from $110 to $125 per month, retroactive from August 1st 1920, on a nine hour forty minutes day all overtime beyond that period being at the rate of 75 cents per hour.

"In addition, the Council pledged itself not to discriminate against any of the strikers. The agreement is to last for one year, but may be cancelled by either side on a thirty days' notice.

"The Ferry Captains are now demanding an increase from $190 to $200 per month, and have signified their intention of walking out on September 23rd. If their demand is not met. The Mates are to be called out in sympathy, but there is no dispute over the wages paid these latter. Ten men are involved. The Council holds that the Captains are receiving a fair wage for their services and unless either of the contending parties back down in their present stand, there will be a second tie-up in the ferry service".

3. Gas Workers' Strike

A report on general conditions in Vancouver concerning the Gas Workers' strike states that:-

"The employes of the Victoria Gas Company, numbering 22, went out on strike on 8th September.

"The point at issue is the demand for time and half for Sunday work. The company are determined not to accede to this demand, and have given the strikers an ultimatum to the effect that if they do not return to work immediately, they will not be reinstated".

A later report from Vancouver says:-

"The Company served notice on its individual employes that unless they reported for work on 10th September they would automatically be discharged. It was reported on the 11th September, that none of the men went back to work".

4. Strike of International Jewelry Workers' now ended

We are now advised that:-

"The strikers of the Vancouver Branch of the International Jewelry Workers' Union are now back at work and no further trouble is anticipated.

"The meetings between the employers and employes were conducted in a very friendly spirit".[5]

5. Typographical and other Unions Amalgamated

An agent at Vancouver advises that:-

"The typographical and other newspaper unions have amalgamated into a sort of One Big Union. I am informed by a well-known labour printed. Eighteen organizations of pressmen, stereotypers, printers, lynotype operators, bookbinders, etc. have organized in New

Westminster, Vancouver and Victoria. They are 100 per cent strong he says, and the International Headquarters, though objecting, have been forced to give way. This "O.B.U." of the printing trades intends to handle all of its own local affairs without consulting the International. They have already presented demands to the newspaper proprietors for an increased scale, to take effect January 1st, 1921, when the present agreement expires. They will ask for $10 a day straight time, $12 a day for over time and night work, and a 7-hour day.

"Tentative efforts are being made to have reporters affiliate with the printing trades".

Whether this means a definite split from the A.F. of L. and an affiliation with the O.B.U. is hard at present to decide.

6. Dissensions in the ranks of the O.B.U.

A further indication of the strained relations between the two prominent O.B.U. officials, Winch and Midgley, is disclosed in a report to hand from Vancouver. Although they are both attending the O.B.U. Convention at Port Arthur it will be noted they did not travel together. The report follows:-

"Midgley left Tuesday night for the O.B.U. convention at Port Arthur. He asked me on Monday to see if I could find out if Winch was going. Winch told me he was not. I asked Winch of the I.W.W. question would be fought out at Port Arthur, and he said he did not think it would be even touched. This morning (14th September), I saw Midgley and he told me he had seen Winch late Monday and asked him to arrange for an O.B.U. committee to Meet Hon. G.D. Robertson, Minister of Labour, when he came here, and Winch told him he could not as he expected he might be out of town when the minister arrived.

"Late this afternoon Midgley saw me on the street and came up to say "Winch has gone to Port Arthur, he left last night. He went C. N. R. and will stop off at a couple of towns before he gets to Port Arthur'. Midgley seemed quite put out. He said 'I think Winch lied to you about not going to Port Arthur".[6]

7. O.B.U. Declined further assistance to Ukrainians

In a report from Vancouver our agent says:-

"The Vancouver Branch of the Ukrainian organization is not at present making any progress by way of gaining larger following amongst the Ukrainians. The O.B.U. has declined further assistance to their paper, the last number of which (No.11) appeared on September 19th.

"Tom Tomashewsky, the Editor of Truth and Freedom, stated that on account of insufficient funds and disharmony amongst the members of the group, he could not make headway with the paper at present, and would cease to publish it. He intended, however, to publish a humourous bi-monthly illustrated journal sometime this winter. He would be the sole owner and avoid politics".

8. Charles Lestor Collecting funds to go to Moscow

From an outside source we are informed that Charles Lestor, socialist agitator of Vancouver, has secured by subscription about $500.00 for his transportation to Moscow, and is leaving for England en route to that point.

9. Socialist Party of Canada, Vancouver Branch

A meeting was held under the auspices of the Socialist Party of Canada at the Empress Theatre on 12th September. The Chairman introduced Mr. J. Harrington, the speaker of the evening. Then he spoke briefly explaining the objects of the meeting as follows:-

"Comrades and fellow workers; I suppose you all know what these meetings are held on Sunday nights for: mainly offer the education of the working class and also to put before the working class what stand they should have in social life. We hold these meetings, also on the corner of Carrall and Cordova streets on Mondays, Thursdays and Saturdays.

"We have another way of educating the working class by the distribution of literature, especially the "Western Clarion" which you should all subscribe to.

"We are also, starting classes on the 1st of October; any member (especially the younger members) who wish to learn more about socialism, should get into these classes".

Mr. Harrington then spoke in part as follows:-

"We saw by the newspapers that the big fight between the Soviet and Poland has quietened down. Of course we can't believe them. They tell us it was the bloodiest battle ever fought. It appears that some people like to fight their battles on the front page of the "Province" newspaper. This Bolshevist trouble is like the Mississippi or Fraser River. It runs along and there are farms and all kinds of successful industries along the banks, and all of a sudden, these rivers rise and threaten to destroy the wealth which is being produced from the lands, and all the people rush and blockade the water, but it only leaks out in another place. So you can see that when all the Capitalists rushed to stop the trouble in Russia, it broke out in Italy.

"The Catholic Church has great power, and power is what counts; it is what always counted, and it will count now for the labouring class of today throughout the world has the power, and through that power they will maintain their object".

The meeting was well attended. Literature was sold and a collection amounting to $71.00 was taken up.

An agent reporting on local No. 1. Socialist Party of Canada, Vancouver, states:-

"The offices, meeting hall and library of this organization are situated at 401 Pender St. E., where a disused chapel is rented for that purpose. The Secretary is one Jack Shepherd, and the librarian George Haig. The committee consists of 5 or 6; they have informed meetings almost daily, in one of the larger rooms of the basement. Here a large quantity of the "Western Clarion" and other radical literature is stored.

"Open air meetings are held 2 or 3 evenings a week, where popular speeches are held on subjects appertaining to Socialism. At time as many as 100 gather to listen, but it is estimated that 75% of them are either already members or otherwise initiated. The organization has grown only little of late, and the committee is anxious to expend their field of activity and influence.

"A financial statement, issued by the committee of Local No. 1 of the Socialist Party of Canada to members reads as follows 9 for six months):-

	Dr.	Cr.
Dues acct...............	$ 373.00	.... $ 86.00
propaganda..............	1948.00	.... 1560.00
Literature..............	1560.89	.... 1395.40
General.................	19.45	.... 806.35
Library.................	3.00	.... 3.00
Soviet relief...........	59.00	.... 20.00
	3963.45	3870.75
Balance.................	3870.75	
	92.70	
Dr. Balance June 1	275.39	
	368.09	
Difference unacctd	31.40	
Balance in Bank	563.55	
Outstanding cheques	164.06	
	399.19[8]	

10. Chinese Nationalist League sending funds to China

The Officer Commanding at Vancouver reports that:-

"The Chinese Nationalist League is very active just now in the matter of collecting funds for transmission to China. Our informant learns that $10,000 had recently been subscribed in British Columbia and sent to China through this league.

11. Chinese Esperanto School Vancouver

An agent who visits the Democratic Academy at 210 Pender St, Vancouver, informs us that he meets there Hong Sum, the secretary, who says the address of the Esperanto teacher was changed to Room 525 Canada Hotel, 514 Richard St.

He also says the Academy was established by the Chinese Labour Association for educative purposes, and the membership is 200 strong. The school is amateur, with classes in English, book-keeping and political economy. Only about a dozen students attend regularly. A portrait of Tolstoi appears on the walls of the schoolroom.

12. Labour Conditions Swanson Bay

An agent who visited the Pulp, Lumber and Shingle Mills at Swanson Bay says in part:-

"There are employed at this Plant at present about 400, with about equal numbers of Whites, Japanese and Chinese, a large number of whose families are on the place.

"I would mention a point to show the inconsistency of the O.B.U. members at this camp, which was brought to my notice: one of the workers' demands was for equality in pay with Whites and Orientals, yet this month one of the sawyers, speaking for three others as well, asked the manager for extra pay, saying he did not think it right that a Chinaman working alongside him, should get the same pay as they did, and two of these men, were men who were at the camp during the May strike, and apparently were in perfect accord with the demands for equality".

13. British Columbia Detachment Reports West Kootenay

A report from West Kootenay concerning Michael Casey, O.B.U. organizer says:-

"Casey seems to be holding down his job as secretary of the O.B.U. by soliciting for a few new members, he is not doing much on account of there being so many returned soldiers in the Penticton District.

"There are some 425 men all told, working on construction on the Government irrigation works, of this number the check up shows about 200 O.B.U. members, at least 80 per cent of these O.B.U. members come from the Slocam Mining District where they went out on strike some few months ago."[9]

Stewart

Apart from the Premier Mine there is very little activity in this district at present. A patrol was made to the Premier Mine on the 9th September, and found everything progressing in the usual way.

Grand Forks

Labour conditions in this district still remain good and there is no appearance of unrest. The majority of the mines and mills have been visited by mounted patrols and everything is reported quiet.

Chakawana (Coastal Patrol)

There is considerable labour unrest at Ocean Falls district, but nothing serious has occurred up to the present.

Esquimalt

Commander H.E. Holme took over the command of the sawmill and shipyard in full swing. Labour conditions favourable.

Cumberland

All logging concerns and sawmills are working full swing with a few exceptions.

A machine gun battery has been formed in Courtenay and are equipped with Vickers Guns, Rifles, equipment and uniform. The city of Cumberland has been presented with war trophies, two German light machine guns have arrived, and there is a 77 MM field gun on the way".

14. East Kootenay

An agent who visited the East Kootenay district reports:-

"I attended a miners' smoker on 14th September. Richardson, ex-M.P. from England addressed the meeting on Prohibition only, but the men would not give him a hearing.

"I also attended a Sunday night's meeting called by the U. M. W. of A. About 35 men were present. A motion was passed to circulate District 18 for the purpose of calling a convention. It would be called by the U. M. W. of A., but the O.B.U. would try and get all O.B.U. men as delegates to over rule the U. M. W. of A. The chief reason or as a pretex of calling a convention is that the low wage men have not had the increase, that is to say, a man had $6.00 and a man at $4.00, the $6.00 a day man is getting more per day on the increase, some claim the increase should be all alike.

"Wm. Sherman made the statement that the U. M. W. of A. would not last any longer than the last of October. It was also said at the meeting that the men are not ready for to strike now.[10]

In forwarding the report the Officer Commanding East Kootenay District remarks:-

"This man Sherman mentioned above is one of the worst agitators, and was one of the delegates to the O.B.U. Convention at Calgary. They are undoubtedly going to stir up trouble but whether they will succeed in calling a strike is difficult to forecast just now".

15. Miscellaneous Notes

A visit by the "Chakawana" on 21st August to Ocean Falls has resulted in a report that the labour conditions there are good. It is noted that by free use of overtime some men there work 500 hours a month, the average wage being 65 cents an hour.

Attention has been drawn to a man named David Dion, now a forman in a lumber camp near Ocean Falls. This man last February was an O.B.U. agitator; now he poses as anti-O.B.U. The discrepancy is being investigated.

Richard Higgins, Vancouver, a somewhat prominent member of the L.W.M. is on his way to Port Arthur. He is a delegate to the O.B.U. Convention, and in addition will organize in that district. He speaks French and Italian.

16. First Annual Convention of the G.A.U.V.

The first annual convention of the G.A.U.V. was held at their Club rooms, 570 Granville St., Vancouver on 8th and 9th September. The newly elected officers were:-

M. A. Oxford, Provincial President

J. L. Miller, First Vice President

R. A. Webb, Secretary

The Association is entirely a political one and purpose working in connection with the Farmers and Labour organizations. At present there are about 400 members in the Vancouver Branch. There is also a Ladies Auxiliary.

There are 9 units of this organization. Delegates from only six attended the convention. Four did not attend because of lack of funds. Fifty cents a head was collected from everybody who attended the Whist Drive. Before this organization can make headway with their objects, they will need to get more funds than they have at their back at present.

II. ALBERTA

17. Convention of Miners held at Calgary on 10th and 11th September

Full reports of the O.B.U. Miners' Convention at Calgary are now to hand. Proceedings on the whole seem to have been rather tame, its chief result is embodied in a circular issued on the 16th September by the district secretary which reads as follows:-[11]

"District No. 1. Mining Dept. O.B.U.".

"Arthur Evans, Dist. Sec.
P.O. Box 1650, Calgary.

September 16th, 1920

"To the officers and members of the former District No. 18 U. M. W. of A.

Fellow Workers:

"The following resolution was given to me for circularizing the district with. It was passed at a meeting of the West Commercial Miners' Unit, after having been on strike against the U. M. W. of A. check-off and intolerable conditions.

> 'We the members of the West Commercial Miners' Unit of Wayne, call on mine workers to notify their respective employers that unless the U. M. W. of A. check-off is removed and negotiations opened for a new agreement by Oct. 1st 1920, they will take whatever action is necessary to bring about the removal of the check-off and the

opening of negotiations for a new agreement!

Signed on behalf of the West Commercial
(Signed) A.P. Picco, Sec.
R. Roberts, Chairman.

"The convention held there in Calgary was of the opinion that unless the miners in this district take action against the check-off in the next few weeks, nothing practical could be done about it until this time next year.

"At the same time the convention was of the opinion that the present scarcity of coal is a factor in our favour, and that all other things being considered, the present time is the most opportune for forcing the issue, not only of the check-off but also of the wages and conditions around the mines of the whole district.

"The first action to be taken is the notification of the employers that unless the U.M.W. of A. check-off is removed and negotiations opened up for a new agreement by Oct. 1st., you will act in whatever way you consider necessary. (Should you do this, and the employers turn you down, your action will depend on the sentiment of the rest of the district. This office will inform you of that).

"This circular is being sent to all camps in the district. I, successor to Sec. Ed. Browne, should be notified of your attitude and actions promptly. You will be informed as to all happenings.

"THIS IS A RANK AND FILE PROPOSITION, WE HAVE SUBMITTED LONG ENOUGH TO THE CHECK-0FF AND ENFORCED AGREEMENT. LET US ACT".

(signed) Arthur Evans
District Secretary, No. 1. Mining Dept. O.B.U.

"HAVE THIS TAKEN UP AT YOUR FIRST MEETING, OR CALL A SPECIAL MEETING AND IMMEDIATELY NOTIFY DISTRICT SECRETARY OF RESULTS."

The delegates did not seem confident of the support they would receive from the miners in case a strike was called. No delegate was appointed to the O.B.U. convention which is about to assemble at Port Arthur.[12]

18. Meeting of Central Council of the O.B.U. at Edmonton

At a meeting of the Central Council of the O.B.U. on 11th September Carl E. Berg gave a report of the miners convention in Calgary as follows:-

"The miners had decided that the Drumheller valley was the one to start the fight against the check-off and that if a majority of the miners in the Drumheller Valley thought that it was to their interests to go on strike it was up to them to call one and that if they did the rest of the miners would not be affected at the start but that on a date that was set at the convention, but was not made public, the rest of the miners in the whole of District 18 would go out on strike. Berg pointed out that the reason the date was withheld was that it would keep the bosses guessing and that they would be tied up at the time that they probably least expected it, as there would be no notice given when the rest of the district came out in support of the miners in the Drumheller Valley. He also stated that it was the firm decision of the miners that the check-off must go".

"The miners who have to lose a half days' work to attend the meetings of the central council gave notice of motion that at the next meeting they were going to move that the Central Council meetings be held on Sunday afternoon instead of Saturday.

Our report continues:-

"Berg reported that the miners are going to make a gigantic effort to organize all the mines in the Province that are not at present organized and that the miners are going to send out returned soldiers, who are members of the O.B.U. to break the ground for organizers and that by the spring they hoped to have the whole of the Province 100% organized".

19. The O.B.U. in the Drumheller Coal Fields

Our investigator, who recently visited the Drumheller district, was impressed with the renewed activities of the O.B.U. element in that area. His report in part is as follows:

"If the Drumheller mines come out on strike, steps are at once to be taken to call out the remainder of the District not later than October 1st 1920.

"I find there is considerable amount of agitation in Drumheller on behalf of the O.B.U. Geo. Palmer the secretary of the O.B.U. at Drumheller, being the prime mover. He is working very hard on behalf of this organization and doing everything within his power to stir up trouble. I had several conversations with Palmer in which he told me that the O.B.U. element was in the majority in the Valley and that they were determined to defeat the operators and the U. M. W. of A; that the miners, as a whole, had no grievances, whatsoever, so far as wages and working conditions were concerned, but that they would not abide by the "check-off". He intimated to me that the operators would have a lot of trouble on their hands,[13] within the next few weeks, in the way of strikes, that the feeling of the miners was running so high that they are determined to strike and force the operators to recognize the O.B.U. In regards to this feature, it is problematical as to want success they will, have in pulling the men out on strike and it greatly depends upon the tactics they will devise.

"In reference to the operators stand in this matter, I am a little doubtful. The Red Deer Valley Coal operators Association held a meeting at Drumheller on the afternoon of the 7th to discuss the situation and from what I am informed, they decided to stand firm and beat the O.B.U. However, when you get one or two operators individually and discuss the situation with them privately in their homes, one can easily notice that their chief desire is to keep the mines running by any means whatsoever, as they feel they cannot afford a strike. The operators, upon whom we can rely as being absolutely genuine in their intentions of standing firm, are Messrs. Gouge of the Newcastle and A. B. C. mines, A. H. Gibson of the Premier and Tupper of the Rosedeer mine at Wayne. These men can afford to hold out against a strike and furthermore their mines do not need the care and protection in the event of a strike that the others do, but with the other operators, I am afraid they, if the strike lasts for any length of time, are apt to weaken, as they cannot stand the expenses of keeping their mines in repair. For instance, S. L. McMullin of the Midland Mine, Drumheller, informs me that owing to the fact that this mine is wet, it cost him a mater of between three and four thousand dollars a month to keep it in proper condition, in the event of a strike. Furthermore, some of these operators appear to have the idea that a local Union at each mine is the best principle to work on and to dispose of both the U. M. W. of A. and the O.B.U.

"I gather that they have come to this conclusion through the bad example set them by the Monarch Mine owned by the North American Collieries. This mine has been running continuously, but is an O.B.U. mine in to .

"As regards the North American Collieries: this company is not a member of the Western Coal Operators' Association and therefore do not come under the agreement made by the latter organization with the U. M. W. of A. and the order of Coal Commissioner Armstrong as regards the check-off, with the result that they employ any and everybody, regardless of what union they may belong, so that their mine, the Monarch, is a breeding ground of the O.B.U. at Drumheller. The general public and miners as a whole do not understand this and the opinion has been expressed to me a good many times as to why the Government does not force them to abide by the order of Coal Commissioner Armstrong; if this gentlemen's order has any power behind it at all. They do not realize that technically the Government has no power to enforce this order upon the North American Collieries, as they are not included in the above mentioned agreement. While on this subject, I might mention that although the North American Collieries were not included in the agreement for reasons stated above and do not abide by the order in reference to the check-off, at the same time they have taken advantage of the increase in cost of coal, the said increase being granted by an order of Coal Commissioner Armstrong on the strength of the agreement between the Western Coal Operators Association and U.M.W. of A. so that I do not see why this company should abide by one portion and not the other. The operators who are not in a financial [14] position to stand a strike have told me that they do not see why they should not take the same stand as the North American Collieries, which have been able to keep their mine open all the season; they do not see why they should fight the O.B.U. element at a loss, temporarily, while the North American Collieries are allowed to run their mine under the system they have adopted. It is practically impossible to judge just exactly what stand the majority of the operators would take in the event of a strike or what success the O.B.U. will have in pulling a strike.

"There is a shortage of labour in the Drumheller field, however, the operators as a whole do not appear to be worrying themselves to any extent, as they claim the same conditions occurs every year during the harvest period.

"The organizers for the U.M.W. of A. appear to be doing their best in this field and they are of the opinion that they will control the situation eventually, if the operators will only support them, which remains to be seen, as I have already stated".

20. Christophers at the Calgary O.B.U. Miners' Convention

Christophers was in attendance at the O.B.U. Miners Convention held at Calgary on the 10th and 11th September and returned to Blairmore on the evening of the 11th.

An extract from a report dated 13th September concerning Christophers says:-

"Christopher was the only delegate that wanted to use sabotage as a weapon with which to fight the U.M.W. of A. check-off. He advocating that the delegates should go back to their respective mines and get the men to produce the coal and turn it out in rotten shape, and to turn out as little as possible, stating if they did this, then they would be hitting at the pocket of the miner owner, and they would gain their ends. The convention as a whole was absolutely against this line of action. He further made statements to the effect that if the miners came out without the Railway workers behind them they would be sure to lose out. He stated that in Winnipeg, there were enough men in the O.B.U. there to tie up the whole of the country if necessary. Christopher further advocated that a series of strikes pulled throughout the district would be an effective weapon against the operators".

21. Alderman A. G. Broatch

A. G. Broatch, City Alderman and Chairman of the Railway Transportation Unit No. 1. O.B.U. Calgary, has been appointed delegate to attend the O.B.U. convention at Port Arthur on September 20th, 1920.[15]

22. Report of J.F. Maguire, O.B.U. Organizer

J. F. Maguire, organizer for the O.B.U. in Edmonton in submitting his weekly report, after stating that the men in the C.P.R. yards seem antagonistic to the new movement says:-

"During my two weeks' organizing I have visited almost every job in town. The railroads shops, freight sheds and building construction, and have found among the rank and file a fearful lack of understanding of the O.B.U. and in many instances a complete lack of knowledge of the labour movement in general. In my opinion before a great increase of members takes place we shall have to carry on a more active propaganda. Every job I visited every man I approached I had to explain in detail the difference between the A.F. of L. and the O.B.U. and the invariable answer was "it sounds all right", but I will have to think it over". Under these conditions it is impossible in my opinion for an organizer to make expenses by new initiations only.

"During the week I talked with a few cooks, bakers, and waiters and it may be possible to start a small unit along this industry; as most of them are quite in favour of the O.B.U. However, a little work will be necessary before a unit can be materialized."

23. Meeting held by Building trades Unit O.B.U. Edmonton

At a meeting of the Building Trades Unit of the O.B.U. Calgary a letter was read to the meeting from James Law, secretary of the Winnipeg Defence Committee.

The letter in part was as follows:-

"Fellow workers reorganization of the above Committee (Winnipeg Defence Committee) will be taking place soon. At the present time we are actively engaged in cutting down expenses to the lowest minimum...............We have on hand a supply of the following books;- Pritchards' Address to the Jury, Dixon's Address and the History of the Winnipeg Strike. The former price of these books were $18.00 and $23.00 per hundred respectively. The committee has reduced the price of these books to 10 cents per copy and we suggest that the different organizations throughout Canada order sufficient quantities to issue to their membership. No workman's home should be without these books. There has also been a persistency call from the different cities in Western Canada for the Winnipeg Defence Committee to issue a defence fund stamp, valued at 25 cents. This scheme after being discussed by the committee has been adopted. We have them in 10 cents and 25 cents denominations which can be affixed to your due cards, or receipts. Instruct your secretary to get a supply of these stamps which will be charged to your local. These stamps can also be sold to the people outside your own local [16] and will also act as receipt for money collected by your local collectors. Now fellow workers we call upon you to co-operate with us in this matter and assist us in our fight for freedom and liberty for the workers. Several instances have arisen recently where the workers have been persecuted, locked out and threatened eviction for carrying union cards, arrested and railroaded for two years in jail, etc. Until this committee hearing of the above cases immediately took action and are still fighting cases of the above nature. Through the prompt action of this committee the kidnappers of Christopher have been arrested by the Attorney Generals' Department of Saskatchewan and sent up for trial at the October assizes and are now out on $18,000.00 bail each. These are only a few of the cases handled by this committee. You all know the work we have done in connection with the now famous State Trials held in Winnipeg early this year. These men are still in jail for fighting your fight. The fight for better conditions for the workers. Don't forget that the wives and families of these men have to be supported and it is up to your fellow workers to see to this".

Yours for the case of the workers.

(Signed) James Law, Secy.

On discussion of this letter the following motion was passed "That the Secretary be instructed to order twenty of "Pritchard's address to the Jury, and twenty-five of "The History of the Winnipeg Strike".

24. Mass Meeting of Ukrainians at Red Water, Alberta.

A report from Edmonton advises that a meeting of Ukrainians were held at Red Water, about 600 people were present from the district. The report follows:-

"The Meeting opened at 8 p.m. Melnyk occupied the chair and introduced three speakers, M. Glowa, and Mechailychyn from Edmonton, Madiara from Fedora. All three speakers spoke along the same line about the Ukrainian movement in Ukrainian, especially about the fighting between the Ukrainians and the Poles. The speakers said it did not matter with whom Ukrainia was united they should fight until they gain their independence. The speakers idea of Bolshevism was that it was much more favourable to the Ukrainians than Polish rule, and that is why the Ukrainians fight together with the Bolshevists against the Poles. In Canada we should have a National Ukrainian Homes all over the Dominion where the Ukrainian spirit could be fostered. The Ukrainian language and songs should be dear to all Ukrainians and such homes is the only place where the children can be properly trained and educated in such to become true Ukrainian Nationalists.

"The Speakers did not refer to the assimilation with the Canadian race or the fostering of Canadian ideas in the educating of their children, advocating only Ukrainian Nationalism".[17]

25. Tom Richardson

In a report to hand from Calgary we are advised that:-

"Tom Richardson, who is an ex-member of Parliament of the House of Commons, England, will speak at the convention of miners at Calgary on the 10th September. Lawson is also trying to arrange for him to address a meeting of radicals on the following Sunday".

26. Ben Spoor Arriving from England

Ben Spoor, a friend of Tom Richardson, who is expected to arrive here from England about 17th September on his way to a convention in Washington, U.S.A., is to address meetings in Toronto, Montreal and Winnipeg.

As this man is a fanatic of Prohibition, Lawson is trying to arrange for a meeting to be held under the auspices of the Prohibition League. Lawson stated that Spoor's lecture would be entitled "Prohibition and the working man" and said "that quite a little "Red" stuff would be thrown in and that he would advertise the meeting and see that all the 'Good Reds' in town were there".

III. SASKATCHEWAN

27. O.B.U. Northern Saskatchewan

Extracts from a report concerning the L. W. I. U. of the O.B.U. in Northern Saskatchewan are as follows:-

"Apparently the O.B.U. centre all their hopes in the Pas District, as attempted organization at Big River, Hudson's Bay Junction and other points proved a failure and a waste of money".

"Tehter said that Noggy Mackintosh, O.B.U. delegate is working at a lumber mill at Merritt, B.C. where he is getting $9.00 a day as a lumber piler. Tehter intends to get work of a similar nature if possible, when he gets to Vancouver".

"Tether seems to greatly regret that they did not go to the Pas to organize in the first place, instead of having office at Prince Albert, where the O.B.U. spent around $5,000 on organization work to no purpose whatever".

The Officer Commanding in commenting on this report says:-

"I feel quite satisfied that the O.B.U. is not so solid as Tether makes out. I feel sure though that a last effort will be made to organize at the Pas this winter when the camps commence operations".[18]

A further report of the O.B.U. activities in Northern Saskatchewan states in part:-

"George Tether, secretary for the Prince Albert District of the L.W.I.U. had left the Pas on Sept. 1st and had gone to Vancouver, and that one John R. Leith is now in charge of the District".

"Leith has been in and around the district for some three months as a delegate of the L.W.I.U. and it would appear that he knowing that Tether was more or less discouraged and wanted to leave on account of his wife's illness, had planned not only to hasten Tethers' departure, but to secure his position.

"One thing that Leith did was, while away on his last two trips, which covered a period of some six weeks, he sent in numerous reports stating that he was not meeting with any success and forwarding only an occasional new name for membership during this period and brought back with him over $800.00 for dues etc. He withheld the names of new members secured and the money received until Tether had turned over the office to him. For, as he stated, if Tether knew how well he did he might not have left."

It continues:-

Yesterday afternoon I assisted Leith in checking up the number of members in good standing in the district, there has been all told 1,682 members signed up in this district, of which 714 have either taken transfer cards to other districts or have failed to pay their dues, leaving a balance of 968 up to date members.

"Leith on his last trip covered the districts of Ruby Lake, H.B. Junction, Tisdale, Star City, Melfort and Bozeman, it was on this trip that he secured 300 new members".

28. General Conditions in Southern Saskatchewan

The Officer Commanding Southern Saskatchewan in his weekly report for 11th September says:-

"Employment. During the week there has been a marked shortage in the labour market. This applies to ordinary labour, building trades and railways as well as to the more acute shortage in harvest help. Wages have jumped from $5 and $6 a day to $7 and $8. The situation should improve within the next ten days."

"O.B.U. Activities. From what I can learn Regina is being avoided by leaders in the movement. There is a general impression that they are closely watched in this city. In any event they appear to be dead here".

29. Harvesters and I.W.W. Literature

An agent in conversation with some harvesters in Regina states:-

"According to their statements they entered Canada legally, one gave his name as Peterson stating to me that he bought a "whole bunch" of I.W.W. literature along with him, which he distributed after landing at Brandon. On my request for some of this I.W.W. literature he proceeded to the Waverley Hotel and brought me a copy of the Industrial Workers and a copy of a pamphlet entitled "I.W.W.", and [19] remarked this is the best of out literature. They informed me about the progress of the I.W.W. in the U. S. A. and certain things concerning the movement in the United States and they also expressed the hope that one day the O.B.U. and the I.W.W. will amalgamate.

The G.A.U.V. at Regina are trying to get F. J. Dixon, M.L.A., to address them.

IV. MANITOBA

30. Meeting of Running Trades Union of the O.B.U. Winnipeg

A report from Winnipeg advises that the fortnightly meeting of the Running Trades' Union of the O.B.U. was held on a Sunday.

In part the report states:-

"The meeting was then opened for general discussion, under which the strike of last year was brought up.

"Mr. Stephenson declared that the Running Trades were the ones who had the doing of things if they wanted to.

"As an instance, he gave an illustration of what took place last year, in front of the City Hall, declaring that the machine guns and ammunition was brought up from Toronto, and that the Brotherhood of Railway Trainmen and the B.T. of R.E. International organizations had been notified of their coming, but took no steps to prevent it.

"A motion was put before the International Brotherhood he declared in an endeavour to have the arms delayed, but it was turned down, and a few weeks later, the very same guns were turned on the men and their wives in front of the City Hall.

"Mr. Stephenson said this was where the Running Trades would have to play their part in case of any trouble that might arise in the War against Capitalism which was now in progress, and it would be up to the Running Trades next time to see that no such merchandise was carried on the train they were running.

"But he further stated that it was not the intention as far as he could find out of the O.B.U. to use the strike as means of beating the master, unless it was absolutely necessary.

"The O.B.U. he declared, used the boycott system and he believed that when the organization was properly built up, it would be preventing strikes instead of making them, as there was no worker who really could afford to strike, at any time, and when he did, he lost, even though he gained the object he was on strike for."

"Comrade L. Goucher stated that arms and ammunition were coming into the City over the C.G.R. and C.N.R. where he was working every [20] day, and he guessed the Capitalist class was getting ready to kill some more people when another strike took place.

"He further declared that the working class could make no headway while the Capitalist class was allowed to import such means to prevent the workers from using their power."

31. Ukrainian "Canadian Farmer"

In the Ukrainian "Canadian Farmer", dated 10th September, the following article has been printed:-

"Everyone thought up till now that in Asia or in all the Mohammedan World in general, the Bolsheviki could not count on many supporters. In reality it is not so Mohammedan factions of the "Eastern Commissariat Department of Foreign Affairs" opened a "Union to liberate Islam". The Union gets from the Soviet Government a support in the sum of 5 million roubles in gold for the purpose of the safeguarding and maintaining of the Mohammedan uprisings against the European rule".

32. Swystun, Ukrainian Labour Party

Swystun, of the Ukrainian Labour Party, in his lecture on 12th September at the National Home, Winnipeg, gave a full account of Russia, its republics and their Governments, and finally stated that the Ukrainian Independence, their safety and help lay in the hands of the Bolsheviki, and the only means for the Ukrainians to obtain all that, would be to ally themselves with the Bolsheviki Government.

V. Ontario

33. Convention of Dominion Trades-Congress

The following is an extract from a letter received from an outside source regarding the convention of the Dominion Trades Congress at Windsor, Ontario:-

"We are pleased to be able to again report this year the re-election of all officers of the Dominion Trades Congress. While there was considerable doubt as to whether we would be able to carry the whole ticket, this was eliminated after Premier Meighen's speech on Tuesday which had the effect of creating a good deal of thoughtfulness on the part of the milder type of radicals and by Wednesday morning we were so sure of our ground that we thoroughly organized to give the Reds the trimming of their existence. No doubt you have read the press reports of what happened to the Toronto leader of the radicals, Jimmie Simpson, and his resolutions from the Toronto Trades Council when we used all of our heavy weights to show up his and the Toronto Trades Council's work in the [21] labour movement for the last couple of years".

"The idea of sending the Convention to Winnipeg, after being thoroughly discussed, was that the different International organizations are going to flood the West with organizers to combat the O.B.U. and the best thing to do next year would be to show them that we were not afraid to go out there and give them a fight for the offices in their own territory and at present it looks as if this is a safe policy and will go a long way toward killing O.B.U. influence in the west".

"There was less socialistic and revolutionary bunkum at this convention than there has been to my personal knowledge for six or seven years back."

"The reason assigned by the Butcher Workers' International for not giving Braithwaite the office of Canadian organizer was due to his statements on different occasions that he favoured the O.B.U. as the best form of organization for Canadian workers".

34. The arrest of Two I.W.W.'s - John Currie and Aaron Webber

The I.W.W. faction were active in distributing literature amongst delegates to the Convention of the Dominion Trades Congress held at Windsor. As a result of these activities John Currie and Aaron Webber, both members of the I.W.W. were apprehended and have been remanded to the Sandwich Jail until the 27th September. Our report in this connection reads in part as follows:-

"On Friday night, 17th September, John Currie and Aaron Webber, both of Detroit, Mich. U.S.A. members of the I.W.W. crosses to Windsor and commenced to distribute I.W.W. pamphlets amongst the delegates attending the Convention. The two agitators met with a hostile reception. Most of their literature was collected by the delegates and set fire to in front of the Armouries. The two men were arrested about 10 p.m. the same night, by the Immigration Inspector and turned over the City Police. The following morning they were arranged before Magistrate Meyers and remanded to the Sandwich Jail until 27th inst., bail being refused."

35. O.B.U. Meeting at Toronto addressed by P. Leckie

A belated report from Toronto states:-

"That at a propaganda meeting of the O.B.U. P. Leckie told the audience that they are on the way to Windsor as delegates to the Dominion Trade Congress. He said they are going to the Congress as Reds and to show Tom Moore what Reds can do and it is going to be a [22] big battle between the Reds and the A.F. of L. and we will sure beat them. He said that the workers will never get anything from the present Government. Canada is the rottenest place in the world for the workingman and we are going to have a revolution here very shortly. He agitated them to throw over the present Government and take away everything from the Capitalist and divide amongst the working class the same as they did in Russia and what they are doing at the present time in Italy". He spoke for two hours and there were about 600 persons present".

The final outcome of the Convention must have been very disappointing to Leckie and his associate "Reds".

36. Russian Workers School. Toronto

Lika Goldberg in conversation with an operative stated that there were not enough students attending the Russian Workers' School for her to teach. She is therefore helping Dadokin in the school three nights a week because the students refuse to have Morris Nestor for a teacher as he is a capitalist and owns a business.

Morris Nestor of the Russian Book Store, 185 Dundas Street, Toronto, has arranged with the New York Book Stores that they will not sell certain Russian literature except himself in Toronto.

37. Shapiro and the Jewish Socialist Revolutionary League

A meeting of the Jewish Socialist Revolutionary league was held on 18th September. There were 32 members present and a committee was formed for the purpose of collecting $450 from the Jewish Workers to furnish a new place and to obtain literature.

One of the members named Shapiro proposed that from 1st to 30th October will be the 'Red month' that will be for collecting the above sum of money and to distribute propaganda and get new members.

Shapiro is never working and is supplied with plenty of money. He is a very busy men, at all radical meetings. He is organizer for the above party in Toronto. He contributed $30.00 for the new place.[23]

38. Educational Press Association, at 182 St. Catherine Street, East, Montreal.

Further information is now to hand regarding the "Education Press Association" of Montreal. It would appear that one Isidore Boltuck, an Austrian, who is reported to be one of the most influential men in the radical movement of Montreal, is the originator of the "Educational Press Association" idea. In 1919 Boltuck was apprehended for making seditious utterances while addressing a radical meeting in Montreal. Since that time he has discontinued appearing upon the platform at public meetings. In order to carry on his radical activities, he apparently, conceived the idea on starting a small book-store in Montreal, for the purpose of distributing radical literature. This he called the "Educational Press Association and all radical publications distributed by the "Educational Press Association" are stamped with a stamp bearing that name.

A Mrs. Carmen Gonzoles takes charge of the book-store during the day and poses as a public stenographer. During the evening Boltuck and his associates sell literature at the various radical and labour meetings held in Montreal. Quantities of radical newspapers and pamphlets are imported from France, England and the United States by Boltuck and resold at the book-store.

So far the venture has not been a financial success and it is reported that Boltuck is called upon each week to donate money out of his won pocket in order to keep the book-store going. There are no indications that

Boltuck is receiving any financial assistance from outside sources.

Boltuck is a supporter of the O.B.U. and no doubt he considers he is furthering the cause of that organization by his activities in distributing radical literature.

39. O.B.U. Quebec District

The Officer Commanding Quebec District, Montreal, remarks:-

> "There is lack of harmony existing amongst the O.B.U. element here at Montreal and even those who pose and are active as its leaders are not familiar with the O.B.U. constitution, particularly in so far as the appointment of delegates to conventions is concerned. As it appears that W. E. Long will not be able to attend the convention, Rebecca Buhay will attend in his place.
>
> "The meeting referring to at which it was understood Joe Knight would speak on Fletchers' Field on Sunday afternoon the 12th instant was not held owing to inclement weather which prevailed. I understand Joe Knight has returned to Toronto."

40. "Society for Technical Aid to Soviet Russia"

An informant who attended the celebration of the Society for Technical Aid to Soviet Russia at 641 Frontenac St. Montreal on 11th September, states that about 500 to 600 persons were present, most of [24] whom were foreigners. The walls of the hall were decorated with red flags and banners bearing the Bolshevik emblems and different kinds of revolutionary pictures from the present Bolshevik movement.

The celebration was commenced by the singing of revolutionary songs. About 9 p.m. they played a drama entitled "Before the Victory". The main plot of that is drama was the last fight between the labour and capitalist governments in which war labour gained a victory. The main characters of this drama were Premier Lloyd George, the leaders of the revolutionary army, capitalists, etc. This drama caused much enthusiasm amongst the people.

W. Revenko, secretary, then spoke about the improvement and enlargement of this organization and continued:-

> "By order of the Russian Soviet Ambassador Ludwig K. Martens from New York, U.S.A. this organization came into being on 7th September, 1919, under the name of "Union of Russian Engineers and Workmen. At the beginning this organization consisted of 20 members. At that time the Russian colony of Montreal did not believe in the success of this organization because previously there were several similar organizations that all disappeared under oppression and arrests from authorities. Our organization is on the way to success and has great prestige outside of Montreal; also our meetings, automobile school and evening classes of Russian language and other subjects are very popular. He advised the people to send their children to this school to get real education.

He then spoke about the purpose of the organization and said:-

"To get labour people together and give them education and knowledge about Soviet system. We already have passed through the bitter experience of the Capitalistic system, now we must solve the problem of establishing regular relations between all labour people".

Zdarovetz, instructor of the automobile school, read the report concerning the financial condition of the organization. At the end of his report he proposed that they should play and sing The Revolutionary Dead March in Memory of comrades who died for the revolutionary cause and that every person stand up.

Our agent continues:-[25]

"The Celebration came to a close by Secretary Revenko, making his second speech. He went back to the early days of the Bolshevik movement in 1917. In this strong speech he described how Bolshevism was born and started in Russia and has been spread all over the world. He said that "Bolsheviki made dead blow to Capitalistic governments". Further, he explained that 'Bolshevism is not only a Russian movement, but it is an international movement, it depends and will give liberation to all labour people". He continued saying 'that during three years of great activity the Bolsheviks already had good results, that the Italian workmen had arisen and made revolution, also the labour organizations in England are adopting the Bolsheviki system and tactics. The same movement of revolt amongst labour is still going on throughout Canada and the United States'. In the last part of his speech he gave high tribute to Lenin and he called him "The Famous Immortal Leader". He said that 'Lenin is a man who will bring the world revolution and dictatorship of the proletariat, also he made remarks about Lenin Trotsky as here and organizer of the Great Red Army. He closed his long speech with a loud exclamation "Long live the World Revolution", "Long live our leader N. Lenin, Long live our hero Leon Trotsky". The people were so enthusiastic at the end of his speech that they made a great noise and applauded him, with the result that he called the people to stand up and sing the Internationale (Revolutionary Anthem).

Our agent says:-

"Revenko, the secretary of this organization, has very good ability as a public speaker and has great influence among the foreigners. His speeches and agitation would do a great deal of harm amongst labour".

VII. HALIFAX

41. Halifax Stevedores and Longshoremen

A report from Halifax says:-

"Up to the present there is absolutely no signs of a movement by Irish sympathizers to induce the Longshoremen to cease work on British ships.

"The S.S. "Coronia" arrived last night at 5.30 from Liverpool. This is the first British Ship in port for some time. After she discharged her cargo and passengers she proceeded to New York.

"There was absolutely no signs of any one endeavouring to stop the Longshoremen from working on this ship. Apparently no one has yet arrived, or their presence would have been discovered among the Longshoremen, who were awaiting all afternoon for the Coronia to dock."

ROYAL CANADIAN MOUNTED POLICE HEADQUARTERS

Ottawa, 30th September, 1920.

SECRET

NO. 43

NOTES OF THE WORK OF THE C. I. B. DIVISION FOR THE WEEK ENDING 30TH SEPTEMBER

Table of Contents

1. Characteristics of the Period

For some time past our attention has been directed to the activities of the O.B.U. in the Southern Alberta Coal fields. The actions of the O.B.U. officials in that area indicated that plans were being prepared to bring about a trial of strength between the mine operators in the Alberta fields and the O.B.U. on the questions of the recognition of the O.B.U. by the operators and the compulsory check-off to the U. M. W. of A.

As this report is being prepared information comes to hand advising that the threatened strike is to be called by the O.B.U. on or about 1st October, 1920. The organizers for the O.B.U. have concentrated their efforts on the Drumheller section, apparently working on the theory that should they be successful in inducing Drumheller to lead the way and come out on strike a good proportion of the remainder of the District will follow suit.

O.B.U. circulars are making their appearance in different sections of the country, warning men to keep away from the Alberta coalfields, as a dispute is taking place in that section and a strike will likely be called.

A careful review of the facts before us at the present time regarding the situation in the Alberta coalfields point to the probability of the O.B.U. being successful in bringing out a large percentage of the miners in the Drumheller section. What effect this will have on the remainder of the District and what proportion will follow the action of the Drumheller men, is difficult at present to estimate. There is one outstanding fact in connection with this proposed strike in the Alberta coalfields and that is the lack of funds in possession of the O.B.U., with which to carry on a strike for any lengthy period.[3]

On the other hand there is a pressing demand for coal, which fact, no doubt will have its effect on the action of the operators.

I. BRITISH COLUMBIA

2. Gas Workers' Strike, Vancouver

Our agent at Vancouver reports on the Gas Strike as follows:-

"One of the volunteer workers at the gas works told me that he did not see how the plant could continue operation. The work is being done by clerks who volunteered from the B. C. Electric offices. They do their office work and then go nights to the gas plant. The chief engineer, Mr. I. Keiller, got only six hours sleep in 48. The engineers, who are union men, had to refuse to continue at work when the gas workers went out and strike-breakers were hired. The strikers do not look upon the office men as strike-breakers, figuring they are only temporary employes. But new men are considered so, as they are going in to take permanent jobs. As soon as the company began to taken on permanent men, the engineers had to quit. Now the company is seeking gas workers and engineers.

"The pickets on the outside of the plants are on the qui vive, and use only verbal arguments so far. However, they are growing more bitter toward any actual "scabs". The intimidate, in a sense anyone who approaches with the intention of asking for a job. About 20 pickets are on duty around the plant all the time. The company sends its shifts to the works in automobiles that speed up and dash through the gates.

"Thus far the company has been able to get only about a dozen men, and some of them have been reached by the strikers and persuaded

to quit, I am informed.
"My informant, whose sympathies are entirely with the company, said it was "God's own blessing that the 'green' workers had not already brought on a more or less serious explosion".
A later report says:-
"The street railway men who are employed by the same company as the Gas Workers are about demanding increased rates of pay, and whilst the situation is bristling with possibilities, yet I do not think it is likely that the Street Railway men will go out, but I have an idea that the whole situation will result in an amicable settlement between the employer, the Street Railwaymen and the Gas workers, with a strong possibility of increased street car fares".

2. The Street Railway Employes' Demands

A report concerning the Street and Electric Railways Union states:-[4]
"Since my last report, the proposed demands of the men for more pay have been lying more or less dormant but the matter is being stirred up now, owning to the fact that their co-workers, the Gas Company's employes are out on strike, and look like losing out on their case.
"The Street Railwaymen realising this delegated their business agent to meet the Company on behalf of the Gas Workers, with a view to alleviating their present position, which is that of having been "fired" for non-compliance with the Company's wishes i.e. that they should go back to work without more fuss.
"On 24th September, the Street Railwaymen's Committee is to meet to decide the new scale of wages for linesmen, conductors, motormen, shopmen and maintenance-of-way men. The committee includes representatives of employes from New Westminster, Victoria and Vancouver. It is believed that the Company will refuse their demands as they have done in the Gas Workers' Case, and just what will be the outcome of that is difficult to say just now, but I hardly think it will result in a strike, which will have far reaching effect, much as the O.B.U. and other radical elements would wish it so.

4. B.C. Printing Trades Council

A special agent informs us that:-
"Printers, Lynotype operators, bookbinders, stereotypers, and pressmen of New Westminster, Vancouver and Victoria, have organized or amalgamated in one district body, I am told, called the "B.C. Printing Trades Council". They are all International Organizers.
"Hitherto, the International headquarters have always insisted on governing the action of local unions. Now, however, the Printing trades have decided not to be controlled by the head offices, but to carry out their own negotiations and agreements in a manner

deemed advisable by the organizations in the immediate district affected. For this reason they have amalgamated and prepared a scale.

"They are not affiliated with the O.B.U. direct, and if they are with the A.F. of L. they are not all advocates of the body. For instance, one of the strong men of the B.C. Printing Trades Council is W.R. Trotter, a man of O.B.U. sympathies.

"What they really established is an O.B.U. of their own, in a sense. They have decided to settle their local differences locally without interference from officers in some distant part. The officers in those distant parts have apparently consented to this being done, otherwise the International relations would have been severed. This has not happened and is not likely.

5. O.B.U. Finances

A report dated 21st September, from Vancouver says:-[5]

"I am led to believe that the O.B.U. is getting into bad shape financially, and many of the members are not keeping up their dues.

"The Hicks Employment Agency, connected with the B.C. Loggers' Association, has for a long time been throwing its wrenches into the machinery of the O.B.U., and the latter organization, especially the L.W.I.U. is beginning to recognize that it cannot continue to organize successfully in face of the opposition of the B.C. Loggers' Association.

"It is likely that a convention of the O.B.U. may be called here shortly, the main object of it being to arrange for a series of strikes in the Lumber Camps, in order to force the B.C. Loggers' Association to slow down on their methods, and to further organize the workers not to ship out through the Hicks' Employment Agency".

6. O.B.U. East Kootenay

A report concerning the O.B.U. activities in Fernie, dated 20th September says:-

"A mass meeting of the miners was called for 19th September, the meeting was called by the new secretary of the U.M.W. of A., Robert Draper. When the meeting was called to order there were exactly 35 present out of a membership of between 800 and 900, these representing the O.B.U. element among the miners.

"Wm. Hunter, the President of the U.M.W. of A. was the chairman, and he opened the meeting by stating that the rank and file of the miners were not satisfied with the new agreement which had recently been concluded between the operators and the U.M.W. of A. and that they were called together for the purpose of discussing ways and means of remedying this state of affairs. After considerable discussion it was decided that ballots would be printed and that a vote would be taken among the miners on the two questions; "Are you in favour of an increase in wages for the low-wage men" and "Are you in favour of the check-off"?

"Now the low-wage men referred to in the first question are what is known as the 'company men' and these are in the majority. Now those responsible for this resolution know perfectly well that the company men are in the majority and that they will all vote in favour of an increase and as a natural consequence all vote against the check-off as the leaders are already preaching that it would be impossible to get the increase so long as they retain the check-off as the check-off makes them members of the U.M.W. of A. and that this body is satisfied with the existing agreement.

"I have been given to understand that this scheme was planned out and laid before the O.B.U. here by Christophers of Blairmore".[6]

7. Patrol Report

An extract from a report dated 16th September from Ocean Falls is as follows:-

"Generally speaking, the men are quite satisfied with conditions at camps operated by the Pacific Mills Company and I look for no serious trouble. During my, visit, I saw no sign of the I.W.W. organizing nor any attempts at sabotage".

8. British Columbia Detachment Reports

"Chakawana" (Coastal Patrol)

"Labour conditions along the Coast patrolled by the Chakawana are quiet at present, with the exception of slight bickerings between employer and employes in the Ocean Falls District. Both the supply and demand of labour is good".

Nanaimo Detachment

Coal Mines

"All mines working to full capacity, at the same rate of pay, and no trouble at any of the mines, with their labour".

General "Everything is quiet and settled in all mining, milling and logging camps and there is no trouble anticipated by any of the companies with labour at the present time".

Merritt

"There seems to be little or no attempt in O.B.U. matters here. The hall is dark most of the time and fewer O.B.U. buttons are noticed on the streets".

Kamloops

"The labour situation is at present very quiet; there doesn't seem to be any unemployed hanging around the town, as there is plenty of work on the ranches and lumber camps."

II. ALBERTA

9. O.B.U. Coalhurst

A report concerning the O.B.U. at Coalhurst says:-

"The mines are now running up to full strength there being about 400 men employed. In my report dated 16th August I stated there were about 100 men working out on the farms who were all expected back at the mines before 1st September in order to draw their retro-active pay from the 1st April, 1920. Most of these men returned in time to get this pay and a few stayed on the farms harvesting. It is estimated that there are about 75 per cent O.B.U. men amongst the Miners at Coalhurst mines at present. There is a small percentage of U.M.W. of A.

"The general opinion of the miners at the above camp seems to be that there will be a strike all over the district about 1st October, 1920".[7]

10. O.B.U. Commerce

A report to hand from Commerce states:-

"The Chinook mines are at present running up to full strength. There are about 170 men employed. The majority of the men who were harvesting during the strike have returned to work. It is estimated that although all the men at present are paying dues to the U.M.W. of A. 25 per cent are O.B.U. and 25 per cent are U.M.W. of A. the remaining 50 per cent do not care to which union they belong. All they want is to be left alone and allowed to work, but, in the event of the O.B.U. gaining power they would undoubtedly be willing to pay their dues to the O.B.U."

11. O.B.U. Meeting, Lethbridge

An important O.B.U. meeting was recently held at Lethbridge by prominent O.B.U. officials. There is no doubt this meeting was called for the express purpose of inducing the miners in the Lethbridge area to also walk out should the men in the Drumheller field go on strike. The importance of this meeting has impelled me to quote hereunder full extracts from our reports.

"On adjournment of the meeting "James Slocan, President of this local announced that P.M. Christophers, Henry Beard, G. Palmer from Drumheller and Walter Clark from Coalhurst, all O.B.U. advocates were here to address the men. G. Palmer then took the floor and said that he was an O.B.U. man and that he had come down from Drumheller and was out to advocate O.B.U. principles, and that they were going to make a jump either one side or the other as he considered this the most opportune time to get rid of the obnoxious check-off. He said he was an enthusiastic O.B.U. man and that it was the only industrial organization that was going to benefit the workers of Canada, and that the boys in Drumheller District were forced to sign the obnoxious check-off against their will before they would be allowed to resume work in the mines. They had the wool pulled over their eyes then because they were told that the operators and the Government would not recognize the O.B.U. but instead they classed it as a Bolshevik movement sprung up from Russian propaganda distributed broadcast throughout the North American continent. Since then he said we had the wool pulled from our eyes and the men were beginning to see and think for themselves. At the present time the Miners in the Drumheller District were 90 per cent O.B.U. and what they want at the present time is the check-off repealed and that Drumheller Valley be recognized as an O.B.U. District. At a meeting there of the U.M.W. of A. to discuss important business there were only four members who attended the meeting and one was an International organizer and one a company man".[8]

"He said that two days afterwards the O.B.U. called a meeting and that there were 400 members in attendance that was the stand of the men in Drumheller. The O.B.U. could not do much for the (men) workers at this stage as it was only in its infancy yet, but regardless of that the workers in certain districts were depending on the Drumheller men making the first move towards maturing the O.B.U. and other districts expect that when it is matured it will be handed to them on a plate. At the present time the O.B.U. is like a newly hatched chicken and you can't expect it to lay eggs right away. He hoped that when the time came that the Lethbridge Miners would be men and come out and help the Drumheller miners. He remarked that there never was a more opportune time than right now to get rid of this damned check-off.

"In concluding he said "I want you boys to think this thing over and think it seriously if you want to free yourselves from this bondage and I have no doubt that Lethbridge boys will be just as strong O.B.U. as we are up in Drumheller. Some of you fellows are a little nervous and scared but there is nothing to be scared of, get your courage up for this fight and fight it to a finish. There will be no date mentioned as to when it would come off but he could assure then that it would be in the near future and I hope you boys will be solid behind it. I don't know the feeling of this meeting, he said, as it is under the auspices of the U.M.W. of A. but I assume you are all O.B.U. by the attitude and reception you have given us in this meeting. This concluded Palmers speech.

"Henry Board then took the platform. He read some statistics from the Labour Reader to show that there were 1,000 delegates representing labour at a convention in England to discuss the Russian Question, he announced "the resolutions passed at this convention which asked for the recall of the British Navy from blockading Russia and the withdrawal of the British Troops in that Zone of War. He said that the O.B.U. had made great progress since he was here last, but he hoped they would find some better means of communication between the camps so as to put the different camps wise as to what was taking place. He then went on to relate the success they had at Coalhurst and Monarch. He said that the O.B.U. had been recognized by the Government, as he had a letter here which had been sent to Secretary Spencer of the Coalhurst Local from the officials at Ottawa, asking for information re unemployment there, it was addressed to U.M.W. of A. Local Coalhurst, because of this Spencer returned the blank form to Ottawa saying 'that they was to address this local as O.B.U. in future. Then he read the reply which read "O.B.U. Local Coalhurst" from Ottawa. He then dealt on some of the subjects that Palmer dealt with re Drivers wages in Drumheller district. He concluded his speech something similar to Palmers.

"Then P.M. Christophers got up and said that he knew most of the boys here were O.B.U. and hoped they would show themselves up as well at Drumheller when the time came.

"He also said that there was no time like the present, as never in [9] the history of Canada was there ever so great a shortage of coals at the present. He said that there was no date specified as to when it would come off but it would come off in the near future and with short notice.

"He said he was going to-morrow to a convention at Port Arthur where they would discuss questions pertaining to this camp and on his return he would speak here, he said he would notify Peacock to post up notices around to give the members notice of this meeting. He said that when he was at Bob Russell's trial in Winnipeg he heard more lies told there in ten minutes then he had heard in half a life-time. He went on to say the Government was issuing pamphlets and distributing them as fast as the mails could carry them as there were thousands of them in Calgary when he left but was sorry he could not obtain one before he left. He said that Gideon Robertson, Minister of Labour, was a bigger liar than Annaias. He then dealt with contract prices for certain work in the Michel Mines and went on to show in figures where this new arrangement had reduced wages per square yard from 70 cents to $2. below the old agreement.

"He remarked that it was the rottenest agreement he had ever heard of. He said they were out for the repeal of this check-off and that they were going to get it if it took him 20 years. Christophers and the rest of them were having a conversation from James Sloan outside the door and I heard Beard say they were getting some printed posters to read:- "Sign the Check-o? and you have nothing to lose but your brains". They are going to distribute them around the mines. He said that about the 1st of October they would come out at Drumheller or the first week in October, and that would be the signal, for the rest of the camp to act. And that when they came out at Drumheller he would bring all the O.B.U. organizers down here and endeavour to bring them out here to.

"Clark of Coalhurst spoke a few minutes dwelling mostly on the success they have had with the O.B.U. at Coalhurst. He says there is not a man that is dissatisfied now since they got the O.B.U. There agreement at Coalhurst with the management calls for the Miners to give the management 30 days notice prior to any strike but he said there would be no 30 days as they would down tools without any notice. He then went on to relate how they did in the Yorkshire mines during the big strike when the Government had to use the Royal Navy to sabotage the pumps to keep the mines from ruin. He advocated for O.B.U. and that was all he had to say. This concluded the meeting".

12. <u>O.B.U. Calgary</u>

The following circular letter was sent out by Arthur Evans, District Secretary, O.B.U. Mining Dept. No. 11. to various points in Canada and the U. S. A.:-[10]

"To the Transient Wage Worker in Canada and U.S.A."

"Fellow Workers:-

"There is an industrial dispute taking place in the Coalfields of Alberta and South Eastern British Columbia, (formerly Dist 18. U.M.W. of A.) and coal miners and others are therefore requested to keep away.

"If you wish to help the miners here, do your bit by keeping away from this district, thereby permitting the workers to wage their fight against the enforced check-off of the U.M.W. of A., and intolerable conditions existing in this district.

"The larger the surplus of the labour in Alberta, the greater will be the mine owners' resistance to the workers' demands; do not be misled by statements in the capitalist press to the effect that there is no trouble in this district. A strike may be called at any time.

"Even you can co-operate in this struggle of you will keep away from this district".

13. <u>Lawson and the "Searchlight"</u>

The N. C. O. in charge of Canmore Detachment, reports as follows on a public meeting held at that point:-

"The object of the meeting was to collect money in order to keep the <u>Searchlight</u> going, both speakers spoke on the part the <u>Searchlight</u> had taken in assisting the Miners to get the increase and that the labour organization was very much handicapped without a newspaper, Editor Lawson said he had been running the paper at a loss and that he was going from camp to camp to get assistance financially from the workers. Canmore had not supported him in his enterprise as they should have done. He stated the camps in the Crows' Nest Pass and Drumheller Field were all from 75 to 90 per cent O.B.U., and said to watch all from 75 to 90 per cent O.B.U., and said to watch their movements in the next 2 or 3 weeks, stating they were going to make the operators release them from the check-off system and advised Canmore to line up."

14. Miscellaneous Notes

An extract from a pamphlet entitled "Freedom", a Ukrainian weekly, is as follows:-

"We get authentic information from reliable parties that the Bolsheviki Ambassador in America, spends large sums of money to disorganize the Ukrainian Nationalists, and for the publication of Ukrainian papers, the "Ukrainian Labour News" (Winnipeg, Man) "Ukrainian Daily News" (New York, U.S.A.) and other publications to support Bolshevism, in North America. There are many Bolsheviki agents, Jews and Russians employed on the staff of these papers and publications".[11]

At a recent meeting of the Labour Church Edmonton, the Chairman announced that no further openair meetings would be held this season, but that the committee was trying to arrange for a theatre for the winter, to hold concerts and meetings in, if successful it would be announced at a later date through the press.

The O.B.U. Bulletin was distributed as usual during the meeting.

Wasyl Swystun, Ukrainian agitator, is arranging for a big convention of the Ukrainian National Church (in Canada) at the end of the present year, when Dr. Kopachuk is to be elected Bishop of that Church.

III. SASKATCHEWAN

15. Activities of the L.W.I.U. of the O.B.U. at The Pas, Man.

In a report dated 18th September, concerning the activities of the L.W.I.U. of the O.B.U. at the Pas, Man, the following passage occurs:-

"New members are being enrolled daily by Leith, secretary of the L.W.I.U. and he is making side trips to adjacent camps in an effort to secure new members and to revive interest in the L.W.I.U. among the old members. He is meeting with considerable success and there has been more O.B.U. talk among the workers at The Pas during the week than ever before. There are a few who speak unfavourably towards the O.B.U. but by far the greater majority are in favour of it. Regular meetings are to be held in future and as soon as a few more members are obtained the district will 'take over' for itself, that is, instead of having a secretary appointed by the Central Executive at Vancouver and all money being sent to Vancouver the district will by vote elect their own Secretary, Executives committee, etc. and only a portion of the money obtained by dues etc. will be forwarded to Vancouver. Once this is done and the members are conducting their own affairs, a far greater interest will be taken by the members, which will greatly strengthen the Union. No definite time has been set as to when they will attempt to enforce their demands as this will depend entirely on the time it takes to secure sufficient members to make a strike an assured success. Leith figures that it would be best to wait until the logs are ready to be skidded to the river, for at that time the Company would have to grant their demands at once or lose their entire season by not getting their logs to the water in time for the drive".[12]

IV. MANITOBA

16. Assistance to Soviet Russia Meeting

A meeting was held in the Strand Theatre, Winnipeg, on 19th September. Dr. Johannesson presided. The meeting was called for the purpose of opening a campaign for the collection of funds for the purchase of medical supplies for Soviet Russia.

Dr. Johannesson spoke in part as follows:-

"It is our misfortune, said the chairman, 'that we are always watched by spies. Some time ago, you could see the taking notes in their seats, but now they are afraid but as soon as the meeting is ended, they will go into some neighbouring hotels and write whatever they think will be of interest to the Government, and whenever opportunity comes, as the strike trial of last Fall, they will use these notes as evidence against some of the gentlemen and ladies who will address you today".

The first speaker was Ald. A.A. Heaps. Our report says:-

"In his speech he stated that the workers, though they belong to a greater class of people are always subdued by a smaller class of Capitalists, and whatever wrong or disgraceful thing is done in a country, the blame is put on the workers. How long will the workers stand this?

"The Capitalistic papers of Winnipeg are daily filled up with news concerning the atrocities of the Bolsheviki in Russia; that the people are suffering from want of food, clothes and many other necessities of life. Canada, he said, is a country governed not by Bolsheviki, but by Capitalists, and still there are so many of you who do not know how you are going to get your coal for winter or the clothes for your family, or what you are going to get your children to eat. And still here in Winnipeg there are thousands of tons of coal, thousands of stores with clothes and great abundance of food supplies. Is this atrocity smaller than in Russia, where such things are not to be found?"

Miss Smith was the second speaker. She described the great shortage of medicines and medical instruments amongst the doctors in Russia. One doctor, she said, had to take out a soldier's eye, and the instrument he used was a razor.

The third speaker was Mr. Houston, who invited the audience to a hearty donation.

Mr. Gage (who recently returned from England) gave a lively speech on the progress and organization of the workers in England. He [13] said that he was in England at the time a certain man returned from Russia and was to give a lecture at the Albert Hall.

He said:-

"The Hall contained ten thousand people, and about 40,000 Russian sympathizers were outside the hall, singing radical songs and giving loud applause to Russian Soviet. The police, he said, could not do anything, and had to remain quiet. It is impossible, said he, for England to wage war against the Russian Soviet, because as soon as England sends out an army to fight the Russian Soviet another thing that she will find will be the Soviet Government in England (Loud applause).

Workers, he said, 'are to be content at least with this that the British Government without the workers consent would be paralyzed if they did anything against the interests of this class".

A returned soldier and Mr. Stewart (who spoke at the "Hands Off" Russia meeting) also spoke at this meeting.

A collection amounting to $287.00 was taken up, $21.00 of this amount being contributed by the six speakers on the platform. Socialistic and Bolshevik literature was sold to the value of $100-$150.

Resolutions were passed that the workers will continue to make campaigns in order to raise funds for the assistance of Soviet Russia.

17. Strike of Lake Shipping Seamen

The men employed on the Great Lakes went on strike for an increase in wages on 15th September. There is no disorder and the crews are awaiting the settlement of their demands which are being considered in the East.

The increase asked for amounts from 20 to 30 dollars additional per month.

A report regarding the O.B.U. convention at Port Arthur, dated 21st September, says:-

"The above mentioned convention which was scheduled to commence on the 20th starts at 10 a.m. to day, 21st inst. owing to the non-arrival of certain delegates. The meetings are held in the Finn Hall at Port Arthur and ow? to this place being chosen instead of either of the Labour Temples at the head of the lakes, a considerable [14] amount of adverse criticism has been aroused.

"I am informed that owing to the O.B.U. inactivity many of the most radical members among the Finns have dropped out of the organization and are looking for some organization that aims at revolution".

V. ONTARIO

18. O.B.U. Convention, Sudbury

From a reliable source we are informed that the O.B.U. Convention at Sudbury on 6th-9th September, was a failure due to internal dissension based on suspicion that the Finns were trying to obtain control of the O.B.U. for furtherance of I.W.W. or Socialistic schemes of such a Radical complexion as to conflict with the policy laid down for O.B.U., which recognizes that any extreme Radicalism is likely to result in legislation which will interfere with O.B.U. growth.

This informant says:-

"The Finns are the most dangerous part of the O.B.U. in this district, they have associations within themselves of a revolutionary nature and are only using the O.B.U. for their own purposes: I am convinced that they are in close touch with European Bolshevists and that they know better than to confide in their O.B.U. confreres, unless they happen to be Finns. It is well known that the most secret O.B.U. matters leak out sooner or later; but a good deal goes on among the Finns that is closely associated with European Politics".

19. Plan to establish O.B.U. paper in the East

A correspondent at Hamilton writes that on the 16th September he accompanied Roberts to Toronto, where they saw Mrs. Knight, who said "the O.B.U. had plans for some time to try and establish an O.B.U. paper in the East and that Cascadden would probably have charge of it; that this paper might be located in Hamilton or Toronto, and that Joe Knight had already secured the promise of subscriptions for bundle orders from various locals and internationals to support him when in danger of it having to close down for lack of support. This matter is to be brought up at the O.B.U. convention. Mrs. Knight seemed to be quite certain that it would meet with approval.[15]

He continues:-

"As far as I can make out from Mrs. Knight, Joe Knight will have a good deal to do with the establishment and management of the paper and will also act as a free lance organizer for the O.B.U. Mrs. Knight said that if their plans carried Joe would spend a great deal of his time in Hamilton and vicinity and do everything in his power to make the Hamilton local a success".

20. The Russian Workers' School, Toronto

A lecture was delivered by M. Dodokin in the Russian Workers' School, Toronto, on 19th September. All the audience were Anarchist-Communists.

The subject of his lecture was a review of the World-wide Labour movement. He began with conditions in Russia, stating that the workers had achieved much, in comparison with former conditions. He expressed satisfaction at the recent Italian movement.

Concerning England he said "England is an Empire which from his viewpoint, is gradually losing its dominating position amongst the Great Powers: India is in open revolt, Ireland is struggling for independence and the Dominion are to be regarded as seriously that a conflict may occur at any time".

21. Moses Almazoff at Meeting of the Jewish Socialist League, Toronto

A meeting of the Jewish Socialist League was held at 194 Beverley Street, Toronto, on 24th September.

Our report states:-

> "The Committee brought a report that they interviewed Jim Simpson and others and they asked him to organize a new Social Democratic Party. He refused because he is the Secretary of the F. L. P. and he promised to help them if they form a radical organization after the discussion. They formed a committee which would get into communication with all radical organizations in the Province and asked them to send two delegates to a special meeting which is going to beheld at the end of next October. Besides the committee has to work out a new platform and constitution. The constitution will be submitted for acceptance, if they do not agree with the constitution then the league will go ahead with their work. After the discussion the president introduced a man named Almazoff from Winnipeg. He [16] spoke to the audience saying that he was in jail last year for his radical activities in Winnipeg. He said 'I am still a radical as I was before and that he is going to stay in the city for a time. He promised to give a lecture next Friday at the above place and he is going to help to organize".

22. Plebbs' League, Toronto

A new organization, called Plebbs League, was started on 19th September on the corner of Shuter and Yonge Street, Toronto. The programme of this organization is to educate the proletariat as to class consciousness and to understand their political power. Their ultimate purpose is the overthrowing of the capitalistic system of Government.

Three speakers were addressing the crowd on the same principles as we have heard from the Socialists, Labour Party and O.B.U. speakers.

23. Miscellaneous Notes

An extract from a report dated Welland, 23rd September states:-

> "On Sunday, 3rd October, a meeting will be called at Welland of the real active reds in that city to hear a report of the convention, but as Winding stated there will be certain points publicly discussed. An

executive meeting will be held. Zeegar, when going to Toronto will stop either at Welland or Niagara Falls to give them inside information as to the results of the Congress".

An extract from a report dated Hamilton, 24th September, is as follows:-

"Roberts received a letter from Los Angeles local of the O.B.U. stating that one of their members was arrested some time ago and after two trials he is slated for a third trial on 4th November. In both trials the jury failed to agree and in the meantime he and several others are touring the United States appealing for funds to aid in fighting the case to a finish, as they claim that the authorities are making a test case of this and if the O.B.U. should lose, their member, whose name is Blossom, will be sent to jail; that this would be the beginning of the smashing of the O.B.U. in that part of the country. The letter asks the Hamilton local to try and arrange a meeting for one of their speakers and to also help them financially. They are trying to arrange for one of their members to tour Canada".[17]

VI. QUEBEC

24. Meeting of Society for Technical Aid to Soviet Russia

On September 19th a meeting of the Society for Technical Aid to Soviet Russia was held. A report by Kaverga was read concerning his negotiations with U. Binette.

According to this report U. Binette of the O.B.U. agreed with the plan to organize a special committee to raise funds for Soviet Russia, and promised helped and contributions, but stated that he (Binette) had received special letters from Ludwig R. Martens (Soviet Ambassador at New York) and Dr. Mendelson (Secretary of Soviet Relief Fund at New York) in which letters it was stated that Dr. Mendelson and another representative would be in Montreal at the end of September or the beginning of October in connection with this matter; and Binette advised that they should not organize until the arrival of the aforementioned representatives.

They decided to call a meeting inviting the leading men of the local labour organizations, and also to send a letter to Dr. Mendelson.

There was quite a hot discussion about the New York explosion. W. Revenko, secretary, and some other members expressing their opinions that the bomb outrage was done by the U.S. authorities or their agents as an act of provocation so as to turn the public against all labour movements, but the majority of the members are still thinking that this explosion was done by Anarchist-Terrorists (the most extreme fanatic party, amongst all the radical organizations) as an act of revenge to Governments for political prisoners.

A further meeting of this Society was held during the week and our correspondent writes:-[18]

"Secretary W. Revenko read a letter from Dr. Mendelson, secretary of Soviet Russia Medical Relief Committee, New York, in which he was asked to collect money from labour in Montreal to aid Soviet Russia.

"He gave a speech on conditions in Soviet in which he stated that 'The population were suffering from the murderous blockade of England". At the end of his speech he proposed a special committee for that purpose, and decided to ask other radical labour organizations for contributions for Soviet Russia. After discussion it was decided to select a committee from the members, also to appoint two delegates to confer with leaders of the O.B.U. about this matter. A committee of our were chosen from Medical Relief for Soviet Russia, with Dr. Nighthours as secretary; two delegates were also chosen, namely Kaverga and Selan, who will give a report on this matter next Sunday.

"Sec. W. Revenko notified the members that comrade Paradovsky had left for Soviet Russia on 18th September.

"Paradovsky is an active member of this association. He is well-known as a translator of Bolsheviki pamphlets from Russian to Ukrainian. He also is a clever painter. Many of his sketches of Bolsheviki revolutionary movements are used as decoration for the hall of this organization".

25. O.B.U. Metal Trades Unit

A meeting of the O.B.U. Metal Trades Unit was held at the Labour Temple, Montreal, on 16th September. About 20 members were present and John O'Cane was elected Chairman.

Rebecca Buhay took the floor; her subject being the "Class Struggle". Part of her speech follows:-

"So we find today a small minority of one class of people who possess and don't produce, through virtue of laws and militia, holding fast on that big class who produces and do not possess, because somehow or other, this small class has been able to gain control of the machine of industries, they have also united their forces to such extent until they have become so powerful that they do dare the working class to wrest that power from them."

A. Saint-Martin was the next speaker, who spoke in part as follows:-

"We have reached the day when it is necessary to take over the industries of the country and run them for the benefit of all people instead of only a few. I want you to remember this word; plant the seed of the verb "Take" into the mind of your fellowworkers, water it occasionally so that it may flourish and some day in the very near future, we will be able to "take" the industries of the country in our hands and run them as they should be run.[19]

The report continues:-

"Under the order of "The good and welfare of the movement" W.E. Long, secretary-treasurer of the Metal Trades Unit stated that the Amalgamated Society of Engineers of Maisonneuve, as the result of the meeting held by Joe Knight on the 11th September, have decided to join the O.B.U. in a body, and owing to the fact that the Amalgamated Society of Engineers' Hall is rented and paid for until the 1st may 1921, it would be advisable for the Metal Trades to join forces with the Amalgamated Society of Engineers and hold the meetings at Maisonneuve instead of the Labour Temple, it will curtail expenses and it would be much better for those workers who live in the North and East of the city.

"A long and heated discussion took place over this report U. Binette stated that if the Metal Trades Unit was going to join forces with the Amalgamated Society of Engineers, it would be much better also to employ the General Workers' Unit, until such time as they would be able to function independently.

"Long also stated that the Amalgamated Society of Engineers were coming into the O.B.U. as a unit, every member will carry an O.B.U. card after 22nd September.

26. Dissension in the O.B.U., Montreal

An O.B.U. meeting was held at the Labour Temple Montreal, on 23rd September. In a report concerning this meeting dated 27th September, the following passages occur:-

"O. Cahrette, Secretary-treasurer of the O.B.U. general workers' Unit, in giving a financial report, stated that the General Workers' Unit are about $859.00 in the hole".

"A. Saint-Martin then moved the following resolution:- 'Is it advisable for the O.B.U. to have a permanent headquarters in Montreal?' When the motion was put to a question, U. Binette delivered a long speech opposing the motion, stating that the O.B.U. was not in a position to keep a permanent headquarters and that it was ridiculous to try to make the workers and people in general believe that the O.B.U. is a strong organization financially or morally. We must face the facts whether we like them or not, do not let us deceive ourselves nor let us deceive the memberships for some day they will learn the truth and call you "bluffs".

"Saint-Martin in reply to Binette's remarks stated that it was very stupid and reactionary for Binette to make such statements, such statements as Binette's have the tendency to decrease instead of increasing the O.B.U. membership and such action should be fought with every weapon in order to prevent such opinions from being expressed. Binette, he continued, is always coming to throw his cold water on our enthusiasm".[20]

Our reports continues:-

"The storm broke once more, every one wanted to speak but not until the chairman threatened to call the meeting off, the amendment was put to a vote which was lost".

The meeting dispersed at 11.15 p.m. in disorder.

27. French Socialist Communist Party

A meeting of the above organization was held at the Labour Temple, Montreal, on 26th September, 60 members were present.

A Saint-Martin spoke in part as follows, before proceeding to the temple:-

"That the Police and authorities are responsible for the terrible New York explosion. He further stated that in order to make this remark clear to everyone, he will explain why the police have committed such a terrible crime. He continued by stating that the authorities are using every tactic with the view to create an ill feeling against the Communists, which is the only way they will be able to gain support, but asked those present, not to believe that the 'Reds' are capable of such acts.

He then requested the crowd to follow him to the Labour Temple. As soon as they reached the Labour Temple, and the crowd had taken their seats, Gottsell proceeded with the meeting by reading from a French publication regarding the conditions of Soviet Russia and that stand taken by the Allied Power with the view to crush Russia.

After Gottsell was through reading, a few questions were asked by the members present but none of any importance, Gottsell answered all the questions.

A Saint-Martin was the next speaker.

"He dealt on economics and requested those present to organize, educate and prepare themselves for the coming revolution, stating, "If you are not organized you will be made to suffer, you want to educate yourselves and know just what you are expected to do, when the opportune time arrives".

He concluded his speech by saying:-

"That there is a social revolution taking place today in all countries of the world and it's the duty of every toiler to organize for the cause"[21]

VII. MARITIME PROVINCES

23. Strike at Reserve Mine, Cape Breton

400 men were idle owing to a strike in the Collierie Nos 8. and 10 Reserve Mine, Cape Breton.

Our report says:-

"The men went on strike on account of a checking system which means that when the men put their lamps in the checking room they have to receive a check bearing the same number which is on their lamp, and when he receives his lamp in the morning he must deposit his check with the timekeeper in order to get his day's pay.

"The men claimed that receiving and depositing this check was a loss of time to them, consequently a strike was called and about 400 men went out but they received no support from the U.M.W. of A. and they were obliged to go back to work on September 17th under the same checking system".

Extracts from a report concerning the Royal Commission Convention in Glace Bay, dated 20th September are as follows:-

"The delegates present were in every way pleased with the finding of the Royal Commission, and are not much in love with the remarks, and the way some of the other men are acting; they are all fair minded, and only want to do what is right; some others I have found, are very radical and trying to do all in their power to raise what ever trouble they can in the rank and file of the U.M.W.

ROYAL CANADIAN MOUNTED POLICE HEADQUARTERS

Ottawa, 7th October, 1920.

SECRET

NO. 44

NOTES OF THE WORK OF THE C. I. B. DIVISION FOR THE WEEK ENDING 7th OCTOBER.

Table of Contents

Rumoured visit by Mr. Smillie.
" 11. B. C. Detachment Reports.
" 12. The Drumheller Situation.
Feeling among the Miners.
Replies to Evans' circulars.
Lawson and Evans in charge; Christophers etc. holding aloof.
Scheme to obtain pretext for Switchmen's strike.
" 13. Affairs in the Crow's Nest Pass.
Referendum at Fernie.
Conditions at Blairmore.
" 14. Notes from the Coalfields.
E. Browne's resignation.
Dishonest statements by Arthur Evans.
Conditions at Taber.
Conditions at Lethbridge.[2]
" 15. The Calgary O. B. U.
Dissension appearing.
Shop Stewards Movement languishing.
" 16. The Edmonton Labour Church
Ritchie's Plans.
" 17. Ukrainian Opposition to Canadianization.
" 18. Miscellaneous Notes.
Ukrainian Church quarrel at Sheho.
The Radville O. B. U.
No O. B. U. at Gravelbourg.
" 19. Winnipeg O. B. U. in Difficulties
Building Trades Unit losing its fight.
Gains by the Running Trades Unit.
" 20. O. B. U. leaders at Winnipeg.
" 21. R. E. Bray's speech.
" 22. Socialists and the Third International.
" 23. Another Ukrainian Dispute.
" 24. Miscellaneous Notes.
Identity of "W. Gordon"
Lake Shipping strike settled.
" 25. Negotiations between Factions at the O. B. U. Convention
" 26. The Plebs League.
Praying for Distriess next winter.
" 27. Activities of Foreigners.
Russian Workers' School.
Almazoff's activities.
Jewish Socialist League.
Shapiro's activities.

1. Characteristics of the Period

The strike at Drumheller seems to have had a bad start. Our latest information by mail indicates that the preparations for it were inadequate, that Lawson and Evans, who were promoting it, were not very confident, and that several of the leaders, such as Christophers, Beard and Browne, were taking little or no part in the arrangements.

A telegram received on 6th October, however, announces that some 1,200 men have struck in Fernie, the citadel of the O. B. U. in the mining community.

Evidence from several sources suggests that the L. W. I. U. is experiencing some decline, possibly in membership, and certainly in power. The change in the market is putting the employers in a stronger position, and the men are not nearly so ready to provoke conflicts.

A curious development in British Columbia is the disposition of a number of agitators to support Prohibition on the ground that it increases discontent. Several reports to this effect have come in this week. In one case a local clergyman was moved by this attitude to speak from an O. B. U. platform.

In Winnipeg the fight in the Building Trades between the O. B. U. and the Internationals seems to be going in favour of the latter. The O. B. U. unit is in a depressed condition.

One more small revolutionary society has been formed in Toronto. It is called the Plebbs League, and it is as unpromising and as unamiable as the others. Its leading spirit, Morris Spector, at a recent meeting prayed earnestly for a hard winter, with a bread line.

Revolutionists in various parts of the country have been attributing the Wall Street bomb outrage to the authorities, or to the police or detectives.[4]

The Russian organization in Montreal is interesting in the fidelity with which it conforms to Bolshevist policy in Russia. It seems to be under close direction from New York.

1. BRITISH COLUMBIA

2. The L. W. I. U.

The N. C. O. in charge of C. I. B. work in East Kootenay has made the following report upon conditions in the logging industry in South Eastern British Columbia:-

"Regarding the strength of the L. W. I. U. there has been a distinct falling off in the number of members employed in this district in the past two months. Out of a total of 2,500 members that were in the district at the end of July last, about 600 have departed to Alberta and Saskatchewan for the harvest season, about 1,700 are distributed amongst 12 large mills at present operating in the district, and about 200 scattered amongst small operators.

"There is a distinct shortage of labour in the lumber camps, and very little bush work is going on. Conditions are unfavourable for a strike in all camps except the C. P. R. Mills at Yahk, where 300 men are employed, where the product taken up by the C. P. R. co. The market is very low, the mills have been working on their last winter's out steadily during the present summer, very little has been shipped, and the yards are all piling up lumber. The lumbermen are prepared to close down at any time and wait for a better market, and therefore any action on the part of the employees to call a strike would be met by the employers by an instant closing down of operations, which would be disastrous only to the strikers.

"The L. W. I. U. although organized solidly throughout the district, are not strong enough to dictate to, or make demands of the employes, and can only deal with the employers as employes of the respective firms by whom they are employed. This condition has existed throughout the present year, and has worked satisfactorily to all concerned.

"It is considered that by the end of October next the loggers at present on the prairies will have returned, and conditions will be much better".

Reports from an outside source as to conditions within the L. W. I. U. at Vancouver suggests that the union is feeling less powerful now. A good many agitators find that they are black listed, and are experiencing some agitation on their own account.[5]

Before the recent Port Arthur Convention Winch was rumoured to be seeking a place on the Provincial Compensation Board. This presumably was to ensure a retreat if he were displaced.

Although the L. W. I. U. are $2,000 behind with their per capita tax to headquarters, and in consequence had trouble at the Port Arthur Convention they voted $500 to aid the Vancouver gas-workers in their strike.

An agent who is well acquainted with the affairs of the L. W. I. U. in Vancouver, says under date of 25th September that

"He believes that the long talked of split between Midgley and Winch has finally come to a head at the Winnipeg Convention. The last edition of the Federationist shows that the coast delegates refused to be seated in the convention under the conditions imposed by the credentials committee and operator believes he can see in this the hand of Midgley working to eliminate Winch and his bunch. Alexander was the only coast delegate who took a seat in the convention under the conditions imposed and it is well know that there is little love lost between him and Winch".

3. O. B. U. Notes

A report on conditions in Victoria dated 28th September remarks that feeling is strong against the O. B. U. and that the O. B. U. is making no great headway among the returned soldiers' organizations.

However, the Building Trades Council has recommended its locals to reduce their entrance fee from $30 to $10.

Information has been received that at Anyox the O. B. U. have added from 150 to 200 members. This is represented as being a local rally, and not as due to any special incursion of organizers from outside.

Last June V. R. Midgley issued circulars commending the Shop Stewards movement, and trying to arrange a tour for Alex M. Robertson of the Scottish Labour College, Glasgow, whose movements have been noted. Robertson's address is given as in New York. The circular met with [6] little response, and the attempt to arrange a tour failed.

Paul Meadows, an "old-timer", has been made secretary of the O. B. U. at Merritt. His pay is said to be $40 a month. He is of mediocre ability and is not regarded as a dangerous agitator.

Michael Casey, an O. B. U. organizer at Penticton, has fled owing to a warrant being issued for his arrest on a charge of boot-legging. He has sought refuge in the United States and the Immigration authorities have been asked to prevent his return to Canada.

This man seems a general bad character, being a reputed card-sharper. He instigated several strikes in the mines and lumber camps of Southern British Columbia.

The Revd. D. T. McClintock of Nelson, B.C. has come into prominence lately by his utterances on the labour question. After preaching in his own church in a friendly way of the O. B. U. on 9th September he addressed a meeting at Silverton under the auspices of the O. B. U. Womens' Auxiliary. His address, which included an attack on the pamphlet issued by the Labour Department, greatly pleased the O. B. U.

4. Agitators and Prohibition

A curious development in Vancouver is a disposition on the part of leading agitators to support Prohibition, in the belief that it fosters discontent. Among these are R.W. Trotter, A. S. Wells, V. R. Midgley, and E. Winch. somewhat contradictory stories are told as to efforts to effect an alliance between labour men and the "Drys", to the effect that the extremists are trying to induce the Internationals to take part in the movement. A passage in our report on the subject, (which is written by a well-informed agent) is:-

> "Winch thinks that if Canada goes dry it will accelerate the general unrest that is what the Radicals want".[7]

In this connection the following note on W. R. Trotter, secretary of the Federated Labour Party of Vancouver may be quoted:-

> "In company with others he spoke at the Broadway Theatre, in this city, on the 26th instant. He is reported to have said that in 1916 the labour men considered the question of prohibition as none of their affair. They thought it merely a trick on the part of the Capitalist class to create greater production in the factories and mills through increased sobriety, but today the heads of organized labour are lamost to a man in support of it, and before its adoption it was impossible for the organizers of labour to obtain even a hearing among the lumber-jacks. Largely as a result of prohibition they have since had time and clear brains to organize into a body 19,000 strong.
>
> "Trotter concluded with the remark that if the present social unrest should result in anything approaching revolution, it would be very desirable to have a sober proletariat."

It is noted that Thomas Richardson is busying himself in advocacy of prohibition. In this connection the N. C. O. in charge of C. I. B. work in Vancouver remarks:-

"There is a feeling among local radicals that a 'bone-dry' condition in the country will strongly enhance their opportunities for causing general unrest".

At Prince Rupert on Sunday 26th September a debate was held on Prohibition under the auspices of the Central Labour Council of the O. B. U. W. P. Lynch, Queen Charlotte Islands, attacked Prohibition, advocating Government control and sale. Revd. W. Stevenson upheld Prohibition; he quoted the utterances of Messrs. Wells, Woodsworth and Trotter, which already have been quoted, and adopted their line of argument.

5. The Labour Church

The movement to establish a Labour Church in Vancouver was formally launched on 26th September, when a meeting was held. The chairman, J. Clarke, said that to avert the criticism that they taught economics under the name of "Church" they would call it the "People's Sunday Night Meeting". Mr. J. S. Woodsworth described the methods followed in the Labor churches in Winnipeg and Brandon. He said that:-[8]

> "They must develop an Institution which will function as the Workers' Church, College and Club, all in one, and all in sympathy with the Movement are invited to associate themselves with it; he also stated that, in future, they intend to have Music and Hymns suitable to the occasion, and that very soon he would preach a sermon from the text for which he was arrested and charged with sedition".

He devoted some attention to replying to the criticisms contained in the pamphlet issued by the Department of Labour.

The attendance was small. Our report says:-

> "It was quite noticeable that the class of people who attended are, or have been, Church-going people and they expected more of a religious meeting".

6. "The Friends of Freedom for India"

A report from Vancouver dated 28th September says:-

> "There is also a movement going on among Hindus of Vancouver called "The Friends of Freedom for India". This, he (Tom Doyle) stated was backed up financially to a certain extent by de Valera, so-called president of Ireland. The movement is getting strong in the U. S. and Mr. Urquhart the secretary of Provincial Branch, will have an interview with these Hindus and try and get them to co-operate on the Irish question".

Strangely enough, the June report of the Intelligence Service at Singapore, which was received this week, notes the appearance in Farther India of evidences of the work of this body. Its New York address is the Rand School of Social Science. No. 7 East 15th Street, New York, which affords hospitality to so many subversive societies.

7. Chinese Societies

A survey of the Chinese Societies in Vancouver, after remarking that special life if highly developed among these people, and that numerous club, societies and tongs exist which for the most part have no anti-governmental tinge, mentions three that engage in political action:-[9]

1. The Chinese Labour Association of Canada. It has two subsidiary organizations, the Chinese Shingle Workers' Union of Canada and the Democratic Academy. It publishes a small bi-monthly pamphlet, the Labour Movement. It is noted that the Academy (which has 15 pupils and no salaried teachers) has classes in Esperanto, but no revolutionary significance seems to

attack to this.

2. The Chinese Empire Reform Association. This is described as "Ultra democratic", and to be a body with branches in the United States, Mexico, Australia, Japan and Hawaii. It has some association with the Chinese Times of Vancouver. Apparently it is concerned with politics in China.
3. The Chinese National League. This opposes No. 2. The Victoria Branch of No. 3 is inactive. Its membership is approximately 400.

8. Charles Lestor

Charles Lestor delivered his valedictory address in Vancouver on 26th September; he stated that he would be absent for three or four months.

He attributed the Wall Street bomb explosion to some detective agency.

Part of the report is:-

"The 'Daily Herald's refusal of Soviet gold is one of my reasons for going .... When I heard that the paper had refused to take £75,000, I knew I must go. The British workers have been trained to think of a matter or action as right or wrong, according to the capitalist moral code ...... If we (the S. P. of C.) can get this or any other Soviet money, we won't hesitate to take it, knowing that we are going to put it to good use. Winston Churchill spent secretly £20,000,000 trying to defeat the Soviets. He used the British workers money, so the workers are quite justified in using Soviet money in trying to defeat Churchill and the capitalist class".

In conversation he said that his purpose in going to England was "to educate his ignorant fellow-workers in England". He stated that he intends eventually to go to Petrograd, to observe Communism in actual operation, and to form an opinion whether the Bolshevist methods are applicable in the Western World. He has about $500 not a large sum for so ambitious a project.

9. Soldiers' Organizations

The principal soldiers' organizations in Vancouver number approximately as follows:-[10]

G. W. V. A. ...... 5,000, Army and Navy ... 3,000
Imperial Veterans 1,400, G. A. U. V....... 400
Gunners and Sappers 300

An effort is being made to organize these for political purposes. On 4th September a meeting was held in the City Hall of the United Soldiers' Council of Vancouver, the organizations represented being the Amputation Club, the Army and Navy Veterans, the G. W. V. A., the Imperial Veterans of Canada, the G. A. U. V. and the C. A. S. A. After discussion it was decided that the U. S. C. as a whole would take no action; but the G. A. U. V. were to communicate with the various organizations and ask their support.

On 19th September the G. A. U. V. held a well-attended meeting at the Empress Hotel, at which the $2,000 gratuity was demanded, the Federal Government was denounced, and the election of soldiers' representatives was urged. The audience was sympathetic. Some of the speeches bordered on the revolutionary.

The society known as "Comrades of the Great War" in Vancouver, which has been inactive for some time, now seems to have come altogether to an end. A chattel mortgage against its effects has been foreclosed, and everything has been sold at a bailiff's sale.

An "Ex-Soldiers' Labour Council" has been formed in Victoria, composed of representatives of:-

(1) Great War Veterans Association.

(2) Comrades of the Great War.

(3) Grand Army United Veterans.

(4) Metal Trades Council.

(5) Trades and Labour Council.

The local O. B. U. unit applied for representation, and the Trades and Labour Council on 15th September decided in favour of the application and the G. A. U. V. on 21st September voted against it.

10. Miscellaneous Notes

Conflicting reports are received as to the likelihood of the [11] striking gas-workers of Vancouver being supported by the Street railwaymen in a sympathetic strike. The balance of probability seems to be against this. The strikers seem to be losing.

Concerning the dispute between the Shipyards in Vancouver and their men, a well-informed agent declares that "The companies are stalling for time".

The B. C. Printing Trades Council are asking the newspapers in Victoria for $10 for a 7-hour day, day-work, and $11 a day, night work. The newspapers are unlikely to agree.

The movement to include reporters in this body is not meeting with success.

A report from Prince Rupert states that the appeal for medical aid to Soviet Russia is receiving no support whatever in that district.

A report from Vancouver is that a few copies of Alberta Inkpin's Communist, the organ in Great Britain of the Third International, are received by individual agitators. It is not sold on the news-stand.

Track has been obtained of several meeting places of the Finns of Vancouver. The agent who is in charge of this aspects of the situation says:-

> "That he has been watching these people pretty closely and is in touch with many of them, and, whilst they are nearly all socialists of the ultra-radical order, yet they seem generally to be very inac-

tive. The O. B. U. makes but very little headway with them".

Mrs. Rose Henderson has been living in Vancouver for a time. She is expected to arrive in Winnipeg early in October, to deliver an address. A report from Vancouver says:-

> "This woman is a regular fire-brand, and whilst here has been interesting herself in O. B. U. affairs, social and otherwise, and has also addressed meetings held under the auspices of the Federated Labour party.
>
> "Mrs. Henderson has also actively interested herself in the affairs of the Self Determination for Ireland League at this point, but the [12] best authorities say she is not very conversant with the question".

A patrol from Hazelton eastwards to Telkwa, Moricetown Smithers, Round Lake and Aldermere showed labour matters to be very quiet. The districts visited were very orderly.

A rumour is in circulation in Vancouver that Robert Smillie may visit Canada.

11. British Columbia Detachment Reports

Stewart, 18th September

Nothing to report as to labour activities or labour unrest. The autumn exodus beginning.

Prince George, 11th September:-

"The Labour situation is very quiet; all labourers in this district are quiet and no agitation whatever".

Port Alberni, 18th September:-

"District quiet and orderly. Camps and mills working without any signs of unrest.

"District quiet and orderly ..... No outward indications of disturbances in labour circles locally, matters in this regard being very quiet".

Ocean Falls, 18th September:-

"Labour element assuming normal conditions again".

Merritt, 25th September:-

Owing to a cessation of lumber orders, probably caused by the increased freight rates, the mill of the Nicola Pine Mills Co. Merritt, has been forced to let out some 150 men. The married men are being retained, for the most part, in hopes that orders will come in. As this town is largely dependent upon the mill, this lack of orders has a far-reaching effect. The logging camps will not be running at full capacity unless the situation improves".

Grand Forks, 18th September:-

"Labour conditions are good at present in the district and there is no appearances of any unrest".

II. ALBERTA

12. The Drumheller Situation

Reports from Drumheller dated 22nd September are to the effect that the feeling there was far from being unanimous in favour of the strike. One report from a very confidential source in describing meetings held in Drumheller said that at one of them only 190 men voted [13] out of 250 present. No ballot was taken, the vote being by a show of hands. This observer's estimate is that the Drumheller miners are thus divided:- 55 per cent for the resolution; 25 per cent against it; 20 per cent waiting for the outcome before they take sides.

Another report, after stating that "A great number of the strikers are not in favour of the strike movements, they being more or less in financial difficulties, though at the same time in sympathy with the O. B. U.", goes on to give an amusing account of a meeting at Wayne which was addressed by two men, one of whom is named Feumach:-

> "Feumach urged the men to hold out against the operators. This meeting I was informed was only lukewarm and many in the audience asked questions 'as to where the finances were coming from if they went on strike'. Feumach answered that they would to stick it with backbone. He however asked that a collection be taken up to defray his expenses to the convention and the answer came back 'that it would have to be backbone too'.

By 29th September Arthur Evans had received only six or seven replies to his circular on the Drumheller strike; of these only three were in writing and of these only one (from Michel) actually stated that the abolition of the check-off had been demanded.

Lawson and Evans seemed to be managing the preliminaries of the Drumheller strike; it was remarked on that date that neither Christophers, Beard and Brown had visited the Drumheller area, not had they given active support. The Officer Commanding Calgary reports that Lawson and Evans seemed to be getting cold feet.

We have received information that a scheme was formed whereby the railway switchmen in the Drumheller area would pretend to fear violence, with the hope that the R. C. M. P. would be directed to remove any O. B. U. pickets; and that the switchmen then would refuse to work "under military surveillance".[14]

13. Affairs in the Crow's Nest Pass

At Fernie the referendum ordered by the O. B. U. men working through the local U. M. W. of A. machinery resulted thus:

In favour of the checkoff 88
Against the check-off 431
Spoiled Ballots .... 14 total 533
In favour of increase for day workers 451
Against increase for day wage workers 59
Spoiled ballots 13

This referendum was framed to appeal to the "company men" i.e. those who draw the lowest wage.

Our report, which is dated 27th September, adds:-

"The miners here expect Beard or Christophers to come and advise them as to what action to take. Up to the present I understand no word has been received from either of these two men, but indications are that in all probability a strike will be called on October 1st if the operators do not grant the men's request".

A report from Blairmore dated 25th September, after noting that the situation in the Pass was quiet, that Christophers was absent, and that "Rod" McDonald, the local O. B. U. secretary was working at ordinary industry, adds these remarks:-

"From information gathered at the present time, the miners are not in favour of striking, and such men as Christopher and other leaders of the O. B. U. seemed to have lost favour, the men considering that they are grafting at their expense, and doing no work, and I believe this is one reason that R. McDonald has been working for the last two weeks. On the other hand the miners are sore about the last check-off.

"There was some talk amongst the men at Hillcrest, that should the miners in England go on strike, they might consider going out in sympathy with them, but this is not general, and the larger majority of the men do not favour a strike".

14. Notes from the Coalfields

Edward Browne has resigned as Secretary of "Mining District No. 1., O. B. U.". One Arthur Evans has succeeded him.

Evidence is in our hands as to dishonest methods pursued by the O. B. U. in their attempt to foment a strike in the Alberta coalfields. Arthur Evans, who has succeeded Ed. Browne as District secretary, has sent out circular letters to locals, asking for action,[15] and asserting that "the following local have endorsed the Western Commercial resolution etc". The lists that follow differ widely, and all include names of mines where the resolution in question has not been passed. This constitutes circulating false statements with a view to bring about a strike.

A meeting of the Canada West Mine Local at Taber on 22nd September showed that Taber was not expected to strike in sympathy with Drumheller and that conditions in Taber did not justify a strike.

The regular weekly meeting of Local No. 5741 U. M. W. of A. Lethbridge, was held on 21st September. Our report says:-

"There was no talk of a strike at the meeting but I heard if voiced around the mines that there would be a strike. I presume there will be 60 per cent of the miners work if they call a strike. P. M. Christophers will address the men upon his return from the Port Arthur convention of the O. B. U."

In commenting on an uneventful meeting of the Lethbridge local held on 28th September the N. C. O. in charge of C. I. B. work in Southern

Alberta expresses the opinion that there was not much danger of trouble in that particular locality.

15. The Calgary O. B. U.

Dissension is appearing among the Calgary O. B. U., and their prospects are clouding. (1) The organization of shop-stewards reported a while ago, seems to be losing its energy; if it dies out, the O. B. U. probably will lose ground in the C. P. R. shops. (2) Two members of the O. B. U., Turner and Burns, were criticised severely at a meeting held recently and Turner was ejected from the body. (3) The resolutions sent by the Transportation Unit No. 1. to the Convention were uncompromising; there were summarised thus:-

"1. That the Union do away with all travelling organizers
2. That organizers must act on the job.
3. That all members who are in business for themselves be expelled from the Union.
4. That all members belonging to committees or delegates must not be of a political nature, therefore, belonging to no political party whatsoever".[16]

16. The Edmonton Labour Church

Revd. Mr. Ritchie is planning to carry on his Labour Church agitation in Edmonton during the coming winter, on a larger scale. The report continues:-

"He has also formed a new 'Independent Labour Party', radicals, a branch of the Dominion Labour Party of this city, who will put their own representatives in the field at the forthcoming civic elections this fall.

"At the present time Ritchie is contracting on carpenter work, as he cannot get a job himself with the contractors in the city on account of his radical principles, and connections with the O. B. U.".

17. Ukrainian Opposition to Canadianization

On 25th September the Ukrainian Greek Catholic Association known as "Shewchenko" gave a play in Edmonton. O. Shyber, the president, delivered an address, which is thus reported.

"He said that the Ukrainians in Ukrainia would fight hard for the independence of our dear Ukrainia. He also said 'I don't care on what side they fight, with Bolshevists or against them, so long as they fight for the independence of Ukrainia. We are with them, and through Ukrainian national schools, songs and theatrical plays, in this country, we will prevent our children from assimilation with the English and train them for patriotic Ukrainians who will go to Ukrainia and be leaders among our people'. The speaker also appealed strongly to the public to attend every such theatrical play and help financially support every Ukrainian cause".

III. Saskatchewan

18. Miscellaneous Notes

The activities of the Peter Mohyler Institute of Saskatoon, with which Wasyl Swystun is connected, continue to attract attention. There has recently been established a Ukrainian Greek Orthodox Theological Seminary at Saskatoon, the Revd. Lazor Herman or Gherman being rector. Some time in June or July the last-named got into a fight at Sheho, which ended in prosecutions before a magistrate. Herman and his faction apparently tried to displace the priest established there, and a scuffle endued. To some extent it was a matter of the older men, who speak Bukowinia standing by the old priest, and of the younger men supporting Herman and his doctrine of the Ukrainian language, Ukrainian [17] schools, teachers and priests, and "Ukrainian flag".

A recent investigation at Radville shows the O. B. U. unit there to be very quiet.

Investigation at Gravelbourg shows that while wages for threshers are high, owing to scarcity of men, there is no O. B. U. talk.

IV. MANITOBA

19. Winnipeg O. B. U. in Difficulties

The Building Trades Unit, O. B. U. Winnipeg, held a discouraging meeting on 27th September. The following were the principal features:-

1. It was admitted that three quarters of the membership have fallen away, and returned to the Internationals. The nominal membership is 800; only 200 are left who are paying dues. This was mentioned several times, in different terms.
2. The fight with the Internationals is going adversely for the O. B. U. At the instigation of the former, O. B. U. men are cojtinually are being dismissed from jobs; the O. B. U. organizers contemplated arranging a strike of painters and electricians to counter this, and found these trades so disinclined to such a course that they did not venture upon the step.
3. The unit is in a bad financial position, many members having fallen into arrears.
4. A dispute is in progress concerning the organizers. Two are now on salary; the money in hand does not seem sufficient to pay them; a proposal to have only one was discussed without a decision being reached.
5. As an aggravation, the secretary has absented himself from several meetings and has neither vouchsafed an explanation nor turned in the books.

"Someone suggested that the Unit was going to the devil, and several agreed that it was a fact.

"The meeting then dispersed".

As an offset to this a meeting of the Running Trades Unit O. B. U. Winnipeg, on 26th September it was declared that about 30 accessions to the ranks had been booked during the fortnight just past.

20. O. B. U. Leaders at Winnipeg

A mass meeting was held in Winnipeg on Sunday 26th September under the auspices of the Central Labour Council, O. B. U. to hear [18] O. B. U. delegates returning from the Port Arthur Convention. Speeches were made by Joe Naylor, V. R. Midgley, and Ald. Broatch of Calgary, and also by R. E. Bray who has just been released from jail. The attendance was about 700, and enthusiasm was shown.

The speeches of Naylor and Midgley were of the usual description, extolling the O. B. U. and assailing the International. They declared that the convention had been successful, and one passage in Midgley's speech is thus reported:-

> "He stated that further resolutions had been passed at the last convention for the betterment of the One Big Union; that now even the highest paid official, which was the general secretary, could not do anything without the consent of the workers, who were members of the organization, and even this official could be fired from his position at any time that the workers become dissatisfied with any of his actions".

21. R. E. Bray's Speech

Bray's speech was more interesting. It was of a revolutionary tone, but contained some significant passages. He complained that the support given to him and his comrades in jail had been limited to cheering.

> "The boys at the prison farm had come to the conclusion that the workers were divided by the old psychology having left most of them, and that they were being still controlled with the one idea 'If we go on strike we will lose our jobs".

The report continues:-

> "He declared that the workers of Winnipeg had taken a step back at this controlling idea when their leaders were convicted last spring, and it had always been the boys' idea that the workers would demand their release, or else lay down every tool and go on strike until they were released, but they had been disappointed in this idea, which went to show that the workers were afraid of losing that job of theirs, and would rather let their leaders put in time instead of losing it, or run the chance of so doing".

After stating that the prisoners would not accept release on any terms which would give credit to the Internationals he renewed his complaints:-

> "'We believe', he stated 'that to a certain extent we have been overlooked. The workers were either afraid or unable to fight by means of the strike, and were unwilling to advise what steps we should take, whether to go out or stay in, and he himself felt that the

workers of Winnipeg should write and tell the boys just what they thought of the situation."[19]

Another interesting passage was an onslaught upon Englishmen:-

"He laid great stress on labour conditions in England years ago in his father's time and declared it was always the Englishman who did the scabbing, and the Englishman who was the traitor to the labour movement of the world, and he was not ashamed to say so, although it was to be remembered that he was a good Welshman himself.

"The average Englishman he declared made fun of Russians or Italians, calling them the bohunks, but it had been shown that these same bohunks would not have thinks struck over them like the Englishmen, as could be seen by both Russia and Italy, both countries being involved in a general strike condition against the Capitalist system."

For the rest his oration was of the usual socialistic nature. It also included a tribute to the conditions in the jail farm, where the latter part of his confinement had been spent.

22. Socialists and the Third International

The N. C. O. in charge of C. I. B. work in Winnipeg makes the following report under date of 2nd October:-

"I am in receipt of information that the Socialist Party of Canada has been asked by the Third International to join up with them. If they do so, it will mean that they will be binding themselves to immediate militant action in a revolutionary movement, so I am informed.

"The matter was discussed at a recent meeting of the Socialist Party, and it is said that it is very unlikely that the Canadian Party will join with the Third International. The majority of members take the stand that joining the Russian organization would mean binding themselves to immediate militant action in a revolutionary movement, and that such would be inadvisable now, and as long as the working class of Canada is indifferent to class consciousness.

"This situation is under discussion in all Socialist locals throughout the Dominion. No other party, I believe, is eligible to join the Third International, for the Executive demand that organizations joining with it, be of the most revolutionary class".

23. Another Ukrainian Dispute

Another Ukrainian church squabble is reported, this time from Sifton, Man. It is of the usual type; the local priest found his preserves poached upon by an interloper of the Swystun faction and there was a quarrel. The newcomer, Revd. Nykola Kopachuk, was very impudent [20] when a warrant was served on him and there was a fight and some litigation. He seems to have served during the war as a chaplain in the Austrian army, to have been in Canada only 3 months, and to have entered in an irregular manner. Particulars as to his entry are being looked up.

24. Miscellaneous Notes

"W. Gordon", the writer of certain Bolshevistic letters to the press, has been identified. He is a Russian name Fred Gordienko, who calls himself Gordon. He lives in Winnipeg, is a member of the Ukrainian Labour Temple Association, and his domestic circumstances are irregular.

The strike of lake shipping men was settled at Fort William on 24th September. The companies granted about 10 per cent increase and the men agreed. On 23rd September the companies successfully brought in strike breakers, who evaded the pickets. Three boats thereupon left port, and this killed the strike.

V. ONTARIO

25. Negotiations between Factions at the O. B. U. Convention

It appears from information obtained in Eastern Canada that at the O. B. U. convention at Port Arthur conference were held between the representatives of the O. B. U. of the I. W. W., and of the Communist Labour Party. Upon the outcome of these negotiations the immediate future of these factions in the Toronto-Hamilton-Niagara region seems to depend. The O. B. U. and the I. W. W. may fight each other, or may form a closer alliance. One project entertained is to organize locals under the name of the Communist Labour or Communist Party, with the I. W. W. in control in the background. Interminable and obscure negotiations seem to be on foot in the matter.

26. The Plebs League

To the list of small revolutionary societies in Toronto had [21] been added "The Plebs League", which has as its address 28 Wellington Street, the abiding place of the "Ontario Labour College". The first meeting at which it was broached was held on 12th September, and organization was completed on 27th September. The officers are:- Secretary, Swift; -Marks or Marx, Committee, Mrs. Florence Constance Bell and Morris Spector. A new chairman is selected for every meeting. The members number 25 to 30. Persons also associated with it are Max Armstrong and one Berg.

Apparently the cause of the formation of this body is dissatisfaction with George Wilshow and his followers of the Ontario Labour College, on the ground that they have not accounted for the collections taken up at their openair meetings. The new league is pledged to voluntary work.

Some opposition was offered to the move on the ground that it would injure the O. B. U.

The reading matter circulated (largely in foreign languages) is of an incendiary nature.

The Workers' Recreation Club, which is one of these small bands, and which is considering amalgamation with the Plebs League, on 31st August had a budget of $197; the heaviest disbursements was $100 for rent.

Another meeting of the Plebs League was held on 3rd October, the attendance being about 50. It was decided to hold street corner meetings, care being taken to avoid interfering with the O. B. U. A speech by Morris Spector, who is a leading spirit in the body, is thus reported in part:-

> "The P. L. is teaching the working class communism directly, and not trying to get more wages, only more action and the above speaker said that the purpose of the Plebs league is the direct duty to spread revolutionary propaganda under the direction of the 'Third Internationale' and he said that he expects to be in direct communication with Moscow and anybody of the members who knows what communism is must spread the knowledge among the Trade Unions, and other radical organizations so that they would be ready to act when the time comes".[22]

Questioned as to the outlook for the winter he said:-

> "Will pray that something happens like 1914, when people depend on the 'bread line', then we could do some good work amongst them".

Two delegates from the Jewish Socialist League asked unsuccessfully for English-speaking lecturers; the Plebs League has no speakers for its own meetings.

27. Activities of Foreigners

Reports continue to be received on the Russian Workers' School, 111 Dundas Street, Toronto. It now has been in existence about a month, with V. Dadokin in charge. It is thoroughly Bolshevistic. A meeting held there on 25th September was attended by 130 people. A Russian whose name so far has not been obtained spoke somewhat as follows:-

> "Comrades we are living in Canada as prisoners, no freedom of speech or print is allowed in this Country. We are assembling in the cellars like rats, so that the spies if possible, could be avoided. When will the time arrive when we shall feel freedom as they do in Russia".

Almazoff, formerly of Winnipeg, consorts with these people, but does not seem to be doing much overt agitating. He does some teaching at the school.

Dodokin, discourages Russians who intend to return to Russia from learning English, holding that they should study their own language, and arithmetic, history, geography, etc.

The Jewish Socialist League of Toronto on Sunday 26th September held an openair meeting, at the corner of Dundas and Elizabeth street, an incendiary speech being delivered by one Brown, in Yiddish. He urged the formation of Soviets on the line followed in Russia and Italy.

A leading man in this league is one Shapiro, a reporter on the Yiddish daily paper published in Toronto.

A meeting place for Russians has been discovered in Hamilton. These gatherings are camouflaged as "educational classes". They meet in a room on the premises of a Jewish firm.[23]

28. Miscellaneous Notes

We have information to the effect that the A. F. of L. is organizing in Toronto a serious attempt to combat the extremist element in the Trades and Labour Council of that city. The first overt move probably will be made in the Bricklayers' Union, that being the leading union in the city.

Splits have occurred in Toronto in the Electrical and Butcher Workers' organization, with a possibility of litigation. Rumour charges Braithwaite, the business agent of the Butcher workers, and an advocate of the O. B. U., with considerable deflacations, and an action in the courts might reveal some of the O. B. U. ramifications.

The Toronto local of the Socialist party of Canada on 28th September had only four members at its weekly meeting, and decided to discontinue its meetings for the winter. Its attendance has been dwindling for some time.

John Currie and Aaron Webber, the men who tried to circulate I. W. W. reading matter in Windsor, appeared in Police Court on 27th September. Doubt being entertained as to whether a conviction would be under Section 97A or B of the Criminal Code, the Crown Attorney dropped the charge on condition that the accused promised not to circulate I. W. W. reading matter in the Province. This undertaking was readily given and the men were discharged.

J. Donovan, an I. W. W. agitator, has been in Niagara Falls for some time, having entered at Windsor.

Jim Branton, alias Jim Brady, a bricklayer from Butte, Montana, left Toronto on 23rd September to go to England. He is an O. B. U. and I. W. W. agitator.

J. R. Knight was in Toronto from 26th to 29th September, and left for the north.

Peter Leckie of Ottawa had begun to stir about as an O. B. U. speaker. On 25th September he spoke at an open-air meeting in Toronto. He acted as chairman for Ald. Heaps and Dunn when they spoke in Ottawa, [24] and is fond of addressing long letters to the Ottawa Citizen. He is not a man of much ability, and seems to have little standing among the trade unionists of Ottawa.

VI. QUEBEC

29. Conditions in Montreal

The Officer Commanding Quebec in his confidential monthly report says:-

"Conditions in Montreal and district may be considered as good, especially as regards common labourers, the demand for exceeding the supply. The same, however, cannot be said of some of the trades, especially the shoe operators. At the present time there are 8 of the largest factories at Montreal entirely closed down, and the remainder are only working from 25 to 35 per cent capacity. This is said to be due to the markets being overstocked and the reluctance of the public to pay the high prices for footwear. This will likely be remedied by a drop in prices to conform with other reductions in the H. C. of L.

"Clothing factories are also very quiet and the same conditions to a lesser extent apply in these trades".

Concerning the O. B. U. he says:-

"This organization is not making any headway in Montreal, notwithstanding what the supposed leaders may say to the contrary. There is no sale of their literature, and what is being distributed has to be given away free. There is more or less petty jealousy rife amongst the leaders, and as far as gaining membership, very few appear to be enrolled.

"Joe Knight when here attempted to get the Amalgamated Society of Engineers to join the O. B. U. in a body, and while he was successful in getting a few members to join, the majority of the members would have nothing to do with him or the O. B. U.

"Other radical associations, such as the French Socialist Communist Party, and the proposed Independent Socialist Communist Party of Quebec, do not appear to be gaining much headway. The former are holding meetings every Sunday at noon at the Labour Temple and the speakers are the same ones on every occasion......................
With regard to the latest movement, it appears to have died a natural death, as the sponsor of the movement, F. W. Gerrish, is looked upon by the radicals as being an aspirant for political appointment, and has not the interest of the workers at heart.

30. Russian Bolshevists in Montreal

We have an interesting report of a meeting of the Society for Technical Aid to Soviet Russia, which was held on Sunday 26th September. The proceedings were in Russian. The secretary and leader, W. Revenko,[25] delivered what appears to have been an able and well-informed addressed, the point of which was the distinction between the "Socialist-Communism" and Anarchist-Communism". He apparently regarded the latter of these theories as the ultimate goal, but the former (which prevails in Soviet Russia) as a necessary stage. Some objections were made to this by some anarchists present, and Hvat, or Hvatoff (who has been noticed before) made an effective speech on the same line, Anarchism, he said, is the next step after Socialist communism but they were not ready for it; Socialist and Anarchists still are fighting for the same object, the dictatorship of the proletariat.

The significant thing about this is that Revenko and Hvat were careful to expound and extol the exact doctrine which Moscow just now is putting forth. As that doctrine has changed rapidly, and as there is a welter of theories from which to choose, their course argues close and recent direction from the Russian Government.

31. Incitements to Violence

Apart from this, the utterances of these men were incitements to revolution of the most violent sort. The labourers Revenko said, should seize the machinery of production industries, plants, factories, railways and banks. Especially should they seize the banks. Hvat applauded the action of the Italian workmen, but considered that they had "made a mistake by not seizing the direct power of authority and support of the peasants". He also expected revolution to come soon in England.

One incident is illuminating. One of the dissident anarchists criticized the iron system and discipline of Lenin and Trotsky, whereupon Revenko spoke in rebuttal. "He said", according to our report, "That he might be anarchist himself, but under present condition, labour must obey orders of leaders and learn and carry strong military discipline to crush imperialistic capitalist Governments and, [26] he said, we must use organized power against power, to get what we want, he said that opposition of the anarchists was an act of treachery, against labour's movement".

32. Revolutionary Discipline at a Public Meeting

The public meeting held in Montreal on 1st October, ostensibly to collect money for medical aid to Soviet Russia, was attended by 175 persons, of whom only, 10 were French or English; the rest were Russians or Jews. The collection was $367. The tone was intensely revolutionary. Buhay, Binette, Alex Schubert, Wm. Revenko and Maurice Frager were the speakers.

An amusing feature of the gathering was that Michael Buhay announced that "soldiers of the Revolutionary Army are well disciplined", and on the strength of this forbade any of the audience to leave until the end, or even to speak to their neighbours.

33. Miscellaneous Notes

The proposed Labour College at Montreal is hanging fire. Little money has been collected, and the executive committee has not met for four weeks. Anna Buller the moving spirit, is anxious to get to work, presumably to provide herself with a position, but few seem to share her anxiety.

The "Reds" in Montreal are busy asserting that the Wall Street Explosion was engineered by the United States Government to discredit the cause of revolution.

The French Socialist Communist Party held a meeting in Montreal on 3rd October, the attendance being small, no new faces being seen, and the usual stuff being talked.

VII. THE MARITIME PROVINCES

34. Situation in the Coalfields

Apprehension exists lest a cessation of work occurs in the Cape Breton Coalfields over the Royal Commission's report. Apparently the men are disposed to strike rather than accept three clauses in the [27] report, relating to the sliding scale, the right to arbitrate, and long term contracts. At Inverness the managers seem inclined to agree with the men. It remains to be seen whether the Dominion Coal Company will try to force the men to adopt the report; if they do, a lock-out will follow. The Coal Company for their part are anxious to avoid a fight, as they have important orders to fill, but if they do fight will press it to a finish.

The Officer Commanding Maritime Provinces is of opinion a show-down must come sometime.

Small squabbles leading to short strikes continually are being reported from Cape Breton.

ROYAL CANADIAN MOUNTED POLICE HEADQUARTERS

Ottawa, 14th October, 1920.

SECRET

NO. 45

NOTES OF THE WORK OF THE C. I. B. DIVISION
FOR THE WEEK ENDING 14th OCTOBER.

Table of Contents

Coleman and Blairmore unlikely to strike.
Bergs remark about financing the miners.
Attempted Strike at Cardiff.

" 15. The Searchlight
" 16. The O. B. U. in Northern Alberta.
" 17. The Edmonton Labour Church.
" 18. Miscellaneous Notes.
Edmonton Street Railwaymen and the O. B. U.
Farmilo's Attack on the O. B. U.
R. E. Bray's tour.[2]
" 19. Saskatchewan: Sambrook's attitude towards Reforms.
" 20. "Bible Students" preparing the way for Revolution.
" 21. Manitoba: The Central Labour Council O. B. U.
Anderson's precautions against misquotation.
Flowers, the California Seditionist.
The Drumheller Strike.
R. E. Bray's Credentials.
" 22. Western Labour News on the O. B. U.
" 23. Winnipeg Comment on the Coal Strike.
Lumber, Agricultural and Construction Camp Unit O. B. U.
" 24. Dominion Labour Party and the O. B. U.
" 25. The Winnipeg Labour Church.
" 26. The Foreign Communities.
Ukrainian Red Cross.
Collections for medical aid to Soviet Russia.
Ukrainian Labour Party.
Rumoured in rush of revolutionary Finns.
" 27. Conditions in Western Ontario.
" 28. Extremists in Toronto.
" 29. Miscellaneous Notes.
Unemployment in the Niagara District.
- Kennedy.
George Evans
Ludowski.
" 30. Quebec: Seditious speeches at Montreal.
Preiger on the execution of Lloyd George, Wilson and Millerand.
" 31. Miscellaneous Notes.
The French Communists and the Worker
Charges against Binette.
The Labour College.[3]

1. Characteristics of the Period

Interest this week is divided between the coal strike in Alberta and the revelations of the proceedings at the Port Arthur Convention.

The Alberta strike continues in a dragging way, parts of the Crow's Nest Pass being the only places to strike in sympathy with the Drumheller O. B. U. The principal thing about the developments is the evidence which has been obtained as to the dishonest methods of Arthur Evans, the successor of Ed. Browne as District Secretary. To locals in Drumheller he wrote that the North and South had pledged themselves to strike in sympathy; to the South he wrote that the North and Drumheller were pledged; to the North he wrote in a similar vein about the South and Drumheller. The whole affair has an air of light-headedness.

Information which has come in during the week shows that the quarrel between the Winch and Midgley factions at Port Arthur was so deep and so bitter that a split in the O. B. U. seems likely. It has blazed up in numerous places; at Vancouver the B. C. Federationist is publishing Winch's side of the case, in Edmonton Carl Berg had a stand-up fight with Midgley and Naylor at a public meeting and in Winnipeg and Montreal the echoes are resounding. The immediate prospect now is for an attempt by the L. W. I. U. to take over the rest of the O. B. U.; Winch already has begun to subsidize the Searchlight and to pose as the real friend of the Alberta miners. For this project Winch already has an organization, and perhaps somewhat larger monetary resources. The whole affair is so important, and information comes from such widely separated places, that the news from the several provinces is assembled in the following paragraphs.[4]

I. THE PORT ARTHUR CONVENTION

2. Unseating of Winch and his partisans

The Convention at Port Arthur was marked by an open quarrel between the L. W. I. U. and the rest of the O. B. U. Victory rested with Midgley, who threw Winch out of the Convention, at the price of the withdrawal of the L. W. I. U. delegation. An *ex parte* account of the affair is published by the O. B. U. Bulletin of 2nd October in the form of a long report from the Credentials Committee.

The means adopted by Midgley were clever and tortuous and he seems to have outwitted Winch. He devised a means of seating delegates, on the basis of payments of per capita tax, which would compromise the L. W. I. U., whose finances at present are low largely as a result of earlier conventions. He enunciated this in a circular which was so worded that Winch does not seem to have noticed the full effect of the rules; at all events he did not protest. Then the Credentials Committee found the L. W. I. U. some $2,100 in arrears, seated those delegates who represented the Coast District (which is more or less critical of Winch) and threw out Winch, Cowan and Neale on the ground that they did not represent specific districts. As usual, the issues were much complicated by details. Eight of these seated seven L. W. I. U. men and Carl Berg left the convention, which retained only one man W. A. Alexander of the largest unit. The convention thus reduced is stated to have comprised 31 members, though only 19 can be traced.

The foregoing is an outline of occurrences. Evidence accumulates as to the depth of the split. J. R. Knight was on the side of Midgley, as the L. W. I. U. delegation, if they had been seated, would have attacked his management of affairs in Eastern Canada, as well as Midgley's handling of the head office. Midgley controlled the [5] credentials committee, which resorted to courses which the loggers' union greatly resent; for example, the committee simultaneously disqualified the L. W. I. U. for being in arrears with per capita, and seated a Thunder Bay delegation which represented a district at once in arrears with its per capita and heavily in debt to the L. W. I. U. but which was antagonistic to Winch and L. W. I. U.

Contradictory reports of the Convention have appeared in the O. B. U. Bulletin, which favours Midgley, and the Worker of Montreal, and B. C. Federationist which are controlled by the L. W. I. U. The account in the Worker is very bitter, and even so, by the statements of Walter Cowan, suppresses much of what took place.

The executive committee of the O. B. U., elected at the Port Arthur convention, is:- W. A. Pritchard; R. B. Russell; F. Woodward (Winnipeg); W. A. Alexander (Vancouver); P. M. Christophers (Crow's Nest Pass). Alternate for Pritchard and Russell are Joe Naylor (Cumberland) and J. R. Knight (Toronto). The executive may be increased (if a proposed amendment carries on referendum) by giving an additional member to each district council which has a membership of 2,000. It will be noticed that Winch disappears.

3. Resolutions passed by the Convention

On 4th and 5th October O. B. U. meetings were held in Winnipeg at which a good deal of news got out. the important occasion was that of 5th October, the fortnightly meeting of the Central Labour Council, O. B. U., F. Woodward being the principal speaker.

First, some bits of miscellaneous information were given among these being:-[6]

The organization apparently has been given the power "to dismiss any member of the O. B. U. who belongs to another hostile organization". (This conceivably could be used as a purge against the L. W. I. U.)

It had been decided to move the general head office from Vancouver to either Calgary or Winnipeg, preferably the latter.

"Owing to financial weakness", Tom Cassidy is to be withdrawn as official general organizer at Chicago.

No more general travelling organizers would be employed.

No official could hold an "officially paid position" in the O. B. U.

for a longer term than one year.

The struggle to obtain the release of the convicted strike leaders should be continued.

The system of per capita tax payments is to be reformed in some way, a way which the general executive is to devise.

A general head office is to be established in the United States, probably in Chicago. This should be followed up by a convention of U. S. members.

Funds are very low, the organization having only $162 to its credit after defraying the expenses of the convention.

Concerning these items it may be noted that the resolve at once to open offices in Chicago and to drop the organizer there seem inconsistent. The resolutions as to general travelling organizers and limited tenure of office require elucidation, as all the paid officials and organizers seem to be at work as usual.

4. Echoes of the Quarrel

Next comes echoes and disclosures of the quarrels of the convention.

P. G. Anderson, whose affiliations probably are with the L. W. I. U. charged that the convention was composed almost if not quite wholly of paid officials. Reluctance was shown to answer this charge.

Woodward's references to the L. W. I. U. are thus reported:-

"The Lumber Workers' Industrial Union of the O. B. U. brought up a considerable amount of discussion at the Convention, it was stated, and the opinion had been that these members would have to either change their attitude or keep apart by themselves as they were [7] running far too differently from the other units of the organization.

"This, however, it was stated was not put to any motion, only the delegates were requested to notify the officials of that unit what attitude they should adopt."

Less information of a general nature, but more about the quarrel, came out at the earlier meeting, which was one held by the Building Trades Unit, O. B. U., also at Winnipeg. Here the speaking was done by Cottrell and Hammond, two of the five Winnipeg delegates. Their statements may be quoted at some length. The first to speak was Cottrell. He mentioned the General Secretary's report. This, he said, disclosed

"that a little over one half the members of the O. B. U. were keeping their dues paid up.

"The miners have dropped back considerably in their per capita tax, he stated, and likewise the Metal Trades Industry Unit, the only unit keeping anywhere within its old standing being the Railway Shop Units, and even they had fallen back considerably in their per capita payments.

"He said it might be stated that four individuals had tried to stick one over the O. B. U. members of the convention, their names being Cowan, Neale, Winch and Hanmor, but on finding they had no credentials, and refused to state who they represented, the four were refused admittance to the convention seats. These delegates were either Police officials or International members, Mr. Cottrell stated, and they thought it better to keep them away as mistaken reports would have been issued.

"He stated that considerable trouble had ensued with the Lumber Workers' Unit; the outcome of which he could not definitely state, as the general Secretary's report had not been received, but it was his opinion that this Unit would be separated from their affiliation with the Central Council if they did not act differently in the future.

"The expenses of all unite, he declared, disclosed the fact that they were barely existing, and it was a hard proposition to see a clear way to build up the organization unless the workers themselves put more interest in their work for their respective units.

"The Winnipeg Units he claimed, had been the best paid up units in the organization, and those of Vancouver the poorest.

"Further statements regarding financial affairs, he stated, would be issued in the General Secretary's report, which was expected any day".[8]

5. The Financial Situation

Hammond's report dealt largely with finance.

"The financial statement he stated, of the entire organization showed only a little over $160 to their credit, and this matter although it could be worse was very serious, he said, as last year things were in a far better condition at the Calgary Convention.

"The expenses of the two general organizers were something damnable, he said.

"J. R. Knight had put in expenses totaling to three thousand, three hundred and ninety some odd dollars from December 1st 1919, up to August 24th 1920; nearly one thousand of this amount was for transportation charges, another thousand for expenses and nearly all the balance for salary.

"P. M. Christophers were somewhat less, he stated, being two thousand one hundred and thirty odd dollars in all, from February 1st to August 14th, 1920 of which amount one thousand, one hundred, was salary.

"The correct figures could not be stated at present, he said, although he had them in a book somewhere.

"These figures were thought to be pretty extravagant, but could not be helped owing to the amount of travelling and good work these two men were doing for the organization, he stated".

6. A Row at Edmonton

A mass meeting of the O. B. U. held in Edmonton on 1st October to hear about the Port Arthur Convention ended in an uproar after a bitter quarrel. Naylor and Midgley addressed the meeting on orthodox lines. When they had finished a logger asked why the L. W. I. U. delegates had been excluded. Midgley's explanation was resented by Carl Berg, and a fierce and prolonged debate ensued. Midgley said that the loggers "had never been true members of the One Big Union" and inveighed against the various measures taken by the L. W. I. U. to preserve their identity as against the general mass of the O. B. U. A woman in the audience denounced Berg as "a coward, a highly paid nuisance, and a traitor to the cause of labour in Edmonton". Berg retorted in kind.[9]

While the meeting swayed from side to side as points were scored, the general feeling seemed to be that Berg has lost his influence and soon will be out of the O. B. U.

7. Winch's Probable Course

A delegate who has talked a good deal about the affair is W. Cowan, who now is the O. B. U., or rather L. W. I. U., organizer in Montreal. As is explained later, he has succeeded Binette.

In the first of these conversations Cowan stated that the L. W. I. U. will recommend to their members that they refuse to recognize or be bound by any decision of the convention. Cowan's remarks merit rather full quotation:-

> "During the long conversation Cowan stated that the Lumber Workers have no intention of breaking away from the O. B. U., stating that the stand taken by the Lumber Workers' delegation at the convention will be decided, whether they were right or wrong, when the referendum is taken amongst the Lumber Workers, and if the majority of the Lumber Workers endorse the stand taken by their delegates at the Convention, it will necessitate calling another general convention, and compel the convention to give the Lumber Workers' delegates the power to represent an "Industrial Unit" and also the power to divide their votes equally amongst the delegates. On the other hand, if the rank and file of the Lumber Workers' Unit, decided that the stand taken by their delegates at the O. B. U. convention was wrong, then they might, or they might not throw in their lot and abide by the decision of the majority of the convention.
>
> "Cowan further stated that no matter what will happen, the harmony amongst the leaders of the O. B. U. is now broken; the arguments which arose at the O. B. U. convention plainly showed that there was more than a mere fight of opinions in progress; it was a fight to decide whether the real workers were to be in control of the O. B. U. or whether the Anarchists were to control it.
>
> "He further stated that such men as Joe Knight, who so dearly loves to be called a labour leader, do not work in the best interest of the

workers; Knight's ideals and views are purely anarchist, and owing to the fact that he never was a worker and does not understand the psychology of the rank and file, and fails to understand that the real work is on the jobs and in the shops and that the O. B. U. must first organize along 'Industrial lines' before the workers [10] could be sufficiently educated to become class conscious and form a 'Class' organization like Knight wishes to form, to stir up a revolution, and if the Industrial Form is not followed the O. B. U. will never be able to function.

"Cowan further stated that owing to the fact, that Knight is a good orator, he has been able to convince most of the ignorant O. B. U. workers to support his ideas, but he too must see the end of the O. B. U. but is too stubborn to give in.

"Knight also knows, Cowan continued, that once he commences to lose ground in the O. B. U. it won't take the rank and file very long to boost him out and that as soon as the Winnipeg strike leaders are released, Knight will be put where he belongs".

A few days later, on 9th October, Cowan remarked in conversation that the O. B. U. is on the surface of a volcano which at any moment might blow it out of existence. The interview proceeded thus:-

The L. W. I. U. are $2,100 behind with their per capita. The reason is that the union, though affiliated with the O. B. U. is an industrial union governed by its own executive, which is elected by a rank and file which constitutes the heart and soul of the O. B. U.; this executive, with its officials and organizers, works independently of the Central Executive of the O. B. U. The L. W. I. U. executive cannot understand why the majority of an organization should be dictated to by a minority; at Port Arthur the delegation of the L. W. I. U., representing 23,000 members, were forced to retire by delegates who represented a little more than 10,000 members.

The L. W. I. U. neither can nor will pay their per capita for the following reasons:-

1. They cannot see why they should give it to Midgley, who represents a minority of the membership, and does not know what the workers need, as he never was a worker.
2. Their funds are exhausted. They are supporting the following papers:- B. C. Federationist, Searchlight, O. B. U. Bulletin and Worker. Further, when the O. B. U. was formed the L. W. I. U., then affiliated with the A. F. of L., advanced $1,800 to Midgley; this money really belonged to the International. The advance never has been paid.[11]
3. The L. W. I. U. have spent all their money in propaganda, offices having been established in Vancouver, Fort William, Le Pas, Sudbury, Montreal, etc. Some of these have been expensive.
4. They will not submit to dictation from "people who do not

understand the needs of the workers". The L. W. I. U. might take control of the organization and ruin it to suit themselves.

Cowan further said that Knight and Midgley had exaggerated the numbers of the O. B. U. In Vancouver it had been asserted that Montreal had 5,000 members, in Montreal it had been stated that the Winnipeg Street Railway had gone O. B. U. in a body. Joe Knight had avereed that there was 4,000 in Toronto, etc.

He repeated that the L. W. I. U. would gain control of the O. B. U. and hoist Knight and Midgley out of it.

8. Repercussions in Montreal

One effect of the uproar touches Montreal. The L. W. I. U. at Vancouver now find themselves unable to maintain the Montreal office; they asked their organizer there, U. Binette, to carry on gratuitously for a while, and he promptly left. He is returning to his trade (he is a carpenter) but he is likely to join the Internationals in attacking the O. B. U., as, despite his resignation, he seems annoyed at a successor having been appointed. That successor is Walter Cowan, who is trying to keep things together. Binette apparently is a thoroughly mercenary man; he has been taking part in sundry meetings of foreigners of a most seditious nature, and in particular on 1st October spoke at a meeting at which Freiger (or Preiger) prophecied the execution of Mr. Lloyd George, President Miller and President Wilson.

A small item in the affair is the bad impression produced at the convention by Rebecca Buhay, who was a delegate. Apparently she was long-winded and incoherent, and she elicited some very uncerimonious reprimands.[12]

II. BRITISH COLUMBIA

9. Lefeaux under Suspicion

It now appears that W. W. Lefeaux is under suspicion by his revolutionary associates. According to information gathered in Vancouver, something in his actions in Winnipeg during the trials of the strike leaders caused him to be distrusted. Our report says:-

"Towards the end of last year he went to New York and saw several Soviet representatives, with a view of securing a position on their mission. He asked the S. P. of C. for credentials, but was refused same. A stenographer with above law firm, had told one of the S. P. leaders that she has seen correspondence passed between the firm and Lefeaux, requesting him to return to Vancouver, but he had declined and proceeded on to England. He is supposed to have gone from there to Petrograd. The S. P. of C. leaders here, who know the herein mentioned, suspect that Lefeaux went to Russia as a secret agent of the British Government, but under the guise as a communist".

It will be recalled that Lefeaux, who acted as "devil" for the defence counsel, drew from the Defence Fund an exorbitant remuneration for times as much as the person who (with far higher qualifications) performed the same service for the Crown Counsel.

10. Thomas Richardson

Thomas Richardson has accepted the Labour nomination in the Yale bye-election. His campaign apparently is to be made under the auspices of the Federated Labour Party. Locals of this body have been organized in Penticton and Vernon, and Mrs. Rose Henderson is campaigning for him.

An attempt to effect al alliance with the United Farmers has failed. The notice in the B. C. Federationist of the United Farmers' convention is so bitter as to suggest great disappointment. The convention apparently was influenced by a rancher named Makovski who sometime ago opposed Pritchard in a debate on "Bolshevism".

11. Individual Agitators

Frank Cassidy of Vancouver has been sent out on an organizing [13] and speaking tour by the Socialist Party. He has been in Southern British Columbia, and he proposes to go by the Crow's Nest Pass to Calgary.

It now appears that Michael Casey was acquitted of the charge of selling liquor which was laid against him, (which was mentioned last week) and that he continues to reside in Penticton.

One J. Clarke is conducting a class in Esperanto in connection with the Chinese Labour Association of Vancouver. The class comprises 10 Chinese and 2 whites. It is avowedly revolutionary, the text book being the Communist Manifesto.

Esperanto is being actively pushed by the revolutionary elements.

J. Smith was the principal speaker at the Socialist meeting in Vancouver on 3rd October. He criticised the demands of the G. A. U. V., saying that if all were obtained conditions would be no better. Instead of asking the Government for changes, they should form a Government of their own.

W. R. Trotter has resigned his position as Secretary of the Federated Labour Party, and is now a paid speaker for the Prohibitionists. He is touring the Province of British Columbia.

Mrs. Rose Henderson spoke on Sunday 3rd October at the "People's Open Forum" in the Federated Labour Party, Vancouver. Her address was a violent attack upon the Canadian Government, and a declaration that all Governments were "on their last legs".

The Vancouver Labour Church met on Sunday 3rd October, J. Clarke being chairman and J. S. Woodsworth the principal speaker. Mr. Woodsworth's text was the one from Isaiah which was mentioned in his indictment in Winnipeg. He argued that what he had said in Winnipeg had not been seditious.[14]

12. Miscellaneous Notes

Some dissension has been caused among the longshoremen by the action of the men in Vancouver in loading vessels with munitions for Russia. Resentment was expressed at a meeting of the Vancouver longshoremen at the strictures of the B. C. Federationist, but a resolution to discontinue their subscription to the paper failed.

The strike of the Vancouver Gas Workers has failed completely. The B. C. Federationist blames them for the failure, on the ground that they acted by themselves, as a craft.

The mines at Merritt are working only two or three days a week. The town naturally is feeling the effect of the short time.

The Victoria General Workers' Unit, O. B. U. on 1st October, resolved to have nothing further to do with the Soldier-Labour Council. The meeting was small, only 14 persons attending.

II. ALBERTA

13. The Coal Strike in Drumheller

A report from Calgary dated 1st October describes the situation in the Drumheller field thus:-

Four small mines completely out.

Four large mines with all their men working.

Five mines with from half to three quarters of their men working.

Two mines with one third of their men working.

Altogether from 55 per cent to 60 per cent of the men were at work.

> "Evans has not received the support and co-operation of Christophers and Baird, and, for that matter, few, if any, of the other so-called O. B. U. leaders in the South and North districts".

Beard, the district chairman, arrived on 1st October in Calgary from the south, and on learning how things stood in Drumheller expressed great dissatisfaction. He decided to go to Drumheller, though Evans tried to dissuade him.

Fresh evidence has come to hand of the dishonest nature of [15] Arthur Evans' strike-propaganda in the Drumheller area. On two occasions he assured meetings of miners that "all" or "practically all" of the locals in the District had promised action. In the case of the Monarch mine these false statements had an effect in deciding the men, who had been doubtful as to what course to pursue.

14. The Situation Elsewhere

On Sunday 3rd October P. M. Christophers addressed a meeting of Miners at Lethbridge on the Drumheller situation. He made false assertions as to the number of men out in Drumheller, at one time saying that not 60 men were at work, and at another saying that the field was out solidly. He urged the Lethbridge men to strike for a week, return to work for a few days, then strike again, and so on; in this way they would avoid monetary strain and would not need financial help from the unions. The Lethbridge men seemed unimpressed.

This advice illustrates forcibly the weakness of the O. B. U. in trying to accomplish strikes without a treasury.

Reports dated 7th and 8th October indicate that Christophers was not very successful in rallying Lethbridge and Taber to the support of the Drumheller and Fernie strike. Lethbridge was particularly apathetic.

A report dated 1st October describes certain manoeuvering between the Fernie Local and the U. M. W. of A. office at Calgary. The local is nominally U. M. W. of A. and in reality under O. B. U. control. Theoretically a proportion of the obnoxious "check-off" money is turned over to the local union, and the Fernie local was most anxious to obtain possession of this, presumably to finance their projected strike against the U. M. W. of A. The Calgary office, however, was holding this back on sundry pretexts, and further was objecting to certain men, including William Sherman, being elected by the local to office.[16]

A report from Fernie dated 6th October attributes the strike there wholly to William Sherman. Out of 763 men only 100 reported for work on the 6th. The men are described as not very enthusiastic.

The total number out on 6th October at Fernie and Michel was 970.

The total payroll at Michel is 520, this including office staff, coke oven employes, and lumbermen. The men who struck numbered 307, these including all the actual miners.

Walter Clarke of Coalhurst, a strong O. B. U. man, spoke at North Lethbridge on 8th October. Posing as a returned man he made a number of statements as to the treatment given the soldiers in the Army such as that they had to exist for six weeks on a biscuit a day. He was howled down by returned men in the audience, who shouted "liar", and even coarser expressions. He finally had to stop.

The men at Coalhurst went on strike on 7th October, the pretext being their objection to the "check-off". They returned to work the same day, after a heated argument at a meeting. This issued in a secret ballot which resulted in a vote of 160 for working, and 92 for striking.

A report dated 2nd October, expresses the opinion that the miners in Coleman and Blairmore would not strike.

In his quarrel with Midgley and Naylor at Edmonton Carl Berg said that if the O. B. U. could not finance the coalminers in their strike the loggers would.

An abortive attempt at a strike was made at the Alberta Coal Mining Company's mine at Cardiff, Alberta. Five foreigners presented a demand for higher wages. This was resisted, and the attempt collapsed. The mine is an open-shop one. The five men who formed the deputation on the 24 days before their action had earned from $275 to $305.[17]

15. The Searchlight

Lawson is behind $800 with the company which prints the Searchlight. He got out an issue on 1st October by Winch giving him $140 or $150.

This action by Winch, when he is pinched for money, suggests that he is disposed to fight with Midgley for the leadership of the O. B. U. in the coalfields. With this may be compared Berg's promise to the miners.

16. The O. B. U. in Northern Alberta

In Northern Alberta on 30th September the strength of the O. B. U. was estimated thus:-

Lumbermen and Agricultural Workers	300
Miners	275
General Workers	175
Transportation Workers	325
Building Trades Workers	150
Total	1235

In addition, unions sympathetic to the O. B. U. had 555 members; unions hostile to the O. B. U. had 3,311; and neutrals had 216. These figures show a slight increase in the O. B. U. during the last three months. The N. C. O. in charge of C. I. B. work remarks:-

> "The number of miners who are working in this district, which also includes Nordegg, is estimated at 2,000. Out of this number there are 275 bona fide O. B. U. members. Of the remaining 1,725 the majority are, on the surface, members of the U. M. W. of A. and antagonistic to the O. B. U. but as the O. B. U. are endeavouring to stage a strike in the near future, a considerable number of the individual members of the U. M. W. of A. will no doubt join the strikers if they can be persuaded and assured that there will be any hope of a successful strike, but it is impossible to begin to estimate the percentage who are actually in sympathy with the O. B. U. and therefore in the above table the 1,725 are classified as antagonistic to the O. B. U.".

17. The Edmonton Labour Church

The Edmonton Labour Church reopened on Sunday 3rd October, Mr. G. L. Ritchie taking charge. He read extracts from Scott Nearings book "Religious Socialism", and spoke on "The outlook for labour". His address was principally an attack on the pamphlet issued by the [18] Department of Labour. He also complained of the disciplinary action taken against him by the Methodist Church.

In the discussion Senator Robertson was savagely assailed, one man laying down the doctrine that it was unconstitutional to appoint a Senator to be a Minister of the Crown.

18. Miscellaneous Notes

The Street Railway Employes of Edmonton have joined the O. B. U. retaining certain features of sick benefits, life insurance etc. which they had before.

A. Farmilo, the International organizer at Edmonton, has made a sharp attack upon the O. B. U. in the Edmonton press. Analyzing the figures and facts which have become public, he describes it as in a bad way, and thoroughly corrupt.

R. E. Bray is making a tour of the prairies. He spoke at Taber on Friday 1st October and on Sunday 3rd October at North Lethbridge. His Taber meeting was poorly attended and he made a bad impression. A fairly full report of his North Lethbridge meeting discloses nothing beyond his usual vein of complaint and abuse.

IV. SASKATCHEWAN

19. Sambrooks attitude towards Reforms

Joe Sambrook, the Regina leader of the O. B. U., attended a meeting of the People's Forum held on Sunday 3rd October. The subject was Proportional Representation. Sambrook spoke as follows:-

"Why all this useless talk of Proportional Representation? It is only another little thing got up by the powers that be to fool the working class and to make them think that the boss is giving them something for nothing; but the working class will not gain anything by it as the worker will always find himself in the same fix so long as the present system exists".

20. "Bible Students" Preparing the way for Revolution

W. T. ("Bill") Crawford of the I. B. S. A. spoke on 3rd October at Prince Albert. For the most part he attacked the Churches, [19] but part of his address took the line of predicting revolution. Our report says:-

> "With reference to industrial matters, he skillfully tried to show that 4/5th of the labour and work in the world today was useless to the people as a whole; but that all this would change under the new era now at hand, when the workers would work for his own benefit, instead of slaving for others. This part of his speech was practically advocating the doctrine of Sovietism. He used scripture profusely to back up his arguments and closed his speech leaving the audience with the impression that a time of great trouble and upheaval was at hand, had in fact commenced, when all nations would be swept away, but not to lose heart on account of this, but rather rejoice, as out of the chaos, Christ's Kingdom would appear on earth, to bring peace and goodwill to mankind".

V. MANITOBA

21. The Central Labour Council O. B. U.

Some of the general business transacted at the meeting of the Winnipeg Central Labour Council O. B. U. on 5th October (which is reported in Part I.) merits notice.

During the discussion of the quarrel between the L. W. I. U. and the official organization of the O. B. U., it was noted that a young woman was taking shorthand notes. P. G. Anderson announced that it was at his instance, as his statements had been garbled and he wished to guard against his being done in connection with the discussion on hand.

It was decided to countenance a visit from Flowers, the California O. B. U., who is the object of legal prosecution in his own State. He is to lecture and take up a collection.

It was decided to stop the education classes, these not having been a success. Propaganda will be carried on this winter by public meetings.

Great dissatisfaction was expressed at the dearth of news from the Drumheller strike, and the O. B. U. Bulletin was required to put forth greater efforts to obtain information on the subject.

A curious incident was the discovery that R. E. Bray who was supposed to be Vice-President of the Central Labour Council, never had [20] had any official credentials, and had been in arrears with his membership card when he was arrested.

22. Western Labour News on the O. B. U.

The Western Labour News, which now is antagonistic to the O. B. U., says in its issue of 8th October:-

> "No accurate information has been issued from any authoritative source giving, from the proceedings of the convention at Port Arthur, any coherent idea of the actual position of the One Big Union. This convention was held behind closed doors. The result has been that a good deal of information has leaked out, of which if a tenth part is true, there was ample justification for holding the convention behind closed doors. Indeed, in addition to closing the doors, it might not have been inappropriate to have put the shutters up".

23. Winnipeg Comment on the Coal Strike

Comment upon the Alberta Coal strike among O. B. U. circles in Winnipeg, reported on 4th October, was of a curious character, suggesting ignorance of the actual situation. They seemed, for example, to expect the U. M. W. of A. to help the O. B. U. to strike. Two significant paragraphs from this report are:-

> "O. B. U. officials admit they know what a crisis a general strike of the mine workers will be apt to bring about in Canada, but declare that the miners must use all possible means for bettering their conditions, as they have always been beaten at any of their attempts in the past.
>
> "News reached the Roblin Hotel (the O. B. U. headquarters) that Red flags were being flown by workers in the Drumheller coal mines. This was considered a good joke by O. B. U. officials".

The Lumber, Agricultural and Construction Camp Unit, O. B. U. of Winnipeg was noticed a while ago. A report dated 2nd October was that it included some miners in its membership, and that it was keenly interested in the Alberta coal strike. It was helping by keeping miners away from the troubled region, and that it conceivably might embark on a sympathetic strike.

It was noted that this unit was enrolling a number of loggers, the Secretary, P. G. Anderson having reported considerable success.[21]

> "The one drawback to this Unit is, however, (the report adds) that they cannot keep track of their members, and unless the member be an O. B. U. at heart, only his initiation fees are received."

24. Dominion Labour Party and the O. B. U.

The latest development in the fight between the Winnipeg Trades and Labour Council and the local O. B. U. brings in the Dominion Labour party. The new move is to strengthen this party to enable it to outvote the O. B. U's. The O. B. U. Bulletin for its part is challenging the Council, and editorial in the issue of 2nd October being a signal for hostilities. Our report says:-

> "The D. L. P. is divided at present into three divisions right, centre and left. The right is composed of International Trades Unionists, the left of radical thought and O. B. U., and the centre of men who do not or cannot belong to either of the other groups. It is hoped through the foregoing Editorial to influence the centre against the left, and finally life them out of the Party. About 200 Internationals compose the right wing. This promises to be very interesting for the next two months".

25. The Winnipeg Labour Church

The Winnipeg Labour Church service on Sunday 3rd October, was attended by about 400 persons. There was present a choir of about 20 voices, a pianist and a violinist. The address was given by G. B. Currie, his subject being "What's wrong with the World". It was an advocacy of Marxian Socialism, with the usual attacks on Capitalism and the usual laudation of Soviet Russia. Under international Socialist rule the country could be run perfectly without capitalism. Among his utterances were:-

> "You carpenters, you bricklayers, you electricians, you plasterers all you workers who are connected with the building houses," he said, "you build the most beautiful mansions, and yet you live in some dirty little house, away back in the dirt of the city, and leave the large, grand house which you made with your own skill to the hands of some Capitalist hound, who is making his profits out of the workers".
>
> "You tailors and weavers of cloth", he said "you weave the finest clothes and tailor the finest suits worth over a hundred dollars, and more, and yet you go to some little dugout of a second hand Jew store and buy a poor shady suit for ten or so dollars and leave the good suits for the Capitalist class".[22] Under International Socialism, he declared, there would be "lots for all" and "All for lots".
>
> Incidentally he denied that Socialism was antagonistic to marriage.

26. The Foreign Communities

The Ukrainian Red Cross in Winnipeg has now in the Bank $10,972.08 and $2,000.00 has been sent lately to Lemberg to the executive of the Ukrainian Red Cross in Eastern Galicia. Funds are being refused still.

The amount collected in the Ukrainian Labour Temple on Sunday 3rd October for aid to Soviet Russia comes up to $528.00.

The total amount is over one thousand in Winnipeg alone.

The "Soviet Russia Relief Commission" during the four months April to July, inclusive, received $11,459. Of this $7,000 was expended for medical supplies, and the balance on hand on 1st August was $2,845.

A meeting of the Ukrainian Labour Party was held in Winnipeg on Sunday 3rd October to raise funds for the medical relief of Soviet Russia. It was addressed by one Cory, who spoke in English, and by Popowich and Deviatkin. The speeches were violently pro-Bolshevist and anti-British. Cory's speech also was violently anti-religious.

From Fort William, where we have a considerable Finnish Colony, about two thirds of which is socialistically inclined, comes a report that the revolutionary elements in Finland are actively promoting emigration of revolutionists from Finland to Canada. A number of these immigrants are said to be arriving in Fort William already. The movement in Finland centres in Tammerfors.

VI. ONTARIO

27. Conditions in Western Ontario

The Officer Commanding Western Ontario in his confidential monthly report for September makes the following remarks:-[23]

> "There is a noticeable reaction among labour men against the O. B. U. and other radical organizations, and labour leaders are realizing that the teachings of the extremists are doing the cause of labour more harm than good. The 'Red' sympathizers are slowly being eliminated from the ranks of labour officials and their places filled by men of moderate and conservative views.
>
> "It is possible that there may be some trouble in the district during the winter months on account of unemployment. There are a considerable number of unemployed in the City of Toronto at the present time, and the number will be increased as some firms shut down. On the other hand there is plenty of employment at the lake cities, and it is hoped that the demand for men in other parts of the Province will offset the unemployment situation in Toronto.
>
> "In Toronto the O. B. U. is very weak and very little activity among its members is apparent. Some activity is reported in the hamilton and Thessalon districts.
>
> "Closely allied the Jewish Socialist Revolutionary League, referred to above, are the two new groups known as Plebs League and the Russian Workers' School, which have recently come into being in

Toronto .... So far nothing of importance has transpired at their meetings".

28. Extremists in Toronto

Despite the failure of the O. B. U. to win membership in Toronto, we receive warnings that the condition of Labour politics there is threatening, resembling those in Winnipeg before the strike. The Toronto Trades and Labour Council is in the hands of extremists, and in general labour machinery is in undesirable hands. The leaders of the extreme element include John W. Bruce, James Simpson and Fred Bancroft the two last named being writers on the Toronto Star.

The International leaders have taken alarm and are preparing to deal vigorously with this situation.

29. Miscellaneous Notes

A survey of the Niagara district shows an appreciable amount of unemployment and consequent discontent. At Welland it was stated that 1,700 or 1,800 men were out of work, many being married men who found it hard to leave town. Much discontented talk was heard and either Joe Knight or his wife was expected to visit the place.[24]

Conditions in Thorold were similar.

A Vancouver Socialist named Kennedy has appeared in Toronto, has associated himself with the Plebs League, and has spoken at one of their open-air meetings.

We now hear of one George Eavens as active about St. Catharines etc. He is described as a strong radical and believer in direct action. He is associated with Mrs. Custance and the Ontario Labour College.

Ludowski recently has been sojourning in Welland, stirring up discontent among the foreigners there. The prospects there are for unemployment during the winter, and he proposes to avail himself of it.

VII. QUEBEC

30. Seditious Speeches in Montreal

On 1st October a meeting was held in Montreal to raise money for medical aid to Soviet Russia. The attendance was only 200-300, and the chairman, Michael Buhay, expressed disappointment. The societies represented included the society for Technical Aid to Bolshevist russia, the Jewish Socialist Bolshevist Party, and the One Big Union. The speakers were M. Buhay, U. Binette, until lately the local O. B. U. organizer (who spoke in French) W. Revenko (who spoke in Russian) Schubert (in Yiddish) and one Preiger or Freiger (in English). The collection was $328, its size being due to the impression produced by Freiger's speech.

Revenko in his speech expressed the hope that the British Capitalistic Government will be overthrown and a Soviet Government established in England.

Preiger or Freiger attacked the Governments of the Allies and evoked loud applause by the following passage:-

"Believe me comrades, I tell you that the time will come soon, is coming now, when Lloyd George, Wilson and Miller and will be under the death sentence of workers' tribunals, and they will be thrown to the scaffold for execution".[25]

31. Miscellaneous Notes

Following upon Binette's resignation, the French Communist Party have made propositions for the editing of the French portion of the Worker which amount to the acquisition of that periodical by the Communists. Cowan, who is in charge at Montreal, is disposed to accept, despite the hostility of St. Martin and Gottsel, the leaders of the French Communist Party, to the O. B. U. The decision will lie with Winch.

Charges of being "a labour fakir, a reactionary, a spy" etc. have been anonymously made against U. Binette. At a meeting of the Metal Trades Binette unsuccessfully demanded an investigation, and on A. St. Martin praising him Binette retorted by accusing St. Martin of being his accuser.

Anna Buller has made some progress with her scheme for a Labour College. A room has been rented, and work was to begin about 15th October. The meeting at which the decision was made was attended by eleven persons.

ROYAL CANADIAN MOUNTED POLICE HEADQUARTERS

Ottawa, 21st October, 1920.

SECRET

NO. 46

NOTES OF THE WORK OF THE C. I. B. DIVISION FOR THE WEEK ENDING 21ST OCTOBER

Table of Contents

Ben Legere at Lawrence, Mass.
Winnipeg Labour Church.
" 17. ONTARIO: J. R. Knight
" 18. The Labour College.
At Toronto
At Hamilton
" 19. The Jewish Socialist League
" 20. Almazoff's Activities
" 21. Foreigners in Hamilton.
" 22. QUEBEC: More News of the O. B. U. Convention.
The resolutions passed.
The quarrel with the L. W. I. U.
" 23. General Workers' Unit in Low Water.
" 24. "The Worker".
" 25. Miscellaneous Notes.
Hvat on the Third International
A. S. E. join the O. B. U.
Guson
Anna Buller
" 26. MARITIME PROVINCES: Coal Strike possible.

1. General Characteristics of the Period

The strike in the Alberta coalfields drags on. In the Drumheller area our latest reports describe a general drift back to the miners, though it is noted that news of sympathetic strikes elsewhere would give the spirits of the men a fillip. In Fernie and Michel the strike also persists, but it had not spread down the Pass. Press reports state that the strike in the Pass has come to an end.

The quarrel in the O. B. U. is not so much in evidence in this week's reports, though some additional particulars have come to light. It appears, however, that the decision to move the headquarters to Winnipeg was definite; whether the change is to be immediate, or is to depend upon a referendum, has not been made clear. Further, the "Class" system was definitely adopted.

Recent reports suggest very strongly that the O. B. U. is a declining force. Its quarrel with the Loggers' Union puts it into a position of antagonism with a body which so far has been considered the heart of the whole movement; the Lumber Workers have the largest membership of any constituent body, they have spent more money in missionary work than any others, and on the whole they have more influence with the revolutionary press then Midgley and his associates have. Simultaneously, in Winnipeg its fight with the Internationals is going badly; in the third quarter of the year its membership there declined from 12,500 to 9,200, and its meetings now wear an air of discouragement.[4]

I. BRITISH COLUMBIA

2. The Federated Labour Party

Contradictory reports have been rendered to us lately upon the Federated Labour Party. The more favourable one says in part:-

"This body was organized about 2 years ago, and is composed of those members of the International Trade Unions who desire participation in politics as a labour organization. While the Trades and Labour Council adopts an attitude of indifference towards parliamentary etc. campaigns, the F. L. P. seeks acquisition of influence through representation in the Legislative Assembly."

It is added that many O. B. U. and S. P. of C. members belong. The present secretary, one MacInnes, who succeeded W. R. Trotter a couple of months ago, gives the membership as 3,000, and says that in the coming Provincial election the party will contest about 20 seats, including 4 in Vancouver.

The other report says:-

"It appears that through disorganization and opposition the Federated Labour Party is not at the present active, nor in good standing in Victoria.

"No meetings have been held by this Party here since 10th April, 1920".

3. In the Loggers' Union

A report on the L. W. I. U., dated Vancouver 30th September, says:-

"There is a good deal of discussion in the Hall and out of it about the impending split in the affairs of the O. B. U. This refers to the split between Midgley and Winch. Operative found out that Logan, who was chairman of the Convention at Port Arthur, had referred to the Loggers with some contempt and slurred them and their occupation and openly showed his regard for them as being an ignorant and illiterate set of men. This had made quite a deep impression on a lot of members of the Loggers' Union here. Winch is being extensively inquired about now".

Winch, it appears from other sources, was making a somewhat leisurely journey homewards, visiting outlying centres of activity as he went.[5]

4. The Vancouver Labour Church

The Vancouver Labour Church met on Sunday 10th October, Mrs. Rose Henderson being the principal speaker. The title of the organization was changed to "People's Sunday Evenings". Mrs. Henderson's topic was "Criminals in the Making", and was based on her experiences as a member of the Juvenile Court in Montreal. "The deductions made by her were, that the existing order of society, and economic conditions were responsible for ill-bred children and criminals. The ruling class, she said, sins according to the Code, and does not get punished, but the poor people sin against the Code, and are mercilessly being punished".

5. Individual Agitators

J. Edward Bird, who is legal adviser to the O. B. U., and has acted on behalf of the I. W. W., presided at a meeting of the G. A. U. W. which was held in Vancouver on 3rd October.

J. S. Woodsworth addressed the Socialist meeting in Vancouver on 10th October. His address was on "the history of the human race", and was of an academic cast. The audience numbered only 18.

J. Stack, who was made chairman of the future policy committee at the Coast convention of the L. W. I.U., has left that body altogether to do I. W. W. agitation. He denounces all the O. B. U. men Winch, Midgley, etc.

Another report describes this man as too heavy a drinker to be an effective agitator.

J. A. Greider, a very active agitator, is holding meetings in Southern British Columbia, in and near Nelson.

J. Kavanaugh was the speaker at the Socialist meeting in Vancouver on 10th October. He said nothing important.

6. Miscellaneous Notes

The strike in the steel shipyards of Vancouver is among the [6] plumbers, sheet metal workers and steamfitters. It affects from 75 to 100 men.

The annual fair at Prince Rupert attracted a considerable number of Indians, and the local O. B. U. signed up about 100 of them. Special concessions were made to them in the matter of dues.

Inquiries at Prince Rupert, Prince George, Hazelton, Ocean Falls, Nelson, Midway, Grand Forks, Trail, fail to show any activity in these places on the part of the Chinese Labour Association.

The Pile Drivers and Wooden Bridgemen of Vancouver have abandoned the Internationals and joined the O. B. U. This affects about 150 men.

II. ALBERTA

7. The Strike in the Coalfields

A review of the Drumheller situation dated 12th October dealt with 16 mines. On 30th September before the strike began, these mines had 1,582 men at work, this number being not quite sufficient; on 6th October they had 562; on 12th 858. On the 6th six mines were completely shut down; on the 12th only ne, and it a mine which is in financial difficulties. The strike was at its height on the 4th, when fewer than 500 men were on duty; on 5th October the men began to drift back. On the date of the survey the general opinion was that the men would gradually return to work unless sympathetic strikes occurred in the South and North; and this was doubtful.

A report from Fernie dated 11th October states that a plan was on foot to procure a secret ballot on the question of returning to work; such a ballot, it was stated, would result in a decision to return. However, the company was understood to have decided to refuse employment [7] to one or two agitators, more especially to William Sherman, the local leader who engineered the strike.

On 11th October picketing began at Michel, some men who wished to work being turned back. The pickets all are office-holders of the U. M. W. of A., so completely has the local of that body been captured by the O. B. U.

Reports from Coalhurst on 12th, 13th and 14th October showed a steady increase in the number of men at work. On 11th October 225 men were at work, and by the 14th the number had increased to 285. The strikers were fewer than 100.

A report upon Blairmore and Hillcrest dated 9th October states that at the former place men were returning to work, and that at Hillcrest a vote resulted in 138 for a strike and 150 against it.

8. The Closed Shop Order

Last April the O. B. U. took action against Fuel Commissioner Armstrong's closed-shop order, on the ground that it was a violation of the Lemieux Act. This action was dismissed by the Police Magistrate and an appeal was taken. On 7th October the appeal was dismissed by the Appellate Court of Alberta. The ground for the dismissal was that Mr. Armstrong's approval and the Order in Council under which it was issued, had been violated by an Act of Parliament passed last session. However, any subsequent order of the sort by Mr. Armstrong will be open to legal proceedings.

9. The Edmonton Labour Church

The Edmonton Labour Church on 10th October was addressed by Rev. Geo. L. Ritchie, the subject being "Why a new Social Order". He referred to Mr. Mackenzie King's speech at Edmonton, saying that if he [8] (Ritchie) had said as much six months ago he would have been sent to jail. He said that the Militia and the R. C. M. P. were being trained in Edmonton and every other city in street fighting. Capitalism was supported by bayonets. "Laws were made for the protection of property, not life, there was no protection to life, i.e. to the life of the children against disease and hunger".

10. Edmonton Notes

The Edmonton local of the Socialist Party of Canada is practically dead, its place having been more or less taken by the Labour Church.

At Edmonton the Building Trades Unit O. B. U. has withdrawn from the Central Labour Council, O. B. U.

III. SASKATCHEWAN

11. The O. B. U. in Northern Saskatchewan

A survey of the O. B. U. situation in Northern Saskatchewan as of 30th

September shows 560 men who belong or are friendly to the O. B. U., and 2,300 who belong to unions hostile or indifferent to it.

The two centres of O. B. U. influence are the lumber industry and Saskatoon. In the former conditions are changing owing to the closing of some mills and camps and the shifting operations to other places. In the neighbourhood of the Pas about 1,500 men will be employed in the bush during the winter. Until some time in September the O. B. U. were very quiet, but lately a new secretary, John R. Leith, who has succeeded Tether, has been active, and the membership in this region has increased by about 40 per cent.

Elsewhere, outside of Saskatoon, the O. B. U. is practically dead. In Saskatoon it has about 160 members, or half of what it formerly had; these are of an inferior class of labour. The English-speaking members dislike the manner in which the dues are used up in ineffective attempts to increase the membership.[9]

Except at the Pas a reaction is in progress against the O. B. U. Even there it is doubted whether all of the nominal members of the L.W.I.U. would follow the organization if a strike were called. The leaders are planning to organize the men in the winter and hold up the drive in the spring.

It may be worth noting that the O. B. U. membership at the Pas all belong to the L.W.I.U.

IV. MANITOBA

12. O. B. U. losing ground in Winnipeg

A survey of the trade union field in Winnipeg as of 30th September confirms the view that the O. B. U. are losing ground. Their numbers have dropped from 12,505 on 30th June to 9,200; those of unions hostile to the O. B. U. have grown from 12, 521 on 30th June to 13,935. Unions sympathetic to the O. B. U. have dropped from 3,000 to 2,600; unions in dispute between the two elements have increased from 1,078 to 1,500. The Street Railway Union, 1,945 strong, is counted neutral; it has failed to go over to the O. B. U. as was expected.

13. Cross Currents in the O. B. U.

Indications multiply of heart-searching among the Winnipeg radicals. For instance, two conversations with Mr. Willcocks, secretary of the Labour Church have been reported to us. This man's son is business manager of the O. B. U. Bulletin. The elder Willcocks has become highly critical of William Ivens; he disputes Iven's title to be the founder of the Labour Church, claiming that distinction for himself, and he calls Ivens an adventurer and opportunist. One passage is:-

> "He (Ivens) is not the recognized Pastor of the Labour Church. He was appointed official speaker, but that was only in recognition of his work. He is not in good standing with the Executive of the Church or the male members of the Church. He is still much in

> favour with the women members. He will not have the standing in the church when released that he had before his trial. Willcocks was a hero-worshipper of his before his trial, but not now. He signs [10] his letters 'Your Loving Pastor' that is all rot, and all for effect".

Willcocks also describes Iven's illness, which caused his removal from the Jail Farm to the Jail as a trick.

After allowing for personal jealousy, and a possible business rivalry (for the Western Labour News and the O. B. U. Bulletin are bitter opponents) this remains an interesting suggestion that Iven's influence is waning.

However, Mr. Willcocks' regard for the O. B. U. also is on the decline. In another conversation he is quoted thus:-

> "He also said he had very little use for the O. B. U. organization and felt than an organization such as the Dominion Labour Party was of more benefit to the workers, claiming that the O. B. U. members would soon be realizing this and coming over to the Dominion Labour Party.
>
> "He acknowledged, however, that his ideas used to run along with the O. B. U. until lately, when the organization seemed to have lost all interest, and was going down hill, while the Dominion Labour party was going up.

14. The Dominion Labour Party

Currently, the affairs of the Dominion Labour Party are stirring. The new activity for the moment assumes the form of an internal quarrel, which may result in a dissipation of its energies at the coming, municipal election. The secretary, Robert Ringland resigned at a meeting held on 13th October; this was accepted, but a vote of confidence was passed in him, in circumstances which constituted a censure on the extremist party, who attacked him; and Ringland will carry on. The quarrel is based on the conflict between the Internationals and the O. B. U. The former have made an effort to capture the organization; they had added over 100 to the membership and now have a majority of the Executive Committee. A counter effort by the O. B. U. element may now be expected.[11]

15. O. B. U. Dissensions in the Press

The two Winnipeg papers contain some signs of the internal quarrel which is troubling the O. B. U. The O. B. U. Bulletin of 16th October makes no editorial references to the matter, but prints an angry onslaught upon Carl Berg with reference to the dissensions in Edmonton. The Western Labour News of 15th October publishes particulars of an editorially exults in the rift. It describes the peculiar position of the loggers' union, and the accompanying personal jealousies, and says:-

> "For practical purposes the foundation of the One Big Union is inherently unsound. The only merit it possesses is as a platform from which the tenets of the Socialist Party of Canada could be preached,

> and that this is a merit is by no means admitted by its own members. This peculiar attitude towards their own organization of most of the leaders, and nearly all the literature of the O. B. U., has not been calculated to retain in a condition of efficiency as an industrial organization, and has caused its constitutional weakness to declare itself sooner than might otherwise have been the case".

16. Miscellaneous Notes

Ben Legere now appears as the General Secretary of the Lawrence local of the Amalgamated Textile Workers of America. In that capacity he is sending out circulars asking for aid to the strikers at Lawrence Mass. One paragraph reads:-

> "It is important that the workers no longer be taught the false doctrine that the way to power lies in organizing 'along the line of the industry'. Winnipeg demonstrated that organization as a class in the strategic centres of capitalism is the real need".

The O. B. U. and kindred unions are attacked as offering "no more hope for the workers than does the A. F. of L.".

Apparently these circulars are a move in an internal fight, for he speaks of "the gang of sky-pilots that control this union" i.e. the A. T. W. of A.

The Winnipeg Labour Church meeting at the Strand Theatre on 10th October was addressed by F. J. Dixon, M.L.A. on "The Old Order and
[12] the New". The attendance was 1,000. Mr. Dixon attacked the existing order and demanded the release of the strike leaders.

V. ONTARIO

17. J. R. Knight

Joe Knight in conversation on 10th October explained his being dropped from the Executive Committee of the O. B. U. by stating that he had been kicking all the year that an organizer should be sent to Eastern Canada, whereas the others wanted to keep him in the West. Also he and "Secretary Mitchell" (presumably Midgley) "have not got along very well".

> "The present plans of Joe Knight are to tour the Eastern part of the country and he proposes to tour between Winnipeg and Niagara Falls and take a percentage of the collections received at each meeting also half the initiation fee of each new member".

The foregoing gives a new view of the personal relations of the O. B. U. leaders. Knight sides with Midgley against Winch, but none the less there is bad blood between him and Midgley.

Knight on 11th October addressed 60 people in Occident Hall, Toronto. His speech, while an advocacy of the O. B. U., was purely revolutionary; he dwelt on the revolutions in France, and apparently made some remarkably inaccurate statements about them. Revolution was sure to come, he said. Asked if the capitalistic Government of Canada would collapse as had happened in Russia, he said that he did not know its exact end, but if peaceable overthrow would not be possible, force was likely.

18. The Labour College

In conversation on 10th October Mrs. Custance gave an account of the affairs of the Ontario Labour College. Last year, "although they did not have a success financially yet they had about $43 left over at the end of the term". This year they should do better, as certain initial expenses would not recur. So far 30 pupils have registered for [13] the new term.

The leading spirits of the college are Mrs. Custance, Spector and Bell. They impress upon their students the difference between the two classes of society, "and that the only way they will or can get justice is by might". She criticised the O. B. U. for first taking in workers and then trying to teach them.

A project is mooted to establish a Labour College in Hamilton. Kristoff is interested in it.

Mrs. Custance, Knowles, and Roberts of Toronto have promised to help with this scheme.

19. The Jewish Socialist League

The Jewish Socialist League of Toronto is making progress. At a meeting held on 8th October about 60 were present and it was decided to rent a hall which would accommodate more people. This hall is to be the Provincial headquarters, and the distributing office for revolutionary reading matter.

After comparing the constitutions of the Third International and the British Communist Party the meeting decided to adopt the former.

A local agitator named Essor said that as the British Communist Party can work openly he could not see why they should not follow suit. He would try to ascertain the legality of such a course; if it should prove illegal they could work under cover. All members of the League who belonged to trade unions must propagate communism in their union meetings. They also should organize small communist units.

20. Almazoff's Activities

Mention has been made in earlier issues of Almazoff's arrival in Toronto; he is a very seditious person, who at the time of the Winnipeg strike had a narrow escape from deportation. He now has begun to stir about in Toronto, and his first steps seem to be to make things [14] uncomfortable for Dodokin, or Dadokin, the organizer of the Russian Workers' School and the keeper of the foreign bookshop at 111 Dundas street; hitherto Dodokin seems to have been the leader of the foreign revolutionists in Toronto, but Almazoff has an air of challenging this leadership.

Dodokin not long ago organized "social evenings" at his premises; Almazoff speaks frequently at them. On Saturday evening one of these took place, and there was a breeze between the two. Dodokin, as an Anarchist-Communist, criticised the Bolshevist government and Almazoff defended it on opportunist grounds. Almazoff gave an address embodying the communist interpretation of the development of society. The attendance was 65.

Next day, on 10th October, there was another affair, at the same place. Almazoff spoke on "Freedom", and we have two reports of what took place. According to one of these accounts, after Almazoff had finished his disquisition Dodokin "said that he did not see any freedom in Russia. He said that the Communist Party is in authority and that any party who has the authority will preserve it at any cost. Literature and letters are censored more than in any other country, etc. In answer to that Almazoff said that Russia is in such a condition that no other country has ever experienced". Apparently he represented present evils as accompaniments of the period of transition. Dodokin stuck to it that Bolshevist rule was arbitrary.

The other account, which describes the occasion as a meeting of the Jewish Socialist League, and says that about 160 persons were present, dwells rather upon Almazoff's utterances. He made a considerable impression. He declared that the workers in Canada were not free, and said: "Let us organize a strong proletariat army with a [15] dictatorship and discipline". They should use the paper guns and bullets which the Bolsheviki had found so effective. "The Jews in Canada should firmly hold together, form a strong organization and in such way there is a secure and bloodless victory". This victory Almazoff expected would come "very soon perhaps six months or a year". "Do not be afraid if the newspapers call us foreigners or aliens. We are at home everywhere".

Almazoff, also spoke on the same day at a Russian meeting called by the Russian Progressive Library; his subject was "Life and Science", and was not of a revolutionary cast. The presiding officer, Mrs. Maria Nekolayeva, urged all the Russians to form one big radical society, so as not to dissipate their energies. However, she dislikes Dodokin because he is a Anarchist-Communist, while she and her husband are orthodox Bolshevists. The Nekolayevas are new-comers in Toronto, having formerly lived in Western Canada.

21. Foreigners in Hamilton

Mention has been made of a know of foreigners who hold meetings in Hamilton. This group is discussing the question of organization; proposals which are mooted are joining the Socialist Party of Canada in a body, forming a Russian local of the S. P. C., and joining the O. B. U. as a separate unit. One of them, Kristoff, told our informant that what they really would like to do was to form a local of the Communist Party, but that they were afraid to do so because of the law; he proposes to ask the Department of Justice what the legal position is.

VI. QUEBEC

22. More News of the O. B. U. Convention

Rebecca Buhay reported on the Port Arthur Convention to the Metal Trades Unit, O. B. U., Montreal on 7th October. Her account of [16] the resolutions passed was as follows:-

1. That the O. B. U. headquarters be moved from Vancouver to Winnipeg. A referendum to decide.
2. That the Central Executive be empowered to demand the disbandment of the L. W. I. U. i.e. the closing of their general office, and the abolition of their separate organization and membership; all per capita and supply fund to be handed to the General Financial Secretary.
3. That the O. B. U. adopt the "Class" form of organization.
4. That a general organizer be sent to Quebec to organize all railway workers.
5. That the effort to release the Winnipeg strike leaders be continued.
6. That membership and receipt cards be in French and English, and a French paper be published in Montreal as soon as possible.
7. That the Central Executive be empowered to appoint a "Council of Action" on the plan followed in England.
8. That the "Council of Action" be empowered, in the event of a general strike in England, to "use their economic power" to convey food to the workers in England.

The foregoing is an approximation, Miss Buhay and our informant both having relied on their memories in the absence of copies of the resolution.

Miss Buhay in her account of the quarrel was antagonistic to the L. W. I. U., saying that they had tried to force their views upon the convention, to capture it or break it up. The L. W. I. U., she said, had been working independently of the Central Executive Council, having their own headquarters, organizers, local offices and a separate membership card. They had sent organizers out of their jurisdiction to "grab off" every member and every dollar they could get.

Walter Cowan objected vigorously to this hostile description of his unit. He defended the "industrial" type of organization, declared that the L. W. I. U. were the only part of the O. B. U. who did any work, and spoke satirically of Joe Knight and his pretensions.[17]

W. E. Long declared that the L. W. I. U. had gone to Port Arthur with 3 objects:-

1. To keep headquarters at Vancouver.
2. To get rid of Joe Knight.
3. To get rid of Midgley.

Miss Buhay gave some information as to membership. The membership cards issued totalled 71,606, but only 19,000 members had paid their dues from 1st January to 1st September.

At the close of the meeting an odd incident showed how poor a creature the Buhay woman is. Cowan engaged her in conversation, and she admitted that the L. W. I. U. had been right, but had lost because they were not strong enough to force their view on the convention. "Remember, Cowan", she said "under the system we live under everything is decided by power whether right or wrong".

23. General Workers' Unit in Low Water

The General Workers' Unit, O. B. U. of Montreal met on 14th October, 19 members attending. The financial Secretary reported that there were no funds in the treasury, that bills amounting to $19 were pressing, and that he "was through with the organization", and was resigning. It also developed that the unit was responsible for $50 for the expenses of the delegate to the Port Arthur convention.

The small attendance at these meetings is stated by our informant to be due to the incessant collections which are made. To attend regularly at the numerous gathering means spaying three or four dollars a week, and this is too severe a drain for most of them.

At this meeting Binette, the retiring organizer, adopted a very sulky and recalcitrant attitude.

24. The Worker

W. Cowan and the French Communist Party have come to terms as to the French portion of The Worker. Articles used are to be translated [18] and shown to Cowan, and the Communists are to buy and distribute a stipulated number of copies. Cowan at the interview expressed himself as anxious to work with the Communists. Our reports says:-

> "Cowan stated that the aims and objects of both organizations are identical; both are working towards the emancipation of the workers and the establishment of a proletarian dictatorship Government, and although, they might differ in opinion as to the best way to organize the workers with the view to be successful, yet they should be fair enough to leave their opinion open for discussion with the view to reach the best decision, and not to say I'm right and you wrong, and if they agree in opinions they will be able to do good work and avoid corruption in the rank and file of the O. B. U."

A later report states that Cowan has stipulated that the paper must keep neutral as between "class" and "industrial" types of organization until the L. W. I. U. have decided on which course to take. The editorial committee probably will consist of 2 L. W. I. U., 2 French Socialist Communists, 2 General Workers, O. B. U. and 2 Metal Trades O. B. U.

25. Miscellaneous Notes

On 3rd October Hvat, alias Hvatoff lectured at the Society for Technical Aid to Soviet Russia on the Third International. His address was an historical sketch of the three "Internationals", and he strongly advocated Lenin's Third of Moscow International. He attacked the programme of the American Socialist Party, and urged the cause of revolution. Only the left path would lead the workers to liberty, "we workers cannot gain this liberty and possess all wealth until the last Capitalist is destroyed".

At the conclusion there was one of the debates, now becoming frequent, between the believers in the pure Anarchist doctrine and the defenders of Bolshevism. Revenko finally had to intervene to quiet the discussion.

The Amalgamated Society of Engineers in Montreal, who have about 800 members, have joined the O. B. U. Their object seems to be to [19] force the works where they are employed to allow them to have shop stewards.

A new agitator has begun to speak in Montreal, his name apparently being Guson. He read a two-hour address at the usual Sunday meeting of the French Socialist Communist Party on 10th October.

Investigation shows that Anna Buller was borne in Rumania, probably of Jewish parents.

VII. MARITIME PROVINCES

26. A Coal Strike Possible

The coal mining situation in Cape Breton is described as serious, a strike being nearly inevitable unless the operators grant all the men's demands.

ROYAL CANADIAN MOUNTED POLICE HEADQUARTERS

Ottawa, 28th October, 1920.

SECRET

NO. 47

NOTES OF THE WORK OF THE C. I. B. DIVISION FOR THE WEEK ENDING 28TH OCTOBER

Table of Contents

---

1. General Characteristics of the Period

Fuller details of the collapse of the strike in the Alberta Coalfields emphasize two points. One is the reckless lying and callous leadership of the junta of the O. B. U. heads who brought about the strike. By the third day they were alarmed about money, by the end of the first week they realized that things were going badly with them, and they knew that the struggle was hopeless some time before they would admit it. The men must have lost a good deal. The leaders were exceptionally untruthful in the statements they made, and incidents of the later days of the struggle were the sending of delegations from Fernie and Lethbridge to Drumheller to see for themselves what the conditions actually were. The other point is the disposition of the leaders to indulge in mutual recriminations.

Two consequences are beginning to appear. One is the imminence of the extinction of the Searchlight. The other is the adoption by the mine-operators of a distinctly more aggressive attitude; a number of O. B. U. men are being refused employment.

Details of the split in the O. B. U. continue to be received. They contain no additional facts of importance, but they make it clear that the quarrel is deep-seated and that a bitter struggle may be expected. This week's development favour Midgley as against Winch; the former has got a measure of support from the B. C. Federationist, and the latter seem rather isolated. In British Columbia the impression seems to be that the O. B. U. is beginning to disintegrate.

Reports continue to be received to the general effect that a coal strike is likely to occur in Nova Scotia.[4]

I. BRITISH COLUMBIA

2. The O. B. U. Referendum

The O. B. U. have made public the clauses of the referendum which is to be taken as a result of the Port Arthur Convention. These number fifteen, and are strongly adverse to the L. W. I. U. Among the questions circulated are:-

No. 1. That in the preamble of the constitution the words "not according to craft but according to industry" be deleted.

No. 6. To prevent overlapping and disputes the approval of the General Executive Board must be obtained in conducting organization work in new territory, and the opening up of affairs in new districts. (This clearly is aimed at the L. W. I. U. incursions into Saskatchewan, Manitoba, Ontario and Montreal).

No. 9. A section in arrears for per capita tax for three months shall be suspended. Every branch must be in good standing for 30 days before the Convention, in order to secure representation.

No. 12. If any unit, council or body fails to send in a financial report, the next highest authority may audit its books. (This is particularly aimed at the financial autonomy of the L. W. I. U.)

No. 13. Every section of the One Big Union must use the official membership receipt, issued by the General Executive Board. (The L. W. I. U. have a separate receipt).

Another proposed change takes the General Secretary out of the General Board and makes him its servant.

3. B. C. Federationist against Winch

Another development in the situation is that the British Columbia Federationist, despite its nominal control by the L. W. I. U., has declared editorially against Winch. In its issue of 15th October it deals with the question of industrial organization and pronounces against it and for district organization. The former, it says, would make the O. B. U. a mere federation of industries, and is not far removed from craft unionism. It also contends that the purpose in [5] organizing the O. B. U. in March 1919 clearly was not industrial. It describes the present quarrel as one among a few officials, whom it rebukes in the name of the rank and file.

4. O. B. U. Losing Ground

Commenting upon the foregoing, a well-informed agent says:-

"The general impression among labour men is that the organization is losing steadily. Midgley refuses to state what the membership is. On every hand I hear that there is a weakening. For instance J. H. McVety (the leader of the Internationals) in speaking of the recent strike of gas workers, told me that the strikers -- who went out as an O. B. U. organization -- approached him after the strike had been going on for some time and offered to come back in the International fold if he would get their jobs back for them. He said he got Sir Henry Drayton and Hon. G. Robertson, Minister of Labour, to see George Kidd, general manager of the B. C. Electric Railway Company, parent company for the gas works. Kidd refused to entertain any proposition of conferring with the strikers".

"I asked McVety if the Internationals were going to let the O. B. U. people come back. He said some, not all. The radicals would never be permitted in again. A clause in the constitution of the Vancouver Trades and Labour Council had been changed since the O. B. U. was created, which permitted exclusion of the 'reds'.

"I asked him where the rejected ones would go, where they could join any organization. He said the only thing left them would be the socialist party.

"McVety laughed at any likelihood that the Third Internationals would ever get a dangerous footing here. The labour men would not stand for it".

This agent further quotes a conversation with a number of shipyard workers, all Scotchmen, and all apparently good types of reputable workmen. "During our talk", he says

"we touched on the O. B. U. They said it had weakened, partly due to poor leadership, but rather deplored its failure. They said it had some good principles, if properly led. What appealed most to them was the aim to get free from domination of United States. They favoured a true Canadian or all-empire organization. They did not like the American colouring to the Internationals and the A. F. of

L."[6]

5. Midgley's Explanations

On his return to Vancouver Midgley spoke freely in private conversation. He argued that the real membership of the O. B. U. is about 38,000; in addition to the 19,000 paid-up members there were 5,000 members in Alberta who were excused paying because of their fight with the U. M. W. of A.; Vancouver had been let off temporarily to pay for their new hall; and the L. W. I. U. had never paid up to full strength.

His explanation of the withdrawal of the loggers was that the I. W. W. element was in control; he hoped that the saner men of the loggers would repudiate this element. Winch, he said, had fought the I. W. W. until he saw that they were too strong, and then had switched; now the I. W. W. look upon him with suspicion and the saner men will reject him; he would be a "dead one" as soon as the I. W. W. executive felt strong enough to oust him.

Midgley was very bitter against Carl Berg, whom he described as "a syndicalist of the rankest hue".

He also expressed the opinion that in the present juncture strikes are folly. They should organize for a more auspicious time.

The N. C. O. in charge of C. I. B. work in Vancouver regards the foregoing as mere special pleading.

6. Strength of the O. B. U. in British Columbia

The N. C. O. in charge of C. I. B. work in Vancouver has furnished an estimate of the O. B. U. as in September. He regards the organization as on the verge of disintegration. The records are in a chaotic state, owing to the tendency of districts to default, so that figures are difficult to compile. However, he recalls previous estimates of the membership in British Columbia thus:-[7]

On 16th July 22,050
" 10th August 13,357
" 20th September 16,522

This last estimate was made up as follows:-

L. W. I. U. 13,357
Other Units 3,165

As the loggers have seceded, the real O. B. U. membership accordingly should be placed at 3,165, with the 13,357 loggers in an anomalous position, not exactly hostile, and not sympathetic.

Labour bodies friendly to the O. B. U. are placed at 7,726; those hostile or indifferent at 13,275.

A decrease in the number sympathizing with the O. B. U. is expected.

7. Alexander Attacking Winch

At the Port Arthur convention W. A. Alexander, one of the L. W. I. U. organizers, deserted Winch, and sided with the Midgley faction. On 13th

October he held a meeting of the O. B. U. at New Westminster, at which he advocated the Midgley plan of district organization. Only 20 attended, out of about 200 who were not more than six months in arrear with their dues.

It was agreed on all hands that all the units were out of money, and that the members were badly in arrear. The meeting decided to ask T. A. Barnard, who was the labour candidate in the recent bye-election, to become district organizer.

Our report says:-

> "He (i.e. Alexander) then told a few facts about the O. B. U. convention and said that, as a result of the stand he took there, he expected to be let out of his job as an O. B. U. official in about a week's time. There were too many officials in the O. B. U. at present, and the majority of them are striving jealously for power that is why he took his stand in favour of the District Organization system in opposition to their plan of Industrial organizing. He said he came very close to blows with some of them and had to order Carl Berk out of his room, and the struggle is [8] still going on, and an agreement will not probably be made until it is voted upon, as it will be shortly".

8. O. B. U. Notes

Mention was made a while ago of the enrolment of some Indians in the O. B. U. at Prince Rupert. It now appears that those people were enrolled in the "Fisheries and Water Products Unit, O. B. U." The younger Indians are mixing a good deal with whites as labourers and are somewhat prone to join such organizations; in the Prince Rupert case they had sleeping in the O. B. U. hall and probably thought that the paying of a dollar was a return for hospitality.

The Fisheries and Water Products Unit has the following membership:-

Trollers and Deep Sea Fishermen	190
Cannery Hands	200
Fish Packers	70
	460

The O. B. U. metal miners of the Skeena district held a convention at Prince Rupert on 4th October. Hitherto they have belonged to the General Workers' Unit, they now see, disposed to form a unit of their own.

While particulars are lacking as yet, it is understood that they evinced great dissatisfaction with the Port Arthur convention.

A Shipyard Workers' Unit of the O. B. U. has been formed in Prince Rupert. It began with about 40 members.

On noting the presence of Winch at the revolutionary-prohibitionist meeting at Vancouver our informant remarks on his aloofness from his fellow agitators. "He sat alone behind the circle, and as far away as he could get from Midgley". After speaking he left the meeting.

A report from Midway states that the O. B. U. is losing ground in the Okanagan Valley. Michael Casey (whose alcoholic activities have [9] been noted already) has ceased to be the salaried organizer; he has gone to work, to escape a charge of vagrancy, but he sooner or later will be convicted of boot-legging.

His successor as local secretary is a man named Wm. Whritson.

9. Revolutionists as Prohibitionists

On Sunday 17th October a curious prohibition meeting took place in Vancouver. It was in the hands of the extremist element, the chairman being Thomas Richardson and the speakers including R. P. Pettipiece, E. Winch, V. R. Midgley, W. H. Cottrell, W. R. Trotter and a number of other "Reds". The only speaker not associated with this element was a woman, a member of the British Columbia Teachers' Federation. The theme of all the speakers was:-

> "The dawn of Social Revolution is approaching, and its accomplishment will be speeded up by the advent of total prohibition".

There was the usual abuse of everybody; in addition to attacks on those who opposed prohibition there were references to the Provincial Premier, and the R.C.M.P. who were termed "Stoolpigeons". Some of the remarks made may be noticed.

Winch said that he was governed by self-interest.

> "He believed his interest would be advanced when all were total abstainers. The employers benefited the workers when they brought in prohibition. They sought during the war to increase efficiency for their individual profit; and now their class interest as capitalists was menaced by prohibition. Total prohibition would not come, no matter what Act was passed, until such time as the workers of the World controlled governments.

R. P. Pettipiece dealt largely with present conditions in Russia, which he said had been brought about by the prohibition of vodka. He had voted "wet" before, but this time he would vote "dry".[10]

W. R. Trotter said that if revolution was to come, the people needed to be sober, so that they could take hold of things.

All the speakers except the woman and Charles Cassidy, representative of the International Boilermakers, talked revolution.

At a meeting of the Moderation League (the party opposed to prohibition) Sir Hibbert Tupper referred to the "Soviets" as being lined up with the clergymen who were for prohibition, and he was interrupted by a number of men who resented criticism of the Soviets.

10. Revolutionary Meetings

Dr. Currie was the speaker at the people's Open Forum" at Vancouver on Sunday, 10th October. His subject was "Production for use", and he illustrated it with charts which he said come from a book which had been suppressed by the United States Government. He declared that his subject was seditious. He states that in the Steel trade in the 30 years from 1870 to 1900 the production per man per year had risen from 60 to 360 tons; the wages per man per year from $400 to $900; and the profits from $300 to over $900. He said:-

> "What would happen if a crowd of working men wanted to build houses for themselves, and in doing so, took possession of one of our large lumber mills? They would immediately have the Police after them most likely the Mounted Police, 'Yellow Legs' as they are called. If the Police could not stop them, then the Militia would be called out and the consequences would be that the working man would be worse off than ever. If we want to produce for our own use, we must do away with this social parasite class, and take over the industries on a co-operative basis amongst ourselves".

J. Harrington was the speaker at the Socialist meeting held on Sunday 17th October in Vancouver. The meeting was not very successful, the attendance being smaller than usual and the speaker not impressing the audience. [11] Harrington made the surprising statement that since the revolution in Russia the projected canal to connect the Baltic and Black seas has been completed. "This was to prove that the working class could manage without the boss".

11. Miscellaneous Notes

Further reports on the Chinese Labour Association seem to show that it is mainly confined to Vancouver. The Esperanto classes which are taken by one J. Clarke seem to have much to do with it; and they are revolutionary in tendency, the text-book being the "Communist Manifesto".

Uncertainty exists at present as to who and what J. Clarke is. He may be a cog in the Bolshevist machine.

In reporting that Thomas Richardson has accepted the Labour nomination for the bye-election in Yale, the V. C. O. in charge of the Midway detachment says that he will have very little support. His campaign manager is one J. W. S. Logie of Summerland, a druggist whose ideas on social questions, religion etc. are regarded as peculiar.

There is reasons to believe that the B. C. Federationist is contemplating a change of policy, in the direction of moderation.

A weekly detachment report from Cumberland contains the following remark:- "All workers seem anxious to hold their present jobs in anticipation of a hard winter".

Another weekly detachment report, this time from Kamloops, describes the loggers as seeming satisfied with the conditions under which they are working.

At a meeting of the Vancouver Longshoremen on 15th October a letter was received from the Secretary of the Seattle district, couched in pessimistic terms.

At Vancouver the B. C. Street Railway has settled with the union on a basis satisfactory to the men. Increases are given to various classes of labour.

Frank Cassidy is continuing his speaking tour. On 8th October [12] he spoke at Yahk, B. C., and proceeded by way of Cranbrook to Fernie.

II. ALBERTA

12. The Story of the Strike

We are in possession of a record of proceedings at the O. B. U. headquarters in Calgary during the coal strike; they show that the leaders guided the men into disaster. The strike was called on 1st October; on 2nd October the leaders at Calgary were in good spirits; on the 3rd they began to be troubled about money; on the 4th Evans, Beard and Ormond began a tour of the Crow's Nest Pass; on the 8th when they had returned it was understood that things were going ill. Evans, the Secretary, left on the 10th for a tour in the north, his real object apparently being to collect enough to pay his own salary of $200 a month. By the 13th the Fernie men had sent a delegation to Drumheller to see the facts for themselves; Bray, who was there, told them that the strike was lost. Yet the struggle was allowed to continue. There was much mutual recrimination among the leaders.

13. Lawson's Speech

A belated report of a speech by Lawson on 1st October to the Transportation Unit of the O. B. U. at Calgary shows that he utters two characteristic observations. One was a statement that the had authoritative information that the coal handlers at Port Arthur and Fort William "had only to be notified" and they would tie things up there. The other was that the Drumheller miners might sign the check-off because "it was too early in the year to pull a steam coal strike". "They would wait until Senator Robertson got nicely settled in Ottawa, and then, boys, look out for the trouble".

He also gave a curiously incorrect account of the quarrel at Port Arthur, representing Berg as assailing the loggers union.[13]

This singular speech seems to have been delivered before the coal strike had begun.

14. Strike Notes

An interesting episode at Taber on 17th October was the co-operation of mine-management and union in sending a man to Drumheller to ascertain the true state of affairs. The management paid expenses and half wages.

The N. C. O. in charge of the detachment observes:-

> "The general feeling was that the men do not resent the check-off. But they object to a union which is not their choice and also the fact that dues and assessments go to the different headquarters of the U. M. W. of A. in the States. They were satisfied here and wished to remain in agreement with Howard, (the manager who made the

arrangement described). But they felt they had an interest in these other camps and if need be would back them up".

A report upon the Drumheller strike by the N. C. O. in charge of C. I. B. work in Southern Alberta lays stress upon the part played in it by the foreigner led by English-speaking agitators. About 60 per cent of the miners went out; of these nine-tenths were foreigners.

A report upon conditions in Wayne (in the Drumheller area) dated 13th October is to the effect that the strike leaders were not having a very comfortable time. A meeting of 1st October was broken up by the heckling of U. M. W. of A. men; on 2nd October another meeting developed hostility towards the leaders, who had a narrow escape from violence.

On 18th October the miners at Fernie decided to return to work. Full notice was given that the management would refuse to employ certain men. One of these was Wm. Sherman and some disposition to resent this was shown. On 19th October 289 men reported for work i.e. about half the regular shift. Five or six men have been "discriminated against".[14]

The troubles at Coalhurst flamed up again on 21st October, when the men struck because the management had refused to employ six or seven men who had been active advocates of the O. B. U.

Considerable restlessness on the part of the coal-miners at Lethbridge is reported.

On 19th October two developments appeared at Michel; the strike showed signs of weakening over 100 underground men reported for work --; and the coal company dismissed all the O. B. U. leaders. The last action caused indignation among the strikers.

A strike at Nordegg, which involved about 400 men, began on 9th October and ended on 15th October. It was due to resentment at the "check-off" and a desire to co-operate with Drumheller, the local secretary, James Bewsher, being principally responsible. It ended upon a prospect of increased wages and the news that the majority of the other mines in the district were working.

15. The Searchlight

The failure of the O. B. U. strike in the Alberta Coalfields probably will mean the demise of the Searchlight, and a move by Lawson to fresh fields. A proposal was made by him by R. E. Bray and David of Winnipeg that the Searchlight and the O. B. U. Bulletin unite, the new paper to be known as the O. B. U. Searchlight, with Lawson as its editor; Lawson declined to entertain this idea, probably because he expects the O. B. U. leaders to be arrested soon and fears to identify himself with the organization. He is anxious to go to Nova Scotia to spread O. B. U. propaganda there; he has telegraphed to J. B. McLachlan, but so far has received no reply. He is very short of funds.[15]

16. R. E. Bray

On 13th October R. E. Bray addressed a meeting of strikers at Drumheller. It comprised 400 or 500 men, nine-tenths of them foreigners. As a direct aid to the strikers it was not much, being a recital of his personal experiences in the Winnipeg strike and in the trial. It contained, however, much preaching of class hatred, and a strong insinuation that the jury at Winnipeg had been bribed, with the connivance of Judge Metcalfe and Mr. Andrews. The fact that the audience was largely composed of foreigners increases the seriousness of such a speech.

At the meeting Bray made a personal attack upon Sergt. Waugh, who was present, using very scurrilous language about him and the R. C. M. P., and indeed laying himself open to a charge of assault.

Bray spoke at Canmore on 15th October. His address did not interest the audience, and he gave the impression of being anxious to get money.

17. Miscellaneous Notes

The Ukrainian Society "Samo Obrazowania" of Edmonton on 9th Edmonton put on a play named "The Striker". It was revolutionary propaganda, the principal part being taken by John Klybanowski. It made a considerable impression upon the audience, which numbered about 160. The play seems to be a stock piece of propaganda, having been performed elsewhere.

A report upon Uus Ilm, an Esthonian paper printed in New York, shows it to be thoroughly Bolsheviki, and very dangerous. It apparently is the only paper printed in this language on the Continent.

Inquiry as to the resignation by Edward Brown of the post of Secretary of the O. B. U. "District, No. 1" shows that it was [16] principally due to domestic trouble.

Frank Cassidy's address at Fernie on 14th October was a failure, there being present fewer than 20 people all foreigners, and mostly Germans.

III. MANITOBA

18. Violent Speeches at an O. B. U. Meeting

An O. B. U. meeting was held in the Ukrainian Labour Temple in Winnipeg on Sunday, 17th October. One G. B. Currie and M. Popowich were the speakers.

Currie's speech was very violent. He boasted of the progress made by revolutionary unionism in Great Britain, and after asserting that shipments of munitions to Poland had been stopped, said:-

> "The great body of workers is classed in three divisions, that is, Miners, Manufacturers and Railway men. If these unite together, England will be paralyzed, which I hope will come soon. The miners are on strike. They strike not on account of the High Cost of Living nor because their labour is worth more than they get, but they strike to crush the Capitalistic employers and to get the operation of that industry into their own hands, which is only just, because that Industry should be operated not for profit but for use".

He continued:-

"'I am glad', says Robert Smillie, 'that the miners' strike is on because it will put a crimp into the little game of France'. Coal, coal was what France wanted and England was the country to supply her, as she was unable to get it anywhere else. Imagine, therefore, what will happen if the strike lasts about seven days! Famous Lloyd George and Churchills have exerted all their means to overcome the strike, but in vain. Councils of Action are established in every village and town amongst organized workers, and the Government is unable to stir, through fear of its own existence. All the efforts of Lloyd George, Millerand and other Italian and Polish Statesmen, are of no avail".

Other expressions used by him were:-

"Think it over, and let us use all weapons to sweep away and eradicate the profiteering Capitalists, and turn all the industries of the world into use of everybody, rather than that they should remain for the profit of a few only". [17]

"My coming to Canada, and my speaking here before you would not be vain were you all strongly united in one body, mind and soul, and not idly awaiting the promises of your bosses. Rise, and join your hands with your brothers over the ocean for the whole of Europe is boiling and chances offer themselves to you to challenge your enemies for emancipation, to own and operate the industries you produce for your own use".

Popowich spoke in Ukrainian, his speech consisting of an attack on the press, on the ground that it did not tell the truth, with the usual moral that revolutionary papers should be read. One interesting passage was:-

"In order to fabricate their news, they go even so far as to make damage to the public to make their news the more exciting, and the more horrible. You are all aware, I suppose of the explosion of a bomb on Wall Street in New York? What was the purpose of that explosion! Well, it has been found through investigation that it was done by the Capitalists simply to have their papers filled with news, and this news to be used as a weapon upon the workers".

Little is known as yet about Currie.

19. Misinformation about the Alberta Strike

At a meeting of the Socialist Party held in Winnipeg on 17th October F. Woodward, who is a member of the O. B. U. Central Executive Committee, spoke about the Alberta Coal Strike. Statements that the strike was nearly over were an absolute falsehood. "Telegrams had recently been received by him, direct from the strike committee, both at the Drumheller and other mines, stating that fourteen mines were at present completely tied up, and that the men had been offered a dollar and a half a day raise in wages, if they would only return to work, but as yet they had declined the offer, as they were out this time to make a job of the situation". He added some incorrect statements as to the Bienfait situation, describing the strike as still in progress, and called for help for the Alberta men. The concluding portion of his speech is thus reported:-

> "He commented on how solid the Capitalist walls were built, and stated that no means could be too severe to be used against this system, when it became time for the workers to control industry".[18]

20. O. B. U. Notes

The Winnipeg and District Branch of the O. B. U. met on 20th October in the Ukrainian Labour Temple. Apparently it was a Ukrainian meeting.

P. Anderson, who was a delegate at the Port Arthur convention, secured approbation of his action in withdrawing from it. His reason for withdrawing was that the committee refused to pass a resolution to the effect that the "United Workers of Canada" should join with "all the workers beyond the oceans".

Delegates were appointed from the Ukrainian Unit, O. B. U. to the relief committee for Soviet Russia.

A possibility exists of trouble on the Winnipeg Street Railway caused by the O. B. U. unit refusing to work with members of the International Unit.

21. Charles Lestor

Charles Lestor, who is on his way to England, spoke at the Socialist meeting in Winnipeg on Sunday 17th October. After a disquisition on the iniquity on the Capitalistic system, he predicted the coming or revolution.

> "The strike of the miners now in progress in Great Britain, he said, was very probably the start of the abolition of this system. It had not as yet gone far enough to say for sure just what the miners meant, but one thing sure, they would accomplish what they were out for.
>
> "If the strike continued to grow, it would be armed revolution like that in Russia very probably, he said, because he felt quite sure that the Capitalist system would not go out of business without a fierce struggle because they had all the Army, Navy and Police at their disposal.
>
> "In Great Britain herself, he said, they were quite confident of success in the final struggle, because the workers were organized to such an extent that a general strike would completely paralyze the country's industry, but it was the United States which held the firm hand of Capitalism and they stamped out any of the Labour movements with terrific vengeance".[19]
>
> "Revolutions were sure to take place in all countries, Great Britain, France, Italy, Spain, United States, but he would not say in Canada, for he would not be safe in so doing".

Other remarks of his were that in the United States the private spies and detectives blew up public buildings to create a disturbance; and that he wished that Napoleon had won against England, because Waterloo had been followed by the employment of child labour to pay the war debt.

Another statement was that when the Socialist Party gained power they would "mete out proper punishment" to Judge Metcalfe and Mr. A. J. Andrews "and all others of their kind and their followers". "You know it will not be a difficult task to hand a jury of workers who will probably take care of the situation".

The attendance was 700.

Another report of this speech contains the following passages:-

> "When the final time did come, and the workers had captured Political power, which they would be forced to do, if people were to be kept alive in the world, he said, the question seemed to be, 'What would be done with the Capitalist Class?'
>
> "The same would be done with them in Russia, he declared. They would be out selling papers on the streets, and out working with the workers.
>
> "As a joke, he said, when this change of Political power took place, he was going to be a Magistrate, and when any of the Capitalist class came before him, he would say, twenty years, regardless of the crime, and if the individual began lamenting and asking for leniency, he would say, ten years more for contempt of court, because all this was coming to this class when the workers once got their chance".

IV. ONTARIO

22. O. B. U. NOTES

Investigation of the labour situation at Kirkland Lake about the middle of October showed conditions to be satisfactory. For some time the O. B. U. have been inactive. The mines report a shortage of labour, high wages paid in the bush attracting many men; nevertheless, [20] the men seem aware that the exaction of higher wages would result in the mines closing down. This feeling results in neglect of the O. B. U., which is not of immediate service to them.

The O. B. U. is keeping its office at Kirkland Lake open and has a secretary, one S. Kirk; he has little weight.

J. R. Knight has announced that he will remain permanently in Toronto. He now is tampering with the Street Railway Union.

Knight has been urging the Hamilton local of the O. B. U. to get to work on its projected campaign for increased membership.

A "Brass Check Club" has been formed in Hamilton. it is comprised of radicals and is to circulate the book of that name and other revolutionary matter.

23. The Extremists

The Jewish Socialist League has appointed a committee to instil communist ideas among Jewish Trade Unions. The members are Almazoff, Wolf, Esspr, Shapiro and Russkin.

Complaint is made that this league is not receiving any radical reading matter from the United States.

At a meeting held on 1st October Almazoff said that he had formed a Jewish Communist Party in Montreal.

The Plebs League of Toronto have affiliated with their namesake in England. They also have decided to act under the direction of the Third International.

On 15th October the group of Russians which meets in Hamilton discussed the formation of a local of the Communist Party. A proportion of the 50 or 60 persons present were afraid to do so, apprehending imprisonment and deportation, and the meeting failed to come to a decision.[21]

The Russian Progressive Library in Toronto at a special meeting on 20th October decided not to form a school for agitators, but to keep the library for reading only.

Considerable unemployment is noted at Welland, with the men getting very hard up and rather in the mood for disorder.

V. QUEBEC

24. Miscellaneous Notes

On 17th October at a meeting of the Society for Technical Aid to Soviet Russia Revenko judged it necessary to argue at length against the anarchist point of view. He gave a thorough-going defence of the course of the Moscow Government in shooting persons who did not agree with it.

A travelling agitator from New York named Platonoff also spoke on "Revolution and Government".

There are in Montreal several allied societies, the Esperanto Club, the Theosophical Society and the Universal Library. A preliminary investigation goes to show that they have no connection with revolutionary agitation.

VI. MARITIME PROVINCES

25. The Coal Mines

In reporting upon the prospects of a coal strike in Nova Scotia, one of our informants draws attention to the course pursued by J. B. McLachlan, the Secretary-treasurer of the District. McLachlan is strongly for a strike, of the most extreme description; and this in spite of the fact that the district treasury is ill-supplied for a struggle. He adds:-

> "I have often heard it said that McLachlan has kept the treasury empty by holding so many meetings, conventions, conferences, etc., and that he had a sinister motive behind this, namely:- that in event of a strike the International officials of the U. M. W. of A. would fail to supply money enough to pay a substantial strike allowance. This would then create dissatisfaction in the ranks of the U. M. W.

and cause a split among the miners, and perhaps the miners of District 18, O. B. U. section would come to their rescue, and therefore organize McLachlan's pet idol the O. B. U. in District [22] 26. This is what McLachlan has been secretly working for ever since the split in District 18, but he has been extremely cautious and careful since the O. B. U. show down at the convention in Truro last April".

The chances of District No. 18 (Alberta) helping with money are uncommonly remote.

On 13th October a strike occurred in Dominion No. 1. Mine, Cape Breton. The cause was a small and local grievance, and the men acted in defiance of the labour agreement, and of their own chiefs.

A mass meeting at Glace Bay on 17th October seemed strongly in favour of a strike.

ROYAL CANADIAN MOUNTED POLICE HEADQUARTERS

Ottawa, 4th November, 1920.

SECRET

NO. 48

NOTES OF THE WORK OF THE C.I.B. DIVISION FOR THE WEEK ENDING 4TH NOVEMBER

Table of Contents

" 13. Miscellaneous Notes.
Ukrainian Play at Edmonton.
Ukrainian at Coalhurst.
Mr. and Mrs. Pullan.
John Boychuk.

" 14. The Labour Church.
Bray's meeting broken up.

" 15. SASKATCHEWAN: Miscellaneous Notes.
The Paris Hotel.
The People's Forum.
Free O.B.U. Reading matter.

" 16. MANITOBA: The O.B.U. on the English.

" 17. The *Western Labour News* and the O.B.U.

" 18. G. B. Currie.

" 19. Labour Dissensions.
The Dominion Labour Party.
Internationals *versus* O.B.U.
W. D. Bailey.
W. H. Hoop.

" 20. The Labour Churches.
Winnipeg Church Declining.
A. E. Smith not so extreme.

" 21. The Foreign Revolutionists.
Sava Zura.
Popowich.
A seditious Scandinavian Poet.

" 22. ONTARIO: The Situation in Toronto.

" 23. The O.B.U. in the Lumber Camps.
Investigation at Thessalon.

" 24. Conditions in the Niagara District.
Investigation at Welland
Exploiting unemployment.

" 25. O.B.U. affairs.
Address by Mrs. J. R. Knight.
Meetings in Toronto
Tom Cassidy again in Windsor.
Windsor O.B.U. weak.
Harry Roberts.

" 26. The Hamilton Extremists.
Proposed Labour College.
Circulating reading matter.

" 27. Friction among Foreign Revolutionists.
Almazoff heckled at Welland.
Faction's at Welland.

---

1. General Features of the Period

No outstanding features present themselves.

In Vancouver it is becoming apparent that the L.W.I.U. are in difficulties; the position of the union has been weakened, there appears reason to expect a dangerous attack upon it by the operators, and the men are showing disaffection towards the management, i.e. towards Winch. The prospects of unemployment in the winter among the loggers are considerable; and open shop may be declared.

It develops that the disorder at Mr. Meighen's meeting in Vancouver was premeditated, and that it was hoped to prevent him from speaking.

Investigation in Southern Alberta shows that in the last three months the O.B.U. have decreased form 10,000 to 8,000 members.

The leaders of the unsuccessful O.B.U. strike now are breaking up into three factions. At Winnipeg the O.B.U. in admitting the defeat of the strike declared that it had been exceedingly badly managed. They took occasion to attack the English-speaking workingmen in Drumheller with much bitterness.

The Winnipeg Labour Church is declining. Mr. A. E. Smith's attitude is much less radical than it was before his election to the Manitoba Legislature.

In Ontario there is an increase in the friction between the several factions into which the foreign revolutionists are divided.

The extremists are looking forward with satisfaction to the prospects of unemployment, as they think it will bring grist to their mill.

I. BRITISH COLUMBIA

2. Winch's Account of the Quarrel

Winch's version of the quarrel in the O.B.U. now is, to hand; it was given in a conversation from which some extracts may be made:-

"'The camp and lumber workers are still the O.B.U.', said E. Winch to me today. 'But Midgley must go. He will go. The only reason he won out this time was that he and his gang framed us. The camp and lumber workers have a membership of twenty thousand paying dues. We do not pay per capita tax on all, because there are many units that are not yet self-supporting. I do not think the entire organization of the O.B.U. has over 35,000 paying dues. There is very much less paying per capita'".

"'Ballots have already been sent out to our members for their expression on our action. Results will not be in for two or three weeks at best, and the camps are, widely scattered. But I have confidence our action will be supported. Midgley and his friends [4] changed the constitution to fit their needs after we withdrew. Midgley knows he is done. Carl Berg of Edmonton is a strong man and he is now on our executive'".

"'What about the I.W.W.?' I asked him".

"'That organization has done wonders for the loggers, as anyone will admit', he said. 'They will grow in strength because they have evolved a new policy. They have decided to no longer fight other labour bodies, but to devote all effort to fighting the bosses and getting better and better conditions'".

Winch added that he had been asked if he wanted Midgley's job, but had refused it. Midgley's wages, he said were $50. a week.

"He said the Federationist was against them because Wells thought or feared they would get control of the paper. Consequently while admitting privately that Winch and his associates were right in withdrawing from the convention, Wells would not do so openly in the paper. However, Winch thought the time would come when the Federationist would support the loggers more definitely.

"He said he had been 'roped in' for the prohibition meeting. He thought the majority of loggers would go for moderation, as they thought it would be nearer prohibition than the present silly statute."

The most interesting passage in this interview is the defence of the I.W.W.; it tends to bear out Midgleys statement that Winch is swinging to that organization. Winch's explanation of the attitude of the Federationist also is interesting; the L.W.I.U. nominally possess a moiety of the stock, but have paid only $100 on it. It must be observed that Well's article in the Federationist defending Midgley's view against Winch's is moderately expressed and strongly put; from the standpoint of an industrial unionist, his arguments seem very cogent.

3. Winch's Troubles

Despite Winch's assertions, the indications now point to his organization being in a precarious position. A series of reports from an outside source on the L.W.I.U. covering the period from 7th to 22nd October describes the internal conditions of that body as serious. The loggers are becoming uneasy over news that the logging camps may close down for a period in order to cut wages; they are grumbling at the extent to which they have sacrificed work and pay in obeying numberous calls for strikes, and are anxious to continue steadily at work. A recent development has been an influx of loggers from the east who do not belong to the O.B.U. or to any other labour organization; these men seem to be preferred by the companies, and this, and the number of unemployed who now are willing to work in the woods adds to the anxiety of the men.

Dissension has appeared between the English speaking element and the Swedes and Finns over the contract system; they have been [5] several fights in connection with this matter, and there is a growing willingness to take contract work, whether the O.B.U. likes it or not. The chances are said to be favourable to a general split between the English speaking element and the Finns.

As so often happens at such a juncture, the men now are exceedingly critical of the management of the unit. The particular point of criticism is finance, there being dissatisfaction among the ordinary members over the failure to build up a treasury although much money has been coming in. Cases have occurred of men tearing up their cards.

Winch in fact, seems to be in difficulty with his organization.

The Officer Commanding British Columbia in this connection remarks:-

> "The L.W.I.U. will require careful handling to pull through the coming winter, and this fact is well known to the Loggers' Association. This latter organization may be depended upon to take full advantage of conditions, and they no doubt will enforce "Open Shop" and cause a reduction in the scale of wages paid in all branches of the Lumbering industry".

The financial statement of the L.W.I.U. from September 24th to October 7th shows the following summary:-

Balance on hand September 23rd 1920	3,737.39
Receipts..	2,801.37
	6,538.76
Expenditure..	4,336.01
Balance on hand	2,202.75

The largest item of expenditure is $1,653 per Capita tax to headquarters, and $1,635 described as part of the O.B.U. convention expenses.

4. Prospects of Unemployment among Loggers

Confirmation of the apprehensions of the men comes from another quarter. An agent submits the following report:-

> "Several thousand loggers are out of work, and within the next few weeks there will be hundreds more out on account of the camps closing down.
>
> "The first reason for the closing of camps is because the mills have no orders for lumber; and the second is that the B.C. Loggers' Association is going to try to break up the L.W.I.U. and the I.W.W.

element which has been causing so much trouble in the logging camps during the past year.

"The above mentioned organizations are short of funds, and by closing down a number of these camps, most of the loggers will be 'broke', and when the camps re-open, the association will endeavour to enforce "Open shop"".[6]

"I visited several Employment Offices, there are very few jobs on the boards, and a number of men hanging around looking for work. A great many of these men are from Eastern Canada who came west for the harvest and did not return, having figured on lots of employment in logging camps at the coast."

5. The B.C. Federationist

In a former issue appeared a surmise that the B.C. Federationist might adopt a more moderate attitude. The last issue to hand prints under the heading of the L.W.I.U. page the following disclaimer:-

"This page is paid for by the Lumber, Camp and Agricultural Workers' Department of the O.B.U. Opinions expressed therein are not necessarily endorsed by the Federationist".

The N.C.O. in charge of C.I.B. work in Vancouver is disposed to regard this as a symptom of the expected change of attitude.

6. O.B.U. Notes

J. H. McVety, the leader of the Internationals in Vancouver, in conversation lately declared that the O.B.U. were "in bad shape". One remark of his merits notice:-

"On the subject of Carl Berg, he declared that Berg was a disrupter, and his presence on the executive of the loggers would result in an explosion and continual troubles. Berg was too radical, although very clever. His methods were not ones that would meet general favour, and his desires to dominate would result in clashes with other strong men of the organization".

A report upon the Building Trades Unit, O.B.U. Prince Rupert, places its nominal membership at about 100, but adds that fewer than 50 are in good standing, they usually have difficulty in getting enough members to hold a meeting. While the unit is under the control of the local Central Labour Council O.B.U., its moving spirit is a Scandinavian named A. O. Morse.

A report on the general work of the O.B.U. Penticton, states that it has approximately 170 members in good standing. They are employed upon construction work.

It is noted, in connection with a matter upon which information is required, that "since Midgley returned from the East, he has been singularly uncommunicative".

7. The Insult to the Prime Minister

Reports dated 26th and 27th October show that as early as on that date the G. A. U. V. of Vancouver were arranging to interrupt Mr. Meighen's meeting. The plans laid were for a procession of members of this body to march to the place of meeting, for a delegation to present to the Prime Minister certain questions concerning the treatment of [7] returned soldiers, and to demand that he answer those before speaking on any other subject; and "in the event that the Premier is unable to give satisfactory replies to the delegation, the rank and file would cause such disturbances as could effectually make the continuance of the meeting impossible".

8. Miscellaneous Notes

The two rival International locals, Nos. 313 and 310, of the electrical workers in Vancouver still are fighting, with the former in difficulties. It is in bad financial condition, most of the members having ceased to contribute the per capita tax. It is asserted that No. 310 was created at the instigation of the B.C. Telephone company, to split the men. If such is the case, the object was attained, as there has been much litigation over charters etc. between the two bodies.

An incident of the affair is that Isaac Rubinowitz, the barrister who defended the Russians whose deportation was ordered, extracted a few of $3,000 from No. 213 for representing it in court. It was this that crippled the union.

At the Vancouver Labour Church meeting on Sunday 17th October, the subject was prohibition. J. S. Woodsworth and Miss Chesney were the speakers; both advocated prohibition from the revolutionary standpoint. Miss Chesney saying that the Capitalists were trying to give liquor back to the people to keep their minds muddled.

The audience was not large, and was divided; several persons objected to what the speakers said, the meeting became a debate, and the audience seemed rather to incline to the opposition.

J. S. Woodsworth spoke on 24th October, at the Vancouver Labour Church on the "Passing of the Old Religions". The attendance was only about 100, but those present paid close attention to the speaker.

The quarterly report of the Ukrainian Labour Temple at Vancouver shows that branch has 35 members; it met on 11 occasions during the quarter. It spent on reading matter nearly $100 and had on hand a little over $20.

T. O'Connor was the speaker at a Socialist meeting in Vancouver on Sunday 24th October. He ridiculed the recent referendum on Prohibition, and is quoted as saying:-

> "We Socialists don't believe in Moderation, Prohibition, or even elections of any kind. We have no time for little things like these; we believe in production for use and doing away with the Capitalist and Master-class. You will be no better off for votes, elections or anything in that line; you are slaves and always will be until you understand your social standing in this world".

O'Connor predicted a hard winter with parades of the unemployed.[8]

II. ALBERTA

9. O.B.U. Weaker in the South

An estimate of the strength of the O.B.U. in Southern Alberta and South Eastern British Columbia as on 30th September shows a weakening. The figures given are:-

Sub-district	O.B.U. or Friendly	Hostile or Indifferent
Calgary	1,461	4,292
Lethbridge	916	254
Medicine Hat	-	915
Taber	295	-
East Kootenay	3,925	1,335
Macleod	1,056	1,056
Banff	455	260
	8,108	8,112

The estimate of the O.B.U. for 30th June placed their numbers at 10,116, so that there has been a decline of 2,000.

Any estimate is difficult because of the enforced membership in the U. M. W. of A. and accompanying preference for the O.B.U. Two of the remarks of the Officer Commanding District merit attention:-

> "If a good all-Canadian organization could be started, exclusion of radical agitators, it would, in my opinion meet with general favour from all the different branches of labour in the country".
>
> "The O.B.U. shows every sign of weakening in this District, and I believe would have remained on strike for an indefinite period, but for the fear they could not continue to pay the men 'strike pay'. The indications are that the organization is in a bad way from a financial point of view, and a good many members are not paying their dues regularly."

10. Echoes from Drumheller

Investigation shows that it is quite possible to produce evidence to convict Arthur Evans, the new O.B.U. District Secretary in the Alberta Coalfields, of circulating false information in circulars which he sent out to stir up the recent strikes.

On 24th October Arthur Evans and George Palmer addressed an O.B.U. meeting in Drumheller. There was some dispute about the hall, which was occupied forcibly against the protest of the trustees. At Evans' instigation it was resolved to strike again on 1st November if the men who had been discriminated against were not reinstated. This was regarded as little more than a method of beating a retreat; the strike has not materialized.

A feature of Evans' address was his assertion that the half hearted manner in which the strike at Fernie was prosecuted was due to the posting of telegrams stating that Drumheller had not gone out. He attributed to others his own policy.[9]

P. F. Lawson on Sunday 17th October spoke in Calgary. He declared that he coal strike in reality had been a victory for the O.B.U., because it had shown their strength, and had proved that the mine operators were afraid of them. "If the people thought the trouble was over they were badly mistaken, as it had only just started".

He spoke of Nova Scotia, saying that J. B. McLachlan was wholly in sympathy with the O.B.U., and prophesying that he shortly would be arrested.

Up to 21st October McLachlan had not replied to Lawson's appeal (mentioned last week).

Evans called a meeting of the O.B.U. board on 25th October, the object being to discuss the possibility of financing the Searchlight, by means of a rather fantastic plan. This was that the miners should join the U. M. W. of A., and pay the check-off; under this each member is assessed $1.50 a month, and of this sum 45 cents is retained by the local; O.B.U. sympathizers would be elected officers of these U. M. W. of A. locals, and should use 10 cents per member per month of these local resources to keep the Searchlight going.

The indications are that the leaders of the O.B.U. in the coalfields are breaking into three parts; the factions are:- (1) Christophers and Beard; (2) Palmer, Lawson and Evans; (3) Clarke of Coalhurst, Sherman of Fernie and the delegates from the north.

P. M. Christophers has been boasting that he and the other O.B.U. agitators have defied the injunction served on them by continuing the speak in the coalfields. The facts of the case are that the plaintiffs who served the injunction are the operators of the Red Deer Valley Coal Association, and that the injunction only covers the mining camps in the Red Deer Valley, otherwise Drumheller and Wayne; thus Christophers and others affected are at liberty to address meetings in any other district. Since the injunction Christophers has not spoken in the Drumheller area, and the other defendants have modified their activities.

Evans recently visited the northern coal-mining camps; collecting for the O.B.U. He obtained about $300; but in conversation he explained that out of this was to come his salary of $200, and his expenses; so that the O.B.U. treasury would not be greatly fattened. Evans and Palmer now are competing for a post as travelling organizer, and Lawson's support of Palmer in this matter has caused friction between Lawson and Evans. In short, there is a fair amount of dissension among the local leaders of the O.B.U.

11. Elsewhere in the Coalfields

A report from Blairmore dated 16th October describes conditions as satisfactory. It says:-

"Several local meetings were called by the O.B.U. during the week, with a view to discussing the possibility of going out on strike, these meetings were very poorly attended, and which later resulted in the agitators being discharged and most of them leaving the [10] district to seek work elsewhere; this was brought about by loyal workers of the U. M. W. of A. in the Blairmore and Coleman localities, and which I am informed on reliable authority, has broken the dangers of any strike of the miners in this locality during the present fall and winter.

"I have also been informed on reliable authority, that, owing to the complete break-down of the O.B.U. in this district, P. M. Christophers O.B.U. organizer, and R. McDonald O.B.U. Secretary, have severed their connections with the O.B.U. and that today, Christophers was seeking work at Coleman."

A report from Blairmore dated 23rd October states that the position there seem satisfactory, that there is no talk of striking, and that both P. M. Christophers and R. McDonald, formerly One Big Union organizer and secretary respectively, are engaged in construction work on new buildings and apparently are doing no agitation.

The Fernie strike was officially called off on 18th October, and work was fully resumed on the 21st. The men gave the company and the U. M. W. of A. ten days, expiring on 31st October to adjust the matter of the discrimination against William Sherman and the other trouble-makers; however, there was little likelihood of a further stoppage of work, and any trouble which might occur was regarded as likely to be but temporary.

At Michel the men returned to work on 20th and 21st October. As in Fernie certain agitators were refused employment, and the men gave the company ten days to adjust the matter. The Officer Commanding Fernie, says:-

"From the present indications I do not think that there will be any stoppage of work as the rank and file of the miners are only too satisfied to be back once more at work".

The last strike at Coalhurst near Lethbridge came to an end on 26th October. Seven agitators were dismissed, and are believed to have left the vicinity.

12. The O.B.U. Depressed

At an O.B.U. meeting at Calgary held on 15th October, H. Davis of Winnipeg spoke on an organization tour he has made. Saskatoon, he said, was at a standstill; Drumheller had been more satisfactory than he had expected, and on his return trip he would enrol the majority of the switchmen; Lethbridge and Coalhurst were "doing time". He urged them to keep the Searchlight alive.

The N.C.O. in charge of C.I.B. work for the District in commenting on this observes that his information concerning the switchmen in the Drumheller region is, first, that the O.B.U. were unsuccessful in their efforts to enlist them; and secondly, that the C. N. R. officials would welcome any joining of the union by these men,[11] "as it would give them an opportunity they desire of discharging them and have a new crew shipped in".

Concerning Ald. Broatch, who was a delegate at Port Arthur, he reports:-

> "A. Broatch appears to be very pessimistic about the success of the O.B.U. with the result that he is in disfavour with the O.B.U. members and the impression is that Broatch is trying to gracefully retire from the organization".

13. Miscellaneous Notes

The Samo Obranowicz Society in Edmonton recently put on a revolutionary play in the Ukrainian Greek Catholic Hall named Batraky (Transient Workers). As usual John Klybonsky played the leading part.

Ukrainian miners at Coalhurst on 26th September organized a local of the Ukrainian Labour Temple some 25 members signing on the first night. It was noticeable that 18 of these were unable to pay the full amount of the membership fee.

A Jewish couple named Pullan have opened a general store in Manville, Alberta. This already has become a meeting place for the foreigners of the vicinity, and a centre of infection for revolutionary agitation. Mrs. Pullan is a sister of Popowich's wife.

John Boychuk, the Ukrainian agitator, who recently left Vancouver, now is living in Vegreville. He continues to agitate, and in particular is busy with the collection for medical aid to Soviet Russia.

14. The Labour Church

The Edmonton Labour Church on Sunday, 24th October, was addressed by H. H. Hall, secretary of the Socialist Service League, upon Prohibition. No other subject was discussed.

R. E. Bray spoke at the Edmonton Labour Church on Sunday evening 17th October. His address was of the usual sort, but the proceedings were varied by an odd row. He was describing the jury in the Winnipeg trial, and said that there were on it sons of Presbyterian ministers, sons of Methodist ministers, sons of lawyers and such people, and Jews. Forthwith there was an uproar, a number of Jews present interrupting and forcing him to quality his statement. It broke up the meeting. The audience was 300, and the interest and collection both were small.

It is to be observed that the report from which this is abridged cannot be wholly accurate, for Bray's remarks could hardly be made about the Jury. They might apply to the counsel for the prosecution, one of them being the son of a Methodist minister, and one a Jew.

III. SASKATCHEWAN

15. Miscellaneous Notes

Information has been received that the Paris Hotel in Regina [12] is the headquarters of the local O.B.U. Austin Stanley, who now is, organizing in that district, stays there and uses this hotel as his office. The hotel-keeper, one McCarthy, is the president of the local Sinn Fein organization.

The Honourable W. L. MacKenzie King was invited to address the Regina People's Forum on Sunday evening, 24th October. He was unable to be present, and George Broadley delivered a socialist address.

The O.B.U. in Regina are supplying a news stand with O.B.U. reading matter free, so that any sales will be clear gain to the proprietor.

IV. MANITOBA

16. The O.B.U. on the English

An O.B.U. meeting was held in Winnipeg on Sunday, 24th October, at which defeat in the Drumheller strike at last was admitted. The speakers were H. Davis and F. Woodward, who had returned from a visit to the scene of the strike. Our report says:-

> "The speakers admitted defeat in the mining District, and placed the responsibility at the door of the state, the mine owners and the International unions, U. M. W. of A. They claim that 99 per cent of the workers do not belong to the International movement, but he (sic) also said that all of the 99 per cent did not belong to the O.B.U. either. Woodward said the 'check-off' was responsible for much of the trouble in the mines".

An interesting passage is thus reported:-

> "'The British workers' said Woodward, 'were the most despicable of men'. They created racial prejudices in Drumheller the same as they did at Bienfait, and they were not worthy to be called union men. They enjoyed the distinction of being born under the British flag (laughter-sneers) but to him it did not make any difference where a man was born, so long as he was a worker and class conscious".

Woodward also said that the strike in the Drumheller Valley was the worst organized and conducted of any he had any knowledge of; that had had something to do with their defeat.

David also attacked the English:-

> "At a certain camp, he stated, there was a bunch of dirty Englishmen in control, who were voting on going back to work. The foreign speaking people were strictly against this, and made several protests against the others going back to work, but as usual the Englishman got his way, and the foreigners who were married got orders to be at work in the morning or more out of their houses".[13]

The attendance was about 500. Both speakers complained bitterly of the small attendance and lack of interest.

17. The Western Labour News and the O.B.U.

The Western Labour News in its issue of 22nd October quotes the utterances of the B.C. Federationist on the quarrel among the O.B.U. and draws the following conclusions:

"One of these is that nine-tenths of the propaganda oratory and literature used to advance the O.B.U. in Winnipeg is either dishonest or ignorant of its true basis and purpose.

"Another is that the O.B.U. is mainly dependent upon the Lumber Workers, Miners and Railroad shopmen where industrial unionism is a fact. The O.B.U. is not an absorbent of these industrial unions, it is a parasite living on them, devouring their vitals and paralysing their energies either to benefit their own members or the labour cause in general".

The same issue contains Mr. Tom Moore's denunciation of the Bolshevist attack on International and craft unionism.

The Press Committee of the Trades and Labour Council of Winnipeg met on 26th October to outline a policy for the Western Labour News. The decision was that it is to adopt an aggressive attitude towards the O.B.U.

18. G. B. Currie

G. B. Currie addressed a mass labour meeting in Winnipeg on 22nd October, his speech being of a very revolutionary nature; it dealt largely with conditions in England and Scotland, with which he declared himself familiar.

Currie apparently is organizing the Agricultural and Lumber Workers' Unit, O.B.U. in Winnipeg.

The attendance was 200; the meeting was under the auspices of the Young Labour League.

Currie is a Scotchman by birth, about 26 years of age. He has been in Canada only about 4 months; he has mentioned having been in the United States and having been warned away. He may have been in the British Army. He is an exceptionally good speaker and agitator.

19. Labour Dissensions

The Dominion Labour Party of Winnipeg held a meeting on 27th October. The attendance was the largest in its history amounting to 400. Despite the presence of a strong delegation from the Street Railway Unit, O.B.U., the Internationals were in the majority and controlled the meeting.

The proceedings developed the fact that the extremist element intend to run "Class Conscious" candidates in the approaching municipal elections. This is almost certain to cause a split in the labour ranks, and may result in the labour candidates being defeated in the approaching municipal elections.[14]

A recent move in the war in Winnipeg between the Internationals and the O.B.U. was the refusal by the trustees of the Trades Hall to allow its use by the O.B.U. Unit of the Street Railway. Much ill-feeling resulted.

Wm. D. Bailey, M.L.A. recently elected to the Manitoba Legislature in the Labour interest, has come out definitely as an advocate of the O.B.U.

W. H. Hoop has been engaged as organizer by the International Association of Stationary Engineers, Oilers etc. for the Winnipeg district.

20. The Labour Churches

A report upon the Winnipeg Labour Church describes it as practically at a standstill. The different branches meet regularly every Sunday evening, and are addressed by more or less prominent speakers, but the attendance has greatly fallen off. The nominal membership continues to increase, as new members join from time to time, but many give nothing except their initial dues; thus the list continues to grow while the active members are decreasing in numbers.

Mr. Willcocks, who now is described as President, remarked in conversation that very few members have been secured for the last six months and added, "Were it not for the energetic work of the women the Church would be going down hill fast". The present nominal membership is about 2,800.

The branch in Transcona has practically come to an end, and the Weston branch is falling behind.

A feature of the situation is that the increase of socialist opinion tells against the Church; the O.B.U. are antagonistic to all churches and take little interest in the Labour Church.

The report ends with the following remark:-

"The Labour Church is making practically no progress in Winnipeg. It is badly in need of finances, and has practically no hold on the general run of radical workers".

Since A. E. Smith, M.L.A., was elected to the Provincial Legislature his radical activities have ceased, and the services in the New People's Church have been of a more moderate nature. A report on its meetings on 10th, 17th and 22nd October shows that the Prohibition referendum was discussed at all these meetings; Mr. Smith spoke at the two first and a Mr. Olson of Brandon College addressed the last one. At none of these meetings was there revolutionary talk.

21. Foreign Revolutionists

Sava Zura, who was sentenced to imprisonment for having prohibited reading matter in his possession, has been released on parole from the penitentiary and has returned to Fort William. He has promptly resumed his revolutionary agitation.[15]

Sava Zura believes that another foreign-born agitator, Luka Ilschuk, caused his imprisonment by informing on him. Ilschuk has moved to Toronto and the Russian Community thinks that he did so out of fear of Zura.

Information has been received that Popowich, who for some years was manager of the Ukrainian Labour Temple in Winnipeg, now is the secretary of the Winnipeg local of the O.B.U., this is a more highly paid position. Popowich is anxious to go to Russia as soon as he can, being under the impression that he will be rewarded for his services to Bolshevism in Canada by a high position there.

A curious incident has occurred in Winnipeg. Stephan G. Stephansson, an elderly farmer living at Markerville, Alberta, has published a book of poems, apparently in Icelandic; the work is on sale at Icelandic bookstores in Winnipeg. Mr. Thomas Johnson, Attorney General for the Province of Manitoba, has taken the ground that the poems are seditious and that the book should be suppressed and the sale forbidden.

V. ONTARIO

22. The Situation in Toronto

A survey of the general field of agitation in Toronto shows the following elements:-

(a) The Plebs League. This is making slow progress. Its principal members also belong to the Ontario Labour College, as already noted, it subscribes fully to the Third International, and has affiliated with the Plebs league of England; it stands prepared to take orders from Moscow. It is a centre of distribution of radical literature in Toronto, receiving it from England, and from I.W.W. sources in the United States. It supplies the O.B.U. with their surplus reading matter. The leaders are Moris Spector; Bell; Armstrong; Swift; Conny; Marks; and Mrs. F. Custance. Their activities are:- (1) Agitation at public meetings; (2) Distribution of revolutionary reading matter; (3) Educational methods.

(b) The Jewish Socialist League. This also has made slow progress, the revolutionary Jews being divided as to their attitude; some are ready to avow their revolutionary tendencies, and others are afraid. There are about 5,000 Jewish workers in various unions in Toronto, but very few of them are willing to join this associations. The league numbers only about 50 at present. Its financial sources are meagre, and its propaganda has been hampered by the difficulty of obtaining English speakers for its street meetings; speeches in foreign languages are now allowed on the streets. The leaders are:- Almazoff; Shapiro; Edelman; Sosnovich; Temkin; Brown; Miller; Stroham; Weiss; and Dianoff.

(c) The O.B.U. Progress is still very slow. The extent to which it is falling under foreign influence is shown by the fact that it proposes to hold a celebration on 7th November of the Third Anniversary of the beginning of Bolshevik rule in Russia. The weekly business meetings are attended by about 7 to 10 members; the street meetings on Saturday and Sunday, however, usually draw considerable crowds. They also distribute [16] some reading matter. They suffer from an insufficient number of speakers. The local leaders are:- J. R. Knight and Mrs. Knight and one McKnight, whose sobriquet is "Scotty". Their financial condition is described as being "complete broke", the membership is stationary, some of the members are in arrear with their dues and the organization depends upon the collections at street meetings to pay its bills. An interesting point is that the O.B.U. had 14 Bulgarian members but that these have seceded and joined the Plebs League.

(d) The Ukrainian Bolshevik Society. This also is weak; it has about 500 members, but their activities seem confined to attending street meetings. However, the organization has a considerable amount of revolutionary reading matter which comes from Austria and the United States; this is sold at the Ukrainian bookstore in York Street. Its principal members are:- Stefanitski; Boichuk; Samchuk; and Korchuk. These men apparently visit towns in the vicinity of Toronto.

(e) The Russian Workers' School. This also has made slower progress than was hoped for by its founders. It has only 35 members. Its school course is purely educational, but the lectures on Sunday usually are revolutionary propaganda. However, dissensions exists in this, as the anarchist element led by Dodokin has come into conflict with the Bolshevist advocates led by Almazoff. This is the one place in Toronto where anarchist reading matter is sold.

(f) Spujnia. The Polish National Society. This seems not to be so radical.

While these various radical agitators have failed to gain a great amount of support, it is remarked that a certain desire to see revolution in Canada can be observed among the working people.

23. The O.B.U. in the Lumber Camps

An investigation has been made of the lumber camps worked from Thessalon and Deal Lake, on the Soo line of the C. P. R. There are 13 camps, from 30 to 70 miles north of Dean Lake, and 1,275 men are employed. Two O.B.U. agitators, Brunette and Rainville, have been working in these for some time, with the result that the unrest has been considerable. One of the three companies concerned has a labour turnover of 100 per cent a month; three-fifths of the men are French-Canadians, and as the new men come from the Province of Quebec each man costs the company $30 before he begins work. The company's complain that the O.B.U. will not come to them and state what is wrong, but stir the men up to discontent. It is to be noted that living conditions have been considerably improved of late.

24. Conditions in the Niagara District

A report on general conditions at Welland dated 26th October brings out the close connection between labour agitation in Canada and Great Britain. The point of the report is the effect of the growing unemployment on the minds of the men; they are being sedulously informed [17] that it is merely "a move upon the part of the Capitalist class to crush the workers and make them migrate to other centres where labour is not so plentiful" such as the mines and lumber camps. Winding, who is, operating in that district hopes that conditions during the winter would "help the workers to wake up" and was hoping that a successful strike in England of the

Triple Alliance "would have a tremendous effect on work throughout the world".

25. O.B.U. Affairs

Mrs. J. R. Knight on 25th October spoke in Occident Hall, Toronto on "Brotherhood". Her speech was bitterly anti-religious, and was an attack on brotherly love.

> "Churches and brotherhoods have preached brotherly love for ages, but such love is meant only amongst the slaves; they must love each other, but foremost the imaginary God. This God was the means to drive great fears into minds of the slaves and by such means were the slaves kept in subjugation. The slaves were bound to fight for their masters and for interests of masters, and the slaves were taught to believe that if they do not obey they are bound to find themselves in hell at last".

The O.B.U. in Toronto have arranged to hold weekly propaganda meetings in the Empress Theatre on Yonge Street. The pamphlets to be circulated are "Lenin" by Zenovieff with the O.B.U. preamble on the cover. One Rosenthal is helping with the printing.

The O.B.U. in Toronto seems confined to the foreign element.

Tom Cassidy, the O.B.U. agitator, has reappeared in Windsor and the neighbouring towns.

The O.B.U. there are in a poor way. A meeting which Cassidy called on 21st October was attended by only four or five persons. The local lodge has no regular meeting place. The local press apparently refuses to print O.B.U. announcements; this action was attributed by an O.B.U. sympathizer in the course of conversation to the influence fo the Trades and Labour Council not to "the Capitalists".

A note on Harry Roberts, the Hamilton agitator, who is so frequently mentioned in these summaries, states that he is an Englishman of about 48 or 49 years of age, who spent his earlier life in London and came to this continent about 15 years ago. He worked in various parts of the United States, in the coal mines of Sydney, N.S. and in the mines at Cobalt and Black Lake, Quebec. He has been settled in Hamilton for some time. He is a bricklayer and has been active in union matters; he was practically the first man to join the O.B.U. when it was started in Hamilton, and is its most vigorous member.

26. The Hamilton Extremists

Arrangements are under way whereby the Ontario Labour College in Toronto will help to establish a Labour Hamilton. Mrs. Custance, [18] Bell and Armstrong will take turns to go to Hamilton to teach. In Hamilton an attempt is to be made to interact the Amalgamated Clothing Workers.

An attempt is to be made to bring Scott Nearing to Toronto to deliver a series of lectures.

The Hamilton revolutionists have had a spurt of activity in circulating reading matter. One pamphlet which they are putting about is L.C.A.K. Marton's reply to the pamphlet issued by the Department of Labour.

27. Friction among Foreign Revolutionists

The increasing friction amongst the several factions of foreign revolutionists is illustrated by an incident which occurred on Sunday, 24th October at Welland. A meeting there, attended by about 200 persons mostly Russians from Thorold, St. Catharines and Port Colborne, was addressed in English by Almazoff. It is remarked that:-

> "His speech was delivered in such eloquent English that it was understood by only a few, and many left the hall before it was over".

When he had finished the lecture, a dispute took place between the Russian Communist-Anarchists under the leadership of one Medinsky of Welland, and the Ukrainians; Almazoff was asked questions as to the nature of democracy of Soviet Russia, where anarchists were arrested and shot. Almazoff apparently was disinclined to engage in a dispute. The Ukrainians resented the action of the Anarchists in heckling the speaker, and there was a quarrel over the use of the hall, the Anarchists complaining that it had been built by all the workers and should be used by all the workers; apparently the Ukrainians turned the Anarchists out.

Confirming the foregoing in some respects is another report concerning revolutionary activities at Welland. The heads of it are as follows:-

1. Two parties have developed; a strong Ukrainian Communist or Bolshevist Party, and a Russian Communist-Anarchist Party. These have continual disputes.
2. The Ukrainian Communists receive at irregular intervals a secret revolutionary paper; which is printed in the United States. It apparently is issued fitfully.
3. An Ukrainian agitator who recently visited Welland, and St. Catharines is one Dymtryshyn, alias A. D. Jaholnecki and A. D. Hobeolenko. His present whereabouts are unknown to the Welland revolutionists.
4. The Communists of Toronto, Hamilton and Welland are said to have collected over $8,000. This is to be expended in printing a book in Vienna; the edition is to consist of 10,000 copies, of which 3,000 are to be distributed in Canada and 7,000 in Galicia and Bukowinia.[19]

28. The Foreign Extremists

The Jewish Socialist League of Toronto held a special meeting on 22nd October. The following business was transacted:-

1. They refused to collect for the James Simpson Defence Fund.
2. Asked to collect for medical aid for Soviet Russia, they decided to ask Martens of New York for further information. A rumour is abroad that the money collected in Toronto has not all reached the relief fund.

3. They discussed, and apparently agreed upon, a proposal by Essor to create a new party to be termed "The International Socialist Party of Canada". This name, is was expressly stated, is but camouflage; what they would like to call it is the Communist Party, but they are afraid to do so. Essor said that if they were "on the doorsteps of a revolution" they would not mind calling themselves Communists", but the revolution is far off in Canada yet. We cannot risk being arrested".

Word has come from the Niagara district that some time ago a man named Ladan (or Ladau), former leader of the Ukrainian Socialists in the United States and editor of the Robitnyk of New York, went to Europe under orders from the Soviet Government by way of Canada; he stayed over one night in Welland. He stated that he had received a letter from Lenin directing Ukrainian and Russian radicals not to try to return to Russia but to stir up trouble in the United States and Canada. He also stated that the Ukrainian Daily News of New York received some financial support from the Soviet Government.

The date of the foregoing information is uncertain.

A Jewish agitator in Toronto named Samson Koldofsky has been attracting attention. About two months ago he left for Europe with Henry Dworkin. he is the head of the Jewish Garment Makers' Union, and also one of the leaders of the Bolshevik movement in the city. He was the principal agitator in the strike of Garment Makers about a year ago in Toronto.

He collaborated with Dworkin in the suspicious meetings which followed Dworkin's first visit to Poland. The better class of Jews dislike him as a dangerous agitator.

A foreign-born agitator named Michniewicz of Hamilton has undertaken to collect for the fund for medical aid to Soviet Russia. he has been authorized to do so by a letter from a man named Povalski of Winnipeg.

VI. QUEBEC

29. Miscellaneous Notes

The Society for Technical Aid to Soviet Russia is planning a celebration in Montreal on 7th November of the 3rd Anniversary of the establishment of Soviet Government in Russia. A project is under way for a street parade of a symbolic nature, and public meetings will be held. Apart from that, there is to be present a man named Jacob Hartmann of New York, who is described as the right hand of L.C.A.K. Martens, and as the editor of Soviet Russia. He is to explain matters concerning the collection of Soviet funds now in progress throughout the United States and Canada. He is to be tendered a banquet, at which he may make an important statement. [20]

This society is co-operating with the extremists in toronto in the matter of circulating revolutionary reading matter.

A survey of the situation at Sherbrooke describes the conditions there as satisfactory; there is steady work for all the population, and no labour discontent is known to exist. Most of the few foreigners in town are Jews. However, at Coleraine, Thetford, and Black Lake, where asbestos is mined, a considerable number of foreigners are employed, mostly Russians, and there is always more of less trouble there.

VII. THE MARITIME PROVINCES

30. The Miners

A report from Springhill, N.S.; puts the number of men employed in the vicinity at 1,500. All are members of the U. M. W. of A., but the report says:-

> "The miners in this district are of a very susceptible and unsteady type. They usually drift from one extreme to the other. There have been twelve strikes in the last fifteen years, and one of them lasted two years.
>
> "At times there are strong O.B.U. sentiments among some of them. They were unsatisfied with the old P.W.A. and gave it up to join the U. M. W. of A. Now there is a certain amount of dissatisfaction in their ranks, and hot O.B.U. discussions are a common occurrence in their locals.
>
> "There is a strong feeling at the present time for a strike in order to have their demands granted."

A report from Inverness dated 24th October says:-

> "The men are beginning to lose faith in their leaders, and they have bitterly attacked Mr. J. J. McNeil of Inverness".

A man named L. E. Graham, described as representing the Boston Bible Tract Society, spoke at Inverness on Sunday 24th October, in a strongly socialistic vein.

ROYAL CANADIAN MOUNTED POLICE HEADQUARTERS

Ottawa, 11th November, 1920.

SECRET

NO. 49

NOTES OF THE WORK OF THE C.I.B. DIVISION FOR THE WEEK ENDING 11TH NOVEMBER

Table of Contents

Beattie, Cartwright and Jordan join Sinn Fein.
Dandineau
E. Robinson.
" 14. ALBERTA: Conditions in Drumheller
Agitators Blacklisted.
Temper of the men.
Threat of a renewal of the Strike.
Nationalities at Drumheller.
Legality of the Injunction.
" 15. Other Collieries.
Fernie
Brazeau.[2]
" 16. Miscellaneous Notes.
Bray at Edmonton.
G. B. Williams, International Bible Students
Edmonton Labour Church.
" 17. The Searchlight
" 18. SASKATCHEWAN: Miscellaneous Notes.
O.B.U. at Saskatoon.
O.B.U. at Moosejaw
Bray under suspicion.
Mrs. D. Carter
Conditions in Regina.
" 19. MANITOBA: The Ukrainian Labour Temple.
Differing Stories as to Finances.
Educational Activities.
" 20. Miscellaneous Notes.
The Young Labour League.
John Houston
Crittendon
Kohn.
The Municipal Elections.
A. E. Smith, M.L.A.
" 21. ONTARIO: The situation in Western Ontario.
O.C's Monthly report
Strikes on Algoma Central Railway.
Survey of the O.B.U.
Survey of other revolutionary agencies.
" 22. The O.B.U. in the Sudbury Region.
Cowan and the Soo Finns.
E. Guertin
D. Rainville.
Patrol on the Algoma Central
Strike at Neimi's Camp.

General Characteristics of the Period

Slack water still prevails; the revolutionary unions, associations etc. are in a depressed condition, and unemployment, while feared by labour men, has not become serious, and is not causing noticeable discontent. Cases are occurring of acceptance by employes virtually without complaint of reductions in wages. In particular, the One Big Union is so weakened by successive defeats and internal quarrels; and the Communist groups are so small in numbers: that any danger which may threaten during the approaching winter will come from genuine unrest caused by lack of work, and not from effective agitation by extremists. Should distress become general, the extremists of course will exploit it eagerly; but their organization for conducting such exploitation is at a lower point than has been the case since the ending of hostilities. They also are short of money perhaps more so than for a couple of years.

In this week the principal development is the obtaining of further information about the break in the One Big Union. We now have sufficiently full information as to the quarrels: the matters of interest now are the extent to which Winch can retain his hold upon the Lumber Workers;

the outcome of his fight with Midgley; and the result of the Midgley referendum, with its proposal to move the One Big Union headquarters to Winnipeg.

In Eastern Canada revolutionary agitation seems more than ever to be withdrawing into the ranks of the foreign language workmen; and schism is growing among them, the Anarchists proper resenting the opportunism of the Moscow Government, which is upheld by the Communists.

I. The Quarrel in the O.B.U.

2. Midgley's Official Report

The official report of the O.B.U. convention at Port Arthur now is available. Much of it is occupied with the quarrel with the [4] Lumber Workers, the facts of which already are well known. Some of the other passages contain fresh information.

The report of the General Executive Board gave particulars of the work done in the United States. J. R. Knight paid visits to "some independent unions in New York City", which had invited him to do so, and "assisted in giving them information with regard to our movement, and also assisted in gathering together a number of independent and unattended labour organizations". T. S. Cassidy was kept in Chicago from April to 14th August, "when lack of funds compelled the Board to discontinue their assistance".

Up to April last O.B.U. Units had been established in the following places in the United States:-

Chicago	Los Angeles
Milwaukee	San Francisco
Neihart	Oakland
Toledo	Seattle
Butte	

In January the Executive Board asked the O.B.U. local in the United States to appoint a member to represent the United States on the General Executive Board. this soon proved impracticable, and at a convention held in Chicago in April a General Executive Board was elected for the United States, and all of the membership south of the International boundary was turned over to it. "This Board is working in harmony with the Canadian G. E. B., and are issuing supplies similar to those issued by this Board".

Reference is made to the Alberta Coal Strike; the units there were excused payment of their per capita tax for April and the succeeding months.

3. Membership Figure

Midgley's official figures as to membership are, in brief, that during 1919 the number of cards issued was 41,394 and that in 1920 from 1st January to 31st August 30,212 more were issued making a total [5] of 71,606; the highest number being 6,950 in January; after March, when 5,630 were issued, there was a steady decline to 2,375 in August. The report goes on to say:-

"Unfortunately the financial statement does not reflect in the per capita receipts the actual membership. The detailed figures according to the per capita paid show that the average membership for the five months from January to May was 19,510, which compared with the seventy one thousand memberships that have been issued, indicates that per capita has been paid to the Board on only a portion of the membership. Some districts have failed to pay on even a portion of their membership for several months, and if the average was taken for the eight months the comparison would be more surprising".

Midgley made the following proposal:-

"That the local units pay their per capital direct to the General Executive Board, instead of through the central labour councils and district boards. It will be noticed that nearly all of the isolated units are paid up to date. The reason that the Board has not received the revenue due is not through the failure of the local units to pay but it is because the Central councils and boards have in several cases used the funds for their own purposes instead of paying their obligations to the G. E. B."

This was approved.

4. The Financial Statement

The financial statement shows a budget of not quite $13,000; the receipts were $12,929,34, almost wholly from per capita tax ($12,803.73). The expenditure was $12,803.04, the principal items being $3,326 for the head office and $9,379 for organization expenses. The balance was $126.50.

The detailed report of the per capita tax receipts shows that the number paying in January was nearly 28,000; that in the four ensuing months it stood at from 18,000 to 20,000; and that in June it dropped abruptly to fewer than 7,800, and in July to fewer than 5,800, rising in August to 6,200. The drop is due largely to the disappearance in June and the following months of the Lumber Workers. Omitting them from the whole statement, the numbers in the first quarters never were fewer than 10,000 or as many as 12,000, and during April and May were 3,200 and 8,800.

In short, 1920 has been a steady decline in payments.[6]

Midgley has issued a circular appealing for funds. The General Executive Board is issuing an organization fund stamp which will be sold to members at 25 cents each and attached to their membership cards.

5. O.B.U. Headquarters in Difficulties

Under date of 23rd October Midgley wrote from Vancouver to Arthur Evans, the O.B.U. District Secretary in the Alberta Coalfields, apparently in response to a request for further credit for supplies. The letter was a refusal, Midgley stating that the uproar provoked at Edmonton by Carl

Berg "had naturally hit our credit with the local bourgeoisie, and the people who manufacture our supplies are not giving us further credit". Midgley stated that his headquarters owe the bookbinder who makes the cases for O.B.U. cards $1,700; and the bookbinder insists on a payment before he will provide any more. He also reminded Evans that in addition to the Alberta district owing headquarters some $300, a number of locals also are in debt to the General Executive Board for supplies. He added:-

> "The failure of the lumber workers to contribute to the support of the G. E. B. for the last five months has been the main cause of our financial difficulties.
>
> "The Lumber workers who have been the most prosperous section of the organization, and the section that has derived the most from the O.B.U. propaganda should have, by paying their little ten cents per capita, enabled the G. E. B. to have extended your district greater support during the fight that has been forced upon you.
>
> "However, it was perhaps necessary that this question should be settled, and the matter is now before the membership to settle. The O.B.U. constitution gives the members control of their own organization, and they must learn to discipline themselves, all the officials should do is to faithfully perform the wishes of the membership. At least that is what I am endeavouring to do although the difficulties are at times very disheartening".

Another remark by Midgley is as follows:-

> "As I informed you yesterday it is as much as we can do to keep Christophers going, and I think it is the desire of the Board to keep him going as long as we can meet his bills".[7]

In connection with the remarks about Christophers, it will be recalled that a few days later he obtained work in the Crow's Nest Pass; so that it would appear that the stringency at headquarters continues.

6. Squabbles at Edmonton

The internal fight in the O.B.U. was active in Edmonton during October. Davis and Bray, the Winnipeg delegation, touring the Prairies, sided with the Midgley faction against Carl Berg; a meeting of representatives of the Building Trades Unit and Transportation Workers was held on 18th October to devise means of combatting Borg's fight to control the Edmonton Transportation workers. It was decided to call in the help of J. R. Knight. Arrangements were made to prevent Berg diverting money from the Midgley office to the L.W.I.U.

The quarrel in Edmonton has had a curious result. One of the Midgley faction sent a letter to the B.C. Federationist describing the meeting at which Berg made public the facts of the dispute; this report incidentally contained unfavourable references to Mayor J. A. Clark. Mayor Clark addressed a heated reply to the Federationist. The editor sent a copy of the letter to the Edmonton O.B.U., and it was considered at a meeting of the O.B.U. on 27th October; a somewhat shuffling rejoinder was despatched to the B.C. Federationist and it was decided to draft a further letter to the press attacking the Mayor on the grounds that he on the surface favoured labour but worked against it underground.

The O.B.U. officials who engineering the coal strike in Alberta are carrying their personal quarrels before the public. The following is an extract from a report of an O.B.U. meeting at Edmonton on 27th October. The Evans concerned is Arthur Evans, who succeeded Edward Brown as District Chairman, and so mismanaged the strike:-

> "On Evans gaining the platform he proceeded to give an account of the recent miners' strike and said the strike could have been won if [8] it were not for the tactics of P. M. Christophers, Beard, Clarke, and a few more of the O.B.U. men who were afraid to use force to gain the demands of the miners. He stated that questions in dispute that were asked Christophers and Beard were answered by them that it was a question for the rank and file. He (Evans) claimed that they should have stayed in the parts where the miners would not come out, that it was nothing to do with the rank and file, but that it was for the officials of the O.B.U. to force their membership out and keep them out. He then attacked the building Trades Unit for breaking away from Berg and going off by themselves, so as to cause dissension among the rest and damage the industrial movement. He was an I.W.W. and always would be one, and the O.B.U. ought to be a movement on the same lines. It was only a few reactionaries like Joe Knight, Midgley and a few others that were opposed to the I.W.W. idea that were causing good men like Berg trouble, and splitting the movement. He got mad and tore into the Building Trades Unit for coming into the meeting and tearing a good 'Wobbly' like Berg to pieces, instead of inviting Berg to come up and discuss it with them in a friendly spirit. He stated that he was going up to Coalspur and tell the miners up there what was what, and that we would hear from him in the near future. Bros. Coombs then replied and told him what this unit knew about Berg, and then things got interesting; such phrases as "you're a God damned liar" etc., being common. It was developing fast, and only finished on account of Evans having to catch the train for the West".

On Sunday 31st October J. R. Knight addressed the O.B.U. in Edmonton, his speech being principally devoted to combatting the influence of Berg, and the cause of the Lumber Workers in the split with the O.B.U.

It is remarked that Knight's speech was much milder than his earlier utterances in Edmonton.

7. The Lumber Workers' Referendum

The referendum which the L.W.I.U. are circulating asks three questions:-

1. Do the members approve the action of their representatives at Port Arthur?
2. Do they desire the L.W.I.U. to vote in the O.B.U. referendum?
3. Do they favour maintaining a "Lumber, Camp and Agricultural workers' department of the O.B.U.", and retaining the right to maintain their own headquarters?

8. The O.B.U. "Attacked from Within"

Midgley has issued a circular which is being addressed to all units of the O.B.U. Purporting to deal with the situation at large, it devotes special attention to the split. Two passages are as follows:-[9]

"We have even observed instances where some groups of workers have endeavoured to bring their craft union machinery and craft union psychology into the O.B.U. with them and have been surprised to find that it did not work. Merely placing O.B.U. cards into the pockets of the members of a craft union will not make that union function more effectively than before. The workers must place their interests as members of the working class above their petty craft interests, in other words they must become Class-conscious instead of craft-conscious."

"Now, however, the O.B.U. is being subjected to an attack from within, not from those who desire O.B.U. but from those who wish to build a number of distinct industrial unions, each with its separate headquarters, officials and organizers, which would result in confusion, duplication of effort and the expense that we are trying to leave behind us with the craft unions".

9. Utterances in the Labour Press

Two internal feuds of the organization are being freely ventilated in the extremist press.

The Western Labour News of 29th October attacked the O.B.U. vehemently, describing it as a failure, as having injured the cause of labour, and as having "inherent constitutional defects". One of those is "a fatal weakness in the form of organization", which is illustrated by the quarrel with the Lumber Workers. It says:-

"The dispute there existing is not a casual dispute such as may occur in any body, but one which must arise sooner or later between every large body of organized workers and the governing forces of the O.B.U. The Lumber Workers could not be represented in the organization as Lumber Workers; because then they would exercise a virtual control, so the attempt was made to introduce the ward principle of representation by which they lost their identity as lumber workers. The central clique says they should lose their identity as Lumber Workers if they are to remain in the O.B.U. As they have no intention whatever of losing their identity as Lumber Workers, the only course left for them is to get out of the O.B.U.

The Building Trades Unit of Edmonton and the National Railway Workers' Unit have seen the point and also withdrawn. The point is that the same trouble not only will but must arise with regard to every large body of men in a basic trade industrially organized which affiliates with the O.B.U., and, if they do not withdraw in a body, they will certainly withdraw individually. This process of disintregation is already very seriously affecting the association in Winnipeg".[10]

The Alberta coal strike is mentioned as a failure "in contact with external conditions":-

"The O.B.U. engineered the strike without any organization to sustain it, or for any object that was worth while. The O.B.U. put its members among the miners up to making a fight for the O.B.U., but when the fighting began, it was not in the line itself but in some organizer's mouth and pocket at a distance. And even if the loyalty of these men to the O.B.U. can stand this treatment, they face the same position later on as the Lumber Workers are in just now, which is rather a bad lookout for them".

In conclusion, the Western Labour News says:-

"The serious matter for organized labour as a whole in the ill-fated business is that just when a universal drive in favour of the open shop is on, Labour is in a bad position to meet it, precisely to the extent in which the propaganda in favour of the O.B.U. has been a success".

Elsewhere in the same issue the Western Labour News describes the coal strike thus:-

"The event showed that as a grievance the checkoff is a good deal like death and taxes, things everybody claims a constitution/right to grumble about.

"As a strike the whole proceedings were ridiculous. There was no organization and no solidarity, and the cause for which war was declared was not to improve the wages of conditions of the men, but to break up a rival organization which is the only one which has ever been able to function in the interests of the men".

The significance of the remark about the open shop is to be found in the fact that elsewhere in the same issue appear several paragraphs to the effect that a general attempt is to be made by employers in Canada and the United States, this winter to break the unions and to institute openshop.

The O.B.U. Bulletin of 30th October has a general air of depression, and in its editorial column shows embarrassment. It discusses "Industrial or Geographical organization" in a gingerly way, its clearest statement being the following:-

"There is a tendency to fight and divide over the question of Industrial vs. Geographical form of organization. This is pure foolishness. Both forms of organization are needed and overlapping is bound to occur. Sensible men cannot make a fight on these lines. The miners, the railway workers, the building trades, the textile [11] workers, are bound to come together, to consider their needs as workers, in their own industries. Industry, itself is not simple; it is complex. There will come a time when the workers in a given community will require the aid and support of their immediate neightbours of every industry, when the class interests are uppermost. Both the industrial and the community, or geographical, forms of organization will be required".

The B.C. Federationist of 29th October has columns dealing with the internal quarrel. So far as this particular is evidence, the fight seems to be going adversely to Winch and the L.W.I.U.; two or three camps have declared against him, and the Coast district seems hostile.

The Lumber Workers' Unit of the O.B.U. in Winnipeg is very bitter against the local Central Council O.B.U. in having threatened to decry in the foreign-speaking papers. Popowich, who is the editor of the Ukrainian Labour News, also is secretary of this unit.

10. Within the Lumber Workers' Unit

A report from Vancouver dated 4th November contains the following paragraph:-

> "I heard, also that J. Kavanaugh is running hard for Winch's job, and that the mine workers in the East are backing up the L.W.I.U. in their quarrel with the O.B.U.".

A report upon the L.W.I.U. dated Vancouver 4th November, contains the following passages:-

> "After investigation at all local employment offices, I find a great many men looking for work; from what I learn from Employment Agents there is very little work coming in on account of camps closing down. As a rule, most of the camps close down during the Winter for repairs, but this year, they are closing on account of the lumber market being so poor, and as near as I could find out about 80 per cent of the Logging camps are shut up for an indefinite time. Several large lumber mills are, also, closed down owing to having nearly a year's supply of cut lumber on hand, with no sign of a market from the Prairies yet.
>
> "I ascertained that 90% of the Shingle Mills have shut up also, on account of poor markets.
>
> "I interviewed Mr. Weaver, manager of the Brooks, Scanlon and O'Brien Lumber Company, and had a talk on the Labour question. He informed me that the reason for closing down in the logging industry was on account of the poor market and the high wages being paid, and [12] that the association was going to close all camps and try to open later with a cut in wages, with more production; he

could not say for what length of time these camps would be closed. From a general idea, I gather that the question of unemployment is going to be a serious one this winter, as so many harvesters from the East have come to Vancouver, figuring on obtaining work in the logging camps for the winter."

II. BRITISH COLUMBIA

11. The Slocan Strike

An investigation into the strike in the Slocan conducted on 21st October shows that at that date the conflict still was in progress but that signs of weakening were beginning to show among the O.B.U. members in the district. Their numbers had declined, and of the miners at work about half were O.B.U. the rest being either Internationals or non-union men.

Picketting in the O.B.U. is still carried on, and this makes it difficult for the mines to secure new men.

Sandon still is closely organized by the O.B.U., under the guidance of T. B. Roberts.

Roberts appears to be working with the Midgley faction of the O.B.U.

12. Miscellaneous Notes

R. P. Pettipiece spoke at Vancouver under the auspices of the Federated Labour Party on 31st October. His subject "Politics and the Liquor Referendum"; he expressed regret at the victory of the Moderates on the ground that prohibition aided the cause of the revolutionists. The meeting was not well attended and the audience was not unanimous.

Jack Kavanaugh addressed the Socialist meeting in Vancouver on Sunday 31st October. The meeting was well attended and the audience interested. He declared that "this Capitalist class will never be thrown out of business by the use of the ballot".

An investigation of certain small lumber camps near Kitchener in the East Kootenay sub-district goes to show that in that region [13] little interest is taken now in the O.B.U. A delegate at one of them told our informant that he was tired of the post. At this camp roughly half the men are O.B.U.

A sentence in the report is:-

> "Wages have been cut all along the line, but there is very little kick as the men expected it".

A detachment report from Ocean Falls states that labour conditions are more settled there than has been the case for many months past. The large logging camps are expected to close down before Christmas owing to ice and snow.

Seditious Indian literature is once more coming into British Columbia including copies of Ghadr (Mutiny), the principal anti-British organ of Hindu revolutionists. The tone of this paper continues violent.

13. Individual Agitators

Three agitators have come to our attention at Nanaimo: Thomas Beattie, who up to about 8 months ago was active in the Crow's Nest Pass, and was boycotted there by the miners; James Cartwright, who lately has been boycotted in Nanaimo owing to his persistence in agitation; and Arthur Jordan, who has served jail sentences in New Zealand in connection woth labour troubles. All three of these men have join the Self-Determination for Ireland League.

Mention was made some weeks ago of the sudden disappearance, on being questioned by the R.C.M.P., of an O.B.U. agitator in the East Kootenay sub-district named Dandineau. He has returned to Kitchener from the prairies, but has refused to resume work as a delegate. Our informant states that he "is apparently scared stiff".

It is worth noticing that this man who belonged to the L.W.I.U. does not wish to see it break away from the O.B.U. but advocates the withdrawal of the per capita tax until the L.W.I.U. are given full voting power at conventions.

An O.B.U. organizer named E. Robinson has been trying to [14] organize the lumber miller at Yahk. He was unsuccessful, getting only one new member, and failing to induce anyone to take the job of delegate. His collections for dues barely paid his expenses.

III. ALBERTA

14. Conditions in Drumheller

The strike in Drumheller has been followed by the blacklisting of about 100 men by the Red Deer Valley Coal Operators' Association. Among these are a number of men like Christophers, Carl Berg, Sherman and Evans who have not been associated with the Drumheller region; others like Joe Ormond and Mike Lumich are local agitators. The attempt to renew the strike because of this seems to have failed.

Our information is that most of the men are satisfied with the new rate of pay and conditions. Further, a considerable number of English speaking miners have returned from the harvest fields seeking employment.

The O.B.U. Bulletin in its issue of 30th October prints a statement by H. Davis concerning the Alberta coal strike, in which the following sentences appear:-

> "There is a certainty of another strike in the Alberta fields .... There is not a satisfied miner in that country ...... That the unrest will produce a shut down and it will be when the country is bare of coal. The workers of Winnipeg should understand the situation and be prepared".

A careful survey of the Drumheller area shows that on 22nd October the total of men at work, was 1,948. There were of the following nationalities:-

English-speaking ....989 - 50.7 per cent
Austrians ....358 - 18.3 " "

Italians ....134 - 6.8 " "
Russians .... 119 - 6.0 " "

and small numbers of Danes; Norwegians; Serbs; Belgians; Dutch; Hungarians; Ukrainians; Germans; Swedes; Spaniards; Bohemians; and Chinese.

On 28th October George Palmer visited Lethbridge for the purpose of consulting H. Ostlund, the O.B.U. lawyer, as to the [15] legality of the Drumheller injunction. Apparently Ostlund advised him that it was illegal.

15. Other Collieries

A report from Fernie dated 1st November states that the threats of renewing the strike if William Sherman was not taken back by the Coal company had come to nothing. The report says:-

> "Since the passing of this resolution there has been a considerable change of heart on the part of the coal miners and the leaders find that they are not so ready now to lay down their tools at the first word, with the result that although the men discriminated against have not been reinstated, the miners have made no effort to go on strike. As already stated in previous reports the rank and file of the miners do not want any further stoppage of work and it is only among the haulage hands that there appears to be any possibility of a stoppage of work. However, at the present time everything is quiet and the indications are that the mines will continue working steadily".

The Brazeau Collieries are working full time again, with conditions practically normal. Men are constantly arriving at the camp and by 25th October they had over 500 on the pay roll. The N.C.O. in charge of the detachment reports:

> "Everything appears to be going along very quietly, but the majoritt of miners in this camp are not in favour of the U. M. W. of A. check-off. This may cause trouble at any time".

16. Miscellaneous Notes

Bray spoke at the Dunvegan shops in Edmonton on 19th October; he encountered considerable opposition from the Berg faction of the O.B.U. As usual, his speech was merely an account of his experiences in the Winnipeg strike and in the subsequent trial. One statement which he made was of interest; it is reported thus:-

> "He stated that on the day that the verdict was returned, at 11 o'clock there were three of the jurymen strong for acquittal and they were dismissed to bring in a verdict at 2 o'clock. When they came in at 2 o'clock they were all agreed on the verdict of "guilty" and one of the three who was in financial difficulties was able, directly after the trial to pay off his debts and retire. It was similar in the other two cases as they had not had to work since the trial, and that the Judge had warned them what had happened in the Juryroom was

sacred to themselves".[16]

Another address by G. B. Williams of the International Bible Students' Association is reported from Edmonton; it was delivered on Sunday 31st October. In it he predicted the coming of revolution and anarchy.

G. L. Ritchie addressed the Edmonton Labour Church on 31st October on Luxury and Poverty". His speech was a denunciation of the existing form of society.

17. The Searchlight

Another issue of the Searchlight jas been got out, dated 22nd October, Lawson is over $800 in debt to his printers.

Mention was made in No 48 of a wild scheme for financing the Searchlight which was devised by Evans. The meeting of the District Board which he called to consider it came to nothing, as only one member of the Board besides Evans took the trouble to attend.

IV. SASKATCHEWAN

18. Miscellaneous Notes

A report on the O.B.U. at Saskatoon states that Mill, the local organizer, gave information as to the conditions of the organization. Our report is:-

> "It appears that there are 330 names on the books at the present time. Subscriptions are bot all paid uo and many remained unpaid so far back as June last. There is a growth of 30 members since mid-summer, but these are all practically harvesters (classed as General Workers) with a few C. N. R. men (unskilled labour). In reality the mivement has lost ground as those oeing dues to the organization might be termed deserters quite reasonably, although Mill is still outwardly optimistic".

A further paragraph in the report is as follows:-

> "Mill states that the miners at Drumheller (O.B.U. men) are going to take "vacations" of two weeks and a month at a time, and this I understand is the weapon now to be used to hinder the output of the mines".

An investigation at Moose Jaw shows the O.B.U. cause there to be stationary. McAllister, the local leader there, said:

> "We have not had a meeting for months; we are getting a few members now and again, and we have about 200 O.B.U. men in Moose Jaw at the present time".[17]

One remark by McAllister of Moose Jaw is significant:-

> "That man Bray of Winnipeg, is in bad with the head men of the O.B.U. there; they seem to think he has been paid money by Government agents to supply information of the O.B.U. doings".

A Mrs. Dorothy Carter is co-operating with Austin Stanley in trying to organize the O.B.U. in Regina. Her assertions do not lack for hardihood; one of them is that the O.B.U. number 300,000. She advocates the Soviet Form of Government. She is a hotel waitress, who is separated from her husband, apparently in circumstances not wholly devoid of scandal.

A report on conditions in Regina dated 1st November states:-

"For the average labourer in Saskatchewan there is still plenty of work, on farm by season contact; in the woods or on railway construction".

V. MANITOBA

19. The Ukrainian Labour Temple

With reference to a report from Ontario (see para 24.) that the Ukrainian Labour Temple at Winnipeg cost $76,000, investigation shows that the building permit put the cost at $40,000; any additional cost would have to be reported to the building inspector, and added to the original permit. The building inspector expressed the opinion that the structure may have cost more than $40,000 because of the high price of labour. However, all the men who worked on the building were sympathizers with the cause, so that it would be reasonable to conclude that some work was given free.

This discrepancy recalls earlier suggestions that the affairs of the Temple were a great deal of mystery, and that money was being poured into it without satisfactory accounts being rendered.

Another report which has been received is that the total cost of the building was $70,000, that of this $42,000 has been paud; leaving $28,000 unpaid. The present debt, which was the subject of discussion [18] at a meeting on 2nd November, includes the sum of $1,800 which the Temple owes to individual members who wish to return to Europe, and accordingly want their money. An effort is to be made amongst the Ukrainian workers in the city and in the Western provinces to raise this money. Another debt which apparently causes soje concern is one of $10,000 for building materials.

In addition to serving as a place of entertainment, the Temple accommodates an "after 4o'clock school" when the Ukrainian language and literature are taught to about 100 pupils free. A school for adults for teaching Ukrainian and English is contemplated.

20. Miscellaneous Notes

An organization termed the "Young Labour League" has recently been launched in Winnipeg to educate the young workers regarding the class struggle. It is comprised almost wholly of, Ukrainians, Russians and Poles. While it has held a few meetings, the attendance has been small, the collections have been insufficient to pay for the rent of the hall, and it consequently is about $120 in debt. The members will appeal to the older organizations for help, and if these do not respond generously the organization probably will dissolve.

This League held a "Mass Labour Meeting" at Liberty Temple, Winnipeg, on 29th October; about 30 people attended, half of whom were young girls. John Houston gave an address on Labour organization which included a friendly account of the I.W.W.

One Crittendon also gave a Socialist speech at this meeting. He spoke favourably of the Soviet system and of the withdrawal of rights from persons who do not belong to the working class.

A person named Kohn was the speaker at the Socialist meeting held in Winnipeg on Sunday, 31st October; he was introduced as a well-known member of the Socialist Party of Great Britain. His speech was an account of labour conditions in Great Britain in a strongly [19] revolutionary vein.

In connection with the pending municipal elections in Winnipeg, it is reported that many of the International labour men are beginning to think that it would be better for their own men to be defeated at the polls than to allow the radical members of the party to be successful.

Mr. A. E. Smith, M.L.A. addressed the New People's Church in Brandon on Sunday 31st October; about 100 persons were present. Mr. Smith's subject was "Labour in Political Development", and he does not seem to have said anything of a revolutionary nature.

VI. ONTARIO

21. Situation in Western Ontario

The Officer Commanding Western Ontario in his confidential monthly report for October notices the strong action being taken by several prominent men in Labour circles to offset the O.B.U. and radical propaganda, and in particular to drive the "Red" element out of the District.Trades and Labour Council in Toronto. "It cannot be disguised", he writes, "that there is a strong radical element here, but reports from agents, etc. point to the fact that the majority of Labour is beginning to realize that they are being exploited by their 'red' keaders". He continues:-

> "There have been small strikes among the employes in five camps along the Algoma Central Railway, during the past month, and a strike of 250 men in Neimi's camp at Ruel is threatened. The men are asking for higher wages and an 8-hour day. The trouble can be laid at the door of the O.B.U. So far there have been no disturbances, and the managers of the camps affected, hope to replace the dissatisfied men. They do not intend tosubmit to their demands. The situation is being kept in touch with.
>
> "The main trouble along the Algoma Central is among the Finns employed in the camps. They are mostly O.B.U. members and a radical bunch. A patrol from the Sault Ste. Marie detachment is now in progress along this line".

The Officer Commanding Western Ontario proceeds to give a general survey of the O.B.U.:-

> "As stated above, the discontent among the various camp workers is caused by the activities of the O.B.U. agitators, several of whom are busy in the Algoma district. There is a split in the ranks of the O.B.U., caused by the Finns desiring to form a local of their own,

not contro led by H.Q. of the O.B.U. in Vancouver. The outcome [20] of this dispute is being watched with interest.

"There has been a certain amount of activity in Hamilton lately, the principal agitator being one Roberts.

"In Toronto the O.B.U. have been holding their usual open air meetings each week, but do not appear to be getting a great deal of support. At their business meeting arrangements have been made to hold weekly meetings in the Empress Theatre, Toronto, during the winter months. The leaders of the O.B.U. appear to be anxiously awaiting developments of the trouble in England".

Dealing with other revolutionary agencies, he says:-

"The man Almazoff, late of Winnipeg, is apparently keeping very quiet, and nothing suspicious has transpired during the past month, although he is being kept under surveillance. Most of the members of the S. P. of C. which is almost defunct in this City are now members of the Russian School, Plebs League or the 'Zluka'.

"An attempt is being made to get the Russian Bolsheviks and the Ukrainians to unite into an anarchist group, but the two parties are antagonistic and always quarreling among themselves. The meetings of the 'Zluka' are poorly attended and no definite plan of action has been arranged by the members. With regard to the Russian School, most of their meetings are in the form of social events but Dodokin Siniloff and Almazoff, who are interested in tjis School, are dangerous men.

"Plebs League is a branch of the Anarchists Communist Party, the principal organizers being, Bell, Armstrong, Berg and Mrs. Custance. At their last meeting only 17 persons were present. The league is a new one here, and is apparently an offshoot of a similar league in England. Their programme of propaganda has not yet been decided upon".

22. The O.B.U. in the Sudbury Region

A report from Sudbury states that Walter Cowan has been much disturbed over the threatened withdrawal of the Sault Ste. Marie Finns from the Sudbury district, O.B.U. in the event of the coming referendum favouring the retnetion of the administration in Vancouver. Our report says:-

"The Finns demand the retnetion of the per capita tax in the East and failing that will form a separate O.B.U. organization at Sault Ste. Marie comp sed entirely of Finns. (This will be a pretty radical branch of the O.B.U. without doubt.) The Finns here also intend to form a separate organization".

Eugene Guertin apparently has succeeded Cowan as secretary-treasurer in the Sudbury district. Cowan's headquarters, as has been noted in previous summaries now are at Montreal. Our report says:-[21]

"About all that is known of Cowan here is that he is a native of Scotland, a quiet fellow who has had his hands full in keeping the foreign element of the O.B.U. here from getting the O.B.U. prosecuted as an out and out Bolshevist organization his policy has been one of quietly organizing".

Dave Rainville, who was associated with E. Guertin for some time as organizer formthe O.B.U. in Northern Ontario, apparently has abandoned this occupation and proposes to work as a trapper and hunter during the coming winter. A report upon the situation says:-

"There are getting to bemore and more French Canadians in the O.B.U. and I cannot help thinking that these Frenchmen are enjoying a little of the joys of town life and railway travel at the expense of the O.B.U. I think a good many of them are humhubs and that the Finns see through their little game hence their anxiety for a separate union".

A patrol is being made along the line of the Algoma Central Railway. The report of the first week's work shows that visits were paid to about a dozen camps employing about 200 men. The O.B.U. is powerful on this line and has won several successes.

Several reports have been received concerning the strike in Neimi's camp, mentioned above by the Officer Commanding Western Ontario. The camp is near Haileybury. According to one report, the strike occurred among the Finnish labourers. The working strength of the camp was 210, and of these 140 left. The company decided to fight it out, and the prospects were that the men would be beaten. The N.C.O. in charge of C.I.B. work in the Cobalt sub-district remarks that the O.B.U. evidently had been deceived by the victory they had won in the Algoma Central Railway strike and had been nonplussed when this company showed fight.

An earlier report, from Sudbury, dated 1st November, says:-

"The Spanish River Pulp Company evidently intend to put up a fight and as it is just what the local O.B.U. needs to give impetus to a recent revival in recruiting here there is likely to be trouble particularly as 60 or 70 per cent of the men involved in Neimi's camp are Finns, who have also the present incentive to say 'we are the only members of the O.B.U. who have ever had the courage to start something, and now that we have go rid of Cowan and his anti-radical policy, we are going to make the O.B.U. something to fear in the Sudbury district'".[22]

The report goes on to say:-

"It is just possible that the result of the Referendum voting which closes today may have a very great influence on local O.B.U. matters the Finns are expected to secede and form a branch of O.B.U. of their own in the event of the Referendum favouring the continuation of the allegiance to O.B.U. headquarters at S.S. Marie and can be depended on to set a hot pace for the more conservative English speaking branch here and it is predicted among that latter that the Finns will have this District in the lime light from now on".

23. Extremists in Toronto

A man named MacKenzie spoke on 30th October at an open-air meeting of the O.B.U. in Toronto, his subject being "The Miners' Strike in England". He expressed the strongest desire to see a struggle. One passage in his speech is thus reported:-

"Why is it that Russian Workers have advanced to first place, when they are not so well educated as the English workman? Becsue there was no compromise between the Capitalists and the Labouring class. In other countries, where strikes are allowed and there is a policy of give-and-take, the wreckage of the Capitalist,system has been avoided".

At a meeting of the Plebs League on Sunday, 31st October T. Bell lectured on the "Downfall of the Second International". Our report says:-

"His explanation of the cause of the downfall was the absence of the dictatorship which would establish discipline in the rank and file of the proletariat and thereby concentrate their united power against the enemy.

"The Socialists, he said, cannot be Called Communists because they are not violent in doctrine and not revolutionary enough: their moral teachings alone cannot obtain control over the country, and unless they apply force they will never reach the goal. There are I.W.W., Independent Labour Parties and other similar organizations who are radical, but they are not communists because they are not revolutionary enough".

Asked if the Irish Transport Workers were revolutionary enough to be called communists Bell replied in the negative "because they were not trying to overthrow the Government".

The meeting was small; the audience comprised only 17 persons.

24. Foreign Born Revolutionaries

A meeting of Zluka was held in Occident Hall, Toronto, on 31st October. A man whose name apparently is Volmenko, spoke on behalf of [23] the Russian Soviet medical relief fund. He described himself as an anarchist; the agitator Stefanitski opposed him from the Bolshevist point of view. Our report of the incident is as follows:-

"Stefanitski, a lab our agitator, got up and told the speaker that he did not understand the nonsence of the Anarchists, who are preaching their ideals but who never explain themselves without dictatorship, He said that such statements as "take what you need" is ridiculous. If anyone can take what he needs, then naturally someone will take more than he needs, while you cannot prevent him doing it and there will be the same capitalist greed in existence.

Again, he continued, how would you explain the term need? One needs one loaf of bread a day, while another needs three, and there can be no hard and fast rule as to the needs of each individual. Then about power. How can you express your power if you have no discipline? What is any organization without a dictator? Dictatorship only can lead to victory. Communism under proletariat dictatorship can distribute the produce among its members, and then everyone will get what he wants to live on, ever one will be a worker and be useful to the community".

This is one more example of the quarrel which is developing between the two factions of revolutionists.

Michniewicz and several others are trying to form in Hamilton a local branch of the Ukrainian Labour Temple, the headquarters of which are at Winnipeg. He places the cost of the new temple recently built there at $76,000. He states that about 100 foreigners had pledged themselves to collect money to undertake a similar building in Hamilton, but had been obliged to postpone action for a while.

A report upon Welland dated 2nd November states that no grest activity prevails at present among the Ukrainian Socialists there, nor is there a Russian Communist party in existence there at present. In this locality the Communists and Anarchists are strongly opposed to each other; the Communists uphold the proceedings of the Moscow Government.

25. Martens' Offise Heard from

A Russian named Volzt visited Hamilton on 5th November on his way to Winnipeg. He described himself as a confidential clerk in Martens' office in New York, and he seems to have some connection with the collection of funds for medical supplies for the Soviet Government.[24]

According to his statement, the appeal has been made broadcast throughout the United States as well as Canada, and he placed the amount so far collected at about $43,000; he expects to collect that much more within the next month. While his exact business was not ascertained, it appears that he will visit some of the prominent revolutionists there, including the management of the O.B.U. Bulletin, to ask for support in this connection.

Volzt described Martens' Office as intending to open a branch in Canada with the idea of placing large orders for various sorts of materials with important firms, thereby averting unemployment, and so obliging the Government to treat the Soviet representatives in a more lenient manner.

26. Miscellaneous Notes

Examination of Molot, an Ukrainian publication issued in New York, shows it to be maintaining its revolutionary nature.

Additional information has been received as to Koldofsky. Two stories are in circulation among the Jewish Trade Unionists in Toronto concerning him. One is that he has gone to Poland to obtain first hand knowledge as to conditions there; the other, which it is not easy to understand is that he is there in the interests of the Garment Workers' Association. It is suggested that he may be a courier for Dworkib.

Information has been received from an outside source that Dworkin is under arrest in Poland, charged with smuggling men through for the Soviet Government; that two of his associates have been shot, and that he is awaiting trial.

VII. QUEBEC

27. Conditions in Montreal

The Officer Commanding Quebec in his confidential monthly report for October states that there was not much activity among the radical element in the city during October. He notes that the plumbers of Montreal have been on strike during the whole month; a recent move in this has been the invocation by the masters of the clause in the [25] Criminal Code forbidding picketing.

One episode, which has been the subject of angry comment in the extremist press in Western Canada, is thus reported:-

> "The textile and boot and shoe trades are still working short time, and one of the largest boot factories in Montreal has made an offer to the employes to accept a reduction of wages to enable the factory to keep running, with the alternative of closing down. The employes have accepted the reduction in good spirit realizing what the factories are up against under the extraordinary conditions in the money market prevailing at this time. It is expected that other industries will have to follow suit in the near future, or else there will be a great deal of unemployment here this winter. Navigation closes at Montreal on 26th instant, this will release a large labouring class, but a large number will be absorbed by the lumbering industry where there is still a big demand for men".

28. Thetford Mines

An investigation at Thetford mines shows that there is no danger of revolutionary unionism there. Such labour troubles as exist are in the form of a conflict between the International Union and the National Catholic Unionp the organizer of the former, a man named Bastien in reality is a man of conservative tendencies, but is proniunced by the National Union as a radical.

29. Miscellaneous Notes.

At the instigation of recent arrivals from the United States, the Jewish Socialist Party of Montreal met on 29th October to discuss the formation of a Communist Party which should yield full allegiance to the Third International. Amongst those attending were Schubert, Michael Buhay, Isidore Boltuck, Freiger and St. Martin. After a sharp discussion the majority decided to form the proposed party. The committee of organization consists of St. Martin and two others.

An All-Soviet convention is to be held in New York on 28th November. The Society for Technical Aid to Soviet Russia in Montreal is to send two representatives, Zarrovetz and Gurin.

According to revolutionists in Niagara Falls, Ben Legere intends within the next few weeks to visit Montreal.

A woman agitator known as Miss B. Hall. is reported at work in Montreal. She is a graduate of the Rand School of Economics in New York and desires to become a teacher at the projected Montreal Labour [26] college. The institution is to be held in St. Joseph's Hall, which is above the premises occupied by the Educational Press Association.

VIII. MARITIME PROVINCES

30. Possibilities of Trouble

A report from Halifax, from the O. C. Maritime Provinces, dated 8th November describs the labour situation in Cape Breton as serious. Once more apparently the U.M.W. of A. executive would prefer a settlement, but were afraid of their men; meanwhile, the operators were prepared to fight the union, and were taking steps looking to that end.

An earlier report upon labour conditions at Sydney Mines, New Waterford, Glace Bay and Birch Grove states that the mines are running in full blast and that every one seems fairly well satisfied. The prospects now are adverse to a strike in these localities during the coming winter.

The Officer Commanding Maritime Provinces in his confidential monthly report for October makes the following observations:-

> "Generally speaking labour conditions in the Maritime Provinces are very quiet now, and the attitude of labour has been much more normal.
>
> "The Independent Labour Party of Nova Scotia have established a labour temple in one of the Relief Commission's old buildings on Sackville Street, and by the admission of women hope to have their party 10,000 strong before the next Federal election".

He adds, however, that recent civic bye-elections have been very discouraging to these people.

Discussing the recurrent reports of trouble in the Cape Breton coal mines he observes:-

> "Living conditions are very bad indeed in most of the mining towns in Cape Breton, and although being established for years, the towns of Reserve and New Waterford have no water or sanitary arrangements of any kind. This feature has much to do with the prevailing unrest, and were living and social conditions improved there would be less food for discontent".

He adds that there is considerable unemployment in Halifax and that labour circles are anticipating a hard winter and unemployment.

ROYAL CANADIAN MOUNTED POLICE HEADQUARTERS

Ottawa, 17th July, 1926.

SECRET

NO. 327

WEEKLY SUMMARY

NOTES REGARDING REVOLUTIONARY ORGANIZATIONS AND AGITATORS IN CANADA

REPORT

(No Report was issued for the week ended 9th July).

The Communists are preparing to take an active part in the pending General Election. The Ontario Section of the Canadian Labour Party (which is wholly under their control) is to hold a convention in August.

Some space is given in this issue to the official report of the seventh convention held by the Ukrainian Labour Farmer Temple Association, covering the year 1925. Particularly interesting features are the close organization and firm discipline, and the progress made in regard to seditious schools, a sort of Normal School of agitators having been held.

Fresh evidence is given in this issue of the bitterness with which the Ukrainian agitators disparage the public schools.

An example of the extent to which the Ukrainian Communists rely on music as an avenue of propaganda is the projected tour through the prairies of a mandolin orchestra of about 20 young girls trained by the Ukrainian Labour Farmer Temple Association in Winnipeg.

The One Big Union is making some progress in Cape Breton; the miners are disgusted with the United Mine Workers of America, and are in a state of uncertainty as to their future course in matters of organization.[2]

APPENDICES

TABLE OF CONTENTS

APPENDIX NO. 1. GENERAL

"Humour and Truth"
Mandolin Orchestra on Tour.

" 9. Progress made by the One Big Union in Nova Scotia.
" 10. O.B.U. Attack upon "Canadian Friends of Soviet Russia."
" 11. Canadian Defence League and the Ku Klux Klan.
" 12. Attempted French Communist Paper in Montreal. L'Ouvrier Canadien
" 13. Communists Notes.
Y.C.L. on Work in Unions.
Der Kamf's attack on the Workmen's Circle
Malcolm Bruce in Detroit.
" 14. An Anti-British "Chinese Society of Canada" Projected.

APPENDIX NO. II. REPORTS FROM DISTRICTS

" 15. ALBERTA: Communist Party Notes.
Edmonton Party dislike new organization.
Quiet in Drumheller
Canadian Labour Party
English Children not attending seditious schools.
Party short of money.
" 16. The Ukrainians:
Drumheller agitation low.
Frank Zozuk expelled
Visit to Smoky Lake
Sundry Meetings.[3]
" 17. I.W.W. and O.B.U.
Sam Scarlett
F. Roberts.
" 18. SASKATCHEWAN: Communist Activities
Agitation in Regina, Moose Jaw & Sturgis.
Attitude to the Furrow.
Trouble among the Pioneers.
Cyril Harding suspended.
Steve Kolatch, Willowbrook.
"Section of Youth" at Regina.
" 19. The G.B.U.
Nutana and Humboldt units.
Fred Lake.
" 20. MANITOBA: Communist Notes.
Book Store Closed.
Y.C.L. leaderless.
Jews and the Cloak-makers and Furriers

APPENDIX NO. 1: GENERAL

1. Ontario Communists and the General Election.

The Ontario Section of the Canadian Labour Party, which is completely under Communist control, will gold a Convention on 7th August in Toronto, to prepare for the coming Federal and Provincial elections. Candidates will be selected, and a platform decided upon. Our informant says:-

"This will be the first convention of its kind ever held by the Labour movement in Ontario and providing that funds are sufficient no doubt quite a number of candidates will be placed in the field. I believe that the bulk of the candidates will be selected for Constituencies in Northern Ontario.

"In conjunction with this, the Toronto Central Council of the

Canadian Labour Party will hold a Convention on 19th July to nominate candidates in Toronto, if they decide to contest any of the Constituencies."

---

2. Methods of Approaching Foreign-Language Farmers.

Illustrating one method of agitation among immigrant farmers, M. Rozen, an active Communist of Edmonton made an interesting statement at a business meeting of the Communist Party held in that city on 3rd July. It is thus reported:-

"During the month of June I have been travelling through the district on my personal business buying poultry and eggs from farmers. I have done all I could for the Party. The farmers are coming to understand that the Capitalist class have been robbing them all the time. As far as I can tell we have 60 percent of the farmers in the left-wing movement."[5]

---

3. The Ukrainian Labour Farmer Temple Association in 1925.

It will be remembered that the seventh convention of the Ukrainian Labour Farmer Temple Association was held in Winnipeg on 25th 27th January last. An official report has been issued, and a translation of this contains some passages of interest, in addition to what was noted at the time.

The financial report of the "Workers-Farmers' Publishing Society", the dummy company which issues the Ukrainian revolutionary newspapers, showed that the general income during 1925 was $42,734.97; the general expenditure having been $40,365.72, the balance this being $2,369.25; as the balance from 1924 was $4,484.36, this makes a total favourable a balance of $6,853.61. One expenditure was $1,050.65 sent to Europe to pay for the publication of a translation of Karl Marx's "Capital" into Ukrainian.

The circulation of the Ukrainian revolutionary press was reported to be:-

Ukrainian Labour News	6,800
Robitnitsia	5,800
Farmers' Life	2,500

The income of the largest of these, the Ukrainian Labour News, was about $25,000, and of this half, or $12,851.87 was received in the form of subscriptions, and half, or $12,634.94, as gifts. It is fair to note that no receipts from advertisements are listed.

The Central Executive Committee of the society during 1925 had a general income of $11,157.48, and general expenses of $10,199.33. The balance thus was $958.15, and as the cash balance from 1924 was $603.81, the year 1926 was begun with a cash balance of $1,561.96.[6]

The largest expense was $1,873.30 for the "Higher Educational Course"; another considerable item was $1,787.50 for "Short term loans", and yet another of $1,702.12 is described as "return of loans". The debt during the year was $4,990.04, and as $1,702.12 was paid on this, the debt on beginning 1926 was $3,287.92.

4. Size of the Society

Figures as to the membership etc. show 64 branches, with a membership composed of 1870 men, 902 women, and 1637 pupils in the children's schools. Other figures are:- Dramatic Circles, 43; choirs, 21; orchestras 38. The value of the property is shown at $410,572.80 of the branches 40 had buildings; these either had been transferred to the Central Committee, or were in process of being transferred.

The report of the Central Executive Committee contains an account of the "Higher Educational Course" which at the time of the holding of the convention was in progress; in part it is as follows:

> "There are 40 students, 17 of whom are kept at the cost of the organization, and 23 are paying for themselves. All students are living in one building and eat in one restaurant, and study collectively. There are two teachers, and besides, from time to time other comrades lecture on organizational matters. The technical matters of the Higher Educational Course are managed by a board of three comrades students. Two inspectors are appointed to look after the teaching. The whole programme of the Higher Educational Course is managed by a board of five inspectors. Two inspectors, one representative of the Central Executive Committee, one teacher, and one of the students board. Reports about the proceedings of the teaching will be submitted by the inspectors, teacher, and the representative of the students. Although the Higher Educational Course will cost the organizations very much, it will be worth while. However, in the future we have to think about, instead of spending money for housing to erect for it a proper building, and to create a steady Labour University."

Considerable attention was paid to the process of centralization whereby the ownership of all the property of the sixty-[7]odd locals is to be vested in the headquarters organization. This work has made progress, but had not been completed at the time of the convention.

5. Efforts among Women and Farmers.

A subsidiary body which has made progress is the Women's Section; during 1925 it increased by five branches; the total standing at the convention at 36 branches. The income during the year was $1,701.90, and the expenditure was $1,720.88.

The magnitude of the plan to Belshevize the farmers is shown by a report made by Ml. Sawyak, who travelled as an organizer in rural districts in Saskatchewan and Alberta. Complaint is made that slackness by the

Alberta Provincial Executive Committee interfered with the full success of his tour, the report continuing:-

"The plan was to visit at least 40 farm villages, but only 11 were visited because of sickness. The farmers in general were very favourable to the organizer. Even there where some part of the farmers were in the beginning in enmity, after the speech greeted the organizer."

The situation in Ontario was described as unfavourable, a passage in the report being:-

"The general situation of our organization in Ontario, notwithstanding our best efforts, is not of the best. In some of the branches is to be noticed carelessness, lack of energy and sincerity in the work. Some of the branches did not think it even important to come in contact with the P.E.C., and the latter often have to ask the services of private sources in order to find out about the work of these branches."

///

The issue of Rebitnitzia of 1st July contains the following statement of principal branches of the Women's Section of the Ukrainian Labour Farmer Temple Association:-

"Place"	Membership
1. Winnipeg, Man.	321
2. Timmins, Ont.	69
3. Fort William, Ont.	66
4. W. Fort William, Ont.	59[8]
5. Transcona, Man.	52
6. Edmonton, Alta.	50
7. Vancouver, B.C.	50
8. Fort Frances, Ont.	50
9. Port Arthur, Ont.	40
10. Sudbury, Ont.	40
11. Calgary, Alta.	30
12. Lethbridge, Alta.	28
13. E. Kildonan, Man.	19
14. Coalhurst, Alta.	16
15. Regina, Sask.	13
16. Hamilton, Ont.	11
Total	815

In addition there are village branches.

6. Further Plans in Alberta.

According to a statement made by Ivan Symbay at a special meeting held in Edmonton 7th July, the provincial convention recently held in Alberta passed a number of resolutions, the more important being reported as follows:-

(1) "A resolution to establish educational Institutions in Edmonton, so all farmers of the Province of Alberta will send their children to be educated in the Proletariat movement, also attend High Schools from the Labour Farmer Institution.

(2) "A resolution that children from 8 to 18 years be organized as a section of the Labour Farmer Temple Association.

(3) Organizers to be sent out in the Province amongst the farmers and labourers, organizing them and their children."

---

7. The Workers' Benevolent Society

The Ukrainian Labour News of 10th July contains the financial statement of the Workers' Benevelent Society for the second quarter of 1926. This shows receipts aggregating $6926.11 and expenditures amounting to $4421.13, leaving a balance of $2,454.98. The sum brought forward on 31st March was $1,3087.83, so that July begins with $15,542.81 on hand.[9]

In the figures formerly given for the first quarter of 1926 an error of $15. occurred in addition. This is reproduced in this statement, suggesting that the accounting work of this society is badly done.

In the expenditures of the society are noted appropriations of $200 for the "Higher Educational Course" and $150 for the "Press Fund, Ukrainian Labour News."

In connection with this society which in reality is a stalking horse under which Ukrainians not in sympathy with revolution are drawn into touch with the agitators it is of interest to note that A. Wojtyshyn, the Calgary organizer, addressed the Calgary branch of the Ukrainian Labour Farmer Temple Association on 20th June, assailing ordinary insurance companies and urging his hearers to join the Workers Benevolent Society. Our report of his speech in part is as follows:-

> "It has paid to the members insurance since in existence about $13,000.00 and $12,000.00 cash remains on hand at present. Capitalists' insurance makes millions every year and some has billions in the banks at present. We have about 300,000 Ukrainians in Canada. If only 100,000 of the workers and farmers join this society we will get about $12,000.00 from them per year. Out of this sum we pay about $6,000,000 to the members and administration and another $6,000,000 will be left for the disposition for any good cause of the working class. It is the duty of every working man and woman to be a member of this society instead of supporting capitalists insurance who use their money, very often, against the workers."

He proceeded to advise this course on Communist grounds.

The audience numbered about 150 and seemed to be impressed.

---

8 The Agitation among the Ukrainians

The minute control exercised over the branches of the Ukrainian Labour Farmer Temple Association is shown by a circular [10] recently sent out. Our account of it comes from a report of a business meeting of that body held in Edmonton on 30th June, and is as follows:

"The Secretary, Ivan Symbay, read a letter from the Executive at Winnipeg as follows:-

"That all U.L.F.T. Associations in Canada are to send us a full report of all work done during the last six months:-

1. How many children are attending the Association Schools.
2. How many Picnics.
3. How many shows.
4. Business Meetings.
5. Propaganda Meetings.
6. How many lecture meetings.
7. How much literature was sold.
8. How many new members were taken into the Branch.
9. How many members dropped out.
10. How many children are organized in the Association."

Ivan (or John) Symbay, the Ukrainian intellectual who recently conducted the "Higher Educational Course" at Winnipeg, is making his presence felt in Edmonton, where he is sojourning at present. The Officer Commanding the R.C.M.Police in Northern Alberta in his confidential monthly report for June makes the following remark concerning this man:-

"Before J. Symbay came to Edmonton there were 35 children attending the class at the Temple now there are 75. At Beverly, Alberta, where Symbay also teaches, there are 42 pupils."

At a meeting of the Edmonton branch of the Ukrainian Labour Farmer Temple Association held on 20th June Symbay said:-

"Comrades, there are many of our children that are keeping out of school. Every Labour child should go to school, that will stop them from going to the Street Walkers' School. The working class child must be educated to know the capitalist class and the working class. The children that are going to the Public Schools do not get the history of the working class. All they know is that the Kings are Gods over the people. The people are under the control of the Kings and the ruling class. So send your children to be educated, not for the benefit of the Capitalists, but for the working class. They are to become the ruling class of the world and to become the ruling class they must know the constitution of the two classes."[11]

In a meeting held by the same society on 22nd June in the course of the recent Provincial general election held. Finally, a labour candidate in Edmonton, is reported as saying:-

> "There is one thing that I want to tell you and that is that many Ukrainians have been refused naturalization papers because they are in the working class movement. If you elect Labour into the Provincial House, I will tell you that you will not have to go through any 'red tape'. They will not let you become naturalized as long as you are labourers, because they know that you will not vote for their class. So, let us stay together; the time will come when the working class will control the constitution of this country and the rest of the world."

From time to time we have noticed the activities of one Ivan Gnyda or Hnyda, a Ukrainian revolutionist who carries on a precarious business in Montreal publishing seditious books, pamphlets etc. Not long ago the head office of the Ukrainian Labour Farmer Temple Association in Winnipeg gave him some pecuniary assistance. A recent enterprise of his is the issue of a number of books ostensibly educational, but of revolutionary trend. We now learn that Ivan Kulyk, the member of the Russian Soviet Trade Delegation who pays particular attention to Ukrainian affairs in Canada, is showing much interest in Gnyda's affairs.

Both the Customs Department and the Post Office Department have forbidden on grounds of blasphemy, the entry into this country of "Humour and Truth," the revolutionary Ukrainian weekly published in New York. We learn that the management intend to smuggle it into Canada.

The Centrol Executive Committee of the Ukrainian Labour Farmer Temple Association at Winnipeg intend to send a mandolin orchestra of 21 [12] young girls on an extensive tour through the West. The Ukrainian Labour News of 3rd July publishes an article by L. Shatkulsky on it, describing this organization as occupying a very prominent place in the Ukrainian revolutionary agitation. The tour is to cover some 2,500 miles. It was to begin at Brandon on the 6th July, and the party are due in Edmonton in August. This is an example of the use made of music in propaganda.

---

9. Progress made by the One Big Union in Nova Scotia

We have received a report on the General Workers Unit of the One Big Union at Sydney. In 1924, when Ben Legere was active there, this organization had a membership of about 600; it collapsed, however, and at one time only 12 members paid their monthly dues regularly. Another attempt has been made to organize the Steel Workers, but Foreman Way, the O.B.U. organizer, has repeated the tactics of 1926, working principally among the miners and thus leaving the steelworkers unit to shift for themselves. Our report says:-

> "At the present time the O.B.U. unit in Sydney is comprised of 20 members, known as 'the Old Guard' and most of these men are not working at the steel plant. The Sydney unit has its headquarters, consisting of an office and hall, on the corner of Charlotte and Prince Streets, but they hold only business meetings, for members only, and every Saturday night a social with card games and prizes. These socials are attended by large numbers of steelworkers."

We also have an account of the O.B.U. coalminers unit in New Aberdeen. This was formed by Thomas Wooler and Jack Clancy, in October 1925. It has numbered as high as 200 but at present only some 40 or 50 members are paying their monthly dues. The secretary and local leader, [13] for a time was one Frank White; this man was convicted in connection with the food raids in Glace Bay last winter and is now in prison; his place has been temporarily taken by one Joe McKinnon, but this man who has organization work in other towns, can give little time to the New Aberdeen work nd the unit is making little progress. It is meeting with obstruction from both Communists and the United Mine Workers of America.

We have received a note on the formation in May last of an O.B.U. unit in Florence in Cape Breton. This was effected very quietly; so far about 50 miners have joined, the remainder having declined to attach themselves to the O.B.U. though alleged to be much disgusted with the United Mine Workers of America.

We also learn that the O.B.U. have gained a footing in Dominion No. 1 and Dominion No. 6 mines in Cape Breton, though no units have as yet been formed there. The miners generally are disgusted with the United Mine Workers of America. In addition to Forman Way and Joe McKinnon, the O.B.U. have put two more organizers into this district, one being Foster of Winnipeg and the other being St. Andre of Montreal.

At a mass meeting recently held in New Waterford 160 miners signed application cards for the O.B.U. however, no unit has yet been formed there. Forman Way and Joe McKinnon were the speakers.[14]

---

10. O.B.U. Attack upon Canadian Friends of Soviet Russia

Not long ago the O.B.U. Bulletin drew attention to the fact that when the Home Bank collapsed a sum of nearly $5,000 was lying to the credit of the "Canadian Friends of Soviet Russia", this being part of the moneys raised for famine relief in Russia, though the famine by that time was over. The "Canadian Friends of Soviet Russia" was one of the numerous subsidiary organizations created by the Communists in order at once to carry on agitation under cover and to gain funds which they could manipulate for their own purposes. The revelation, which was accompanied by the unkind words in the use of which the O.B.U. Bulletin excels, clearly drew blood. The Maritime Labour Herald of 3rd July devotes a good deal of space to a reply, the gist of which is that the total sum raised for the Russian Famine Relief in Canada by the Canadian Friends of Soviet Russia was about $125,000; that the over-head expenditures were very small; and finally:

> "The reason why $4700. was our balance at the time of the collapse was because new activity was being organized and developed for the benefit of the victims of the famine the orphaned children.
>
> "It was not our fault, although our unfortunate experience, to have all our plans for this new undertaking, namely, the permanent maintenance of a Children's Home in the U.S.S.R., frustrated by the failure of the Home Bank. This was an anxiety and a disappointment in itself."

In the meantime, the O.B.U. Bulletin in its issue of 24th June has renewed its criticisms, publishing a rejoinder to Mrs. Florence Custance, who had addressed a protest to it. The Bulletin says in part:-

> "The famine started in 1921; in 1922 the effects were felt worst of all, yet the Home Bank did not fail until 1923. When we donated to the Famine Relief Funds, in our simplicity, we took it for granted, that these funds were to be forwarded directly in cash or kind, to Russia. We subscribed this money along with the rest of [15] the workers, to feed hungry men, women and children AT THAT TIME NOT YEARS AFTER.
>
> WHY THE LONG SILENCE?
>
> "When we come to think of it, it is rather strange that, to our knowledge, no statement has been issued by the Canadian Friends of Soviet Russia in connection with this amount of money that was in the Home Bank. We have searched our files and made numerous enquiries, but have been unable to find one person who has received a statement concerning this question."

---

11. Canadian Defence League and the Ku Klux Klan

A report from Calgary dated 28th June states that the Canadian Labour Defence League now has 24 branches in Canada.

This Party is circulating a leaflet issued by the Socialist Labour Party of the U.S.A. which denounces the Ku Klux Klan as an organization fostered by capitalists to contend against labour. One passage in this is as follows:-

"Let there be no mistake about the role the Ku Klux Klan is and will be playing in America. That organization together with all the others of like character and tendencies, in the measure that the rule of American capitalism is going to be challenged, will become part of the Pretorian Guard of capitalism, an extra-legal force to be used for purposes which the legal repressive forces of the political state cannot well serve without flying too brazenly in the face of historic tradition. In the nature of things and in line with the developments to come, that force will be used to browbeat the working class, to impede its efforts toward better organization by means of provocative methods and counter organization and in every possible manner frustrate its striving toward its own emancipation."

---

12. Attempted French Communist Paper in Montreal.

On 25th June a special meeting was held of the members of the [16] McGill Research Club and the French Branch of the Communist Party of Montreal; those present numbered 6 students and ten members of the French Branch. Tim Buck also was present and spoke. It is decided to publish the journal L'Ouvrier Canadien. Jean Paulin, a student was appointed Editor, the committee being Tim Buck, C. Paquette, Banel (Jewish student) and one Smith. Paulin at present is working for a New York paper, and will use extracts from it for L'Ouvrier Canadian. This paper will be published monthly; half the cost will be defrayed by the City Central Committee of the Communist Party of Montreal and half by the headquarters of the Communist Party at Toronto. It is to be distributed free.

---

13. Communist Notes

The headquarters of the Y.C.L. in Toronto have sent out a bulletin on Trade Union work. It contains the familiar demand that all Y.C.L. members join Trade Unions, and gives directions for the formation of "fractions" in the Unions.

A special warning is given against the danger of allowing these Communist fractions to become segregated.

The issue of Der Kamf of 2nd July contains an interesting attack upon the Executive of the Workmen's Circle. The governing body of this society has been driving the left-wing out of it, and apparently by way of reprisal, Der Kamf asserts that its insurance business is being carried on illegally.[17]

The Agitprop Department of the Communist Party is sending out from Toronto, a syllabus of 13 lessons in Leninism to be used during the period of "Red Recruiting" about December next.

Malcolm Bruce is said to be now living in Detroit.

---

14. An Anti British "Chinese Society of Canada" Projected.

A statement appeared in the Public Press not long ago that a Chinese named Edward Shuey Bing Lee, in Montreal, has been advocating the formation of a chinese Society of Canada. Enquiries show that this movement eminates from the Kue Min Tang, or Chinese Nationalist Society, a revolutionary and anti British organization. A report from Montreal says:-

"Edward Shuey Bing Lee, is, I understand, a student at McGill University, where he is studying railway systems and methods. This man holds no office in the organization, but is merely an ordinary member. His name is familiar in the local newspapers as he not infrequently writes in the correspondence columns, letters of a highly instructive nature upon economic conditions in China. His phraseology and apparent command of the English language, and his excellent style leads one to believe that he is very highly educated, both along general lines and interior economy of the country whence he hails.

"Nevertheless, Edward Shuey Bing Lee is no other than the Edward Lee who, in conjunction with Ing Feng, was prosecuted by us for conspiracy in connection with the planting of decks of drugs in this city some years ago."

This "Edward Lee" case was a very mean one. Having been ejected from a rooming house for not paying rent, the two Chinese placed narcotics in the house and accused the landlady of being concerned in the narcotic drug business.

ROYAL CANADIAN MOUNTED POLICE HEADQUARTERS

Ottawa, 23rd July, 1926.

SECRET

NO. 328

WEEKLY SUMMARY

NOTES REGARDING REVOLUTIONARY ORGANIZATIONS AND AGITATORS IN CANADA

REPORT

The most interesting development in the week has been the decision of the Communist Party to take as active a part as possible in the general election now in progress. The line to be taken is to attack His Excellency the Governor General on the ground that he has acted unconstitutionally, and to use that as a ground for demanding severance from the British Empire.

The Maritime Labour Herald has ceased publication. This leaves J. B. MacLachlan at a loose end, and he may move to Northern Ontario to organize for the Mine Workers' Union. He may be a candidate in one of the seats in that region.

The Communists, indefatigable starters of new newspapers, have two fresh journals in process of incubation, the Woman Worker in Toronto and L'Ouvrier Canadien in Montreal. Their Yiddish paper, Der Kamf, momentarily is in financial distress.

According to an Edmonton revolutionist, the recent immigrants who came from the Ukraine are of revolutionary temper.[2]

TABLE OF CONTENTS

APPENDIX NO. 1: GENERAL

APPENDIX NO. II: REPORTS FROM DISTRICTS

Jean Corbin on the group system.
A. Wojtyshyn
Schoeppe, ex-detective
Ukrainians visit Mundare
E. R. Fay.

" 8. Sam Scarlett's New Tack.

" 9. SASKATCHEWAN: Doukhobors again Being Urged to go to Russia.

" 10. MANITOBA: Communist Activities
The Railroad Shop Man
Y.C.L. & Pioneers Inactive
Conference of Paper Mill Workers.
D.L. Broadhurst, Brandon.
Bunda.

" 11. Proposed German Branch of the Communist Party

" 12. I.W.W. and O.B.U.
O.B.U. and railway shopmen
J.A. McDonald (No. 2)

" 13. ONTARIO: Notes.
London Communists
Ukrainians raise $1097 in Detroit and Windsor.

" 14. QUEBEC: Notes
A.E. Forget
Society for Cultural Relations with Moscow
L'Ouvrier Canadien
Mrs. Falken (or Sokolicht)
Canadian Labour Defence League
Montreal O.B.U. Collapse
St. Andre short in his accounts.[3]

APPENDIX NO. 1: GENERAL

1. Communists and the General Election

The Central Executive Committee of the Communist Party has issued a circular letter to the various branches, reading as follows:-

"The Central Executive Committee is desirous of gathering as much information as possible of the opportunities that present themselves throughout the country, of having our Comrades as Candidates in either the rural or industrial constituencies.

"Opportunities that fall into three categories may present themselves:-

"(1) Straight Party Candidates. This may be possible where there is no Canadian Labour Party organized; where if organized they do not intend contesting the election, or even where if organized and contesting the election another constituency might be contested by the Party on an understanding with the Canadian Labour Party.

"(2) Candidates of the Canadian Labour Party where Party members can secure nomination. Every attempt should be made to make this possible.

"(3) In rural constituencies where our Comrades may secure the nomination of Farmers' Organizations, such as the United Farmers of Alberta, Farmers' Union of Canada etc., our Comrades should make a thorough convass of the possibilities here and no opportunity should be missed of having our Comrades selected.

"The situation and the possibilities should be reviewed immediately and full details reported to the Central Executive Committee Secretary directly. We must act and act quickly in this matter. We must lose no opportunity of having our Party Comrades chosen as the standard bearers of the Workers and Farmers in this election. The inclusion of a few Communists in the Labour and Farmer Representatives in Parliament would do much to increase the prestige and strength of our party in Canada. Make a full report of this as soon as possible."[4]

---

2. J. B. MacLachlan A Possible Candidate

The Maritime Labour Herald has suspended publication, the issue of 10th July being the last.

It will be remembered that sometime ago our informant in the Cape Breton field prophesied that the paper would have a short life, and would be employed to provide an occupation for J.B. MacLachlan and one or two others as long as the money held out.

We have received from Toronto the following report regarding MacLachlan:-

"The above person, who was editor of the Maritime Labour Herald, is out of a position now, that publication being extinct.

"He will be leaving Nova Scotia in a short time and will go to Northern Ontario to become Organizer of The Mine Workers' Union of Canada.

"There is also a possibility that he may participate in the Federal Election and become the Labour Candidate in the North if J. MacDonald does not accept the nomination."

---

3. Communist View of the Election Issues

The Toronto Worker in its issue of 24th July attacks His Excellency the Governor General for his action in the recent political events. One article, signed M.L.J., contains the following passages:-

"Just as Sir John McDonald is known as the father of Confederation, so Lord Byng will be known as the Father-in-Law of Independence. MacKenzie King will of course dispute the title, but the question now agitating the minds of the voters is a question of law, of Constitution and Byng's the boy who made that agitation [5] possible. In fact he's one of the last of the line of British Governors-General in Canada. He listened sympathetically to Meighen, and because he was a sympathetic listener, his place is assured in Canadian as well as Empire history."

"We stand for independence of Canada. We will work for it. It belongs to our programme. We are Canadians. All right, then, we must be something more. We must be internationalists, united with workers, in every country of he world for the overthrow of our common enemy, capitalism. We must learn to understand the world movement of labour and the world movement of anti-labour. That knowledge will enable us to see through the moves of finance imperialism, and not be blinded as to our class interests by any capitalist politician that ever came down the pike waving the Union Jack or the Maple Leaf."

An editorial in the same issue headed "Whither Canada?" also demands independence of Canada. One passage is:-

"The legal and constitutional relations of the Dominion are out of step with the forces shaping her real destinies. Byng's action has simply brought these into high relief. The struggle is now on to give public and constitutional expression to these forms. What are they? What is the destiny of the Dominion in the next few years? Why has Byng, representing the home government, decided by a stroke of the pen to combat these forces? There was no longer room for phrases. It is a part of the dissolution of one Empire and the ascendancy of another. It is the turning point in a great struggle between England and the United States."

---

4. Communist Newspapers

At a meeting of the Winnipeg City Central Committee held on 15th July, a report from the Jewish Branch contained the remark the Der Kamf is in a bad condition financially.[6]

A report from Toronto says:-

"Under the auspices of the Federation of Women's Labour Leagues a newspaper has been published in magazine form known as 'The Woman Worker.'

"The first issue was published one week ago and it is intended to publish it every month.

"Mrs. F. Custance is the Editor."

5. Revolutionist Prophesying a Japanese-American War.

J. A. MacDonald (No. 2) the I.W.W. orator who suddenly has appeared in Winnipeg, addressed an open air meeting at the market place there on the evening of 14th July, dealing principally with unemployment. Our report says:-

> "Alluding to wars and the class war in particular, the speaker drew the audience's attention to the fact that war may break out at any time now between the U.S.A. and Japan. The Federal Secret Service of the U.S.A. a month ago succeeded in obtaining possession of the full war plans of the Japanese Government for an offensive against the U.S.A. At present the United States Government was putting into operation the means whereby the population of the U.S.A. could be placed on a war footing mobilization of the whole of the populace, rationing etc. He also said that Canada, with the connivance of the Imperial authorities, would give consent to the passage of American troops across the imaginary boundary line, and he warned his audience not to be misled by the 'Yellow Peril' slogan that the Capitalist class would raise. There was only one war that the workers must recognize and that was the Class War."

This wild talk is an unusually livid example of the manner in which these agitators are perpetually trying to keep the lower elements of the population in a ferment of expectation. With it may be compared Sam Scarlett's assertion at Calgary (mentioned in Appendix No. 11) that the British General Strike had been on the point of success when the labour leaders hastily ordered its cessation.[7]

6. The Ukrainians

The Ukrainian Labour News of 10th July publishes an appeal, signed by the Central Committee of the Leningrad Young Communist League of Soviet Russia, addressed to the Young Workers of Canada, asking them to visit the Soviet Republics. It is suggested that the delegation consist of young people working in different organizations or in chops and factories. It may be expected that the matter will be taken up seriously by the Ukrainian and Finnish groups of the Communist Party and by the Ukrainian Labour Farmer Temple Association.

At a meeting of the Edmonton branch of the Communist Party held on 11th July, John Klybanowsky, who had just returned from a propaganda trip to smoky Lake, said:-

> "I have talked to many of the immigrants as to whether they like this country. The immigrants that have come from Galicia are Czecho Slovakians. They said that this country is much better, but

the immigrants that have come from the Soviet Republic they are more for the proletariat movement."

ROYAL CANADIAN MOUNTED POLICE HEADQUARTERS

Ottawa, 5th August, 1926.

SECRET

NO. 330

WEEKLY SUMMARY

NOTES REGARDING REVOLUTIONARY ORGANIZATIONS AND AGITATORS IN CANADA

REPORT

Appreciations of the present state of the revolutionary schools are to be found in this issue from Montreal, Ottawa, and Edmonton. In Edmonton a teacher named John (Ivan) Symbay is doing much mischief, as he is unusually well educated.

The Communist International, through a subsidiary body in Europe named the Educational Workers' International, has made a tentative effort to get into touch with the Canadian Teachers' Federation.

The One Big Union is trying to reestablish itself in Winnipeg by putting Charles Lester forward, without admitting the fact that he is in their pay.

Both Lester and some I.W.W. agitators are making threats about the western harvest. Lester suggested to the railway shop workers that they strike during the crop moving season.[2]

APPENDICES

Table of Contents

APPENDIX NO. I: GENERAL.

APPENDIX NO. I: GENERAL

1. Revolutionary Schools in Edmonton.

We have received from Edmonton a survey of the present condition of the revolutionary schools maintained in that city and vicinity. The Officer Commanding the Royal Canadian Mounted Police there says:-

"The Ukrainian Labour Farmer Temple Association conduct two educational schools in this districts Edmonton and Beverly. Beverly is a suburb of Edmonton, the residents being mainly coalminers. The latest figures, and we have a good source of information here, as to the attendance, are as follows:- Edmonton, 120 pupils; Beverly, 56 pupils. These figures have increased greatly in the last few months, chiefly owing to the fact that one John Symbay, a student of the educational course at Winnipeg, is in charge. He is a well educated man, a fluent speaker, and is imbued with revolutionary ideas.... Above all, John Symbay is exceedingly well thought of by the Ukrainians generally, and must be regarded as a dangerous man; he, by his teachings being utterly opposed to the Canadian Constitution and decidedly in favour of a Soviet system of Government.

"Practically the sole attendance at these schools or classes are Ukrainians; at Edmonton, for instance, there are three Russian Jews and three Russians the balance are Ukrainians; at Beverly, every student is a Ukrainian no English-speaking children are attending these schools.

"The school is in session at Edmonton and Beverly three times a week, with lectures almost every Sunday afternoon.

Discussing the subjects taught, he says that the main subject taught is the Ukrainian language, and proceeds:-

"English is not taught, Symbay's great line being to tell the children of the alleged awful conditions of the workers in Russia under the Czarist regime, and how the workers overthrew the capitalist class in Russia, and how the workers in Canada are now preparing to overthrow the capitalist class in Canada, and how much better off, they, the workers, will be when they have control of the Government. They are also taught not to believe in religion or royalty; that the red flag is the God of the workers. Symbay also tries to teach them everything possible of the Soviet constitution, and of the great benefits to be derived from such a Government, and what a fine thing it would be for the workers if they had a Soviet Government here in Canada.

"In connection with the Ukrainian Labour Farmer Labour Temple Association of Edmonton, there is also the Orchestra; there are 26 children in same; they give concerts, assist in shows, etc. and also accompany organizers into the foreign farmer settlements on organizing campaigns. The larger part of the programme of this orchestra are revolutionary songs and marches.[5]

"As regards the Finnish race we have several settlements of Finns in this district notably at Red Deer, Alberta, a large number of whom have socialistic or revolutionary tendencies; they are a very clannish race and it has been found very difficult to get reliable information as to their propaganda. I am satisfied, however, that as regards this district the Finns are not affiliated in any way in their socialistic or revolutionary aims with any other race, but keep strictly to themselves in their various farming communities."

"With respect to the Jewish race; I have never received any information that the Jewish element of this district had any serious revolutionary aims; as a matter of fact the Jewish settlement here is small, mainly composed of small business men, lawyers, etc., and appear to be a quiet, law abiding people."

2. Revolutionary Schools in Ottawa.

For some time we have been aware that the revolutionary element in the Ukrainian community in Ottawa maintain a school. A new report has been procured upon it, and our investigator states that it is situated in the residence of one Nicholas Hopchuk at 523 Arlington Avenue; it has two grades, and as many as 38 children have been registered at it. The reports says:-

"This school goes under the name 'Ukrainian Workers' Party';

and a fee of one dollar per month is charged. Photographs of the late Russian Bolshevist Lenin, and other leaders of the Bolsheviki, are hung on the walls of this school room. Michael Chopowick and Peter Takubowski, Communist whose activities have been reported on by this office previously, are the leaders of this school."

The subjects taught are the same as elsewhere.

3. Revolutionary Schools in Montreal.

Another report is from Montreal, an agent writing:-

"At present these schools have closed down but they open again in September. The following schools are in the city:-

"The Ukrainian and Russian school is at 12 Market Place and from 33 to 38 children attend here. The school is held in the evenings from 5 to 8 p.m. and the teachers are Mrs. Bourarkeff and two other women. One of the delegates from 212 Drummond Street (Russian Soviet Trade Delegation) also sometimes comes down and gives instruction.

"At the Frontenac school 20 to 24 children attend, the school being held in the afternoon. I was informed that a delegate from Drummond Street gives instructions here.

"35 to 43 children attend the school in the afternoon of the Young Pioneers at the Labour College, at 70 Mance St. The teacher is Mrs. Julia Cohen and the school is conducted by the Young Communist League.

"The Lachine school has closed.

"The Finns as yet have no school."[6]

It may be added that the children attending the school in Market and Frontenac Streets are Russian and Ukrainian; at 70 Mance Street the children are Jewish.

4. Communist Notes.

George Latham has been nominated by the Canadian Labour Party as Labour candidate for East Edmonton.

The Canadian Labour Party in Edmonton, while not entirely Communist, is under Communist influence, the Communists usually managing by adroit caucus work to obtain the decisions they desire. Latham himself is not a Communist.

We have information to the effect that the Educational Workers' International, an organization with its seat in France, but entirely under the direction of Moscow, is making efforts to get into touch with the Canadian Teachers' Federation. The Third International is exceedingly anxious to get hold of the teaching profession, so as to introduce its influence into the state school. The E.W.I. has begun by addressing to the Canadian body an innocent-looking questionnaire about salaries.

We have received a copy of the first issue of the Young Comrade, a mimeographed paper issued for the Pioneers. It is strongly Communistic.

The Central Executive Committee of the Communist Party are circulating a broadsheet, entitled "Lessons of the British General Strike". It contains the usual abuse of the British Labour leaders, and argues that the course of the general strike has proved its value against capitalism.

The Edmonton branch of the Communist Party has received orders from Toronto directing "every Communist to be on the job amongst the immigrants. During this year there will be a hard winter for the slaves."[7]

---

5. Charles Lester's O.B.U. Campaign in Winnipeg.

Charles Lester has been very busy addressing audiences in the Market Place and at the railway shops in Winnipeg, and has impressed those who have heard him with his skill as a speaker. To some extent he has been occupied in denouncing religion. When speaking on economics, while he avoids open advocacy of the O.B.U., he follows the general line taken by that body. His whole course in Winnipeg is an example of underhand campaigning.

Lester addressed an open-air meeting of the C.P.R. shop gates at Weston on 23rd July. Our report says:-

> "He earnestly pleaded with them not to take any notice of announcement that the time was not suitable for negotiations, and pointed out that now was the time to act. The crop would have to be moved in a few weeks time, and the workers, if they remained united and solid, could force the issue at this period, but there must be solidarity. The speaker was given an attentive hearing from about 150 men.
>
> "There is no doubt that there is great dissatisfaction among the shopmen. The Division No. 4 Committee has failed them, and although the men of the American Federation of Labour do not look upon the way the O.B.U. is trying to control the situation, with favour, it is extremely probable that conditions are coming to such a pass that they will be forced to take direct action, irrespective of any union.
>
> "A ballot has been taken but no announcement has been made yet. The men of the O.B.U. are ready to go right ahead, but the members of the A.F. of L. unions are somewhat reluctant. They have not faith in the O.B.U. and think this organization is having altogether too much to do with it, although lately the O.B.U. organizers have studiously refrained from butting in, at least publicly. Possibly this is the reason Lester is in the city. Officially he has no

connection with the O.B.U. He is a Socialist, but he speaks along O.B.U. lines.

"The situation is at present somewhat tense. The men are quite well aware that they can tie up traffic in the crop moving period, this will just about approximate the time when a large number of I.W.W. agitators and members are in the city, and this bunch make no bones about declaring that they intend to set the wage scale for harvesters, and are prepared to cause trouble of a serious kind.[8]

"All the different organizations are aware of the crisis approaching, and the red element are out to get theirs. There will be an effort to get the building trade labourers out, but this may be difficult as large numbers of them are declaring their intentions to leave the building jobs and go harvesting, they are hard to organize. It all depends on what the shopmen do.

"Bartholomew of the Communist Party is supposed to be in town. All this, taking into consideration that a general election is approaching promises to make the month of August a period of unrest."

In reporting another speech of Lester's at the C.P.R. shop on 28th July, an agent, after remarking that Lester is careful in his speech not to mention anything about the O.B.U., adds that the ordinary organizers of the O.B.U., Sykes, Clancy, etc. ceased their propaganda in this neighbourhood as soon as Lester came to town.

In commenting upon this report the Officer Commanding the Royal Canadian Mounted Police in Manitoba says:-

"The shop gate meetings from some time have been the favourite stumping ground for the O.B.U. crowd. Evidently they are leaving the field open to Lester to see what he can do. As a matter of fact the Baltimore and Ohio scheme is said to be working very efficiently at present, which tends to make it much harder for the O.B.U. to gain ground in the shops."

A further report, dated 30th July, says:-

"Lester is still on the job. He was at Transcona yesterday. This man is undoubtedly speaking on behalf of the O.B.U. He travelled down on the O.B.U. organizers' car. Clancy is in Calgary. Sykes was in Winnipeg last week but has not been around this week.

"Lester never mentions the O.B.U. in his speeches, but the men are fully aware of whom he speaks for."

In this connection it may be remarked that there have been of late several small strikes in the coalmines in Cape Breton, called by the United Mine Workers of America, protesting against work being given to members of the O.B.U. There is some ground for the belief that these strikes will be kept up until the company refuses to employ O.B.U. [9] members.

6. The Canadian Labour Defence League and Antonina Sokelicz

Much activity, at present centering principally in Winnipeg, is being shown in booming the Canadian Labour Defence League, an organization designed, like so many revolutionary bodies, to appeal to non-communistic labour while in reality held in strict control, more or less secretly exercised by the Communists. The Canadian society is a branch of the international Communist organization known in Moscow as M.O.P.R. and by Ukrainians as M.O.D.R. (International Prisoners Aid); in the United States it is styled the International Labour Defence and in Canada as the Canadian Labour Defence League. It sometimes is called the Red Aid. According to the Ukrainian Labour News it is established in 33 countries and has a membership of 6,500,000.

Antonina Sokelicz (Falken) at present in Canada, was active in this organization in Poland, and her visit to Canada, apart from her mission to organize Polish Canadians into Communism, has had to do with the recruiting of this League.

As an example of the co-ordination which marks these people's work, it may be noted that in preparation for her coming the Ukrainian Labour News printed a series of articles in advocacy of the League; the sixth of the series appeared in the issue of 24th July.

As a result of Antonina Sokelicz's activities, the following branches of the Canadian Labour Defence League have been formed in Winnipeg: Polish, about 55; Ukrainians, about 300; Jewish, about 35. The Ukrainian branch, by the way, lost no time in passing a resolution demanding an amnesty in Poland.

The Jewish branch of the League began as a "United Aid Committee for strikers". This draws its membership from [10] The Jewish branch of the League began as a "United Aid Committee for Strikers". This draws its membership from the Workmen's Circle, the National Workers' Society, the Jewish Branch of the Communist Party, the Right and Left wing of the Poale Zion, the Liberty Temple Association, the Mother Society of the Workers' National Institute and the Jewish Guild Society. It will be seen that by this device the Communist are drawing non-Communist Jewish organizations into the Communist enterprise.

One of Antonina Sokelicz's lectures was held in the Liberty Temple, a Jewish meeting place, and another in the Ukrainian Labour Temple.

The City Central Committee of the Communist Party in Winnipeg are trying to manoeuvre the Independent Labour Party into helping to form an English branch of this body.

7. Agitation Among the Foreigners.

Definite information has been received from Kamsack that 17 Doukhobor families, comprising 54 people, are expected to leave that place for Russia on 14th August. Their departure is not absolutely certain; the number of families depends upon whether final settlement will have been made for their farms; it is understood that deductions from the purchase price of the land will be made to cover transportation to Russia. This is the outcome of several provincial agreements between the Ukrainian Immigration and Colonization Association and the Doukhobors. Mr. Ivan Kulyk addressed the Doukhobors in several places.

We have received a report of a meeting of the Fort William branch of the Ukrainian Labour Farmer Temple Association. After Wasyl [11] Peruniak had demanded that every member of the party and every workingman must regularly attend all picnics and all concerts, and Peter Chepesiuk had spoken to the same effect S. Kamaranski gave a speech which is thus reported:-

> "I know comrades we suffer and die from hunger, but we, the labourers must keep faith because there is a great number of us and we are a great power. Let us collect money to support our labour organizations. He gave $14 Peruniak $10 Chepesiuk, $10, and some more tens. And some there gave a dollar cash. Kamaranski collected at that concert meeting $172.50."

The Officer Commanding the Royal Canadian Mounted Police in Manitoba remarks:-

> "It will be noted in the last paragraph of this report that quite a respectable sum of money was collected from men said to be dying of hunger."

The Edmonton branch of the Ukrainian Labour Farmer Temple Association on 24th July, presented a play entitled "Always Revolutionist". An account of this given by our correspondent is as follows:-

> "In the first act, a revolutionist was going amongst the workers telling them they should not work for the boss and get nothing for their work, and so the workers quit work.
>
> "In the second act the revolutionist came out and called propaganda meetings amongst the workers and gave a speech, saying that if all workers would stay by him the revolution would be here any time, and the capitalist class will be put out of control.
>
> "In the third act the leaders were busy amongst the workers preparing them for the revolution. One of the crowd acted that he was against them and he put the police on the job and the leaders were arrested and the movement was broken up, but the leaders stayed on the job and organized for a new start."

The attendance numbered about 60.

8. The I.W.W. and the Harvest

A man known as J. Sharp has been appointed by the I.W.W. head office, Chicago, as General Organizer for Western Canada, with instructions to open I.W.W. halls at Moose Jaw, Saskatoon and Winnipeg.[12]

Apparently Moose Jaw will be his first stopping place. He will be paid $4 a day and expenses.

Sam Scarlett, who still is at Calgary, has been laid up by an accident, and in his absence a man named Keith addressed an I.W.W. meeting in Calgary, on Sunday, 25th July.

A correspondent says:-

> "Since the Agricultural Industrial Union, No. 110 organized in Western Canada, over 4,000 members have been recruited for I.W.W. organization.
>
> "The majority of the I.W.W.'s members going away from the Prairie Provinces leave after the harvest, but generally return each year for the harvest."

ROYAL CANADIAN MOUNTED POLICE HEADQUARTERS

Ottawa, 12th August, 1926.

SECRET

NO. 331

WEEKLY SUMMARY

NOTES REGARDING REVOLUTIONARY ORGANIZATIONS AND AGITATORS IN CANADA

REPORT

The Communists are trying to influence the course of the general election in several parts of the country. Reports from Toronto and London in this issue show once more how treacherous their course invariably tends to be.

Another example of the combination of thirst for power and of treachery which so characterizes the Communist is afforded by a report of a plot which is in progress to oust Gerald Dealtry, the founder of the revolutionary paper, the Furrow, and substitute formal Communist ownership. Bartholomew who in some respects is the most effective Communist agitator now at work so far as the English-speaking element is concerned is revealed in a particularly mean and odious light in this affair, as he is lending himself to betray a benefactor.

The break-down of the group organization of the Communist Party proceeds apace. Regina has been allowed formally to repeal it, and in Toronto it has reduced the membership materially.[2]

APPENDICES

Table of Contents

APPENDIX NO. I; GENERAL.

APPENDIX NO. II: REPORTS FROM DISTRICTS.

APPENDIX NO. I: GENERAL

1. Effect of the Communist Reorganization in Toronto.

The reorganization of the Toronto Communist Party into shop and area groups took place in April last. We have received, under date of 4th August, a survey of the situation as it has been effected upon reorganization. The report is as follows:-

"It appears that the party has lost a number of members; only 50 per cent of the total dues have been paid which means at least 15 per cent of the members have not attended shop or area group meetings. According to groups reports, the chief trouble comes from the Finnish members.

"In some groups the Finnish members have not attended and they claim that they are only members of the Finnish Society, and not members of the Communist Party, therefore will not attend meetings of groups of the Communist Party.

"Another important point is the language question. In some groups they cannot understand each other. This also tends towards members becoming disgruntled.

"But although the members are becoming disinterested the power of the Communist Party is still the same in the Labour Party and Trade Unions.

"The same apathy, I am informed, exists throughout the country, so it appears that the Communist Party is not as strong numerically now as it was before reorganization."

2. Regina Abandons the Group Form of Organization.

The members of the Communist Party living in Regina held two meetings at the Ukrainian Labour Temple in that city on Sunday, 1st August, the up-shot of their deliberations being a decision to abandon the group system and form themselves into an International Street Group. The matter was principally discussed at a meeting in the afternoon, but the decision was reached at a meeting in the evening, which was attended by T. Ewen of Saskatoon, who represented the Central Executive Committee.[5]

Our report of the afternoon meeting says:-

"In the discussion on the motion it was pointed out that the group system had failed and hope was expressed that if the party would be reorganized in conformity with the motion, the party would become active again and its activities better co-ordinated. One or two Ukrainian members wanted to have the party reorganized on a language basis. The prime movers in the attempt to have the party reorganized and put on an efficient footing were the Ukrainians. The City Central Committee came in for some considerable criticism for failing to function and for failing to properly lead the groups. Members of the City Central Committee stated that the inactivity of the Committee was a reflex of the inactivity of the groups, and consequently, it was not the City Central Committee that was to blame but the groups themselves."

At this meeting nearly everyone present agreed upon the need of reorganizing the party. Dealing with the evening meeting the following is said:-

"T. Ewen, apparently had been commissioned by the Central Executive of the party to come to Regina with the object in view of reorganizing the party. The action of the Central Executive was more or less in consequence of complaints made by the Ukrainian Agit Prop Committee to the effect that the groups and the City Central Committee were inactive and could or would not function.

"The second meeting was called to order at 10.45 by T. Susiak with T. Ewen of Saskatoon present. There were 14 members present, and T. Susiak was appointed chairman for the meeting.

"After having briefly outlined to him the circumstances surrounding the party, T. Ewen addressed the meeting and stated that the meeting in the afternoon agreed upon a wise course of action and supported the motion. The motion was then put and unanimously adopted."

3. Communist Intrigue in Labour Party Affairs in London.

The Communist group in London has been playing the usual game in labour party politics. The London Branch of the Labour Party decided on 16th July to hold an opening convention on 28th July to nominate a candidate for the pending elections. During the interval the Communist Party was busy, its efforts being particularly directed towards the members of the Canadian Brotherhood of Railway Employes. This union met on 26th July and L.R. Menzies, the Communist agitator, urged the members to be present at the convention. Our reports says:-[6]

"He mentioned A.C. Avery, as a man who could be trusted to look after the interests of Labour if nominated and elected. (Members of the local Communist Party know well that Avery has no chance of being elected, but want his name on the lists for propaganda purposes.)"

The convention broke up in a quarrel, the chairman insisting that only delegates should take part in it, and Menzies leading a violent demand that it be an open one. The chairman was sustained, and Menzies made sundry remarks, one being that "The London Labour Party was being run by a bunch of crooks."

At a meeting of the Executive of the London Labour Party an apology was demanded from Menzies on pain of his expulsion from the Labour Party. Our report says:-

"If Menzies is expelled from the London Labour Party it is more than likely that the Canadian Brotherhood of Railway Employes will also withdraw and if this happens it will probably mean the disintegration of the L.L.P. Menzies was urged to explain that he did not intend to charge the leaders of the L.L.P. with being dishonest and it is possible that he may modify the charge, but he says positively that he will make no apology for what he said.

"The opinion of the leaders of the Communist Party here is that they will have to break with the L.L.P. eventually and that it would be to the advantage of the Communists to do so. The policy to be followed, however, is to pretend to maintain the United Front at all costs and let the other party take the responsibility for weakening the resistance which a United Labour Party could oppose to oppressive capitalism.

"Comrade Hazelgrove is still addressing large crowds at the Market Square Saturday evening meetings. The Sunday meetings at the Federal Square were not well attended and are not being held regularly at present."

4. Amenities Between Communists and Socialists at Toronto

As stated in the public press, the Central Council of the Canadian

Labour Party at a meeting held on 6th August decided to put forward two candidates in Toronto, John MacDonald in Centre West Toronto and James Simpson in Northwest Toronto. In doing so it was resolved to "have no truck or trade with either of the Capitalists Parties". An intimation came that "if J. MacDonald ran in Centre West Toronto then the Jewish Socialists would not support him."[7]

On 7th August a special election convention was held by the Ontario section, Canadian Labour Party, to prepare the election manifesto. Our report says:-

"There were over a hundred delegates present with Communist Party delegates in the majority.

"Heated discussions took place over the question of complete self determination of sovereignty for Canada; it was moved by J. Simpson to have Self Determination struck out.

"During the argument Simpson was called a crook, a traitor and was told by James Muldowney that he hunted with the hounds and ate with the ducks. Muldowney stated that he could not possibly belong to the same party as Simpson in the future, as the latter had endeavoured to intimidate labour in this Federal election, and therefore he was resigning as Vice President, Ontario Section, C.L.P., President of Toronto Central Council, C.L.P., and member of Earlscourt Branch of the Canadian Labour Party; as Simpson told him to join the Communist Party where he belonged.

"After several other insults had been thrown at Simpson he threatened to resign as secretary and leave the room, but Spector withdrew the amendment, striking out Self-determination, leaving it Complete Sovereignty for Canada, which Spector states is exactly the same because, if you have complete Sovereignty you have Self-determination.

"The other demands in the Manifesto are the usual, Old Age Pensions, Abolition of Cadet Training in Public Schools, Repeal of British North America Act, Immigration, National Health Insurance, etc."

5. Communists Plotting to Capture The "Furrow".

On 16th July a secret meeting was held in Saskatoon of Communist members who were attending the Farmers' Union Convention; the meeting was called by T. Ewen to discuss the relationship of the Furrow to the Communist Party. Ewen acted as the representative of the Central Executive Committee of the Communist Party, and read a letter which he had received from that body on the subject.

Our report proceeds:-

"Briefly speaking, in the letter, the Central Executive Committee explained that, although a party member is editing the paper, the party has no control over the paper and consequently, the paper could not be endorsed by the party as a left wing paper. Jack MacDonald, over whose signature the letter was written, stated, however, that the Central Executive Committee could not find any [8] fault with the policy of the paper and asked the meeting to discuss the whole matter with the end in view of whether or not the paper could be brought under the control of the party and if not, if some other left wing paper could be got out. MacDonald also stated that Bartholomew started to edit the paper without consulting the National office of the party and that no permission was given to him to proceed with the publication of the said paper.

"After the letter having been read, Ewen gave a more detailed account of as to how the paper was started blaming Bartholomew for going into partnership with Gerald Dealtry, whom he characterised as a reactionary trickster. He also accused Bartholomew of having broken the discipline of the party by not consulting the National Office. He said that Bartholomew came up from Winnipeg with the intention of going into partnership with Dealtry, and that they (Saskatoon Branch) only heard of the affair after the first issue, edited by Bartholomew, appeared.

"The explanation given by Ewen brought Bartholomew to his feet, who informed the meeting that the whole matter had been discussed between him and the District Executive Committee prior to his leaving Winnipeg. He stated further that while no official permission was given to him by the members of the D.E.C. in Winnipeg, it was understood that he was to go to Saskatoon and to edit the paper. He especially referred to M. Popowich, who greatly favoured the proposition, and who promised that he would take the matter up with the National Office upon his arrival in Toronto. Bartholomew also stated that he had written to the Central Executive immediately after his arrival in Saskatoon, informing them of his intention, and that he has a copy of that letter in his office.

"Following Bartholomew's remarks, Ewen spoke and disagreed with some of the statements which he made. Bartholomew replied to what Ewen had said, maintaining that his statements were correct.

"It was at this juncture when some of the outside members interfered, some wanting to have the meeting adjourned in order to give Bartholomew time to procure the copy of the letter, and some suggested that the meeting be proceeded with in view of the fact that a meet had been called in the Bijou Theatre, commencing at 10.30p.m. at which Bartholomew was to speak. Most of the farmer members stated that they had endorsed the Furrow, and that it would be bad policy to tell the people to whom they had sold subscriptions that they should not support the paper. It was also stated that the left wing conference of the farmer delegates to the conventions had endorsed the Furrow as the official organ of the Farmers' Progressive Educational League, and that it would react in a very unfavourable way if these arrangements would be upset.

"After some discussion it was agreed that in view of the difficulty and in view of the wide publicity that had been given to The Furrow, the question before the members was 'how to bring the paper under party control.'[9]

"It must be stated that on one occasion Bartholomew made the statement that should the meeting decide that he should cease to edit the paper, he would do so because he wanted to live up to the discipline of the party.

"After some considerable discussion, Bartholomew was asked as to what his equity in the paper was. Bartholomew explained the status of the Furrow Publishers as follows:-

"The Furrow is owned by G. Dealtry and himself, each holding a technical equity of $500; that the putting up of these sums was only on paper in order to get the legal documents fixed up; that in reality neither Dealtry nor he has any money invested; that the paper has been financed by Dealtry; that the office furniture and fixtures is all owed by Dealtry for which he charges rent; that the paper has no assets, and that the paper owed about $60 to the printers.

"Bartholomew also explained that in order to keep the paper going it was necessary to sell space to advertise. Advertisements thus far have practically covered the printing costs.

"When asked if Dealtry would care to sell his share in the paper, Bartholomew thought the he would not, at least as long as there were any prospects of bringing the paper on a paying basis. Bartholomew was of the opinion, however, that should the paper experience financial difficulties, Dealtry would be only too willing to take in another partner, who would be in a position to put up the share in case, namely $500. This, he said, would mean that there would be three shareholders then, each holiding $500 shares. If the Communist Party, through some party member, would put up the $500, in such a manner so that it would not arouse the suspicion of Dealtry, the paper could easily get in control of the paper.

"It was agreed then, after some discussion, that the plan suggested by Bartholomew be adopted, namely, that Bartholomew continue to edit the paper and when the opportunity presents itself he shall notify the party, and the party will then through some party member purchase his share in question.

"It may be pointed out that a number of party members could be called upon to advance the necessary money if needed. Two of these whose names were mentioned are Marte and Fred Ganong of Sturgis.

"The time in which the paper is liable to find itself in financial difficulties was stated to be during the early part of October or perhaps sooner than that.

"It was also suggested that in the event of the paper acquiring that share it would be a comparatively easy matter to induce or force Dealtry to hand over his share thereby bringing the paper under complete control of the party.

"In the course of the discussion it was stated by Bartholomew that about 200 subscriptions were started up during the convention week, most of which were collected from Farmers' Union delegates."[10]

The incident vividly show the constant atmosphere of intrigue and treachery which envelopes the Communist movement. Dealtry, whom Bartholomew is plotting to betray, came to his assistance when he was in great need, having apparently hardly had enough to eat.

6. Women's Sections Formed in the Communist Party.

A report from Toronto, dated 7th August, says:-

"Women's Section have been formed in the Communist Party for some time amongst the English-speaking section, although it is not a separate organization, being purely for the purposes of extending Communist influence. No membership cards are required, but members must belong to the Communist Party.

"The chief work which is done by them is in the Women's Labour League and is purely socialist in character.

"Before the last convention, the Ukrainian Section of the Communist Party did not admit women at all into their section, but now they are admitted and have organized a women's section.

"Nowhere as far as I know have they adopted any other name except 'Women's Section of the Communist Party.'

"Mrs. F. Custance is their representative on the Central Executive Committee and is in charge of the work, but is not a paid official."

7. Trying to Perform Revolutionary Plays in Halifax.

The Communist Group in Halifax is trying to set up a revolutionary drama, Hugh Pynn, the Communist, who at present is chairman of the Trades and Labour Council, having proposed that that body co-operate in this enterprise. Our report of the meeting held on 27th July, says:-

"Before closing the meeting, Pynn proposed that they should present a revolutionary stage play which would express the working class ideology; he strongly recommended for this purpose two particular plays; one 'Singing Jailbirds' by a Socialist writer named Upton Sinclair, and the other 'The Strike'. He said that the latter would be the more suitable of the two for staging, and would give a real impression of the workers' struggle. Pynn suggested that if

> this play could only be staged successfully, that they might organize and establish a permanent workers' theatre in Halifax, which would specialize in revolutionary drama, and thus spread Communist ideas and make them more attractive to the workers."[11]

The Trades and Labour Council, however, rejected the idea, and it is unlikely that the scheme will prove effective.

This is another example of the clever and persistent way in which the Communists try to get other people to do their work for them.

It was decided at a meeting of the Edmonton Branch of the Ukrainian Labour Farmer Temple held on 4th August to set on foot a collection to aid the striking coalminers. In connection with this J. Stukoluk, the Vice President of District 18 of the Miners' Federation, addressed the meeting, his speech including a statement that in the week just passed he had "stopped 33 scabs from going to work."

The Edmonton Branch of the Ukrainian Labour Farmer Temple Association gave a picnic on 2nd August, for the benefit of the striking miners at Beverly. The crowd was small, only about 75 in number; there was much talk in resentment of the recent policy on the decision that the miners had no right to picket.

13. The Ukrainians

The Ukrainian Labour Farmer Temple Association Mandolin Orchestra in its performance at Fernie, on 29th July, did not disclose its full character. According to a Polish citizen who attended, the programme, both vocal and instrumental was of a fairly high order, with nothing of a revolutionary nature; the songs were nearly all old Ukrainian folk songs, some being rendered in Ukrainian and others in English. "O Canada" was rendered at the beginning of the evening, but the National Anthem was omitted at the end.

The Ukrainian Communists in Edmonton still are worried over the difficulty they experience in getting their members naturalized. Orders from headquarters for revolutionary aliens to become naturalized are imperative, and the fact that the police from time to time show that they are aware that a given applicant is identified with revolutionary [12] agitation has caused alarmed resentment. At the meeting of the Edmonton branch of the Ukrainian Labour Farmer Temple Association on 4th August, a measure of organization was set on foot, a member of the party being appointed to help revolutionary aliens who wish to be naturalized by making out papers, etc.

8. The Ukrainians

An incident at a business meeting of the Edmonton Branch of the Ukrainian Labour Farmer Temple Association held on 4th August illustrates the strength of the grip which this organization is getting on its members, and the authoritative attitude it is assuming. Our report says:-

"The question of the children's schools was taken up, and it was decided that every member of the Association was to be taxed 75 cents a month to help keep the school going. Those parents who have children at the school and are not members of the association, must pay $1 a month.

"It was decided that more shows and concerts are to be given to help provide funds for lectures and schools."

The head office of the Ukrainian Labour Farmer Temple Association at Winnipeg has issued the following appeal:-

"We are asking all sections of the Ukrainian Labour Temple to stay by the Building Committee at Winnipeg; we have started to build the new school room and press room, which will cost $36,000; we have collected $10,000, we must have $26,000 more to complete the job; you have that money, let us have it and save the interest from going to the capitalist class. Every section in Canada should donate a sum of money by giving concerts, etc."

A report of the School Committee of the Edmonton branch of the Ukrainian Labour Farmer Temple Association submitted on 4th August states that 133 children were attending school three times a week and that 33 "members", i.e. adults, were attending a course school half an hour each time. Our report adds that a propaganda lecture is given to the members and children by J. Symbay, the school teacher.[13] The Regina School during July had an attendance of 44 pupils, senior and junior.

The Moose Jaw school had an attendance of 35 during July; it being the holidays for the public schools, classes were held nearly every afternoon.

9. A Sample of Mischief-Making by Moriarty.

William Moriarty addressed an open-air meeting at South Porcupine on 31st July, under the auspices of the Mine Workers' Union of Canada. He criticised local labour conditions, our report saying:-

Moriarty predicted a scarcity of miners by the fall on account of those whom are declared to be in a tuberculose stage here; either to quit or come up to the surface. Every man has to pass an examination by the Government doctor, and if he is declared to be in the first stage of consumption, second or third, he has to come out of the mine. Next fall would be the time for the men to ask for better conditions and a raise of wages if the workers were properly organized."

10. Trouble with the O.B.U. in Cape Breton

The Officer Commanding the Royal Canadian Mounted Police in the Maritime Provinces in his confidential monthly report for July, makes the following remarks regarding conditions in Cape Breton:-

"At the end of the month, considerable local unrest is occurring in various mines where O.B.U. men have been employed by the operators. The U.M.W. called a strike and the mine stopped working but work continued two days when the O.B.U. men joined the U.M.W.

"Two collieries at Sydney Mines are out for the same reason and the president of the M.W.U. is making every effort openly to drive out the O.B.U.

"The British Empire Steel Corporation refuses to take any part in the matter and leave the responsibility to the U.M.W. It is anticipated that the U.M.W. will win out and make the mines a 'closed shop.'"

He adds that the O.B.U. are getting their forces together in Cape Breton.

The series of local strikes in Cape Breton, according to a correspondent, have issued in a victory for the United Mine Workers of America; all the working miners have been formed into that body.[14]

It may be worth while noting in this connection that the Citizen, the Halifax labour paper of somewhat extreme views, which has been assailing the Communists, has now opened fire upon the O.B.U.

ROYAL CANADIAN MOUNTED POLICE HEADQUARTERS

Ottawa, 19th August, 1926.

SECRET

NO. 332

WEEKLY SUMMARY

NOTES REGARDING REVOLUTIONARY ORGANIZATIONS AND AGITATORS IN CANADA

REPORT

The Communists still are trying to get some advantage out of the general election. In Winnipeg they are trying to get concessions from the Independent Labour Party by threatening to run separate candidates, and in Alberta they have seized the opportunity to get signatures to petitions for clemency, or a new trial, for Lewis McDonald (Kid Burns).

At Drumheller the Ukrainian revolutionists are trying to complete their separation from the Church by holding Communist funerals.

The O.B.U. agitation has spread to Edmonton.

An appreciation of that unquiet district, the Crow's Nest Pass, shows conditions among the coal-miners to be unusually peaceful. In some camps the Mine Workers' Union of Canada predominates; in some the British Columbia Miners' Union; and in one place the mines are open shop.[2]

APPENDICES

Table of Contents

APPENDIX NO. I: GENERAL

APPENDIX NO. I: GENERAL

1. Winnipeg Communists and the General Election

At a meeting of the Winnipeg City Central Committee held on 12th August, the local political situation was considered again, apparently with an eye to forcing their way into the labour campaign. Our report says:-

> "From the discussions it appears that the Executive Committee of the City Central Committee planed to force the Independent Labour Party to a United Front by calling a conference of labour organizations to endorse the candidate of the Independent Labour Party otherwise to scare the Independent Labour Party by putting M. Popowich up as a candidate of the Communist Party to split the labour vote.

"A telegram was sent to the Central Executive Committee to Toronto asking if Popowich would come here and to pay his railway expenses and to answer by wire. As no answer was received, it was the opinion of the delegates of the City Central Committee that it was too late for calling the mentioned conference."

The Officer Commanding the Royal Canadian Mounted Police in Manitoba in commenting on the foregoing says:-

"It was previously decided that the Communist Party would not put up a candidate for the forthcoming Federal elections, and in all probability a belated idea of sending Popowich was only done to annoy the Independent Labour Party and to bring them up to the mark in connection with the Canadian Labour Defence League.

2. Canadian Labour Defence League's Campaign for Lewis McDonald

Under instructions from the head office in Toronto, the Canadian Labour Defence League is active in Drumheller, and in Alberta as a whole, working for the release of Lewis McDonald, (Kid Burns); petitions are being circulated and, owing to present political conditions, are being signed rather widely. A report says:-

"The leaders of the Canadian Labour Defence League are expecting that there will be enough signatures on their petition which will compel authorities to grant another trial for L. McDonald by a jury. They are also of the opinion that if another trial was granted by a jury, McDonald may be let free, or will be sentenced only for a few months. This is the hope of the Canadian Labour Defence League at present. The Canadian Labour Defence League is absolutely under the control of the Communist Party, so that if McDonald gets free from jail, the Communist Party will try to claim all the credit for their activities in this case."[5]

3. Trying to Stir up Discontent

The headquarters of the Communist Party at Toronto have sent out a circular on Unemployment and Immigration. A translation of the Ukrainian version is:-

"Every group of the Communist Party should prepare themselves for the coming winter, to be on guard amongst immigrants; there will be destitution this winter for the working classes, every worker and immigrant must look after the Communist movement; every member of the party that goes out harvesting, must be sure and spread Communist propaganda amongst immigrants. Times will be hard this coming winter, and all immigrants and workers should be brought into the left wing movement against the capitalist class. The army of unemployed will have to be looked after and prevented from being exploited by the Capitalist class. This work must be carried out by the Communist Party."

At a meeting of the Edmonton Branch of the Communist Party which was held on 8th August, M. Rosen in commenting on the foregoing letter said:-

> "The more immigrants that we put into Canada, the better it will be for the Communist movement and the end of the capitalist class will be nearer, and it will help the Communist Party to organize the farmers against the capitalists class. There will be more soup houses than ever in Canada this year."

4. Agitation Among Ukrainians at Drumheller.

We have received a survey of the situation among the Drumheller Ukrainians which shows renewed activity of communist agitators among them. Our agent mentions a play which was presented on Sunday, 1st August, in the Ukrainian Labour Temple at Drumheller, under the title "Past and Present System of Rule in Russia." He says:-

> "This play was very interesting from the Bolsheviks' point of view; it represented the most miserable life of the working class under the capitalists' system in Russia, and after this a change took place in that country the workers possessed all the wealth, and used the same for their own benefit. There were about 150 present, composed of Ukrainians and a few Russians and Jews."

On 2nd August the Winnipeg Ukrainian Labour Farmer Temple Association Mandolin Girls' Orchestra gave a concert: our report observes:-
[6]

> "No Bolshevik songs were sung or played, so as not to offend the English public. There were about 200 present composed of Ukrainians, some English, Jews, Italians and others.
>
> "On 3rd August the same orchestra held a concert in the Ukrainian Labour Temple, New Castle, West Drumheller. This concert was opened and closed by playing the 'International' and every second song was of a Bolshevik character.
>
> "N. Charyk make a brief speech about the orchestra from Winnipeg, stating that if the workers can produce such musical talents, they can rule the country as well, if they have the same chance as the Russian workers had in Russia."

The attendance at this concert was about 200, mostly Ukrainians.

The Ukrainian revolutionary school in Drumheller closed down during July, but was to be reopened early in August with W. Nykyforuk, who attended the Higher Educational Course in Winnipeg last winter, as a teacher.

5. A Communist Funeral.

The report contains the following passage which probably has considerable significance:-

> "On 11th July, a very interesting funeral took place in Drumheller. One member of the Ukrainian Labour Farmer Temple Association, W. Samotiuk, had died on 9th July, and his funeral

ceremony was held in the Ukrainian Labour Temple. The coffin of the late W. Samotiuk was placed in the middle of the hall, and the members sang and played the mandolins, playing 'Bolshevik's Dead March'. N. Charyk made an address and then all marched to the cemetary, where J. Stefuniuk made another speech, and the members repeated once more the Dead March.

"This is the second Communist funeral to be held in Drumheller. Last winter L. McDonald (Kid Burns) acted as high Communist priest, at the funeral of communist Schwartz, but from information I obtained, it looks as if there were two Communist priests at the funeral of W. Samotiuk. The reasons I mentioned about this funeral is that the Bolsheviks and Communists are trying to separate their members from the Church and religion for ever. The members of the Ukrainian Labour Farmer Temple Association are practically prohibited to attend any Church service. Many of them live together only on a marriage license, and none of them baptize their children. Now they start a new form of funeral, exactly the same as the Communists in Russia."

6. Ukrainian Notes.

The Ukrainian Labour News of 12th August announced that on [7] 9th August a beginning was made at the erection of the new building for the Ukrainian Labour Farmer Temple Association in Winnipeg. It is to cost $36,000, and the usual appeal is made for funds. The paper says:

"The following is the plan of the building: the basement, the windows of which will be on the surface, will be for the printing plant; the first floor will be the hall for the children's school, a kitchen and some rooms for the printing plant; the second floor will be the offices of the administration of the editors, of the General Board and library."

In commenting upon this the Officer Commanding the Royal Canadian Mounted Police makes the following remark:-

"It has been stated that the new building will be also used to accommodate classes for the schools and that the additional accommodation will provide for a very large increase in the number of scholars, as it has been lack of accommodation that has prevented the attendance being much larger than it is at present."

An interesting and characteristic remark in a report received from Fort William, on 10th August, is that a picnic attempted by the West Fort William branch of the Ukrainian Labour Farmer Temple Association for the Sunday, 8th August, failed "on account of there being no music."

According to the Ukrainian Labour News of 12th August The Workers' Benevolent Association have bought a farm of 38 acres near

Winnipeg, to serve as a shelter for old and crippled members and for orphans; for this purpose a tax of 50 cents has been imposed upon the membership. The land was bought for $1,800 at a tax sale.

7. Communist Notes

The Ukrainian Labour News in its issue of 5th August publishes a list of affiliations of the Communist International. This enumerates 50 territorial sections of the International, No. 1 being the U.S.S.R. (the Russian Communist Party.) The Communist Party of Canada appears as No. 41 in the list, directly after the Communist Party of Bekhara.[8]

The Officer Commanding the Royal Canadian Mounted Police in Montreal in his confidential monthly report for July, remarks that the City Central Committee of the Communist Party there have decided to reorganize the party by districts.

Annie S. Buller has issued a circular letter, under date of 5th August, asking for a vigorous celebration of International Press day on 3rd October. A special issue of the Worker is to be got out for that day and efforts are to be made to get new subscribers.

Dealing with the Soviet Russian Trade Delegation the Officer Commanding the Royal Canadian Mounted Police in Montreal says in his confidential monthly report for July:-

> "Ivan Kulik of this delegation and his secretary, A. Kladkow, returned this month after visiting various Doukhobor settlements in the west, their object being to persuade 300 families to return to Russia. Difficulty is being experienced in getting them to leave Canada the Doukhobors being apparently aware of the real state of the peasants in their native country.

According to statements in the Polish paper Tribuna Robotnicza, there are now 56 members of the Polish branch of the Canadian Labour Defence League in Winnipeg, and 15 in the branch in St. Catharines.

8. The O.B.U. Agitation

We have received a further report from Sydney dealing with the series of local strikes by means of which the United Mine Workers of America have been fighting the One Big Union. Our informant states that in some mines these tactics have succeeded and that the miners have joined the U.M.W., but he states that in other places the O.B.U. have shown a determination to be free from the United Mine Workers. He adds:-

> "The conditions of the miners appear to be one continual struggle. First against the coal company, Besco, later against the present executive of the U.M.W. and now they are quarrelling among themselves. On the one hand there is growing sentiment [9] towards the O.B.U. and on the other hand their is an equal degree of alarm

on the part of the executive of the U.M.W., who have now started a campaign against the O.B.U. Conditions are thus becoming more complicated every day.

"In this warfare there is also a third party the Communists, with their 'no splits, no secession' policy, and this group blame the present executive of the U.M.W. and John W. McLeod for all the trouble. They accuse the executive of the U.M.W. with having fallen into the hands of Besco and assert that they are in the employ of the Conservative party of Nova Scotia.

"J.B. MacLachlan is against the O.B.U. and his present hatred of the party is due to his understanding of the danger of a split among the miners.

"The U.M.W. of A., once a powerful organization of the miners in Nova Scotia, has now been split up into many different groups, each of which is fighting for control of the miners."

Our informant adds that it is unlikely that the miners will throw up their present two years' contract with the coal companies.

J. Clancy, the O.B.U. agitator, has appeared in Edmonton having addressed a mass meeting of railway workers on Sunday, 8th August, he declared that he was on a tour from Halifax to Vancouver, in the interests of the O.B.U., trying to induce the railway workers of Canada to close their works irrespective of craft unions into a solid front and demand 10 cents an hour increase in pay or go on strike and tie up the railroads before the crop movement starts, forcing the railroads to meet their demands.

In advocating this Clancy declared that another made the following declaration:-

"Another crash is coming when the capitalist class pick up where they left off in 1918 and you will be conscripted into a one big union of workers.

He succeeded in getting the following three resolutions carried:-

"1. Railroad workers! Are you willing at this time to close your ranks irrespective of your craft union, and if not organized, are you willing to support an increase in wages at this time. Carried.[10]

"2. Railroad Workers! Are you willing to elect a Committee from this meeting to recommend the shopmen for an increase in wages. Carried.

"3. Railroad Workers! Realizing that the time is so short when the railroads will have us at their mercy, are you willing to have a ballot printed and put in the hands of every shopman that they can vote 'yea' or 'nay' on this question. Carried.

The Committee referred to was not appointed in public. Our report says:-

"There was little enthusiasm evidenced by the workers at this meeting, in fact, more than half of the audience of about 200, left the hall before the meeting was over."

The Non-commissioned officer in charge of this work in forwarding this report notices the appreciation of another information who was present at this gathering as follows:-

"The Committee referred to in the second resolution herein, is going to be appointed privately. Further, that the Communist Party of Canada and the Ukrainian Labour Farmer Temple Association are solidly against the O.B.U. and will do anything to block their efforts.--- was also of the opinion that the railroad workers were not at all enthusiastic at this meeting."

9. The I.W.W. at Winnipeg.

Reports from Winnipeg regarding the I.W.W. state that a number of men belonging to that organization are drifting into town. The wages offered for harvesters at the time of reporting were low $3.50 a day. A report, dated 10th August, says:-

"There is no open agitation as yet, although there is quite an undercurrent of unrest and dissatisfaction but so far it has not been serious enough to take notice of. As a matter of fact the numbers of I.W.W. in town at present are not enough to create a great deal of trouble amongst the large number of harvesters that are bound to arrive soon from the east."

A report, dated 12th August, says that the influx of harvesters from the east had begun, and that the I.W.W. members were out to meet them and were distributing tracts. The number of harvesters are so great that only a small proportion could be approached by the small number of I.W.W. men acting as agitators.

A man named M. Manchier is acting as secretary on the Winnipeg branch at present.[11]

An earlier report from Winnipeg, dated 9th August says:-

"There have been large number of members of the I.W.W. arriving in town. So far they have been quiet. The idea is to have scouts at the different railroad depots and labour offices, but so far there are not enough harvesters in town.

"They intend to make as many men as possible members of the I.W.W. In any case their intention is to dictate what wages will be paid in the harvest fields.

"During the week quite a large number of them hung around the headquarters in Main Street, but during the week-end very few were there.

"Those fellows are not going out to jobs as yet. They are waiting till the excursions arrive. So far there is little scope for their activities. About the 15th is the date set for their activities."

A report dated 15th August described the I.W.W. as not aggressive.

10. The Ku Klux Klan at Fredericton.

According to the Fredericton Gleaner the Ku Klux Klan has made an appearance in New Brunswick. Large fiery corsses were displayed in the vicinity of Fredericton, on 10th August, and 26 candidates are said to have been admitted to membership. The particular faction working there is the Ku Klux Klan of Kanada.

The proceedings seem to be under James S. Lord, M.L.A., of St. Stephen, who is described as Imperial Klaliff.

ROYAL CANADIAN MOUNTED POLICE HEADQUARTERS

Ottawa, 2nd September, 1926.

SECRET

NO. 333

WEEKLY SUMMARY

NOTES REGARDING REVOLUTIONARY ORGANIZATIONS AND AGITATORS IN CANADA

REPORT

(Note. No Summary was issued for the week ending 26th August.)

The Communists are busy in the elections in several constituencies, but to little purpose. Money is short, and in several places their activities seem principally directed to the embarrassing of the campaign of normal Labour candidates.

A ten-page bulletin has been issued on the election, apparently designed to be a sort of speakers' handbook. Beyond noting its definite demand for separation from the British Empire it is unnecessary to attack much weight to it.

The Young Communist League is preparing for an International Youth Day on 5th September.

I.W.W. attempts to influence harvesters seem to have met less than their customary trifling success.[2]

APPENDICES

Table of Contents

APPENDIX NO. I: GENERAL

APPENDIX NO. I: GENERAL

1. Election Activities of the Communists.

Timothy Buck is busy in Montreal, instructing them in election operations. This is to help Michael Buhay in his candidacy.

We have a report of a mass party membership meeting held by the Communist Party in Toronto, on 24th August; very few party members attended, though the purpose was to stir up interest in the political campaign. Maurice Spector and John MacDonald were the speakers; the latter stated that if they did not procure $400 by 4th September one of their candidates in Toronto must fall out.

William Moriarty has relinguished his project of running as a candidate in North Temiskaming. Until recently the Canadian Labour Party, the Mine Workers' Union of Canada and the Communist Party spent a good deal of time and energy in trying to arrange for Moriarty's candidacy.

The London Labour Party on 13th August expelled L. R. Menzies for his refusal to apologize for his assertion that "the London Labour Party was being run by a bunch of crooks." After describing the circumstances of the expulsion, our report says:-

> "Mr. Menzies remained as a visitor and delivered a short speech in which, he said 'he regretted the action of the London Labour Party in expelling him as a cause of possible injury to the cause of the workers in general', and stated that he would ask his local union, the Canadian Brotherhood of Railway Employees not to withdraw their delegates from the party. Said he, 'As Communists, we must always stand for solidarity and the united front, within the party no matter at what cost. Such action as has been taken here tonight we regard as part of the struggle of a young party and it will not affect our work and policy.' Comrade Menzies is the only London member on the executive of the Ontario Section of the Canadian Labour Party."

Despite this Menzies was put forward as a candidate for the nomination to contest the London riding in the approaching election; his [5] opponent, Robert Foxcroft, secured a majority, and Menzies asked that the nomination be unanimous. Our report adds:-

> "The intention of the left wing was to nominate A. C. Avery but this was changed at the last minute as Avery is again out of employment and expects to get a job on the C. P. R. and though he would not get this if he was advertised too much as a Communist. Comrade Menzies was therefore urged to stand for nomination and agreed to do so."

Later on Foxcroft withdrew his candidacy, with the result that there is a bitter quarrel in progress between the London Labour Party and the Communist Party.

A. E. Smith, who has received the Labour nomination for the Port Arthur-Thunder Bay constituency, is secretary of the City Central Committee of the Communist Party in Toronto. During his absence in the campaign his wife will carry on his duties in Toronto.

Members of the Finnish Association have declared that Smith's chances for election are excellent.

The Communists of Winnipeg held a general meeting of the Party members on 25th August to consider various things relating to the elections. The first item on the programme was to arrange a collection for the "Agit Prop" Committee funds, and concerning this our report says:-

"In the first point of the agenda, J. Kahanna explained that the National Executive Committee is short of funds, and propaganda, leaflets cannot be printed, also an organizer be sent where there is a need of such. The aim of the Agit Prop is the sum of $2,000, and the quota for Winnipeg is $300 which have to be collected immediately."

Arrangements were made to raise this sum.

It was decided to print a leaflet attacking the Independent Labour Party for its stand upon the united front as regards the Canadian Labour Party and the Canadian Labour Defense League, but nevertheless advising the workers to vote for its candidates on the ground that this is the best that could be done at present.[6]

On the following day the City Central Committee after some disagreement ratified the decision to try to form a "united front" with the Independent Labour Party. It is hardly likely that the latter body will take any notice of the request of the Communists, which is little more than an attempt to edge in upon their campaign.

James Lakeman, who has been nominated by the Canadian Labour Party in East Edmonton, is chairman of the Communist Party in that city. The Ukrainian Labour Farmer Temple Association in Edmonton is working hard to assist him; and the work is being prosecuted in trade unions and by the Canadian Labour Party. Nevertheless, Lakeman in an address to the Canadian Labour Party at Edmonton, on 24th August, complained that his campaign was going too slowly, and that they had no money; he urged that "they start to do something." It was decided to make an house to house collection for funds.

2. Communist Election Propaganda.

John MacDonald has issued as propaganda reading matter for the present election what is described as a monthly bulletin. It is a mimeographed pamphlet of ten pages, dealing wholly with the general election. In the opening portion the Central Executive Committee defines the party attitude thus:-

"The party is anti-parliamentary in the sense that fundamentally we believe parliament can never be used for the abolition of the Capitalists' system. Parliament is essentially a part of the apparatus of capitalist Government and will be replaced in the course of the Social Resolution by the Council form of government. Nevertheless, during the period that the workers are still mobilising their forces to challenge the parliamentary system, we must avail ourselves of every platform, every forum and every tribunal to declare our views to the masses and also by practical legislative proposals in the House itself, show up the limitations of Parliamentary Democracy. For that reason, the Communist Party considers parliamentary activity as of great importance at the present time, although we do not judge the strength and possibilities of the Workers' movement purely or even chiefly, by the number of representatives it has in the House."[7]

Passing on to its relations with the Canadian Labour Party, the bulletin says:-

"The Party is everywhere supporting the common candidates chosen by the convention of the Canadian Labour Party. There is an instance however, in Montreal, where the party is running a straight Communist candidate. This is due, not to our desire, so much as to the force of circumstances. Our party has been expelled from the Quebec section of the Labour Party. On that account however, we cannot allow the standpatters to wipe their feet on us. If the party is to be treated in this way, we must fight back. For that reason, we have decided to put up a candidate of our own, but throughout the rest of the country our Party candidates are running on the Labour ticket."

Dealing with the extent to which the Communists support the programme of the Labour Party, the bulletin says:-

"Our support of the Labour Party is intended to develop independent political action. At the same time, the Communist candidates have it as their duty in the campaign not only to represent the minimum programme of the Labour Party but also to interpret that programme in the light of the Communist programme as a whole. Thus, for example, after a heated debate, the Ontario section of the Labour Party agreed to raise the constitutional issue in the election to the extent of demanding the complete self-determination and sovereignty of Canada. Reformists like James Simpson have declared that they will interpret this demand as realizable within the framework of the Empire. The Communists can only interpret this demand as implying specifically the abolition of the British North America Act, and separation of Canada from the Empire and complete independence.

A large proportion of the document is taken up with the denunciation of the constitutional issue. An early passage says:-

"From our viewpoint the Constitutional issue is of great importance to the working class. It is a very narrow-minded viewpoint that the Reformists take in separating the political from the social issues. This is not so much a Socialist way of looking at things in the light of a class struggle as a desire to evade the class struggle and particularly the struggle against capitalist-imperialism. In the last analysis men of the type of Simpson are afraid to rouse the strong imperialist prejudices against themselves and are desirous of maintaining the present fabric of the British Empire which they are pleased to call the British Commonwealth."

After some words expressing the writer's dislike of the British Empire the bulletin continues:-

"We follow the Leninist policy of demanding the complete self-determination and independence of the Colonial and semi-Colonial peoples within the British Empire. Only when people are [8] free from foreign and capitalist domination can we hope to achieve a true and greater federation of all people on a basis of fraternity and equality. These are the matters which actuate the party in emphasizing the constitutional issue which we interpret as something more than the mere prerogatives of the Governor-General. Canada at the present time is one of the weak links in the chain of the Empire. Both in the interests of our fight against imperialism and our struggle against capitalism, it is necessary that we take a clear-cut stand in favour of the independence of this country."

The details of the constitutional issue occupy six closely typewritten pages, which call for little comment. A rather brief section of the bulletin is devoted to social legislation and the Senate, this including a denunciation of the rejection of the Old Age Pensions Bill, a demand for the legalization of picketing, etc. It demands the abolition of the Senate.

Another section is headed "The Workers' and Farmers' Government." It includes the following:-

"As a measure although a partial one, in this direction of partial socialization, the party demands the nationalization of the mines and railways without compensation."

A further passage in this may be of interest:-

"During the life of the last Parliament Mr. Woodsworth often talked and wrote about so-called 'Co-operative Government' as the alternative to the present party form of Government. The Communist Party warns against this conception as being simply a veil for coalition Government and class collaboration on the parliamentary field. The concessions for labour must be forced from the capitalist class by parliamentary and extra parliamentary pressure while retaining absolute independence of any co-operative arrangement with the capitalist parties."

3. The Young Communist League.

The "Politcom" of the Young Communist League in Canada has issued from its Toronto headquarters somewhat pretentious instructions about the celebration of International Youth Day, which is to take place on 5th September; the celebration is to begin on 30th August and to continue throughout the week. Members of the League are urged to make the celebration important as well as enthusiastic, and a number of suggestions are made, the most interesting being as follows:-[9]

"This year Youth Day will be celebrated in Canada during the heat of the Federal Election Campaign, a week before the voters go to the polls. Accordingly, the National Executive Committee has come to the conclusion that we have a most excellent opportunity for combining our Youth Day slogans with the immediate demands of the working-class youth in the elections campaign."

The methods suggested are the familiar ones of lectures, articles in extremist newspapers, the circulation of leaflets, the holding of open-air meetings, socials, dances, etc. This beating of drums is somewhat discounted by the following passage:-

"Groups have not been very ready to send in donations from the proceeds of summer entertainments. This is very poor policy. The National Executive Committee and Young Worker suffer severely from almost complete lack of funds. Therefore, the groups will have to strictly adhere to the decision that half the proceeds of the Youth Day demonstrations go to the National Office where it will be divided between the National Executive Committee and the new Young Comrade, which is very much in need of funds, being a new paper. Send reports of Youth Day to the National Office promptly."

The circular also includes what appear to be notes for addresses. These include the following passage:-

"Denunciation of pro-Fascist organizations of youth. Exposure of hypocrisy of the League of Nations. We must point out our position of uncompromising opposition to all capitalist wars. We are not pacifists but anti-militarists. We oppose capitalist wars with the class war. We demand the cessation of all military training in the schools and cessation of further expenditures by the Provincial, Municipal or Federal Governments for military training. The main feature of Youth Day must be our anti-militarist campaign. Especially at this period can we place our position better before the young workers and make an issue of it. The part of Canada in the British Empire reduces her to a position where the young workers of this country must sacrifice their lives in every war of British Imperialism. We must back the labour party and the Communist Party in their election demands for the Independence of Canada and the abolition of military preparations and training."

Under the heading of "Economic Demands" there is included the following:

"Vocational training for young workers at expense of employer, under trade union management, and ensuring a living minimum wage, for young workers of both sexes."

International Children's Day also is to be celebrated on 5th September, the programme for that including the following items:-[10]

> "Down with reaction in schools, the Boy Scouts, Cadet training, bourgeois children's organizations. Out of these join the Young Pioneers; we must begin our recruiting with children's day and call for members to join up from the platform."

4. Communist Notes.

Moriarty, who has given up hope of being a candidate in Timmins, has left that place for Kirkland Lake, Cobalt, Silver Centre and other places. According to one report, he may ultimately go on to Vancouver to organize.

Timothy Buck is to remain in Montreal, to the end of September according to one report, to the middle of October according to another.

An incidental proof of the closeness with which the Canadian Labour Defence League is dominated by the Communists is given by an occurrence in Winnipeg. Mrs. Sokolicz (Falken) recently organized there a Polish branch of that body. At a meeting of the City Central Committee of the Communist Party held on 26th August the Ukrainian branch of the Communist Party recommended that a Polish branch of the Communist Party be formed, to control the Polish branch of the Labour Defence League. It was decided to try to induce the Polish society "New Life" to transform itself into a Communist Party branch.

At the same meeting of the City Central Committee the Young Communist League reported that it proposed to form an auxiliary branch composed of Jewish youths, who have recently arrived from Europe, and who cannot join the Young Communist League because of their ignorance of English; it appears that there are 15 of these youths ready to join. It was decided to sanction this on condition that as soon as these lads are sufficiently acquainted with the English language they are to transfer [11] to the Young Communist League. The Jewish branch of the Communist party concurred in this arrangement.

According to reports given by the Jewish Branch of the Communist Party to the Winnipeg City Central Committee on 26th August, Der Kamf is in a bad financial position.

The Jewish branch of the Communist Party in Montreal recently collected over $800 for this paper.

An agitator known as Jack Young of the Canadian Labour Defence League in Toronto has spent some time in Montreal. Mrs. Custance may visit Montreal to help to organize the Canadian Labour Defence League.

5. The Ukrainians

Some differences of opinion seem to be manifesting itself in Edmonton between the Ukrainian Labour Farmer Temple Association and the Communist Party with regard to the Youth Section of the Temple. Pressure is being brought to bear to have this body affiliate with the Young Communist League, and the Ukrainians seem disposed to resist this, on the ground that they desire to keep control of their Youth Section. So thorough-going is this opposition that Klybanowsky has taken this stand, and the matter has been referred to the Central Executive Committee at Winnipeg.

A Ukrainian paper named Zhalo, or Sjhalo (Sting) has been observed in circulation in Edmonton and Fort Frances. It is published in New York, and may be a continuation of Smik y Pravada (Humour and Truth) under another name; the latter paper has been forbidden entry to the country.

Ivan Kulik of the Soviet Russian Trade Delegation is contributing a series of articles to the Ukrainian Labour News.[12]

---

6. The I.W.W. Unprosperous

A report from Winnipeg, dated 27th August, is to the effect that the I.W.W. agitation in Winnipeg is going slowly; there is some talk of discontinuing the office there. The Officer Commanding the Royal Canadian Mounted Police in Manitoba makes the following remark in this connection:-

> "The class of harvesters who have been passing through Winnipeg have been of a very much superior type than usual and the I.W.W.'s have found it difficult to make any headway with these men, consequently they have been rather discouraged, and now the fact that high wages are being paid there will be nothing left for them to agitate for, all of this accounts for the situation being quiet."

Other reports from Winnipeg point to a fall in the I.W.W. there.

James Sharp, the man who is carrying on the I.W.W. organization in Saskatoon this autumn, has been unable by reason of lack of money to occupy the premises used by Sam Scarlett last year; and has taken less advantageous quarters.

Sharp's excuse for not having the money was that one Brady, an upholder of the I.W.W. at Calgary had absconded with $200.

ROYAL CANADIAN MOUNTED POLICE HEADQUARTERS

Ottawa, 9th September, 1926.

SECRET

NO. 334

WEEKLY SUMMARY

NOTES REGARDING REVOLUTIONARY ORGANIZATIONS AND AGITATORS IN CANADA

REPORT

An interesting note upon the Ukrainian Labour Farmer Temple Association in Edmonton appears in this issue. Careful examination of statistics given for successive years suggests the suspicion that the organization during the last two or three numerically has stood still. The Edmonton reports confirms this, but says that its influence over the general Ukrainian community is increasing, and that the Ukrainian Workers' Benevolent Association has proved to be an admirable recruiting ground.

Another interesting report deals with revolutionary schools in Winnipeg and the vicinity.

Communist support of the Independent Labour Party in the election in Winnipeg is of the usual back-stabbing sort.[2]

APPENDICES

Table of Contents

APPENDIX NO. I: GENERAL

APPENDIX NO. II: REPORTS FROM DISTRICTS

APPENDIX NO. I: GENERAL

1. Membership of Ukrainian Labour Farmer Temple Association.

In examining at headquarters the official reports made at various times by the Ukrainian Labour Farmer Temple Association, it was noticed that while assertions of progress are incessant, the figures actually quoted showed no progress for the last two or three years. The attention of several Officers Commanding districts has been drawn to this, and we have received from Edmonton the following comments and appreciation:-

"After investigation of the matter as is available I find that the membership of the Edmonton Branch of the Ukrainian Labour Farmer Temple Association at the present time is 96 on whom a per capita tax of 15 cents is paid into the headquarters at Winnipeg. (N.B. This is a slight advance on the figures of January, 1926).

"With respect to the Edmonton District, the membership has actually declined since 1922-23. This is mainly accounted for by the fact that during that period a move was made to turn titles of property, etc. of the various branches over to the trustees of the parent body at Winnipeg, Manitoba. This caused bitter controversy, with the result that when by ballot it was decided to turn these deeds over to the headquarters, a large number resigned.

"The Edmonton Temple of this Association has been fully paid for and is the property of the Organization with no encumbrances. The Edmonton Branch has some three hundred odd dollars in the treasury.

2. Ukrainian Workers' Benevolent Association a Recruiting Ground

"Without hesitation I would say that the influence of this Association and its subsidiary societies, over Ukrainians, is on the increase, due in a great measure to the fact that a Benevolent Branch has been organized. Any Ukrainian, whether or not a member of the organization may join the society, but it is noticed that it is a great recruiting source for membership to the Ukrainian Labour Farmer Temple Association; for example, several of those who dropped out in 1922-23, who have joined the Benevolent Organization, have again been drafted to the U.L.F.T.A. At the present time there are 2,600 members enrolled in this Benevolent organization.[5]

"In connection with the Youth Section of the Association, while they are not officially allied to the Communist Party of Canada, their aims and objects are identical. The schools in this district are conducted by one J. Symbay, a very able man.

"I am told that the purpose of these schools is to teach not only the younger generation to read and write, but also the elder members, many of whom are illiterate, in order that they may read the revolutionary literature that is issued from time to time. There is no question but what the major portion of the classes are along the lines of preparing the members thereof for a revolution, with the Soviet System of Government as their objective.

"I should add that as far as I can gather greater care prevails now in keeping their accounts and rolls in a more businesslike manner, thus showing the progress the erstwhile illiterate foreigners are making."

The astuteness with which the revolutionary agitation among the

Ukrainians is conducted is revealed in the foregoing paragraphs. As soon as they perceived that the "Temple" had reached its peak of development they organized the Benevolent Society, at once to provide a "legal" organization in case proceedings should be taken against them and to inveigle into the movement Ukrainians who otherwise would remain aloof from the professedly seditious body.

3. Revolutionary Schools in Manitoba.

The Officer Commanding the Royal Canadian Mounted Police in Manitoba has furnished us with an appreciation of the present condition of the revolutionary schools maintained in that Province. He says:-

"The new figures obtainable show a slight gain, and it is very probable that the coming fall and winter work along the lines of organizing the children and youth will give a considerable increase, as a certain amount of preparatory work being done by these who took the Higher Educational Courses at the Ukrainian Labour Farmer Temple Association in Winnipeg last winter, will have had time to materialize.

"It has been stated by the leaders of the Ukrainian Labour Farmer Temple Association here that at least 1,000 scholars have made application to enter the schools, of which number only 350 have been able to be accommodated, and owing to this lack of room (which is being met by the erection of a new building already started) the work has been held back considerably. The number of children attending the U.L.F.T.A. school at the present are as follows:

"Winnipeg 350. divided into 5 classes.

From 1st July until further notice the hours will be as follows:-
1st Class Monday, Tuesday, Wednesday, Friday and
Saturday from 10 a.m. till noon.[6]
2nd Class Thursday from 10 a.m. till noon and
Monday, Wednesday and Saturday from 2 to 4 p.m.
3rd and 4th Classes Monday and Wednesday from 4 to 6,
and Saturday from 3 to 5 p.m.
5th, 6th and 7th Classes Tuesday, Thursday and Friday
from 2 to 5 p.m.

" East Kildonan - 75

" Transcona- 80

From July 5th until end of August.
1st, 2nd and 3rd classes from 3 to 4 p.m.
4th and 5th Classes from 9 a.m. to noon.

" Port Arthur - 47

" Fort William - 55

" West Fort William - 83

" Fort Francis - 43 (no change since last return)

"In addition to the above the formation of the Ukrainian Children's Schools of the Ukrainian Labour Farmer Temple Association is being put into practice. In many of the Rural Ukrainian settlements, such as Brightstone, Red Deer, Brokenhead, Janow, Gonnor, Bread Valley, Fisher Branch districts. It is in those localities that organizers are working principally in connection with the Ukrainian Workmen's Benevolent Association. In the Fort William District (Port Arthur) the Finns have an O.B.U. school of some 200 children, which is held on Sundays only, the teacher being one Arnberg. No particulars are obtainable at present on the subjects taught.

4. Finnish, Jewish, Russian and Lettish Schools.

"There is also an O.B.U. Finnish school at Fort William, the teacher being David Aho; but we have been unable to ascertain the number of scholars, which will probably be less than the Port Arthur School. Similar schools are said to be operating at Nipigon and Intolla and to be well attended, but the number of scholars is now known to us.

"At Lettinia, in the Lac du Bonnet district, which is a Lettish community, a young folk's class and Sunday school was started early in the year, but definite particulars are not available, but the fact that Communist literature was distributed would tend to show that it is under Communist influence.

"The school conducted by the Workmen's Circle (Jewish) at the Liberty Temple shows that for the past two years very little progress has been made, as the scholars at the present time number 240 at the school classes, and 50 children attend the Kindergarten.

"It has just been learned that there is also a Russian school for children, the attendance being about 35, hold at the Liberty Temple. Jacob Penner being the teacher. This is held three days a week. The fact that the teacher is well known to us as a communist would enable us to guess the kind of teaching.[7]

5. Nature of the Teaching.

"The following, which were examination compositions of the different classes in the Workmen's Circle School, will show the influence that the teaching exerts on the children:-

"Did God Create Mankind, or Mankind Create God?" by a 13 year old boy (this boy is at present a leader amongst the Pioneers, and his brother, a boy of 17, also a graduate of the Workmen's Circle School is a leader in the Young Communist League.)

"The cause of Immigration," by a 13 year old boy.

"Why do the large Industries swallow the Middle Class," by a 14 year old boy.

"The Band" (A Jewish Revolutionary Party of Former Russians), by a 15 year old girl.

"The Pohale Zionist school, better known as the 'Peretz' school, shows a steady increase, and the most recent figures are as follows:-

No. 1. Peretz Institute	360	in the School classes
	50 "	" Kindergarten.
No. 2. King Edward Branch	65 "	" school classes
No. 3. Elmwood "	40 "	" " "

" Taking the Peretz School, the following are a few examples of the examination compositions:-

"A Short Biography of a Russian Revolutionary Girl," by a girl of 13.

"Coal: How this dangerous work is very poorly paid," by a boy of 13.

"The First of May: Its Importance for the Workers," by a boy of 10.

"The Labour Problem," by a girl of 12.

"The Only Remedy against Crises," by a girl of 13.

"Working Men and Bosses," by a boy aged 12.

"Can there be peace between the workman and the Boss?" by a boy of 15.

"The Boy Scouts" (Opinion Expressed to do away with the Boy Scout movement), by a girl of 15."

6. "Young Worker" advocating Civil War.

The issues of the Young Worker for September contains a story, signed A. J. Clarke, entitled "On the Barricades." It is a clear case of representing civil war as the goal at which those young people aim. It represents the government of the day discussing a revolution and ordering a field marshall to crush it. One passage represents the field [8] marshal as saying:-

"Gentlemen, we have one cure, the cure of the Paris Commune, that is, wipe out the workers' revolt in a sea of blood, workers' blood. Hobilize every loyal citizen and drown their revolt in their own blood."

It then describes street fighting and the defeat of the soldiers, and concludes thus:-

"The sun, lighting the streets in the ruddy glow of dawn, shone on a scene of destruction. In the roadway, a group of bodies encircles a disabled armoured car, the bodies of the two soldiers in its wrecked interior, a field marshal and its driver.

"Upon its steel turret, a flag of red, in its centre, three golden letter Y.C.L."

The August issue of this periodical asserts that the Montreal police fired upon strikers picketing a shop.

7. Communist Election Manifesto in Winnipeg.

The Communist Party in Winnipeg has issued an election manifesto which contains one or two passages of some interest. Upon the constitutional issue it says:-

"The action of the Governor General in granting dissolution of Parliament to Meighen and refusing it to King shows clearly which way the wind is blowing. Canada is still the slave of the British Crown, and the constitutional issue shows that not only have the Canadian workers to struggle with Canadian capitalists, but with British capital also. The British North America Act is the constitution of Canada, and we are subjects, in the final analysis, of the British Imperialists. The B.N.A.A. has been consistently used in the past to block any social legislation, such as the 8-hour day, that the workers have been able to wring from the Canadian capitalists. It has been used to deny the workers' relief, the unemployed, and higher wages. Until this act is abolished and Canada becomes independent, the workers can hope for no amelioration of their lot. Demand the annulment of the B.N.A.A. and a complete declaration of Canadian independence."

Dealing with its relations with the Independent Labour Party and the Canadian Labour Party it says:-

"Confronted with the many bitter defeats and attacks that the workers have been forced to submit to because they are divided and poorly organized industrially and politically to defend their rights and to beat down the attacks of the Boss class, here in Winnipeg, as elsewhere, the Communist Party has repeatedly attempted to bring about a United Front of all labour political organizations and trade unions to form an all-embracing C.L.P. which would be controlled by the majority vote and which could in the present stage of the working class express the political aspirations of the workers.[9]

These attempts of the Communist Party to bring about the Canadian Labour Party have been steadily sabotaged by the Independent Labour Party.

"In this election like in previous ones, the I.L.P. has gone ahead and rushed the nomination of their candidate, A.A. Heaps, in the North Constituency without any attempt to consult labour, and the labour organizations whom they call upon to support their candidate. The I.L.P. forced the Communist Party to face the alternative of putting a candidate of their own into the field and thus splitting the labour vote and killing the chances of a Labour candidate going to Ottawa, or, of abstaining from the election and permitting the I.L.P. candidate, who represents only a certain section of the workers in the North Winnipeg constituency, to stay in the field as the only Labour candidate. The Communist Party chose the second alternative, because it sees the imperative need of a United Front to fight the boss and not to put any obstacles in the way of the Canadian

Labour Party.

"The Communist Party will continue to work and fight for the C.L.P. and will break in the end all sabotage of the office seekers and officialdom of the I.L.P. certain that the rank and file workers are for a united front of all labour organizations in the struggle with the Boss class. The workers are beginning to see the additional strength that a C.L.P. will mean to them and know that a candidate elected to the Federal House by the C.L.P. is there to represent the interests of Labour, and not the constituency as a whole, which consists of different classes."

The Central Executive of the Communist Party has issued several leaflets; one is entitled "Federal Elections and the Constitutional issue; another is described as an "Election Manifesto and a third is a leaflet on "The Senate and Social Legislatic .

The leaflet on the constitutional issue contains the following passage:-

"The issue is: 'Why is Lord Byng here at all to govern as the appointee and representative of an outside power-- the British Imperial Government?' 'Why is Canada still in leading strings?' Plainly the 'constitutional issue is the issue of the Constitution of Canada."

In the course of a campaign speech delivered on 29th August at a picnic held by the Ukrainian Labour Farmer Temple Association at Edmonton, James Lakeman, the Labour candidate in Edmonton, said:-

"I am a Communist and I am proud of it, and proud of everyone who is out to help the slave get out under the capitalist system."[10]

8. Appeal from the "Worker".

A.S. Buller, the business manager of the Worker, has issued an appeal for help which betrays some anxiety. A "Sustaining Fund Campaign" was to have been undertaken in October, but it has been delayed until December, "due to the fact that our Finnish comrades in the United States and Canada will be engaged during October in a drive for the Communist Press of the world. This you will realise will hamper our 'drive' as our Finnish comrades have always supported the Worker and co-operated to make our work successful." It is stated that this will affect the work seriously, and non-Finnish comrades are urgently asked for help.

9. Ukrainian Notes

The issue of Robitnitsia of 1st September contains a statement that the section of Youth of the Ukrainian Labour Farmer Temple Association at present has 20 branches, with 1,062 members. The branches and the membership are as follows:-

Winnipeg, Man. 308	Edmonton, Alta............ 49
Port Arthur, Ontario ...40	Moose Jaw, Sask 26
Fort William, " 66	Thorold, Ont................. 23
Transcona, Man. 74	Vancouver, B.C...... 45
Regina, Sask. 26	E. Kildonan, Man.... 31
Lethbridge, Alta. 28	Hamilton, Ont. 11
Sudbury, Ont. 40	Drumheller, Alta. 51
Fort Frances, Ont. 50	Calgary 36
Timmins, Ont. 68	Medicine Hat, Alta....... 17
West Fort William 59	Winnipeg Beach, Man. 14

There also appears a statement that a new branch of this body has been organized in Ford City with 32 members. This branch seems to be composed of young women.

According to a letter from Medicine Hat, published in the Robitnitsia of 1st September, the Working Women's Branch of the Ukrainian Labour Farmer Temple Association there has been galvanized into activity by the visit of Anna Moysiuk, a Winnipeg woman, who was active with the mandolin orchestra in its recent tour.

Examination of the Ukrainian comic paper Zhalo (Sting) tends to confirm the impression that it is Smik y Pravada, (Humour and Truth),[11] issued under a new name in order to avoid prohibition. The "new" paper continues a correspondence the earlier portion of which appeared in the "old" one, and there are acknowledgements of subscriptions which must have been sent when the "old" paper was in existence. Zhalo at present is edited with a good deal of restraint so as to avoid a fresh prohibition.

A leaflet called "Support the British Miners" is being circulated in Winnipeg, apparently in both the Ukrainian and Yiddish languages. It is signed "United Workingmen's Aid Committee." The only thing worthnoting in it is the following sentence:-

> "In 1921, when the British miners lost their strike, the wages of the workers all over the world were reduced."

10. I.W.W. and O.B.U.

James Sharp recently returned to Calgary from an organization trip in Saskatchewan and Manitoba; he gave a report of his proceedings at a business meeting of the I.W.W. held on 29th August. One interesting statement was that the former I.W.W. secretary at Winnipeg was a bootlegger, this accounting for the poor progress made there; he hoped for a better showing now that they have a new man there. He was sanguine with regard to prospects in Moose Jaw and Saskatoon, and remarked that the I.W.W. have about 200 delegates in the three prairie provinces. Another remark of his is thus reported:-

> "He also stated that a lot of I.W.W. delegates collected some

> money last year who never turned in the money to the organization, we should take direct action against these members and compel them to return the money which belongs to the organization, I am not saying where, when or how we should take this action, but he will do it somehow."

Sam Scarlett has been asserting in Calgary that prospects in Drumheller are good; he is developing an attack against the check-off system which, according to him, is oppressive there and is resented. Our report says:-[12]

> "His ambition is to get at least one operator in Drumheller to sign an agreement with the I.W.W. and this will be the first time in Canadian history where an operator has signed an agreement with the I.W.W."

We have received a copy of the Organizers' Report periodically issued by the General Executive Board of the One Big Union, covering the week of 24th July. This shows that agitation is proceeding in Vancouver, Edmonton, Calgary, Nova Scotia and the Minto area,N.B., and of course, Winnipeg. Practically all the activities described are those of visits to works and the spreading of leaflets, etc. It resolves itself into an attempt to induce international labour men to secede and join the O.B.U.

Thomas H.Dunn, who is contesting the Springfield constituency in Manitoba in the Federal elections as a candidate for the Independent Labour Party, is an active member of the O.B.U. He signed the report quoted in the preceding paragraph, describing himself as secretary.

PART 2:
CHIEF AGITATORS IN CANADA

Compiled by Public Safety Branch of the Department of Justice

"A"

AHO, ARTHUR Address unknown. Alleged I.W.W. worker in B.C.

AINGER, FRANK Address unknwon. Alleged I.W.W. worker in B.C.

ALDRIDGE, F. Box 531, Prince Rupert, B.C. Secy. Longshoremens' Union. Subscriber to "Solidarity".

ANDERSON, NELS Address unknown. Alleged I.W.W. worker in B.C.

ALPATOFF, B. 143 Powell St., Vancouver, B.C. Arrested on October 19th, 1918, charged with attending illegal meeting and with having objectionable matter in his possession. Pleaded guilty to charge of attending meeting and fined $10.00 on Dec. 23, 1918. Other charge withdrawn.

AHLQVIS, JOHN Toronto, Ont. Charged in October 1918 with having objectionable literature in his possession. Arrested at Sudbury, Ont.

AJOLA, JOHN Sudbury, Ont. Charged in October 1918 with having objectionable literature in his possession.

"B"

Bargman, Andrew Camp 2, Port Alberni, B.C., Alleged I.W.W. worker in B.C.

Benstrom, L. I.B. Camp, Knox Bay, B.C. Alleged I.W.W. worker in B.C.

Blom, John Kinman Camp, Jackson Bay, B.C. Alleged I.W.W. worker in B.C.

Bodner, Bill Abbotsford, B.C. Alleged I.W.W. worker in B.C.

Boulger, Jim Address unknown. Alleged I.W.W. worker in B.C.

Boyd, J.W. Grand Prairie, Alta. Address in book found at I.W.W. headquarters at Chicago.

Bradshaw, R. Drumheller, Alta. Secy. Drumheller Local United Mine Workers of America. Reputed to be a strong I.W.W. agitator and bad man.

Broadhurst, Thos. Drumheller, Alta. President Drumheller Local United Mine Workers of America, and alleged I.W.W. agitator.

Burdick, J. Formerly of Box 85 Nippon St., Seattle, Wash. Alleged

I.W.W. worker in B.C.

Budzey, Nikijer Vancouver, B.C. Arrested October 19th, 1918, charged with attending illegal meeting. Fined $10. Dec. 23, 1918.

Beech, W. 1912 address was Victoria, B.C. In 1912 was Secretary I.W.W. Local #328.

Bainbridge, Issaac 363 Spadina Av., Toronto, Secretary Social Democratic Party and Editor "Canadian Forward" which was suppressed October 5th, 1918. Was arrested and charged with printing objectionable matter and allowed out on suspended sentence. Address also given as 14 Milicent St., Toronto.

BELIKI, ALEXANDER Charged at Timmins, Ont., with having prohibited literature and in an enemy language in his possession. Found guilty December 5, 1918. Fined $200. or three months hard labor.

BOZINSKY, THOMAS 516 Queen St. W., Toronto, Ont. Charged in October 1918 with having objectionable literature in his possession.

BLASLKY, MATNEY 98 McCaul St., Toronto, Ont. Charged in October 1918 with being a member of an unlawful association.

BERG, EDWARD Con. 7, N.E.H. Charged in October 1918 with being a member of an unlawful association.

BOBE, ANGUS 57 Glengary Ave., Windsor, Ont. Charged with attending a meeting where the Russian language was being used and having papers in his possession in the same language. Case remanded until November 21, 1918. Convicted Dec. 23rd, 1918, and fined $100.00

BUDZEJ, NIKIFOR Vancouver, B.C. Charged in October 1918 with having objectionable matter in his possession. Dec. 23, 1918, pleaded guilty to charge of attending an unlawful meeting. Fined $10.00. Other charges withdrawn.

BUSHNIL, FRANK Humboldt, Sask. Charged in October 1918 with sedition, found guilty and sentenced on the first three counts to two years hard labor, to run concurrently; on count four to a fine of three hundred $300. dollars, or six months in jail, same to commence at end of above term; and on count five also to a fine of $300., or six months to commence at the end of imprisonment referred to in count four.

"C"

CACCHEONI, (Italian) Wayne, Alta. President Wayne Local United Mine Workers of America. Reputed to be bad-type agitator.

CARLSON, AUG. Camp 17, Ocean Falls, B.C. Alleged I.W.W. worker in B.C.

CARNEST, L. (Austrian) Morden, B.C. Employed by Pacific Coast Coal Mines Ltd. Alleged I.W.W. worker in B.C.

CHAPMAN, THOS. Address unknown. Alleged I.W.W. worker in B.C.

CHURCH, I.L. Co., Oxford Bay, Bute Inlet, B.C. Alleged I.W.W. worker in B.C.

COLE, C. 804 1/2 Spruce St., Alleged I.W.W. worker in B.C.

CONOSFVITCH, F. 142 Pearl St., Brantford, Ont. Subscriber to "Solidarity".

CROCKETT, VAL. V. Anyox, B.C. Subscriber to "Solidarity".

CURTIS, W. Address unknown. Alleged I.W.W. worker in B.C.

CONNELL, W. 1912 address was Kamloops, B.C. In 1912 was Secretary I.W.W. Local #327.

CONNELL, W. 1912 address was 34 Cordora St., Vancouver, B.C. In 1912 was Secretary I.W.W. Local #45.

CHARITONOFF, MAX. Sentenced October 1918 to three years Manitoba Penitentiary for having objectionable matter in his possession.

COLODY, GEO. 22 Gerrard St., W., Toronto, Ont. Charged in October 1918 with being a member of an unlawful association. Also with having objectionable matter in his possession. Sentenced to 12 months in jail.

CHEWONUK, MAX 14 Cameron St., Toronto, Ont. Charged in October 1918 with being a member of an unlawful association.

COLE, WILLIAM 258 Queen St., Stratford, Ont. Charged in October 1918 with being a member of an unlawful association.

COOK, WILSON Con. 7, N.E.H. Charged in October 1918 with being a member of an unlawful association.

COOK, AARON Lot 18, Con. 6, N.E.H. Charged in October 1918 with being a member of an unlawful association.

COOK, HARRY Lot 18, Con. 6, N.E.H. Perth County. Charged in October 1918 with acting as an officer of an unlawful association. Fined $300. or 4 months in jail. Dec 19/18

COOK, WILLIAM Lot 18, Con. 6, N.E.H. Charged in October 1918 with allowing his premises to be used as meeting place for an unlawful association.

CHABASK, LUCIN 224 Droullard R., Ford, Ont. Charged with attending a meeting where the Russian language was being used and having papers in his possession in the same language. Case remanded until November 21, 1918.

CHRESHAN, J. Timmins, Ont. Charged in October 1918 with having objectionable literature in his possession.

CAASHUIR, NICK (Cooshnir) Sault Ste. Marie, Ont. Charged in October 1918 with being a member of an unlawful association and fined $2500. or three years in goal.

CUZMITCH, A. Brantford, Ont. Secretary Russian Social Revolutionary Group. Charged with having objectionable matter in his possession. Convicted and fined $500. or 12 months in jail.

CHEESEMAN, HENRY 236 River St., Toronto. Charged with having objectionable literature in his possesion. Found guilty Jan. 8th, 1919. Remanded for one week for sentence. Jan. 16, 1919, committed to Ontario Industrial Farm, Burwash, for six months.

"D"

DAHLBERG, A. Kurzinan, Alta. Address in a book found at I.W.W. headquarters in Chicago.

DEALMARK, WM. (Austrian) 41 Hastings St. E., Vancouver, B.C. Employed by Pacific Steel Co. Ltd., Eburne, B.C. Alleged I.W.W. worker in B.C.

DELL, W. LEO. alias John Jaschuk, at Timmins, Ont. Charged with having prohibited literature and in an enemy language in his possession on December 5, 1918; found guilty and fined $200.

DOERING, WILMOT Lot 20, Con. 6, N.E.H. Charged in October 1918 with being a member of an unlawful association.

DOERR, GORDON Lot 17, Con. 7, N.E.H. Charged in October 1918 with being a member of an unlawful association.

DAHMER, WILLIAM Lot 11, Con. 7, N.E.H. Charged in October 1918 with being a member of an unlawful association.

DECKER, ALBERT Con. 7, N.E.H. Charged in October 1918 with being a member of an unlawful association.

"E"

EINGRON, ALBIN Morson via Sleeman, Ont. Subscriber to "Solidarity".

ELLIOTT, J.H. Box 16, Shawnigan, B.C. Alleged I.W.W. worker in B.C.

ERICKSON, OLAF. 35 Cordova St., W., Vancouver, B.C. Alleged I.W.W. worker in B.C.

ESLIN, J. Prussia, Sask. Subscriber to "Solidarity".

EVTICHOFF, NICK 14 Camden St., Toronto, Ont. Charged in October 1918 with being a member of an unlawful association.

EALAREGA, PANTELY 224 Droullard R., Ford, Ont. Charged with attending a meeting where the Russian language was being used and having papers in his possession in the same language. Case remanded until November 21, 1918. Dec. 1918, Fined $100. and costs or six months.

EMROSE, P. Toronto, Ont. Charged with wearing a button of the

Socialist Party of the United States. Sentenced to 9 months in jail.

ELOYNIK, EVODKIN Ford, Ont. Charged with being in possession of prohibited literature. Case dismissed December, 1918.

"F"

FLOOT, GUST. c/o Louie Knutson, Rock Bay, B.C. Alleged I.W.W. worker in B.C.

FOURBIER, HELMUTH Port Alice, B.C. Aleged I.W.W. worker in B.C. (German)

FRANZEN, J. Camp 17, Ocean Falls, B.C. Alleged I.W.W. worker in B.C.

FILLMAN, EMIL 52 Cordova St., E., Vancouver, B.C. arrested October 19th, 1918, charged with having objectionable matter in his possession.

FRASER, MATT 1912 address was P.O. Box 1594. In 1912 was Secretary I.W.W. Local #58.

FILSINGER, MOSES Charged in October 1918 with making "Seditious utterances" in the village of Mildmay, Ont. Found guilty by Magistrates Chapman of Port Elgin and McIntosh of Southampton, and fined $300. and costs.

FITZGEORGE, JAMES 208 Wellington St., Stratford, Ont. Charged in October 1918 with being a member of an unlawful association.

FORESOV, GEO. Vancouver, B.C. Charged in October 1918 with having objectionable matter in his possession.

"G"

GARRISON, AUG. Camp 17, Ocean Falls, B.C. Alleged I.W.W. worker in B.C.

GERDO (or Gerds) MIKE
Camp 19, Ocean Falls, B.C. Alleged I.W.W. worker in B.C.

GRAVETT, J.E. Address unknown. Alleged I.W.W. worker in B.C.

GREEN, H. Port Moody, B.C. Smith & Dollar Co. Alleged I.w.W. worker in B.C.

GUMMESON, ADOLPH Wabigoon, Ont. Subscriber to "Solidarity".

GREEN, JOHN 205 Carrall St., Vancouver. Summoned October 1918, charged with having prohibited literature in his possession.

GRUE, LOUIS Committed for trial at Brockville, Ont. December 9th, for having seditious literature in his possession. Liberated on $2000. bail. To appear at the assizes in January, 1919.

GOURILSHUK, METROPAN 145 Palmerston Ave., Toronto, Ont. Charged in October 1918 with being a member of an unlawful association.

GLAVATIKY, SAM or (Klavislky) 101 Cadillac St., Ford, Ont. Charged with attending a meeting where the Russian language was being used and having papers in his possession in the same language. Case remanded until November 21, 1918. Convicted Dec. 23rd, 1918, and fined $100.

GRIHORASH, HARRY (Grehash) 68 Albert Rd., Ford, Ont. Charged with attending a meeting where the Russian language was being used and having papers in his possession in the same language. Case remanded until November 21, 1918. Convicted Dec. 23rd, 1918, and fined $100.

GERYLEQYCH, ALEX Sault Ste. Marie, Ont. Charged in October 1918 with being a member of an unlawful association and fined $4000. or five years in goal.

"H"

HADLEY, GUS OR GEO. Discovery Passage, B.C. (Burnetts Camp). Alleged I.W.W. worker in B.C.

HARDIN, HEDLEY V. Louis Creek, Alta. Subscriber to "Solidarity".

HARDY, GEORGE Was Secretary-Treasurer of Marine Transport Workers Industrial Union #200 March 1917 to June 1917, then went to B.C., thence to Seattle, Wash. Sentenced to imprisonment in U.S. Pen. at Leavenworth, Kansas, for one year and one day, fine of $30,000.

HARDY, FRED Born in Liverpool, England, lived in Canada, left Canada for U.S. in 1908. Alleged to have been one time a member of the 38th Canadian Regiment. Formerly secretary of the General Recruiting Union of the I.W.W. 1001 Madison St., Chicago. Now reported to be in Canada.

HARTMAN, J.C. Victoria Hotel, Brampton, Ont. Subscriber to "Solidarity".

HIGGINS, R. c/o Comox Logging Co., Headquarters, Courtenay, B.C. Alleged I.W.W. worker in B.C.

HILLERY, JOHN (English) Rosedale, Alta. President of Rosedale Local United Mine Workers of America. Reputed to be an I.W.W. and bad-type man.

HJELT, OLE Instow, Sask. Address in book found at I.W.W. headquarters in Chicago.

HOBER, JULIUS 10329 101st St., Edmonton, Alta. Subscriber to "Solidarity".

HOPKINS, Drumheller, Alta. Organizer of United Mine Workers of America. Reputed to be bad agitator.

HUNGERFORD, O.M. Vancouver, B.C. Alleged to be "very active" I.W.W. worker in B.C.

HARRISON, J.W. 1912 address was 630 Columbia St. New Westminster, B.C. In 1912 was Secretary I.W.W. Local #80.

HNATIUK, P. 1912 address was 723 Flora Ave., Winnipeg, Man. In 1912 was Secretary I.W.W. Local #47.

HAMANIUK, GEORGE 26 Third St., Cobalt, Ont. Charged in October 1918 with having publications in his possession in an enemy lanugage.

HARBATUKE, TOM 224 Droullard Rd., Ford, Ont. Charged with attending a meeting where the Russian language was being used and having papers in his possession in the same language. Case remanded until November 21, 1918. Convicted Dec. 23, 1918, and fined $100.

HALUHANSKY, JAKOS (Jekos Halishansky) 224 Droullard Rd., Ford, Ont. Charged with attending a meeting where the Russian language was being used and having papers in his possession in the same language. Case remanded until November 21, 1918. Convicted Dec. 23rd, 1918, and fined $100.

HAWLAN, NIKITA (Niketa Hallan) 224 Droullard R., Ford, Ont. Charged with attending a meeting where the Russian language was being used and having papers in his possession in the same language. Case remanded until November 21, 1918. Convicted Dec. 23rd, 1918, and fined $100.

HARJU, KNUTTI Sudbury, Ont. Charged in October 1918 with having objectionable literature in his possession.

HONCHAR, JOHN 75 Maitland St., London, Ont. Charged with being a member of an unlawful association and having objectionable literature in his possession. Suspended sentence. October 1918.

HONCHERICK, FEODER 504 Philip St., London, Ont. Charged with being a member of an unlawful association and having objectionable literature in his possession. Suspended sentence. October 1918.

HOBIN, TOM (Holm) Sault Ste. Marie, Ont. Charged in October 1918 with being a member of an unlawful association and fined $2500. or three years in goal.

HAAKKALA, AUGUST Sault Ste. Marie, Ont. Charged in October 1918 with being a member of an unlawful association and remanded.

"I"

IVENO, REV. W. Editor Winnipeg Labor News, formerly Minister of Methodist Church, Main St., Winnipeg. Present address Labor Temple, Winnipeg, Man.

"J"

JOHNSON, A. Box 252, Port Arthur, Ont. Address in book found at I.W.W. headquarters in Chicago.

JOHNSON, A. Address unknown. Alleged I.W.W. worker in B.C.

JOHNSON, ANDREW Grading Camp, Pimpkish Lumber Co., Alert Bay, B.C. Alleged I.W.W. worker in B.C.

JOHNSON, E. Lamb Lumber Co., Wolfshun Bay, B.C. Alleged I.W.W. worker in B.C.

JOHNSON, E. Land Lumber Co., Laing Bay, B.C. Alleged I.W.W. worker in B.C.

JOHNSTON, ANTON Union Bay, B.C. Alleged I.W.W. worker in B.C.

JOHNSTON, FRED Stays at Irving Hotel when in Vancouver, B.C. Alleged I.W.W. worker in B.C.

JOHNSTON, P. Address unknown. Alleged I.W.W. worker in B.C.

JOHANSON, S.G. 1912 address was 34 Cordora St.W., Vancouver, B.C. In 1912 was Secretary I.W.W. Local #322.

JASCHUK, JOHN alias W. Duchuk, at Timmins, Ont. Charged with having prohibited literature and in an enemy language in his possession on December 5, 1918; found guilty and fined $200.

JARVIS, JACOB Sudbury, Ont. Charged in October 1918 with having objectionable literature in his possession.

JUNTUNEN, HENRY Sudbury, Ont. Charged in October 1918 with having objectionable literature in his possession.

JOHNSTON, EMILE Sudbury, Ont. Charged in October 1918 with having objectionable literature in his possession.

JACKARKEW, DYONIZY Sault Ste. Marie, Ont. Charged with having objectionable literature in his possession. Convicted and fined $1000. or 3 years in jail.

"K"

KAAIRO, BURNO 601 Hamilton St., Vancouver, B.C. Alleged "very active" I.W.W. worker in B.C.

KAMPO, ANDREW Camp 19, Ocean Falls, B.C. Alleged I.W.W. worker in B.C.

KELLY, G. Address unknown. Alleged I.W.W. worker in B.C.

KIPKO, G. (Austrian) Trail, Age 40. C.M.&S.C. Alleged I.W.W. worker in B.C.

KOLBERG, C.E. Flat Creek, Alta. Subscriber to "Solidarity"

KERITENTIKO, J. (Keritenko) Columbia Hotel, Vancouver, B.C. Arrested October 19th, 1918, charged with attending illegal meeting. Pleaded guilty Dec. 23, 1918, fined $10.00. Other charges withdrawn.

KOLYNICK, THEODORE 516 Queen St. W., Toronto, Ont. Charged in October 1918 with having objectionable literature in his possession.

KAPUSTAK, BILL 70 Droullard Rd., Ford, Ont. Charged with attending a meeting where the Russian language was being used and having papers in his possession in the same language. Case remanded until November 21, 1918. Convicted Dec. 23rd, 1918, and fined $100.

KULIK, JOHN 50 Kildare Rd., Walkerville, Ont. Charged with attending a meeting where the Russian language was being used and having papers in his possession in the same language. Case remanded until November 21, 1918.

KRAMARUK, J. Timmins, Ont. Charged in October 1918 with having objectionable literature in his possession.

KOWALIAWSKI, J. Timmins, Ont. Charged in October 1918 with having objectionable literature in his possession.

KOLJONEN, DR. H. Sudbury, Ont. Charged in October 1918 with having objectionable literature in his possession.

KATAINEN, PETER Sudbury, Ont. Charged in October 1918 with having objectionable literature in his possession.

KOZEL, PAUL 504 Philip St., London, Ont. Charged in October 1918 with being a member of an unlawful association. Suspended sentence.

KERETANKO, JOHN Vancouver, B.C. Charged in October 1918 with having objectionable matter in his possession.

KOW, DYONIZY JACKAR Sault Ste. Marie, Ont. Charged in October 1918 with being a member of an unlawful association and fined $1000. or three years in goal.

KEVAIS, MIKIAL Windsor, Ont. Charged with having prohibited literature in his possession. Convicted Dec. 23, 1918, and fined $200.

KLAVISLKY, SAM (or Glavatiky) Ford, Ont. Charged with having prohibited literature in his possession. Convicted Dec. 23, 1918, and fined $100.

KOVALENKE, PAVEL Ford, Ont. Charged with having prohibited literature in his possession. Dec. 23, 1918, fined $200. and costs or six months.

"L"

LARSEN, LOUIS Discovery Passage, (Burnetts Camps) B.C. Alleged I.W.W. worker in B.C.

LARSEN, R. Address unknown. Alleged I.W.W. worker in B.C.

LARSON, JOHN I.T. Camp, Campbell River, B.C. Alleged I.W.W. worker in B.C.

LARSON, L. Watt Camp 19, Ocean Falls, B.C. Alleged I.W.W. worker in B.C.

LATONRAKI, SAM. Address unknown. Alleged I.W.W. worker in B.C.

LEBICK, MIKE (German)Copper Mountain, B.C. Alleged I.W.W. Worker in B.C.

LEWIS, GEO. 11th St. and Hendry Ave., North Vancouver, B.C. Alleged I.W.W. worker in B.C. (very active).

LIND, GUST Barbara Camp, Britannia, B.C. Alleged I.W.W. worker in B.C.

LINDELL, J.F.M. c/o Alex. Ramsey, 536 Prior St., Vancouver, B.C. Alleged I.W.W. worker in B.C.

LOTSKAR, Address unknown. Alleged "very active" I.W.W. worker in B.C.

LUCKEN, IVER Camp 2, Stave Falls, Ruskin, B.C. Alleged I.W.W. worker in B.C.

LUNDIN, ASKER Camp 4, Massett Timber Co., Fort Clements, B.C. Alleged I.W.W. worker in B.C.

LINDBERG, E.F. 569 Hamilton St., Vancouver, B.C. arrested October 21st, 1918, charged with having objectionable matter in his possession, sentenced to five weeks in jail and fined $100. or in default of fine, 2 months additional imprisonment. Charged with being an officer of an unlawful association.

LATCHEM, E.W. Now under indictment and arrest at Omaha, Nebraska. In 1912 was Secrtary I.W.W. Local #327.

LARSON, GUST 425 Kinistino Ave., Edmonton, Alta. In 1912 was Secretary I.W.W. Local #82.

LUND, JACOB (Jacko)Peter St., Cobalt, Ont. Charged in October 1918 with being a member of the Social Demoratic Party and of the Finnish Socialist Association of Cobalt, and with having objectionable literature. Fined $200.00

LUPPA, CHAS. (Lippa) 106 Lang St., Cobalt, Ont. Charged in October 1918 with having publications in his possession in an enemy language. Fined $200.00.

LANTZ, JOHN Lot 18, Con. 7, N.E.H. Charged in October 1918 with being a member of an unlawful association.

LASSPUK, M. Timmins, Ont. Charged in October 1918 with having objectionable literature in his possession.

LEHTI, WARIO Sudbury, Ont. Charged in October 1918 with having objectionable literature in his possession.

LUOMA, WALTER Sudbury, Ont. Charged in October 1918 with having objectionable literature in his possession.

LINKEVIT, ANTONE 75 Maitland St., London, Ont. Charged with being a member of an unlawful association and having objectionable literature in his possession. Suspended senetence. October 1918.

LADOVSKY, STEVE 523 Simcoe St., London, Ont. Charged in October 1918 with being a member of an unlawful association. Suspended sentence.

LESKOW, HARRY Sault Ste. Marie, Ont. Charged in October 1918 with being a member of an unlawful association and fined $200. or one year in goal.

LICKOFAY, GEORGE (or Lichopoy) Windsor, Ont. Charged with having prohibited literature in his possession. Convicted and fined $200. Dec. 17, 1918.

LOOKY, EDWARD Windsor, Ont. Charged with having prohibited literature in his possession. Convicted and fined $200. Dec 17, 1918.

"M"

MAGNUSON, ANDREW Camp 16, Ocean Falls, B.C. Alleged I.W.W. worker in B.C.

MAGISSON, or MAGNUSON A.Camp 16, Ocean Falls, B.C. Alleged I.W.W. worker in B.C.

MAHLER, HERBERT (Canadian) Sentenced August 1918 to imprisonment in U.S. Penitentiary at Leavenworth, Kansas, for five years and fined $25,000. for being I.W.W. worker.

MARIAN, A. Logash, Man. Subscriber to "Solidarity."

MATTI, K. Formerly of 356 Taylor Ave., Astoria, Ore. Alleged I.W.W. worker in B.C.

MEARD, JOHN Powell River Lumber Co., Kingcome River, B.C. Alleged I.W.W. wokrer in B.C.

MEDERES, CHAS. 11th St.E., North Vancouver, B.C. Alleged "very active" I.W.W. worker in B.C.

MEGAR, or WEZGAR, JOHN Brooks Bidlake Mill Co., Powell River, B.C. Alleged I.W.W. worker in B.C.

MEJER, JOHN c/o Brooks Bidlake, Powell River, B.C. Alleged I.W.W. worker, in B.C.

MMARD, JOHN Powell River Lumber Co., Kingcome River, B.C. Alleged I.W.W. worker in B.C.

MOSS, R. 271 Nelson St., Brantford, Ont. Subscriber to "Solidarity."

MELINCOFF, NICK 738 Jackson Ave., Vancouver, B.C. arrested October 19th, 1918, charged with attending illegal meeting.

MELINCOFF, NICK 738 Jackson Ave., Vancouver, B.C. arrested October 21st, 1918, charged with having objectionable matter in possession.

MORSE, A.O. 1912 address was P.O. Box 917, Prince Rupert, B.C. In 1912 was Secretary I.W.W. Local #326.

MATTELAINEN, SOFIA (Mrs) (Matlelinen) 106 Lang St., Cobalt, Ont. Charged in October 1918 with having publications in her possession in an enemy language. Fined $200.00.

MORROW, JAMES 26 Sackville Place, Toronto, Ont. Charged in October 1918 with having objectionable literature in his possession.

MADRASHUK, PHILIP 104 Denison Ave., Toronto, Ont. Charged in October 1918 with being a member of an unlawful assocation.

MEISTRENKO, SAM 104 Denison Ave., Toronto, Ont. Charged in October 1918 with being a member of an unlawful association.

MOROZ, MIKE 67 Denison Ave., Toronto, Ont. Charged with being a member of an unlawful association in October 1918.

MANCE, W.W. 13 Woolpreg Ave., Toronto, Ont. Charged in October 1918 with being a member of an unlawful association.

MELNIK, ALEX 224 Droullard Rd., Ford, Ont. Charged with attending a meeting where the Russian language was being used and having papers in his possession in the same language. Case remanded until November 21, 1918. Convicted Dec. 23, 1918, and fined $100.

MELNIK, MIKE (Pelepuk) 115 Droullard Rd., Ford, Ont. Charged with attending a meeting where the Russian language was being used and having papers in his possession in the same language. Case remanded until November 21, 1918. Convicted Dec. 23, 1918, and fined $100.

MALICK, E. Timmins, Ont. Charged in October 1918 with having objectionable literature in his possession.

MARKEVITCH, A. Timmins, Ont. Charged in October 1918 with having objectionable literature in his possession.

MANNINEN, DAVID Sudbury, Ont. Charged in October 1918 with having objectionable literature in his possession.

MOROYUK, THEORDORE 523 Simcoe St., London, Ont. Charged in October 1918 with being a member of an unlawful association. Suspended sentence.

MATTSON, EMIL South Porcupine, Ont. Charged in October 1918 with being a member of an unlawful association.

MELNIKOFF, NICOLAI Vancouver, B.C. Charged in october 1918 with having objectionable matter in his possession.

MAKARIVITCH, WM. Windsor, Ont. Charged with having prohibited literature in his possession. Convicted and fined $200. Dec. 17th, 1918.

"Mc"

MCAINISH, CO., 4 12 College St., Toronto, Ont. Address in book found at I.W.W. headquarters in Chicago.

MCBAIN, B. P. 631 McBain St., Ft. William, Ont. Address in book found at I.W.W. headquarters in Chicago.

MCINNES, ED. Union Bay, B.C. Alleged I.W.W. worker in B.C.

MCFARLANE, WILLIAM Joyceville, Ont. Up on two charges of

making seditious statements. Found guilty on first charge and fined $50.00 and costs. On second charge let off on suspended sentence and costs of court. Ordered to put up 2 bonds of $500. each as a guarantee of good behavior in future. He is president of the Joyceville branch of the United Farmers of Ontario.

"N"

NAGY, L. (Hungarian)Michael, B.C. Age 41. Alleged I.W.W. worker in B.C.

NEDERLEE, O.K. Vancouver, B.C. Alleged I.W.W. worker in B.C.

NELSON, JOHN Crown Hotel, Vancouver, B.C. Alleged I.W.W. worker in B.C.

NIPOLES, Address unknown, Alleged I.W.W. worker in B.C.

NIXON, INNES Address unknown. Alleged I.W.W. worker in B.C.

NORMAN, MARTIN Camp 4, Massett Timber Co., Fort Clements B.C. Alleged I.W.W. worker in B.C.

NAYLOR, JOS. formerly president of B.C. Federation of Labor. Anti-conscriptionist. Formerly president B.C. Trades & Labor Council Socialist 1917 address P.O. Box 415, Cumberland, B.C.

NIEMINEN, DAVID 106 Lang St., Cobalt, Ont. Charged in October 1918 with being a member of the Social Democratic Party, and of the Finnish Socialist Association of Cobalt, and with having objectionable literature. Fined $200.00.

NIEMINEN, (Mrs.) DAVID 106 Lang St., Cobalt, Ont. Charged in October 1918 with being a member of the Social Democratic Party, and of the Finnish Socialist Association of Cobalt, and with having objectionable literature. Withdrawn.

NEWMAN, WILLIAM 55 Cherry St., Stratford, Ont. Charged in October 1918 with being a member of an unlawful association and with being a representative of said unlawful association.

NYKIFORUK, MIKE Cobalt, Ont. Charged with having objectionable literature in his possession. Fined $500.00.

NEBIS, MICHIAL Windsor, Ont. Charged with having prohibited literature in his possession. Dec. 17th, 1918, fined $200. and costs or six months.

"O"

O'BRIEN, PAT Wilson & Brady Camp, Heriot Bay, B.C. Alleged I.W.W. worker in B.C.

OLSEN, A. Camp 2, Massett Timber Co., Port Clements, B.C. Alleged I.W.W. worker in B.C.

OLSEN, W. c/o H. Seaton, R.R., Victoria, B.C. Allcged I.W.W. worker in B.C.

OLSON, CHAS. Box 135, Powell River, B.C. Alleged I.W.W. worker in B.C.

OUTIS, W. Address unknown. Alleged I.W.W. worker in B.C.

OTTA, JOHN (Otto) 12 Larose St., Cobalt, Ont. Charged in October 1918 with having publications in his possession in an enemy language. Fined $100.00

ORLETZKI, W. Timmins, Ont. Charged in October 1918 with having objectionable literature in his possession.

OSTEPCHUK, J. Timmins, Ont. Charged in october 1918 with having objectionable literature in his possession.

ORGNIK, GEORGE 502 Philip St., London, Ont. Charged in October 1918 with being a member of an unlawful association and having objectionable literature in his possession. Suspended sentence.

OLEGNICK, EVDOKIM 245 Droullard Rd., Ford, Ont. Charged with attending a meeting where the Russian language was being used and having papers in his possession in the same language. Case remanded until November 21, 1918.

OLEARAGA, PANTILY Ford, Ont. Charged with having prohibited literature in his possession. Convicted and fined $100. Dec. 23rd, 1918.

"P"

PARTUCH, RUDOLPH (German) Port Alice, B.C. Alleged I.W.W. worker in B.C.

PATRITI, A. 528 McPherson St., Ft. William, Ont. Address in book found at I.W.W. headquarters in Chicago.

PATRITTE, B. 631 McBain St., Ft. William, Ont. Address in book found at I.W.W. headquarters in Chicago.

PATULLI, B. 631 McBain St., Ft. William, Ont. Address in book found at I.W.W. headquarters in Chicago.

PETERSON or PATTERSON, E. Port Alberni, B.C. Alleged I.W.W. worker in B.C.

PERKINS, HARRY 65 Bain St., Toronto, Ont. Charged in October 1918 with being a member of an unlawful association.

PELIPUP, MIKE
(Pelepuk) 230 Cadillac St., Ford, Ont. Charged with attending a meeting where the Russian language was being used and having papers in his possession in the same language. Case remanded until November 21, 1918. Convicted Dec. 23, 1918, and fined $100.

PUGACK, FODEY (Pujack) 305 Droullard Rd., Ford, Ont. Charged with attending a meeting where the Russian language was being used and having papers in his possession in the same language. Case remanded until November 21, 1918. Convicted Dec. 23, 1918, and fined $100.

PUHOSKY, PAUL 245 Droullard Rd., Ford, Ont. Charged with attending a meeting where the Russian language was being used and having papers in his possession in the same language. Case remanded until November 21, 1918. Case dismissed Dec. 1918.

POLIEKO, K. Timmins, Ont. Charged in October 1918 with having objectionable literature in his possession.

PANCHENKO, M. Copper Cliff, Ont. Charged in October 1918 with being a member of an unlawful association.

PROKASAK, W. Vancouver, B.C. Charged in October 1918 with having objectionable matter in his possession. Dec. 23, 1918, pleaded guilty to charge of attending an unlawful meeting, fined $10.00. Other charges withdrawn.

POLOCHNUK, ESA Windsor, Ont. Charged with having prohibited literature in his possession. December 1918, fined $200. and costs or six months.

"Q"

QUELL, CHARLES Amulree, N.E.H. Charged in October 1918 with being a member of an unlawful association.

QUELL, FRED Amulree, N.E.H. Charged in October 1918 with being a member of an unlawful association.

"R"

ROGERS, GEO. Address unknown. Alleged I.W.W. worker in B.C.

ROWAN, JAMES (English) During 1913 and 1914 was Secretary of Local 82 of I.W.W. in Edmonton. Latter part of 1914 was arrested and charged with murder at Lac la Biche 150 miles N.W. of Edmonton. In 1917 was Secretary I.W.W. at Portland, Ore. (Local 339). August 1918 sentenced to imprisonment in U.S. Penitentiary at Leavenworth, Kansas, for twenty years and fine of $20,000.

REID, JAMES N. 208 Harvie Ave., Toronto, Ont. Charged in October 1918 with having objectionable literatue in his possession. Suspended sentence.

ROSSITER, ERNEST 299 Queen St., Stratford, Ont. Charged in October 1918 with being a member of an unlawful association and with being a representative of said unlawful association. Fined $100. or two months in jail. Dec 19/18

RUBANETZ, W. Timmins, Ont. Charged in October 1918 with having objectionable literature in his possession.

ROHOVICK, ALEX 502 Philip St., London, Ont. Charged in October 1918 with being a member of an unlawful association. Suspended sentence.

ROBERTS, T.B. Silverton, B.C. Charged with making seditious statements and acquitted. Is Secretary of Silverton Miners' Union. October 1918.

"S"

SANDQUIST, ALEX Port Alberni, B.C. Alleged I.W.W. worker in B.C.

SCOW, 7th Ave. & 16th St., New Westminster, B.C. (Without naturalization papers). Alleged I.W.W. worker in B.C.

SIEMENS, E.K. Box 246, Arcola, Sask. Subscriber to "Solidarity."

SINCLAIR, ARCHIE (Canadian) Sentenced August 1918 to imprisonment in U.S. Penitentiary at Leavenworth, Kansas, for ten years and fine of $35,000. for being I.W.W. worker.

SMITH, JIM Address unknown. Alleged I.W.W. worker in B.C.

SMITH, GEO. 1415 8th Ave., New Westminster, B.C. (Without naturalization papers). Alleged I.W.W. worker in B.C.

SMITH, B.E. Address unknown. Alleged I.W.W. worker in B.C.

SMITH, MERVYN 82 Shanly St., Kitchener, Ont. Address in book found at I.W.W. headquarters in Chicago.

SMITH, Rosedale, Alta. Secretary Rosedale Local of United Mine Workers of America. Reputed to be bad agitator.

SODERBERG, A. c/o Alberni Pacific Lumber Co., Port Alberni, B.C. Alleged I.W.W. worker in B.C.

SOMENUK, T. (Austrian) Michael, B.C. Alleged I.W.W. worker in B.C.

SOUSIE, NEIL Grahams Island, Spruce Camp, B.C. Alleged I.W.W. worker in B.C.

SOVIANTE, A. Wolfson Bay, B.C. Alleged I.W.W. worker in B.C.

STEADMAN, ARTHUR 11th St. E., North Vancouver, B.C. Alleged I.W.W. worker in B.C.

STONE, CHARLES Address unknown. Alleged I.W.W. worker in B.C.

STROMBERG, K.P. c/o A.P. Allison, Grassie (Grassy) Bay, B.C. Alleged I.W.W. worker in B.C.

SWANSON, ANDREW c/o Smith Dollar & Co., Port Moody, B.C. Alleged I.W.W. worker in B.C.

SWANSON, ADOLPH Camp 11, Ocean Falls, B.C. Alleged I.W.W. worker in B.C.

SWANSON, ANDREW Camp 2, Massett Timber Co., Port Clemens, B.C. Alleged I.W.W. worker in B.C.

SWANSON, A. Address unknown. Alleged I.W.W. worker in B.C.

SWANSON, W. Address unknown. Alleged I.W.W. worker in B.C.

SMITH, Miss L.M. 1912 address was 923 Caledonia Ave., Victoria,

B.C. In 1912 was Secretary I.W.W. Local #44. (Textile Workers).

SCHELKING, BARON EUGENE DE Native of Baltic Provinces of Russia. Expelled from Russia Diplomatic Service for financial irregularities--. Arrived Vancouver, B.C. March 23, 1918 accompanied by German wife.

STOCKMAN, REV. O. Lutheran Minister. Tavistock, Ont. Age 32, Wife's age 36, both registered at Tavistock, Ont., as alien enemies.

SHUMOVITCH, DANCharged at Timmins, Ont., with having prohibited literature and in an enemy language in his possession. Found guilty December 5, 1918. Fined $200. or three months hard labor.

SPENCE, REV. BEN. H. Charged 1918 with having objectionable matter (The Parasite) printed. True bill returned by Grand Jury at Summer Assizes. Case dropped October, 1918.

SALMEN, WAINO (Wino) 82 Helen St., Cobalt, Ont. Charged in October 1918 with being a member of the Social Democratic Party and of the Finnish Socialist Association of Cobalt. and with having objectionable literature. Fined $200.00.

SALMEN, (Mrs.) BETTY 82 Helen St., Cobalt, Ont. Charged in October 1918 with being a member of the Social Democratic Party and of the Finnish Socialist Association of Cobalt. Withdrawn.

STROWZYUSKI, MIKE 30 Second St., Cobalt, Ont. Charged in October 1918 with having publications in his possession in an enemy language.

SAWCHUK, P. 10 Helen St., Cobalt, Ont. Charged in October 1918 with having publications in his possession in an enemy language. Fined $200.00.

STROM, LOUIS 11 Murrey St., Toronto, Ont. Charged in October 1918 with being a member of an unlawful association.

SHEW, THOMAS E. 221 Victoria St., Toronto, Ont. Charged in October 1918 with having objectionable literature in his possession. Suspended sentence.

SLEEP, JOHN 280 Waverley Rd., Toronto, Ont. Charged in October 1918 with being a member of an unlawful association.

STEPANITOKY, JOHN 516 Queen St. W., Toronto, Ont. Charged in October 1918 with having objectionable literature in his possession.

SVIGACH, AGNEW 75 Grange Ave., Toronto, Ont. Charged in October 1918 with being a member of an unlawful association. and for having objectionable matter in his possession. Sentenced to 3 months in jail.

SMIMOW, ALIX 54 Richmond St. W., Toronto, Ont. Charged in October 1918 with being a member of an unlawful association.

SOMICA, KONRAD 104 Denison Ave., Toronto, Ont. Charged with

being a member of an unlawful association October 1918.

SCHMIDT, EDWIN N.E.H. Perth County. Charged in October 1918 with being a member of an unlawful assocation.

SCHNEIDER, SIEBERT Amulree, N.E.H. Charged in October 1918 with being a member of an unlawful association.

SCHOENHALS, GEORGE Lot 18, Con.7, N.E.H. Charged in October 1918 with being a member of an unlawful association.

SKIDMORE, ARTHUR 44 Louise St., Stratford, Ont. Charged in October 1918 with being a member of an unlawful association. Sentence, fined $500. and 30 days, or in default of fine at end of 30 days, 6 months' in jail. Dec 19/18 Released Dec. 31, 1918.

SAVTCHOUK, BASIL (Santchouck) 224 Droullard Rd., Ford, Ont. Charged with attending a meeting where the Russian language was being used and having papers in his possession in the same language. Case remanded until November 21, 1918. Convicted Dec. 23, 1918, and fined $100.

SHKILEUTZ, UFANASY 169 Droullard Rd., Ford, Ont. Charged with attending a meeting where the Russian language was being used and having papers in his possession in the same language. Case remanded until November 21, 1918.

SIFKIN, ABRAM 9 Parent Rd., Windsor, Ont. Charged with attending a meeting where the Russian language was being used and having papers in his possession in the same language. Case remanded until November 21, 1918.

SVATOSHUK, JOHN 245 Droullard Rd., Ford, Ont. Charged with attending a meeting where the Russian language was being used and having papers in his possession in the same language. Case remanded until November 32, 1928. Case dismissed December, 1918.

SOCAL, STEPHEN (Sokan) 4 Francis St., Ford, Ont. Charged with attending a meeting where the Russian language was being used and having papers in his possession in the same language. Case remanded until November 21, 1918. December 1918, Suspended Sentence.

SAVTCHOUK, BASIL (Santchouck) 224 Droullard Rd., Ford, Ont. Charged with attending a meeting where the Russian language was being used and having papers in his possession in the same language. Case remanded until November 21, 1918. Convicted Dec. 23, 1918, and fined $100.

SHENIUK, J. Timmins, Ont. Charged in October 1918 with having objectionable literature in his possession.

STANETZKI, G. Timmins, Ont. Charged in October 1918 with having objectionable literature in his possession.

SODOVISKY, WEEKENTY 502 Philip St., London, Ont. Charged

with being a member of an unlawful association and having objectionable literature in his possession. Fined $250. and costs or six months in jail. October 1918.

SHISHII, KRILL Windsor, Ont. Charged with having prohibited literature in his possession. Convicted Dec. 17, 1918, and fined $200.

SEEDON, ISIDORE Ford, Ont. Charged with having prohibited literature in his possession. December 1918, fined $100. and costs or six months.

"T"

THOMPSON, GEO. Address unknown. Alleged I.W.W. worker in B.C.

TRUSSOFF, GEO. 736 Jackson Ave., Vancouver, B.C., arrested October 19th, 1918, charged with attending illegal meeting.

TRUSSOFF, GEO. Arrested October 21st, 1918, charged with being Officer of Unlawful Association.

TRUSSOFF, J.F. (see below) 736 Jackson Ave., Vancouver, B.C. Arrested October 19th, 1918, charged with attending illegal meeting.

TRUSSOFF, GEO. Dunlevy Rooms, Vancouver, B.C. Arrested October 21st, 1918, charged with having objectionable matter in his possession.

TREEHUBA, FRED 523 Simcoe St., London, Ont. Charged in October 1918 with being a member of an unlawful association and having objectionable literature in his possession. Fined $250. and costs or six months in jail.

TREEHUBA, WILLIAM 523 Simcoe St., London, Ont. Charged in October 1918 with being a member of an unlawful association and having objectionable literature in his possession. Suspended sentence.

TREEHUBA, HARRY 523 Simcoe St., London, Ont. Charged in October 1918 with being a member of an unlawful association. Suspended sentence.

TORSSOV, JOHN FRED (Trussoff) Vancouver, B.C. Charged in October 1918 with having objectionable matter in his possession. Dec. 23, 1918, pleaded guilty to charge of attending an unlawful meeting, fined $10.00. Other charges withdrawn.

TUOMI, OTTO Sault Ste. Marie, Ont. Charged in October 1918 with being a member of an unlawful association and fined $2500. or three years in goal.

TORTILLA, AUGUST Sault Ste. Marie, Ont. Charged in October 1918 with being a member of an unlawful association and discharged.

TREITAK, ANDREW Brantford, Ont. Found guilty January 14th, 1919, of being member of an unlawful association. Remanded until January 20th, 1919, for sentence.

"U"

ULACUK, PETE 305 Droullard Rd., Ford, Ont. Charged with attending a meeting where the Russian language was being used and having papers in his possession in the same language. Case remanded until November 21, 1918. Convicted Dec. 23, 1918, and fined $100.

ULEASODECH, STEVE 93 Aylmer Ave., Windsor, Ont. Charged with attending a meeting where the Russian language was being used and having papers in his possession in the same language. Case remanded until November 21, 1918. Convicted Dec. 23, 1918, and fined $100.

"V"

VANSAND, AUFIN Crown Hotel, Vancouver, B.C. Alleged I.W.W. worker in B.C.

VOINVICH, DAN (Austrian) Phoenix, B.C. Alleged I.W.W. worker in B.C.

VARYION, SERGIJ (Varyon) Vancouver, B.C. Arrested October 19th, 1918, charged with attending illegal meeting. Also having objectionable matter in his possession. Dec. 23, 1918, pleaded guilty to charge of attending an unlawful meeting fined $10.00. Other charges withdrawn.

"W"

WATTS, TOM Menzies Bay, B.C. Alleged I.W.W. worker in B.C.

WESTBERG, H. Camp No. 4, Stillwater, B.C. Alleged I.W.W. worker in B.C.

WESTER, L. New Kistle Lumber Co., Alert, B.C. Alleged I.W.W. worker in B.C.

WEZGER, or MEGER, JOHN Brooke Mill Co., Powell River, B.C. Alleged I.W.W. worker in B.C.

WHEELER, J. Coughlans Shipyards, Vancouver, B.C. Alleged I.W.W. worker in B.C.

WILLIAMS or WILLIAMSON, WM. North Vancouver, B.C. Alleged I.W.W. worker in B.C.

WILLIAMS, GEO. Formerly Secy. Lumber Workers Industrial Union, Seattle, Wash. Alleged I.W.W. worker in B.C.

WILSON, MRS. Has been corresponding with E.J. Chamberlain an I.W.W. leader at Seattle, requesting him not to send any more I.W.W. matter to Saulte Ste. Marie, Ont.

WINTER, A. or O. Camp No. 2, Abbotsford, B.C. Alleged I.W.W. worker in B.C.

WHYLDMAN, C.E. 1912 address was 1349 9th Ave. W., Calgary. Alta. In 1912 was Secretary I.W.W. Local #79.

<u>WAHRN, WAINA</u> 280 Waverley Rd., Toronto, Ont. Charged in October 1918 with being a member of an unlawful association.

<u>WAGNER, THEODORE</u> Amulree, N.E.H. Charged in October 1918 with being an officer of an unlawful association.

<u>WIRTU, JOHN</u> Copper Cliff, Ont. Charged with having objectionable matter in his possession. October 1918.

<u>WILSON, JOHN J.</u> Sault Ste. Marie, Ont. Charged in October 1918 with being a member of an unlawful association and fined $1000. or three years in gaol.

<u>WASELINCHUK, STEFAN</u> 149 Beverly St., Toronto, Ont. Charged in October 1918 with being a member of an unlawful association.

<u>WATSON, CHARLES</u> 467 Parliament St., Toronto. Charged with having "The Red Terror in Russia" and other objectionable literature in his possession. Found guilty Jan. 8th, 1919. On Jan. 9th, 1919, sentenced to three years in Kingston Penitentiary and fined $500.00, or in default of payment, to an additional six months.

"Y"

<u>YOROSCHUK, BASHON</u> 9 Toko St., Toronto, Ont. Charged in October 1918 with being a member of an unlawful association.

"Z"

<u>ZEGAR, EVAN</u> 245 Droullard Rd., Ford, Ont. Charged with attending a meeting where the Russian language was being used and having papers in his possession in the same language. Case remanded until November 21, 1918. Convicted Dec. 23, 1918, and fined $100.

<u>ZAKARAK, JOHN</u> Sault Ste. Marie, Ont. Charged in October 1918 with being a member of an unlawful association and fined $4000. or five years in gaol.

<u>ZAKRZENSKI, JOHN</u> Windsor, Ont. Charged with having prohibited literature in his possession. December 1918 fined $200. and costs or six months.

PART 3: RCMP PERSONAL FILES REGISTER, 1919-1929

No.	NAME	ADDRESS	COMMENTS
1	Armstrong, Geo.	Winnipeg	
2	Armstrong, Mrs. Geo	Winnipeg	
3	Burick, Paul	Taber	
4	Baker, Samuel	Regina	
5	Burge, Dick	Vancouver	
6	Ballarin, Andrew	Mountain Park Mines	
7	Cuthbutson, Mrs.	Blairmore	
8	Christopher, J.P.	Calgary	
9	Caccioni, J.	Drumheller	
10	Dumpe, Petro	Mountain Park Mines	
11	Fortman, William	- do -	
12	Gosden, Robert		
13	Knight, J.R.	Edmonton, Alta.	
14	Knight, Mrs.J.R.	Edmonton, Alta	
15	Kingsley, E.T.	Vancouver	
16	Luopa, Nestor	Manyberries	
17	Macdonald, Archie		
18	Paulson, Owen H.	Calgary	
19	Peacock, Chas.	Lethbridge	
20*	Rutka, Joe		
21	Queen, (Alderman)	Winnipeg	
22	Ross, (- do --)	Calgary	
23	Russell, T.E.W.	Edmonton	
24	Shannon, Tom		
25	Sartory, Louise	Mountain Park Mines	
26	Semanoff, Paul		
27*	Susnar, Alex	Brule Mines	
28	Stigler, Max	- do -	
29	Vincer, Guiseppi	Mountain Park Mines	
30	Yardsley, Geo.	Taber	
31	Maguire, J.P.	Edmonton	
32	Ivens, Wm.	Winnipeg	
33	Nugent, Bernard	Taber	
34*	McCutcheon, R.J.	Winnipeg	
35	Bradshaw, R.L.	Drumheller	
36	Rees, David	Vancouver Island	
37	See 175P/12		

No.	NAME	ADDRESS	COMMENTS
38	Shadel, John		
39	Potter, John	Fernie	
40*	Levitt, Robert	Bellevue	
41	Johnson,	Coleman	
42	Hunter, William	Fernie	
43	Lestor, C.	Vancouver	
44	Blumenberg, Sam	Winnipeg	
45	Erickson, Oscar	Fernie	
46*	Winch, Ernest Edward	Vancouver	
47	Green,	- do -	
48	Charles, E.F.	- do -	
49	Kavanagh, Jack	- do -	
50*	Roska, Pete	Bellevue	
51	Nickefor, Nick		
52	Kelly, Gordon J.	Vancouver	
53	Needleands, R. H.	- do -	
54*	Gutteridge, Helena R.	- do -	
55	Trotter, W. R.	- do -	
56	Boyak	Coalhurst	
57	Puzul, Geo.	- do -	
58	Bessetti, Steve	- do -	
59	Karcho	- do -	
60	Manning, J.		
61	Brown, Ed.		
62	McQuoid, Wm.		
63	Lefeaux, W. W.		
64	McMillan, John	Cumberland, B.C.	
65	McMillan, Wm.	- do -	
66	Russell, Hugh	- do -	
67	Little, David	- do -	
68	Bruce, Preston	Beaver Camp	
69	Braes, Wm.	Cumberland	
70	Vonara, Victor		
71	Tatezuk, Nick	Crows Nest Pass	
72	Stephanovich, Nick	-- do --	
73	McWilliam, Mrs. Jean	Calgary	
74	McKenzie, J.E. or W.	Vancouver	
75	Lewin, R. W.	Calgary	
76	Sangster, C.	- do -	
77	Emery, R.	- do -	
78	DePerrier, E. A.	- do -	
79	Lawson, J.R.	Calgary	
80*	Radical Conditions	Vancouver, B.C.	Trans. to 175/1732
81	Fields, J.M.	Powell River, B.C.	
82	Midgeley, V.R.	Vancouver	
83	Mcvitty,		
84	Rogers, Dan	Coleman	
85	Barker, John	Medicine Hat	

No.	NAME	ADDRESS	COMMENTS
86	Kimball, J.H.	Baraca, Alta.	
87	Kent, J.	Wayne	
88	Beard, H.	Michel, B.C.	
89	Naylor, J.	Vancouver Island	
90*	Johns, R.J.	Winnipeg	
91	Pritchard, W.A.	Vancouver	
92	Erickson, Oscar	Fernie	see 175P/45
93	Maurice, S.E.	Drumheller	
94*	Irvine, William (Rev.)	Calgary	
95	Smitten, Walter		
96*	Popowich, Mathew	Winnipeg	
97	Krat alias Krutt, Paul	Toronto	
98	Shusko, (Doctor)	Winnipeg	
99*	Mutch, E.M.	Regina	
100	Lewis, J.H.	Saskatoon	
101	Parkhouse alias Barkhouse, Jack		Lethbridge
102	Ray, Alex	- do -	
103	Lundberg, Ernest	Vancouver	
104	Higging, Richard	Vancouver	
105	Parkyn		
106	Allman		
107	Grogan		
108	Transferred to 175P/23		
109	Razanoff, Theodore		
110	Baron, Paul	Coleman	
111	Cottrell, Wilfred Harry	Vancouver	
112	King,	Seattle	
113	Phillips, W.B.		
114	Robson, W.B.		
115	Biggs, Thos.		
116	McDonnell, Pete		
117	McMurphy, George D.		
118	Price, Thos.	Hillcrest	
119	Jackson, Charles	Calgary	
120*	Moysiuk, Dmytro	Winnipeg	
121*	One Big Union		
122	Kinshep	Eckville	
123	Budka, (Bishop)	Winnipeg	
124	Taylor, J.	Esquimault, B.C.	
125	Foreman, L.	Surf Inlet	
126	Korbaly, Mike	Vancouver	
127	Kelt, J. alias Dikoyske	- do -	
128	Noslorozski, Pete alias Natraski		- do -
129	Goloyen, Teodor	- do -	
130	Mounsey, Wm.	- do -	
131	Davis,	Calgary	
132	Chekoeff, Geo.	Vancouver	
133	Diakoff, John	- do -	

No.	NAME	ADDRESS	COMMENTS
134	See 175P/271		
135	Snow,	Coalhurst	
136	Rhurmier, A.H.	- do -	
137	McConnell	Blairmore	
138	McGillis, Archie	Deadman's Island	
139	Stephenson, C.	Vancouver	
140	Tessler, M.	Winnipeg	
141	Nykorah, Leon	- do -	
142	Broatch, A.T.	Calgary	
143	Corse, Mrs.Geo.S.	- do -	
144	Hooley, J.S.	Calgary	
145	Fisher, John	Lac-du-Bonnett	
146	Walker, Robert	Cumberland	
147	Jura, Sava	Fort William	
148	Ilschuk, Luka	- do -	
149	Nerberg, O.	Calgary	
150	Mariot, Mark	Vancouver	
151	Fulcher, Edward	Brandon	
152	Berlinsky	Fort William	
153	Moran, Jack	Vancouver	
154	Ledgerwood, J.	- do -	
155	Leonard, Charles	- do -	
156	Joffre, Joseph	Drumheller	
157	King, Andrew	Vancouver	
158	Guikuno(Jenkins), J.	- do -	
159	Anderson, Paul	- do -	
160	Gruder, Jack		transferred to 175P/972
161	Jacques, W.	- do -	
162	Mark, Chas.	Drumheller	
163	Transferred to 175P/93		
164	Scown, Isiah	- do -	
165	Homberg, Lars	- do -	
166	Garven, A.	- do -	
167*	Charitonoff	Winnipeg	
168*	Lobaj, Danilo	- do -	
169*	Almazoff, Moses	- do -	
170	Henderson	- do -	
171	Burton	- do -	
172	Parsky, M.	Calgary	
173	Lee, John	Lethbridge	
174*	Sullivan, Frank	- do -	
175	Krozer, John	Calgary	
176	Fraser, John or Bill	- do -	
177	Green, Richard	Drumheller	
178	Hughes, B.	Vancouver	
179	Burgess	Vancouver	
180	Harvey,	Vancouver	
181	McEwan alias McKeown	Vancouver	

No.	NAME	ADDRESS	COMMENTS
182	Sparks	Vancouver	
183	Chapman	Vancouver	
184	Smith, W.	Vancouver	
185	Moore, Kelsey	Vancouver	(I.W.W.) 186
187	Millward, Edward	Vancouver	(I.W.W.)
188	Taylor, P.	Pocahontas	
189	Lamont,	Vancouver	
190	Zak, Albert	Commerce, Alta.	
191	Spencer, Percy	Coalhurst, Alta.	
192	Lewis, Geo.	S. Vancouver	
193	Morris, Wallace T.	New Westminster	
194	Vincent, J.	Vancouver	
195	Dennis, J.	- do -	
196	Campbell, John	Vancouver	
197	Beagrie, Geo.	Swalwell	
198*	Russell, R.B.	Winnipeg	
199	Logan, W.H.C.	- do -	
200	Baker, F.J.	Brandon	
201	Lovatt, W.H.	Winnipeg	
202	Roberts, H.H.	St. Vital, Man.	
203	Scobell, A.	Winnipeg	
204	Transferred to 175P/198		
205	Crapper, F.	Moose Jaw	
206	McMurtry, Jas	Saskatoon	
207	Monroe, Wm.	Moose Jaw	
208	Sawbrook, Jas	Regina	
209	Hazeltine, R.	- do -	
210	Kolling, (Koelling), Wm.	Brule Mines	
211	Marshall, J.	Calgary	
212	McNabb, Donald	Lethbridge	
213*	Berg, C.E.	Edmonton	
214	Wells, A.S.	Vancouver	
215*	Sinkaroski, W.M.		
216	Oneski, Frederick		
217	Porrin, Michael		
218*	Chropko, Timothy	Edmonton	
219*	Yakymchek	- do -	Transferred 175/652
220*	Lutchok, I.	- do -	Transferred 175/650
221	Klybanowski, John	- do -	
222	Samotiuk, J.	- do -	
223	Sitik, Stack	- do -	
224	Slobodian	- do -	
225	Morsa, Nick	- do -	
226	Budnyk, Mike	- do -	
227	Pike, J.B.(Rev.)	Montreal, Que.	
228	Dzwonar	Edmonton, Alta.	
229	Kureychuk	- do -	
230	Prokopnick, Nick	- do -	

No.	NAME	ADDRESS	COMMENTS
231	Yanicki, W.		
232*	Danyluk, Nick		
233	Martin, Harry	Fernie	
234	Scarpelli, C.	Corbin	
235	McDonald, R.	Blairmore	
236	Brooks, John	Bellevue	
237	Lote, Frank	Hillcrest	
238	Sapan, S.		
239	Spiridon, Waldimir		
240	Kaverczak, Dimitri		
241	Keckrasoff		
242	Karoba, Sava		
243	Starikoff		
244	Murphy, Pat	Castelgar, n. Nelson BC	
245	Kourbatoff		Transferred to 175/P1439
246	Mareeff		Transferred to 175/P1436
247	Mateveoff		
248*	Nickson, Nicolas		
249*	Basanoff, Fred		
250	Cihovic, Peter		
251	Nekita (The Sailor)		
252	Perochjoff		
253	Broberg, Matt	Prince Rupert	
254	Erichuchovich, T.	Edmonton	
255	Nickaloef, Mrs.Mary	- do -	
256	Kariarinsky, Thrati	Fort William	
257	Koroluk, Takov	- do -	
258	Whesorkun, Misha	- do -	
259	Moore, Fred C.	- do -	
260	Davidovich, Heokey	Parry Sound, Ont.	
261	Werrier, Misha	Winnipeg	
262	Dworkin	- do -	
263	Matlin	- do -	
264	Bay, Sergt Jacob		
265	Geller, Louis		
266	Gordon, Geo.		
267	Brier		
268	Molitowski, Misha		
269	Morrison, Edward	Vancouver	
270	Korseloff	- do -	
271	Zouriff, Boris	- do -	
272	Trousoff, Sr.	- do -	
273	Trousoff, Jr.(Younger Brother)		- do -
274	Belak		
275	Miller, J.	nr. Cloverdale, B.C.	
276	Hartnell, J.S.	Vancouver	
277	Karpovich, E.	- do -	
278	Orloff	- do -	

No.	NAME	ADDRESS	COMMENTS
279	Cassidy, W.D.	- do -	
280	Morey, Charlie	- do -	
281	Wachtin, G.V.		
282	Devyatkin, B.	Winnipeg	
283	Leaman, Alex.F.	Redcliff, Alta.	
284	Legros, Wm. Ernest	- do -	
285	Smith, Harry	Calgary	
286	Gill, Albert	Kimberley	
287	Peebles, Wm. Henderson	North Lethbridge	
288	Transferred to P325		
289*	Lescarbeault, Augustin	Winnipeg	
290	Abramowitch, A.S.	- do -	
291	Hirsch	- do -	
292	Shaien	- do -	
293	Reel, Geo.	- do -	
294	Mitchell, Eddie	- do -	
295	Sutton, Mrs. E.	Victoria	
296	Stevens, W.	- do -	
297	Donnachie, R.	- do -	
298	Dakers, J.	- do -	
299	Davies, A.M.	- do -	
300	Woodward, E.S.	- do -	
301	Morrison, F.	- do -	
302	Berry, A.	- do -	
303	Hall, L.	- do -	
304	Smith, P.R.	- do -	
305	Horovenko, Wm.	Calgary	
306	Terril, John	- do -	
307	Nyman, Karl	Port Arthur	
308	Koski, Matti	- do -	
309	Heino, Otto	- do -	
310	Finklestein, Sam	Winnipeg	
311	Katainen, Peter	Port Arthur	
312*	Dworkin, Leo	Calgary	
313	Pritchard, H.K.	Vancouver	
314	Freiberg, J.P.	Edmonton	
315	Dahlstrom, Adolph	- do -	
316	Waldman, Kalman	Winnipeg	
317	Kousinoff, Jack	- do -	
318	McLughan, Robert	Vancouver	
319*	Dworkin, B.	Calgary	
320	Burns, Thomas	Vancouver	
321	Mace, Thomas	Prince Rupert	
322	McInnis, Jim	- do -	
323	Gothard, Sam J.	Vancouver	
324	Pressa, Evert	Manyberries	
325	Clark, Geo.A.	Lethbridge	
326	Adams, Geo.	Elmwood	

No.	NAME	ADDRESS	COMMENTS
327	Onisinoff	Ft. William	
328	Bohdanovisch, Karol	- do -	
329	Saltzman, H.	Winnipeg	
330	Bird, J.Edward	Vancouver	
331	Thompson, Thomas	Lethbridge	
332	Rukin, Samuel	Calgary	
333	Boiko, Wasyl	Port Arthur	
334	Suchman, J.	- do -	
335	Mcafee, C.	Redcliff	
336	Greenberg, Joe	Winnipeg	
337	Bodnar	- do -	
338	Lechtzier	- do -	
339	Timkoff	- do -	
340	Rosenthal, Sam	- do -	
341	Pidrucki	Drumheller	
342	Waskan	Edmonton	
343	Derysh, Mike	Drumheller	
344*	Rudak, George	Edmonton	Transferred to 175/P3771
345	Sinclair, Pete	Vancouver	
346	Newman, B.E.	Cloverdale, B.C.	
347	Casparson, C.J.F.	Vancouver	
348	Cyganoff	Victoria	
349	Draiman	- do -	
350	Bernstoff	- do -	
351	Nordstrom, O.	La Glace, Alta.	
352	Nelson, Geo.	Neobe, P.O., Alta.	
353	Pendass, Slim	Sexsmith, Alta.	
354	Pronin, Michael	Lethbridge	175P/217
355*	Thachuk, Nicolas	Canmore, Alta.	
356	Broadhurst, H.C.L.	Brandon	
357	Bunker, A.H.	Calgary	
358	Hill, Albert		
359	Thomas, Geo.		
360	Ward, Wm. H.	Moose Jaw	
361	Chadwick, Richard	- do -	
362	McAllister, Wm.	- do -	
363	Wurstone, Alexander	Vancouver	
364	Allen, Jos Henry	- do -	
365	Wheatley, Frank	Bankhead	
366	Lawson, P.F.	Fernie	
367	Sivertz, C.	Victoria	
368	Dooley, T.	- do -	
369	Varney, F.	- do -	
370	Nikoloff, N. & Wife	Morningside, Alta.	
371	Shydlowski, Mike	Brule Mines	
372	Nimick, John	Edmonton	
373*	Hudema, John	- do -	
374	Smith, M.C.	Vancouver	

No.	NAME	ADDRESS	COMMENTS
375*	Kalmusky, John	Saskatoon	
376	Bennett, Tom	Regina	
377*	Gryszczuk, Wasyl	Saskatoon	
378	Sochynsky, F.	- do -	
379	Broadley, Geo.	Regina	
380	Musselman, J.B.	- do -	
381	Katras	Regina	
382	Falk, F.M.	Weyburn	
383	Sturdy, Geo.	Regina	
384*	Mutch, E.M.	Regina	Trans. P175/99-See P.HF 99
385	Konstantine		
386	Steiner, John	Vancouver	
387	Watts, Walter	Calgary	
388*	Casey, George B.		
389	Kouznitzoff, Paul		Transferred 175P/1441
390	Colodin, G.		
391	Wasyl,	Vancouver	
392*	Smith, Albert E.	Brandon	
393	Hanson, AJ	Saskatoon	
394	Mayes, Walter	Vancouver	
395	Konovalon, Paul	Calgary	
396	Poasonin, John	Vancouver	
397*	Curry, William Jamieson	- do -	
398	McKay, Gordon	- do -	Transferred to 175/P2001
399	Marsoff, D.	Saskatoon	
400	Kolomiez	- do -	
401	Avie, Kalle		
402	Schwifft, Moses	New York City	
403	Harrington, J.	Regina	
404	Paine, Heiman	Winnipeg	
405	Mew, Chester W.	Brandon	
406	Powell, Percy	Calgary	
407	Suchman, Sarah	Port Arthur	
408	Fils	Winnipeg	
409	Yaronko, Ivon	Brule Mines	
410	Deachman, R.J.	Calgary	
411	Shurley, A.E.	Vancouver	
412	Orr, Wiley	Seven Persons	
413	Watson	Vancouver	
414	Bartholomew, Heff	Brandon	
415	Pelto, Waino	Ft. William	
416	Gerber	Winnipeg	
417	Briugman, Herbert		
418	Miklossy, Alfred Louis		
419	Shciypanski, P.	Vegreville	
420	Dutka, Mike	Edmonton	
421	Werenko, G.		
422	Bursukow	Wahasto	

No.	NAME	ADDRESS	COMMENTS
423	Simpson, Bert	Vancouver	
424	Mason, Joe	- do -	
425	Falk, Ernest Frederick	Regina	
426	Cantrill, A. W.	- do -	
427	Hnidan, Drytro		
428	Torniak, Yourko	W.Edmonton	
429	Wakaluk	Briseton, W.Calgary	
430	Slater, James	Bondiss, Alta.	
431	Rostotzki, D.	Duvernay	
432*	Harrington, Thomas	Regina	
433*	Bringman, Fritz	Winnipeg	
434	Radis	- do -	
435*	Martin, Fritz	- do -	
436	Richmond	- do -	
437*	Penner, Jacob	- do -	
438	Veitch,	- do -	
439	Heaps, A.A.	- do -	
440	Wind, Carl	- do -	
441	Schloms, Victor	- do -	
442	See 175P/431		
443	Miller, Thomas	Kimberley, B.C.	
444	Doyle, Thomas	Vancouver, B.C.	
445	Shaw, Fred	Prince Rupert	
446	Montgomery, Wm. H.	- do -	
447	Hamilton, James	Vancouver, B.C.	
448	Erkkella, Herman	Indola, Ont.	
449	Smith, J.E.	Ft. William	
450	Bonice (Bohenks), Bill	- do -	
451	Petras, Matthaes	Lethbridge	
452	Gawryluk, J.	Fernie	
453	Tomage, Steve	Corbin	
454	Marsh, John	N. Lethbridge	
455	ONeil, Jack	Victoria	
456	Gorst, James	Vancouver	
457	Filistans, Felix	Drumheller	
458	Messera, Octave	- do -	
459	Borney, Joe	- do -	
460	Matlak, Mike	- do -	
461	Ratchford, Joe	- do -	
462	McLeod, Jerry	- do -	
463	Drakous, Steve	N.Battleford	
464	Green, M.	Winnipeg	
465*	Kimmel, J.G.	- do -	
466	Seifert, Paul	- do -	
467	Sachs, Curt	- do -	
468	Burdette, W.	Seattle	
469	Johnson, J.A.	- do -	
470	Harris, W.B.	- do -	

No.	NAME	ADDRESS	COMMENTS
471	Young, C.B.	- do -	
472	Filewire, W.C.		
473	Robertson,		
474	Matter, J.	Lethbridge	
475*	Sawiak, B.M.	Canora, Sask.	
476	Burton, John	Abernethy, Sask.	
477	Donnally, Mrs. W.R.		
478	Harvey, James	Regina	
479	Constantine, Pte.E.K.H.	Vancouver	
480	Smith, D.W.	Brandon	
481	Brudwig, Sam	Cranbrook	
482	Casey, Michael	- do -	
483	Brindley, Mike	Fernie	
484	Brunner, Math.	Regina	
485	Fraser, David	Calgary	
486	Defilippi, Domenico	Edmonton	
487	Costello, John	Brule Mines	
488	Alexandres, N.	Regina	
489	Parcovich, Nick	Fernie	
490	Werwig, F. Evans	Prince Rupert	
491	Roseburgh, W. Alex	Brandon	
492	Madden, W. H.	Vancouver	
493	Miller, Geo.	- do -	
494	Hatch, Geo.	Princeton	
495	Holmes, E. J.	Edmonton	
496	Chrapko, Nick	Lanuke	Transferred to 175/P3185
497	Bellis, C. E.	Edmonton	
498	Sakowski, John	Lanuke	
499*	Humen, Wasyl	- do -	
500	Johnson, Frank		
501	Markiewicz, Paul (Rev.Father)	Winnipeg	
502	Webster, George	Vancouver, B.C.	
503	Earven, George	Syleton (Man.)	
504	Smith, Dan	- do -	
505	Bray, R.E.	Winnipeg	
506	Burns, Edward	Vancouver	
507	Viette, Maurice	Calgary	
508	Dohan, Sam	Redcliff (Alta.)	
509	Davis, G.Morgan	Redcliff (Alta.)	
510	Zebrauska, George	Redcliff (Alta.)	
511	Current, Walter	Redcliff (Alta.)	
512	Schwabe, Goddhiff	Redcliff, (alta.)	
513	Santavsky, George	(Southey Sask)Regina	
514	Vix, B.Solomon	Vancouver	
515	Pettipiece, R.Parm	Vancouver	
516	Mercer, E.F. (Rev)	Edmonton	Transferred 175/P705
517	Tietz, John	Regina	
518	Nakonechny, Teodor	Calgary	

No.	NAME	ADDRESS	COMMENTS
519	Leslie, William	Lillydale, P.O., Sask.	
520	Hangen, Agnes	Edmonton	521
522	Nichols,	Lethbridge	Transferred to 175/P624
523	Simps, Peter	Yorkton	
524	Balesta, Basil	Canora, Sask.	
525	Fuhr, Conrad		
526	Dorch, M.S.	Lethbridge	
527	Bunker, A.H.	6 Miles N., Manyberries	Transfered to P/357
528	Engelking,	3 Miles S.E., Manyberries	
529	Horad, Prank		
530	Laney, Edward	Vancouver	
531	Babcock, Nat	Red Deer, Alta. or Corbin, B.C.	
532	Gravett, James E.	Vancouver	
533	Mcginnes, James	Prince Rupert	Transferred to 175/P322
534	Hertel, Rudolph	Winnipeg	
535	Zummack, Charles F.(Rev)		Edmonton
536	Notman, John	Nelson, B.C.	
537	Beattie, W.E.	South Vancouver	
538	Campbell, Sam	Vancouver	
539	O'Connor, Thomas	Vancouver	
540	Brennan, Charles	Vancouver	
541	Mckay, Jordon(Dr.A.)	Vancouver	Transferred P398
542	Stean, Charles	Highland Park, Burnaby, B.C.	
543	Ollikkala, Edward	Fort William	
544	Ollikkala, Kalle	Fort William	
545	Malinowsky	Fort William	
546	Airola, Wille(Big Bill)	Fort William	
547	Munroe, Claude	Lethbridge	
548	Wingfield, Henry	Calgary	
549	Johnson, Bert (A.V.H.)	Vancouver	
550	Sealtritti, Fortunate	Wiggan, Coalhurst	
551	Sloan, James	Coalhurst House	(No. I)
552	Todd, Robert	Vancouver	
553	Young, R.H.	Vancouver	
554	Leach, Robert	Vancouver	
555	Verandor, Frank	Vancouver	
556	Zukin, John	Calgary	
557	MacHadden, Louis	Taber	
558	Hardek, Philip	Yorkton	
559	Harrington, J.	Vancouver	
560*	Hirschfield, David Boris	Calgary	
561	Dompe, John	Calgary	
562*	Stoll, Henry	Regina	
563	Stoll, Ludwig	Regina	
564*	Stoll, Fred (Fritz)	Regina	
565	Merchel, William	Regina	
566*	Lundgard, Peter (O C)	Nr. Sundial, Alta.	
567	Ormond, Joseph	Brule, Alta.	

No.	NAME	ADDRESS	COMMENTS
568	Hnatiuk, Peter	Taber	
569	Wyrostak, Peter	Lethbridge	
570	Hood, William	Vancouver (may move to Rosedale)	
571	Fox, Arthur	Calgary	
572	Townsend, C.	Calgary	
573	Sash, John	Frederick Island, B.C.	
574	Kornishoff	Fort William	
575	Rauk, John	Hays Creek,	
Prince Rupert B.C.			
576	Sungard, Chirst	Nr.Sundial, Alta.	
577	Sungard, Oscar A.	Nr.Sundial, Alta.	
578*	Wyrostak, George	Lethbridge	
579	Cherlenko, Nick	Hardieville	
580	Paladiezuk, Mike	Yorkton, Sask.	
581	Smith, Eddie J.W.	Regina	
582	Haseltine (Hazeltine), Ralph		Regina
583	Alley, George	Regina	
584	Rukin, Samuel	Calgary	
585	Henderson, H.	Vancouver	
586	Niketa,	Vancouver	Transferred to 175P252
587*	Baceda, Giuseppi Joe	Lethbridge	
588	Baroldie, Arthur	Lethbridge	
589*	Farmes, George	Lethbridge	
590	Zummack, (Rev.)Charles F		
591	Walker, John	Regina	
592	Borodowski, Mike	Victoria	
593	Read, Ambrose	Vancouver	
594*	Woodsworth, J.S.	Hollybush, Vancouver West	
595	King, Oliver		
596	Kushner, Wm. (Bill)	Edmonton	
597	Millward, Charles	Goodfire P.O. Via Hythe Alta.	
598	Millward, Frank	- do -	
599	Millward, Ralph	- do -	
600	Millward, Edgar	- do -	
601	Carletts, Jesse F.	- do -	
602	Carletts, Nell	- do -	
603	Unknown	Winnipeg	
604	Salm, F.Ludwig	Grayson, Sask.	
605	Edwards, Charles	Vancouver	
606	Mahone, John	Vancouver	
607	Albo, Romeo	Vancouver	
608	Irvine, Wm. H.	Edmonton	
609	Denick, James	Wronton, Sask.	
610	Hlanoff	?	
611	Anton, Harry	Yorkton	
612	Rappaport, David	Calgary	
613*	Papperny, Leo	Calgary	
614	Wright, W.	Coleman, Alta.	

No.	NAME	ADDRESS	COMMENTS
615	Atkinson, John	Coleman, Alta.	
616	Bell, W.	Coleman, Alta.	
617	Sakella, Mike	Paasburg, Alta.	
618	Skalb, Karl	Hillcrest, Alta.	
619	Beatty, Thomas	Coleman, Alta.	
620	Eccleson, Richard	Bellevue, Alta.	
621	Campbell, Harry	Bellevue, Alta.	
622	Chapman, Wm.	Coleman, Alta.	
623	Marcelango, Dominic	Hillcrest	
624	Nicholls, Charles	Calgary	
625	Harris, E.S.	Calgary	
626	Boothman, George	Calgary	
627	Dorch, J.	Lethbridge	
628	Dorch, P.	Lethbridge	
629	Clark, George A.		Transferred to P325
630	Ecomornay, Guss	Regina	
631	King, William	Gen. Del. Vancouver, B.C.	
632	Hartlieb, F.J.	Megronne, Sask.	
633	Conomowski, Pete	c/o Emir Sevier, Ebrurger, Sask.	
634	Kirpuiski, Fred.	Yorkton	
635	Hoornaerts, Tony	Norwood	
636*	Saprunoff, D.	Blaine Lake	
637	Donhanink, Victor	Harry Hill, Alta.	
638	Bushall, J.S.	Vancouver	
639	Desmond, Paddy	Vancouver	
640	Chekuda, Anani	Saskatoon	
641	Piotoski, Mike	Lethbridge	
642	Roberts, Joe	?	
643	Nelson, John	Port Arthur	
644	Laine, Frank	Port Arthur	
645*	Boychuk, John	Vegreville, Alta.	
646	Gottschlick, Hugo	Lacombe, Alta.	
647	Alschin, John	Vancouver, B.C.	
648	Richter, Franz	Winnipeg, Man.	
649	Budomyk, Konstantyn	Edmonton	
650*	Lutchak, Joseph	Edmonton	
651	Stanki, Omyerst	Rhein, Sask.	
652*	Yakimchuk, Mike	Edmonton	
653	Prokapnik, Nick	North Edmonton	
654	Prokapnik, John	(12 miles N.E.) Vegreville, Alta.	
655	Tatisholes, F.	C/O Tom Remman, Allen, Sask.	
656*	Centazzo, S.	Edmonton, Alta.	
657	Keitel, Albert	Lacombe, Alta.	
658	Moser, Constantine	(Box 270), Wiggin Coalhurst	
659	Finewack, Mike	Wayne, Alta.	
660	Grupa, August	Wiggin, Coalhurst, Alta.	
661	Eastham, Howard	Edmonton	
662	Koelling, William Frederick	Brule Mines, Alta.	

No.	NAME	ADDRESS	COMMENTS
663	Barnett, Herbert H.	Calgary	
664	Baningartuis, Karl	Oak Bluff, Man.	c/o J. Henderson
665	Reiner, K.	Edmonton	
666	Dorfman, Moses	Winnipeg	See PHF2471 Duplicated
667*	Dorfman, Gabriel	Winnipeg	
668	Dorfman, Michail	Winnipeg	
669	Mysk, Nick	Winnipeg	
670	Poprowicz, Ben	Winnipeg	
671	Bercovitch, A.(Doctor)	Winnipeg	
672	Kalichman, George	Winnipeg	
673	Danyluk, Nick	Brule, Alta.	
674	Fulker, Frederick	Rabbit Lake, Alta.	
675	Reid, Roy	Rabbit Lake, Alta.	
676*	Morrison, William	Rabbit Lake, Alta.	
677	Welsh, William		
678	Rybeck, Harry	Vermillion, Alta.	
679	Hansen, Otto	Sydley, B.C.,	c/o Porters Camp
680	Brown, William Alexander		Traners, Alta.
681	Stein, Charles	Wiggin, Coalhurst	
682	Smith, Peter	Wiggin, Coalhurst	
683	Verochick, Veroschuk	500 blk, Air "2", Saskatoon	
684	Chraschevsky,	Fort William	
685	Brightwell, James	#2 - 5th Ave. W.Vancouver	
686	La-France, John	Morse, Sask.	
687*	Swystun, Wasyl	Saskatoon, Sask.	
688	Lindsay, W.	Mary St. W, Fort William	
689*	Searle, Wm.	Russoborough, P.O. Elrose	
690	Schneider, Frederick	Morse, Sask.	
691*	Saari, Jalmar	Port Arthur	
692	Noble, Thomas M.	P.C. 182, Vancouver, B.C.	
693	Johannesson, S.J. (Dr)	Winnipeg, Man.	
694	Neiderover, Anton	Taber	
695	McKenzie, Alec	Vancouver	See File 175.P.74
696	Cobb, Fred	Banff	
697	Boyce, Agitator	Vancouver	
698	Okihiro, Masukichi	Vancouver	
699	Campbell, J.C.	Trail, B.C.	
700	Shorts, Chas.	Rocky Mountain House, Alta.	
701	Distzenko, Thomas	Vancouver	
702*	Bringman(Brickman), Fritz		
703	Hertel, E. Mrs.		
704	Veitch,		See File 438
705	Mercer, Francis E. (Rev)	Edmonton	
706	Kaufman, C.	Edmonton	
707	Beier, Peter	Edmonton	
708	Babuka, Tudor	Edmonton	
709	Grant, J.	Fort William	
710	Swaniston, Ralph	Calgary	

No.	NAME	ADDRESS	COMMENTS
711	Kiderviski, or Kuderuyski, John	Moose Jaw	
712	Popoff, Constantin	Slocan City, B.C.	Transferred to 175P2257
713	Weismer, J.	Fort William	
714	Kuzman, Wasyl	Fort William	
715	Roenicke, William	6 miles N.E. of Euchant	
716	Fraser, Alex		
717	Sauck, Timofey	Fort William	
718	Sova, John	Saskatoon	
719	Pugh, Thomas	Cranbrook (or Vancouver)	
720	Swidesky, B.	Vancouver	
721	Yoshy, Frank	Vancouver	
722	Stirling, R.E.	Regina	
723	Staley, Thomas	Ribstone, Alta.	
724	Lawrence, W.J.	Edmonton	
725	Nolte, Bob	Moose Jaw	
726	Schull, Charles	Moose Jaw	
727	Hall, Murray	Eyebrow	
728	Forsman, Pat	Barons, Alta.	
729	Bolam, Peter J.	Trail, B.C.	
730	Daly, T.J.	Vancouver	
731	Untinen, Jonas (Sr)	Carmangay, Alta.	
732*	Untinen, Jonas (Jr)	Carmangay, Alta.	
733*	Stewart, Donald	Fort William	
734	Balancheff, L.	Vancouver	
735	Smith, Harry	Drumheller, Alta.	
736	Sara, Gabriel	Wayne, Alta.	
737*	Shalagan, Mike	Clover Oak, P.O.	
738	Jabalos, Jack	Ebenezer, Sask.	
739	Hinks, Robert	Calgary	
740	Thomas, John	Creston, Kitchener	
741	Mangles, Joseph	Michel	
742	Billingsley, Charles		
743	Wiitasaari, Lauri	Port Arthur	
744	Howard, John	Hanna, Alta.	
745	Brennan, John B. Francis	Port Alberni, B.C.	
746	Keryl, Harry	Edmonton	
747	Abramovitch, Max	Edmonton	
748	Thompson, Jimmy	Cranbrook	
749*	Cheryk, Alex	Fort William	
750	Desebrock, Hans	Raslo, B.C.	
751	Duncan, Jas. A.		
752	Saget, H.L.	Brandon	
753	Nenwrith, John	Nr.Rosedale between Jackpine & Robin Hood Mines	
754	Melyshenko, Wasyl	Yorkton, Sask.	
755	Sazaruk, Takor	Fort William	
756	McLellan, Bruce	Silverton & Nelson, B.C.	
757	Grant, J.	Winnipeg	
758	Henwell or Henewell	Brandon, Man.	

No.	NAME	ADDRESS	COMMENTS
759	Gothard, Samuel James L/Cpl.	Vancouver	
760	Iwasuk, Spiradou	Fort Qu'Appelle	
761	Jowett, Holmes	Lethbridge	
762*	Godwin, Sydney	Pennant	
763	Roberts, T.B.	Silverton	
764	Boates, Mckenzie John	Sandon, B.C.	
765	Nesteruk, Martin	Fort William	
766	Koivisto, Alli	Port Arthur	
767	Reedar, F.M.	Silverton	
768	Dingwall, George	Rossland, B.C.	
769	Navak, George J.	Trail, B.C.	
770	Bayliss, Robert	Crawford Bay, B.C.	
771	Donnelly, Jack (alias Slim)	Yahko, B.C.	
772	Harte, Angust	Crawford Bay, B.C.	
773	White, Thomas		
774	Mcgregor, James Edward	Crawford Bay, B.C.	
775	Kitchen, George	Vermillion, Alta.	
776	Bannister, Harry	Beaver Crossing, Alta.	
777	Schraba, Irvan	Flat Lake, Alta.	
778	Pinski, George	Cold Lake	
779	Kalvin, Robert F.	Vancouver, B.C.	
780	Herms, Ernest Frederick	Orion, Alta.	
781	Zimmer, George	Crawford Bay, B.C.	
782	Mortimer, James	Silverton, B.C.	
783	McDonald, Allen	Beaver Crossing	
784	Chisty, Lary	Beaver Crossing	
785	Hatherley, N.N.		
786*	Clarke, G.G.J.N.		
787	Dahlgren, Arthur	Fort William	
788	Moir, Joseph A.	? Silverton, B.C.	
789	Landry, A.F.		
790	Redel, George	Taber	
791	McFegan, Alex	Blairmore	
792	Nelson, A.	Goddard, Alta.	
793	Krause, Herman	Lethbridge	
794	Zeith, John	Taber, Alta.	
795	Connors, Tom	Vancouver	
796	Sungreen, Knut	Goddard, Alta.	
797	Kangas, August	Goddard, Alta.	
798	Kangas, Math	Goddard, Alta.	
799	Paivia, Frank	Rowan, Ont.	
800	Begley, W.C.		
801	Bjorkman, Wanio	Nr. Rowan Tp. of Conmae, Ont.	
802	Ceddy, A.M.	Sutherland	
803	Dixon, James	Fort William	
804	Federick, Nicolai	Taber, Alta.	
805*	Freyman, Ernest	Hewitts Landing, Sask.	
806	Korejezukor or Rosezechuk, Timothy	Edmonton	

No.	NAME	ADDRESS	COMMENTS
807	Zahrandnik, Moyk	(Provincial Jail), Lethbridge	
808	Hess, Samuel	Vancouver, B.C.	
809	Taylor, Mrs. H.G.	Vancouver	
810	Richardson, Thomas	Vancouver	
811	Hamilton, James H.	(Provincial Jail), Regina	
812	Haiduk, Michael	Fort William	
813	Morrison, V.	Medicine Hat, Alta.	
814*	Barnard, Thomas Alfred	New Westminister, B.C.	
815	Blumberg, John	Vancouver	
816	Hourwitz, D.	Winnipeg	
817	Dixon, F.J.	Winnipeg	
818	Le-Dell, Wm.	Vancouver	
819	Legere, Benjamin	New York	
820	Mazinak, Kyrte		
821	Zula, Wenzyl	Edmonton	
822	Cowan, Walter	Port Neville	
823	Johnson, Erick	Kimberley	
824	Atkinson, Fred	Kimberley	
825	Hagwall, Theobold	Kimberley	
826	Burnell, Patrick Saxavary		
827	Haidick, Ivan	Fort William	
828	Daerries, Heinrich Carl Wm.	Weyburn	
829	Gasso, Steve	Wayne, Alta.	
830	Mitchell, C.W.	Hazelton, B.C.	
831	Jacobi, Charles		
832*	Bjormason	Wynyard, Sask.	
833	Oddson, Sveinn	Wynyard, Sask.	
834	Odzuski	Fort William	
835	Andreopulos	Fort William	
836	Smith	Fort William	
837	Padre, Paul	Fort William	
838	Roma, Santo	Redcliff, Alta.	
839	Horne, Robert Wm.	Redcliff, Alta.	
840	Crow, Jerry F.	Redcliffe, Alta.	
841	Flye, F.		
842	Watson, A.V.		
843	Kannasto, Sanna		
844*	Navizivskey alias Prokopetz	Winnipeg	Transferred to 175/P1852
845	Stechyshyn	Winnipeg	
846	Stirling, George	Tappen	
847	Stockman, Andrew	Waddington, Alta.	
848	Kalvin, George	Medicine Hat, Alta.	
849	Rudolph, Fritz	Medicine Hat, Alta.	
850	Guither, Fritz	Waddington, Alta.	
851	Kaly, Peter	Waddington, Alta.	
852	Herman, Peter	Waddington, Alta.	
853*	Heino, Otto	Port Arthur	Transferred to 175/P309
854	Mavahea, A.	Port Arthur	

No.	NAME	ADDRESS	COMMENTS
855	Baccari, Frank	Port Arthur	
856	Lubinski, Adolph	Port Arthur	
857	Clemens, J.	Port Arthur	
858	Maine, M	Fort William	Transferred to 175/P2235
859	Lund	Lovett, Alta.	
860	Presdoehl, C.H.C. (Rev.)	Landstren, Sask.	
861	Struit, George		
862	Alcin, R. (Max)		
863	Lahti, John	Intola	
864	Olson, P.N.		
865	Moyle, Wm. M.		
866	Bell, Charles T.		
867	Bogel, A.	Winnipeg	
868	Schwaitzfeld, N.	Regina	
869	McKinnon, John		
870	Wellbrook, Dietrick	7 miles S. of Gouvenour, Sask.	
871	Warkentin, Isaac	Winkles, Man.	
872	Lehto, Julius	Fort William	
873	Bojapolos, J. (or Pojapolus)	Fort William	
874	Burgard, Isidor	Fort William	
875	Werrett, Bernard	Fort William	
876	Tiboni, John J.	Fort William	
877	Dixon, Julius (alias Shorty)	Port Alberni, B.C.	
878	Kinney, F.	Winnipeg or Vancouver	
879	Mann, Otto	NE 1/4 31.34.30 W1St	
880	Scotland, George	Regina	
881	Kirk, Mrs. John	Winnipeg	
882	Zeitter, F.	Winnipeg	
883	Brown, Alf	Deloraine	
884	McLaren, J.	Terrace, B.C.	
885	Hoyer, A.J.	Central Butte, Sask.	
886	Galloway, James	Edenwald	
887	Labell, Y.J.	Edmonton	Transferred to 818
888	Grod, Frank	Mcbride, B.C.	
889	Mead, Geo. G.	Lethbridge Jail	
890	Fanthorpe, Richard	Victoria, B.C.	
891	Pilgrim, Thomas	Nanaimo, B.C.	
892	Cartwright, James	Nanaimo, B.C.	
893	Brickman, A.	2 Miles N. of Kenora, Ont.	
894	Bartosh, Frank	Kenora, Ont.	
895	Heilmann, Richard	Kenora, Ont.	
896	Schroeder, Aldoph	Kenora, Ont.	
897	Katz, I.	Kenora, Ont	
898	Morris, Charles	Kenora	
899	Watt, F.J.	Winnipeg	
900	Gretzenger, Karl	Medicine Hat, Alta.	
901	Spence, W.D. (Rev.)	Victoria	
902	Holowanichuk, Fred	Edmonton	

No.	NAME	ADDRESS	COMMENTS
903	Kerester, William	Punnicky	
904	McRoberts, Alex	Taber, Alta.	
905	Brett, William	Lethbridge	
906	Stevenson, William (Rev.)		
907	Munroe or Mandryk		
908	McCormick, John	Drumheller	
909	Kingdom, Charles H.	Lethbridge	
910	Burde, John M.C.	Port Alberni	
911	Alexandreff, Rev. (Russ. Priest)	Seattle	
912	Fairhurst, Timothy	Taber	
913	Dower, or Power, R.	Prince George	
914	Robinson, Jas	Vancouver	
915	Schwetze, Mrs. Elizabeth	Winnipeg	
916	Golden, James	(Transient)	
917	Henderson, Ed	Ocean Falls, B.C.	
918	Devine, James M.	Ocean Falls, B.C.	
919	Martin, Thos.	Ocean Falls, B.C.	
920	Johnson, John	N.K.	
921	Sykes, or Sikes, Wellington Wm. J.	N.K.	
922	Mclernan, Pte	Victoria, B.C.	
923	Spitzoka, John	Provincial Jail, Moosomin	
924	Hebenik, Alex	Barons, Alta.	
925	Delea, Tremica, (Dr. Rev)	Lethbridge	
926	Whitehouse, Sam	Fernie, B.C.	
927	Halzer, Joe	Leipzig, Sask. (moving to B.C.)	
928	Colbourne, Albert		?
929	Nozey or Nozy, George	?	
930	McKnight, Joe	N.P.A.	
931	Oucher, Fred	?	
932	Poupard, Daniel Wm.	Victoria	
933	Pierce, W.E.	Victoria	
934*	Andrichuk, Andrew	?	
935	Keane, M.J.	?	
936	Hobbel, Frank		
937	Beyers, Fritz	S.W. 1/4.36.28.17	
938	Gusekus, Frank	Leipzig, Sask.	
939	Molner, Steve	S.W. 1/4 24.27.18W 2nd	
940	Gyorfi, Vincent	S.W. 1/4 34-26-18-W 2nd	
941	Hodgkinson, James	Nanaimo, B.C.	
942	Stephanik or Stefanik	Winnipeg	
943	Zwaryck, Wasel	Mountain Park, Alta.	
944	Costalarin, Dan	Nordegg, Alta.	
945	Jackson, John Leslie	Salmon Arm, B.C.	
946	Dribyt, Ikow	Fort William	
947	Langle, Stewart	Penny, E. of P. George	
948	Ironson, O.	(Transient)	
949	Graves, John	(transient)	
950	Spietz or Spietzl, Jack	1 Mile from Terrace, B.C.	

No.	NAME	ADDRESS	COMMENTS
951	Spietz or Spietzl, Joe	Terrace, P.O.	
952	Chabun, John	Rochester P.O., Alta.	
953	Inglis, Bob	Fort William	
954	Taylor, W.	Regina	
955	Smith, G.B.	Regina	
956	Randall, Geo.	Regina	
957	Dunnett	Regina	
958	Kinsella, F.	Regina	
959	Stokes, J.P.	Regina	
960	Sturdy, Geo.	Regina	
961	Perry (Alderman)	Regina	
962*	Bruce, Malcolm	Regina	
963	Dipke, George	Winnipeg	
964	Cattle, J.E.	One mile W. of Kiddon G.T.P.	
965	Barker, Frank	Nanaimo, B.C.	
966	Allen, Richard	Prince George	
967	Rawluck, Harry	(Transient)	
968	Murdock, John	(Transient)	
969	Wilson, Henry Lee	Barons, Alta.	
970	Merritt,		
971	William, Mick (McWilliams, P.)	Campbell River, B.C.	
972	Greiser, Jack	Vancouver, B.C.	
973	Freeman, Samuel	Edmonton	
974	Svndynsky, Mike	N.Lethbridge	
975	Charny, alias J.Black	Jail, Lethbridge	
976	Day, Wm.	Vançouver Island	
977	Mitchell, Sid	Victoria, B.C.	
978	Hawrys, W.	Edmonton	
979	Combe, W.	Edmonton	
980	Mitchell, Robt.	Edmonton	
981	Walquiss, W.	Vancouver, B.C.	
982	Youngish, R.W.	Vancouver, B.C.	
983*	Keenan, Joseph	Mount Olic	
984	Maser, Chas. B.		
985	Cameron, D.S.	Prince Rupert	
986	Marshall, Stanley	(Transient)	
987	Lynn, Thomas	Lethbridge?	
988*	Mojsa, John	Edmonton	
989	East, James	Edmonton	
990	Murray, Wm.G.	Edmonton	
991	Lysness, John	Fort William	
992	Wagner, C.H.	Thought to be Peace River dist.	
993	Clarke, Wm.	Mount Olic, B.C.	
994	Johnstone, Wm.	Vancouver, B.C.	
995	Hess, E.E.	Brouse, B.C.	
996	Guyet, Paul	Brouse, B.C.	
997	Dimmock, Harry H.	Silverton, B.C.	
998	Austin, Irwin A.	Nelson, B.C.	

No.	NAME	ADDRESS	COMMENTS
999	Moe, John Barney	Hazelton	
1000	Wood, John Christie	Vancouver, B.C.	
1001	Skehar, Wasyl	Nordegg, Alta.	
1002	Helberg, Gunna	S.W. 2-71-10-W. Halcourt, P.O.	
1003	Rudolph, Jacobi		
1004	Carl, Jacobi		
1005	Schlay, Carl	Winnipeg	
1006	Young, George	Regina	
1007	Mutch, R.C.	Smithers	
1008	Carson, James	Smithers	
1009	McCabe, Arthur Patrick		
1010	Chapman, Martin	Regina	
1011	Allan, Frank	Nanaimo, B.C.	
1012	Babyn, Nicholas	A.B.C. Mines	
1013	Rabuka, M.J.	Perdin, Sask.	
1014	Zastovony, Theordor	Saskatoon	
1015	Mounsey, J.E.	Winnipeg	
1016	Evenson	Camrey, Alta.	
1017	Kusnitzoff, Peter	Arran, Sask.	
1018	Kusnitzoff, Phillip	Sopoff, Sask.	
1019	Shaw, Neil A.		Socialist
1020	Dean, Andrew	Nanaimo	
1021	Christer, Matt	Nanaimo	
1022	Rogers, Jack	Nanaimo	
1023	Houston, J. or W.		
1024	McDougall, Kenneth	Winnipeg	
1025	Hendrickson, Gust	Port Arthur	
1026	Lockhead, Rupert	Port Arthur	
1027	Bishop, Arthur John	Vancouver, B.C.	
1028	Boreland, Mrs.Andrew	Vancouver, B.C.	
1029	Saderberg, Andrew	Spokane, Wash., U, B.C.	
1030*	Shatulski, M.	Edmonton	
1031	Funk, John	Runnymede, Sask.	
1032	Cashuba or Rashuva	Courtenay, B.C.	
1033*	Kon, Louis		
1034	Skraastad, O.O.	Bingville, Alta.	
1035	Sikes, O.	Fort William	
1036	Hughes, Thomas	Blairmore, Alta.	
1037	Patterson, W.	Balirmore, Alta.	
1038	Beale, J.	Bellevue, Alta.	
1039	Smith, J.B.	Edmonton	
1040	Johnson, Nels	Lucerne, B.C.	
1041*	Williams, Enoch	Bellevue, Alta.	
1042*	Evans, A.	Lucerne, B.C.	
1043	Scheepmaker, W.M.	Edgewood, B.C.	
1044	Mcecheren, Dan	Kimberley, B.C.	
1045	McLehnan, George	Kimberley, B.C.	
1046	Abedeoff, Simeon	Buchanan, Sask.	

No.	NAME	ADDRESS	COMMENTS
1047	Ritchie, G.S.(Rev)	Edmonton	
1048	Hallson, Geo.	New Westminister	
1049	Binder, Anton	Regina	
1050	Off, Frank	Regina	
1051	Ferenz, Wm.	Regina	
1052	Nilson, Brown alias Buster	Courtenay, B.C.	
1053	Marlow, R.H.	Calgary	
1054	Herman, Dr. & Rev	Saskatoon	
1055	Harjn, John Kust	Corbin, B.C.	
1056*	Stratton, Arthur O.		
1057	Boda, John	The Pass, Man.	LWIU of OBU, Delegate
1058	Arkin, John Isaac	Edmonton S.	
1059	James,	Winnipeg	Labour Church
1060	Smith, C.L.	(Transient)	
1061	Burrough, J.H.	Prince Rupert	
1062	Equist, Eric	Trail	
1063	Carnett, H.	Calgary	
1064	Day, E.	Calgary	
1065	Cooke, A.E. (Rev)		
1066	Whitford, Fred	Wayne, Alta.	
1067	Walters, James	Charesholm, Alta.	
1068	McLean, John S.	Edmonton	
1069	Chunlneczki, K.	Edmonton	
1070	Lazarenko, John	Edmonton	
1071	Priti, Sam	Edmonton	
1072*	Evans, Arthur	Drumheller	
1073	McCaffery, J.A.	Edmonton	
1074	Tipp, John L.	Edmonton	
1075	Seeman, Lewis	Edmonton	
1076	Raplin, S.	Edmonton	
1077	Harris, Fred C.	Edmonton	
1078	Laycock, James Gilbert	Swift Current	
1079	Cummings, Wm.	Aerial, Alta.	
1080	Bott, George	Winnipeg	
1081	Knowles, Frank	Prince George, B.C.	
1082	Kraus, Albert Otto	Edmonton	
1083	Law, James	Winnipeg	
1084	Retroschuk, Jafran	Erickson	
1085	Hornobin, John	Coleman, Alta.	
1086	Burns, Robert	Calgary	
1087	Zabinski, Jos.	Coleman	
1088	Clarke, J.A. (Mayor)	Edmonton	
1089	Nelson, Israel	Edmonton	
1090	Laflecke, Joseph	Edmonton	
1091	Dwyer, I.H.	Vancouver	
1092	Hillquist, G.	Vancouver	
1093	Roberts, A.	?	
1094	Stevens, W.	Ladysmith Timber Lumber Co., Vancouver	

No.	NAME	ADDRESS	COMMENTS
1095	Atkinson, Peter		
1096	Israel, Simon	Edmonton	
1097	Skatz, Samuel	Edmonton	
1098	Nichol, R.D.	?	
1099	Trucott, W.	Blackfoot, Alta.	
1100*	Springford, C.W.	Blackfoot, Alta.	
1101	Regan, J.E.	?Regina, Sask.	
1102	Souttan, (Delegate)	?	
1103	Fishback, James		
1104	Bockus, Forrest		
1105	Stokes, M. (alias Whitey)	Grand Prairie	
1106	Gleason, M.		
1107	Chisholm, Thomas		
1108	Fritz, J.P.		
1109	Melton, Monty		
1110	Renand,		(175/476)8/1/20
1111	Lemoine		(175/476)8/1/20
1112	Wickstrom, N.P.	Might be at Prince Mine	
1113	McPhee, Dan C.	Prince Edward Island	
1114	Howey, George	Trail, B.C.	
1115	Donovan, Paddy	Vancouver, Stratford Hotel	
1116	Kauznitzoff, Phillip (Agitator)	Barrows Station, Man.	
1117	Thivierge, Ernest	The Pass, Prince Albert	
1118	Laggira or Laggina, Pete Denis	The Pass	
1119	Manley, Steve	Dome Creek	
1120	Papioziou, A.W.		
1121	McNab	Silverton	
1122	Hartman, Carl	Vancouver	
1123	Carleitiou, George	Edmonton	
1124	Shuler, Sam	Edmonton	
1125	Neilson, Sam	Edmonton	
1126	Maloney, Joe K.	Edmonton	
1127	Huculak, Mike	The Pass	Transferred to 175/P2196
1128	Muzuryk, George	South Saskatoon	
1129	Taylor, G. Fred		OBU Agitator
1130	Makovaz, Mike		
1131	Jacklin, Mrs.	Beansfield	
1132*	Black, John	Winnipeg	Bolshevist
1133*	Rogomon, Moses	Saskatoon	
1134	Craig, Joe	Vancouver	
1135	Martinos, J.	Wayne, Alta.	
1136	Lauchick, Peter	?	
1137	Gunn, Robert or Robert Eccles (Mack the Tailor)	Cranbrook, B.C.	
1138*	Gallagher, J.		Agitator
1139	Johnston, J.F.		Delegate LWIU
1140	Goldman, Issac	Edmonton	
1141	Brown, Geo. R.		Socialist
1142	Celli, Angelo		OBU Organizer

No.	NAME	ADDRESS	COMMENTS
1143	Guenther, Herman Oscar		Alleged
1144	Melville, George	Regina, Sask.	
1145	South, John	Regina, Sask.	
1146	Sergishuk, Mike	The Pass, Man.	
1147	Gehrke, Herman	Govan, Sask.	
1148	Lingas, James	?	
1149	Spailos, George		
1150	Woods, Jack	Vancouver	
1151	Strauss, Oscar	Nakusp, B.C.	
1152	Deljans, Herbert	Edgewood, B.C.	
1153	Banks, Robert S.		
1154	Carmichael, Bruce	Ladysmith, B.C.	
1155	Goldsmith, J.L.		
1156	Killet, Harry	Campbell River	
1157	Meadows, Paul	Merritt, B.C.	
1158	Jakinson, Antonio	Vancouver, B.C.	
1159	Doyle, James	Vancouver, B.C.	
1160	McPherson, Martin	?	
1161	Smith, Harvey	Nakusp, B.C.	
1162	Peterson, James Louis	?	
1163	Luigert, Bertnolt Lang	Sask.	
1164	Howland, H.	Campbell River	
1165	Osterberg, Alex	Quathiaski Cove, B.C.	
1166	Wintrip, J. Welbore	Channel, B.C.	
1167	Erickson, Herman	Heriot Bay, B.C.	
1168	Mckinnon, A.	?	
1169	Parres, N.	? Quebec	
1170	Springer, Thomas	Bainbridge, B.C.	
1171	Pare, Frank	Vovenley, B.C.	
1172	Barton, Wm.	(Camp Hdgs, Comox Logging)	
1173	Oleson, Andy	Duncan Bay	
1174	Rindfleisch, Herman	Winnipeg	
1175	Black, Mike	Coleman, B.C.	
1176	Young, Fred	11 miles from Faulkners Camp	
1177	Laycock, Thos.	Nelson	
1178	Zerebko, Orest	?	
1179	Donovan, G.C. (MD)	Winnipeg	
1180	Clark, Walter	Coalhurst, Alta.	
1181	Blakely, A.W.	Wyath Batbs	
1182	Heller, Harry		175/1881
1183	Parker, Ad		175/1881
1184	Batt, Walter	Vancouver	
1185	Dickie, Andy	Merritt, B.C.	
1186	Lorimer, Mrs. Christina	Vancouver, B.C.	
1187	Beltuer, Rudolph	Box 73, Merritt, B.C.	
1188	Guiney, Neil		
1189	Nelson, S.	Vancouver	
1190	Hyslop, Major	Coleman, Alta.	

No.	NAME	ADDRESS	COMMENTS
1191	Holmston, E.A.		OBU Agitator
1192	Galloway, Thomas		
1193	Johnston, Hugh A.	Drumheller	
1194	Reigh, Oswald	Trail, B.C.	
1195	Hanson, Hugo	?	
1196*	Palmer, Geo. Henry		
1197	Hlady, John	Moose Jaw, Sask.	
1198*	Stepcoff, Alex (alias Stemkowski)	Moose Jaw, Sask.	
1199*	Babych, Geo.	Moose Jaw, Sask.	
1200	Hryceniuk, Fred	Moose Jaw, Sask.	
1201	Ceser, Henry		
1202	Novak, Mike	Mountain Park	
1203	Letcher, Robert	Mountain Park	
1204	Roberts, R.B.		
1205	Ehrlich, Arthur	Winnipeg	
1206	Howard, "Bert" (alias Freeman)	Vancouver	
1207	Cooper, Elijah	Routledge, B.C.	
1208	Homer, Bert	Vancouver, B.C.	
1209	Berg, Charles E.	Sproat Lake, Alberni, B.C.	
1210	Kamienski, P.	Winnipeg	
1211	Davidchenko, Mrs.	Saskatoon	
1212	McBeth, E.M.	Nelson	
1213	O'Neil, P.J.	Penny, B.C.	
1214	Elliott, Albert	Stewart or Hyden	
1215	Tapert, F.G.		
1216	Robinson, Ald.	Winnipeg	
1217	Hagstrom, John	?	
1218	Anderson, Ferndans	?	
1219	Rolak, W.	Moose Jaw	
1220	Makar, Pete	Nordegg, Alta.	
1221	Reid, Jack	Port Alberni	
1222	Skehor, Steve	Nordegg, Alta.	
1223	Mooney, J.L.	Vancouver	
1224	Collins, C.A.	--	
1225	Sineloff, Simon (alias Sinilon)	Toronto	
1226	Anderson, Oscar	Wilson Brady Camp, Heriot Bay, Valdes Island	
1227	Millington, Samuel Mark	S.Vancouver	Cancelled see 175/P1244
1228	Nedin, Nels	Sandon, B.C.	
1229	Burt, W.E.	Sandon, B.C.	
1230	Massie, Ely	Sanniel Arm, Victoria, B.C.	
1231	Charlton, Jack (alias Slim Sharlton)	Last known at Drumheller	
1232	Hill, Tony K.	Fernie, B.C.	
1233	Prewachuk, Gregory	The Pas, Man.	
1234	Grace, Steve	The Pas, Man.	
1235	Beitz, Jacob	Medicine Hat, Alta.	
1236	Picard, Edward	Nakusp, B.C.	
1237	Thomas, Levi	Courtenay, B.C.	
1238	Plain, Jesse	Courtenay, B.C.	

No.	NAME	ADDRESS	COMMENTS
1239	Kalma, Steve	Bankbreak, Alta.	
1240	Steele, Stewart	Prince Rupert, B.C.	
1241	Dewar, Rodney	Sandon, B.C.	
1242	Baker, Fred	Victoria, B.C.	
1243	Anderson, Oscar	Heriot Bay Walder S. B.C.	Cancelled see 175/1226
1244	Millington, Samuel Mark	Vancouver, B.C.	
1245	Kiellgen, Heinrich	Goddard, Alta.	
1246	Wolton, George	Arrow Park, B.C.	
1247	Mitchell, E.D.	Brandon, Man.	
1248	Gage, Sydney E.	Winnipeg, Man.	
1249	Clarkson, Wm.	Beaverdale, B.C.	
1250	Malchow, Gus E.	Stavely, Alta.	
1251	Jancoe, Tour	Pocahontas, Alta.	
1252	Horwick, John	Vancouver, B.C.	
1253*	McLachlan, J.B.	Springhill, N.S.	
1254*	Buhay, Rebecca	Montreal, Que.	
1255	Boltuck, Isidor	Montreal, Que.	
1256	Mendelsohn, Mrs. Ray	Montreal, Que.	
1257	Morrison, C.F.	Wayne, Alta.	
1258	Scaia, Joseph	Edgewood, B.C.	
1259*	Vaara, Arvo	No 2 Camp, Comox Log Co.	
1260	McCarthy, D.J.	Vancouver, B.C.	
1261	Dougherty, Thomas	Vancouver, B.C.	
1262	Rawka, Louis	Amyox, B.C.	
1263	Reuther, Michael	Winnipeg, Man.	
1264	Urquart, Andrew	Eburne, B.C.	
1265	Currie, Percy Charles	Medicine Hat, Alta.	
1266	McWhinnie, James	Cascade, B.C.	
1267*	Fay, E.R.	Cranbrook, B.C.	
1268	McLennon, Malcolm	Alberni, B.C.	
1269	McTear, Alfred	Nelson, B.C.	
1270	Switch, William(Swede)	Vancouver, B.C.	
1271	Clement, Louis	Dauphin, Man.	
1272	Roy, Charles	Dauphin, Man.	
1273	Erb, Ferdinand	Yellowgrass, Sask.	
1274	Jaster, Emil	Lang, Sask.	
1275	Wilke, A.G.	Yellowgrass, Sask.	
1276	Dreigher, August	Lang, Sask.	
1277	Graves, Emil	Lang, Sask.	
1278	Graves, Frederick	Lang, Sask.	
1279	Teske, Will	Lang, Sask.	
1280	Realrich, John	Lang, Sask.	
1281	Dawes, Gustave	Lang, Sask.	
1282	Jaster, Leus	Yellowgrass, Sask.	
1283*	Mallard, Marie (Mrs. Joseph)	Edmonton	
1284	Bussiau, August	Winnipeg	
1285	Hedin, Nels	Box 168, Sandon, B.C.	

No.	NAME	ADDRESS	COMMENTS
1286	Slobozian, Augus	Nordegg, Alta.	
1287	Carlson, Ocsar	Beaver Lake, Alta.	
1288*	Miller, Paul	Nordegg, Alta.	
1289	Burt, W.E.	Sandon, B.C.	See P/H 1229
1290	Dreigher, Edward	Lang, Sask.	
1291	Flynn, J.Harry	1 Alice St, Toronto	
1292	Zschiedich, Walter	Winnipeg, Man.	
1293	Brandt, Paul	Winnipeg, Man.	
1294	Werner, Paul	Winnipeg, Man.	
1295	Logan, Matthew	Lethbridge	
1296	Thompson, F. Willard	Halifax, N.S.	
1297	Dove, Fred	Otosquen, Sask.	
1298	Hole, James	Medicine Hat, Alta.	
1299	Muigford, T. (alias Mugford, F.)		New Westminister
1300	Hooff, G.	Medicine Hat, Alta.	
1301	Barrow, Robert	Nelson-Cranbrook, B.C.	
1302	Alison, Peter F.	Nakusp, B.C.	
1303	Heinke, Gustaf	Nakusp, B.C.	
1304	Roberts, Thomas	Nelson, B.C.	
1305	Neuwauk, Karl	Nakusp, B.C.	
1306	Baxter, Robert	Princeton, B.C.	
1307	Cottrell, T.R.	Victoria, B.C.	
1308*	Mckenzie, James	Edmonton, Alta.	
1309	Barnard, William	Regina, Sask.	
1310	Studevaus, James P.	Evesham, Sask.	
1311	Brundize, J.S.	Regina, Sask.	
1312	Long, W.E.	Montreal	
1313	Klein, W.A.	Regina, Sask.	
1314	Dympsey, W.D.	Mafeking, Man.	
1315	Grant, Donald	Hillcrest, Alta.	
1316	Quigley	Coalhurst, Alta.	
1317	Alvensleben, Alvo Von		
1318	Baillie, William Hugh J.	Saskatoon, Sask.	
1319	Towash, Ren		
1320	Sudworth, Rock	Michel, B.C.	
1321	Murphy, James	Lethbridge, Alta.	
1322	Alexander, W.A.	Vancouver, B.C.	
1323	Freeman, Jack	Vancouver, B.C.	
1324	Davies, John G.	Brandon, Man.	
1325	Singh, Harbar	Vancouver, B.C.	
1326	Klewak, Mike	Vancouver, B.C.	
1327	Golden	Vancouver, B.C.	Cousin of James Golden, P.916
1328	Binnette, U.	Montreal	
1329	Millikan, Dr.	Regina, Sask.	
1330	Zaskipery, Steve	Moose Jaw, Sask.	
1331	Moore, William	Ocean Falls, B.C.	
1332	Sidaway, John	Vancouver, B.C.	

No.	NAME	ADDRESS	COMMENTS
1333	Macinnes, Angus	Vancouver, B.C.	
1334	Jackson, Amos	Big River, B.C.	
1335	Forrest, D.	Squirrel Cove, B.C.	
1336	Travis, Owen M.	Winnipeg, Man.	
1337	Purich, W.M.	Regina, Sask.	
1338	Muir, David	Big River, Sask.	
1339*	Crandell, Ed	Big River, Sask.	
1340	Patterson, Adam	Big River, Sask.	
1341	Mackintosh, Fred	Big River, Sask.	
1342	Mackintosh, Noggy	Tisdale, Sask.	
1343	MacDonald, Michael	Big River, Sask.	
1344	Poirier, H.	The Pas, Man.	
1345	Hart, G.I.	Edmonton, Alta.	
1346	Holm, Sam	Port Arthur, Ont.	
1347	Bryan, Harry		
1348	Eckert, Frank	Sheraton, B.C.	
1349	Frannsen, J.	Swan River, Man.	
1350	Estan, Rosie	The Pas, Man.	
1351	Bidder, Fred	Cranbrook?, B.C.	
1352	Boyd	Vancouver, B.C.	
1353	Doyon, J.	Ocean Falls, B.C.	
1354	Casey, Patrick	Prince George	
1355	Moore, Robert M.	Regina	
1356	Jareuia (Yarevia) Stephen	Winnipeg, Man.	
1357	Bewsher, James (alias James Barcke, alias Bucher, Jas)	Nordegg	
1358	Ratkowski, Joseph	Petie River, Man.	
1359	Pappas, Theodore	Prince George, B.C.	
1360	McRae, Jim H.	Coalhurst, Alta.	
1361	Kennedy, Bruce	Brandon, Man.	
1362	Olafson, Carl Oscar	Merritt, B.C.	
1363	Turner, Edwin	Merritt, B.C.	
1364	Nicholson, William	Merritt, B.C.	
1365	Hughes, Eli F.	Stoppington, Alta.	
1366	Stopp, Alvin	Stoppington, Alta.	
1367	Miller, Bill	Stoppington, Alta.	
1368	Weirtz, H.A.	Stoppington, Alta.	
1369	Daniels, John W.	Brandon, Man.	
1370	Strochien, E.	Prince George, B.C.	
1371	Richardson, Hank (H.B.)	Vancouver, B.C.	
1372	McPherson, J.D.	Vancouver, B.C.	
1373	Bogaert, Andree	Montreal, Que.	
1374*	Buhay, Michael	Montreal, Que.	
1375	Pasco, Gregory (alias Nesberko, alias Grishka)	Stave Falls, B.C.	
1376	Clark, Mrs. James Allan	Vancouver, B.C.	
1377	Robertson, J.D.	Vancouver, B.C.	
1378	Barnett, John W.	Edmonton, Alta.	
1379*	Tether, George	Prince Albert, Sask.	
1380	Svendsen, Oscar	Quesnel	

No.	NAME	ADDRESS	COMMENTS
1381	Larson, Fred	Merritt	
1382*	Shubert, Joseph	Montreal	
1383	Pilon, Gustave	Montreal	
1384*	Scott, Nearing	New York	
1385	Hoey, L.	Calgary, Alta.	
1386	Brownfield, E.C.	Big River, Sask.	
1387	Tomashewski, Thomas	Vancouver	
1388*	Armstrong, Maxwell	Toronto	
1389	Hansen, William M.	Victoria, B.C.	
1390	Jacias, Edward	The Pas, Man.	
1391	Brotherton, Ralph	Merritt, B.C.	
1392	McGuiness, John	Vancouver, B.C.	
1393	Salewich or Salewicz, Mike	Moose Jaw, Sask.	
1394	Hanson, Andrew	See 3.I P4 RGE 7 W2	
1395	Motruk, M.	Moose Jaw, Sask.	
1396*	Stelp, Julius	Qualicum Beach, B.C.	
1397	Harvey, William	Ladyswith, B.C.	
1398	Rafter, Robert	Vancouver	
1399	Nordegg, Martin	Nordegg (now in New York)	
1400*	Inglis, Dr. F.	Gibsons' Landing, B.C.	
1401	Carpenter, Adelburg Louis	Humbolt, Kingsgate, etc.	
1402	Hart, Tom	Orsville, Wash., USA	
1403	Brown, William	Alice Arm, B.C.	
1404	Sawyer, Gilbert	Fernie, B.C.	
1405	Carey, Henry	Fernie, B.C.	
1406	Clemetson, Elmer Lawrence	Rockford, B.C.	
1407	Bart, Louis	Vancouver, B.C.	
1408	Mickalowski, Harry	Taylorton, Sask.	
1409	Watson, Tom	Vancouver, B.C.	
1410	Pinkerton, John	Chase, B.C.	
1411	Hatch, William	Vancouver, B.C.	
1412*	Kostuk, Fred (alias Fred Shupok)	Medicine Hat, Alta.	
1413	Black, Bert	Queen Charlotte Is, B.C.	
1414	Stewart, Alec (alias Sandy Stewart)	Calgary, Alta.	
1415	Pine, Thomas (alias Shorty Pine, alias Shorty Nugget)	Moose Jaw	
1416	Winchester, James	Weyburn, Sask.	
1417	Wiley, George	Winnipeg	
1418	Henricson, John	Sault Ste. Marie, Ont.	
1419	Relf, Leo	Regina	
1420	O'Dea, Jim	Rrince Rupert	
1421	Morris, Charles	Smithers, B.C.	
1422	Mazai, L. (alias Massoi or Majai)	Alice Arm, B.C.	
1423	Yair, George	Big River, B.C.	
1424	Welch, Bob	Alice Arm, B.C.	
1425	Smith, Walter	Calgary, Alta.	
1426	Smith, Malcolm	Vancouver	
1427	Mullin, J.A.	Fort William?, Ont.	
1428	Hogg, James	Vancouver	

No.	NAME	ADDRESS	COMMENTS
1429	Rigby, Robert Erington	Vancouver	
1430	Smith, A.	Swift Current	
1431	Mouzuchenko, Anton	Vancouver	
1432	Enoff, Andrew (Andrie)	Vancouver	
1433	Dehteroff, Semen	Vancouver	
1434	Kashuba, Nicholas	Vancouver	
1435	Smith, Mark	Beaverdale, B.C.	
1436	Makeef, Philipp	Amyox, Granby Bay	
1437	Voronoff, Andria (alias Voronin, alias Verenchin)	Vancouver, B.C.	
1438	Drazoff, Andrea	Vancouver, B.C.	
1439	Kourbatoff, Mike (Michael)	Vancouver, B.C.	
1440	Gritzencko, Efim	Vancouver, B.C.	
1441	Kouznetzoff, Paul	Pelly, Sask.	
1442	Kustar, Pete	Moose Jaw, Sask.	
1443*	Kossick, Joe	Moose Jaw, Sask.	
1444	Bolton, Homer	Vancouver, B.C.	
1445	Farmer, S.J.	Winnipeg, Man.	
1446	Sutherland, Jack	Hyden?, Sask.	
1447	Achieff, Gus (alias Gaza)	Vancouver, B.C.	
1448	Gagne, Jeff	Usk, B.C.	
1449	Zaharoff, William	Vancouver, B.C.	
1450	Wolfram, Gustav	Vancouver, B.C.	
1451	Norton, C.W.	Victoria, B.C.	
1452	Wilkie, W. Mcnab	Victoria, B.C.	
1453	Petrie, R.	Vancouver, B.C.	
1454	Fawkes, Thomas	Ford City, Ont.	
1455	Halliwell, Thomas	Oxbow, Sask.	
1456	Henry, A.	Fort William	
1457	Hartt	Montreal, Que.	
1458	Davidson, John	Moose Jaw, Sask.	
1459	Donald, Charles	Medicine Hat, Alta.	
1460	Benson, Samuel	Redcliff, Alta.	
1461*	Tipping, Fred G.	Winnipeg, Man.	
1462	Dunn, Tom	- do -	
1463	Hall, Ed	Hazelton, B.C.	
1464	Gooding, R.	Hazelton, B.C.	
1465	Isserlis, Abraham	Vancouver, B.C.	
1466	Ilyow, J.	Regina, Sask.	
1467	Nykolock, Peter	Regina, Sask.	
1468	Watters, James Cameron	Sydney, Cape Breton	
1469	Tranquillini, F.L.F.	Victoria, B.C.	
1470	Smith, James	Cumberland, B.C.	Irishman
1471	Nedllec, John	Regina	IWW
1472	Spencer, Earl	Weyburn, Sask.	
1473	McKenzie, Sam	Vancouver, B.C.	
1474	Webster, D.I.	Vancouver, B.C.	
1475	Lazare, J.	Montreal, Que.	
1476	Ranns, Rev. Horace Dixon	Carievale, Sask.	

No.	NAME	ADDRESS	COMMENTS
1477	Lubin	Vancouver, B.C.	
1478	Macneil, John J.	Inverness, B.C.	
1479*	Nickson, Agathia (Mrs. Nicholas)	Vancouver, B.C.	
1480	Dompierre, John	Usk, B.C.	
1481	Wilson, W.E.	Prince Rupert, B.C.	
1482	Mogridge, Robert	Edmonton	
1483	Blais, J. Raoul	Montreal	
1484	Simpson, George	Montreal	
1485	Cassidy, Tom	Montreal	
1486	Stanley, Austin	Regina, Sask.	
1487	Robinson, A.F.	Hazelton, B.C.	
1488	Egge, John	Hanna, Alta.	
1489*	Pomonarenko, William	Hanna, Alta.	
1490	Tallis, W.H.	Regina, Sask.	
1491	Olson, Gustav	Yahk, B.C.	
1492	Hokkyo, Junichi	Vancouver, B.C.	
1493	Ryan, August	Coalhurst, Alta.	
1494*	Dzuridzinsky, Kozma (alias Denackie)	Calgary	
1495	Rich, W.D.	Regina	
1496	Bullen, George	Vancouver, B.C.	
1497	Ridsdale, Harold	Moose Jaw, Sask.	
1498	Winton, Edward	Prince George, B.C.	
1499	Goodell, Chester	Carlyle, Sask.	
1500*	Flatman, Fred J.	Niagara Falls, Ont.	
1501	Mueller, Fred	Alameda, Sask.	
1502	Stove, Edward	?	
1503	Revenko, W.	Montreal	
1504	Gerrish, F.W.	Montreal	
1505	Boschi, Torri	Montreal	
1506	Kennedy, Edward J.C., MD	Montreal	
1507	Leslie, A.	Vancouver, B.C.	
1508	Fox, William	Radville, Sask.	
1509	Ellsworth, John	Powell River, B.C.	
1510	Williams, Fred	Powell River, B.C.	
1511	Robertson, Alex. M.	(Transient)?	
1512	Sirak, Frank (alias Krymaic, F.)	Coleman, Alta.	
1513	Hovelsrond, J.	Regina, Sask.	
1514	Ross, F.	Buckley Bay, B.C.	
1515	Choice, John	Vancouver, B.C.	
1516	Fisher, H.	Buckley Bay, B.C.	
1517	McGrath, M.P.	Buckley Bay, B.C.	
1518	Hamilton, L.B.	Buckley Bay, B.C.	
1519	McLeod, John	South Vancouver	
1520	Roberts, J.	Buckley Bay, B.C.	
1521	Logan, Andrew	Buckley Bay, B.C.	
1522	Mcvay, H.L.	Regina, Sask.	
1523	Yamada, Sutiya	Vancouver, B.C.	
1524	Helgeson, Ed	Buckley Bay, B.C.	

No.	NAME	ADDRESS	COMMENTS
1525	Revedeberg, Fred	Radville, Sask.	
1526	Lawrie, James	Trail, B.C.	
1527	Willoughby, E.	Calgary, Alta.	
1528	Pulzer, Leo	Alice Arm, B.C.	
1529	Onishenko, John	Hafford, Sask.	Transferred 175/P2805
1530	Tubbs, W.P.	Bienfait, Sask.	
1531	Elliott, Leonard B.	Radville, Sask.	
1532	Wainright, W.	Powell River, B.C.	
1533	Oakes, A.L.	Raliarice, Sask.	
1534	Orshiwsky, N. (Father of O.Orshiwsky)	Regina, Sask.	
1535	Stossil, I.W.	North Vancouver, B.C.	
1536	Hoop, W.H.	Winnipeg, Man.	
1537	Gonzales, Mrs. Carmen	Montreal, Que.	
1538	Rokwell, Hiram	Vancouver, B.C.	
1539	Irwin, Rev. J.A.H.	Antrim, Ireland	
1540	Crawford, Lindsay	Toronto	
1541	Locosse, George	Vancouver, B.C.	
1542	Stack, James	Vancouver, B.C.	
1543	Sullivan, Paddy	Vancouver, B.C.	
1544	Holowach, William	Regina, Sask.	
1545	Orshiwsky, O. (Son of N. Orshiwsky)	Regina, Sask.	
1546	Clancy, James	Vancouver, B.C.	
1547	Gottsell	Montreal, Que.	
1548	Blanc	Montreal, Que.	
1549	Lust, Jacob	Irvine, Alta.	
1550	Webster, James	Nanaimo, B.C.	
1551	Jordan, Arthur	Nanaimo, B.C.	
1552	Lane, Albert	Nanaimo, B.C.	
1553	Hunter, Charles	Alice Arm, B.C.	
1554	Larsen, Oscar	Alice Arm, B.C.	
1555	McKenna, James	Vancouver, B.C.	
1556	Tuplin, Harry Colvert	Ocean Falls, B.C.	
1557	Collins, Anthony (alias Spike or Tony Collins, alias Francis O'Riley)		Penticton, B.C.
1558	Cassidy, Frank	Vancouver, B.C.	
1559	Reid, W.	Port Alberni, B.C.	
1560	Abbott, Charles E.	Port Alberni, B.C.	
1561*	Uphill, Thos.	Fernie, B.C.	
1562	Horlick, John	Sandon, B.C.	
1563	Hubb	Vancouver, B.C.	
1564	Cox, Sidney V.	Prince Rupert, B.C.	
1565	Booth, N.	Prince Rupert, B.C.	
1566	Donner, Gust	Medicine Hat, Alta.	
1567	Page	Montreal	
1568	McEwen, Duncan	Regina, Sask.	
1569	Larson, Theadore	Stewart, B.C.	

No.	NAME	ADDRESS	COMMENTS
1570*	Edelstein, Hyman	Montreal	
1571	Dandineau, Oliver James	Kingsgate	
1572	Dunnaway, Arthur Cotton	Kamsack	
1573	Hamill, William	Montreal, Que.	
1574	Doyle, Peter	Montreal	
1575	Loye, John	Montreal	
1576	Collier, John	Montreal	
1577	Mott, Charles	Bowser, B.C.	
1578	Husar, Peter	Taylorton, Sask.	
1579	Frazer, Maurice		
(alias	Waldman, alias Reger)	Montreal, Que.	
1580	Morsolins, (unknown)	Montreal, Que.	
1581	Skogland, E.A.	Alice Arm, B.C.	
1582	Dowling, Daniel	Montreal	
1583	Bourke, D.D.	New Westminister, B.C.	
1584	Kelly, E.	Ocean Falls, B.C.	
1585	Delcroix, Frank	Ocean Falls, B.C.	
1586	George, S.	Ocean Falls, B.C.	
1587	Johnson, C.	Ocean Falls, B.C.	
1588	Bodinan, Stanley	Ocean Falls, B.C.	
1589	Webster, William	Ocean Falls, B.C.	
1590	Goldberg, Mrs. Sonia	Toronto, Ont.	
1591	McCarthy, John	Regina, Sask.	
1592	Hughes, Miss Kathleen	(Transient)	
1593	Kernuhan, C.C.	Vancouver, B, C.	
1594	Loughran, H.J.	Vancouver, B.C.	
1595	Sheehan, P.E.	Vancouver, B.C.	
1596	Diaczun, Dan	Taylorton Dist.	
1597	Saint-Martin, A.	Montreal	
1598	Robinson, Ed		
(alias	E.J.Robinson	Wycliffe	
1599	Gibbs, William	Kamsack, Sask.	
1600	Graham, Johnson	Bienfait, Sask.	
1601	Romanovich, Peat? (Pete)	Coleman, Alta.	
1602	Pepperman, Mon	Montreal	
1603	Cincina	Montreal	
1604	Miller, Charles L.	Vancouver, B.C.	
1605	Wilson, James	Vancouver, B.C.	
1606	Dunn, Robert W.	Vancouver, B.C.	
1607	Currie, J.H.	Vancouver	
1608	Wilson, Bert	Ocean Falls	
1609	Linder, Charles	Ocean Falls	
1610	Galer, John	Ocean Falls	
1611	Bundy, Frank	Ocean Falls	
1612	Lee, Karl	Hutton, B.C.	
1613*	Buller, Anna	Montreal	
1614	Molloy, John	Atlin, B.C.	
1615	Grace, Joe	Vancouver, B.C.	

No.	NAME	ADDRESS	COMMENTS
1616*	Butler, John R.	Vancouver, B.C.	
1617	McLaren, J.B.	Vancouver, B.C.	
1618	Archer, W.H. (Captain)	Vancouver, B.C.	
1619	Grey, William	Estevan, Sask.	
1620	Caulfield, C.	Vancouver, B.C.	
1621	Egan, N.J.	Vancouver, B.C.	
1622	Wilson, Burl	Lafleche, Sask.	
1623	Devalera, Eamon	New York	
1624	Henderson, Mrs.Rose	Montreal	
1625	MacDonald	Vancouver, B.C.	
1626	Simpson, William V.	Vancouver, B.C.	
1627	Pitt or Pettit	Vancouver, B.C.	
1628	Reilly, T.	Thompson, River Sound, B.C.	
1629	Price, G.B.	Vancouver, B.C.	
1630	Phelan, W.J.	Vancouver, B.C.	
1631	Hennessy, W.E.	Vancouver, B.C.	
1632	Gillespie, F.J.	Vancouver, B.C.	
1633	Bailey, A.D.	Vancouver, B.C.	
1634	Garvey, Michael	Ottawa	
1635*	Fort, Paul	Montreal, Que.	Transferred to 175/P2534
1636	Sawchuk, Peter	Winnipeg	
1637	McNaulty, J.	Prince Rupert, B.C.	
1638	Currie, G.B.	Transient from England	
1639*	Custance, Florence Ada (Mrs.)		Toronto
1640	Solodka, S.	Manville, Alta.	
1641	Smith, Arthur J. (alias A. Smith)	Ocean Falls, B.C.	
1642	Roberts, H.	Hamilton	
1643	Sudeburg, Decon (alias Von Seedeburg)	Sydney, Cape Breton	
1644	McDonald, Mike	Nelson, B.C.	Transferred to 175/P1343
1645	Barnes, A.	Prince Rupert, B.C.	
1646	Kennedy, Dr. Walter G.	Montreal, Que.	
1647	Whritson, William	Penticton, B.C.	
1648	Morse, Andrew Olsen	McCaulay Island, S. of Prince Rupert	
1649	McClintock, David Turner	Nelson, B.C.	
1650	Flinn, Albert	Coalhurst, Alta.	
1651	Flinn, Charlie	Coalhurst, Alta.	
1652	McMahon, Martin	Lethbridge	
1653*	Belkin, Simon	Montreal	
1654	Pribags, A.	Sherbrooke, Que.	
1655	Ludowsky	St. Catherines	
1656	Shapiro	Hamilton	
1657	Palmer, E.T.	Edmonton	
1658	Carter, Mrs. Dorothy	Regina, Sask.	
1659	Charlton, O.L.	Vancouver, B.C.	
1660	Simpson, James	Toronto	
1661	Quinn, Thomas J.	Lethbridge	

No.	NAME	ADDRESS	COMMENTS
1662	Smith, Thompson	Vancouver, B.C.	
1663	Reilly, John or Jack	Vancouver, B.C.	
1664	Browett, Douglas	Vancouver, B.C.	
1665	Fritz, John	Dysart, Sask.	
1666	Werchola, Wasyl	Prince Albert, Sask.	
1667	Knowles, George	Hamilton	
1668	Kaplan, Fred W.	Winnipeg, Saskatoon	
1669	Ivy, James	Ladysmith	
1670	Elick, Geo.	Ladysmith or Comox	
1671	Stafford, W.B.	Amyox, B.C.	
1672	Hart, John	Amyox, B.C.	
1673	McAuley, W.F.	Amyox, B.C.	
1674	Beaulec, D.	Vancouver, B.C.	
1675	Derry, William H.	Prince Rupert	
1676	Ellis, Edward	Victoria & Prince Rupert	
1677	McDonald, John Donald	Victoria	
1678	Morrison, Charles F.	Prince George, B.C.	
1679*	Collins, Archie	Sudbury, Ont.	
1680	Watts, Henry William	Vancouver, B.C.	
1681	North, P.H.	- do -	
1682	Cassidy, C.S.	Vancouver, B.C.	
1683	Robinson, H.S.	U.S.A.	
1684	McGrath, Jack	Vancouver, B.C.	
1685	McDonald, Joe	Oyen, Alta.	
1686*	Guthrie, Samuel	Oyster Dist (Ladysmith P.O.)	
1687	Radford, John H.	Coalhurst, P.O., Alta.	
1688	Engler, John	Chinook P.O., Alta.	
1689	Millar, J.L.	Vancouver, B.C.	
1690	Henry, Patrick J.	Winnipeg	
1691	Yamchuk, John	Saskatoon	
1692	Mellieux, Tom	Toronto	
1693	Hvatt (Hvatoff)	Montreal	
1694	Boult, James N.	Vancouver	
1695	Corfield, Charles or E	- do -	
1696*	Fraser, Charles	- do -	
1697	Clarke, John	- do -	Esperanto Teacher
1698	Earp, Sydney	- do -	
1699	Cullen, Thos P.	- do -	
1700	McMannis, Charles	B.C.	
1701	Stanovitch, Steve	B.C.	
1702	Carrie, John H.	Windsor, Timmons, Detroit, Vancouver	
1703	Watson, "Red"	Vancouver	
1704	Bloor, Leieur Ella Reeve Dolly Touring Canada	New York, Winnipeg	
1705	Brigden, Beatrice	Brandon, Man.	
1706	Jordan, Sam	Winnipeg, Man.	
1707	Morgan, G.		
1708	Bardorff, Charles Frederick	Montreal	

No.	NAME	ADDRESS	COMMENTS
1709	Boshko, Peter	Saskatoon	
1710	Gordon, Lockhart	Toronto, Hamilton, Etc.	
1711*	Bell, Thomas	- do -	
1712*	Spector, Maurice	- do -	
1713	Jacques, E.E. or R.J.	Hamilton	
1714	Nuttall, Rev. T.P.	Prince Rupert	
1715	Abraham, G.W.	Vancouver	
1716	Campbell, Raymond	Barnes P.O., Alta.	
1717	Pickering, Wm.	Regina	
1718	Liang, Yik Ko	Vancouver, B.C.	
1719	Costello, M.J. Or N.J.	Seattle or Vancouver	
1720*	Foster, W.Z.	USA	
1721	Mcbride, Isac	USA Transient in Canada	USA Journalist
1722	Steward, Bernard	Vancouver	
1723	Schiller, Richard	- do -	
1724*	Goodstone, Albert I.	- do -	
1725	Telford, Robert (MD)	- do -	
1726	Woodward, F.	Winnipeg	(Sec. Central Labour Council)
1727	Byers, James Mark	Prince George, B.C.	
1728*	Hasslem, Edgar Cecil	Hamilton	
1729	Scribbins, Walter James	Vancouver, B.C.	
1730	Kohn, A.	Winnipeg	
1731	Long, Ewart Elliott	Vancouver	
1732	Smith, James (Jimmy)	- do -	
1733	Daly, Patrick	Stewart, B.C.	
1734	Eastman, Dr. Mack		
1735*	Jamieson, Mrs. Stuart		
1736	Spiers, James	Vancouver	
1737	Octavia, Otto	- do -	(Finn)
1738*	Mojsiuk, D.	Hafford, Sask.	Transferred to 175/P120
1739	Bunker, John Charles	Victoria	
1740	Seminoff	Hamilton	
1741*	McDonald, John	Toronto	
1742	Nelson, George	Prince George, B.C.	
1743	McClusky, Mrs. Libertia nee Miss Muskat		Wayne, Alta.
1744	Mayo, J.	Regina, Sask.	
1745	Parker, J.F.	- do -	
1746	Skilbeck, C.	- do -	
1747	Mann, Tom		(English Labour Leader)
1748*	Mariner	Hamilton	
1749	Counsell, J.	Hamilton	
1750	Smith, Mervyn	- do -	
1751	Riggett	- do -	
1752	Mitchell	- do -	
1753*	Maguire	- do -	
1754	Cunningham, Lawrence	Guelph	
1755	Farrell	- do -	
1756	Aloff	Niagara Falls	

No.	NAME	ADDRESS	COMMENTS
1757	McClelland or McLennan, A.	Oakville, Ont.	
1758	Read	Winnipeg or Montreal	
1759	Nocter, Harry	Terrace, B.C.	(Farm _____)
1760	Chuhay	Montreal	
1761	Dadoken	Toronto	
1762	Fry, O.	Hamilton	
1763	Ivanofosky, Wladimir	Montreal	
1764	Lotosky, Dimitre	- do -	
1765	Danchuk, Alfanssi	- do -	
1766	Schwatt, Barri	- do -	
1767	Stiles, John	Prince George, B.C.	
1768	Williams, Robert J.	- do -	
1769	Tokoi, Oscar		
1770	Hammond, W.	Winnipeg, Man.	
1771	Hardy, George H.	Vancouver, B.C.	
1772	Zimmerman, Theodore	Carstairs	
1773*	Heilingher, R.	Ottawa	
1774	Burey, Micki	Montreal	
1775*	Kolisnyk	Winnipeg	
1776	Pearce, H.	- do -	
1777	Bolingbroke, H.	Princeton, B.C.	
1778*	Derey, Mike	Montreal	
1779*	Palingren, Alfred	Prince George	
1780*	Martin, John Leo	Victoria	
1781	Webb, R.A.	Vancouver	
1782*	Kravenchuk, Y.	Montreal	
1783*	Boychuk, H.	- do -	
1784	Ompu, Charles	Vancouver	
1785	Grumatikoff (Dramatikoff), Stoina	Detroit	
1786	Wilshaw, George	Toronto	
1787	Paul, Wm.	Hamilton	
1788	Drury, R.	- do -	
1789*	Stevenson, John	Victoria	Transferred to 175/ö2883
1790	Hallett	Vancouver, B.C.	
1791	Lewinbu @ Waldeman, Peter	Calgary	
1792	Davis, H.	Edmonton, Winnipeg	
1793	Ivorski, Nemo	Montreal	
1794	Francis	Hamilton, Ont.	
1795	Hardiker, Dr.	Hamilton, etc.	
1796	Price, M.	- do -	
1797	Cooney, Tom	Toronto, Ont.	
1798	Shaw, Walter	Prince Rupert, B.C.	
1799	Tree, Ambrose	Calgary	
1800	Woollacott, Walter	Vancouver	
1801	Cascadden, Gordon	Windsor	
1802	Matheson, John A.	West Lorne	
1803	Nykolajchuk, A.	Saskatoon	

No.	NAME	ADDRESS	COMMENTS
1804	Federyschuk, T.	- Do -	
1805	Gardiner	Regina	
1806	Appleton, Harry C.	- do -	
1807*	Stefink, Wasyl	Vancouver	
1808	Hodgins, Courley	Toronto	
1809	Gorosh, John	Vancouver	
1810	Repchuk, John K.	Saskatoon	
1811	Jenkins, Spencer S.	Vancouver	
1812	Stewart, Charles	St. Vital, Man.	
1813	Breeze, Wm.	- do -	
1814	Goorwitch, Charles Samuel		Winnipeg
1815	Cooper, E.R.	- do -	
1816	Harpman, Jonas	- do -	
1817	Holmes, Mrs. Florence	- do -	
1818	Wooler, Thomas	- do -	
1819	Cooper, C.P.	- do -	
1820	Stephenson, Harry	- do -	Engineer
1821	Kaiser, P.M.	- do -	
1822	Probetts, John	- do -	
1823	Rose, Sydney	- do -	
1824	Brown, Thomas	- do -	
1825	Smith, G.	- do -	
1826	Hampton, J.	- do -	
1827	Duxbury, Wm.H.	- do -	
1828	Shepherd, A.	- do -	
1829	Lumsden, Harry	- do -	
1830	Bukin, C.E.	- do -	
1831	Clancey, Jack	- do -	
1832	Waters, Charles		
1833*	Towle, R.W.		
1834	Foster, Walter	Transcona, Man. (Wpg)	
1835	Logan, Mrs. W.H.C.	Winnipeg, Man.	
1836	See P1792	- do -	
1837	Hammond, Mrs. W.	- do -	
1838	Hancocks, Mrs. Edith	- do -	
1839	Van Kleek, Percy	- do -	
1840	Hiab, (alias Grub, alias Grabowsky, Mike)		Thorold, Ont.
1841	Dachuck, Stanley	- do -, Ont.	
1842	Myers, Henry Ernest	Carlyle, Sask.	
1843	McCowan, Malcolm	Mayo, Y.T.	
1844	Major	Montreal	
1845	Atwood	Hamilton, Ont.	
1846*	Simpson, W.S.	New Westminister, B.C.	
1847	Bruce, Robert	Regina	
1848	Hughes, Charles D.	Winnipeg, Man.	
1849	Cottrell, Harry	- do -	
1850	Mintz, B.	Regina, Sask.	
1851	Harman, F.	Victoria, B.C.	

No.	NAME	ADDRESS	COMMENTS
1852*	Navizwisky, P.	Winnipeg, Man.	
1853	Esmonde, Osmond T. Grattan		Australia
1854	Purcell, Nicholas Thomas	Gleichen, Alta.	
1855	Grunate, Michael or Mike	Crowland, Ont.	
1856*	Blugermann, Jim	Crowland, Ont.	
1857	Pidskalny, Trofyn	Fort William, Ont.	
1858	Kotik, Steve	Fort William, Ont.	
1859*	Pohorilec, J.	Fort William	
1860*	Horniak, J.	Fort William	
1861	Wownenko	Toronto, Welland, etc.	
1862	Bellick, Mike	Crowland, Ont.	
1863*	Ivanchuck, Stefan	Crowland, Ont.	
1864	Foichuck, Steve	Crowland, Ont.	
1865	Korczak, T.	Toronto	
1866	Anderson, G.B.	Winnipeg, (468 Sherbrook St.)	
1867	Anderson, Robert	Winnipeg, (713 Elgin St.)	
1868	Lockhart, George	Kitchener, Ont.	
1869	Gordon, William	Winnipeg	
1870	Novosinskey, George	Montreal or Winnipeg	
1871	Allan, Matthew	Victoria	
1872	Moulton, Richard Wm.	Victoria	
1873	Koldofsky, Simon	Toronto	
1874*	Batren, Samuel	Montreal	
1875*	Horodynski, Mike	Montreal	
1876	Peel, Fred J.	Toronto	
1877*	Gosuliak @ Hucaliuk iuk- do -, Ottawa, etc.		
1878	Hicky, James	Port Clemens, B.C.	
1879	Hancox	Winnipeg	
1880	Ballin, Demian or Dan	Pt. Colborne	
1881	You, Chan Sit	? Vancouver	
1882	Boichuck, Tony	- do -	
1883	Head, Walter	Vancouver	
1884	Billik, Alexander	Toronto	
1885	Cafferty or Cafferkey, Henry		Vancouver
1886	Farnicky, Pete	Toronto	
1887	Jasiniuk, Ivan or John	- do -	
1888	Farnham, James	Vancouver	
1889	Michalowsky, Andrew	Winnipeg	
1890	Frankow	N.Burnaby, B.C.	
1891	Trussell, Aylward J.	Vancouver	
1892	Sullivan, Henry	- do -	
1893	Conn, Wm.	Toronto	
1894	Thompson, Wm.	Melville	
1895	Livingstone, Dan	Sydney	
1896*	Barrett, Silby	- do -	
1897	Toivar, John	Sudbury	
1898	Allman, Sydney	Vancouver	

No.	NAME	ADDRESS	COMMENTS
1899	Murphy, J.	Vancouver	
1900	Caskie or (Kaskie), James	Prince Rupert	
1901	Phizicky, Dr. Henry	Montreal	
1902	Halperin, P.	Toronto	
1903	Forbes, James W.	Vancouver ?	
1904	Parsons	Vancouver ?	Transferred to 175/P1980
1905	Lloyd, Geo.	Montreal	
1906	Meugel, O.	Vancouver	
1907	Bayley, W.D. (M.L.A.)	Winnipeg	
1908	Johnson, Samuel	Nelson	
1909	Gunberg, Lev	Winnipeg	
1910	Mitchell, John Sydney	Toronto	
1911	Syrstuck, Geo. (Yourke)	Edmonton	
1912	Korkishka, David	Coleman, Alta.	
1913	Foley, John	Vancouver	
1914	Coulter, W.H.	- do -	
1915	Gheorghui, Ghenadie	Dysart, Sask.	
1916	Kennedy	Toronto	
1917	Coleman, M.J.	Calgary	
1918	Potocki @ Dunn @ Count	Brockdorf	
1919	Galbraith, Gilbert	Prince George	
1920	Lake, Charles	Stewart, B.C.	
1921	Stillie, Andy	Prince George	
1922	Marks (Markson), Barney	Toronto	
1923	Horsburgh, Mrs.	Vancouver	
1924	Conwell, A.	Vancouver	
1925	Smith, Joshua	Victoria	
1926	Masloff, Mike	Winnipeg	
1927	Spackinski, Mike	Edmonton	
1928	Hagen, W.J.	Vancouver, B.C.	
1929	Inglis, James	- do -	
1930	Kelly, C.O.	- do -	
1931	Jackson, Charles	- do -	
1932	Speed	- do -	
1933	Monk, Edmond	Vancouver	
1934	Cunningham, Miss A.	- do -	
1935	Lipshitz	- do -	
1936	Priestley, Robert	- do -	
1937	Iwanchuk, Iwan	Egremont, Alta.	
1938	Paynton, James	?	Ex RCMP
1939	Romanuck, H.	Montreal	
1940	Kravetskey, Jacob	- do -	
1941	Davie, Harry	Winnipeg	
1942	Bessett, T.W.	Vancouver	
1943*	Wagner, John	Sudbury	
1944*	Peteko, J. or Y.	Saskatoon	
1945*	Zinchuk, Nicolas	Montreal	
1946	Solowsky	Timmins	

No.	NAME	ADDRESS	COMMENTS
1947	Heredotz, John	?	
1948	Stanley, P.C.	Moose Jaw	
1949	Takata, Sotojers	Vancouver	(Jap)
1950	Kanns, Sen	- do -	(Jap)
1951	Toyofuku, Atsushi	Vancouver	(Jap)
1952	Murray	- do - (CNUX Organizer) Transferred to 175/P2091	
1953	Kan, Koh Wing	- do -	
1954	Sung, Lambert	- do -	
1955	Sang, Wong Way	- do -	
1956	Munro, D.C.	Moose Jaw	
1957	McDonald, J.H.	Vancouver	
1958*	Tessler, Thomas	Winnipeg	
1959	Gordon, J.A.	Moose Jaw	
1960	Munro, John	- do -	
1961	Sinclair, Robert	Vancouver	
1962	Hogan, Ed	Baraca, P.O., Alta.	
1963	Laroque, L.	Montreal	
1964	Jackson, Bob	Toronto	
1965*	Simard	- do -	
1966	Petitclerc	- do -	
1967	Lacombe	- do -	
1968	Adamson, Sasha	- do -	
1969	Tutte, Wm.A.	Winnipeg	
1970	Bruychere, Peter	Milk River, Alta.	
1971*	Wihreston, Harry	Edmonton	
1972	Martinuk, Ivan John @ Bruce Jack		Toronto
1973	Jean, A.	Montreal	
1974	Gregoire, H.	- do -	
1975	Hamel, L.A.	Montreal	
1976	Desjardins, Geo.	- do -	
1977	Ouimette, H.	- do -	
1978	Frommager, Albert	- do -	
1979	Aylward	Vancouver	
1980	Parsons, F.C.	- do -	
1981	Shaff, @ Shaaf, Anna B.	Edmonton	
1982	Stockdale, J.	Hamilton	
1983*	Lakeman, J.	Edmonton	
1984	Todd, John Thomas	S.Vancouver	
1985	McLean, Neil	Glasgow, Scotland	
1986	Root, Fred	Vancouver	
1987	O'Keefe, Joseph	Gleichen, Alta.	
1988	Trudeau, U.	Montreal	
1989	Whitham, James	Vancouver	
1990*	Drayton, George	Vancouver, B.C.	
1991	Tgchinsky, John	Niagara Falls, Ont.	
1992	Preston	Toronto	
1993*	Hall, Bella	Montreal	

No.	NAME	ADDRESS	COMMENTS
1994	Mooney, John B.	On Tour (Canada & USA)	
1995	Kitchener, Stanley	Michel, B.C.	
1996	Verville, Adelard	Montreal	
1997	Arconet, @ Arcomet, @ Arcomb, Felix		- do -
1998	Lipchuk, Mike	Trail	
1999	Ponak, Steve	- do - ?	
2000	Burgeira @ Burdega, Nick		- do -
2001*	Morris, Wm.	Itinerant (Eastern Canada Organ of CP)	
2002	Bainbridge, Isaac	Toronto	
2003	Rockeff, Tons___A	Toronto	
2004	Lanchuck, Michail	Toronto	
2005	Corbett, Frederick	Ocean Falls	
2006	Keeling, Sidney R.	Edmonton	
2007	Gagnon, Ernest or Henry	Vancouver	
2008	Semirak, Sam	Edmonton	
2009	Rees, G.	Toronto	
2010	Hayha, Tobi	Vancouver	
2011	Andre, E.	- do -	
2012	Aho, August	?	
2013	Gauthier, Leon	Winnipeg	
2014	Helberg, Eino	?	
2015	Weinberger	Hamilton	71-3-35
2016	Cocks, W.	Regina	
2017*	Moriarty, William	Hamilton	
2018	Matz, Sam	Thorold	
2019	Uhryniuk, Peter	Winnipeg	
2020	Tortilla, August	Sault St. Marie	
2021	Turner, Jack	Vancouver	
2022	Ironberg, Gus	Hamilton	
2023	Nordloff, A.B.	Toronto	
2024	Michaels, Wm.	Montreal	
2025*	Blumberger, Dr. Samuel	Vancouver	
2026	Hamner, Harry	Toronto	
2027	McKenzie, J. (Scotty)	Toronto	
2028	Rychls, Wm.	Halifax	
2029	Navin, Frank V.	Moose Jaw, Sask.	
2030	Holowach, Sam	Edmonton, Alta.	
2031	Kowalsky, John		
2032	Anderson, Frank	Edmonton, Alta.	
2033	Yaswara, K.S.	Vancouver, B.C.	
2034	Rychlo, Steve	Sydney, N.S.	
2035*	Buck @ Page @ Johnston	Toronto	
2036	Slobodian, Mike		
2037	O'Neill, Herbert A.	Vancouver	
2038	Orr	- do -	
2039	Rupert, Geo.	Moose Jaw	
2040*	Stokaluk, John	Coleman, Alta.	
2041	Iwasiuk, Dmytro (Dan)	Hillcrest, - do -	

No.	NAME	ADDRESS	COMMENTS
2042	Wortishin (Wortyshyn), Anthony		Drumheller
2043	Thomas		
2044	Stedman, Leonard Brooks	Victoria	
2045	Tanner, Chas A.	Winnipeg	(MP, OBU, CP of C)
2046	Rubinetz @ Ravence, Geo.		Timmins
2047	Fletcher, W.	Vancouver	(CNUX)
2048	Smith, John Patrick	Toronto	(CNUX)
2049	Levchenko, Vasily	Thorold Park	
2050	Simpson, James	Vancouver	(from Sudbury)
2051	Kilner, T.	Toronto	
2052*	Halina, Stefan	Saskatoon	
2053	Horbatuik, A.	- do -	
2054	Zahariyhuk, D.	Montreal	
2055	Parent, E.	- do -	
2056	Belec, Henry	- do -	
2057	Whitham, Daniel	Vancouver	
2058	Morgan, John	- do -	(ex Imp. Soldier)
2059	Komar (Camar)	Toronto (transient)	
2060	Kristoff (Kustoff), T.A.	Hamilton	
2061	Hanna, John C.	Calgary	
2062	Frey, S.B.	Powell River, B.C.	
2063	James, Wm. Walter	- do -	
2064	Martin, Geo. Alexander	- do -	
2065	Anthony, Morris	- do -	
2066	Lewthwaite, Ambrose	- do -	
2067	Pearson, Clarence L.	- do -	
2068	Morrison, Thomas	Powell River	
2069	Hawchuk, Stefan	Montreal	
2070	Gemchuk, Stef	- do -	
2071	Luhka	- do -	
2072	Reardon, Joe	Vancouver	
2073	Flood, T.A.	- do -	
2074	Mill, Walter	Saskatoon	
2075	Iverson, L.	Vancouver	
2076	Deshlevoy, Mike	Toronto	
2077	Plourde, Alfred	Montreal	
2078	Komende, I.	Montreal	
2079	Yacobchak, S.	Montreal	
2080	McLean, Rev D.R.	Vancouver	
2081	Stelp or Stelt or Stelop, T.	- do -	
2082	Kujoitan, Kost	Welland	
2083	Precautionary List of Prominent Agitators in United Kingdom		
2084	Galich or Gelicz, John, or Joe or Ivan		Toronto
2085	Mysuk, Jim	Calgary	
2086	Haywood, John	Winnipeg	
2087	Hackett, Percy C.	- do -	
2088	Radajchuk, Wm.	Saskatoon	
2089	Mcguire	Edmonton	

No.	NAME	ADDRESS	COMMENTS
2090	Ryder, Martin	- do -	
2091	Murray, Geo.	Vancouver	
2092*	Wilson, Walter		
2093	Kennedy, Patrick	Radville, Sask.	
2094	Mercier, Leo	Montreal	
2095	Mathurin, Henri	- do -	
2096	Temney @ Temnecky, Maron J.	Prince Albert	
2097	Lehto, Nestor	Fort William	
2098	Clark, Frank	Calgary	
2099	McDonnell, J.	Vancouver	
2100	Thompson, F.W.	Calgary	
2101	Parce, Alfred	Vancouver	
2102	Volnenko, Pete	Toronto	
2103	Brainer, A.	Radville, Sask.	
2104*	Duleyk, J.	Saskatoon	
2105	McClusky, Walys @ Frank		(Salvation Army), Winnipeg
2106	Belec, Leon	Montreal	
2107	Mcavoy, D.	Montreal	
2108	McGuire, Wm.	Edmonton	Transferred to 170/P2089
2109	Prystupa, A.	Dana	
2110*	Scott, Charles E.	Itinerant	Transferred, see 175/P2518
2111	Cosgrove, P.S.	?	
2112	Marak, Blashko J.	? Winnipeg Dist.	
2113	Rahim, H.	Vancouver	
2114	Robb, Alec	Vancouver	
2115	Howden	- do -	
2116	O'Brien, Patrick	Winnipeg	
2117	Zwidzinski, Kozma	Calgary, Alta.	
2118	Basiuk, Jurke	- do -	
2119	Crute, P.	Vancouver, B.C.	
2120	Squirrel, W.G.	- do -	
2121	Davis, Bucksaw	Winnipeg, Man.	
2122	Czekaluk, Jakiu	Calgary, Alta.	
2123	Prentor, Mrs. Hector	Toronto	
2124*	Hardy, Geo.	Itinerant	IWW Gen Sec, USA)
2125	Nicholsky, Nicholas	Amyox, B.C.	
2126	Paciak, Valentine	Sault Ste. Marie	
2127	Papazian, Arakel Dicran	Nelson, B.C.	
2128	West, Peter	Winnipeg, Man.	
2129	Charran, Jules	Montreal	
2130	Breeze @ Cheyenne @ Shy, Arthur	Nelson, B.C.	
2131	Lewis, Geo.	N.Vancouver, B.C.	
2132	Potapchuk, Dimitry	Sault Ste. Marie	
2133*	Bennett, W.	Vancouver	
2134	Kruhmin @ Koren @ Kooman @ Klooman, Geo.	- do -	
2135*	Kezyma, Harry	Canmore, Alta.	Transferred to 175/P3195
2136	Aubrey, Geo.	Coombs, B.C.	
2137	Forget, Albert Ernest	Montreal	

No.	NAME	ADDRESS	COMMENTS
2138	Page, H.W.A.	- do -	
2139	Mathieux, Alfred or Arthur		Montreal
2140	Podowsky, P.	Blaine Lake	
2141	Barker, James	Vancouver	
2142	Mitchell, Charles	- do -	
2143*	Martin, John	- do -	
2144*	Birch, Elmer Gordon	- do -	
2145	Smith, W.M.	Vancouver, B.C.	
2146	McCourt, J.J.	Winnipeg, Man.	
2147	Patrick, Mike	Sault St. Marie	
2148	Dobson, F.A.	Vancouver, B.C.	
2149	Brunskill, W.E.	Saskatoon, Sask.	
2150	Kilmer, W.L.	Kamloops, B.C.	
2151*	MacLean, Duncan B.	Edmonton	
2152	Long, W.J.	Edmonton	
2153	Long, W.	Edmonton	
2154	Graham, Pete	Edmonton	
2155	Janvier	Edmonton	
2156	Charnall, A.J.	Saskatoon	
2157	Williams, P.J.	Saskatoon	
2158	Barron, W.	Saskatoon	
2159	Robson, Michael	Winnipeg	
2160	Johnson, Gus	Merritt or Kamloops, B.C.	
2161	Booth, Mrs. Edith	Vancouver, B.C.	
2162	Franske, Sarah Frances	Saskatoon	
2163	Rozetski, Kazmir	Bayview, Sault St. Marie	
2164	Luddes, Wm.	Toronto	
2165	Lehti @ Lehto, Wm. @ Edward		Sault St. Marie
2166*	Furbett, Steve	Sydney, N.S.	
2167*	Arbugash, Edward Jules	Montreal	
2168*	Hayditchuk @ Hardy, Peter		Ottawa
2169	Hoare, W.G.	Vancouver	
2170	Henick, Fred	Halifax	
2171	Dumont, Joseph Arthur	Montreal	
2172	Alairie, Maxieme Edouard	Montreal	
2173	Phillips, R.H.	Vancouver	
2174	Burns, John N.	Winnipeg	
2175*	Hill, A.T.	Toronto	
2176	Beauchemin, Phillipe Alfred		Montreal
2177	Kozar, Mike	Sault St. Marie	
2178	Landry, Timothy	Sault St. Marie	
2179	Ainsley, B.	Toronto	
2180	Stubbs, Joe	Hillcrest, Alta.	
2181	Stack, Nick	Saskatoon	
2182	Johnson, T.L.	Ocean Falls, B.C.	
2183*	Gilbert, W.	Winnipeg, Man.	
2184	Irving, Mrs. Maud	Vancouver	
2185	Tervo, Konrad	Sudbury	

No.	NAME	ADDRESS	COMMENTS
2186	Smith, J.T.	Vancouver	
2187	Clayton, R.	Vancouver	
2188	Smith, C.M.	Vancouver	
2189	Benenson, A.L.	Ottawa	
2190*	Sawchuck, Nick	Fort Frances	
2191	Johnson, Ernie	Montreal	
2192	Lambert, Napoleon Joseph		Montreal
2193*	Elendiuk, George	Port Arthur	
2194	Wilson, Richard	Vancouver	
2195	Premachuk, Harry	The Pas, Man.	
2196*	Huculak, Mike	The Pas, Man.	
2197*	Cholovchuk, Makaryj	The Pas, Man.	
2198	Doreshenko, Fred	Montreal	
2199	Morgan, James	Montreal	
2200*	Davey, Sydney		
2201	Croll, Miss L.	Montreal	
2202	Campbell, Gordon	Vancouver	
2203	Lawson, Harold	Vancouver	
2204	Hawthorn, John R.	Vancouver	
2205	Robotham, Herbert George		Vancouver
2206	Ste Andrew, Joseph	Montreal	
2207	Boderte, Auguste	Montreal	
2208	Sara, Henry	Vancouver	
2209	Donnelly, J.	Vancouver	
2210	Barr, James	Vancouver	
2211	Green, Leon @ Butousky	@ H.P. O'Neil	
2212	Aron, Herman John	Port Arthur	
2213	Grand, Harry	Vancouver	
2214	Donnelly, James	Vancouver	
2215*	West, Mike	Saskatoon, Drumheller	
2216	Favell, Theodore	Saskatoon, Drumherrer	
2217*	Thompson	Montreal, Winnipeg	
2218*	Stewart, Charles McGregor		Vancouver
2219*	Harris, Miss Nancy	Winnipeg	
2220*	Davy, Frederak William	Winnipeg	
2221*	Sutcliffe, John I.	Toronto	
2222*	Harris, Miss Kathleen (Kitty)		Winnipeg
2223	Ridey, Frank	Toronto, Ont.	
2224*	Saunders, Charles	Vancouver, B.C.	
2225	Kuzmenoff, Alexander	Vancouver, B.C.	
2226	Whytall, Ben	Sault Ste. Marie	
2227	Seripnychuk, George	Ottawa, Ont.	
2228	Seiden, S.	Montreal, P.Q.	
2229	Chennoff, Mike	Kitchener, Ont.	
2230	Moskall, Mike @ Mike Soldatt		Kitchener, Ont.
2231*	Derkewsky, J.	Vancouver, B.C.	
2232	Floyd, Philip	Vancouver, B.C.	
2233	Hungafond, Jim	Vancouver, B.C.	

No.	NAME	ADDRESS	COMMENTS
2234	Bates, William	Vancouver, B.C.	
2235	Maine, Matti @ Matti Hunonen		Fort William, Ont.
2236	Allikkala, Charles	Fort William, Ont.	
2237	Falls, William	Fort William, Ont.	
2238*	Padgham, Bert	Vancouver, B.C.	
2239*	Sawula, Pete	Saskatoon, Sask.	
2240	Ugrinovich, Paul	Ottawa, Ont.	
2241	Cancelled, see P1267	Calgary, Alta.	
2242	Owen, J.	Vancouver, B.C.	
2243	Shimkin, Mike	Fort William	
2244	Pidskanly, Osip	Fort William	
2245	Zachansky, Waysl	Fort William	
2246	Hucutiak, Wassel	Calgary, Alta.	
2247	Zoleski, Tony	Calgary	
2248	Lott, James	Vancouver	
2249	Burns, John @ Brooks, @ Peterborough @ White		- do -
2250	Rowny, Anism	Perdue, Sask.	
2251	Boshko, M.	- do -	
2252	Dawson, Leslie Mitchell	Vancouver	
2253	Gulbrandseu, Lorenzo @ Bronson		Ottawa
2254*	Tawanec, Stepan	Louvawe, Sask.	
2255	Laboriuk @ Labor, Anton	- do -	
2256	Wileu, Otto	Fort William, Ont.	
2257	Piroscho, M.	Vancouver	
2258	Toltskson, T.	- do -	
2259	Nylmer, J.	- do -	
2260	Sats, L.	- do -	
2261	Nelson, E.	- do -	
2262	Meroshneck, P.	Vancouver	
2263	Sabanskie, A.		
2264	Stover, H.		
2265	McLeod, Alexander		
2266	Lausenberg, A.	- do -	
2267	Upsrich, Miss Bertha	Montreal	
2268	Foucher, H. Arthur	- do -	
2269	Purser, W.	Toronto	
2270	Romashevsky, A.	Vancouver	
2271*	Nazarkewich, R.	Crowfoot, Alta.	
2272	Gontar, P. @ Hantor	Calgary, Alta.	
2273	Crook, Charles	Vancouver, B.C.	
2274	Dixon, S.H.	USA	
2275	Satas, A.M.	Toronto	
2276	Bogoeff, S.	- do -	
2277	Maltais, Joe	Montreal	
2278	Boivin	- do -	
2279	Malboedif, Jean Baptiste	- do -	
2280*	Swift, Walter	Toronto	
2281	Oredzuk, N.	Saskatoon	

No.	NAME	ADDRESS	COMMENTS
2282	Polibroda, M.	- do -	
2283*	Burpee, Thomas H., alias L. Johnson	Toronto	
2284*	Colle, Miss Beatrice	Montreal	
2285*	Mendelssohn, Sam A.	Montreal	
2286*	Mendelssohn, Nathan	Montreal	
2287	Anderson, Charles J.	Vancouver	
2288	Brandon, Frederick	- do -	
2289	Cochrane, John	- do -	
2290	Ferenyk, Janek	Blaine Lake, Sask.	
2291*	Zaremba, Michaela	Timmins, Ont.	
2292	Kulchycki, Palko	Revelstoke, B.C.	
2293*	Dunn, Arthur	Edmonton	
2294	Leminson, Jacob	Winnipeg, Man.	
2295	Laing, Miss	Vancouver	
2296	Borah, D.	Gifford, Sask.	
2297	Kirk, Robert	Vancouver, B.C.	
2298	Ballard, T.	- do -	
2299	Adamson, Jerome P.	Anthony, Ont.	
2300	Mackenzie, G.	Calgary, Alta.	
2301	Shulman, Jak (Jack)	Winnipeg, Man.	
2302*	Hatfield, Harry	Toronto	
2303	Smolin, George @ Sam Mattrose		Montreal
2304	Salusky, Steve	Montreal	
2305	Wagner, David	Niagara Falls	
2306	Robertson, Henry	Winnipeg	
2307	Conger, T.D.	Tchesinkaut, B.C.	
2308	Dixon, Wm. @ Burns	Montreal	
2309	Valentine, W.A. (W.A. Brown)	Powell River, B.C.	
2310	Ashman, Sam Malatesva Sam		Montreal
2311	Palyew, Albert	Montreal	
2312	Grosberg, George	Montreal	
2313	Woolfesky, Ben	Montreal	
2314	Alynn, Jack R.	Vancouver, B.C.	
2315	Sikorski, Joe	Fish Creek, Sask.	
2316	Alexander, George @ George Poponuik		Montreal
2317	Delangy, William	Vancouver	
2318	Robinson, E.D.	Montreal, P.Q.	
2319	Toffan, Alex	Saskatoon, Sask.	
2320	Jovanette	Montreal, P.Q.	
2321	Blanchette	Montreal, P.Q.	
2322	Beausoleil	Montreal, P.Q.	
2323	Belanger, Wilford, alias Lenine	Montreal, P.Q.	
2324*	Gault, A.	Montreal, P.Q.	
2325	Tkachenco, F.	Ottawa, Ont.	
2326	Aubin	Montreal, P.Q.	

No.	NAME	ADDRESS	COMMENTS
2327	Bates, W.	Timmins, Ont.	
2328	Russells	Montreal, P.Q.	
2329	Taillefer, Tiger (no.783)	Montreal, P.Q.	
2330	Hnyda, John	Montreal, P.Q.	
2331	Laing, Paul	Vancouver, B.C.	
2332	Blumfeld, Abby	Montreal, P.Q.	
2333	Koffman, Arnold Spio	Vancouver, B.C.	
2334	Hunaterek, Steve	Montreal, P.Q.	
2335	Whitaker, Albert	Vancouver, B.C.	
2336	Allen, Thomas	Montreal, P.Q.	
2337	Doyen, alias Gorman	Montreal, P.Q.	
2338	Binet, Hassof	Montreal, P.Q.	
2339	Lonovich, Miss	Montreal, P.Q.	
2340	Beaney, Alfred E.	Vancouver, B.C.	
2341	Fannington, A. & Wife	Vancouver, B.C.	
2342	Dudnivich, John	Ridfield, Sask.	
2343	Lushiski, John	N.Battleford	
2344*	Samchenski, Pete	- do -	
2345	Nelfuiggan, Daniel	Vancouver, B.C.	
2346	Guthrie, George	Saskatoon	
2347	McKay, Julian	Saskatoon	
2348	Newfeld, J. Kiefeld, J.	Saskatoon	
2349	Hepburn, W.	Saskatoon	
2350	Gravelier, Ed	Montreal, P.Q.	
2351	Walywasko, Alex	Prince Albert	
2352	Uhryn, Demetro M.	Wakow, Sask.	
2353*	Uhryn, Demetro	Wakow, Sask.	
2354	Lehkiun, A.	Calgary	
2355	Drummond, Mrs. E.	Vancouver, B.C.	
2356	Bardsley, William	Vancouver	
2357	Duke, B.N.	Winnipeg	
2358	McLeod, Ewen	Vancouver	
2359	Sturd, Peter George	Winnipeg	
2360	Smith, A. G.	Vancouver	
2361*	Lazaruk, Steve (Sr.)	Michel	
2362	Galaway, Mark Vossmer	Vancouver	
2363	Aushiu, @ Willis	Vancouver	
2364	Pritchard		Transferred to 175/P91
2365	Marzolis, Benjamin M.	Calgary	
2366	Greenwood, James	Vancouver	
2367	Dolan, John	Calgary	
2368	St.John, Charles @ Violet	Montreal	
2369	Ryan, William @ General	Ryan	Edmonton
2370	Schaeffer, Richard A.	?	
2371	Muorteva, Santeri		
2372	Danles, W.A. False	Montreal	
2373	Hobart, Ernest Alfred	Winnipeg	
2374	Godin, E. Normandy	Montreal	

No.	NAME	ADDRESS	COMMENTS
2375	Shklar, L.	Montreal	
2376	Dvankin, Meyr	Montreal	
2377	Patterson, Christopher	Vancouver & Edmonton	
2378	Kalmuskey, Mrs. Annie	Saskatoon	
2379	Daskoch, William	Fernie, Michel	
2380	Goldstein, J.	Brandon	
2381	Huhtamaki	Fort William	
2382	Dominik, Steve	Lac du Bonnett	
2383	Bozuk, D.	Saskatoon	
2384	Hula, J.	Moose Jaw	
2385*	Navis, J.	Winnipeg	
2386	Chickley, W.	Port Arthur	
2387	Carpendale, W.	Vancouver	
2388	Sawchuck, William	Vancouver	
2389	Kudenko, H.	Winnipeg	
2390	Spence, H. Or W.	Winnipeg	
2391	Boiveau, Albert alias Marat	Montreal	
2392	Halichenko, Alexander	N.Battleford	
2393	Biznar, John	Saskatoon	
2394	Natson, John	Fort William	
2395	Jacque, Alexis alias Laliberte	Montreal	
2396	Christie, Bob	Fort William	
2397	Manila, Joe	Nipigon, Ont.	
2398	McIntyre, Fred	Moose Jaw	
2399	Dealtry, Gerald	Saskatoon	
2400	Kabzei, Tom	Saskatoon	
2401	Jordan, Alfred McKay	Vancouver	
2402*	Kulyk, Sam	Cando, Sask.	
2403	Sidnik, Andry	Blaine Lake	
2404	Mitario, K.	Vancouver	
2405	Iho, David	Fort William	
2406	Ruthko, Bill	Cando, Sask.	
2407	Bolan, Fred	Sydney, N.S.	
2408*	Polansky, Wasyl	Ft. William	
2409	Panchuk, John	Saskatoon	
2410	Wasylkiw, Anna	- do -	
2411	Woodkowiz, John @ John Woodman		Winnipeg
2412	Korol, Louis	Ft. William	
2413	Crossan, Abe	Vancouver	
2414*	Kaft, Victor	Kamsack	
2415	Fisher	Vancouver	
2416	Modrackoff, Harry	Kamsack	
2417	Luneck, Pete	Kamsack	
2418*	Sachatoff, Boris	Kamsack	
2419*	King, Wasyl	Kamsack	
2420*	Karmen, Metro	Kamsack	

No.	NAME	ADDRESS	COMMENTS
2421	Boulter, A.J.	Calgary, Atla.	
2422	Medwig, Alex	Calder	
2423	Nysyk, Stef alias Forynwik, Stef	Rosedale, Alta.	
2424	Woods	Vancouver	(IWW)
2425*	Conroy, James	Drumheller	
2426	Allen, Albert E.	- do -	
2427*	Romer, Jacob	Toronto	
2428	Bazowich, W. or M.	Edmonton	Transferred to 175/P2750
2429*	Waye, Foreman	Halifax	
2430*	McDonald, Lewis Charles @ "Kid" Burns		Drumheller
2431	Mylyniuk, Wasyl	Saskatoon	
2432	Gass, John	Winnipeg, Man.	
2433	Matheson, W.	Winnipeg, Man.	
2434*	Smith, Michael	Winnipeg, Man.	
2425	Bonneyfay, Joseph	Montreal	
2436*	Jameson, Harry	Winnipeg, Man.	
2437	Welinder, P.J.	Vancouver	
2438	Robertson, Henry	Winnipeg, Man.	Transferred to 175/P2306
2439	Leslie, William	Toronto, Ont.	
2440*	Morris, Leslie	Toronto, Ont.	
2441	Flood, Tom	Ft. William	
2442	McGregor, T.	Winnipeg, Man.	
2443*	Peabody, Jack	- do -	
2444	Hayward, Ernest	- do -	
2445	P.J.Wilender	Seattle, USA	
2446	Tourkewich, D.	Winnipeg, Man.	
2447	Irehan, M.	Russia	
2448	Niemi, Victor	Nipigon, Ont.	
2449	Chojahowski, John	Prince Albert, Sask.	
2450	Machin, J.	Toronto	
2451	Rowan, James	Vancouver	
2452	Larych, H.	Edmonton	
2453	Jeffery, Fred	Vancouver	
2454	Threffalls, F.	- do -	
2455	Jennings, J.	- do -	
2456*	Scarlett, Sam	Vancouver, B.C.	
2457	Bachynski, William	Haileyburry, Ont.	Transferred to 175/P2459
2458	Backynski, Wasyl	Espanola, Ont.	
2459*	Ewen, Thomas A.	Saskatoon	
2460	Etsu, Suzki	Vancouver, B.C.	
2461	Mitarai, Kisaburo	- do -	Transferred to 175/P2404
2462	Takai, Koichiro	- do -	
2463	Yoshida, Ryruchi	- do -	
2464	Sato, Toshiko (Mrs.)	- do -	
2465	Kanno, Len		Transferred to 175/P1950 17/3/26
2466	Peterson, James Louis	Fernie, B.C.	Transferred see P/H/F 1162
2467	Bersin, George	Lac du Bonnet	

No.	NAME	ADDRESS	COMMENTS
2468	Bohdavoich, Kozma	Prince Albert, Sask.	
2469	Taylor, Carl G.	Winnipeg, Man.	
2470*	Wallace, Joseph Sylvester	Wallace Advertising Agency, Halifax, N.S.	
2471	Dorfman, Gabriel	Winnipeg, Man.	
2472*	Bossy, Walter J.	131 1/2 Queen St. West, Toronto	
2473	Dancyt, Alex	Lac du Bonnett, Man.	
2474	Swidersky, Nick	Edmonton	
2475	Yerko, S.	Saskatoon	
2476	Grundberg, Fred	Lac du Bonnet, Winnipeg	
2477*	Thompson, Archibald	Port Arthur	(English Harvester)
2478*	Andreichuk, Steve	32 West Street, Whitney Pier, Sydney, N.S.	
2479*	Peruniak, Trofyn		
2480	Laughland, Rev. J.	Rockcliffe Annex	
2481	Bland, Dr. Salem G.	Toronto	Minister
2482	Kalmin, Alex or Andrew	Lac du Bonnet, Winnipeg	Farmer
2483	Kennedy, Joe	Timmins, Ont.	
2484	Niel, Sulo Gabriel	Toronto, 7 Mortimer Ave.	
2485	Black, Norman	Pelly, Sask.	
2486	Petterson, Oscar	Lac du Bonnet, Wpg.	
2487	Kronberg, Alfred	Lac du Bonnet	
2488	Rosenberg, John	- do -	
2489	Clarke, Joseph A.	Edmonton	Cancelled see 175/P1088
2490*	Ketcheson, Mark	158 North Beaconsfield Ave., Toronto	
2491	Korchee, Paul	Prince Albert	
2492*	Hnatiuk, Steve	Transient	
2493	McCaul, D.C.	Calgary	
2494*	Smith, Stewart	Toronto	Son of A.E.Smith
2495	Latham, George	Edmonton	
2496	Windle, Arthur E.	Timmins	Originally from B.C.
2497	Cunningham, Lawrence, Pat or Lorne		Quelch
2498	McKay, Alex A.	Glace Bay, N.S.	
2499	Trotman, Arthur Stanley	Sydney, N.S.	
2500	Marteniuk, Joe	Humbolt	
2501	Brynoff, J. alias J.Bray	Prud'Homme	
2502	Lathi, Charles	Cobalt	
2503	Communist Party of Canada, Strength of Canada		
2504	IWW Strength of Branches		
2505	Green H.	Toronto	
2506	Belgin, Jack	Lac du Bonnet, Winnipeg	
2507	Backman, John	Lac du Bonnett	
2508	Lymboy	Toronto	Transferred to 175/P2709
2509	Lozina, Doctor Konstantin	Toronto	
2510	Kochmarevsky	Hamilton	
2511*	Pallot, H.J.	Edmonton	
2512	Stefaniuk, Fred	Meacham	
2513	Zukerman, N.	Vancouver	
2514*	Petroff, Mike alias Petrov	Toronto	

No.	NAME	ADDRESS	COMMENTS
2515	Diakunets, Peter	Toronto	
2516	Halliday, James	Vancouver	
2517	Katayama, Sen		
2518*	Scott, Charles E.		Also 175/P2110
2519	White, Robert	Vancouver	
2520	Skulte, Martin	Lac-du-Bonnet	
2521	Brewer, John		
2522*	Drystash, Demi	Hamilton	
2523	Hendrickson, Martin	Mundare, Alta.	
2524	Cameron, Albert E.	Sudbury	
2525	Kozak, John	Ft. William	
2526	Burford, Chas E.	Edmonton	
2527	Knight, Miss	Edmonton	
2528	Mathews, John	Lac-du-Bonnet	
2529	O'Hara, Paddy		Secret
2530	Wolynec, alias Kalynic, Miss Mary		
2531	Bohenko or Bohonex, Wasyl		
2532	Kahana, Joseph	Winnipeg	
2533	Puhtze, Jacob	Lettonia	
2534*	Faure, Paul	Montreal	
2535*	Madinsky, Dan	Sydney	
2536	Tchitcherin, Captain Boris		
2537*	Kostiniuk, Mike	Sudbury	
2538	Kulyk, Ivan		Soviet Trade Delegation
2539*	Chervinsky, Nicoli	Ford City, Ont.	
2540*	Bolton, A.E.	Kelliher, Sask.	
2541*	Harding, Cyril A.	Vantage, Sask.	
2542	Veronetz, L.		
2543	Knysh, Mike		
2544	Abramovitch, Raphael		
2545*	Hollowink, John		
2546	Ross, Jack	Winnipeg	
2547	Siminoff (Seminoff), Sam	Kindersely, Saskatoon	
2548*	Kuzik, S.	Fort William	
2549	McDonald, Dan or Blackie		Terrence, B.C.
2550	Nelson, Ben		IWW Agitator
2551*	Bohayczuk, H.	Hamilton, Ont.	
2552	Mackenzie, D.A.		Ex IWW Organizer
2553	Mortimer, J.H.	Usk, B.C.	
2554*	Edshtein, Abe		
2555	Holtman, Morris		Sec: Workers Party of America
2556	Iyama, I.		Jap
2557	Mabille, Leon	New York	
2558*	Yuriychuk, Steve	Edmonton	
2559	Clarke, Harry G.	Portland	Speaker for IWW Vancouver
2560	Sullivan, James or John	Hutton, B.C.	
2561*	Sawula, Stephen	Edmonton	
2562	Wicklund, Rolph Harold		

No.	NAME	ADDRESS	COMMENTS
2563	Graves, Albert	London, Ont.	
2564	Karolyi, Count Michael		
2565	Steele, Joseph	Sydney	
2566	Chaliapan		
2567*	Strong, A.L.		
2568	Minton, J.	Drumheller	
2569	Gordin, Morris		
2570	McDonald, J.A.	Vancouver	IWW
2571	Franchuk, Wasyl	Goodeve, Sask.	
2572	Gobar, Jatrinda Goba		Hindu Wrestler
2573	Divilkovsky, Maxim Anatoliwitch		
2574	Sawchuk, S.	Edmonton	
2575*	Held, Miss Freda	Toronto	
2576*	Keefe, William	Toronto	
2577	Sarupa, Alex	Lettonia, Man.	
2578	Lakgonoff, E. alias Hasboff, E.	Stewart, B.C.	
2579*	Dempster, Osborne Lieut.	Toronto	
2580	Ball, W.R.	Edmonton	
2581	Schwartz, N.		
2582	Gregg, G.	Winnipeg	
2583	Brodnic, Nick	Corbin, B.C.	
2584	Mourisc, Ludwig	Corbin, B.C.	
2585	Kulney, Louise	Corbin, B.C.	
2586	Purcell, A.	England	
2587	Schelking, Eugene de	Corbin, B.C.	
2588	Wanhela, W.		
2589	Thompson, I.P.	USA	IWW Speaker
2590	Sjitnik, Rabbi	Drumheller	Jewish Lecturer

For subsequent record see 1925 Register of Personal History Fyles.

No.	NAME
2598*	
2602*	
2610*	
2623*	
2633*	
2635*	
2638*	
2649*	
2653*	
2657*	
2663*	
2667*	
2671*	Corbin, Jean (Miss)
2677*	
2688*	
2693*	
2698*	Stokaliuk, John
2715*	

No.	NAME	ADDRESS	COMMENTS
2716*			
2718*			
2746*			
2739*			
2758*			
2759*			
2763*			
2767*			
2769*	Ahlquist, J.W.		
2772*	Forkin, Martin		
2777*			
2786*			
2783*	Chomicki, Dan		
2784*	Lapides, S.		
2788*			
2793*	Matveyenko, Paul		
2795*			
2804*			
2810*			
2812*			
2814*			
2817*			
2818*			
2819*			
2821*			
2822*			
2825*			
2826*			
2829*			
2830*			
2831*			
2834*			
2835*			
2848*			
2850*			
2852*			
2858*			
2859*	Lincoln, Trclictsch		
2861*			
2864*			
2868*			
2869*			
2872*			
2873*			
2883*	Stevenson, John		
2884*	Erenberg, N.		
2885*	Cohen, J.L.		

No.	NAME	ADDRESS	COMMENTS
2888*			
2891*			
2894*			
2895*			
2899*			
2903*			
2912*			
2922*			
2923*			
2924*			
2925*			
2926*			
2927*	Kasian, Yourko		
2931*			
2942*			
2949*			
2952*			
2955*			
2961*			
2967*	Chopowick, Michael		
2972*			
2975*			
2979*			
2984*			
2987*			
2990*			
2991*			
2994*			
2995*			
3001*	Trotsky, L.N.		
3002*			
3003*			
3005*			
3007*	Teresho, Wasyl		
3008*			
3010*			
3013*			
3014*			
3020*			
3021*			
3024*			
3026*			
3028*			
3029*			
3030*			
3032*			
3036*			

No.	NAME	ADDRESS	COMMENTS
3042*			
3044*			
3046*			
3061*	Maguire, Thomas		
3063*			
3066*			
3068*			
3070*			
3074*			
3075*			
3076*			
3077*			
3081*			
3082*	Klapchuk, William		
3083*			
3084*			
3087*	Veregin, Peter		
3092*			
3094*			
3097*	Golinsky, Mike		
3098*			
3101*			
3102*			
3103	Bryson, James		
3109*			
3111*			
3114*	Chopowick, Thomas Edward		
3119*			
3122*			
3125*			
3127*			
3130*			
3134*			
3144*			
3145*			
3146*			
3148*			
3150*			
3151*			
3152*			
3154*			
3158*			
3158*			
3161*			
3162*			
3163*			
3165*	Anderson, George H.		
3169*			

No.	NAME	ADDRESS	COMMENTS
3170*			
3172*			
3173*			
3176*			
3182*			
3183*			
3188*			
3192*			
3194*			
3195*	Kezyma, Harry		
3197*			
3198*	Bilinsky, J.		
3202*			
3203*			
3206*			
3208*			
3209*			
3210*			
3216*			
3218*			
3219*			
3220*			
3223*			
3224*			
3227*			
3231*			
3232*			
3233*			
3235*			
3239*	Gilmore, J.		
3240*			
3243*			
3244*	Sundqvist, Gust (fem)		
3246*			
3247*			
3252*			
3254*			
3263*			
3264*			
3267*			
3271*			
3275*			
3276*			
3278*			
3282*			
3284*			
3290*			
3294*			

No.	NAME	ADDRESS	COMMENTS
3298*			
3299*			
3303*			
3305*	Kizyma, Harry		
3307*			
3311*			
3315*			
3316*			
3319*			
3320*			
3321*			
3325*			
3327*			
3328*			
3330*			
3332*			
3333*			
3345*			
3350*			
3351*			
3353*			
3355*			
3359*			
3363*			
3364*			
3365*	Kleparczuk		
3366*			
3379*			
3382*			
3384*			
3385*			
3392*			
3398*			
3399*			
3400*			
3402*			
3406*			
3408*			
3413*	Janosir, Bela		
3414*			
3418*	Makela, Untuvo		
3419*			
3427*			
3432*			
3438*			
3444*			
3445*			
3448*			

No.	NAME	ADDRESS	COMMENTS
3450*			
3453*			
3458*			
3460*			
3461*			
3466*			
3468*			
3475*			
3476*			
3479*			
3484*			
3485*			
3492*			
3494*			
3500*			
3507*			
3508*			
3510*			
3511*			
3512*	Stewart, Charles		
3521*			
3522*			
3524*			
3526*			
3527*			
3529*	Bjarnason, Paul		
3532*			
3534*			
3538*			
3539*			
3546*			
3562*			
3564*			
3565*			
3572*			
3576*			
3578*			
3580*			
3583*			
3590*			
3592*			
3595*	Ewanec, Steve		
3596*			
3597*			
3598*			
3599*			
3600*			
3610*			

No.	NAME	ADDRESS	COMMENTS
3603*			
3616*			
3624*			
3637*			
3638*			
3643*			
3653*			
3656*			
3660*	Adams, Johm		
3661*			
3663*			
3665*			
3666*			
3668*			
3669*			
3671*			
3673*	Petryk, Dan		
3679*			
3680*			
3681*			
3683*			
3685*			
3689*			
3690*			
3703*			
3706*			
3707*			
3711*			
3712*			
3716*			
3721*			
3725*			
3727*			
3729*			
3730*			
3733*			
3738*			
3742*			
3745*			
3747*			
3748*			
3753*			
3755*			
3756*			
3757*			
3763*			
3765*			
3770*			

No.	NAME	ADDRESS	COMMENTS
3771*	Rudak, George		
3773*			
3774*			
3777*			
3782*			
3784*			
3789*			
3793*			
3801*			
3804*			
3806*			
3808*			
3810*			
3812*			
3813*			
3818*			
3819*			
3821*			
3822*			
3824*			
3829*			
3832*			
3834*			
3838*			
3843*			
3849*			
3856*	Delisle		
3857*			
3871*			
3882*	Melnyk, Frank		
3894*			
3895*			
3896*			
3899*			
3900*			
3909*			
3910*			
3912*	Pollitt, Harry		
3918*			
3930*			
3931*			
3938*			
3941*			
3943*			
3958*			
3961*			
3970*			
3973*			

No.	NAME	ADDRESS	COMMENTS
3977*			
3979*			
3980*	Phillips, Paul		
3985*			
3986*			
3987*			
3995*			
3996*			
4001*			
4011*			
4014*			
4015*			
4018*			
4022*	Goldstick, David		
4029*			
4030*			
4031*			
4032*			
4034*			
4040*			
4048*			
4053*			
4057*			
4059*			
4061*			
4065*			
4066*			
4067*			
4073*			
4075*			
4078*			
4080*			
4088*			
4090*			
4091*			
4094*			
4095*			
4102*			
4103*			
4104*			
4106*			
4107*			
4109*			
4113*			
4116*			
4121*			
4124*			
4130*			

No.	NAME	ADDRESS	COMMENTS
4135*			
4144*			
4145*			
4417*			
4150*			
4153*			
4155*			
4157*			
4160*			
4162*			
4164*			
4165*			
4171*			
4175*			
4176*			
4177*			
4187*			
4189*			
4190*			
4193*			
4195*			
4196*			
4202*			
4204*			
4208*			
4215*			
4216*	Smith, Edward Cecil		
4219*			
4224*			
4226*			
4229*			
4231*			
4233*			
4235*			
4239*			
4242*			
4243*			
4245*			
4250*			
4251*			
4254*			
4265*			
4270*			
4275*	Skarra, Aarne		
4285*			
4289*			
4291*			
4292*			

No.	NAME	ADDRESS	COMMENTS
4297*			
4299*			
4300*			
4301*			
4303*			
4306*			
4319*			
4323*			
4330*			
4331*			
4340*			
4343*			
4347*	Kari, Antti		
4350*			
4355*			
4356*			
4358*			
4361*			
4365*			
4366*			
4369*			
4373*			
4375*			
4376*			
4382*			
4386*			
4388*			
4393*			
4399*			
4402*	Palmer, George H.		
4403*			
4404*			
4405*			
4408*			
4409*			
4415*			
4420*			
4425*			
4427*			
4428*			
4429*			
4430*	McKean, Fergus Adam		
4436*			
4442*			
4443*			
4449*			
4452*			
4457*			

No.	NAME	ADDRESS	COMMENTS
4459*			
4460*			
4462*	Collins, Frederick Allen		
4464*			
4466*			
4467*			
4475*			
4478*			
4487*			
4490*			
4491*			
4492*			
4493*			
4499*			
4500*			
4502*			
4503*			
4507*			
4509*			
4510*			
4511*			
4513*			
4516*			
4517*			
4518*	Bogolowich, Mike		
4524*			
4526*			
4530*			
4532*			
4538*			
4544*			
4545*			
4548*			
4551*			
4552*	Filmore, Roscoe A.		
4555*			
4556*			
4568*			
4570*			
4575*			
4578*			
4580*			
4581*			
4584*			
4587*			
4592*			
4595*			
4596*			

No.	NAME	ADDRESS	COMMENTS
4601*			
4603*			
4605*			
4607*	Miller, Alec		
4609*			
4613*			
4615*			
4617*	Campbell, C.		
4625*			
4626*			
4627*			
4635*			
3647*			
4649*			
4650*			
4658*			
4659*			
4668*			
4674*			
4677*			
4679*			
4680*			
4685*			
4682*			
4694*			
4704*			
4705*			
4707*	Bozeweski, Effan		
4720*			
4723*			
4727*			
4733*			
4738*			
4739*			
4748*			
4752*			
4754*			
4756*			
4757*			
4758*			
4060*			
4761*			
4767*			
4769*			
4770*	Tovanch, Steve		
4771*			
4777*			
4781*			

No.	NAME	ADDRESS	COMMENTS
4785*			
4787*			
4789*			
4790*			
4800*			
4806*			

PART 4:
RCMP SUBJECT FILES REGISTER, 1919-1929

Page 1

No. 175 Classification: Bolsheviki & Agitators

Year 1919

1 SUBVERSIVE ACTIVITIES BY GERMANS GALAHAD DIST. ALTA.

2 ALBERTA FEDERATION OF LABOUR - Conference 7-10, 1919
MEDICINE HAT ALTA.
Transferred to 175/114, 115, 116, 117

3 RUSSIANS DISCHARGED FROM CANADIAN ARMY CANADA
Transferred to 175/3

4 RUSSIANS DISCHARGED FROM CANADIAN ARMY FOR BOLSHEVISM
Transferred to 175/3

5 RUSSIANS DISCHARGED FROM CANADIAN ARMY FOR BOLSHEVISM
(3-4 words blacked out)

6 [entry blacked out]

7 [entry blacked out]

8 [entry blacked out]
(Trans To 175/992)

9 TRADES AND LABOUR COUNCIL WINNIPEG MAN.

10 SOCIAL DEMOCRATIC PARTY - FINNISH SECTION
MAYBERRIES DIST

Page 2

11 [entry blacked out]

12 SOCIALIST PARTY OF CANADA CALGARY ALTA.
(B.F. from 175/64)

13 SOCIALIST PARTY OF CANADA PRINCE GEORGE, B.C.
(Trans. to 175/128)

14 BOLSHEVISM IN WINNIPEG - Investigation re WINNIPEG MAN.
(Trans. to 175/4434)

15 SOCIALIST PARTY OF CANADA - WINNIPEG MAN.
(Trans. to 175/4495)

16 BOLSHEVIST LITERATURE YORKTON SASK.

17 [entry blacked out]

18 [entry blacked out]

19	[1-2 words blacked out] - letter to Calgary Herald	
20	[2-3 words blacked out] Seditious actions of	VANCOUVER B.C.
Page 3		
21	[entry blacked out]	
22	[entry blacked out] (Trans. to 175/123)	
23	BADKA, Bishop of Ukrainian Church	WINNIPEG MAN.
24	[entry blacked out]	
25	[entry blacked out]	
26	[entry blacked out]	
27	ANTI-BOLSHEVIK RIOTING IN JAN 26, 1919	WINNIPEG MAN.
28	[entry blacked out]	
29	[entry blacked out] (Trans. to 175/446)	
30	BOLSHEVIK ACTIVITIES - Situation at coal mines	CARDIFF ALTA.
Page 4		
31	[entry blacked out]	
32	[entry blacked out]	
33	[entry blacked out]	MOOSE JAW SASK.
34	[entry blacked out]	MOOSE JAW SASK.
35	[entry blacked out]	LEADER SASK.
36	[entry blacked out]	LEADER SASK
37	[entry blacked out]	BRITISH COLUMBIA
38	[entry blacked out] (Pt. 2 trans. to 175/4833)	B.C.
39	STAR - Vancouver Paper - first issue [3-4 words blacked out]	VANCOUVER B.C.
40	FINNISH ORGANIZATION OF CANADA	PORT ARTHUR ONT.
Page 5		
41	[entry blacked out]	
42	PROPOSED STRIKE - SHIPYARDS (B.F. from 175/45)	VANCOUVER B.C.
43	BOLSHEVIK ACTIVITIES IN TRADE UNIONS (Trans. to 175/4504) Trans to 175/236	VANCOUVER B.C.
44	SOCIALIST MEETING (Trans. 175/43)	VANCOUVER B.C.
45	LABOUR UNIONS - Membership	VANCOUVER B.C.
46	[entry blacked out]	
47	[entry blacked out]	
48	BOLSHEVIK ACTIVITIES - DETECTIVE AGENCY REPORTS	TORONTO ONT.
49	TRADES & LABOUR COUNCIL	LETHBRIDGE ALTA.
50	SOCIALIST PARTY OF CANADA - Mass meeting at	CALGARY ALTA.

Page 6

51 I.W.W. PROPAGANDA AT DRUMHELLER Complaint [1-2 words blacked out] re Conditions in Mining Area

[3-4 words blacked out]

52 LABOUR CONDITIONS - CROWS NEST, ALTA.

53 CROW'S NEST PASS - Suspected trouble in Alleged Bl.Org. at Hillcrest

54 BOLSHEVIK ACTIVITIES - Suspected agitators and others CROWS NEST,ALTA.

55 [entry blacked out]

(Trans. to 175/1158]

56 FERNIE LEDGER - Re Clippings from

57 RIZZOLI - INTERNATIONAL ORGANIZATIONAL - Suspected trouble FERNIE, B.C.

58 STETTLER DIST SOCIALISM IN SOCIAL ACTIVITIES STETTLER DIST ALTA.

Page 7

59 [2-3 words blacked out] Report re Bolsheviki, Propaganda from

60 [line blacked out] Trans. to 175/2813

Trans. to 175/50

61 Socialist Party of Canada, Attitude of Gt. War Veterans to Alien Enemies, Calgary

Conditions labour - Drumheller, Alta.

62 Socialist Party of Canada, Red Deer Valley Coalfields, Drumheller, Labour Conditions

Bolshevik Activities (Re. Threat against [1-2 words blacked out] Vancouver B.C.

63 [1-2 words blacked out] Re. Anonymous threat against (By Bolsheviki Party)

64 [1-2 words blacked out] Information received from, re Bolsheviki trouble at Prince George B.C.

65 Crows Nest Pass, suspected trouble at [1-2 words blacked out] Russian Bolshevist) Trans. 175/4514

Conditions General - Vegreville

66 Vegreville Dist General Conditions amongst Settlers

Socialist Party of Canada - Edmonton Alta.

67 Knight. J.R. Organizer of Socialist Party of Canada, Edmonton. Transf. to 175/4524.

Bolshevik Activities - Blairmore, Alta.

68 Blairmore, Public Labour Meeting held at on 2-2-19

69 [2-3 words blacked out] Re. Bolsheviki Movement, Trans 175/P7

70 Knight J.R. Trans to 175/P13

71 [2-3 words blacked out] P.O. pro German

72 [entry blacked out]

73 Regina, Bolshevik Organization at [4-5 words blacked out]

Socialist Party of Canada, Calgary, Alta. Trans to 175/50

74 Socialist Party of Canada, Socialist Literature, suspected objectionable matter

Bolshevik Activities - Peace River Dist. Alta.

75 Bolshevists Peace River Dist. B.F. from 175/1030

Labour Conditions - Coughlans Shipyard - Vancouver, B.C.

76 Coughlans Shipyard labour Conditions at Vancouver B.C.
Conditions - Amongst Germans - Daly Creek, Alta.
77 Daly Creek School German language spoken at
78 [2-3 words blacked out] Alleged German propagandists
Page 8
Bolshevik Activities - Eckville, Alta.
79 Gilby, Dist of, Bolsheviki meetings held in Entawan Hall, Bolsheviki Conditions at
80 [entry blacked out]
International Longshoremen Ass'n, Vancouver B.C.
81 Longshoremen at Vancouver reports re continued on 175/4455
Bolshevik Activities - Swift Current Sask.
82 Swift Current Conditions at, re Bolsheviki
Vancouver Sun (Newspaper)
83 Vancouver Sun, Excerpt from re Bolshevist Propaganda
84 Vancouver, General Conditions in Trans. to 175/1732
Revolutionary & Subversive Activities, Fernie, B.C.
85 Fernie, general conditions at re Organizations there
86 Medicine Hat, Unemployment at Transferred to 175/6012 4-11-31
87 Winnipeg, Man Labour Church Service, Winnipeg, Man. trans to 175/4507
Bolshevik Activities - Taber, Alta.
88 Taber, Bolsheviki Conditions at
89 S.S. Monteagle, Russians sailing on, [1-2 words blacked out] Bolshevist
Trans. to 175/304
90 Our Standard, Russian Bolshevik Paper
91 Robert Gosden, Agitator Trans. to 5635
92 [3-4 words blacked out] Re Bolshevism traced to Hun agencies
93 Britannia Mine & Granby. B.C. Austrians & Slavanians at
94 Regina District Bolshevism and General Conditions Trans 175/73
95 [1-2 words blacked out] Cumberland Vancouver Island B.C. Suspect
Trans. to 175/5575
96 [4-5 words blacked out] Possible Disturbances by Bolshevists
97 Mountain Park Mines Alleged Anarchists at [5-6 words blacked out]
Trans to 175/24
Page 9
98 Broule Mines [1 word blacked out] alleged anarchist at
Bolshevik Activities in Trades & Labour Council - Regina Sask.
99 Regina, labour meetings held at [3-4 words blacked out]
100 [1 word blacked out]Rly mail clerk Bolshevist
Great War Veterans Ass'n - Winnipeg Man. Trans. to 175/130
101 Gt. War Veterans Association Wpg Returned soldiers Wpg attitude to alien enemies
Bolshevik Activities - Bellevue Alta.
102 Suspected trouble in Crows Nest Pass Bolsheviki activity at Bellevue Alta.
103 Socialist Party of Canada, Calgary, meeting of socialists in Calgary 4-2- 19

104 " " " " " , Russian Jews Calgary
105 " " " " " , Edmonton Coal Field
106 " " " " " , Socialist Meeting at Calgary 7-2-19, Trans. to 175/103
107 Arms Ammunition explosives Calgary
108 " " " Regina
Bolshevik Activities in Trade Unions - Saskatoon Dist. Sask.
109 Labour and other organizations 1 report from Supt. West
Anarchist Literature - Saskatoon, Sask.
110 Possible Disturbances by Bolshevists re [3-4 words blacked out]
111 Arms ammunition explosives, Edmonton Trans 175/151
112 [1 word blacked out] suspected Bolshevist
Bolshevik Activities - Fort William, Ont.
113 Ft. William Dist, Bolshevism general report Trans. to 175/1433
B.F. from 175/406
114 [2-3 words blacked out] Discharged C.E.F. Russian suspected Bolshevist
115 [2-3 words blacked out] " " " trans. to 175/305
116 [2-3 words blacked out] " " "
117 [2-3 words blacked out] " " "
Page 10
117 [1-2 words blacked out] Dischargd C.E.F. Russian, suspected Bolshevist.
118 [1-2 words blacked out] " " " "
119 [1-2 words blacked out] " " " "
Bolsheviki Activities - Calgary Alta.
120 Calgary, Bolsheviki Organizations at (Transferred to 175/3831)
121 Arms, Ammunition & Explosives, Maple Creek
122 Conditions unrest, Maple Creek, Sask.
123 Drumheller Bolsheviki Organizations at
Trans. 175/4397
124 Socialist Party of Canada, Calgary, mass meeting of held at Re. [word blacked out] agitator
125 [2-3 words blacked out] suspected Bolshevism
126 [4-5 words blacked out] re slanderous statement
127 [word blacked out] Drumheller, suspect. I.W.W. Trans. 175/P60
Bolshevik Activities - Winnipeg, Man.
128 Winnipeg, Dist. Bolshevism in Trans. to 175/356
Bolshevik Activities. Lake Isle, Alta.
129 Lake Isle Bolshevism at
130 Gt. War Veterans Asoc'n & Rtd. Soldiers re Vocational Schools, Wpg.
Bolshevik Activities - Edmonton, Alta.
131 Edmonton, Bolsheviki conditions at
132 Soviet Govt. Agents at Yokohama
133 [word blacked out] socialist at Prince Rupert Trans. to 175/P-112
134 [word blacked out] " " " Trans. to 175/P/1648

Page 11

135 [word blacked out] Socialist at Prince Rupert Trans. to 175/P???

136 [word blacked out] " " "

137 [1-2 words blacked out] Sointula, B.C. - Bolsheviki Literature Trans. to 175/2803

138 Winnipeg Dist Bolshevism in. Re Ruthenian Quarter Million Dollars Fund.
Canadian Ruthenian Weekly paper Pub Winnipeg, Man.

139 " " " Canadian Ruthenian-Bishop Budka's Weekly Organ

140 " " " Trans. to 175/140A

140A Social Democratic Club Winnipeg, Man B.F. from 175/140
Industrial Workers of the World Vancouver

141 Vancouver List of I.W.W. members and suspects at (Trans. to 175/4860)

142 [4-5 words blacked out] Bolshi. Conditions Taber Trans to (unreadable)

143 [1-2 words blacked out] alleged agitator, Bolshevik conditions Taber

144 [1-2 words blacked out] Bolsheviki tendencies Trans. to 175/P13

145 Crows Nest Pass suspected agitato & others. [1-2 words blacked out]
Russ Bolshevik

146 " " " " " " . [1-2 words blacked out] "
"

147 Arms, ammunition & explosives Blairmore & Crows Nest Pass
(Transferred to 175/316)

148 " " " Vancouver, Dist.

149 [2-3 words blacked out] Alleged Misappropriation of Patriotic Funds
Trans. to 175/P/35

150 B.F. 175/ 4791 Labour Conditions (amongst mines at Brule Mines) Brule Alta.

151 Arms, Ammunition & explosives, Edmonton, Brule, Jasper.

152 Souris Coal Mining Area, conditions at re Bolshevism

153 [2-3 words blacked out] Pro German [2-3 words blacked out]

Page 12

Bolshevik Activities - Hague, Hepburn, Waldham, Laird, Rosthern, Sask.

154 Patrol to Hague, Hepburn, Waldham, Laird, Rosthern re Bolshevism.
Convention - Sask. Grain Growers. Regina, Sask.

155 Sask. Grain Growers Convention [1-2 words blacked out] pro German.

156 [1-2 words blacked out] agitator Labour Church Services, Winnipeg.
Trans. to 175/P44

157 [1-2 words blacked out] Scientific Socialist Labour Church Services, Winnipeg.
Trans to 175/P1

158 Hague, Alleged Bolshevism at Trans to 175/154

159 [entry blacked out]

160 U.M.W. of A. 16th Annual Convention of District 18 (17-2-19) Calgary, Alta.
Conditions Amongst Foreigners (Preachers & Newspaper Editors)
Regina, Saskatchewan

161 Foreign Preachers and editors

162 [2-3 words blacked out] Member of U.M.W. of A.

163 Arms Ammunition & Explosives Pocahontas Detach

164 Alleged Pro German Dundern
Bolshevik Activities, Medicine Hat. Alta.
165 Medicine Hat possible disturbances by Bolshevists
166 [word blacked out] alleged Bolshevist
Socialist Party of Canada, Medicine Hat
167 Red Revolutionists Society Medicine Hat
168 Crows Nest Pass. Suspected trouble in, [4 words blacked out] [words blacked out] Ukrainian Bolshevist. Trans to 175/7648.
169 [2-3 words blacked out] Watson suspected of expressing pro German remarks.
170 Bolsheviki Conditions Lembergen and Beaver Hill
171 [1-2 words blacked out] I.W.W. organizer
Vancouver, B.C. formerly U.S.A.
172 [1-2 words blacked out] Bolsheviki agitator

Page 13

173 [2-3 words blacked out] alleged Bolshevist
174 Crows Nest Pass, suspected trouble in, alleged organizer at Coleman Alta. Trans. to 175/354
175 [2-3 words blacked out] suspected Bolshevist
176 [word blacked out] suspect
177 Bolshevism in Winnipeg Dist. Soc. Democratic Club, [word blacked out] Bolshevist leader Trans. 175/5483
178 [2-3 words blacked out] agitators, Brule Mines - Trans. to 175/P28
179 [2-3 words blacked out] agitator & vendor of Socialistic Papers
180 [2-3 words blacked out] agitator
181 [2-3 words blacked out] alleged seditious utterances Trans. to 175/P15
182 [2-3 words blacked out] bolshevist utterances
Bolshevik Activities - Lethbridge, Alta.
183 Lethbridge Bolshevist conditions at
184 [2-3 words blacked out] of Mossbank, Unpatriotic utterances
185 Leaders Sask Arms Ammunitions & Explosives at
186 Herbert, Sask alleged rioting to take place at of Veterans

Notes nos. 187, 188 not used.

189 Western Labour News Copies of 177/4
Continued on 175/4434
190 The Socialist Revolutionary Party of Canada Local #3 Winnipeg Trans. to 175/4434
191 Printing Offices in Winnipeg, Man - key to
192 [2-3 words blacked out] complaint against
193 arms ammunition & explosives, Herbert Sask
194 " " Battleford Sub-Division

Page 14

Transferred to 175 P/71
195 [1-2 words blacked out] Bolshevist suspected trouble in C.N. Pass see Agitators and others
196 [2-3 words blacked out] " " " " " Trans. to 175/P??

197 [1-2 words blacked out] Complaint of alleged violation of Consolidated

198 Soviets at Work, Publication
(B.F. 175/2008 & 175/2123 & 175/2571)

199 General Conditions West Kootenay Dist., B.C.

200 Peace River, arms ammunition explosives

201 [2-3 words blacked out] Sixteenth Annual Conv. of Dist 18 U.M.W. of A.
Trans to 175/P73

202 [1-2 words blacked out] alleged agitator

203 [2-3 words blacked out] of the District Ledger Fernie B.C.
Bolshevik Activities - Hague, Alta.

204 Alleged Bolshevism at Hague (Bierbum - alleged Bolsheviki tendencies)
[2-3 words blacked out] New Norway, Alta.

205 [3-4 words blacked out] suspected agitator (New Norway)

206 Budka, Bishop and his adherents. Winnipeg, Man. Trans to 175/P23

207 Manitoba Trustees Association (Convention)
The Red Flag - (Publication)

208 The Red Flag Censoring of
[3-4 words blacked out] Regina Sask.

209 [3-4 words blacked out] Railway Mail Clerk alleged Bolshevist
Correspondence transf. to 175/P99

210 [1-2 words blacked out] of Regina extreme socialist [1-2 words blacked out]
Rly mail clerk alleged Bolshevist

211 [2-3 words blacked out] of New York - I.W.W. Bolshevist
Disturbance Expected (Map of Dist.)

212 Crows Nest Pass suspected trouble in re map of district Crows Nest Pass, Alberta

213 [1-2 words blacked out] Re distributing the "Soviet"
[1-2 words blacked out] Fernie, B.C.

214 Crows Nest Pass suspected trouble in suspected agitators & others
[1-2 words blacked out]
trans. to 175/P45 Socialist agitator

Page 15

Saskatoon, Sask.

215 [2-3 words blacked out] alleged Bible Students Assoc. propagandist
[3-4 words blacked out] Winnipeg Man.

216 [1-2 words blacked out] Russian Editor - meeting of Trades & Labour Council
Winnipeg - Transf. to 175/P167
[1-2 words blacked out] Winnipeg Man.

217 [2-3 words blacked out] Circulator of Literuare
[1-2 words blacked out] Fernie B.C.

218 Crows Nest Pass suspected trouble in suspected agitator & others [1-2 words blacked out] Fernie Russian Bolshevist
[word blacked out] Winnipeg, Manitoba

219 [word blacked out] Bolshevist Bolshevism in Wpg District

220 [1-2 words blacked out] " " "

221 [3-4 words blacked out] - Bolshevist, Bolshevism in Wpg District
222 [1-2 words blacked out] " " "
Bolshevik Activities
223 Bolsheviki, Gull Lake, Shaunavan and East End.
224 Gull Lake & Shaunavan Arms Ammunition Explosives
Bolshevik Activities
225 Bolsheviki Meetings at Coleman & Fernie
226 Bienfait & District Mines at Particulars of
Foreigners employed at Imperial Oil Co. Regina, Sask.
227 Regina Imperial Oil Works Employment of Foreigners at (Trans. to 175/4548)
[1-2 words blacked out] Winnipeg, Man.
228 [1-2 words blacked out] Bolshevist Re Bolshevism in Wpg Dist Trans. to ???
B.F. from 175/1276
229 Ft. William Dist Re Socialist Literature in B.F. from 175/1729
Russelite Movement, Saskatoon, Sask.
230 Battleford Dist Complaint of [4-5 words blacked out] Battleford Socialist tendencies [word blacked out] NBattleford)
231 Arms Ammunition Explosives Lethbridge, Taber Districts
232 " " " Irvine District Transferred 175/233
233 " " " Medicine Hat District
Mapping of Coal Mining Area - Drumheller, Alta.
234 Drumheller Dist Map of Coal Mines
Page 16
Coal Mines - Maps of
235 Edmonton Dist Map of Coal Mines
Socialist Party of Canada, Vancouver, B.C.
236 Socialists Meeting Vancouver, B.C. "Empress Theatre" (Trans. to 175/4504)

Lumber Workers Industrial Union [3-4 words blacked out]
237 B.C. Loggers Camp Workers Union (61 Cordova St. Vancouver [6-7 words blacked out]
Ukrainian Society, Mundare, Alta.
238 CONCERT of Ukrainian Society held at Mundare Dist
239 Russian Newspaper from Vancouver, B.C. Golos Truzenika (Voice of the Worker) Trans. 177/393)
240 [1-2 words blacked out] Bolshevisk [1-2 words blacked out] Edmonton, Alta.
Trans. to 175/P/657
241 [2-3 words blacked out] " Trans to 175/P/646
242 [1-2 words blacked out] suspect
Conditions Labour at Hedley Shaw Milling Co. Ltd. Medicine Hat, Alta.
243 Hedley Shaw Milling Co. Ltd. Medicine Hat. Threatened Labour Trouble at
244 Federated Labour Party, Vancouver, B.C. B.F. from 175/273
Conditions Amongst Foreigners
245 Vermillion & Manville Dist Conditions amongst settlers

246 [word blacked out] suspect
247 [1-2 words blacked out] suspect Bolsheviki Winnipeg District [1-2 words blacked out]
[2-3 words blacked out] Winnipeg Man.
248 [word blacked out] staff " " Trans. to 175/P/465
249 [word blacked out] (Bolshevism) Inserted in File 321.
Jewish Young Labor League, Wpg Man.
250 Young Labour League
251 [word blacked out] Railway Mail Clerk Alleged Bolshevist
252 [word blacked out] suspect [word blacked out] Rail Mail Clerk alleged Bolshevist 175/P/100
253 [2-3 words blacked out] suspect Trans to 175/282
Bolshevik Activities - Coleville Dist Sask
254 Coleville Dist Bolshevisim in the
255 Russian Labour Union [word blacked out] Leader trans. to 175/P/243

Page 17

256 Socialist Party Local No 1 Vancouver transferred 175/236 (Trans to 175/4504)
257 Arms ammunition & explosives Abbey, Sask
258 [word blacked out] Purchase of Army by
Conditions Amongst
259 Finlanders Vancouver
260 [1-2 words blacked out] Suspected Bolshevists Transferred to 175P/526
Bolshevist Activities - Coalhurst, Alta.
261 Bolsheviki Conditions at Coalhurst
262 Arms ammunition explosives Calgary District Transferred 175/107
263 [word blacked out] suspected agitators Transferred to 175/205
264 [1-2 words blacked out] agitator trans to. 175/P/38
265 [1-2 words blacked out] alleged Bolshevists
266 [3-4 words blacked out] Bolshevist agitator
267 Arms ammunition and explosives Victoria & Esquimalt, B.C.
268 Sabotage in Mining Districts Possibilities of
Ex-soldiers and Sailors Labour Council of Canada Lethbridge Dist. Alta.
269 Soldiers & Sailors Labor Party of Canada, Canadian National Union of Ex-Servicemen (CNUX)
270 Women, Decree Socializing Women in Saratov, Russia
271 Vancouver, Shipyards Aliens employed at
272 Condition amongst Foreigner Prince Albert Alta.
273 Federated Labour Party [word blacked out] agitator - Trans. to 175/244
274 Russian Literature from Vancouver
275 Russian Workers Union Vancouver Trans. to 175/851

Page 19

276 [word blacked out] Bolshevist
278 [entry blacked out]
277 [1-2 words blacked out] Bolshevist Trans. to 175/P/128

279 [word blacked out] agitator

280 9th annual convention B.C. Federation of Labour, Calgary 15-3-19
Albert Gill 175/280 (2) Trans to 175/P286

281 Bol Organization Drumheller [word blacked out] agitator Trans 175/P162

282 [1-2 words blacked out] alleged Bolsheviki

283 [1-2 words blacked out] Trans. to 175/P14

284 Mines & other industries Foreigners employed at D Div Winnipeg Dist

285 " " " " " K Lethbridge Dist

[1-2 words blacked out] Michel B.C.

286 Crows Nest Pass suspected trouble in suspects agitators & others [2-3 words blacked out]

287 Mines & other industries foreigners employed at Maple Creek District

288 Interprovincial Labor Convention Calgary District

289 [word blacked out] Wpg of Simpson-Hepworth Co - suspect Inserted in File 321
Trans. to 175/P/433

290 Appeal to Reason Vancouver Trans. to 175/347

291 Mines & other Industries foreigners employed at Edmonton District G Division

292 [word blacked out] I.W.W. Trans. 175/P/532

293 The Comrade Organ of Comrades of the Great War. Vancouver, B.C.

294 [1-2 words blacked out] suspect [word blacked out] Mail Clerk

295 [1-2 words blacked out] " " " " Trans. to 175/P/ 425

Page 19

296 [1-2 words blacked out] to Commissioner

297 [word blacked out] Prince George District Conditions General Trans. to 175/4520

298 Mines & Other Industries Foreigners employed at E Division Vancouver

299 [1-2 words blacked out] address by at Vancouver 9-3-19 Trans. to 175/P15

Bolshevik Activities U.S.A.

300 Bolsheviki in U.S.A.

301 The Finnish Socialist Organization Port Arthur see File 175/40

302 Finnish Organization of Canada General File Trans. to 175/40

[2-3 words blacked out]

303 Regina Dist. Bolshevism in Meeting at Y.M.C.A. address [1-2 words blacked out]
Trans. to 175/P3??

Literature - Banned - Received by Aliens British Columbia

304 Vernon District Banned literature Russians sailing on S.S. Monteagle [word blacked out] Bolshevist

305 [word blacked out] agitator, Transferred to 175/P81

Bolshevik Activities Amongst Canadian Russian Soldiers.

306 Soldiers Canadian Russian Information from [2-3 words blacked out] The Russian People Winnipeg, Man.

Conditions Labour (Western Canada)

307 Western Canada Labour Unrest in [2-3 words blacked out]

Bolshevik activities Canada General

308 Bolshevism General File Trans. to 175/929

309 Arms ammunition & explosives Shackleton, Forres & Estuary

310 Mines & other Industries Foreigners employed at Cities of Calgary Banff & Canmora.

311 [2-3 words blacked out] East End Exchange, Calgary theft of guns & ammunition from East End Exchange.

Revolutionary & Subversive Activities - Diamond City, Alta.

312 Diamond City Alta Revolutionary Propaganda at

Federated Labour Party

313 Federated Labour Party Victoria Meetings Held under auspices of

314 [word blacked out] Socialist

315 [word blacked out] suspect. Trans. to 175/P4640?

Page 20

(B.F. 175/148)

Arms, Ammunition & Explosives, Vancouver District, B.C.

316 High Explosives extracted from Railway Goods Wagons en route Vancouver consigned to Imperial Govt.

317 "The Soviet" General File

318 The "red Flag" " " Vancouver, B.C.

319* The One Big U ion. (Main File). (This file contains information regarding the O.B.U. which covers the general organization, origin, aims and method of dealing with same etc., and not dealing with our particular district or person.) Canada Generally (Trans. to 175/4498

320 [1-2 words blacked out] suspect Brule, Alta.

321 No. 50's reports re General Conditions Wpg. Man. B.F. 175/4732 & 175/3596

322 [word blacked out] alleged Bolshevist, Saskatoon, Sask.

FOREIGNERS EMPLOYED IN MINES & OTHER INDUSTRIES, WINNIPEG, MAN.

323 Mines & Other Industries Foreigners employed at Winnipeg Dis Trans. 175/284

324 " " " " " Ft. William & Pt Arthur Dist

325 [1-2 words blacked out] (Wpg) Representing Womens Labour League of Winnipeg, Man Trans. 175/527??

GREAT WAR VETERANS ASSOCIATION - WINNIPEG, MAN.

326 Gt. War Veterans & Returned Soldiers Winnipeg branch Trans. to 175/130

CITIZENS PROTECTIVE ASSOCIATION - WINNIPEG, MAN.

327 Bolshevism in Winnipeg Dist Re Citizens Protective Association

328 [word blacked out] complaint of McLeod Valley, Alta.

BOLSHEVIST ACTIVITIES - YUKON TERRITORY

329 Yukon Territory Re possible disturbance by Bolshevist Trans. to 175/370

330 [1-2 words blacked out] agitator Stillwater, B.C.

331 [1-2 words blacked out] agitator Stillwater, B.C.

332 [word blacked out] agitator & alleged Draft Evader Stillwater, B.C.

333 [3-4 words blacked out] Prohibited Publications in Possession of WINNIPEG, Man.

334 [1-2 words blacked out] " " " WINNIPEG, Man.

Page 21

335 [1-2 words blacked out] alleged Bolshevist Edmonton, Alta.

336 Ukrainian Labour News Bolshevist Newspaper Trans. to 177/6 vol. 8

337 Svoboda, Prohibited Newspaper

ONE BIG UNION - Crows Nest Pass Dist., Alta.

338 Blairmore, Hillcrest, Bellevue, Coleman, Conditions at Trans. to 175/360

339 [1-2 words blacked out] suspected agitator Vancouver, B.C.

340 [1-2 words blacked out] Distributing Bolshevist Literature Trans. to 175P/321 (Prince George, B.C.)

CONDITIONS LABOUR - WAYNE ALTA.

341 Peerless Mine, Wayne - Conditions in the Drumheller Coal Field Trans. to 175/7563

342 Trades & Labour Council, Calgary, Alta. (Meetings of) [3-4 words blacked out]

REVOLUTIONARY ORGANIZATIONS - VANCOUVER B.C.

343 Revolutionary Parties, Vancouver

[word blacked out] Winnipeg, Man.

344 Socialist Party of Canada [1-2 words blacked out] Socialist Trans. to 175P/77

345 Arms, Ammunition & Explosives, MacLeod Sub Div.

GRANBY CONSOLIDATED MINING, SMELTING & POWER CO. - CONDITIONS LABOUR AT - ANYOX, B.C.

346 The Granby Milling & Smelting Co. Anyox, B.C. (B.F. 175/7473)

347 Young Jewish Labour League (Meeting of) Winnipeg, Man.

Conditions Amongst Japanese (1919)

348 Japanese Situation 1919 BRITISH COLUMBIA

LITERATURE, DISSEMINATION OF - YMIR, B.C.

349 Ymir, B.C. Bolsheviki Literature Distributed at

350 Salmon Arm Observer (newspaper, Salmon Arm, B.C.

- Foreigners Employed by -

351 Royal Crown Soap Co. Employment of Foreigners by Winnipeg, Man.

LITERATURE - ANARCHIST - DISSEMINATION OF - WINNIPEG, MAN.

352 Prohibited Publications Winnipeg, Man.

INDUSTRIAL WORKERS OF THE WORLD - Fernie, B.C.

353 Fernie, B.C. I.W.W. Propaganda Trans. to 175/5687

Page 22

(B.F. 175/537)

BOLSHEVIK ACTIVITIES, Crows Nest Pass, B.C.

354 Crows Nest Pass suspected Trouble in, suspected agitators & others, [1-2 words blacked out]

355 " " " [2-3 words blacked out] CROWS NEST PASS [1-2 words blacked out] Russian Bolshevist. Trans. to 175/355

BOLSHEVIK ACTIVITIES, Winnipeg, Man.

356 Winnipeg, Socialist & Bolshevist (B.F. 175/963 & B.F. 175/2065 (B.F. 175/128 & 175/2243 & 175/928)

ONE BIG UNION - Cranbrook, B.C.

357 Press Cuttings, Lethbridge & District

BOLSHEVIK ACTIVITIES IN 11th C.G.R. - Vancouver, B.C.

358 11th C.G.R. Suspected Disloyal Tendencies amongst members of

[3-4 words blacked out]

359 [1-2 words blacked out] suspected organizer of Bolshevism

(B.F. 175/1700) ONE BIG UNION, Crows Nest Pass, B.C. B.F. 175/338, 175/453)

360 Crows Nest Pass, suspected trouble in Re O.B.U. Propaganda Blairmore Alta.

FOREIGNERS EMPLOYED IN MINES & OTHER INDUSTRIES - Drumheller Dist., Alta.

361 Mines & other industries Foreigners Employed at Drumheller

[1-2 words blacked out] Saskatoon Sask.

362 [1-2 words blacked out] Alien Enemy, alleged use of language calculated to cause breach of peace. Vancouver, B.C.

363 [word blacked out] (Austrian suspect) Transferred to 175P/125

Winnipeg, Man.

364 The Canadian Farmer Advertisement of Offensive Weapons {2-3 words blacked out] Calgary, Alta.

365 [word blacked out] suspected agitator & I.W.W.

[1-2 words blacked out] CALGARY, ALTA.

366 [word blacked out] I.W.W. agitator Transferred to 175/P131

Labour Defence League - Vancouver, B.C.

367 Labor Defence Police Force Trans. to 175/858

Vancouver, B.C.

368 [word blacked out] (German suspect)

CHINESE & JAPANESE ARRIVING IN - VANCOUVER, B.C.

369 Vancouver, arrival of asiatics at

BOLSHEVIK ACTIVITIES - Yukon Territory

370 Disturbances possible, by bolshevists in Yukon

BOLSHEVIK ACTIVITIES - DEADMAN'S ISLAND, B.C.

371 Deadman's Island and Vicinity, Rendezvous alleged IWW and Bolsheviki

[2-3 words blacked out] Edmonton, Alta.

372 [4-5 words blacked out] - suspected Bols. agent

[1-2 words blacked out] - Redcliff, Alta.

373 [1-2 words blacked out] Bolshevist Trans to 175/P510.

Page 23

374 Miners Strike at Bankhead, Alta.

375 Arms, Ammunition & Explosives. Re. Storage of Explosives at Plant of Rocky Mountain Cement Co. Trans. 175/P2617

376 [1-2 words blacked out] Bolsheviki Suspect Trans. 175/P2617

377 Deadmans' Island & Vicinity. Rendezvous for I.W.W., Bolsheviki. [1-2 words blacked out] Proh Lit. Trans. 175P/185

378 [1-2 words blacked out] Alleged Bolshevik Agent - Edmonton, Alta.

379 [3-4 words blacked out] Alleged agitator - Edmonton Alta.

[2-3 words blacked out] - Deadmans' Island, B.C.

380 Deadman's Island & Vicinity Rendezvous for I.W.W. [2-3 words blacked out] Agitator

[2-3 words blacked out] - Vancouver, B.C.

381 " " " " " trans. to 175/P138

382 [2-3 words blacked out] Bolsheviki Suspect Trans. to 175/P797
[2-3 words blacked out] - Ottawa, Ont.
383 [word blacked out] Chinese Consul General
384 [word blacked out] Agitator Trans. to 175/P210
[3-4 words blacked out] - Drumheller, Alta.
385* Re John or Bill Fraser " Re. One Big Union 175/P176
386 [1-2 words blacked out] " Trans. to 175/P387
GREAT WAR VETERANS ASSOCIATION - Emerson, Man.
387 G.W.V. Assoc. Emerson, Man.
[1-2 words blacked out] - Lac Du Bonnet, Man.
388 [1-2 words blacked out] Bolshevist.
389 [1-2 words blacked out] Trans to 175/P145
CONDITIONS - GENERALLY, Lac Du Bonnet, Man.
390 Lac Du Bonnet. General Situation in Settlement at
CONDITIONS LABOUR - Trail, B.C.
391 Trail B.C. Conditions at Trans. to 175/4522
[2-3 words blacked out] - Cumberland, B.C.
392* One Big Union Re Joseph Naylor - organizer. Trans. to 175/P89
Page 24
LABOUR CONDITIONS - Cumberland, B.C.
393 Cumberland, B.C. Re. Labour Conditions Trans. to 175/5321
CONDITIONS AMONG DOUKHOBOURS - Grand Forks, B.C.
394 Doukhobours Lands (Bolshevism at Grand Forks)
395 Arms, Ammunitions & Explosives Re Theft of Explosives from Rocky Mtn. Cement Co. plant
[word blacked out] - Blaine Lake, Sask.
396 [word blacked out] Russian, Bolsheviki Agitator
"THE CRITIC" (English Paper) Pub. in Vancouver, B.C.
397 Critic The Published at Vancouver, Eng. paper
[word blacked out] - Deadman's Island, B.C.
398 Deadman's Island and Vicinity Rendezvous for I.W.W. & Bolsheviks
[1-2 words blacked out] I.W.W. Agitator
CONDITIONS RE - MENNONITES AND HUTTERITES - Canada
399 Immigration of Mennonites & Hutterites into Canada
CONFERENCE - ONE BIG UNION - United States of America
400* O.B.U., Re Secret Conference, U.S.A. alleged to have been held in U.S.A. later part of March 1919.
ONE BIG UNION, Coleman, Alta.
401 O.B.U. Propaganda Coleman, Alta. (trans. to 175/500)
CONDITIONS GENERALLY - Victoria, BC
402 Conditions Victoria
403 [1-2 words blacked out] Bolsheviki Suspect Trans. 175/P727
404 [word blacked out] suspect - Squirrel Cove, B.C.

405 [1-2 words blacked out] Alleged Bolshevist - Edmonton, Alta.

BOLSHEVIST ACTIVITIES, Port Arthur & Fort William, Ont.

406 Port Arthur & Fort William Russian Bolshevist Society Trans. to 175/113

SOCIAL DEMOCRATIC SOCIETY - Fort William, Ont.

407 Ukrainian Social Democratic Society in Canada - Ukrainian Radical Society of Fort William

UKRAINIAN RADICAL SOCIETY - Fort William, Ont.

408 " " " " " " [1-2 word blacked out] Member

[2-3 words blacked out] 175/P148)

409 Port Arthur & Fort William Russian Bolshevik Society

Page 25

[4-5 words blacked out] B.F. 175/690 Port Arthur, Ont.

410 Port Arthur & Fort William - Russian Bolsheviki Society [4-5 words blacked out] Trans. to 175/P260

411 " " " - Russian Bolsheviki Society [word blacked out] - Secretary Trans. to 175/147

BOLSHEVIST ACTIVITES, Dauphin, Man.

412 Dauphin Dist. Conditions in

413 Arms, Ammunition & Explosives - Yukon Territory

BOLSHEVIST ACTIVITIES, Yukon, N.W.T.

414 Disturbances, Possible by Bolshevists - Yukon Territory Trans. to 175/370

[1-2 words blacked out] - Deadman's Island, B.C. Trans. 175P/53

415 Deadman's Island & Vicinity - Rendevouz or I.W.W. & Bolshevists [2-3 words blacked out]

416 [2-3 words blacked out] agitator Trans. to 175P/154

417 ----- (entered as [word blacked out]) Travelling without permission, --- file cancelled, no cover in drawer

BOLSHEVIST ACTIVITIES, Deadmans' Island

418 Deadman's Island, Austrian Bolshevists at B.F. 175/371

419 Deadman's Island & Vicinity - Rendezvous for I.W.W. & Bolshevists [2-3 words blacked out] alleged agitator Transferred to 175/P157

420 [2-3 words blacked out] Alleged I.W.W. Trans. to 175P/8

[2-3 words blacked out]

421 [1-2 words blacked out] " " Trans. to 175/P836

422 [1-2 words blacked out] " " " " 175/P399

423 [4-5 words blacked out] suspected Bolshevists

424 Socialist Party of Canada, Winnipeg Trans. to 175/4434

425 [1-2 words blacked out] of Kleczkowska - Suspect Trans. to 175/5419

[1-2 words blacked out] - Winnipeg Manitoba

426 Socialist Party of Canada - Wpg - [1-2 words blacked out] - suspect.

FOREIGNERS EMPLOYED IN MINES AND OTHER INDUSTRIES [scratched out] - Emerson, Dist. Man. Conditions amongst foreigners.

427 Mines & Other Industries. Foreigners employed at Emerson Det.

FOREIGNERS EMPLOYED IN MINES AND OTHER INDUSTRIES - Brandon, Man.

428 " " " " " - Brandon Det.
429 Mennonites in Alberta ([3-4 words blacked out]]
Page 26
430 [3-4 words blacked out] - Agitator Trans. to 175/P197
431 [3-4 words blacked out] Bolshevist & agitator Trans. 175/P177
432 One Big Union Drumheller, See 175/123
REDCLIFF ROLLING MILLS - Conditions Labour at - Lethbridge, Atla.
433 Labour Trouble Redcliff Rolling Mills
FEDERAL WORKERS UNION - Calgary, Alta.
434 One Big Union Re Federal Workers Union
435 [2-3 words blacked out] suspect - Regina, Sask.
436 Manitoba Dist. Arms. Ammunition etc
437 Ex Service Men. Dependants & Relations of Sailors, Soldiers Ass of Victora, B.C.
ONE BIG UNION - Victoria, B.C.
438 "One Big Union Meeting" Pantages Theatre Victoria B.C.
439 [2-3 words blacked out] agitator Trans. 175/P364
440 [2-3 words blacked out] " Vancouver, B.C.
441 [2-3 words blacked out] I.W.W. Trans 175/P599
TRADES AND LABOUR COUNCIL - Saskatoon, Sask.
442 North Saskatchewan Leaders, Organizers Delegates Labour Org.
BOLSHEVIST ACTIVITES [3-4 words blacked out]
443 Saskatoon, C.N.R. Depot. Bolshevik pamphlet dis. at Trans. to 175/4448
[3-4 words blacked out]
444 " " " I.W.W. activities at Trans. to 175/443
445 Winnipeg Dist Bolshevism in. Sale. Lit.
BOLSHEVIST ACTIVITES - Cardiff Dist. Alta.
446 Cardiff Mines Alta Bolsheviki prop situation
447 [2-3 words blacked out] I.W.W. Bolsheviki Agitator Trans. 175/P196
448 [2-3 words blacked out] Comrades of the Great War. " 175P/323
ONE BIG UNION - Winnipeg, Man.
449 One Big Union Manitoba Dist. Transferred to 175/4457 [3-4 words blacked out]
Page 27
450 [2-3 words blacked out] Suspected Bolsheviki Tendencies
451 [2-3 words blacked out] suspect Trans. ???
452 [3-4 words blacked out] suspect
ONE BIG UNION - Crows Nest Pass, Alta.
453 Leaders, Delegates, Organizations & Labour Organizations, Crows Nest Pass.
Trans. to 175/360
454 Socialist Party Fort William Transf. to 175/1001
455 Nowe Zycie (New Life) Polish Organization Bolshevism in Winnipeg District
FEDERAL LABOUR UNION @ FEDERAL WORKER'S UNION - Calgary, Alta.
456 Federal Workers Union Re Federal Labour Union
[2-3 words blacked out] - Lethbridge, Alta.

457 [1-2 words blacked out] Member of Social Democratic Party & Federal Workers Union

458 Russian Socialist Anarchist Party - Vancouver, B.C.

459 [word blacked out] I.W.W. Agitator - Vancouver, B.C.

(b.f. 175/2841) B.F. 175/675)

ONE BIG UNION - Redcliff, Alta. [2 words blacked out]

460 Redcliff Labour Meeting at One Big Union

[4-5 words blacked out] - Lethbridge, Alta.

461 [2-3 words blacked out] agitator

CONDITIONS LABOUR - Yukon Territory [3-4 words blacked out]

462 Yukon Territoy Employed Foreigners Mines ????

463 Ukrainian Radical Society of Fort William [2-3 words blacked out] Trans. to 175/P256 Socialist and agitator Trans. to [2-3 words blacked out]

464 Socialist Party at Ft. Wm. [word blacked out] Soc. Agit. [2-3 words blacked out] 175/P257

465 Russian Bolshevist Society of Ft. William & Pt Arthur Re [1-2 words blacked out] Socialist agitator [2-3 words blacked out] 175/P258

466 Socialist Party of Ft. Wm. [word blacked out] soc agit. Trans. to 175/P[word blacked out] 175/P259

467 One Big Union Bulletin - Calgary Alta.

STRIKE [scratched out] - CIVIC EMPLOYEES UNION - Brandon, Man.

468 Brandon Strike of Civic employees at [scratched out]

469 Socialist Bulletin - Winnipeg, Man.

Page 28

REDCLIFF PRESSED BRICK CO. - Medicine Hat, Alta.

470 Redcliff Pressed Brick Co. Re High Explosives at Plant of Trans 175/P171 [scratched out] [word blacked out]

[2-3 words blacked out] - Calgary, Alta.

471 Leaders, Delegate and Organizers & L.O. Calgary Sub-Dist. Trans 175/P471 - C.B. Young

GREAT WAR VETERANS ASSOCIATION - Vancouver, B.C.

472 Avenue Theatre Meetings G.W.V.A. & Trades & Labour Council Vancouver. Trans. to 175/1109

473 [2-3 words blacked out] Letter. Trans. 175/P1302

474A [2-3 words blacked out] Agitator and Bol. Trans. to 175/4458 (Trans. 175/P1161) [scratched out]

474 One Big Union Northern Saskatchewan

475 Powell River Conditions at Trans. 175/5141

ONE BIG UNION - Port Alberni, B.C.

476 O.B.U. Meeting held at Port Alberni B.C.

477 [1-2 words blacked out] agitator Trans. 175/279

BOLSHEVIST ACTIVITIES - RE FORGED BRITISH NOTES - Canada Generally.

478 Forged Notes British French Currency (Transferred to 175/929)

[2-3 words blacked out] Vancouver B.C.

479 [entry blacked out]

480* Re Edward Morrison, agitator see O.B.U. Trans. 175/P269
481 Socialist Party of Canada in Wpg Re Young Jewish Literary Association
482 Socialist Party of Canada re Russian Progressive Club [word blacked out] Trans. to 175P282
483* O.B.U. Drumheller re Joseph Joffre - agitator Trans. to 175/P156
[1-2 words blacked out]
484* " Re Alex Susnar - organizer trans 175/P27
485* " Re James King - agitator Trans 175/P112 trans. 175/P485
486* " Re Louis Gree - Secty Electrical Workers, Seattle Trans. to 175/4895
487 " Southern Saskatchewan Trans to 175/4506
ONE BIG UNION - Fernie, B.C. Trans. to 175/4630
488 " " " Fernie B.C.
ONE BIG UNION - Bellevue, Alta.
489 " " " Ballevue, Alta. Trans. to 175/4630
Page 29
ONE BIG UNION - Southern Alta.
490 O.B.U. Southern Alberta
ONE BIG UNION - Calgary, Alta. Trans. to 175/4656
491 " Calgary Sub District
ONE BIG UNION - Banff, Bankhead & Canmore, Alta. B.F. 175/1182 & 175/1916
492 " Banff, Bankhead & Canmore
ONE BIG UNION - British Columba (B.F. 175/1906_ (B.F. 175/1690)
493 " British Columbia District
ONE BIG UNION - Prince Rupert, B.C.
494 " Prince Rupert, B.C. Trans. to 175/5019
ONE BIG UNION - Calgary, Alta. Trans. to 175/P36
495* " Re David Ree - organizer
496 " Re Meeting C.P.R. Employees, Calgary Trans. to 175/4656
497* " Re James Marshall - agitator Trans. to 175/P211
498* " Re Yohann Bararuk, alias John Barker - organizer Trans. 175/P85
[1-2 words blacked out] - Bankhead, Alta.
499* " Re Steve Kalina - agitator
ONE BIG UNION - Coleman, Alta.
500 " Re. Russian Mail for Coleman, Alta. (B.F. 175/401) [word blacked out]
ONE BIG UNION - Coalhurst, Alta.
501 " Meeting at Coalhurst
CITY POLICE FORCE - Saskatoon, Sask.
502 Russian on Saskatoon City Police, Bolsheviks
LUTHERAN CHURCH - Suspected Subversive Activites At - Yellow Grass, Sask.
503 Lutheran Church Meetings Yellow Grass School
504 Brandon Trades & Labour Council Trans. to 175/992
505 Revolutionary Age General Fyle
COMMUNIST PARTY - Rocky Mountain House, Alta.
506 Rocky Mountain House Bolsheviki

ARMS, AMMUNITION, & EXPLOSIVES - Ben Nevis Mine, Alta.

507 Ben Nevis Mine High Explosives

508 Fort William Dist Labour Conditions Trans. to 175/4380

STRIKE - [4-5 words blacked out] - Princeton Dist. Alta.

509 Princeton, B.C. Strike at

Page 30

ANTI-GERMAN DEMONSTRATION - Prince George, B.C.

510 Prince George B.C. Anti-Alien Riots at

511 Bolsheviks & Soviet Booklet

ONE BIG UNION - Brandon Man.

512 O.B.U. Brandon Sub District

513 [3-4 words blacked out] suspected agitator Trans 175/P383

ONE BIG UNION - Regina, Sask. Trans. to 175/4506

514 O.B.U. Regina

515 City Police Forces Wages of

INTERNATIONAL BIBLE STUDNETS - Winnipeg, Man.

516 International Bible Students (Steadfast)

LITERATURE - Yiddish

517 Bolshevism in Winnipeg Dist Circulation of Bolshevist Literature printed in Yiddish.

518 [2-3 words blacked out] Socialist Organizer Trans 175/525

519 [3-4 words blacked out] I.W.W.

520 [1-2 words blacked out] agitator Trans 175/318

521 O.B.U. Cumberland B.C. Transferred to 175/4545

522 Nanaimo Labour Conditions Transferred to 175/4521

The WORKER @ CAMP WORKER - Vancouver, B.C.

523 "CampWorker" new publication

[1-2 words blacked out]

524 [entry blacked out] - Vancouver, B.C.

525 [1-2 words blacked out] Socialist & agitator - Fort William, Ont.

THE WORLD - Oakland, Calif. U.S.A.

526 WORLD, The Socialist Newspaper

[2-3 words blacked out] - Winnipeg, Man. Conditions Amongst Ruthermans

527 [2-3 words blacked out] Bolshevism in the Winnipeg District, Man.

528* O.B.U. Nicholas Nickoloeff & Wife - agitators Trans 175/P255

TRADE UNION LEADERS - ALTA.

529 Leaders Organizers Delegates, Labour Orgn. S. Alberta

Page 31

[1-2 words blacked out] - Fort William, Dist. Ont.

530 [1-2 words blacked out] Socialist Lit. in Ft. William District

531 Smith A.E. agitator Trans to A.E. Smith 175/P392

532 Jasper Park conditions of Mines see 175/4962 [3-4 words blacked out]

533 [2-3 words blacked out] Agitator Trans 175/819

534 General Strike Vancouver [5-6 words blacked out]

535 [1-2 words blacked out] agitator Trans. to 175/43
[4-5 words blacked out]
536 [1-2 words blacked out] - Calgary, Alta.
??????? Eagle Hill, P.O. Alta. Suspected Socialist
BOLSHEVIST ACTIVITES - Crows Nest Pass, Alta.
537 Suspected Trouble Crows Nest Pass Corresp. transf. to 175/354
538* O.B.U. E.T. Kingsley - organizer 175/P15
539* O.B.U. J.R. Knight - organizer 175/P13
540 Bolshevist Conditions in Winnipeg Dist. Sale of arms amongst aliens.
[1-2 words blacked out] - Edmonton, Alta.
541* O.B.U. Fred Kroot - alleged agitator
542 O.B.U. [1-2 words blacked out] organizer Trans 174/539
543 Pearsons Magazine Proh. Pub. - New York, U.S.A.
BOLSHEVIST ACTIVITIES - North Battleford, Sask.
544 Bols Conditions in the Battleford Sub-District.
BOLSHEVIK ACTIVITIES - Humboldt, Sask.
545 Humboldt, Bolsheviki, Conditions at
546 Winnipeg, Strike of Civic Employees [4-5 words blacked out]
RUSSIAN PROGRESSIVE CLUB - Winnipeg, Man.
547 Socialist Party of Canada in Winnipeg Re Russian Progressive Club
CONDITIONS AMONGST FOREIGNERS - Janow Dist. Man.
548 Janow Investigation re foreigners in
PRO-GERMAN ACTIVITIES BY MENNONITES - Giroux & St. Anne, Dist., Man.
549 Geroux & St. Anne Dist Conditions at re Pro German attitude of Mennonite Settlers
Page 32
CONDITIONS GENERAL - Poplar Field & Chatfield Dist. Man.
550 Poplar Field & Chatfield Districts, conditions at
551 [1-2 words blacked out] agitator and Bolshevik - Hedley, B.C.
552 [1-2 words blacked out] suspected distrubuter of Bolshevist Literature
Trans to 175/P330

SOCIALIST PARTY OF CANADA - Winnipeg, Man.
553 Socialist P of C Wpg Russian Progressive Club. [1 or 2 words blacked out]
Trans. to 175/4434

554 Russian Consuls in Canada. - Standing of -
555 NO ENTRY THIS NUMBER MISSED.
556 [word blacked out] agitator bolshevist B.C. Loggers & C.W. Union
Trans to 175/5809

BOLSHEVIST ACTIVITIES - Regina, Sask.
557 [word blacked out] Re Bolsheviki conditions at Regina Trans. to 175/73
[2-4 words blacked out] - Winnipeg, Man.
558 [1-2 words blacked out] uttering seditious language
559 Ft. William General Meeting of Russians & Ukrainians Trans. to 175/5534
560 [word blacked out] Socialist & agitator Bols Sec of Ft. Wm and Pt. Arthur
Trans 175/P333

561 [word blacked out] " " "
Trans 175/331
562 [word blacked out] " " "
Trans 175/P327
563 [2-3 words blacked out]" "
Trans 175/P328
COUNCIL OF SOLDIERS AND WORKERS DEPUTIES OF CANADA
564 Soldiers & Workers Deputies of Canada Council of
COMMUNIST PARTY OF CANADA - Canada General
565 Communist Party of Canada Programme of [5-6 words blacked out]
566 [word blacked out] suspect Trans to Conf File 872 C.I.B. File
STRIKE - OF MINERS - Lethbridge, Alta.
567 O.B.U. Possible Strike of miners in Lethbridge.
[1-2 words blacked out] - Winnipeg, Man.
568 [word blacked out] Alleged Bolshevik Sympathizer
LITERATURE - Socialist from UNITED STATES
569 Socialist Literature from the U.S.A.
Page 33
DISTRICT LEDGER - Pub at Fernie, B.C.
570 Fernie Dist. Ledger General File Trans. to 175/1158
571 Nelson Daily News "
Conditions Amongst Ukrainian - Edmonton, Alta.
572 Edmonton Dist Ukrainians in
573 Vancouver City Police Force Trans to S.F. 7461
TRADE UNIONS - Paid Officials In - Vancouver, B.C.
574 Leaders delegates & organizers B.C. District
575 O.B.U. [word blacked out] Organizer Trans 175/P39
576 [1-2 words blacked out] alleged agitator trans 175/320
577 [1-2 words blacked out] suspected Labour Agitator Trans 175/P455
578 [2-3 words blacked out] Silverton Miners Union & G.W.V. Ass'n Trans to 175/P763
579 Comox Logging Co Strike at - Comox, B.C.
BOLSHEVIST ACTIVITIES, The Pas, Man.
580 Pas & Dist Bolsheviki conditions
581 Royal Commission on Industrial Relations
582 [2-3 words blacked out] Bols. Literature Trans. 175/592
583 [word blacked out] Russian agitator Trans 175/P349
Conditions Amongst Hungarians - Bakevar, B.C.
584 Bakevar, Sask agitation amongst Hungarians
BOLSHEVIST ACTIVITES - Moose Jaw, Sask.
585 Moose Jaw Dist Bols in
586 O.B.U. Moose Jaw Dist Trans to 175/4760
ILLEGAL PURCHASE OF DYNAMITE - Cloverdale Dist., B.C.
587 Cloverdale Dist Purchase of Dynamite

ANARCHIST LITERATURE - Entering Canada from U.S.A.

588 Mother Earth, The Blast, Subscribers to, Anarchist Publications

THE REBEL WORKER - Pub. in NEW YORK, U.S.A.

589 The Rebel Worker Revolutionary Organ

Page 34

CONDITIONS LABOUR - Kamploops, B.C.

590 Kamloops Dist Unsettled labour Conditions in

591 The Proletarian Socialist Party of Canadian Winnipeg Trans 177/298

592 The Confederate " " " " Trans 177/314

593 Nordegg " " " " Trans 175/4452

STRIKE - COAL MINERS - Lethbridge, Alta.

594 Threatened General Strike in Dist No. 18 U.M.W. of America (Trans to 175/1212)

595 [word blacked out] Organizer B.C. Loggers Union [1-2 words blacked out] 175/P276

596 [2-3 words blacked out] Alleged Bolshevist [2-3 words blacked out] 175/P479 [1-2 words blacked out]

STRIKE - 1919 - Winnipeg, Man.

597 General Strike Winnipeg - [3-4 words blacked out]

597 supp General Strike - [6-7 words blacked out]

STRIKE - Brandon, Man. [6-7 words blacked out]

598 Brandon sympathetic strike at [4-5 words blacked out]

SOCIALIST BULLETIN - Pub. in Winnipeg, Man.

599 Socialist Bulletin, Distributed at Canora

BOLSHEVISTS ACTIVITIES - Vancouver B.C.

600 Russian Bolshevists in Canada Transferred to 175/3406

601 Esquimalt. H.M.C. Dockyard Soc & Proh publications Trans 175/1445

602 [2-3 words blacked out] Japanese laterly of Vancouver [3-4 words blacked out] [1-2 words blacked out] Vancouver, B.C.

603 [3-4 words blacked out]

604 [1-2 words blacked out] trans to 175/P358

605 [1-2 words blacked out] Russian agitator

606 [1-2 words blacked out] I.W.W. Agitator Trans 175/P359

COMMITTEE ON PUBLIC SAFETY - British Columbia

608 Vancouver & Victoria Proposed Committee of Public Safety

STRIKE - Regina, Sask. [2-3 words blacked out]

607 General Strike Regina [5-6 words blacked out]

609 Workmans & Soldiers Council in Winnipeg

Page 35

MEETING OF THE WAR VETERANS - Winnipeg, Man.

610 Winnipeg Meeting of Veterans & Soldiers

611 [2-3 words blacked out] - agitator

612 [1-2 words blacked out] agitator Trans to 175/4701

613 Coalspur District probability of trouble in the Trans to 175/6812

THE SLAVE OF THE FARM - Pub. in Vancouver, B.C.

614 Socialist Party of Canada ("The Slave of the Farm")
THE WAGE WORKER AND THE FARMER - Winnipeg, Man.
615 " " " "s ("The Wage Workers and Farmer")
616 [2-3 words blacked out] alleged distributer of Prohibited Pamphlets Trans 175/723
627 Ocean Falls, B.C. Labour Situation
618 [1-2 words blacked out] Bolsheviki Finlander Trans 175/P396
619 [1-2 words blacked out] Naksup B.C. alleged Bolsheviki
WOODSWORTH J.S. (Rev.) @ WOODWARD, E.S. - Vancouver, B.C.
620 [word blacked out] agitator Correspondence transf. to 175/P694
[word blacked out] ELEVENTH CANADIAN GARRISON REGIMENT - Vancouver, B.C.
621 Vancouver Conditions in 11th Canadian Garrison Regiment
TRADES AND LABOUR COUNCIL - Vancouver, B.C. [2-3 words blacked out]
622 Vancouver meeting under auspices of the Labour Council 175/4811
STRIKE - PORT ARTHUR SHIPBUILDING CO. - Port Arthur, Ont.
623 Port Arthur The Shipbuilding Strike at [2-3 words blacked out]
624 Regina City Sympathetic Strke in Trans 175/607 [3-4 words blacked out]
625 [1-2 words blacked out] suspect 175/700
626 Port Arthur Workmen's and Soldiers Council
BOLSHEVIST ACTIVITIES - Beausejour, Dist. Man.
627 Bols in the Wpg dist Conditions in Beausejour District.
628 S.P. of C. Winnipeg One [word blacked out] Bols Propagandist Trans to 175/P289
629 Labour Leaders Personal particulars trans 175/P300
Page 36
[word blacked out] - Medicine Hat, Alta.
630 [word blacked out] Bolshevik Organizer
631 [2-3 words blacked out] alleged agitators at Kirkcaldy Trans 175/521
[word blacked out] - Edmonton, Atla.
632 [1-2 words blacked out] alleged Seditious utterances
633 British Columbia Hindus in Trans to 175/586
BOLSHEVIST ACTIVITIES - Bondiss, Alta.
634 [word blacked out] Bolsheviki at. [4-5 words blacked out]
635 [word blacked out] Trade Union Organizer Trans 175/393
STRIKE - By Trades & Labour Council - Edmonton, Alta. [2-3 words blacked out]
636 Edmonton General Strike [3-4 words blacked out]
[2-3 word blacked out] - Calgary, Alta.
637 [word blacked out] Red Socialist organizers and speakers
638 Devil, The publication 177/160
639 [word blacked out] Anarchist Trans to 175P/394
640 [1-2 words blacked out] Alleged agitator Trans 175/P215
641 [1-2 words blacked out] agitator Subsequent Correspondence on 175/5085
BOLSHEVIST ACTIVITES AMONGST RETURNED SOLDIERS - Vancouver, B.C.

642 Bolshevik movement among returned soldiers. Bols'k Prop. in 260 Batt. C.E.F.
[2-3 words blacked out] - Dauphin, Man.
643 [word blacked out] Bolsheviki agitator
[word blacked out] - Vancouver, B.C.
644 [word blacked out] agitator File destroyed 13/2/56
[word blacked out] - Saskatoon, Sask.
645 [word blacked out] Bolshevist Enthusiast
TRADES AND LABOUR COUNCIL - Prince Rupert, B.C.
646 Prince Rupert Trades & Labour Council - Transferred to 175/646?
CONDITIONS AMONGST JAPANESE - British Columbia
647 Japanese Report on [3-4 words blacked out]
648 "Der Courier" alleged Bolshevik Pub Trans to 177/15
[2-3 words blacked out] - Vancouver, B.C.
649 [1-2 words blacked out] Bolsheviki Movement among returned soldiers
Page 37
[1-2 words blacked out] - Vancouver, B.C.
650 [word blacked out] Bolshevist Movement among returned soldiers
651 London Morning Post - Extract "The Devils Desciples A Bolshevik Gospel"
[word blacked out] - Regina, Sask.
652 [word blacked out] Bolshevist
[word blacked out] - Regina, Sask.
653 [entry blacked out]
CENSORSHIP OF TELEGRAMS SENT BY AGITATORS - Canada Generally
654 Telegram, agitators re censoring of
DER PLANDERER - Regina, Sask.
655 Der Planderer German newspaper being supplement to Sask. Courier
Transferred to 175/1177
[[word blacked out] - Winnipeg, Man.
656 [word blacked out] suspect
657 [word blacked out] Sask, suspect
STRIKE - (In Sympathy with Winnipeg General Strike) - Regina, Sask
[1-2 words blacked out]
658 Regina sympathetic strike [3-4 words blacked out]
STRIKE - (In Sympathy with Winnipeg General Strike) - Saskatoon, Sask.
[1-2 words blacked out]
659 Saskatoon - " " [4-5 words blacked out]
660 [word blacked out] Strike Leader & agitator [1-2 words blacked out] 175/757
STRIKE - (In Sympathy with Winnipeg General Strike) - Moose Jaw, Sask.
[2-3 words blacked out]
661 Moose Jaw Sympathetic Strike [4-5 words blacked out]
[word blacked out] Winnipeg, Man.
662 S.P. of C. [word blacked out] Bolshevik agitator
[word blacked out] - Winnipeg, Man.
663 C.P. of C. [word blacked out]

664 [3-4 words blacked out] Socialist & Agitator H.S. org. Trans to 175P/401

665 Ex Soldiers and Sailors Labour Council Trans 175/ 269

666 [word blacked out] Wm agitator Trans to 175P/173

667 [1-2 words blacked out] Russian Jew alleged agitator Trans 175/P402

CONDITIONS LABOUR - Yorkton & Melville, Sask.

668 Yorkton & Melville, Sask Labour Conditions

STRIKE - (In sympathy with Regina and Moose Jaw Strikes) Prince Albert Sask.

669 Prince Albert sympathetic strike [4-5 words blacked out]

Page 38

STRIKE - (In Sympathy with Winnipeg General Strike of 1919) - Calgary, Alta.

670 Calgary, Sympathetic Strike [4-5 words blacked out]

STRIKE - (In Sympathy with Winnipeg General Strike of 1919) - Melville, Sask.

671 Melville " " [4-5 words blacked out]

CONDITIONS LABOUR - North Portal Dist. Sask.

672 North Portal Dist Labour Unrest

ANTI-BOLSHEVIST LITERATURE - Boissevain & Brandon, Man.

673 Boissevain & Brandon Anti Bolshevik Literature in circulation in

STRIKE - (In Sympathy with Winnipeg Strike of 1919) - Medicine Hat
[3 or 4 words blacked out]

674 Medicine Hat sympathetic Strike [4-5 words blacked out]

STRIKE - By One Big Union - Redcliffe, Alta.

675 Redcliffe Strikes at (Trans to 175/460)

[word blacked out] - Goodhue, Sask.

676 [word blacked out] alleged agitator & Socialist Propagandist

[word blacked out] - Preeceville, Sask.

677 [word blacked out] " " " "

678 [entry blacked out] Trans 175/P407

FEDERATED LABOUR PARTY - Prince Rupert, B.C.

679 Prince Rupert, Westholme Theatre Meetings Fed. Labour Party B.C.

680 [word blacked out] I.W.W. Agitator Trans to 175/P502

CONDITIONS LABOUR - Assiniboya Dist. Sask.

681 Assinboya Dist Labour Conditions

CONFERENCE - One Big Union - held at Calgary, Alta. June 4/1919)
Canada General

682 Calgary Labour Conference 4-6-19

683 [1-2 words blacked out] Alleged agitator Trans to 175/P443

CONTROL OF GOVERNMENT TELEGRAMS DURING
WINNIPEG STRIKE 1919

684 Correspondence Telegraphic out of Wpg during strike

STRIKE - (In Sympathy With Winnipeg General Strike of 1919) North [1-2 words blacked out]

685 Battleford Sympathetic Strike [4-5 words blacked out]

STRIKE - (In Sympathy With Winnipeg General Strike of 1919) Biggar, Sask.

686 Biggar " " [4-5 words blacked out]

STRIKE - (In Sympathy with Winnipeg General Strike of 1919) Drumheller, Alta.

687 Drumheller " " [4-5 words blacked out]

BOLSHEVIST ACTIVITIES - Mokomon, Ont.

688 [word blacked out] Socialist & agitator Organizer Trans to 175/P574

BOLSHEVIST ACTIVITIES - Mokomon, Ont.

689 Mokomon, Ont Bolsheviki Propaganda

Page 39

690 [word blacked out] alleged agitator Trans to 175/410

[word blacked out] Lethbridge, Alta.

691 [word blacked out] I.W.W. Organizer & Delegate

[word blacked out] - Calgary, Alta.

692 [word blacked out] Bolshevist

[1-2 words blacked out] - Vonda, Sask.

693 [1-2 words blacked out] Alleged Bolsheviki Propagandist

INDUSTRIAL WORKERS OF THE WORLD (List of Members -1919-)

694 Industrial Workers of the World (Membership List -1919) Sub Act Within 175P/2439

695 [word blacked out] Socialist Trans to 175/5690

696 Shawnigan Lake Dist Labour Conditions [1-2 words blacked out]

STRIKE - (In Sympathy with Winnipeg General Strike of 1919) Humboldt, Sask.

697 Humboldt Sympathetic Strike at [4-5 words blacked out]

CONDITIONS LABOUR - Estevan, Sask [4-5 words blacked out]

698 Estevan Labour Unrest

STRIKE -(Proposed, in Sympathy with Winnipeg General Strike of 1919) - Victoria BC

699 Victoria proposed strike at [4-5 words blacked out]

TRIBUNE - Pub. in Victoria, B.C.

700 Tribune, Semi-weekly Victoria B.C.

AGITATOR WANTED BY U.S.A. AUTHORITIES

701 Agitator Wanted by U.S.A. authorities.

702 [entry blacked out] Trans 175/376

LITERATURE - Undesireable - Canada Generally.

703 Undesirable Lit. [2-3 words blacked out]

STRIKE - (In Sympathy with Winnipeg General Strike of 1919) Prince Albert, Sask.

704 Humbolt Strike Sympathetic Trans to 175/697 (scratched out) [4-5 words blacked out]

TROOP TRAINS FOR - Vancouver, B.C.

705 Vancouver Troop train for

CONDITIONS GENERAL - Vancouver, B.C.

706 Vancouver Social Conditions Transferred to 175/1732

707 British Columbia Federationist Subsequent Correspondence on 175/4484

708 [word blacked out] suspect trans 175/P559

[word blacked out] - Calgary, Alta.

709 [word blacked out] Red Socialist

Page 40

[word blacked out] - Calgary, Alta.

710 [word blacked out] Red Socialist

[word blacked out] - Calgary, Alta.

711 [word blacked out] " "

712 [1-2 words blacked out] Greek suspect Trans to 175P385

713 List of agitators suggestion of deportation 175/1060

714 New Life publication Trans 175/P167

715 [word blacked out] anarchist " to 175/5222

716 [word blacked out] " agitator Trans to 175/423

717 [word blacked out] " " See 175/P1209

718 [word blacked out] " Trans 175//P143

719 [word blacked out] " Trans 175/P105

720 [word blacked out] " Trans 175/P142

BOLSHEVIST ACTIVITIES - Wabastao, Alta.

721 Wabastao, Conditions in

722 [word blacked out] Suspect Trans 175/P427

[word blacked out] - Saskatoon, Sask.

723 [word blacked out] alleged I.W.W. organizer BF 176/616

724 Andrew Dist Conditions in Trans 175/7084

CONDITIONS AMONGST FOREIGNERS - Lenuke Dist. Alta.

725 Lenuke Dist Conditions in

726 New People's Church Brandon subsequent Correspondence on 175/4572

727 Federation of Unions of Russian Workers Humboldt Detch.

728 " " " " Pas " Trans 175/7214

729 " " " " Edmonton "

Page 41

730 [word blacked out] suspected I.W.W. agitator Trans to 175P/507

731 [word blacked out] agitator " 175/567

732 [word blacked out] organizer Ex Soldiers & Sailors Union Trans 175/P130

733 Sailors Union Strike 1920 - Vancouver, B.C. Subsequent Correspondence on 175/5456

@ Federated Seafarers Union

734 [word blacked out] Labor Party Local B.C. Trans to 175/P445

735 [1-2 words blacked out] Longshoreman. P.Rupert Trans 175/P446

736 Prince Rupert. Labour Situation 175/6993

737 Grand Army of Canada - Montreal, Que.

738 Mokomon, Ont Bolshevik Propaganda at Trans to 175/689

739 Patriots Pledge circulated in Victoria, B.C.

FEDERATION OF UNIONS OF RUSSIAN WORKER'S - Saskatoon, Sask.

740 Saskatoon Federation of Unions of Russian Workers

741 [entry blacked out]

742 [word blacked out] suspect [1-2 words blacked out] Trans 175/5047

743 [1-2 words blacked out] Letter from to Hon N.W. Rowell re Bolshevism Trans 175/6865

ALBERTA NON-PARTISAN - Calgary, Alta.

744 Non Partisan, Alta

STRIKE - West Kootenay Light & Power Co. - West Kootenay, B.C.

745 West Kootenay, Strike Light & Power Co.

United Mine Workers of America - Strike (1919) (Dynamiting of Houses)

746 Dynamiting of House Coalhurst Re Dist 18 Strike Coalhurst, Alberta

747 Victoria, re Labour Convention at, June 1919 Trans 175/P468

748 [1-2 words blacked out] agitator and distributer of Socialist Literature Trans to 175/P463

749 Censored telegrams

Page 42

750 [word blacked out] Regina suspect Trans 175/P478

751 [word blacked out] suspect - Winnipeg, Man.

ARMS AMMUNITION AND EXPLOSIVES - Fort William Dist., Ont.

752 Finlanders arms, ammunition & Explosives

[word blacked out] - Calgary, Alta.

753 [word blacked out] Bolshevist

[word blacked out] - Calgary, Alta.

754 [word blacked out] russian anarchist

[word blacked out] Frederick - Calgary, Alta.

755 [word blacked out] agitator Trans. to 175/P283

756 [word blacked out] I.W.W. Trans 175/P744

757 This number not used

CONDITIONS GENERAL - Gibsons Landing, B.C.

758 Gibsons Landing B.C. complaint from

VAPAUS - Sudbury, Ont. [3-4 words blacked out]

759 Vapaus Finnish newspaper Trans. to 177/296

760 [word blacked out] Russian Jew suspect - Lethbridge, Alta.

INDUSTRIAL WORKERS OF THE WORLD - Sub Section Nipigon Dist. Ont.

761 Nipigon Dist, Ont I.W.W. Agitators

762 [word blacked out] Alfred alleged Strike Leader - Winnipeg, Alta.

763 [word blacked out] Agitator - Calgary, Alta.

764 [word blacked out] Labour agitator Trans 175/P490

LITERATURE - Bolshevist - Port Alberni, B.C.

765 Port Alberni Distribution of Bolshevist Literature in

766 Lanuke Dist Conditions in the [word blacked out] Trans 175/P498

[word blacked out] - Lanuke, Alta. [3-4 words blacked out]

767 Lanuke Dist, " " [word blacked out] Transf to. 175P/499

768 [word blacked out] Alleged Bolshevik agitator Trans 175P/420

769 [word blacked out] agitator Regina " 175/P500

Page 43

770 Undesirables

771 [word blacked out] agitator Trans 175/P528

772 [1-2 words blacked out] Dom. Labour Party, Edmonton Trans 175/P705

[word blacked out] - Edmonton, Alta.

773 [word blacked out] I.W.W. Propaganda

GREAT WAR ASSOCIATION - Vancouver, B.C.

774 Campaigners of the Great War Association Transferred to 175/1109

775 [word blacked out] Labour agitator Trans 175/P82

[word blacked out] - Winnipeg, Man.

776 [word blacked out] Bolshevik agitator

777 This number overlooked - no entry

[word blacked out] - Lethbridge, Alta.

778 [word blacked out] Supplying Bolshevik literature

779 [word blacked out] agitator Trans 175/P640

BOLSHEVIST ACTIVITIES - Rabbit Lake Dist., Sask.

780 [word blacked out] Bolshevik Meeting Armadale School House Trans to 175/854

781 Waskan Bolshevik agitator Trans to 175/5557

FEDERATION OF UNIONS OF RUSSIAN WORKERS - Peace River Dist., Alta.

782 Fed. Unions of Russian Workers Peace River

783 [word blacked out] suspect Trans 175/P500

784 [word blacked out] Seditious Conspiracy O.B.U. Organizer See 175/P2364

BOLSHEVIST ACTIVITIES - Brandon, Man.

785 Bolshevik Propaganda Brandon Spl. Duty. Detachment

SOCIALIST PARTY OF CANADA - Victoria, B.C.

786 Socialist Meeting Boilermakers Hall, Victoria Transferred to 175/1159

787 List of Agitators should be interned Trans 175/713

788 [word blacked out] Secretary Ukrainian Temple

[1-2 words blacked out] - Medicine Hat Dist,. Alta.

789 [word blacked out] German agitator Transferred to 175/P1143

Page 44

790 [word blacked out] Trans 175/P174

[word blacked out] - Eckville, Alta.

791 Finlanders at Eckville [word blacked out] Alleged agitator Alta

792 Finlanders at Eckville Alta, [word blacked out] Trans 175/P122

CONVENTION - 2nd Annual Convention - INTERNATIONAL LONGSHOREMAN'S ASSOC.

793 Inter. Longshoremen Assoc etc - Victoria, B.C. B.F. from 175/954

794 [word blacked out] Austrian Rioting at Winnipeg Trans 175/796

795 [word blacked out] " " "

796 [word blacked out] " " " BF 175/794

797 [word blacked out] O.B.U. organizer trans to 175/P-90

798 [word blacked out] Returned Soldier, Bolshevist Trasn 175/73 [3-4 words blacked

out]

799 [word blacked out] organizer B.C. Loggers Union Trans to 175/719

[word blacked out] - Lethbridge, Alta.

800 [word blacked out] agitator of Hardieville

[word blacked out] - Hardieville, Alta.

801 [word blacked out] " "

802 [word blacked out] " "

803 [word blacked out] agitator Trans 175/P570

804 [word blacked out] Oscar Socialist in Possession of Proh Lit. Trans 175/P566

805 [1-2 words blacked out] Bols agitator " " " 175/P566

806 Russian Woman, Saskatoon Sask Trans 175/P1211 [word blacked out]

808 [1-2 words blacked out] suspect Trans 175/P711

807 [word blacked out] agitator Trans 175/P556

Page 45

809 Kamsack Agitator Name Unknown agitator suspect Trans 175/P816 [word blacked out]

FEDERATION OF UNIONS OF RUSSIAN WORKERS - Maple Creek, Sask.

810 Fed of Unions of Russian Workers Maple Creek

[word blacked out] - Wayne, Alta.

811 [1-2 words blacked out] of Wayne Local U.M.W. of A.

812 Strike General

813 I.W.W. Fort Frances. Trans to 175/1904

814 [word blacked out] Labour Agitator Trans 175/P595

815 [word blacked out] alleged agitator Trans 175/P689

816 Agitators Winnipeg (Thiel Dect. Agency [3-4 words blacked out] see 175/889)

817 B.C. Loggers Union Re. Chinese Branch - Vancouver, B.C.

818 Soviet Constitution [4-5 words blacked out]

819 [word blacked out] O.B.U. Organizer, Trail B.C. Trans 175/P607

820 [2-3 words blacked out] Bolshevist Trans 175/P1412

821 [word blacked out] Complaint of re agitators - Mullingar, Sask.

[word blacked out] - Winnipeg, Man.

822 [word blacked out] Business Manager People's Printing Co. File #'s up to 822 taken from ledger R.93

[word blacked out] - Windsor, Ont.

823 [word blacked out] alleged I.W.W. Trans. to 175/P1801

"WESTERN LABOUR NEWS" - Regina, Sask.

824 Western Labour News Distribution of

BOLSHEVIST ACTIVITIES - Gimli, Man.

825 Gimli, Man alleged Bolshevism in

LABOUR CHURCH SERVICE - Fort Rouge, Man.

826 Ft. Rouge Labour Church Service.

827 Economy Guss Greek suspect, Regina Trans 175/P630

[word blacked out] - Vancouver, B.C.

828 [word blacked out] Labour agitator Re Wire Stretching to trip Police Horses in Strike Riot) Transf to 175/4013

829 Soldiers & Sailors Council, Wpg Transf to 175/1069

Page 46

830 [1-2 words blacked out] Undesirable family Trans 175/P597

831 Labour Unions [3-4 words blacked out]

832 [word blacked out] alleged Bolshevist - Rosetown, Sask.

BOLSHEVIST ACTIVITIES - Regina, Sask.

833 Majestic rooming house Trans to 175/73 [3-4 words blacked out] [word blacked out]

834 [word blacked out] Undesirable aliens Tfs 3456 [4-5 words blacked out]

835 [word blacked out] Alleged leakage of Telegraphic News (Re Wpg General Strike 175/P439)

836 [entry blacked out] Trans 175/P9

FINNISH SOCIALIST ACTIVITIES - Barons, Alta.

837 Finnish Socialist at Barons

838 [word blacked out] socialist etc Barons Trans 175/P732

839 [word blacked out] agitator Tfs 626 Trans 175/P626

840 Unknown agitator at Elks Dist. B.C. Trans 175/P48 [word blacked out]

SOCIALIST ACTIVITIES - Sundial, Man.

841 Sundial Farmers alleged Soc. Cooperation with Wpg Strikers

THE SOCIALIST BULLETIN -

842 Soc. Bulletin Distributed Yorkton Dist.

843 [word blacked out] agitator, Regina Transferred to 175/P403

844 [word blacked out] " Calgary Trans 175/P319

845 [word blacked out] " trans to 175/P-93

846 [word blacked out] " Trans 175/P357

847 [word blacked out] " Trans 175/P233

848 [word blacked out] " Trans 175/P325

849 [word blacked out] suspect Trasns to 175P400

Page 47

STRIKE - Sympathetic - HANNA, Alta. [3-4 words blacked out]

850 Sympathetic Strike Calgary meeting at Hanna [3-4 words blacked out]

RUSSIAN WORKERS UNION - Vancouver, B.C. Union of Russian Working Men

851 Re. Russian Workers Union bombs in possession Neketa the Sailor

APPEAL TO REASON - Pub. in Girard Kansas, U.S.A. Trans. to 177/347

852 Rev. Newspapers appeal to reason Dis. Yorkton Dist.

853 Soviet, The Bols & Socialist Literature Trans 175/317

BOLSHEVIST ACTIVITIES - Rabbit Lake Dist., Sask.

854 Bolshevist Meeting Armadale School House Rabbit Lake Dist. B.F. 175/780

STRIKE - Belmont Surf Inlet Mine - Surf Inlet, B.C.

855 Surf Inlet. Strike at Belmont Surf Inlet Mine. B.C.

856 [word blacked out] Literature Search was made under Warrant from Winnipeg handed to Asst. Cmmr Trans 175/P653

857 [word blacked out] " [word blacked out] without covers trans to 175P645

LABOUR DEFENCE LEAGUE - Vancouver B.C.

858 Labour Defence League Prosecution of B.F. from 175/367

859 " " " Fernie. B.C.

SOCIALIST PARTY OF CANADA - Redcliff, Alta.

860 S.P. of Canada Meeting at Redcliff.

861 Wpg Gnl Strike [word blacked out] & possible release of prisoners Trans 175/P1.

862 Montreal, Conditions in [2-3 words blacked out]

863 [word blacked out] alleged I.W.W. trans to 175/261

864 [word blacked out] agitator Trans to 175/P261 Trans to 175P663X

865 [word blacked out] I.W.W. from Banff Trans to 175P696

866 [word blacked out] supposed agitator Taber

867 Winnipeg General Strike [word blacked out] agitator prosecution of Trans 175/P505

868 " " " [word blacked out] Prosecution of Trans 175/P439 see 175/5525

869 " " " [word blacked out] agitator prosecution of Trans to 175/784

Last transfer 175P/12

Page 48

870 Winnipeg General Strike [word blacked out] agitator Prosecution of trans 175/P1

871 " " " Russell. R.B. " " " 175P198

872 " " " Woodsworth or (Woodward) J.S. Agitator Prosecution of Trans 175/P594

873 " " " [word blacked out] Agitator - Prosecution of

874 " " " [word blacked out] Agitator " " Trans 175/P44

875 " " " [word blacked out] Bolshevik " " " 175/P167

876 " " " [word blacked out] agitator " " " 175/P109

877 " " " [word blacked out] Bolshevik Propagandist "

878 " " " [word blacked out] Labour Leader " " Trans 175/P32

879 " " " [word blacked out] agitator " " " 175/P21

880 " " " [word blacked out] Agitator " " " 175/P90

881 " " " [word blacked out] Agitator " " " 175/P817

882 [word blacked out] I.B.S. Leader 175/P638

883 Red Flags at Vancouver, Consignment of

884 [word blacked out] suspect Trans 175/P2228

175/???? 175/1799 BF. 175/1851 - Members - Illegal Entry into Canada [word blacked out]

INDUSTRIAL WORKERS OF THE WORLD

885 Pacific Highway I.W.W. proposed illegal entry into Canada (Sub Act. Within)

886 Regina accosting of R.N.W.M.P.

887 [word blacked out] suspect trans to 175/P698 Trans to 175P698

BOLSHEVIST ACTIVITIES - Hampton Pool Room - Vancouver B.C.

888 Hampton Pool Room Vancouver Bolshevist Resort

889 [1-2 words blacked out] re agitators Winnipeg (Thiel Det. Agency) Trans to 175/950

Page 49

BOLSHEVIST LITERATURE - Wakaw, Sask.

890 [word blacked out] of Wakaw Complaint of re Bolsheviki Literature

891 [word blacked out] considered dangerous Trans to 175P632

892 [entry blacked out]

893 Fed of Unions of Russian Workers. Regina

894 [word blacked out] agitator Trans to 175P209

895 [word blacked out] of Taber Socialist - German 175P694

896 Bolsheviki Newspaper the "Russky Golos" Trans 177/287

897 Ex Soldiers & Sailors Labour Party of Canada Wpg & Dist Branch trans to 175/1069 Corr trans to 175/4013

BOLSHEVIST ACTIVITIES - Saskatchewan

898 Northern Sask alleged Bolshevik organization

899 [word blacked out] of Saskatoon suspect Trans to 175P378

[word blacked out] - 175/900

900 [word blacked out] Bolsheviki organizer

901 [word blacked out] " " - Calgary, Alta.

902 [word blacked out] agitator Trans 175/P35

903 [word blacked out] suspect Trans to 175P531

[1-2 words blacked out] Dauphin, Man.

904 Dauphin Dist Re Conditions in [1-2 words blacked out]

CONDITIONS GENERAL - Sifton & Valley River, Man.

905 Dauphin Dist Re " Re Post Masters at Sifton & Valley River being threatened with violence.

906 One Big Union Calgary [2-3 words blacked out] Trans to 175P584

LABOUR DEFENSE LEAGUE - Alberta

907 Labour Defence Force Southern Alberta [2-3 words blacked out]

908 Vancouver General Strike [word blacked out] agitator 175P697

[2 words blacked out] - Trochu, Alta.

909 [word blacked out] suspect

Page 50

910 Revolution The Mother of the Trans to 175/528

BOLSHEVIST LITERATURE - Yukon Territory

911 Y.T. Socialist Propaganda in the

SOKOLOWSKI, Mike - Winnipeg, Man.

912 Sokolowski, Mike Killed in Winnipeg Riots Inquest on Death of

913 [word blacked out] agitator Trans 175/P19

914 [word blacked out] Trans 175/61

915 Brandon Sympathetic Strike re [1-2 words blacked out] Trans to 175P491

[2-3 words blacked out] - Winnipeg, Man.

916 Wpg Distr Bolshevism in re [2-3 words blacked out] suspect [word blacked out]

917 Wpg Dist Bolshevism in re [1-2 words blacked out] suspect "

[2-3 words blacked out] - Vancouver, B.C.

918 Labour Defence League Vancouver [2-3 words blacked out]

919 [word blacked out] Propagandist Trans to 175/P212

[2-3 words blacked out] - Fort William, Ont.

920 Ft. William Labour Conditions [word blacked out] Member G.W.V.A.

921 Stewart, Charles agitator Winnipeg Transferred to 175/P1812

922 Ex Soldiers & Sailors Labour Party of Canada Winnipeg Branch [word blacked out] Trans. to 175P635

923 " [word blacked out]

924 [word blacked out] I.W.W. Branch I.W.I. Union #500 Trans 175/P643

925 [word blacked out] " Trans 175/P644

926 [word blacked out] alleged agitator Trans 175/P740

927 "Soviet Russia" Newspaper

BOLSHEVIST ACTIVITIES - Winnipeg, Man.

928 Wpg Labour Meeting Re Immigration Act Trans to 175/356

BOLSHEVIST ACTIVITIES - Canada General

929 Canada Gnl. Situation Bolshevism in (B.F. 175/478) (B.F. 175/308)

Page 51

930 Tract A Much Needed Warning

[word blacked out] - Winnipeg, Man.

931 Winnipeg alleged Seditious Conspiracy [word blacked out] witness required in connection with

932 [word blacked out] subject for deportation

933 Wpg Strike Leaders [1-2 words blacked out] Re Search of Premiers of Trans to 175P209

934 [word blacked out] Subject for Deportation Trans to 175/P14

BANOWSKY, Sherrer - Winnipeg, Man.

935 Banowsky, Sherrer Killed in Winnipeg Riot Inquest on

936 [word blacked out] suspect Trans 175/P660

937 [word blacked out] " " 175/P682

938 [word blacked out] " " 175P681

[1-2 words blacked out] - Lethbridge, Alta.

939 [1-2 words blacked out] suspect

940 [word blacked out] Con suspect Trans 175/P658

[word blacked out] - Brandon, Man.

941 Wpg Strike Leaders alleged theft of $225 from resident [word blacked out] Brandon

INDUSTRIAL WORKERS OF THE WORLD - Port Arthur, Ont.

(Trans. to 177/421)

942 I.W.W. Branch Lumber Workers Indus Union #500
Lumber Workers Industrial Union #500

943 [word blacked out] suspect Trans to 175P259

944 [word blacked out] Leader I.W.W. Branch Workers Indus. Union #500
Trans 175/P415

[word blacked out] - [1-2 words blacked out]

945 [word blacked out] suspect

946 O.B.U. Movements Kootenay Country Trans to 175/5084

947 [1-2 words blacked out] Objectionable Literature

948 [1-2 words blacked out] Subject for Deportation Trans to 175/4870

949 Russian Socialist Am. Party [word blacked out] Anarchist Trans to 175P242

Page 52

950 [word blacked out] suspect [word blacked out] report Trans to 175P671

951 [word blacked out] agitator etc Lethbridge Trans 175/101

952 [word blacked out] " Trans 175/P28

953 [word blacked out] suspect " 175/P58

CONVENTION - Second Annual Convention International Longshoremen's Ass'n - Vancouver B.F. to 175/793

954 Second Annual Convention Pacific Coast Dist Council 38 International Longhsoremen Assn. Trans to 175/793 Shipyard Labourers Riggers & fasteners

955 [word blacked out] Socialist & Bolshevist Coalhurst Trans 175P136

[word blacked out] - Regina Sask.

956 [4-5 words blacked out] suspect

957 General Strike of District 18 U.M.W. of A.

958 [entry blacked out] Trans to 175/P262

959 [2-3 words blacked out] suspect Wpg Trans 175P722

960 [word blacked out] alleged agitator Trans 175/P659

SUBVERSIVE LITERATURE DISTRIBUTED - Sydley, B.C.

961 Porter, Bros Lumber Mill reputed

BOLSHEVIST ACTIVITIES - Winnipeg, Man.

962 Ex Soldiers & Sailors Labour Party of Canada [2-3 words blacked out] Tpg. Street Rly Transferred to 175/1069 Transf to 175/4013

963 Bolshevism in Winnipeg District [1-2 words blacked out] Transferred to 175/356]

964 Organizer for the O.B.U. at Redcliff [word blacked out] Trns 175/P284

[word blacked out] - Vancouver, B.C. B.F. 175/1421

965 Ex. Soldiers & Sailors Organizations Vancouver [word blacked out] Secretary

966 [word blacked out] suspect trans to 175/5441

967 July 19th Celebrations Regina

[2-3 words blacked out] - Sifton, Man.

968 Bolshevism in Manitoba District Conditions in Manitoba District [3-4 words blacked out] of Sifton

RUSSIAN COMMUNIST - Seattle, Wash. U.S.A.

969 Russian Communists Meeting at Seattle or Union of Russian Workingmen in Seattle

Page 53

970 Bolsheviki Propaganda Bureau - London, Eng.

971 [1-2 words blacked out] Receiving Bolshevist literature from U.S.

972 [word blacked out] Fissing Editor & Agitator Trans 175/P3138

973 One Big Union Medicine Hat Trans 175/P1812

974 [word blacked out] agitator Trans 175/5724

[word blacked out] - Winnipeg, Man.

975 [word blacked out] alleged suspect under investigation [word blacked out] report

[word blacked out] - Winnipeg, Man.

976 [word blacked out] suspect [word blacked out] report

[word blacked out] - Winnipeg, Man.

977 [word blacked out] " "

FINNISH SOCIALIST ORGANIZATION - Intola, Ont. [2-3 words blacked out]

978 Finnish Celebrations at Intola & District [2-3 words blacked out]

979 Finnish Soc organization Port Arthur Re [word blacked out] socialist & agitator 175P448

980 [word blacked out] Ukrainian agitator see 175/4590

981 [1-2 words blacked out] suspect Trans 175/P683

[word blacked out] - Vancouver, B.C.

982 [word blacked out] Bolshevik [word blacked out]

983 [word blacked out] agitator trans to 175/P-116

984 Arms, ammunition & Explosives Morden Dist.

985 Intercepted cables re Strike Situation - 1919

[word blacked out] - Essondale, B.C.

986 [1-2 words blacked out] letter Gt. Britain Navy Officer.

987 [word blacked out] Socialist & Agitator Trans 175/P677

[word blacked out] - Vermillion, Alta.

988 [word blacked out] organizer Ukrainian Society, Vermillion Trans to 175/P678

LABOUR AGITATORS - Brandon, Man. [2-3 words blacked out]

989 Labour Agitator Brandon [2-3 words blacked out]

Page 54

990 [word blacked out] Socialist Organizer Trans 175/P684 Russian Bolsheviki Society of Port Arthur & Ft. William.

[word blacked out] - Winnipeg, Man.

991 [word blacked out] suspect [word blacked out] report

TRADES AND LABOUR COUNCIL - Winnipeg, Man.

992 Meetings of Trades & Labour Council Brandon Transf. to 175/4589

993 [word blacked out] Arthur suspect - Vancouver, B.C.

Corr. transf to 172

994 Bolshevism in Manitoba Dist Conditions in Dauphin Dist. Re Supposed bribery [3-4 words blacked out] of Sifton.

995 [word blacked out] agitator Trans 175/P379

996 [word blacked out] agitator at Coalhurst Trans to 175P57

997 [word blacked out] suspect Trans 175/P350

998 [word blacked out] Socialist. Socialist Party of Canada Ft. William Branch Trans to 175/5482 to 175P/688

999 [word blacked out] Regina suspect Trans 175/P581

TURNERS WEEKLY - Saskatoon, Sask.

1000 Farmers Weekly, July 12th 1919

SOCIALIST PARTY OF CANADA - Fort William, Ont. (B.F. 175/454)

1001 Social Democratic Party of Ft. William

1002 [word blacked out] organizer of O.B.U. Saskatoon see 175/P393 [4-5 words blacked out]

1003 Riot of G.W.V.A. at Medicine Hat.

RUSSIAN WORKERS UNION - Kamsack, Sask. Union of Russian Working Men @ Union of Russian Workmen

1004 Russian Workers Union Re [1-2 words blacked out]

1005 [word blacked out] suspect Trans 175/P404

1006 [word blacked out] et al Seditious Conspiracy - Winnipeg, Man. [4-5 words blacked out]

[word blacked out] - Fort William, Ont.

1007 [word blacked out] Leader I.W.W. Lumber Workers Industrial Union #500 Trans to 175/P691

(Trans to 177/421)

1008 I.W.W. Literature Port Arthur see also 175/942 from which this originates.

INDUSTRIAL WORKERS OF THE WORLD - Yahk, B.C.

1009 Alleged I.W.W. Organizer Yahk, B.C. (Trans to 175/5718)

Page 55

1010 [word blacked out] Bankhead Sec U.M.W.A. Trans 175P/365

1011 [1-2 words blacked out] Vancouver suspect Trans to 175P518

1012 [word blacked out] agitator trans to 173/P-518

[word blacked out] - Drumheller, Alta.

1013 [word blacked out] Russian. Alleged Anarchist. Drumheller

1014 [1-2 words blacked out] Russian agitator Trasn 175/P701

[word blacked out] - Wayne, Alta.

1015 [word blacked out] Russian German Alleged Anarchist Wayne

[word blacked out] - Lethbridge, Alta.

1016 [word blacked out] Socialist & Agitator

[word blacked out] Winnipeg, Man.

1017 [word blacked out] Travelling for Ukrainian Voice Publishing Co of Winnipeg.

FEDERATION OF UNIONS OF RUSSIAN WORKERS - Battleford, Sask.

1018 Federation of Unions of Russian Workers C.I.B. No 51. Batteford Sub-District [words blacked out]

STRIKE LEADERS - Prosecution of 1919 - Manitoba, Dist. [2-3 words blacked out]

1019 Prosecution of Strike Leaders. Wpg. Exect'n of Search Warrant [1-2 words blacked out]

STRIKE LEADERS - Prosecution of 1919 - South Saskatchewan [1-2 words blacked out]

1020 " " " " "

STRIKE LEADERS - Prosecution of 1919 - North Saskatchewan [3-4 words blacked out]

1021 " " " " "

STRIKE LEADERS - Prosecution of 1919 - South Alberta [3-4 words blacked out]

1022 " " " [2-3 words blacked out] S. Alta Dist.

STRIKE LEADERS - Prosecution of 1919 - Northern Alberta
[3-4 words blacked out]

1023 " " " " [1-2 words blacked out] N. Alta Dist

STRIKE LEADERS - Prosecution of 1919 - British Columbia
[2-3 words blacked out]

1024 " " " [4-5 words blacked out] B.C. Dist

STRIKE LEADERS - Prosecution of 1919 - Canada Generally
[3-4 words blacked out]

1025 " " " " " General

1026 [1-2 words blacked out] Russian Agitator

1027 [word blacked out] Socialistic School Teacher.

[words blacked out] - Vancouver, B.C.

1028 [word blacked out] Alleged Agitator

BOLSHEVIST PROPAGANDA (List of persons prosecuted re:) Canada Generally.

1029 Bolsheviki Propaganda. List of Parties Prosecuted in connection with

Page 56

B.F. from 175/2672

1030 [word blacked out] agitator Trans 175P/75.

1031 [word blacked out] agitator Trans 175/P118

TRADES & LABOUR COUNCIL (Bolshevist Activities In) - Vancouver, B.C.

1032 Monies donated. Trades & Labour Council Vancouver for Strike purposes [2-3 words blacked out]

[word blacked out] - Vancouver, B.C.

1033 [word blacked out] suspect

[word blacked out] - Vancouver, B.C.

1034 [word blacked out] suspect

SVENSKA CANADA TIDNINGEN - (Newspaper) - Winnipeg, Man.

1035 Svenska Canada Tidnibgen Swedish Red Newspaper.

"UKRAINIA" (Weekly newspaper) - Winnipeg, Man.

1036 Ukrainian national Weekly Paper "Ukraina"

BOLSHEVIST ACTIVITIES - Gimli, Man. B.F. from 175/825

1037 Bolshevism in Gimli District Re Red Flag at Gimli Manitoba on Old Queen's Cottage

1038 [1-2 words blacked out] Russian suspect Trans to 175P1441

1039 [entry blacked out] Trans to 175/P1436

B.F. from 175/1819

1040 Canadian Ukrainian 18/7/19 Trans to 177/288

1041 [word blacked out] Papers. Ottawa Morning Journal re Report of Speech of
Trans to 175P1462

1042 [word blacked out] Agitator - Trans. to 175/P624

[word blacked out] - Weyburn, Sask.

1043 [word blacked out] Using alleged seditious words suspect

1044 [1-2 words blacked out] alleged sedition - Maple Creek, Sask.

1045 "The New Republic" "Book". Trans to 177/123

1046 [word blacked out] agitator (Bolshevik) Trans to 175P223

1047 [word blacked out] agitator (Bolshevik) Trans to 175P223

1048 Russians in possession of passports supposed to be in Canada still

1049 [word blacked out] agitator (Bolshevist) Trans to 175P223

Page 57

(B.F. 175/1106)

DEFENCE COMMITEE - Winnipeg, Man.

1050 Defence Committee Wpg Circular issued by

1051 Ukrainian Greek Catholic Association Shewichenko Meetings Edmonton Trans to 175/5140

[word blacked out] - Vancouver, B.C.

1052 [word blacked out] President Khaki Labour Club

1053 [word blacked out] Bolshevik Trans to 175P2257

1054 Bolshevism. Wpg District Re [word blacked out] Trans 175/P751

1055 [1-2 words blacked out] subject for deportation - Edmonton, Alta.

LIST OF UNDESIRABLES FOR DEPORTATION 1919 "A" DIST. - SASKATCHEWAN

1056 Undesirables. List for Deportation A Dist.

UNDESIRABLES FOR DEPORTATION "F" DIST. 1919 - SASKATCHEWAN

1057 " " " F "

LIST OF UNDESIRABLES FOR DEPORTATION "K" DIST - 1919 - BRITISH COLUMBIA

1058 " " " K "

LIST OF UNDESIRABLES FOR DEPORTATION "G" DIST - 1919 - ALBERTA

1059 " " " G "

LIST OF UNDESIRABLES FOR DEPORTATION "E" DIST - 1919 - BRITISH COLUMBIA

1060 " " " E " BF FROM 175/713

LIST OF UNDESIRABLES FOR DEPORTATION "Y.T." DIST 1919 - YUKON TERRITORY

1061 " " " Y.T. "

LIST OF UNDESIRABLES FOR DEPORTATION "M" DIST - 1919 - MANITOBA

1062 " " " Man "

1063 [word blacked out] suspect Trans 175P/607 [word blacked out]

1064 [word blacked out] alleged agitator Trans 175/724

1066 [word blacked out] O.B.U. Organizer Trans 175/P76

[2-3 words blacked out] - Vancouver B.C. Trans. to. 175/P252 [word blacked out]

1065 [word blacked out] The Sailor Russian Workers Union Trans to 175/P109 [word blacked out]

1067 [word blacked out] for deportation Trans 175/126

1068 Prosecution of strike leaders General - [4-5 words blacked out]

(B.F. 175/829 & 175/762 & 175/1230)

SOLDIER AND SAILORS LABOUR PARTY OF CANADA - Winnipeg, Man.

1069 Soldier & Sailors Labour Party Winnipeg & District. [word blacked out] Agt.

(Trans to 175/4013)

Page 58

1070 [word blacked out] Swiss Consul - Vancouver, B.C.

1071 Russian Bolsheviki Society of Ft. William & Pt. Arthur [word blacked out] member of Trans 175/P714.

1072 [word blacked out] agitator - Lethbridge, Alta.

1073 Russian Workers Union [word blacked out] Trans 175/P1439
[word blacked out] - Edmonton, Alta.

1074 General Strike Winnipeg [word blacked out]
[word blacked out] - Edmonton, Alta.

1075 One Big Union B.C. Dist [word blacked out]

1076 [word blacked out] for deportation Trans to 175P391
[1-2 words blacked out] - Edmonton, Alta.

1077 [1-2 words blacked out] Deportation
[word blacked out] - Edmonton, Alta.

1078 [word blacked out] "
[word blacked out] - Edmonton, Alta. File Destroyed 3/5/56

1079 [word blacked out] "
word blacked out] - Edmonton, Alta.

1080 [word blacked out] "
[word blacked out] - Edmonton, Alta.

1081 [word blacked out] "
[word blacked out] - Edmonton, Alta.

1082 [word blacked out] "
[word blacked out] - Edmonton, Alta.

1083 [word blacked out] "
[word blacked out] Edmonton, Alta.

1084 [word blacked out] "
[word blacked out] - Edmonton, Alta.

1085 [word blacked out] "

1086 cancelled see 175/942

1087 [word blacked out] suspect - Stortoaks, Sask.

1088 Socialist Party of Canada. Ft. Wm. Branch [word blacked out] Trans 175/P733
[word blacked out] - Winnipeg, Man.

1089 Bolshevism in Wpg Dist. [word blacked out]

Page 59

1090 [word blacked out] suspect Trans to 175P718
One Big Union - Goodwin Aniversary Celebration

1091 Goodwin anniversary Celebration (6-8-19) Cumberland, B.C.
TRADES & LABOUR COUNCIL MEETING Re: ARREST OF RUSSIANS FOR DEPORTATION - Vancouver.

1092 Vancouver Trades & Labour Council Meetings under auspices of. Re Arrest of Russians for [word blacked out] deportation.

ALIENS AND SOCIALISTS IN - British Columbia

1093 Aliens & Socialists in Nelson, Trail, Fernie, & Kamloops

1094 [word blacked out] for deportation Trans to 172/3698

1095 [word blacked out] suspect B.F. from 175/1096 Bf from 175/1097 175/1099 175/1098

1096 [entry blacked out] Trans 175/1098 trans to 175/1095

1097 [word blacked out] suspect Trans to 175/1095

1098 [word blacked out] " " " 175/1095

1099 [word blacked out] " " " 175/1095

1100 [word blacked out] Bolshevik agitator Trans to 175/4213

[word blacked out] - Regina, Sask.

1101 [word blacked out] agitator

1102 Bolshevism in Wpg Dist [word blacked out] Rooming House Trans 175/P747

[word blacked out] - Winnipeg, Man.

1103 " [word blacked out]

1104 Imaginary Conversation at Waterton Lakes

1105 [1-2 words blacked out] suspect Morse Trans to 175P/690

DEFENCE FUND COMMITTEE - Winnipeg, Man. (Transferred to 175/1050)

1106 Socialist Meeting under auspices of Defence Fund Committee

ONE BIG UNION (Transportation Unit) Vancouver, B.C.

1107 One Big Union Re Transportation Unit No. 1 Re Vancouver Auto Union

1108 [word blacked out] see local G.W.V.A. Brandon Re Ex. Soldiers & Sailors Labour Party Brandon Trans 175/P752

B.F. 175/472 & 175/774)

1109 Gt. War. Veterans Ass'n Vancouver

Page 60

1110 [word blacked out] suspect Trans to 175P686

1111 Jack Penner. Edmonton Trans 175P/437

1112 [word blacked out] Grain Exchange suspect Trans 175P/866

[3-4 words blacked out] - Provost, Alta.

1113 Complaint of [4-5 words blacked out] re alleged sedition near Provost

1114 Ukrainian Labour News Re Labay D. Editor Trans 175/P168

1115 [word blacked out] Undesirable Trans 175/P830

[word blacked out] - Prince George, B.C.

1116 [word blacked out] agitator

ALBERNI PACIFIC LUMBER CO. - STRIKE - Port Alberni, B.C.

1117 Strike at Port Alberni Logging Camp BF from 175/2507

[word blacked out] - Winnipeg, Man.

1118 Bolshevism in Manitoba Dist re Conditions in Dauphin Dist [word blacked out] travelling for Wpg Picture Frame Co.

[word blacked out] - Winnipeg, Man.

1119 [word blacked out] Prosecution of Wpg.

[word blacked out] - Winnipeg, Man.

1120 [word blacked out] " "
[word blacked out] - Edmonton, Alta.
1121 [word blacked out] suspect. Bolshevik Transferred to 175/P3421
[word blacked out] - Lethbridge, Alta.
1122 [word blacked out] Chautauqua Lecturer
[word blacked out] - Three Hills, Dist. Alta
1123 Suspicious Literature Three Hills Dist [word blacked out]
UKRAINIAN SICHINSKI SOCIETY - Vermillion, Alta
1124 Ukrainian Society Sichinski in Vermillion [word blacked out]
1125 [word blacked out] agitator Trans to 175P775
BOLSHEVIST ACTIVITIES - Cold Lake and Beaver Crossing, Alta.
1126 Bolshevism at Cold Lake & Beaver Crossing, Alta.
1127 The Communist, paper
"THE TRI-CITY LABOUR REVIEW" - Oakland California, U.S.A.
1128 Tri-City Labour Review
[word blacked out] - Winnipeg, Man.
1129 [word blacked out] report agitator
Page 61
[word blacked out] - Winnipeg, Man.
1130 [1-2 words blacked out] report agitator
UKRAINIAN ALIEN CLUB - Brandon, Man.
1131 Alien Clubs Brandon. Ukrainian Club.
GERMAN ALIEN CLUB - Brandon, Man.
1132 " " " German Club
1133 " " " Sogola Club
[word blacked out] - Winnipeg, Man.
1134 [word blacked out] Bolsheviki agitator
UKRAINIAN ORTHODOX CHURCH - Winnipeg, Man.
1135 Ukrainian Orthodox Church Wpg
1136 [word blacked out] subject for deportation Trans to 172/3648
[word blacked out] - Brandon, Man.
1137 [word blacked out] Bolshevist
1138 [2-3 words blacked out] agtr & Bol'k Trans 175/P450
1139 Meeting of International Bible Students Association Brandon, Man. Trans to 175/6623
1140 General Conditions in West Kootenay Re Boast. [word blacked out] Sec Miners Union of Sandon Trans 175/P764.
1141 [1-2 words blacked out] agitator Trans to 175/5944
1142 [word blacked out] bolshevik agitator Trans 175/P737 [2-3 words blacked out]
LUMBER WORKERS INDUSTRIAL UNION B.C. LOGGERS AND CAMP WORKERS UNION - Crow Nest Pass
1143 B.C. Loggers & Camp Workers Union Crows Nest Pass Lumber Workers Industrial Union
[word blacked out] - Plato, Sask.

1144 [word blacked out] agitator (see also file B.F. from 175/336.)
1145 One Big Union Michel Local B.C. Trans to 175/4652 Trans to 175/1844
1146 [word blacked out] agitator " " 175/366
1147 [word blacked out] I.W.W. Agitator " " 175/5433
1148 [word blacked out] Bolshevist " " 175P934
1149 [word blacked out] Bolshevist agitator " " 175P760
Page 62
1150 [word blacked out] I.W.W. Trans to 175/5738
[1-2 words blacked out] - Turtleford, Sask.
1151 [1-2 words blacked out] Alleged agitator
1152 [word blacked out] alleged Spy Trans F64/1919
1153 [word blacked out] Russian Bolshevik Agitator - Toronto, Ont.
UKRAINSKA GARETA - Pub. in New York. U.S.A.
1154 Ukrainska Gareta (Ukranian Daily) [2-3 words blacked out]
1155 [1-2 words blacked out] O.B.U. organizer Port Arthur Trans 175P/745
1156 [word blacked out] O.B.U. Michel Local B.C. Trans 175/P492
1157 [word blacked out] Agitator " 175/4795
(BF 175/570) (BF 175/56)
1158 The Distict Ledger Fernie B.C.
(B.F. 175/786)
1159 Socialist Party of Canada Victoria Branch
1160 [word blacked out] Socialist & agitator Trans 175/P545
1161 [word blacked out] Socialist & Agitator [word blacked out] Trans 175/P749
1162 International Bible Students Ass'n General File Trans. to 175/4909
BOLSHEVIST ACTIVITIES - Red Willow, Alta.
1163 Bolshevism in Red Willow Dist.
1164 Execution of Search Warrants in Winnipeg Strike Index of Literature [4-5 words blacked out]
1165 [1-2 words blacked out] Report Trans to 175P438
1166 [word blacked out] " " " 175P438
[word blacked out] - Winnipeg, Man.
1167 [entry blacked out]
[word blacked out] - Winnipeg, Man. BF from 175/1188
1168 [entry blacked out]
1169 [entry blacked out] Trans to 172/3699
Page 63
[word blacked out] - Winnipeg, Man.
1170 [1-2 words blacked out] report
STREET AND ELECTRIC RAILWAY UNION - Vancouver, B.C.
1171 O.B.U. & Street Railwaymen. Vancouver transf. to 175/4966
1172 Socialist Funerals in Fernie B.C.
[word blacked out] - Drumheller, Alta.
1173 [word blacked out] Italian Alleged Agitator

1174 Regina Public Library Re Bolsheviki Literature

1175 Intercepted letter re I.W.W. Methods sent to [word blacked out] Trans to 175P/884

1176 [1-2 words blacked out] agitator (Trans to 175/4693) " " 175P804

1177 One Big Union Manitoba Dist Re Winnipeg Central Labour Council of the O.B.U. BF from 175/655

1178 Kurzer. Poliki Polish Newspaper - Milwaukee, Wis., U.S.A.

CO-OPERATIVE SOCIETY (Proposed) - Vancouver, B.C.

1179 Proposed Co-operative Society in Vancouver

[1-2 words blacked out] - Vancouver B.C.

1180 [1-2 words blacked out] O.B.U. Vancouver

[word blacked out] - Victoria, B.C.

1181 [word blacked out] Representing "The Veteran" G.W.V.A. Victora

ONE BIG UNION - Canmore, Alta.

1182 O.B.U. Canmore Trans. to 175/492

1183 Bolshevism in Winnipeg [word blacked out] agitator Trans to 175/5402 Trans to 175P/2481

[word blacked out] - Winnipeg, Man.

1184 [1-2 words blacked out] Socialist agitator [4-5 words blacked out]

RUSSIAN SUSPECT - Grey, Sask.

1185 Report of [word blacked out] Re Russian at Grey Sask, suspect

[word blacked out] Autocrat and Tyrant - Pub. in Vancouver, B.C.

1186 Pamphlet [word blacked out] autocrat & Tyrant

DOMINION LABOUR PARTY - Vancouver, B.C.

1187 Labour Meeting Brandon

1188 [1-2 words blacked out] report trans to 175/1168

1189 [word blacked out] transferred to 172/-3699

Page 64

1190 Veregin, Peter [word blacked out] reports etc from /32 Trans to 175P3087

1191 [1-2 words blacked out] agitator " " 175P174

1192 [word blacked out] Bolshevist

[word blacked out] - Rivercourse, Alta.

1193 [word blacked out] Complaint of Revercourse P.O. Alta Distribution of literature "United Farmers Association".

1194 [word blacked out] Cvijanovik agitator - Calgary, Alta.

1195 [word blacked out] O.B.U. organizer & Agitator Trans 175/P791

[2-3 words blacked out]

1196 [2-3 words blacked out] Bolshevist

[word blacked out] - Winnipeg, Man.

1197 [word blacked out] Alleged Undesirable

ITALIAN ANARCHIST PRINTING ESTABLISHMENT - Vancouver, B.C.

1198 Vancouver Italian Anarchist Printing Establishment

[1-2 words blacked out] - Regina, Sask.

1199 [1-2 words blacked out] Greek.

1200 [word blacked out] suspect Trans 175/P642

1201 [word blacked out] Russian Socialist & Agitator Trans 175/P755

LABOUR DISPUTE - Taber, Alta. - LABOUR CONDITIONS - Taber, Alta. (B.F. from 175/1473) (scratched out)

1202 Refusal to re-instate miners on alleged Government Orders Sub heading to 175/594 (scratched out)

United Mine Workers of America - Strike - in District 18, 1919 Alberta & British Columbia.

1203 [2-3 words blacked out] report (deportation) - Winnipeg, Man.

1204 [word blacked out] - Winnipeg, Man. "

1205 [word blacked out] " " Trans to 175P865

1206 [word blacked out] " " " " 175P864

[word blacked out] - Winnipeg, Man. "

1207 [entry blacked out]

1208 Russian Counter Propaganda Proposed Publishing of Canadian Russian Newspaper.

1209 [word blacked out] alleged agitator - Vancouver, B.C.

Page 65

1210 [word blacked out] Undesirable Citizen (alleged) Trans 175P/780

1211 [word blacked out] Bolshevist Sympathizer (Hamilton, Ont)

1212 Fire at Rock Springs Mine. Taber from File 175/594 (Trans from 175/5041)

BRITISH COLUMBIA LOGGERS AND CAMP WORKERS - Vancouver, B.C. [2-3 words blacked out]

1213 B.C. Loggers & Camp Workers Union Japanese Branch Trans. to 175/449

1214 Willow Lake School District Complaint of G.W.V.A. Trans to 172/3647

1215 [word blacked out] Winnipeg, Man

1216 Batt. Federated Labour Party Trans to 175/-P1184

ALIENS AT - Gunne, Ont.

1217 Aliens at Gimme (Waldorf, Ont) [word blacked out] report

1218 Complaint against Sgt Wilson or his agents in connection with Immigration cases.

VOROLD - (Icelandic Newspaper) - Winnipeg, Man.

1219 Vorold - Newspaper

1220 [word blacked out] agitator - Ocean Falls, B.C.

1221 [word blacked out] " Trans 175/P919

1222 [word blacked out] " Trans 175/P917

1223 New Times (New Publication) - Winnipeg, Man.

1224 [1-2 words blacked out] suspect Trans 175/P758

1225 One Big Union Bulletin Wpg. Trans to 177/8

[word blacked out] - Winnipeg, Man.

1226 [word blacked out] Bolshevist

1227 [word blacked out] Bolshevist - Edmonton, Alta.

1228 [2-3 words blacked out] Delegates to L.W.I.W. Trans to 175/5790

1229 [word blacked out] Longshoreman Vancouver. B.C. " " 175P253

Page 66

1230 Ex-Soldiers & Sailors Labour Party Wpg Re Labour Parade 1-9-19 Transf. to

175/1069

1231 [word blacked out] alleged Bolshi Sympathiser Editor Pennant Observer Trans 175/P7??

1232 Telegrams in connection with strike [3-4 words blacked out]

1233 "The Loyal" Greek Newspaper (Weekly) - New York, U.S.A.

FREE RUSSIA (Daily Newspaper) - Pub. Chicago, Ill.

1234 Daily Free Russia Bolsheviki Newspaper

1235 [word blacked out] agitatress Trans 175/P766

[word blacked out] - Magnet, Man.

1236 Toutes Aides S.D. 1724 Re. Alleged Seditious (Manitoba)

1237 [word blacked out] agitator Trasn to 175P767

GERMAN MINISTERS IN CANADA - Canada General.

1238 German Preachers Wpg [1-2 words blacked out]

- Winnipeg, Man.

1239 Hatke-Bolshevism Wpg Dist [word blacked out] report

1240 [word blacked out] report Trans to 175P440

1241 [word blacked out] "

1242 [1-2 words blacked out] - Winnipeg, Man.

1243 [word blacked out] " Trans to 175P467

1244 [word blacked out] " Winnipeg, Man

Battleford, Sask.

1245 [word blacked out] prohibited literature

Battleford, Sask.

1245 (A) [word blacked out] Alleged Agitator.

1246 Contemplated General Strike Winnipeg. [3-4 words blacked out]

1247 [3-4 words blacked out] socialist & agitator Trans 175/P2948

1248 [word blacked out] Agitator Trans 175P/2948 Trans 175/P782

1249 [word blacked out] " Trans to 175P/736

Page 67

1250 [word blacked out] Agitator Trans. to 175P808

1251 [1-2 words blacked out] organizer O.B.U. Trans to 175/P829

ONE BIG UNION (Scratched out) - Lethbridge, Alta. Bf. from 17??????

1252 Meeting of the Federal Miners at Lethbridge Trans 175/P829 (Scratched out)

[word blacked out] - Edmonton, Alta.

1253 [word blacked out] suspect

1254 [word blacked out] agitator Bolshevist Trans 175/P777

1255 [word blacked out] O.B.U. Organizer " 175/P807

1256 [word blacked out] agitator Trans 175/P783

INDUSTRIAL WORKERS OF THE WORLD (Literature) - Vancouver, B.C. [word blacked out]

1257 Longshoreman Re. I.W.W. Propaganda

1258 [word blacked out] agitator Trans 175/P784

1259 [word blacked out] agitator Trans 175/P800 Trans 175/P800

[word blacked out] - Edmonton, Alta.

1260 [word blacked out] Possession of banned literature

[word blacked out] - Edmonton, Alta.

1261 [word blacked out] "

1262 [word blacked out] " - Edmonton, Alta.

1263 Industrial Union News - Newspaper - Detroit, Mich - Vancouve,r B.C.

1264 La Luce Italian Paper - Pub. Vancouver, B.C.

1265 [word blacked out] O.B.U. Agitator Trans 175/P793

1266 [word blacked out] Alleged Agitator & Bolshevist Trans 175/P355

1267 [word blacked out] Press Agent ILWLWL Organization " 175P787

1268 Dominion Labour Party Protest Meeting - Winnipeg, Man.

1269 Anarchist Movement in U.S.A.

Page 68

CONDITIONS LABOUR (Amongst Postal Clerks) - Regina, Sask.

1270 Postal Clerks Regina

1271 [word blacked out] Agitator Trans 175/P788

1272 [word blacked out] alleged agitator Trans 175/P616

1273 [word blacked out] agitator BF from 175/2311 Trans 175/P789 Bols in Man Dist. Bols in Dauphin Dist.

[word blacked out] - Winnipeg, Man.

1274 [word blacked out] agitator

Trans to 175/21

1275 International Bible Students Assn. Medicine Hat [word blacked out] - Prohibited Literature in possession.)

1276 Prohibited Literature Fort William Trans to 175/229

1277 [word blacked out] Editor of Polish Paper "Czas" Winnipeg.

DOMINON LABOUR PARTY @ INDEPENDENT LABOUR PARTY - Calgary, Alta. Trans. to 175/5499

1278 Independent Labour party. Calgary & Dist Branch (Corr. Heading Dominion Lab. Party. Calgary)

1279 [word blacked out] suspect Trans to 175P868

1280 Tribune. Editorial Police Amalgamation 175/1301

1281 [word blacked out] agitator Trans 175/P790

1282 [1-2 words blacked out] alleged I.W.W. Trans to 175/756

1283 [entry blacked out] Trans 175/P477

[word blacked out] - Red Deer, Alta.

1284 Complaint of [word blacked out]

(Sub Act. Within)

INDUSTRIAL WORKERS OF THE WORLD - Rowan, Ont.

1285 I.W.W. Organization Rowan Ont

UKRAINIAN PROPOGANDA - Canada Generally

1286 Ukrainian Propaganda Distribution and Handling of

1287 [word blacked out] President German Club Victoria

RUSSIAN WORKERS CLUB (Prosecution of Members of) - Vancouver, B.C.

1288 Agitators - Subject for deportation Prosecution of Members of Russian Workers Club

1289 [[1-2 words blacked out] " Trans 175/P243

Page 69

1290 [word blacked out] subject for deportation (Russian Workers Union) Trans to 175P242

1291 [word blacked out] " 175/4514

1292 [word blacked out] " Trans 175/P655

1293 [word blacked out] " Trans 175/P390

1294 [word blacked out] " Trans 175/P109

1295 [word blacked out] " Trans 175/P127

1296 [word blacked out] " Trans 175/P248

1297 [word blacked out] Trial of " 172P757

1298 The Brand, Foreign Publication

[word blacked out] - Fort William, Ont.

1299 [entry blacked out] Trans to 175/P799

1300 International Bible Students Association. Victoria.

1301 Prosecution of members of the Russian Workers Union re objectionable article appearing in the Semi-Weekly Tribune against the R.N.W.P.

1302 [entry blacked out] Trans 175/P486

1303 [1-2 words blacked out] Member of American Red Cross returned from Russia

1304 [word blacked out] Bols Agitator Trans to 175P861

CONGRESS - Russian Anti-Bolshevist - New York, U.S.A.

1305 Russian Anti Bolsheviki Congress to be held in N. York 10-9-19

[word blacked out] - Hardy Bay, B.C.

1306 [word blacked out] suspect

[word blacked out] - Winnipeg, Man.

1307 [word blacked out] Revolutionary Socialist

1308 [2-3 words blacked out] subject for deportation Trans to 175P280

1309 [word blacked out] Delegate [word blacked out] " " 175P801

Page 70

1310 [word blacked out] agitator Trans to 175P802

Central Labour Party - Prince Rupert, B.C.

1311 Meetings under Central Labour Party Labour Meeting at Prince Rupert @ Victoria District Trades and Labour Council

Trades and Labour Council (AFL) Victoria, B.C.

1312 Conditions in Victoria Re Trades & Labour Meeting 3-9-19 [2-3 words blacked out]

1313 [word blacked out] L.W.I.U. organizer Trans 175/P815

1314 [word blacked out] " Trans 175/P822

1315 [word blacked out] Re I.W.W. Cards advocating sabotage Trans 175/P981

1316 [1-2 words blacked out] Bolshevik [word blacked out] report Winnipeg, Man.

1317 [word blacked out] suspect " Winnipeg, Man.

1318 Meetings of Jews at Liberty Hall " Trans to 175/347

1319 [1-2 words blacked out] Berry Creek, Alta Trans 175/P1743
[word blacked out] - Victoria, B.C.
1320 League for Amnesty of Political Prisoners [word blacked out]
1321 [word blacked out] Socialist & Agitator Trans to 175P???
CONDITIONS Amongst Lettish People - Canada Generally
1322 Lettish agitators in Western Canada
[1-2 words blacked out] Wilhelmia, Alta
1323 League for the Amnesty of Political Prisoners [1-2 words blacked out]
1324 " [word blacked out] Winnipeg, Man.
1325 [1-2 words blacked out] Report suspect Winnipeg, Man.
1326 Observer Pennant Sask (Newspaper)
1327 [word blacked out] Socialist agitator [word blacked out] report Winnipeg, Man.
1328 [2-3 words blacked out] report Winnipeg, Man.
Great War Veterans Ass'n. Regina, Sask.
1329 G.W.V.Z. Meeting Regina
Page 71
Conditions Labour (Railway Employees) - Saskatchewan
1330 Railway Employees Unrest S.S. Dist
1331 [word blacked out] Socialist & Agitator Trans 175/P812
One Big Union (Activities in Labour Congress - Hamilton, Ont.
[2-3 words blacked out]
1332 Members of O.B.U. attending Labour Congress at Hamilton
1333 [word blacked out] O.B.U. Organizer Trans. to 175P1020
One Big Union - Vancouver, B.C.
1334 Dodwell & Co Theft of Silk from ship owned by Trans. to 175/4859
[word blacked out] - Vancouver, B.C.
1335 [1-2 words blacked out] subject for deportation
1336 Russian or German Jew suspected Bolshevist Transferred to 175/1374 175/P388
1337 [2-3 words blacked out] subject for deportation Vancouver, B.C. [word blacked out]
1338 [1-2 words blacked out] O.B.U. Organizer Transferred to 175/P921
1339 [word blacked out] Alleged Sedition Rosetown, Sask.
1340 [word blacked out] letter from [word blacked out]
Conditions Labour (Cadomin Coal Mines) Cadomin, Alta [2-3 words blacked out]
1341 Conditions at Cadomin Coal Mines Complaint of [word blacked out]
Conditions Labour (Post Office Employees) - (scratched out) - Vancouver, B.C.
1342 Possible strike of Postal Employees Vancouver (scratched out)
Post Office Employees (Labour Conditions Amongst) Trans. to 175/410
1343 [word blacked out] Socialist
1344 [2-3 words blacked out] of Lang Sask transferred to 172/-3781
1345 [word blacked out] O.B.U. & I.W.W. Advocate Trans 175/P935
1346 [word blacked out] O.B.U. Advocate Vancouver, B.C.
[word blacked out] - Lang, Sask.

1347 [word blacked out] Undesirable

1348 [word blacked out] O.B.U. Agitator or Advocate

1349 Dominion Labour Party Lethbridge Letter from Compt. Trans to 175/6140

Page 72

1350 [word blacked out] agitator Trans. to 175P761

1351 Conditions in Victoria Re Civi Employees Protective Association

1352 Electrical Workers Union Vancouver Trans. to 175/4468

1353 Soldiers & Sailors Labour Party of Canada Trans 175/P757 [word blacked out] secretary

[word blacked out] - Comox, B.C.

1354 Strike at Comox Logging Co. Re [word blacked out]

1355 Special Precautions during coming visit of H.R.H. The Prince of Wales 1919

1356 [word blacked out] et al Seditious Conspiracy Re Mass Meeting held Victoria Park 15-9-19 also in connection with defence fund.

1357 Strike of Metaliferous Miners at Kimberley B.C. Kimberley, B.C.

1358 [word blacked out] O.B.U. Advociate Trans. to 175/P1053

1359 Jasper Park Colleries Co Ltd Peabody Coal Co Ltd Pacahontas, Alta.

1360 International Bible Students Association Calgary Alta.

[word blacked out] - Blairmore Dist. Alta.

1361 Trouble in Crows Nest over International Organizer [word blacked out]

Information Supplied Assistant Director of Coal Operations - Calgary, Alta.

1362 Supplying Information re Agitators to Asst. Director of Coal Operations.

Strike - At Genoa Bay Lumber Co. - Cowichan, B.C.

1363 L.W.I.W. Re Strike at Cowichan B.C. Genora Bay Lumber Co.

Strike - UNDINS LUMBER CAMP - KNOX BAY.B.C.

1364 " [word blacked out] Camp Kox Bay.

BOLSHEVIK ACTIVITIES AMONG FINLANDERS - CARLIN, B.C.

1365 Alleged Bolshevism amongst Finlanders at White Lake Carlin B.C.

[2-3 words blacked out] - Edmonton Alta.

1366 [word blacked out] Alleged Agtr.

[word blacked out] - Rosedale, Alta.

1367 [word blacked out] Operator Rosedale Mine O.B.U.

1368 [word blacked out] O.B.U. Delegate & Agitator Trans 175/P454

1369 O.B.U. Regina Re Scotland O.B.U. Speaker Trans 175/P880

Page 73

1370 The Statesman Official Organ Dominion Labour Party Trans 177/7

1371 [word blacked out] agitator Trans to 175/4609

Conditions Labour at Gibson's Landing, B.C.

1372 Conditions at Gibson's Landing [1-2 words blacked out] Outfit

1373 Cancelled

1374 [1-2 words blacked out] alleged Bolshevist Vancouver, B.C.

1375 Meeting of U.M.W. of A. Dist 18 at Lethbridge. Russian or German Jew suspected Bolshevist (original Heading) 175/4706

(Conditions Labour)

1376 Proposed Strike (scratched out) Wpg Street Railway Employees - Winnipeg. Man.

1377 [word blacked out] Subject for deportation Trans to 175P273

1378 Civic Union, Brandon Manitoba

CONVENTION - Grain Growers - One Big Union Activities In - Regina, Sask.

1379 O.B.U. Propaganda Grain Growers Convention Regina

1380 [entry blacked out] Trans 175/P485

Bolshevik Activities - Stry Dist., Alta.

1381 Alleged Bolsheviki Meetings held in the Stry District.

1382 [word blacked out] alleged agitator Lethbridge, Alta.

1383 [word blacked out] " Lethbridge, Alta.

1384 [word blacked out] organizer Trans 175/P818 BF. from 175/1450

1385 [word blacked out] distributing propaganda for O.B.U. man Winnipeg Dist. Alta.

1386 [word blacked out] suspected importer of Bolsheviki Literature Trans to 175/P1852

Conditions Labour (Steel Industry) Canada Gen. [word blacked out]

1387 Steel Industry General Strike

1388 Blue Diamond Coal Co Ltd Brule Mines [word blacked out]

1389 Wynard Advance Wynard, Sask.

Page 74

1390 [word blacked out] agitator Trans 175/P453

1391 [word blacked out] agitator & Article Writer Trans 175/P867

1392 General Strike Wpg [9-10 words blacked out] deportation proceedings against.

1393 [word blacked out] Taylorton Trans 175/P3670

1394 One Big Union Convention at Chicago Ill Trans 175/P362 [word blacked out]

1395 International Bible Students Prince Rupert B.C.

1396 [word blacked out] agitator Trans to 175P841

1397 [word blacked out] Saxavery Agitator 175/P826

1398 [word blacked out] suspect Trans 175P/591

1399 [word blacked out] suspect Trans 175/P583

1400 [word blacked out] Russian Bolche Scty Ft. Wm Pt Arthur Trans 175/P827

1401 Labour Church Service Edmonton Alta. Trans to 175/4515

1402 Gen'l Conditions in Ft. George & McBrice Dists Alta. [1-2 words blacked out] Re Patrol Reg. No. 4230 Cpl St. Laurent i/c Prince George.

1403 [word blacked out] O.B.U. Organizer & Agitator Trans to 175/P739

1404 Slobodian Anarchist Trans 175/P2036

1405 Polish Veterans of 1914-1918 see Polish Council of Western Canada Winnipeg, Man.

1406 [word blacked out] agitator transferred to 175/1626

1407 King Lumber Co Newton B.C. Strike at

1408 Duncan Bay Lumber Co Duncan Bay B.C. Strike at Lumber Workers Industrial Union

1409 Mirrit Ring Camp Strike at

Merrill Ring Camp - Campbell River, B.C.

Page 75

Lumber Workers Industrial Union - Beaver Cove, B.C. (O.B.U.)

1410 McGoogan & McDonalds Pulp & Paper Mill, Beaver Cove, Strike at (Lumber Workers Industrial Union) (scratched out)

Great War Veterans Ass'n. Calgary, Alta.

1411 G.W.V.A. Mass Meeting at Calgary Re Cash Bonus.

1412 O.B.U. Edmonton Alta. Transferred to 175/4742

1413 [word blacked out] I.W.I.W. Organizer transferred to 175/P1498

1414 [word blacked out] " " " 175P74

1415 O.B.U. Monthly - Literature (Trans. to 177/192)

1416 [entry blacked out] TRANS 175/P831

1417 [word blacked out] organizer wholesale & retail clerks International Protection Asociation 175/P1536

Kinman's Logging Camp - Labour Conditions at - British Columbia

1418 Kinman's Logging Camp

Walen Bros Labour Conditions at - Port Alice, B.C.

1419 No 1 Camp Whalen Bros at Port Alice

1420 [1-2 words blacked out] Organizer Transferred 175/P843

1421 [word blacked out] Agitator Vancouver " to 175/965

[word blacked out] (O.B.U.)

1422 [word blacked out] O.B.U. Agent (This cover is empty, no transfer shown, spelling of name uncertain)

1423 [word blacked out] suspected socialist Fort William, Ont.

1424 O.B.U. Fort William Trans to 175/4568

1425 [word blacked out] distributer of Proh. Literature

British Columbia

1426 [word blacked out] Agitator subject for deportation trans 175/278

1427 [word blacked out] Sec. Turners Weekly & Saskatoon Trades & Labour Council. Sask. Saskatoon,

1428 [word blacked out] I.W.[blacked out]. Organizer

1429 Strike at Panama Lumber co. Camp. Sooke Harbour. Sooke Harbour, B.C.

Page 76

1430 [word blacked out] Ex Editor and article writer Wynyard Advance. Agitator. Trans 175/P3529

1431 [word blacked out] suspect Trans to 175/P833

1432 [word blacked out] complaint addressed to X by [word blacked out] Trans 175/P213

BOLSHEVIK ACTIVITIES AT FORT WILLIAM, PORT ARTHUR. ONT.

1433 Bolshevism in Port Arthur & Ft. William.

Ruthenian Propaganda - Saskatchewan

1434 Ruthenian Propaganda Meetings of Ruthenians at Ituna

1435 [word blacked out] agitator Trans 175/P842

1436 [word blacked out] Closing down of Ladysmith Lumber Co Camp. Trans 175/P842

Federated Labour party - Regina, Sask.

1437 Meeting of Fedt Labour Party of Regina

Conditions General - Terrace, B.C.

1438 [word blacked out] & General Conditions at Terrace B.C.

Co. Chase, B.C.

1439 Strike at Adam's River Lumber Camp

1440 [word blacked out] agitator Trans 175/P2161

1441 [word blacked out] Lettish agitator Trans 175/P408

[word blacked out] - Edmonton Dist. Alta.

1442 [entry blacked out]

1443 [word blacked out] Organizer Confederation of Labour Trans 175/P846 [4-5 words blacked out]

Vancouver, B.C.

1444 International Jewelry Workers Union. Threatened strike of [4-5 words blacked out]

1445 [word blacked out] Bolshevist & agitator. Trans 175/P890. Esquimalt H.M.C. Dockyard

[3-4 words blacked out] Socialist, & Prohibited Publication.

1446 [1-2 words blacked out] Bolshevist suspect. Birnie, Man.

1447 [word blacked out] Riceton, Sask.

1448 Dominion Labour Party Medicine Hat. Alta.

1449 [word blacked out] O.B.U. agitator Canmore trans 175P/619

Page 77

1450 [word blacked out] Organizer O.B.U. & I.W.I.U. Trans to 175/1384 to 175P818

(Swedish newspaper) Publ Winnipeg, Man.

1451 Forum, The [word blacked out] editor

[word blacked out] - Swanson Bay, B.C.

1452 Labour agitators at Whalen Pulp & Paper Mills Swanson Bay

[word blacked out] - Greencourt, Alta.

1453 [word blacked out] agitator

Conditions General - Vancouver Island, B.C.

1454 Conditions in Northern Part of Vancouver Island Trans to 175/1483 Transf 175/1673

1455 [word blacked out] alleged Bolsheivst

1456 [word blacked out] Alleged Bolshevist. Trans to 175/2865

Lumber Workers Industrial Union - Northern Sask. (BF. 15/2156)

1457 Organization of Lumbermen & Millworkers Changed to I.W.W. Organization of, ar[word blacked out]

Hardy Bay Dist., B.C.

1458 [word blacked out] agtr & I.W.W. Delegate

1459 [word blacked out] Allgd agitator Trans to 175P859

1460 [word blacked out] agitator trans 175/P30

1461 [word blacked out] agitator Trans 172/1433

[word blacked out] - Toronto, Ont.

1462 [word blacked out] suspect

[2-3 words blacked out] - Winnipeg, Man.

1463 [word blacked out] Re. Ex-Soldiers & Sailors Labour Party Trans to 175/P1015

1464 Labour Conditions Re. Strikes in England & U.S.A. Trans to 175/2930

1465 [word blacked out] Ukrainian Bolshe

1466 [word blacked out] agtr trans 175/P869

1467 [word blacked out] agtr " 175P87

1468 [word blacked out] Agtr. Trans 175/P62

1469 [word blacked out] editor of O.B.U. Wpg Trans to 175/P1023

Page 78

1470 [word blacked out] R.S. Bolshevist Trans 175/P591

1471 [word blacked out] Chicago, Ill.

1472 Dominion Labour Party Calgary Trans to 175/5499

1473 U.M.W. of A. Dist 18 Re. [word blacked out] Trans to 175/1202

1474 Nation, The New York Trans 177/501

1475 Canadian News Jap Newspaper Vancouver, B.C. (See Jap. paper "The Echo" 175/1560)

[word blacked out] British Columbia

1476 [word blacked out] Russian agitator

[word blacked out] Vancouver, B.C.

1477 [word blacked out] suspect

1478 [word blacked out] " Trans 175/P20

Yahk, B.C.

1479 [word blacked out] Intercepted letter from [word blacked out[to -

Strike - General Proposed (scratched out) - United Mine Workers of America (Dist. 18) (Proposed Strike in Oct & Nov 1919 - British Columbia & Alberta

1480 General Conditions in Mining Camps Dist to U.M.W.A. Rumoured intending strike (scratched out)

1481 [word blacked out] Leader, Finnish socialist Branch, Intola trans 175/P863

Grand Priarie, Alta.

1482 [word blacked out] Alleged agitator

Conditions - General - Vancouver Island - B.C. (Trans to 175/1673)

1483 General Conditions of West Coast Vancouver B.C.

1484 [word blacked out] Alleged agitator Esquimalt Dist., B.C.

1485 [1-2 words blacked out] " " B.C.

1486 [entry blacked out] Trans 175P/901

1487 [word blacked out] suspect 175P/291

1488 [word blacked out] subject for deportation 175P249

1489 Anti-Draft League Winnipeg, Man.

Page 79

1490 [word blacked out] subject for deportation

1491 [word blacked out] suspect, [word blacked out] Trans 175/P883

1492 [1-2 words blacked out] suspect agitator Trans 175/P902

1493 [1-2 words blacked out] at Busby. Allgd Seditious Utterances re [word blacked out]

1494 [word blacked out] suspect See 175/53

1495 [word blacked out] " "

1496 [word blacked out] " "

1497 [word blacked out] " "

1498 [word blacked out] agitator

1499 [word blacked out] "

1500 [word blacked out] "

1501 [word blacked out] O.B.U. agtr

1502 [word blacked out] In possession of Proh Lit Trans to 175/P643

1503 [word blacked out] "

1504 [word blacked out] "

1505 [word blacked out] "

(B.F. 175/2641)

1506 O.B.U. Vancouver Island Sub. Dist Proposed meeting Nanaimo

1507 Meetings under Labour Party, Prince George Meeting held by [word blacked out] Trans 175/P810

1508 [word blacked out] In possession Proh. Lit. Trans 175/P766

1509 [word blacked out] " Trans 175/P307

Page 80

1510 [word blacked out] I.W.W. Subject for deportation. Trans 175/P889

1511 Strike at Rosedale Mine. Drumheller Mining Area.

1512 U.M.W.A. Dist 18 Coalhurst

1513 [word blacked out] Labour agitator Trans 175/P904

1514 [word blacked out] Bolshevist suspect. Trans 175/P942

1515 [word blacked out] " " Trans 175/P1358

1516 [word blacked out] Bolshe Leader

1517 Street Railwaymen's Union. Victoria B.C. [3-4 words blacked out]

1518 [word blacked out] In possession of proh Lit.

1519 [1-2 words blacked out] alleged head of Bolshe in Canada and U.S.A.

1520 League for the Amnesty of Political Prisoners general File

1521 Policemens Protective Association - St. John - N.B. [2-3 words blacked out]

1522 [1-2 words blacked out] subject for deportation

1523 Kavanagh, Jack agtr Trans 175/4654

1524 Russian Workers Union U.S.A. & Canada Trans. to 175/5463

1525 [word blacked out] agtr for O.B.U.

1526 [1-2 words blacked out] suspect alien at Gunne Trans 1754/P895

1527 [1-2 words blacked out] " Trans 175/P896

11528 [word blacked out] " Trans 175/P897

1529 O.B.U. Calgary Twenty seventh consecutive & 4th biennial (scratched out) Convention of UMWA Cleveland Ohio USA 17/9/19

Page 81

1530 [word blacked out] Acting Postmaster suspect

1531 [word blacked out] Sec S.P. of C. Trans 175/P63

1532 [word blacked out] suspect

1533 O.B.U. Dauphin [4-5 words blacked out]

Lumber Workers Industrial Union (I.W.W.) Port Arthur, Ont.
1534 I.W.W. Branch. I.W.I.U. # 500 Re Bushmens Organization Meeting (scratched out)
1535 [word blacked out] agitator trans to 175/4618
1536 [word blacked out] alleged Bolshe
1537 [2-3 words blacked out] Alleged Bolshe
1538 Genl report Re Social & Political Unrest in Canada
1539 [word blacked out] suspected Bolshe Trans 175/P888
1540 Teamsters Union & the OLBLUL Brandon
1541 [word blacked out] subject for deport Trans to 175/P-133
1542 [word blacked out] suspect
Union of Russian Working Men
1543 @Russian Workers Union Meetings at Saskatoon
@Union of Russian Workmen
1544 [word blacked out] Russian Priest, Bolshe
1545 [word blacked out] Property of trans to 175/P911
1546 [word blacked out] agitator trans to 175/5194 Transf to 175P/2290
1547 [word blacked out] suspected agtr Trans 175/P908
1548 [word blacked out] suspect Trans 175/P208
1549 Possibility of racial rioting in Canada.
Page 82
1550 War Obstructionists
1551 India Labour Union of America [word blacked out] Agtr
1552 [word blacked out] alleged Bolshe
1553 [word blacked out] " agtr
1554 Victory Loan Campaign Winnipeg.
1555 [word blacked out] suspect
1556 [word blacked out] "
[word blacked out] report see 175/155
1557 [word blacked out] " trans to 175/155
1558 [word blacked out] Deportation of Trans to G./1919
1559 Conditions at Lovett Mines [2-3 words blacked out]
1560 The Echo Jap Newspaper
1561 The Indicator Trans 177/41
1562 Suspected Proh Lit in Dana & Peterson Dist Trans to 177/45
1563 [1-2 words blacked out] subject for deportation
1564 Rebecca BUHAY Trans 175/P1254
1565 [word blacked out] for Deportation
1566 [word blacked out] "
1567 [word blacked out] Proh Lit
1568 [word blacked out] Proh Lit Trans 175/P840
1569 Conditions at]Stewart, Anyox & Alice Arm Mining Dists [5-6 words blacked out]
Page 83
1570 [1-2 words blacked out] sec U.M.W.A. Gladstone Local Trans 175/P483

1571 [1-2 words blacked out] O.B.U. " " " 175/P926

1572 Idog Swedish publication

1573 Labour Election Propaganda Winnipeg

1574 Unnamed Russian Jew In poss. of Proh. Lt trans to 175/1319

1575 [word blacked out] Organization Committee O.B.U. Trans 175/P976

1576 O.B.U. Convention

1577 National Educational Conference [word blacked out] report)

1478 [2-3 words blacked out] "

1579 [2-3 words blacked out] "

1580 Patrol from Hazelton to Octsa, Francois & Burns Lake & ret by Houston, Telkwa & Smithers (Cpt E.T.W. Colther Hqrs 130-25)

1581 [word blacked out] O.B.U. agitator Trans 174/741

1582 [word blacked out] " Trans 175/P88

1583 [word blacked out] agtr

1584 [word blacked out] agtr Trans to 175/P884

1585 [word blacked out] Revolutionary agitator Trans 175/P852

1586 International Bible Students Assoc'n Lethbridge

1587 [word blacked out] agtr Trans 175/P938

1588 Bolsheviks in office of U.S.A. Govt

1589 [word blacked out] Bolshevik Trans 175/146

Page 84

1590 [word blacked out] agtr trans to 175/4777

1591 [entry blacked out] trans 1st/P721

1592 [1-2 words blacked out] agtr trans 175/P929 [3-4 words blacked out]
Civic Employees Federal Labour Union @ Vancouver ??????

1593 @ Civic Employees Union - Vancouver Civic Employees Union - Vancouver, B.C. Sub Act In [3-4 words blacked out]

1594 [word blacked out] agitator Trans 175/P931

1595 General Condition Ocean Falls

1596 Ocean Falls B.C. Socialistic Lit in Circulation at

1597 [1-2 words blacked out] & Vancouver T. & L. Council.

1598 General Situation Melita

1599 St. Clair Socialist

1600 The Irish Press Newspaper.

1601 [word blacked out] suspect

1602 [word blacked out] suspect

1603 [word blacked out] O.B.U. Trans 175/P943

1604 [word blacked out] Socialist & agtr Trans 175/P946

1605 [word blacked out] agtr

1606 [word blacked out] agtr trans 175/P948

1607 [entry blacked out] trans 175/P949

1608 [word blacked out] agtr trans 175/P969

1609 [word blacked out] O.B.U. Trans 174/P944

Page 85

1610 [word blacked out] complaint of trans to 175/5439

1611 Names found in [word blacked out] ocket book

1612 [word blacked out] agtr & bolshe trans 175/P162

1613 [2-3 words blacked out] suspect

1614 [2-3 words blacked out] "

1615 [word blacked out] suspected receiving proh lit

1616 [word blacked out] suspect [word blacked out] report trans 175/P963

1617 [word blacked out] trans " to 175/P-1005 BF. from 175/2295 175/1671

1618 [word blacked out] proh lit

1619 [word blacked out] "

1620 [word blacked out] "

1621 [word blacked out] " trans 175/1660

1622 Ukrainians in Edmonton District (Trans from Ukrainian Labour News) [1-2 words blacked out] Ukrainian Institute.

1623 [1-2 words blacked out] agtr trans 175/P572

1624 [entry blacked out] trans 175/P912

1625 [word blacked out] Proh Lit Ukrainian Labour News

1626 [word blacked out] "

1627 [word blacked out] "

1628 Logging Industry in B.C. agitation & Unrest

1629 [3-4 words blacked out] anarchist

Page 86

1630 [word blacked out] Labour Agitator trans to 175/P-964

1631 Comrades of the Gt. War Vancouver trans 175/P966 (scratched out)

1632 [1-2 words blacked out] Austrian suspect

1633 [3-4 words blacked out] "

1634 [word blacked out] agtr 175/P966

1635 [word blacked out] labour agtr

1636 [word blacked out] " 175/P970

1637 [entry blacked out] 175/P967

1638 [2-3 words blacked out] agtrs O.B.U. Kootenay 175/P997

1639 [word blacked out] labor agtr trans to 175/4905, also 175/P968 also 175/P997

1640 Conditions in Eckville Dist (Trans. to 175/6058)

1641 [1-2 words blacked out] suspect trans 175/P1054

1642 Strike at Capilano Timber Co. Camp 175/P994

1643 [word blacked out] I.W.W. Illegally entering Canada

1644 [word blacked out] German agtr trans to 175/995

1645 [word blacked out] " trans to 175/P-996

1646 [2-3 words blacked out] suspect

1647 Election meeting Wpg trans to 175/1573

1648 Socialist organization Canmore Alta

1649 [1-2 words blacked out] organizer B.C. Loggers Union trans 175/P1160

Page 87

1650 [word blacked out] suspect friend of [word blacked out] 175/P993

1651 German Bond Issues

1652 Co-operation of German & American Socialistic Revolutionaries

1653 Strike at Yapp & Wheeler Logging Camp Shell Creek, B.C.

1654 [word blacked out] Labour Agitator 175/P992

1655 O.B.U. Central Labour Council Winnipeg trans to 175-1177

1656 Dominion Labour Party Edmonton

1657 [word blacked out] Bolshevik 175/P146

1658 [word blacked out] subscriber Ukrainian Labour News

1659 [word blacked out] "

1660 [word blacked out] "

1661 [word blacked out] "

1662 [word blacked out] "

1663 [word blacked out] "

1664 [word blacked out] "

1665 [word blacked out] "

1666 [word blacked out] "

1667 [word blacked out] " 175-1627

1668 O.B.Union I.W.W. Branch I.W.I.U. No 500 Ft. William 175/6130 (scratched out) [2-3 words blacked out] 175/4570

1669 [2-3 words blacked out] report.

Page 88

1670 [2-3 words blacked out] report. trans: to 175/P436

1671 [1-2 words blacked out] " trans to 175/1617

1672 [1-2 words blacked out] " trans to 175/P-1174
(BF 175/1454) (BF. 175/1483)

1673 Conditions in N.West of Vancouver Island trans 175/P1174 (scratched out)

1674 [1-2 words blacked out] Anti-Propaganda Speech trans to 175/4700

1675 [Golden, Age I.B.S.A. Journal " to 177/27

1676 [1-2 words blacked out] rioting

1677 Roberts Lake Camp strike at

1678 [2-3 words blacked out] "Worker" trans 175/P103

1679 [word blacked out] agtr trans 175/P983

1680 [word blacked out] Bolshevist trans to 175/P-984

1681 [word blacked out] agitator 175/P985

1682 [entry blacked out] 175/P986

1683 [entry blacked out] trans to 175/4809 (scratched out) 175/2143

1684 Searchlight newspaper trans to 177/9

1685 [word blacked out] rioting

1686 [word blacked out] "

1687 [word blacked out] "

1688 Counterfeit Coin from China to be distributed through O.B.U.

1689 [1-2 words blacked out] suspect Re. strike at Capalino Lumber Co. trans to 175/???

Page 89

1690 O.B.U. Hazelton etc (Trans to 175/493)

1691 [word blacked out] suspect

1692 [word blacked out] suspect

1693 [3-4 words blacked out] suspect.

1694 Dorwarts or Vorwarts Proh Pub.
Lumber Workers Industrial Union (OBU - IWW) Keewatin, Ont.

1695 Keewatin Lumber Co I.W.W. Propaganda (scratched out)

1696 [word blacked out] rioting

1697 returned soldiers political action

1698 [word blacked out] Proh List trans to 175/57

1699 Conditions at Mountain Park Mines [2-3 words blacked out] Correspondence continued on 175/47

1700 O.B.U. Crows Nest Pass Transf. to 175/360

1701 Ukrainians in Edmonton Dist. trans to 175/4449

1702 O.B.U. Regina Ukrainian Labour Temple Samo Obrazownia Society 175/4449

1703 I.B.S.A. Vernon B.C.

1704 [word blacked out] Proh Lit. trans to 175/P-1034

1705 [1-2 words blacked out] Sec Bolshe Lodge class 3 trans 175/P1034 (scratched out)

1706 Doukobhours & Mennonites organizations of Re Bolshevism in Wanow Dist

1707 [word blacked out] report

1708 [word blacked out] Bolshe

1709 [word blacked out] subscriber

Page 90

1710 Bolshe & Anarchistic Lit issued by Rand School of Social Science [3-4 words blacked out]

1711 Distribution of Seditious Lit [word blacked out] Regina

1712

1713 [word blacked out] socialist trans to 175/P-548

1714 [word blacked out] alleged I.B.S.

1715 Alleged Perjury [1-2 words blacked out]

1716 [word blacked out] suspect

1717 [word blacked out] suspect

1718 [word blacked out] suspect 175/P375

1719 Parties deported from Gt. Britain

1720 Ukrainian Convention Winipeg

1721 [word blacked out] rioting

1722 Woodsworth. J.S. Seditious libel 175/P594

1723 " contempt of court and sedition 175/P594

1724 I.B.S.A. Vancouver
Industrial Workers of the World Re - Supplies - Vancouver BC

1725 O.B.U. Vancouver Re. I.W.W. Supplies (scratched out)

1726 [1-2 words blacked out] suspect

1727 [1-2 words blacked out] Bolshe agtr alias [word blacked out] trans 175/P623

1728 list of suspected agitators

1729 socialistic literature Ft. William trans to 175/229

Page 91

1730 Pocahontas Mines & O.B.U. Organization

1731 [word blacked out] rioting
(B.F. 175/84 & 175/706)

1732 Conditions report Vancouver

1733 [word blacked out] agitator

1734 [word blacked out] agitator trans to 175/P-1003

1735 [word blacked out] agtr " to 175/P560

1736 Western Canada Colliery Co.
Lumber Workers Industrial Union (OBU) Fernie District, B.C.

1737 I.W.I.U. of the O.B.U. E. Kootenay Sub-Dist (scratched out)

1738 Prohibition - The Factor of Bolshevism

1739 [2-3 words blacked out] report

1740 The Poison in America's Cup 177/3 Littlebrooks Library Series

1741 [entry blacked out]

1742 Strike at Nempkish Lumber Co.

1743 [word blacked out] I.B.S.A 175/P1006

1744 [entry blacked out] trans to 175/P-386

1745 Beaver Cove Lumber & Pulp Co. Conditions at - Beaver Cove, B.C.

1746 The Voice of Labour trans 177/147

1747 [word blacked out] Ukrainian Labour News Subscriber

1748 Alleged Bolshevist Meetings at Fedorah Comp. of [word blacked out]

1749 [word blacked out] rioting & unlawful assembly

Page 92

1750 [1-2 words blacked out] Rioting & Unlawful Assembly

1751 [word blacked out] "

1752 [word blacked out] "

1753 Alleged Russian Propagandists travelling to England

1754 Conditions at Fort Simpson

1755 Supposed German Meeting at Govan

1756 I.W.W. Activities, Vancouver Boundary Line Patrol (Trans to 175/885)

1757 L.W.I.U. Prince George

1758 [word blacked out] agtr & Socialist 175/P1024

1759 [entry blacked out]

1760 [word blacked out] newsagent, Winnipeg

1761 [word blacked out] et al Seditious Conspiracy precautionary measures 175/P32

1762 Workers Herald, The

1763 [word blacked out] I.B.S.A.

1764 Reconstruction meeting at University of Alberta

1765 [word blacked out] & Unrest in China
1766 [2-3 words blacked out] 175/P925
1767 Anarchists Arrest of in Sask
1768 [word blacked out] I.B.S.A. Weyburn
1769 Strike at North West Lumber Co. Camp at Hylo, Alta
Page 93
1770 Socialist Daily, Proposed New Labour Paper
1771 [2-3 words blacked out] Intimidation 175/P2
1772 [word blacked out] I.B.S.A. Poss of Proh Lit.
1773 [word blacked out] " " trans to 177/
1774 [word blacked out] " "
1775 [word blacked out] " "
1776 [1-2 words blacked out] "
1777 [1-2 words blacked out] "
1778 [1-2 words blacked out] "
1779 [entry blacked out]
1780 [entry blacked out] 175/P1830
1781 [entry blacked out]
1782 [word blacked out] suspect
1783 [word blacked out] agtr 175/P1796 (trans)
1784 [word blacked out] O.B.U. Official
1785 O.B.U. Nelson
1786 [word blacked out] suspect 175/1728 (scratched out)
1787 [word blacked out] " "
1788 [word blacked out] subscriber U.L.N.
1789 [word blacked out] " "
Page 94
1970 [word blacked out] Subscriber U.L.N.
1791 Finnish Socialist at Manyberries trans to 175/10
1792 Strike at Canmore Coal Mines 2-12-19
1793 Complaint of [2-3 words blacked out] - agtr
1794 Labour Defence Committee circulars sent to I.W.W. Prisoner
1795 Manitoba Grain Growers Association & Labour
1796 [word blacked out] agtr trans 175/P1917
1797 S.P. of C. Local 3 Wpg [word blacked out] member
1798 (O.B.U.) Strike Fernie proposed (scratched out) Miners Unit Fernie, B.C.
1799 I.W.W. coming to Canada from Idaho. I.W.W. movements from U.S.A. to South Alta Dist. (Trans to 175/885)
1800 Labour trying to gain control at Swift Current 175P1078
1801 [entry blacked out]
1802 [word blacked out] Unlawful Assembly
1803 [word blacked out] "
1804 [word blacked out] "

1805 [word blacked out] "
1806 [word blacked out] "
1807 [word blacked out] " trans to 175/1806 Transf to 175/493
1808 [1-2 words blacked out] labour agitator trans 175/P1446
1809 [word blacked out] suspect
Page 95
1810 [word blacked out] Alien Anarchist deported from U.S.A. BF. from 175/2265
1811 [word blacked out] International Bible Students
1812 [word blacked out] agitator & Bolshevist (O.B.U.)
1813 [word blacked out] Proh Lit.
1814 Jewish Demonstrations in Winnipeg
1815 New World
1816 [word blacked out] Ukrainian Labour News
1817 [word blacked out] "
1818 [2-3 words blacked out] report
1819 Canadian Ukrainian Semi Weekly See 175/1040
1820 Khliel Voila (Bread & Freedom) Newspaper
1821 [word blacked out] telegram in possession re shipment of coffins
1822 O.B.U. Convention Calgary 1-12-19 to 3-12-19
1823 Coal transported across boundary at Gretna, Man
1824 Genl. Conditions Crows Nest Pass trans 175/4453
1825 [word blacked out] suspect agre 175/1728 trans 175/P1013
1826 [3-4 words blacked out] suv Ukrainian Labour News trans 175/P1014
1827 [word blacked out] agtr
1828 U.F.A. Meeting at Etzikon (scratched out) Alberta Federation of Agriculture @ United Farmers of Alberta - Sub Act in Etzikom, Alta
1829 [word blacked out] agtr Birch River
Page 96
1830 Mennonites Gretna District Man.
1831 [word blacked out] proh lit
1832 Conditions in Victoria re Unemployment
1833 [word blacked out] agtr (175/1728)
1834 [word blacked out] "
1835 [1-2 words blacked out] " Correspond [2-3 words blacked out]
1836 [1-2 words blacked out] "
1837 [word blacked out] "
1838 [word blacked out] "
1839 [word blacked out] agtr
1840 [word blacked out] agtr I.W.W.
1841 [word blacked out] propaganda
1842 (O.B.U.) Coleman (Proposed Strike Dist #1 O.B.U. Coleman [scratched out])
1843 [word blacked out] agtr at Taber
1844 O.B.U. Proposed Strike Michel B.C. Previous report Michel O.B.U. (Ord) 175/1145

(scratched out) Trans to 175/4652

1845 Miners Unit (OBU) Bellevue Alta.

1846 [word blacked out] I.B.S.A. Winnipeg

1847 [word blacked out] "

1848 [1-2 words blacked out] " Lloydminster

1849 [word blacked out] I.W.W.

Page 97

1850 [word blacked out] proh lit 177/-23

1851 I.W.W. Movements from U.S.A. to B.C. (Trans to 175/885)

1852 [word blacked out] suspect trans to 175/4930 [word blacked out]

1853 [word blacked out] "

1854 [word blacked out] "

1855 [word blacked out] suspected agitator

B.F. From 175/3165 (Trans to 175/4538)

1856 O.B.U. Calgary meeting of railroad transportation O.B.U. Unit No 1 Calgary.

1857 [word blacked out] suspect

1858 [1-2 words blacked out] agtr & Delegate 175/P1025

1859 [word blacked out] suspect

1860 Grand Army of United Veterans @ United Veterans League - Vancouver

1861 [1-2 words blacked out] Uske B.C. suspected I.W.W. 175/P1136

1862 [word blacked out] Ft. William, subscriber Ukrainian Labour News

1863 [word blacked out] "

1864 [word blacked out] "

1865 [word blacked out] "

1866 [word blacked out] "

1867 [word blacked out] " trans: to: 175/4805

1868 [word blacked out] seditionist agitator

1869 [word blacked out] agtr 175/1728 (scratched out)

Page 98

1870 [1-2 words blacked out] agtr 175/1728 175/P1136

1871 [entry blacked out]

1872 [word blacked out] Brandon trans to 175/P-405

1873 [word blacked out] agtr trans to 175/4821

1874 Datoka Free Press paper printed in U.S.A. trans to 177/26

1875 [word blacked out] agtr re alleged underhand methods used by R.N.W. Police

1876 I.W.W. Activities Canadian Bank of Commerce (Trans. to 175/2368)

1877 [1-2 words blacked out] Bible Student

1877 [1-2 words blacked out] proh lit trans to 177-/

1879 [2-3 words blacked out] proh lit I.B.S.A.

1880 [1-2 words blacked out] Wpg Bolshe 175/P90 (scratched out)

1881 O.B.U. Calgary O.B.U. Supporters Edmonton (Trans to 175/4742)

1882 [1-2 words blacked out] I.B.S.A. trans to 177/42

1883 [word blacked out] I.B.S.A.

1884 [word blacked out] " trans to 177/18

1885 [word blacked out] "

1886 [word blacked out] " trans to 177/19

1887 [word blacked out] " " to 177/17

1888 [word blacked out] agtr 175/1728 175/P1032

1889 [word blacked out] "

Page 99

1890 Calgary Public Library Banned List

1891 [word blacked out] agtr

1892 [word blacked out] O.B.U. organizer trans to 175/5320

1893 [word blacked out] suspect

1894 [1-2 words blacked out] Edmonton 175/6125

1895 [entry blacked out]

1896 [entry blacked out]

1897 [word blacked out] alleged I.W.W. propagandist trans 175/P1067

1898 [word blacked out] O.B.U. agitator 175/P1038

1899 [word blacked out] " 175/P1036

1900 [word blacked out] " 175/P1037

1901 [word blacked out] I.B.S.A. trans to 177/49

1902 Rainy River O.B.U. Activities

1903 Alleged Bolshevistic Meeting in Finn Hall in Township Potts
Industrial Workers of the World - Sub. Act. Within - Fort Frances, Ont.

1904 Alleged Activities of I.W.W. in Ft. Francis Dist. (scratched out) BF 175/813

1905 [word blacked out] poss Proh Lit trans to 177/24

1906 Genl. Conditions W. Kootenay Sub-Dist. activities of (scratched out) O.B.U. (Trans. to 175/493) Sub. Act Within - B.C.

1907 [word blacked out] I.W.W. Trans. to 175/P1091

1908 [word blacked out] O.B.U. 175/P1039

1909 [word blacked out] agtr 175/P1040

Page 100

1910 [1-2 words blacked out] Russian Pianist

1911 [1-2 words blacked out] suspect

1912 Civic Elections. Ft. William and Pt. Arthur 1919

1913 Italian Circular (translation) re O.B.U. element #18. (Trans to 175/3441)

1914 [word blacked out] O.B.U. agtr trans 175/P1041

1915 One Big Union Taber (BG 175/2055)

1916 O.B.U. Bankhead Corresp. transf to 175/492

1917 [word blacked out] OLBBLWL agtr 175/P537

1918 [entry blacked out]
Conditions amongst Germans at Turtleford Sask.

1919 Labour Conditions U.S.A. by [word blacked out]

1920 [word blacked out] alleged contravention of P.O. Act Trans 175/483

1921 [word blacked out] I.B.S.A.

1922 [word blacked out] I.B.S.A.
1923 [word blacked out] agtr 175/P1166
1924 Rumoured Strike. Brule Mines
1925 [word blacked out] Fort William trans to 175/P-921
1926 [word blacked out] proh lit (I.B.S.A.) trans to 177/20
1927 [2-3 words blacked out] proh lit (I.B.S.A.)
1928 [word blacked out] proh lit (I.B.S.A. trans to 177-18
1929 [word blacked out] O.B.U. Regina " to 175/P-1049
Page 101
1930 [word blacked out] O.B.U. Regina 175/P1048
1931 [word blacked out] " " 175/P1050
1932 [word blacked out] agtr & propagandist 175/P1051
1933 [1-2 words blacked out] suspect 175/P910
1934 Rumoured Strike Jasper Colleries
1935 [1-2 words blacked out] subscriber U.R. News
1936 [1-2 words blacked out] "
1937 [1-2 words blacked out] "
1938 Unemployment in Vancouver [4-5 words blacked out]
1939 [word blacked out] suspect
1940 O.B.U. Activities, Ignace
1941 [word blacked out] Anarchist
1942 [1-2 words blacked out] suspect
1943 [1-2 words blacked out] agtr
1944 Labour Situation, Brandon trans to 175/5764
1945 " Winnipeg trans to 175/3645 [3-4 words blacked out]
Industrial Woodworkers of the World
1946 I.W.W. Activities (scratched out) (Vancouver) (175/4860)
1947 [word blacked out] Delegate [1-2 words blacked out] F. William
1948 [1-2 words blacked out] suspect Trans. to 175/P1065
1949 [word blacked out] sec B.C. Loggers Union 175/P1081
Page 102
1950 [word blacked out] suspect agtr
1951 [word blacked out] suspect Transf to 175/40 to 175/4833 [4-5 words blacked out]
1952 [word blacked out] Poss of Proh Lit trans to 177/43
1953 [1-2 words blacked out] suspect
1954 Strike at Ole Hansens Tie Camp Shereton B.C.
1955 Unemployed Veterans in Vancouver [1-2 words blacked out]
1956 [word blacked out] I.B.S.A.
1957 [word blacked out] "
1958 [word blacked out] "
1959 [word blacked out] "
1960 [word blacked out] I.B.S.A.
1961 [word blacked out] "

1962 [word blacked out] poss of proh lit trans 177/
1963 [entry blacked out] 175/P1461
1964 Delegates I.W.I.U.
1965 O.B.U. Proposed Strike Blairmore
1966 [1- 2 words blacked out] I.W.W.
1968 [1-2 words blacked out] I.W.W. agtr trans to 175-P-259
1967 [word blacked out] delegate O.B.U. 175/P1259
1969 Evans A. O.B.U. 175/P1072 175/4882
Page 103
1970 [word blacked out] sub U.L. News 175/P3832
1971 [word blacked out] "
1972 [word blacked out] "
1973 [word blacked out] "
1974 [word blacked out] "
1975 [word blacked out] "
1976 [word blacked out] suspected agtr
1977 [word blacked out] sec M.&S. Lodge O.B.U. Trail B.C. trans to 175/P-699
1978 [word blacked out] Organizer O.B.U. 175/P1061
1979 [word blacked out] O.B.U. & Radical Trans. to 175/P1062
1980 [word blacked out] Vancouver trans to 175/P330
1981 [word blacked out] agtr Trans. to 175/P1063
1982 [entry blacked out] 175/P1064
1983 (O.B.U.) Manitoba Dist Ft. William sub District Local at (scratched out) Nipigon Ont.
1984 Rumoured Strike, Brule Mines
1985 [word blacked out] subscriber U.L.N.
1986 [word blacked out] "
1987 [word blacked out] "
1988 [word blacked out] "
1989 [word blacked out] "
Page 104
1990 One Big Union Hanna Dist (BF 175/2116)
1991 [1-2 words blacked out] agtr & Bolshevist
1992 Labour Conditions at Mines Edmonton
1993 [1-2 words blacked out] agtr
1994 O.B.U. proposed strike Bankhead
1995 [word blacked out] subscriber U.L.N. 175/P1084
1996 [word blacked out] I.B.S.A.
1997 [word blacked out] Golden B.C. I.B.S.A.
1998 [word blacked out] " " trans to 177/33
1999 [word blacked out] " "
2000 [word blacked out] I.W.W. delegate trans to 175/P/1169
2001 [word blacked out] List of suspected agtr 175/P1169 (scratched out)

2002 Labour situation re Bush Work Port Arthur Dist. [3-4 words blacked out]

2003 " Pocanhontas Mines

2004 [word blacked out] seditious Utterances

2005 Conditions at Pr. George Comp of Arthur Transf. to 175/2074

2006 [word blacked out] Alleged agtr transferred to 175/439 Transf to 175P/599

2007 [word blacked out] Estate S.P. of C. Vancouver

2008 Conditions in W. Kootenay Sub Dist Edgewood and Lower Arrow Lake Transf. to 175/199

2009 [1-2 words blacked out] agtr trans to 175/5612

Page 105

2010 [2-3 words blacked out] Report

2011 [word blacked out] German Socialist

2012 [word blacked out] Rosedeer Mine, Wayne, Alta

2013 [word blacked out] M.L.A. Calgary suspect trans to 175/P-22

2014 [2-3 words blacked out] suspect

2015 [word blacked out] subscriber U.L. News

2016 [word blacked out] "

2017 [word blacked out] "

2018 [word blacked out] "

2019 [word blacked out] "

2020 [word blacked out] "

2021 [word blacked out] "

2022 [word blacked out] agtr

2023 Conditions at Merritt B.C. (Transferred to 175/4565)

2024 Buffalo Lakes Lumber Co. Strike at

2025 Industrial System Map of O.B.U. (Pr. Geroge)

2026 [word blacked out] Wpg (Bomb Maker)

2027 Evans A. agitator trans to 175/P-1072

2028 [word blacked out] suspected Agtr

2029 [entry blacked out] "

Page 106

2030 [word blacked out] suspected agtr

2031 [word blacked out] susbscriber U.L. News

2032 [word blacked out] "

2033 [word blacked out] "

2034 [word blacked out] "

2035 [word blacked out] " 175/P2034

2036 [word blacked out] "

2037 [word blacked out] " trans to 175/5521

2038 [word blacked out] " 175/P226

2039 [word blacked out] " 175/P649

2040 [word blacked out] " 175/P228

2041 Progressive Workers of the Pacific

2042 Labour Conditions Medicine Hat for subsequent correspondence [4-5 words blacked out]

2043 [word blacked out] Railway Clerk trans to 175/P-1247

2044 New National Policy Regina

2045 Peoples Forum Regina trans to 175/P-1095 [3-4 words blacked out]

2046 [word blacked out] suspect 175/P1095

2047 [word blacked out] alleged agtr 175/P1094

2048 [word blacked out] anarchist 175/P514

2049 [1-2 words blacked out] Delegate I.W.I.U. 175/P1154

Page 107

2050 [word blacked out] Nat Delegate I.W.I.U. 175/P1154 (scratched out)

2051 [word blacked out] Farmer Agtr

2052 O.B.U. Drumheller Rosedeer Mine, Wayne (scratched out) Miners Unit (OBU Wayne Alta)

2053 [word blacked out] Mayor Edmonton 175/P1088

2054 [word blacked out] Delegate

2055 Canada West Local at Taber (Trans to 175/1915)

2056 [word blacked out] agtr 175/P1066

2057 O.B.U. Members in P.O. Vancouver 175/P103

2058 [word blacked out] agre Trans. to 175/P1086

2059 [word blacked out] Undesirable Alien

2060 O.B.U. In Manitoba Dist Activities in Pyrites Mine Trans to 175/4568

2061 Construction Work C.N. Rly

2062 [1-2 words blacked out] Delegate I.W.I.U 175/P1207

2063 O.B.U. Propaganda Edmonton

2064 [word blacked out] suspect

2065 Bolsheviki Group at Wpg alleged members Transferred to 175/356

2066 [word blacked out] suspect

2067 [word blacked out] suspect Delegate T & L Council Regina

2068 [word blacked out] " " trans to 175/P/1102

2069 (O.B.U.) Proposed Strike (scratched out) Hillcrest, Alta. Miners Unit

Page 108

2070 [1-2 words blacked out] suspect 175/1870

2071 Premier Mine Labour Trouble at

2072 [word blacked out] Labour agitator 175/P1098

2073 Vanderhoof. Ft. Fraser General Conditions at
(B.F. 175/2005)

2074 Prince George East to Dome Creek General Conditions at Trans. to 175/4520

2075 [1-2 words blacked out] Labour agtr

2076 Scott-Neering Socialist 175/P1384

2077 [word blacked out] agtr

2078 [1-2 words blacked out] agtr 175/P1100

2079 Blackfoot Conditions at

2080 [word blacked out] subscriber W.L.N. 175/P1395
2081 [word blacked out] suspect trans to 175/P-196
2082 [word blacked out] subscriber U.L.M. " 175/P-1219
2083 [1-2 words blacked out] undesirable (agtr) 175/P1103
2084 [1-2 words blacked out] suspect 175/P559
2085 O.B.U. Amalgamation Committee (Trans to 175/4859)
2086 O.B.S.A. Edmonton trans to 175/4913
2087 [1-2 words blacked out] agtr 1675/P1113,
2088 [1-2 words blacked out] Stewart B.C. Delegate
2089 (O.B.U.) Gen Workers Unit - Vancouver B.C.
Page 109
2090 [1-2 words blacked out] Delegate
2091 [word blacked out] agtr 175/P1524
2092 [word blacked out] agtr
2093 [1-2 words blacked out] agitator 175/P1116
2094 [word blacked out] delegate I.W.I.U. of O.B.U. 175/P1119
2095 [word blacked out] complt
2096 [word blacked out] member of Ex S & S. L. P of C Wpg Branch
2097 O.B.U. Silverton B.C. General Conditions at W. Kooteney
2098 [1-2 words blacked out] The Pas
2099 Suspected Store of Arms Nelson B.C.
2100 Detroit Reds expected to leave Canada
2101 [word blacked out] Bolshevist Winnipeg 175/P1132
2102 Fort Francis Paper Mill, trouble at
2103 Labour Convention Winnipeg (Strand Theatre)
2104 Ukrainian National Home Assoc Saskatoon trans to 175/5130
2105 [word blacked out] sub. Ukrainian Labour News
2106 [word blacked out] "
2107 [1-2 words blacked out] W. Kootney 175/P1129
2108 [2-3 words blacked out] Distributer of Bolshevist Lit at
2109 [word blacked out] Suspect. agtr 175/P1137
Page 110
2110 [word blacked out] agtr 175/P1138
2111 [1-2 words blacked out] suspect Regina 175/P1144
2112 [word blacked out] suspect Regina 175/P1145
2113 [1-2 words blacked out] subscriber U.L.N.
2114 [1-2 words blacked out] "
2115 [1-2 words blacked out] "
2116 Sheerness & District Conditions at Trans to 175/1990
[3-4 words blacked out]
2117 Alleged Bolsheviki Society at Saskatoon Transferred to 175/4448
2118 [word blacked out] Sec Nordegg Mines Unit O.B.U.
2119 [1-2 words blacked out] Leader Radicals in U.S.A., Chicago

2120 [3-4 words blacked out] suspect

2121 [word blacked out] agtr & Propagandist 175/P287

2122 Mountain Park Alta - Miners Unit (O.B.U.) vs U.M.W.A.

2123 W. Kootenay Conditions at Naksup & Arrow Lakes Transferred to 175/199

2124 [word blacked out] agtr returned from U.S.A. 174/P1188

2125 [1-2 words blacked out] report 175/P416

2126 [1-2 words blacked out] "

2127 [word blacked out] O.B.U. Organizer 175/P1157

2128 [word blacked out] suspect 175/P990

2129 -----------

Page 111

2130 [1-2 words blacked out] O.B.U. Delegate

2131 [word blacked out] Bolshevist

2132 [word blacked out] "

2133 [word blacked out] O.B.U. Organizer 175/P1000
Lumber Workers Industrial Union Vancouver B.C.

2134 I.W.W. Union #500

2135 [word blacked out] Bolshevik

2136 [word blacked out] Letter from to Vancouver Daily Sun

2137 [2-3 words blacked out] report agtr BF. from 175/2459

2138 Hamilton & Acme Mines, Strike at

2139 Hutton Mills & Urling Pit, Genl Conditions at [2-3 words blacked out]

2140 [word blacked out] suspect

2141 Brandon church service, Presby Church

2142 Merritt. B.C. O.B.U.

2143 Ainsworth, B.C. O.B.U. (scratched out) One Big Union - Ainsworth, B.C. [word blacked out]

2144 Princeton & Dist conditions at [3-4 words blacked out]

2145 [word blacked out] organizing agtr 175/P1093

2146 [1-2 words blacked out] report 175/P1284

2147 [word blacked out] "

2148 [word blacked out] suspect 175/P366

2149 [word blacked out] Bolshe

Page 112

2150 [word blacked out] agtr 175/P1087

2151 [word blacked out] "

2152 [word blacked out] O.B.U. agtr 175/P1799

2153 [word blacked out] O.B.U. agtr 175/P1176

2154 [1-2 words blacked out] & I.W.W. 175/P1177

2155 [3-4 words blacked out] Bolshe & I.W.W.

2156 Big River I.W.I.U. organization at (Trans. to 175/1457)

2157 [entry blacked out] 175/P104

2158 [word blacked out] publishing seditious libel trial of 175/P817

2159 [1-2 words blacked out] Bolshe Wpg
2160 [1-2 words blacked out] "
2161 [1-2 words blacked out] "
2162 [word blacked out] alleged agtr 175/P1190
2163 Polish Young Men's Club Cedoux
2164 [word blacked out] paper Mine Conditions Western Coal Co Mine at Wayne Alta
2165 Alberta Temperance Act infraction of by Miners Blairmore Alta
2166 Ross-Saskatoon Lumber Co Strike at Waldo
2167 O.B.U. Convention Jan 26th 1920 Wpg Labour Temple
2168 Ukrainian Dramatic Society Moose Jaw
2169 [word blacked out] Report German
Page 113
(R.24-1-20 [word blacked out] rep) 175/P1205
2170 [1-2 words blacked out] report German Socialist Walter Zschierich
2171 I.B.S.A. Regina
2172 [word blacked out] socialist
2173 [2-3 words blacked out] Ukrainian Dramatic Soc. trans to 175/5356
2174 [1-2 words blacked out] " 175/P1199
2175 [1-2 words blacked out] " 175/1200
2176 [word blacked out] " 175/P1197
2177 Canadian Club proposed formation of
2178 [word blacked out] Bolshe Winnipeg
2179 [word blacked out] Bolshe " [1-2 words blacked out]
2180 [word blacked out] O.B.U. Organizer trans 175/P1194
2181 [word blacked out] suspect
2182 [word blacked out] smuggling I.W.W. Supplies [word blacked out] 175/P1206
2183 [1-2 words blacked out] alleged agtr 175P/213
2184 [2-3 words blacked out] Bolshe 175/P934
2185 [word blacked out] agitator 175/P1092
2186 [word blacked out] Ruthenian agtr trans to 175/5850 175P/475
2187 [1-2 words blacked out] report 175/P1210
2188 [2-3 words blacked out] suspect
2189 Wpg Labour situation [3-4 words blacked out]
Page 114
2190 [2-3 words blacked out] undesirable
2191 [word blacked out] Bolshe
2192 Spector "
2193 [word blacked out] alleged I.W.W.
2194 [word blacked out] suspect Tie Insp C.P.R. trans 175/P1212
2195 [word blacked out] allgd agtr
2196 [word blacked out] Letter from W.J.K. to [word blacked out] 175/P366
2197 [entry blacked out]
2198 Surf Inlet O.B.U.

2199 Ellsi Camp Lombard B.C. Strike at

2200 Skidegate B.C. Genrl Conditions at

2201 [word blacked out] agtr 175/P1122

2202 [word blacked out] agtr trans to 175/5290 175/P91

2203 Skandanava School Neosha Sask Grain Growers Annual Meeting [word blacked out]

2204 [word blacked out] allegd Bolshe

2205 [1-2 words blacked out] suspect 175/P1218

2206 [word blacked out] "

2207 Centre Star Mine, Rossland B.C. O.B.U. Movement Kootenay Dist Trans to 175/3344

2208 Seattle U.S.A. Conditions in

2209 [word blacked out] I.W.W. Suspect

Page 115

2210 [word blacked out] complaint of Warner Alta

2211 O.B.U. (Activities) Fort Francis Ont.

2212 Ukrainian Peoples Council Convention of Saskatoon

2213 [1-2 words blacked out] Sec O.B.U. Wayne

2214 [word blacked out] O.B.U. agtr 175/P1191

2215 [word blacked out] Sec I.W.I.U. 175/P1221

2216 [1-2 words blacked out] Ft. Wm. Branch of Russian Bolsheviks trans to 175/5252

2217 [word blacked out] Surf Inlet agtr

2218 [word blacked out] O.B.U. agtr 175/P1285

2219 [word blacked out] O.B.U. trans to 175/6325

2220 [2-3 words blacked out] undesirable

2221 [word blacked out] agtr 175/P1230

2222 McLachlan. J.B. O.B.U. Sympathizer Springfield trans 175/P1253

2223 Model Cafe Cordova Street - Vancouver

2224 [word blacked out] I.W.I.U. Delegate 175/P918

2225 [word blacked out] O.B.U. agtr

2226 I.W.I.Union (Camp & I.W.I.Union) Convention of Jan 1920

2227 Finnish Soc Organiz'n West Kootenay Dist

2228 O.B.U. Generally statistics on - Canada Trans to HV-28-1

2229 [entry blacked out] 175/P1047

Page 116

2230 [1-2 words blacked out] I.W.I.U. Delegate 175/P1172

2231 cancelled

(B.F. 175/3791)

2232 Cobalt, Ont General Conditions Labour amongst Miners

2233 One Big Union Activities - Porcupine, Ont

2234 [word blacked out] suspect 175/P2046

2235 General Conditions in Sudbury District (trans to 175/5416) BF from 175/2616

2236 General Conditions in St. Thomas District [2-3 words blacked out]

2237 [word blacked out] suspect 175/P1232

2238 [word blacked out] Bolshevik

2239 [word blacked out] agitator

2240 [word blacked out] agitator

2241 [word blacked out] agitator O.B.U. 175/P1512 Bf. from 175/2824
[2-3 words blacked out]

2242 Ukrainian Organization "Fight" (Barotha Struggle

2243 Special Meeting of Reds in Winnipeg trans to 175/356

2244 Trial of Reds in New York State - Police Assistance Asked

2245 Arms, Ammunition & Explosives - Regulations - Policy trans to R-125-1900

2246 [word blacked out] suspect Correspondence transf. to 175P1750

2247 [word blacked out] Serbian - suspect 175/P1750 (scratched out)

2248 O.B.U. of Lumber Mills, Loggers, Teamsters etc Vancouver

2249 Mass Meetings - Auspices Women's Labour League Wpg 175/5270 [2-3 words blacked out]

Page 117

2250 General Conditions at Minto - N.B. [1-2 words blacked out]
(BF 175/2252)

2251 General Conditions in Toronto - Reports [word blacked out] Employers Detective Agency.

2252 General Conditions in Toronto Thiels Detectives (Trans to 175/2251)
(B.F. 175/3062)

2253 " Hamilton " [2-3 words blacked out]

2254 " Thorold, Ont Employers Detective (Trans to 175/2669)

2255 " Hamilton " [2-3 words blacked out]

2256 " Montreal " " (Trans to 175/2696)

2257 " Montreal [3-4 words blacked out] Trans to 175/2696

2258 " Buffalo, N.Y. Pinkerton Detectives

2259 " Windsor & Detroit " (BF 175/2674)

2260 " " Ford [word blacked out]

2261 " Montreal [2-3 words blacked out] (Trans to 175/2696)

2262 Deportation - Russian Bolshevists & Agitators Method & Policy

2263 Bolshevism in Ford City, Ont Complaint of [word blacked out]

2264 [word blacked out] "Reg Agitator" suspect

2265 [word blacked out] Anarchist suspect trans to 175/1810

2266 [1-2 words blacked out] O.B.U. Organizer 175/P1266

2267 [word blacked out] suspect 175/P1269

2268 [1-2 words blacked out] organizer, Ukrainian Labour Temple

2269 Irish National Association, Vancouver Trans to Cont A-283

Page 118

2270 [1-2 words blacked out] agitator - Vancouver 175/P1270
BF. 175/2690

2271 [4-5 words blacked out] Seattle 175/P1307

[3-4 words blacked out]

2272 [entry blacked out]

2273 [word blacked out] agtr 175/P506

2274 [word blacked out] alleged Bolsheviki BF from 173/2317

2275 [word blacked out] alleged agtr

2276 [1-2 words blacked out] agtr trans to 175/5537

2277 [word blacked out] Sec I.W.I.U. of O.B.U. Prince George [2-3 words blacked out]

2278 Peoples Russian Information Bureau Literature issued by

2279 [1-2 words blacked out] O.B.U.

2280 O.B.U. Sarnia, Ont

2281 [1-2 words blacked out] United Farmers Ass'n at Stavely, Alta trans to 175/P-1250

2282 [1-2 words blacked out] Evesham - suspected agtr 175/P1310

2283 [word blacked out] suspect trans to 175/P-1309

2284 [1-2 words blacked out] - Allgd agtr

2285 [1-2 words blacked out] agtr - Mafeking 175/P1314

2286 [word blacked out] suspected O.B.U. agtr trans to 175/5230 175/P1267 (B.F. 175/3604)

2287 Halifax & Dartmouth Labour situation at [3-4 words blacked out]

2288 [1-2 words blacked out] Logging Engineer 175/P1268

2289 Manitoba Provincial Elections 1920 Proposed nomination of Radicals in trans to 175/4984

Page 119

2290 Boundary Falls, Alleged disloyal citizens at

2291 Employment Conditions - Prairie Provinces & B.C. (Summary)

2292 Employers Association of British Columbia trans to 175/4567

2293 [1-2 words blacked out] suspect

2294 [1-2 words blacked out] " 175/P1205

2295 [word blacked out] " trans to 175/1617 Corr. trans to 175P1005

2296 Labour Unions - Mine Workers in Canada "Generally"

2297 [3-4 words blacked out] - suspect

2298 United Mine Workers of Nova Scotia [2-3 words blacked out]

2299 [word blacked out] agtr 175/P1165

2300 [word blacked out] "

2301 [word blacked out] "

2302 [word blacked out] alleged agtr

2303 [word blacked out] agtr

2304 [word blacked out] "

2305 [word blacked out] - Captain German Naval Officer - movements of

2306 [word blacked out] alleged Anarchist

2307 [word blacked out] suspect

2308 Gnl conditions at Prince Rupert, Ocean Falls, Bella Bella 175/899 [word blacked out]

2309 Whittaker & Larsen's Camp strike at

Page 120

2310 L.W.I.U. United Grain Growers Lumber Co. Hutton B.C. Sanitary Conditions at camp

2311 [word blacked out] O.B.U. Delegate to England 175/1273 Corr. transf. to 175P789

2312 Winnipeg, Labour Situation at [1-2 words blacked out]

2313 Wpg Police Force " transf to 175/3645 (scratched out) [1-2 words blacked out]

2314 O.B.U. (Delegates to England) Re R.B. Russell case (scratched out)

2315 [word blacked out] agtr & O.B.U. delegate to England 175/P810

2316 [word blacked out] " " 175/P1248

2317 [word blacked out] alleged Bolshevik, compt of [word blacked out] 175/2274

2318 Prince George east to Penny General Conditions Trans to 175/4520

2319 Prince George South to Stoney Creek " [2-3 words blacked out]

2320 [1-2 words blacked out] alleged Bolshevist

2321 [entry blacked out] trans to 175/P-97

2322 [1-2 words blacked out] suspected Bolshevik BF. 175/2521 175/P1386

2323 [entry blacked out]

2324 [1-2 words blacked out] Bolshevik

2325 [1-2 words blacked out] Canada Generally trans to 175/5463

2326 [word blacked out] O.B.U. delegate 175/P1732

2327 [word blacked out] Int " trans to 175/5005 175/P1771

2328 Federal Mines, Lethbridge 175/1252

2329 Blaine Lake General Conditions at

Page 121

2330 [entry blacked out]

2331 [word blacked out] Re Trades & Labour Council Wpg 175/P1536

2332 [word blacked out] Alleged Pro German (Cancelled) C.I.B.

2333 [word blacked out] " " C.I.B.

2334 [word blacked out] " "

2336 [entry blacked out] C.I.B.

2337 [word blacked out] (File Missing see 175/P1282)

2338 [entry blacked out] C.I.B.

2339 [1-2 words blacked out] suspects Chinese at Vancouver

2340 Toronto, Conditions in, [1-2 words blacked out] (File Missing on 29-13-37) Trans to 175/4103 [1-2 words blacked out]

2341 [word blacked out] suspect

2342 [word blacked out] Bolshevik at the Pas, Man. L.W.I.U. in Sask 175/P1233

2343 [word blacked out] Bolshevik 175/P1296

2344 [word blacked out] suspect

2345 [word blacked out] agtr & Delegate 175/2315

2346 Employment in Canada, Generally, Dept of Labour, Report on

2347 [word blacked out] suspect 175/P1133

2348 [word blacked out] suspect

2349 [word blacked out] I.W.W.

Page 122

2350 [word blacked out] agtr

2351 [1-2 words blacked out] agtr. possible vocational training school 175/P2090

2352 [word blacked out] suspect R.B. Russell Case 175/2314

2353 [word blacked out] suspect trans to 175/1294

2354 [word blacked out] " 175/P1293

2355 [1-2 words blacked out] Ottawa

Ford Lumber Co. - Conditions Within Camp at Smoky River No Address

2356 (scratched out)

2357 Canadian Brotherhood of Stationary Engineers, Alberta, Edmonton 23-2-21 (scratched out)

2358 [entry blacked out] trans to 175/3007 [1-2 words blacked out]

2359 [word blacked out] organizer O.B.U. Correspondence Transf to 175/P1407

2360 [word blacked out] sus. Undesirable Immigrant & agitator

2361 Blank & Co New York

2362 [word blacked out] Sein Fiener alleged agtr in Canada

2363 [word blacked out] agtr O.B.U. 175/P1354

2364 [word blacked out] official Am.Fed. of Lab. in U.S.A.

2365 [1-2 words blacked out] sec Trades & Labour Council Wpg Transf. to 175/4589

2366 [word blacked out] meetings under auspices Socialist Party of Canada

2367 [word blacked out] " " "

2368 O.B.U. & I.W.W. Connection between (BF. 175/1876)

2369 Metcalfe Mr. Justice Threats against. Trial of Strikers at Wpg.

Page 123

Industrial Workers of the World (Literature) Toronto, Ont. [word blacked out]

2370 [word blacked out] Toronto. Possession I.W.W. Literature. (scratched out)

2371 [word blacked out] suspect

2372 [entry blacked out]

2373 [1-2 words blacked out] suspects

2374 [word blacked out] O.B.U. agtr

2375 Cooper Cliff conditions at One Big Union Sub Act Within

2376 Dempseys Camp Strike at

2377 [1-2 words blacked out] Ukrainian Dramatic Society Moose Jaw

2378 Experts in U.S.A. organization of

2379 [word blacked out] Seditious propaganda prohibited literature, Toronto

2380 Arms & Ammunition statistics re Importation trans to R-126-1920

2381 [word blacked out] Prohibited Literature 175/P2124

2382 [word blacked out] I.W.W.

2383 [2-3 words blacked out] (Trans Crime) C.I.B.

2384 Irish Liberty Bond (Loan) Campaign in the U.S.A.

2385 Portage la Prairie International Bible Students

2386 [word blacked out] Tie-Camp. sus. agitators at

2387 [word blacked out] agitator Edmonton trans to 175/5935 175/P1287

2388 Russian, [word blacked out] suspect trans to 175/P1284
2389 [entry blacked out]
Page 124
2390 Regina lbr Conditions
2391 Manitoba Dist alleged I.W.W. Activities in
2392 Britannia Mining & Smelting Co. Conditions Labour At. B.C.
2393 Mill Creek General Conditions
2394 O.B.U. Medicine Hat
2395 [1-2 words blacked out] suspect 175/P134
2396 Seattle U.S.A. Strike of Longshoremen at
2397 Algoma Steel Plant at Sault Ste Marie, Ont O.B.U. Activities at Transf. to 175/2461
2398 I.W.W. Song Book of
2399 [word blacked out] agtr 175/P693
3400 [word blacked out] Bolshevist Foreign
2401 [word blacked out] suspect
2402 Telegraphers Union Wpg Convention March 18/20
2403 [1-2 words blacked out] suspect Communist. Lbr Party
2404 The Pas - Man Telegraph Officer at [word blacked out] 175/P1057
2405 [word blacked out] Telegrapher Operator (in 1920) - suspect OBU The Pas. Man. Transf. to 175/2585
2406 Montreal, P.Q. General Conditions [1-2 words blacked out] (Trans. 175/2696)
2407 " P.Q. " " " " [word blacked out] (trans to 175/2696)
2408 " P.Q. " " " " [word blacked out] (Trans to 175/2696)
2409 O.B.U. Vancouver B.C. Transf. to 175/4859
Page 125
2410 [word blacked out] O.B.U. Agent 175/P1301
2411 [word blacked out] Bolshevist trans to 175/P-464
2412 O.B.U. Goose Bay, Queen Charlotte Islands
2413 [word blacked out] suspect 175/P1405
2414 [word blacked out] agitator 175/P1348
2415 Bricklayers Union Calgary proposed strike
2416 [word blacked out] suspect
2417 [word blacked out] undesirable
2418 [word blacked out] suspect
2419 [word blacked out] undesirable [2-3 words blacked out]
2420 [1-2 words blacked out] undesirable
2421 [3-4 words blacked out] undesirable
2422 [1-2 words blacked out] undesirable
2423 [word blacked out] " [4-5 words blacked out]
2424 [word blacked out] "
2425 [word blacked out] "
2426 [word blacked out] request of from cancelled
2427 [1-2 words blacked out] alleged Bolshevist 175/P1910

2428
2429 East, Alderman Calgary suspected agitator 175/P989
Page 126
2430 [word blacked out] Edmonton Agtr 175/P979
2431 [word blacked out] alleged anarchist (This is not [word blacked out]) 175/P1304
2432 Russian Ukrainian Dramatic Company - Concert Troupe
2433 Farmers Party Portage la Prairie Dist
2434 [1-2 words blacked out] Alleged O.B.U. Agitator 175/P1401
2435 [2-3 words blacked out] alleged Bolshevist agent
2436 O.B.U. Montreal Trans to 175/6251
2437 Windsor, Ont Public meetings in Labour Temple at
2438 [word blacked out] O.B.U. agitator 175/P1251
2439 B.C. Fed of Labour Victoria, B.C. 10th Annual Convention
2440 [word blacked out] suspect, Vancouver
2441 [word blacked out] " The Regina People's Forum 175/P1313
2442 [2-3 words blacked out] Finnish Soc. Organ. Gnl. Agent
2443 Prince George Dist Gnl Conditions West to Vanderhoof B.C. trans to 175/4275
2444 Toronto Baptist Church meetings York St.
2445 [word blacked out] suspected agitator
2446 [word blacked out] O.B.U. agitator
2447 St. John N.B. Labour Situation trans to 175/7390
2448 Ukrainian Society in Goodeve & Ituna
2449 (O.B.U.), C.P.R. Construction Camps Alberta
Page 127
2450 New Brunswick, Federation of Labour
2451 Third International [2-3 words blacked out]
2452 [word blacked out] agtr 175/P1215
2453 Ukrainian Dramatic Society Wpg Man
2454 Drumheller Bolshevic Conditions at
2455 Windsor International Bible Students Assoc
2456 [word blacked out] suspect
2457 [word blacked out] " trans to 175/5007 [word blacked out]
2458 [word blacked out] "
2459 [entry blacked out] trans to 175/2137
2460 O.B.U. amongst Finlanders trans to 175/4543
(B.F. 175/2397)
2461 O.B.U. Sault Ste Marie
2462 Sault Ste Marie General Conditions
2463 [1-2 words blacked out] suspect
2464 [1-2 words blacked out] undesirable
2465 [1-2 words blacked out] "
2466 [3-4 words blacked out] suspect
2467 [2-3 words blacked out] White Slave Traffic

2468 [3-4 words blacked out] undesirable

2469 [2-3 words blacked out] suspect trans to 175/P/2841

Page 128

(File Destroyed on Instructions of Sgt Kells, 21-7-53.)

2470 [entry blacked out]

2471 Canora, Sask Conditions at

2472 Toronto Labour Conditions at 175/4803 [2-3 words blacked out]

2473 Swift Current Political Labr. Party Trans to 175/4836

2474 [word blacked out] agtr

2475 O.B.U. in Hamilton Transferred to 175/5953

2477 [1-2 words blacked out] Delegate & member L.W.I.U. of the O.B.U. Pas Transf. to 175/2585

2476 Canmore Strike at [2-3 words blacked out]

2478 [word blacked out] suspect (believed lost)

2479 [word blacked out] sus. agtr Peterboro, Ont

2480 [word blacked out] suspect 175/P1337 B.F. 175/2565

2481 Swift Current O.B.U. 175/P693 [2-3 words blacked out]

2482 [3-4 words blacked out] Hove, Man. [1-2 words blacked out] Trans to 175/P-613

2483 [1-2 words blacked out] suspect 175/P1311

2484 [word blacked out] " Regina trans to 175/P-1309

2485 [word blacked out] " Drumheller

2486 [word blacked out] delegates & members L.W.I.U. of the O.B.U. Pas 175/P1118

2487 Regina United War Veterans League (Trans to 175/2989)

2488 Cobalt International Miners Union

2489 [word blacked out] suspect Drumheller

Page 129

2490 Cobalt O.B.U. Trans to 175/6416

2491 Lethbridge, Alta O.B.U. Convention March 1920

2492 Edmonton New Economic Class (Transf. to 175/4524)

2493 [word blacked out] suspect

2494 Cobalt O.B.U. Strike at McKinley Darragh Mines

2495 [word blacked out] alleged Bolshevist

2496 Truro N.S. Miners Convention

2497 [1-2 words blacked out] suspect 175/P1320

2498 [word blacked out] suspect

2499 [word blacked out] "

2500 Port Alberni Dist Gnl Conditions trans to 175/ [3-4 words blacked out]

2501 Nanaimo Dist " Trans to 175/4521

2502 [word blacked out] agtr

2503 Hamilton amalgamated Clothing Workers Local trans to 175/4537

2504 [word blacked out] agtr

2505 [word blacked out] Bolshevik

2506 Halifax Strike Coal Workers

2507 Port Neville Strike at B.C. Trans to 175/1117 [1-2 words blacked out]
2508 Melville Ukrainian Labour & Socialistic Society
2509 Mountain Park Labour Conditions in Lovett Branches [4-5 words blacked out]
Page 130
2510 [1-2 words blacked out] O.B.U. trans 175/P1315
2511 [1-2 words blacked out] alleged agtr 175/1494 [word blacked out] 175/P1494
2512 [3-4 word blacked out] alleged I.W.W.
2513 [word blacked out] agtr
2514 Yiddish "Arbeiter Klass", Jewish Labour Class, Montreal, P.Q.
2515 [word blacked out] agtr 175/P1323
2516 [word blacked out] "
2517 [word blacked out] Chaim suspect
2518 O.B.U. Saunders Alta
2519 [2-3 words blacked out] Ukrainian Suspect
2520 Hamilton, S.P. of C. BF. from 175/3736 - 175/2553
2521 [word blacked out] sus Bolshevic trans to 175/2322 Transf to 175P1386
2522 [word blacked out] suspect Hamilton
2523 [2-3 words blacked out] agtr
2524 [word blacked out] agtr 175/P1236
2525 [word blacked out] suspect BF from 175/2567
2526 Labour Party Halifax Re Halifax Citizen trans to 175/4786
2527 [word blacked out] suspect
2528 I.W.W. Button Found in C.I.B. Office Regina - [word blacked out]
2529 Rochester N.Y. alleged Bolshevists in
Page 131
2530 [word blacked out] Canora O.B.U.
2531 Alert Bay B.C. Genl Conditions (Trans. to 175/4632)
2532 Bolshevik Literature Sudbury Dist - [3-4 words blacked out] trans to 175/???
2533 [word blacked out] agtr to 175/P1312
2534 [word blacked out] suspect Correspondence transf to 175P1388
2535 [entry blacked out]
2536 [word blacked out] agtr [word blacked out]
2537 Montreal Social League
2538 [word blacked out] suspect 175/P1761
2539 [entry blacked out] 175/P1358
2540 [entry blacked out]
2541 [word blacked out] suspect
2542 [word blacked out] suspect trans to 175/4801 175/P262
2543 O.B.U. among R.C.M. Police - Bellevue, Alta [2-3 words blacked out]
2544 O.B.U. Sub Act. Within - Exshaw Alberta
2545 [word blacked out] Concert Party
2546 Zluka Bolshevist Party trans to 175/5579
2547 Russian Ukrainian Dramatic Co Kamsack BF 175/213

2548 [1-2 words blacked out] (? & G.W.I. Union) L.W.I.U.

2549 [word blacked out] allgd Bolshevist 175/P1366

Page 132

2550 Toronto Labour Council continued on 175/5585 [1-2 words blacked out]

2551 [word blacked out] suspect

2552 Conditions at Toronto Miscellaneous Reports trans to 175/4803 [1-2 words blacked out]

2553 Hamilton. S.P. of C. 175/2520

2554 [word blacked out] agtr 175/P1066

2555 [word blacked out] " 175/P1361

2556 [entry blacked out]

2557 [word blacked out] suspect

2558 [word blacked out] agtr

2559 [word blacked out] "

2560 [word blacked out] suspect

2561 Minto N.B. Arms, Ammun. in poss Miners & Aliens

2562 [word blacked out] suspect

2563 [word blacked out] O.B.U. agtr

2564 [word blacked out] agtr 175/P1345

2565 [word blacked out] suspect 175/2480 Transf to 175P/1337

2566 Shawnigan Lake Lumber Co Strke

2567 [word blacked out] suspect trans to 175/2525

2568 [word blacked out] O.B.U. agtr trans 175/P1258

2569 [entry blacked out]

Page 133

2570 [word blacked out] suspect 175/P1334

2571 Slocan Dist Gnl conditions in Transferred to 175/199

2472 [word blacked out] O.B.U. agtr trans to 175/P-85

2573 Peoples Forum, Toronto - Sub. Activities Within

2574 [word blacked out] allgd Bolshevist

2575 Winnipeg Strike of Tailors

2576 Alien Agitators Austuan-Schumacher, Ont

2577 Copper Cliff, Ont O.B.U. (Convention held at Copper Cliff, April 1920) Ontario

2578 [word blacked out] Suspect 175P/1255

2579 [word blacked out] "

2580 [word blacked out] "

2581 Murphy & Hanson Lumber Camp

2582 [3-4 words blacked out] Conditions Generally [5-6 words blacked out]

2583 [1-2 words blacked out] I.W.W. 175/P131

2584 [word blacked out] Delegate L.W.I.U. of O.B.U.
(B.F. 175/2477 & 175/2405)

2585 [word blacked out] Lumber Workers Indsutrial Union (O.B.U.) The Pas Man.

2586 Cape Breton N.S. Genl Conditions [word blacked out]

2587 South Saskatchewan Dist Labr Conditions in Re O.B.U. Statistics [2-3 words blacked out]

2588 [word blacked out] sus. lbr organizer & agtr

2589 Bruce, Malcolm suspect [word blacked out] 175/P962

Page 134

2590 [1-2 words blacked out] suspect 175/P1387

2591 Point Levy Dist & Quebec City Gnl Conditions in 175/7371 [1-2 words blacked out]

2592 [word blacked out] agtr 175/P1078

2593 [word blacked out] alleged Bolshevist at Swallwell, Alta

2594 [1-2 words blacked out] agtr

2595 [1-2 words blacked out] suspect

2596 [1-2 words blacked out] "

2597 [1-2 words blacked out] "

2598 [1-2 words blacked out] agtr

2599 [1-2 words blacked out] alleged Bolshevist & anarchist

2600 Ottawa, Ont Labour Conditions 175/6028 [1-2 words blacked out]

2601 [word blacked out] suspect

2602 [word blacked out] "

2603 Prince George Dist Gnl Conditions Aleza Lake-Willow River Transf. to 175/4520

2604 Prince George Dist Gnl Conditions Croydon-Rider " " "

2605 [1-2 words blacked out] suspect

2606 [word blacked out] agtr 175/P1667

2607 [word blacked out] suspect 175/1474

2608 [2-3 words blacked out] agtr & Bolshevist

2609 Private Employment Agencies in Alta

Page 135

2610 [word blacked out] suspect

2611 [word blacked out] "

2612 Pembroke, Ont O.B.U. at

2613 Coal Mine Workers Operators in Western Canada [4-5 words blacked out]

2614 [word blacked out] suspect

2615 [word blacked out] sus agtr

2616 Sudbury Ont O.B.U. trans to 175/2235

2617 G.W.V.A. Convention Montreal March 24th to 28th 1920

2618 L.W.I.U. Convention of Feb 1920 at Pt. Arthur

2619 [word blacked out] Wpg Threatening letter to 175/P808

2620 Winnipeg Ukrainian Labour Party Trans to 175/4490 [1-2 words blacked out]

2621 Bolshevists from Detroit sent to Portage la Prairie, Man

2622 [word blacked out] I.W.W. suspect

2623 C & L.W.I.U. of O.B.U. Montreal - Transferred to 175/7284

2624 Island Union of Miners, Organization of

2625 [2-3 words blacked out] Undesirable

2626 [entry blacked out]

2627 [word blacked out] Russian Subject "

2628 [1-2 words blacked out] undesirable & Bolshevist

2629 [3-4 words blacked out] undesirable

2630 [entry blacked out]

Page 136

2631 [word blacked out] O.B.U. Organizer suspect 175/P1351

2632 [entry blacked out] file destroyed 30-5-55 M.OB.

2633 [word blacked out] organization of file destroyed 30-5-55 M.OB.

2635 Canmore Coal Coy. Writ against Industrial Disputes against

2636 [word blacked out] Bolshevist 175/P1400

2634 [word blacked out] suspect, Montreal trans to 175/2739

2637 [word blacked ou] suspect

2638 [word blacked out] agtr 175P1339

2639 [word blacked out] organizer 175/P481

2640 [word blacked out] Organizer O.B.U. 175/P1364

2641 Merchants attitude of towards O.B.U. Vancouver Island sub Dist. Transf. to 175/1506

2642 [word blacked out] suspect

2643 [word blacked out] " 175/P1356

2644 Windsor, Ont Labour conditions at 175/6886

2645 Toronto, Ont Labour Party, Propaganda of Trans to 175/4495

2646 Irish Freedom Canadian Friends of

2647 [word blacked out] Bolshevist

2648 Finnish Legionaries of, coming to Canaa, Helsingfors

2649 Jewish Socialist Party, Montreal

2650 [word blacked out] agtr Jewish Socialist Party Transf to 175/P1759

Page 137

2651 Montreal May Day Conference and Celebration at Transferred to 175/3949

2652 [word blacked out] suspect

2653 Timmins, Ont O.B.U. Organizers (Trans to 175/2685)

2654 [word blacked out] Russian I.W.W.

2655 Hamilton, Ont Bolshevists at BF. 155/3201

2656 [word blacked out] suspect

2657 [1-2 words blacked out] suspect trans to 175/P/1355

2658 German contact or connections [3-4 words blacked out] trans to 175/P1918

2659 Spugnia Bolshevik Society - Toronto Social Democratic Party

2660 World Hotel, Vancouver Bomb Found

2661 [word blacked out] suspect

2662 [word blacked out] suspect

2663 [word blacked out] "

2664 [word blacked out] O.B.U. Organizer trans to 175/P-1418

2665 Jewish Relief Society, Toronto

2666 C.P.R. Labour Conditions on [3-4 words blacked out]

2667 Toronto, May Day Celebration & Strike Transf. to 175/3944
2668 Rhorold O.B.U. Movement in
2669 Thorold Labour Conditions at (BF 175/2254)
2670 [word blacked out] suspect

Page 138

2671 O.B.U. Sub Act. Within - Esquimalt B.C.
2672 [word blacked out] O.B.U. agtr Transf to 175/75
2673 Anchorage Bay, B.C. Strike of Camp "C" at
2674 [word blacked out] General suspect (Trans to 175/2259)
(B.F. 175/3930)
3675 Hamilton, Ont May Day Strike & Celebration
2676 [2-3 words blacked out] Wpg suspect
Grand Army of United Veterans (G.A.U.V.)
2677 United Veterans League, Ottawa, Ont
Grand Army of Canada
2678 Statistics re Salaried Leaders, Organizers of Different Org
2679 Prince George District Patrol to Hutton & Longworth Transferred to 175/4520
2680 [word blacked out] suspect
2681 American Fed. of Lab. 40th joint annual convention held in Mtl June 1920 Canada
2682 Calgary, The Russian Club trans to 175/7099
2683 [word blacked out] Undesirable
2684 [2-3 words blacked out] agitators
2685 Timmins, Ont Gnl Conditions Reports [word blacked out] (BF 175/2653)
2686 [word blacked out] suspect trans to 175/4835
2687 [word blacked out] "
2688 Lethbridge, Waiters' Union (O.B.U.)
2689 Grand Army of United Veterans, Toronto
2690 [word blacked out] Bolshevist 175/2271

Page 139

2691 [word blacked out] Italian suspect
2692 Toronto, Conditions at Employers Detective Agency [word blacked out] trans to 175/2251
2693 [word blacked out] agtr Trans to 175/P1043
2694 [word blacked out] "
2695 [1-2 words blacked out] agtr
BF 175/2406 175/2251 175/2407 175/2408 175/2261 175/3259)
2696 General Conditions Montreal Que.
2697 [1-2 words blacked out] agtr
1698 Buffalo. N.Y. Communist Lbr Party
2699 [word blacked out] agtr
2700 Truro N.S. Gnl Conditions at
[3-4 words blacked out]
2701 Textile Workers - Sub. Activities Amongst - Montreal, P.Q.

2702 Lund. B.C. Gnl Conditions at
2703 [3-4 words blacked out] agtr
2704 Mainland Cedar Co Closedown of operations Thompson Sound
2705 Buhay, Michael agtr trans to 175/4917 175P/1254
21706 [word blacked out] Bolshevist undesirable
2707 [word blacked out] agtr
2708 Newcastle & Chatham N.B. Labr situation at [3-4 words blacked out]
2709 Sydney N.S. Strike at Dominion Steel Plant
2710 [word blacked out] Russian Communist Labour Party
Page 140
2711 Employment Offices Maritime Provinces
2712 Arms & Ammunition in possession of Aliens Toronto
2713 Montreal Labour College
2714 Winnipeg May Day Strike & Celebration
2715 O.B.U. Class meetings at Calgary, Alta trans to 175/4656)
2716 L. & C.W.I.U. in O.B.U. Convention 18/4/20 at Prince George B.C.
2717 [word blacked out] I.W.W. for Deportation
2718 [word blacked out] O.B.U. agtr trans to 175/P-135
2719 Griffins Camp B.C. Strike at L & C.W.I. Union of O.B.U. 23/4/20
2720 [word blacked out] agtr
2721 [word blacked out] Russian subject Bolshevist
2722 Saskatoon Peoples Forum - Sub. Activities Within -
2723 [word blacked out] O.B.U. Organizer trans to 175/P-825
2724 Toronto, O.B.U. Meeting 175/P825 Trans to 175/4482
2725 Prince Rupert B.C. Gnl Conditions trans to 175/6993 [1-2 words blacked out]
2726 Prince George Dist B.C. Conditions Generally Trans to 175/4520
2727 Cape Breton N.S. May Day Situation
2728 Toronto, Union of Russian Workers
2729 [word blacked out] O.B.U. 175/P1306
2730 [2-3 words blacked out] delegate O.B.U. 175/P1380
Page 142
2731 [word blacked out] agtr 175/P1404
2732 [1-2 words blacked out] O.B.U.
2733 [1-2 words blacked out] agtr
2734 Hazelton Detachment Gnl Conditions at
2735 Merritt Detachment " Transferred to 175/4565
2736 Prince George Det " Transferred to 175/4520
2737 Stewart Detachement " Transferred to 175/4439
2738 Unknwon Agtr on P.A. Train with [3-4 words blacked out]
2739 [word blacked out] suspect
2740 Nalson Detachment Gnl Conditions
2741 Grand Forks " " trans to 175/4626
2742 Cumberland " " Transf to 175/5321

2743 Esquimalt " "

2744 Independent Labour Party Halifax

2745 Montreal, inter. Brotherhood of Blacksmiths, Drop Forgers & Helpers

2746 [word blacked out] agtr [3-4 words blacked out]

2747 [word blacked out] International suspects and Undesirables
[2 complete lines blacked out]

2748 [1-2 words blacked out] L.W.I.U. of O.B.U.

2749 Porcupine, General Conditions at

Page 143

2750 Ukrainian Labour Temple Ottawa, Ont Trans to 175/4433

2751 [1-2 words blacked out] Delegate O.B.U. 175/P1391

2752 [word blacked out] suspect trans to 175P/1225

2753 [word blacked out] O.B.U. organizer trans 175/P1389

2754 Corbin. B.C. Activitiers of Ukrainian trans to 175/6248

2755 [word blacked out] agtr

2756 [word blacked out] "

2757 [word blacked out] " 175/P1385

2758 Ottawa I.B.S.A. [1-2 words blacked out]

2759 [2-3 words blacked out] suspect 175/P1786

2760 One Big Union Movement in New York Bulletin published by the New York International Auxiliary Co. Bulletin

2761 Hebrew Agitator alleged

2762 Vancouver, May Day Strike & Celebration Transf to 175/3996

2763 [4-5 words blacked out] trans 175P/1393

2764 [word blacked out] agtr trans 175/P1456

2765 [entry blacked out]

2766 Glace Bay, N.S. general Conditions

2767 [word blacked out] subscribing for Strike Leaders 175/P1394

2768 Anarchist, Commune Party, Leaders of

2769 Strike Bakery & Confectionary Workers Union

Page 144

2770 Building Industry mass meeting for Labourers engaged in

2771 Ladysmith. B.C. Strike at Eastern Lumber Co.

2772 Zualicum Bech Strike at Lake Lumber Co.

2773 [word blacked out] agtr 175/P971

2774 [word blacked out] suspect

2775 May Day Labour Mass Meeting Edmonton, Alta

2776 Edmonton, May Day Strike & Colebrations at

2777 Israelite Press Wpg Secret Sign trans to 177/463

2778 Midway B.C. Gnl Conditions trans to 175/4975

2779 [word blacked out] Northumberland Co. N.B. Lbr Conditions Trouble between union & Non union men Millerton. N. (Scratched out) Millerton & Derby Junction N.B.

2780 Hearst, Ont Lbr situation at trans to 175/7259

2781 [word blacked out] suspect 175/P46

2782 [word blacked out] delegate O.B.U. trans to 175/4707 175/P1346

2783 [1-2 words blacked out] alleged suspect

2784 [word blacked out] suspect

2785 [word blacked out] O.B.U. Organizer

2786 American Federation of Labour Vancouver

2787 Winnipeg, Local Daily Papers

2788 Swift Curent Dist Mennonites trans to 175/4646

2789 Shipyard Workers Deputation To Parliament Bldgs Ottawa May 5, 1920

Page 145

2790 [2-3 words blacked out] suspect

2791 Kenora, O.B.U. Propaganda Trans to 175/5633

2792 [1-2 words blacked out] Newsdealer Communist labour Party U.S.A. 175/P1465

2793 [entry blacked out] trans to 175/4967 175P/1396

2794 Statistics Re Labour Organizations in Canada.

2795 Bricklayers Strike Vancouver

2796 English Labour coming to Canada

2797 [word blacked out] Delegate I.W.I.U. of U.S.A. 175/P1344

2798 Clair, Sask Unknown agtr at [word blacked out]

2799 Calgary O.B.U. Miscellaneous Unit Trans to 175/4656

2800 Fort Rouge Railway Workers Unit O.B.U. (BG 175/3201, 175/3471, 175/3473 & 175/3472)

2801 Swift Current labour Conditions at trans to 175/7243

2802 Bakers Strike Vancouver

2803 Prince Rupert May Day Strike & Celebration

2804 Sub Act Within Halcourt, Alta O.B.U. [2-3 words blacked out]

2805 [word blacked out] agtr 175/P1414

2806 [word blacked out] O.B.U. Finnish Sec Regina 175/P1419

2807 Kamloops Detach. General Conditions trans to 175/4503

2808 [word blacked out] agtr trans to 175P/2369

2809 [3-4 words blacked out] agtr 175/P1415

Page 146

2810 [word blacked out] agtr 175/P1417

2811 [word blacked out] " trans to 175/1413

2812 Hindus, B.C. O.B.U. Propaganda amongst
(BF 175/60)

2813 [2-3 words blacked out] Vancouver May Day Sit. [4-5 words blacked out]

2814 Winnipeg anarchist Lit. Distribution

2815 Dollar, Robt Camp Union Bay B.C. Strike at

2816 Charter Lumber Co. Strike at

2817 Soldiers affairs. Soldiers Civil Re-Establishment. Vancouver, B.C.

2818 [word blacked out] suspect 175/P1416

2819 Railway Mail Clerks & Civil Servants

2820 Meeting. Non Union Carpenters, Regina

2821 Border Cities. Indust & Lbr Situation [3-4 words blacked out]

2822 [1-2 words blacked out] suspect trans to A296

2823 [word blacked out] alleged Presbyterian Minister from Antrim, Ireland. tour of Canada in interest of Sein Fein. 175/P1539

2824 [word blacked out] O.B.U. agitator trans to 175P1512

2825 [word blacked out] sus. agtr trans to 175/P1430

2826 [1-2 words blacked out] suspect

2827 [word blacked out] Contrav. of Customs Act. trans to A149/20

2828 [1-2 words blacked out] agtr (cancelled) [word blacked out] U.S.A. Communist

2829 [word blacked out] Organizer, A.F. of L.

Page 147

2830 London, Ont Labour Condition. [4-5 words blacked out]

2831 Chakawana "Detch". General Conditions.

2832 Ft. William. Questions Re. Proh. Lit Socialist Songs, flying flags etc by [3-4 words blacked out]

Trades & Labour Council. Ft. William. [word blacked out]

2833 Chatham. N.B. Longshoremans Strike

2834 Inverness. C.B. Lbr Conditions trans to 175/7582

2835 Edmonton, Atla. Building Trades unit of the (O.B.U.) B.F. from 175/2900

2836 [word blacked out] O.B.U. sympathizer 175/P1478

2837 [word blacked out] President of Dominion Trade & Labour Congress 175/P1468 Trans to 175/4966

2838 Street & Electric Rlys Union

2839 Western Fuel Co. Strike 15-5-20 Nanaimo, B.C.

2840 Camp & Lumber Workers Industrial Union (OBU) Swanson Bay, B.C.

2841 Redcliff, O.B.U. at Transferred to 175/460

2842 [word blacked out] agtr - Ottawa, Ont Transf. to 175/P2967

2845 Stewart Detch Gnl Conditions Transferred to 175/4439

2846 [word blacked out] Russian Currency.

2844 [word blacked out] suspect 175/P1248

2843 Organizations, Leaders & Radical Press in U.S.A. War Obstructionists

2847 [1-2 words blacked out] undesirable Citizen 175/P1440

2848 [4-5 words blacked out] 175/P1437 undesirable Russian Immigrant.

2849 [word blacked out] Undesirable Immigrant 175/P1319

Page 148

2850 [4-5 words blacked out] undesirable immigrant 175/P1437

2851 [1-2 words blacked out] Undesirable Russian Immigrant 175/P1438

2852 [2-3 words blacked out] " trans to 175/P/1436

2853 [word blacked out] " trans to 175/P/272

2854 Montreal amalgamated Clothing Workers trans to 175/4624

2855 Montreal S.P. of Canada [2-3 words blacked out]

2856 [word blacked out] suspect

2857 [1-2 words blacked out] suspect

2858 Civil Servants Strike of 175/2819

2859 Moose Jaw, O.B.U. Transportation Unit

2860 Moose Jaw. O.B.U. Hotel & Restaurant Employees. Unit (OBU)

2861 Regina School Teacher

2862 [2-3 words blacked out] Undesirable Russian Immigrant trans to 175/5202 175P/647

2863 [word blacked out] agitator trans to 175/P-1504

2864 [word blacked out] agtr

2865 [word blacked out] undesirable agtr

2866 [3-4 words blacked out] - S.P. of Canada 175/P1550

2867 [word blacked out] Communist Lbr Party trans to 175/5484

2868 [1-2 words blacked out] alleged Bolshevist

2869 Dauphin, Man Independent Labour Party trans to 175/4653

Page 149

2870 [word blacked out] O.B.U. Agitator 175/P1443

2871 [word blacked out] Undesirable Immigrant 185/P1447

2872 Toronto, Ont Ukrainians in trans to 175/4747

2873 Vancouver Civil Servants & Mail Clerks

2874 [word blacked out] agtr

2875 [word blacked out] "

2876 [1-2 words blacked out] suspect

2877 Shipyard Workers - Strike - June 1920 Halifax N.S.

2878 [word blacked out] O.B.U. organizer (Trans to 175/4498)

2879 [word blacked out] "

2880 [word blacked out] "

2881 [word blacked out] Labour agitator 175/P1463

2882 S.S. Dist #20 Gnl Lbr Conditions in 175/P1463

2883 America O.B.U. Movement U.S.A.

2884 [1-2 words blacked out] suspect

2885 [1-2 words blacked out] O.B.U. agitator 175/P824

2886 [word blacked out] suspect

2887 Western Canada Labour Conference

2888 Fifty percent coal Cut

2889 Communist Labour Party Hamilton, Ont [4-5 words blacked out]

Page 150

2890 [2-3 words blacked out] agtr trans to 175/5196 175/P1624

2891 Medicine Hat Teamsters Strike

2892 Winnipeg, Defence Committee

2893 [2-3 words blacked out] of Irish Republic trans to C.I.B.

2894 O.B.U. Shop Steward Movement

2895 Sherbrooke, Que Bolshevists & Propagandists, Complaint of [2-3 words blacked out]

2896 Usk, B.C. Lbr Conditions at
2897 [1-2 words blacked out] agtr 175/P1454
2898 Campbell River Gnl Conditions at
2899 [word blacked out] Alleged agtr 175/P1470
2900 Bldg Trades Unit of O.B.U. Edmonton trans to 175/2835
2901 Alice Arm Strike at
2902 [1-2 words blacked out] Undesirable Citizen 175/P1479 [2-3 words blacked out]
2903 [2-3 words blacked out] agtr
2904 [word blacked out] agtr 175/P1458
2905 Moose Jaw, Sask O.B.U. Miscellaneous Unit (Trans to 175/4760)
2906 [word blacked out] sus agitator 175/P1522
2907 [word blacked out] agtr 175/P1368
2908 [word blacked out] " 175/P1365
2909 [word blacked out] O.B.U. agtr at Hamilton
Page 151
Sub Act. Within
2910 Niagara Falls, O.B.U.
2911 [1-2 words blacked out] suspect 075/P1716
2912 [word blacked out] socialist 175/P1367
2913 Buckley Bay Lumber Camps O.B.U. Strike at
2914 Moose Jaw, Threatened Strike of Civic Employees
2915 Shevlin, Clarke Lumber Co. Fort Francis (Trans. to 175/7549)
2916 Cowichan Lake strike at Empire Logging Co. Transf. to 175/3546
2917 [word blacked out] agtr
2918 [1-2 words blacked out] suspects
2919 [1-2 words blacked out] " trans to 175/P-1009
2920 [1-2 words blacked out] agtr 175/P1009
2921 [word blacked out] Jewish Radical 175/P1410 (scratched out)
2922 [1-2 words blacked out] suspect 175/P1495 (scratched out)
2923 [1-2 words blacked out] Russian agitator 175/P1693
2924 Russian S.P. of C. Montreal, Que
2925 Stellarton N.S. Lbr Situation at [2-3 words blacked out]
2926 New Glasgow lbr situation at
2927 Trenton, N.S. " [4-5 words blacked out]
2928 Westville, N.S. "
2929 St. Catharines, Conditions at [4-5 words blacked out]
Page 152
2930 Saskatchewan, Province Labour [3-4 words blacked out]
2931 Montreal General Conditions at trans to 175/5444 [word blacked out]
2932 [word blacked out] I.W.W. Member trans to 175/P-1471
2933 [word blacked out] F.L.F. suspect trans to 175/P/1469
2934 [word blacked out] O.B.U. Delegate trans to 175/P/1532
2935 [word blacked out] alleged agitator trans to 175/P-1411

2936 Russia & Europe Generally conditions in trans to 175/6024 175P/515
2937 [word blacked out] suspect trans to 175/5266
2938 Sudbury Dist Labour Conditions in Transferred to 175/P/5859
2939 [word blacked out] suspect trans to 175/P1466
2940 [entry blacked out] 175P/1467
2941 Nipissing Dist Lbr conditions
2942 [word blacked out] allgd Bolshevist
2943 [word blacked out] sus. socialist agtr [word blacked out]
2944 [word blacked out] agtr trans to 175/P-1645
2945 [word blacked out] sus O.B.U. agtr trans to 175/P-1472
2946 Detroit 1920 Communist Labour Party Convention May & June (scratched out) July
2947 Hamilton, Ont Social Democratic Party
2948 Algoma Central Rly Condtions Labour On Ontario
2949 Statistics Re Yougoslavs, Serbs, Croats, Bolshevists & agtrs
Page 153
2950 West Cape Breton, Labour Conditions in trans to 175/2982
2951 [1-2 words blacked out] suspect trans to 175/P=1449
2952 Vancouver labour conditions among Japanese at
2953 [1-2 words blacked out] agtr trans to 175/P-1476
2954 [word blacked out] suspect trans to 175/5170
2955 Labor Conditions - West Kootenay District, B.C.
2956 [word blacked out] I.W.W. agtr trans to 175/P-531
2957 Strike at N.S. Steel & Coal Co [1-2 words blacked out]
2958 Camp & Lumber Workers Industrial Union - O.B.U. Sub Act. at Fraser Mills
2959 Neepawaw Russell Dist Gnl conditions at
2969[word blacked out] Methodist Minister
2961 Cadomin Mine, Alta strike at
2962 [1-2 words blacked out] suspect
2963 [1-2 words blacked out] "
2964 [2-3 words blacked out] agtr
2965 [1-2 words blacked out] Ukrainian Organixzer [1-2 words blacked out]
2966 [1-2 words blacked out] " suspect trans to 175/5659 175P/2805
2967 [word blacked out] suspect [word blacked out] Hafford Dist. Sask.
2968 Ukrainian National Home Association at Hafford & ????Sask.
2969 Amalgamated Clothing Workers Union, generally [4-5 words blacked out]
Page 154
2970 [1-2 words blacked out] I.W.W. undesirable [word blacked out]

2971 [1-2 words blacked out] I.W.W. suspect trans to 175/P/1371
2972 [1-2 words blacked out] agtr trans to 175/P/1353
2973 Fraser Mills strike Can. Western Lumber Co.
2974 Chippawa Canal Development, Strike of Hydro Electric Commission
2975 [1-2 words blacked out] Communist agtr trans to 175/5058 175P/845

2976 Marina, Fed of Lbr Re Strike at Naval Dockyard, Halifax

2977 [1-2 words blacked out] O.B.U. Delegate trans to 175/P/1487

2978 Radville. O.BU. at (Trans to 175/4877)

2979 Victoria Mines & Dist conditions

2980 [word blacked out] O.B.U. agtr 175P/1500

2981 Nova Scotia O.B.U. Generally trans to 175/4651
BF 175/2950

2982 Cape Breton N.S. Labour Conditions at trans to 175/5328

2983 Radville, Sask O.B.U. trans to 175/4877

2984 [1-2 words blacked out] " agtr trans to 175/P/491

2985 Ukrainian Labour Temple Association, Regina trans to 175/5558

2986 [1-2 words blacked out] O.V.U. Agitator trans to 175/P-1496

2987 Prince George Dist Strike in Transferred to 175/4520

2988 [1-2 words blacked out] O.B.U. agitator trans to 175/P/1486
(BF 175/2487)

2989 Grand Army of United Veterans @ United War Veterans League - Regina

Page 155

2990 [word blacked out] agtr trans to 175/P/214

2991 Victoria B.C. Policemen's Union (T.L.C.) @ Policemen's Federal Assoc. (T.L.C)
@ City Police Union (T.L.C.)

2992 Moose Jaw Grand Army United War Vet League [1-2 words blacked out]

2993 [1-2 words blacked out] O.B.U. agtr trans to 175/P-1497

2994 Meadows Lumber Camp Strike at C & L.W.I.U. of O.B.U.

2995 [1-2 words blacked out] sus Bolshevic agent [1-2 words blacked out]

2996 Cudworth Gnl Conditions at

2997 [1-2 words blacked out] agtr 175P/159

2998 [1-2 words blacked out] Pro. German tfs from a 143/2

2999 Portage La Prairie, Ruthenians at

3000 [1-2 words blacked out] Socialist 175/P361

3001 [word blacked out] suspect trans to 175/P-205

3002 [word blacked out] O.B.U. agtr trans to 175/P-360

3003 [word blacked out] suspect trans to 175/P-1599

3004 [word blacked out] O.B.U. Organizer

3005 Truuka Ukrainian Organization. Toronto, Ont

3006 [word blacked out] Russian agtr & organizer O.B.U.
[2-3 words blacked out]

3007 Montreal, Que Union of Russian engineers & Workman trans to 175/4796

3008 [1-2 words blacked out] suspect trans to 175/P-207

3009 [1-2 words blacked out] Attorney re Fed. Order of Rly Employees trans to 175/4850

Page 156

3010 St. John N.B. Street Rly Strike
Imperial Oil Co. Conditions Labour (at)

3011 Dartmouth. N.S. (Amalgamated Oil Workers Union [scratched out])

3012 Hamilton. W.I.I.U.

3013 [word blacked out] suspect trans to 175/P/1442

3014 [1-2 words blacked out] suspect trans to 175/P/1499

3015 [1-2 words blacked out] O.B.U. Organizer trans to 175/P-1501

3016 [word blacked out] agtr trans to 175/P-362

3017 [word blacked out] " trans to 175/P-1494

3018 [word blacked out] " 175/P1331

3019 [entry blacked out] 175/P1511

3020 Railways & Mines 1920 Canada Gnl Conditions "Paga" [2-3 words blacked out]

3021 [word blacked out] agtr 175/P1527

3022 [1-2 words blacked out] O.B.U. Delegate 175/P1343

3023 [3-4 words blacked out] agtr

3024 Toronto, Ont Irish agtrs & Revolutionists

3025 Halifax Trades & labour Council trans to 175/6329

3026 P.O. Dept Strike of Civil Service Employees

3027 [word blacked out] O.B.U. agtr 175/P1236

3028

3029 [word blacked out] S.P. of C. trans to 175/3029 175P/795

Page 157

3030 [word blacked out] sus agtr

3031 [word blacked out] Bolsheviki agtr 175/P620

3032 [1-2 words blacked out] agtr 175/P1087

3033 [1-2 words blacked out] " 175/P1085

3034 [1-2 words blacked out] " 175/P51

3035 [1-2 words blacked out] " 175/P1142

3036 [1-2 words blacked out] Bolsheviki agtr 175/P621

3037 [word blacked out] agtr O.B.U. 175/P1508

3038 Lethbridge Brewery Strike at

3039 [word blacked out] I.W.W. agitator 175/P1502

3040 [1-2 words blacked out] Bolshevist

3041 R.C.M.P. agitators among trans to 175/4541

3042 Sydney N.S. Convention of U.M.W.A. 1920

3043 Prince Rupert B.C. C & L.W.I. Union (OBU) @ Lumber Workers Industrial Union Conditions General (Hazelton & Kituanga Region) B.C.

3044 Hazelton to Kituanga, Gnl Conditions [3-4 words blacked out]

3045 [word blacked out] Greek suspect

3046 [word blacked out] suspect

3047 Vancouver, B.C. Strike at, Gas Workers' Union BF from 175/???

3048 Vancouver, B.C. Street & Electric Rly Union trans to 175/4966

3049 [word blacked out] suspect

Page 158

3050 [word blacked out] suspect

3051 Winnipeg, Man, strike of St. rly co. transf to 175/3645 [3-4 words blacked out]

3052 I.W.W. Activities proposed in Canada. Correspondence continued on 175/5081

3053 [word blacked out] suspect

3054 Sheho, Sask Ukrainians at

3055 Education Press Assoc'n, Montreal

3056 [1-2 words blacked out] agtr trans to 175/P/1537

3057 [word blacked out] O.B.U. 175/P1328

3058 [word blacked out] O.B.U. Glace Bay. N.S. Gov. General's Visit to Glace Bay N.S. [word blacked out] & Town Council incident. trans to 175/4633

3059 [word blacked out] agtr

3060 Toronto, Ont Jewish & Socialist Party of Canada (Polia Seion) trans. to 175/3665

3061 Allied Trades & Labour Ass'n & Anti-Loafing Law.

3062 Hamilton Gnl Lbr Conditons transf to 175/2253 [3-4 words blacked out]

3063 [word blacked out] suspect trans to 175/3063 [3-4 words blacked out]

3064 Birch River, Man O.B.U. Activities

3065 Non-Partisan League in Canada. Transferred to 175/3587

3066 Reformers Book Agency Wpg Man.

3067 Transcona, Rly shops Threatened strike at

3068 Prince George B.C. Patrols from Transferred to 175/4520

3069 Hillcrest, Alta O.B.U. [word blacked out]

Page 159

3070 [word blacked out] Organizer O.B.U. 175/P1524

3071 Longshoreman's Strike at Prince Rupert. S.S. Chilkoot

3072 Georgetown & Whales Island B.C. Bnl conditions at

3073 [word blacked out] suspect 175P/1530

3074 [word blacked out] agtr

3075 Windsor, Ont Dom. Trades & Lbr Congress.

3076 [word blacked out] suspect

3077 [word blacked out] I.W.W. 175/P1559

3078 [word blacked out] I.W.W. 175/P1560

3079 [word blacked out] Sein Fein

3080 Montreal, Que Irish Sympathizers

3081 [word blacked out] 175/P1542

3082 National Union of Ex-Service Men.

3083 Mis-Statements in Press

3084 Ukrainian Dramatic Co. Touring Canada.

3085 [word blacked out] agtr

3086 [word blacked out] suspect 175/P1534

3087 [word blacked out] Bolshevik 175/P1535

3088 [1-2 words blacked out] agtr 175/P1453

3089 [word blacked out] " 175/P1490

Page 160

3090 [1-2 words blacked out] agtr

3091 Telegraphers & Maintainance of Ways, Strike of

3092 [1-2 words blacked out] agtr

3093 [1-2 words blacked out] suspect

3094 [1-2 words blacked out] agtr 175/P1543

3095 Regina, Sask Self Determination for Ireland, League of Canada. trans to C.I.B.

3096 Fishery and Water Products Industrial Unit of O.B.U. Port ?????, B.C.

3097 Kamsack, Sask. O.B.U.

3098 Granby Mine, Cassidy's Siding, Strike at

3099 [word blacked out] O.B.U. member

3100 [word blacked out] "

3101 Western Salmon Packing Co. Lted. Conditions Labour Summerville Cannery Portland Inlet B.C.

3102 O.B.U. Bien fait, Sask & Taylorton, Sask

3103 [word blacked out] agrr 175/P1544

3104 [1-2 words blacked out] suspect

3105 [word blacked out] agtr 175/P1545

3106 [word blacked out] O.B.U. trans to 175/P3183 175P/1596

3107 [word blacked out] "

3108 [word blacked out] " 175/P1533

3109 Meat Cutters, P. Burns & Co. Strike of

Page 161

3110 [word blacked out] agtr

3111 Glace Bay, C.B. Royal Commission

3112 [word blacked out] Socialist 175/P1566

3113 Nicola Valley Mine Workers Assoc'n Merrit B.C.

3114 Typographical Union #191 Sub. Act. Within - Winnipeg, Man.

3115 [1-2 words blacked out] agtr 175/P1538

3116 [1-2 words blacked out] I.W.W.

3117 R.C.M.P. among G.W.V.A. at Ottawa, Ont. [2-3 words blacked out]

3118 [1-2 words blacked out] agtr

3119 [word blacked out] agtr trans 175/P390

3120 [1-2 words blacked out] O.B.U. Organizer trans to 175/P/1518

3121 [1-2 words blacked out] O.B.U. agtr

(Ten numbers missings)

3132 [word blacked out] Russian Bolshevist.

3133 N.W. Ontario Lbr Conditions [1-2 words blacked out]

3134 Coalhurst - Alberta Strike of Miners

3135 [word blacked out] Russian suspect

3136 O.B.U. Convention at Vancouver, B.C.

3137 [1-2 words blacked out] I.W.W. agtr 175/P1561 (scratched out) [word blacked out]

3138 Imperial, Oil Co. Regina, Sask Labour Conditions at

3139 [word blacked out] agtr 75/P1561

Page 162

3140 [word blacked out] O.B.U. Agitator 175/P913 BF. 175/3158

3141 [word blacked out] Bolshevist (Ukrainian)
3142 Kirkland Lake Mining Camp O.B.U. at
3143 [word blacked out] agtr & Sein Feiner 175/P1546
3144 [word blacked out] Russian O.B.U. Agtr
3145 Weston, Ont alleged Radical Picnic
3146 Brantford (O.B.U.)
3147 Bell agtr Toronto trans to 175/4686 175P/1711
3148 Welland, Ont Gnl Conditions at 175/5485 [word blacked out]
3149 [entry blacked out] 175/P1549
3150 [word blacked out] Sinn Feiner & O.B.U. agtr 175/P1555
3151 [word blacked out] agtr 175/P1383
3152 [word blacked out] suspect trans to 175/3152, 175P/1547
3154 Maritime Provinces lbr Conditions in
3153 [word blacked out] agtr
3155 [word blacked out] O.B.U. Agtr 175/P1571
3156 [word blacked out] suspect 175/P1568
3157 [5-6 words blacked out] I.W.W. Agtr 175/P1557
3158 [2-3 words blacked out] O.B.U. agtr Transf to 175P912
3159 Winnipeg, Man Irish Situation
Page 163
3160 [word blacked out] suspect
3161 [word blacked out] suspect 175/P1379
3162 Montreal, Que Foreign Radical Organization in
3163 Atlas Mine Drumheller Alta Strike at
3164 [word blacked out] Alleged I.W.W.
3165 Transportation Unit #1 O.B.U. Calgary trans to 175/1856 175/4538
3166 [word blacked out] O.B.U. & I.W.W. Agtr [word blacked out]
3167 [word blacked out] suspect 175/P1775
3168 Portage La Prairie O.B.U. 175/P1505
3169 [word blacked out] suspect trans to 175/P-1556
3170 [word blacked out] O.B.U. Organizer 175/P1598
3171 [word blacked out] agtr
3172 Women's Inter League trans to 175/5044 [2-3 words blacked out]
3173 O.B.U. & Inter. Wpg Debate between (trans to 175/4448)
3174 Finnish Fraternal Soc'y Vancouver
3175 Conditions General (Amongst Finns) Port Moody, B.C.
3176 Smithers B.C. I.W.I.U. of O.B.U.
3177 [word blacked out] Paid Lbr Official trans 175/P83
3178 [word blacked out] Organizer
3179 Moose Jaw, I.B.S.A. at
Page 164
3180 Strike at N.A.C. (Monarch Mine) Drumheller
3181 Allemby Local, Int. Mining Mill & Smeltermen's Union

3182 Copper Mt. Local I.M.M. & S.U.

3183 [word blacked out] O.B.U. Coal Mines, Taylorton, Sask trans 175P/1596

3184 Inter. Bible Students, Convention at Edmonton BF 175/4168

3185 Montreal. O.B.U. Gnl Workers Unit

3186 [word blacked out] suspect. Soviet Medical Relief Committee. 175/P1721

3187 [word blacked out] suspect 175/P1869

3188 [word blacked out] allegd seditious Utterances 175/P227

3189 [word blacked out] O.B.U. Secretary & Delegate

3190 Street Electric Rly Wpg Employees Transferred to 175/4457 [2-3 words blacked out]

3191 Montreal Que Independent Socialist Party

3192 Hands off Russia Movement, Toronto

3193 Spector Morris Russian agtr trans to 175/5062 175P/1712

3194 [word blacked out] Ukrainian agtr 175/P98

3195 [entry blacked out]

3196 Hands off Russia Movement, Wpg.

3197 [2-3 words blacked out] O.B.U. agtr 175/P1578

3198 St. Catharines, Ont Russian Social Democratic Party

3199 Calgary, Alta Flour & Cereal Mill workers unit of O.B.U.

Page 166

3200 Moose Jaw, Strike of C.P.R. Shop Labourers.

3201 Winnipeg, Man O.B.U. Running Trades Unit. (Trans to 175/2800)

3202 [word blacked out] O.B.U. Agtr trans to 175/P-1578

3203 Gowganda, Ont O.B.W. at " " 175/6415

3204 Toronto Veterans Educational Platform

3205 [1-2 words blacked out] Bolshevist 175/P765

3206 [1-2 words blacked out] agtr

3207 [word blacked out] O.B.U. Secretary

3208 Western Exchange Ltd Edmonton suspect

3209 Unknown Member of Soviet Government, visit to Hamilton trans to 175/2655

3210 [word blacked out] Russian Deportee

3211 [word blacked out] O.B.U. Organizer 175/P631

3212 Riondel B.C. strike at

3213 New Waterford Dist Lbr Conditions [3-4 words blacked out]

3214 Commerce, Alta O.B.U.

3215 Harvesters O.B.U. Among

3216 Hamilton Trades Lbr Council [3-4 words blacked out]

3217 Hands off Russia Movement Canada Generally

3208 [word blacked out] O.B.U.

3219 Burrard Camp Bowser B.C. Strike at

Page 167

3220 [1-2 words blacked out] Alleged Bolshevist

3221 Metal Trade Unit (O.B.U.) Montreal, Que

3222 Hands off Russia Movement; Montreal
3223 Winnipeg, (O.B.U.) Building Trades Unit.
3224 [word blacked out] agitator 175/P1589
3225 Winnipeg Telegram 19/8/20
3226 Pacific Mills Camp. Strike at
3227 [word blacked out] agtr
3228 Sub Act Within Iroqois Falls O.B.U.
3229 [word blacked out] suspect
3230 [2-3 words blacked out] I.W.W.
3231 [1-2 words blacked out] - I.B.S.A. suspect
3232 [1-2 words blacked out] - I.W.W.
3233 [1-2 words blacked out] I.W.W. Organizer trans to 175/P-137
3234 Yorkton, Sask I.B.S.A. at 175/P137 (scratched out) [word blacked out]
3235 [word blacked out] suspect
3236 Sydney. N.S. Conditions at
3237 Ontario Labour College, Toronto [1-2 words blacked out]
3238 [2-3 words blacked out] Imperial Pressman.
3239 [word blacked out] agtr Toronto
3240 Dominion Coal Company. German Labour Imported by. Caledonia Mines #4
Page 168
Labour Trouble at #10 & #11 Collieries (scratched out)
3241 Reserve Mines - Strike at No. 10 Colliery in 1940 Cape Breton Nova Scotia
3242 Toronto, Ont Gnl. Foreign Lbr. Conditions in trans to 175/4083
3243 Welland, labour Conditions in 175/5465
3244 Niagara Falls, Gnl Conditions 175/P1645 [1-2 words blacked out] 175P/1645
3245 Toronto. Ex Soldiers & Sailors Labour Union (Trans. to 175/4150)
3246 Hamilton Foreign. Lbr Conditions in 175/4471 [2-3 words blacked out]
3247 St. Catharines. Foreign Lbr conditions in 175/5666 [2-3 words blacked out]
3248 Thorold. "
3249 British Columbia. South. Alta Lbr Conditions in mines at (Trans to 175/3445)
3250 Federated Press.
3251 [word blacked out] agtr
3252 Workers Educational League trans to 175/5108
3253 Toronto, Ont Gnl Conditions trans to 175/4083
3254 [word blacked out] suspect
3255 Sion Polia @ Jewish Anarchist Communist Party.
3256 [1-2 words blacked out] Russian Jewish 175/P1590
3257 Detroit U.S.A. Society of Technical Help to Soviet of Russia.
3258 [word blacked out] suspect 175P/1590
3259 [word blacked out] agtr
Page 1569
3260 [word blacked out] suspect 175/P1372
3261 [word blacked out] agtr Canora, Sask.

4262 [word blacked out] suspect [word blacked out] suspect

3263 [word blacked out] agtr 175/P244

3264 Shop Steward's Movement (O.B.U.) Calgary

3265 [word blacked out] agtr 175/P1577

3266 [3-4 words blacked out] suspects

3267 [word blacked out] organizer

3268 [word blacked out] agtr

3269 Cumberland. B.C. (O.B.U.) Chinese Unit.

3270 Hamilton, Ont Hands off Russia Movement

3271 Toronto, Labour Day in

3272 Coalmont, B.C. General Conditions at

3273 Halifax- Darmouth Labour Day Activities

3274 Bulgarian Socialist Party, Toronto, Ont [3-4 words blacked out]

3275 [3-4 words blacked out] agtr 175P/1601

3276 [word blacked out] agtr 175/P1552

3277 [1-2 words blacked out] O.B.U. Organizer 175/P1600

3278 Russian School, Toronto

3279 [word blacked out] suspect trans to 175/4604 175P1180

Page 170

3280 Longshoremens Strike - 1920 New York & Boston

3281 Gas Workers Union Strike trans to 175/3047

3282 [word blacked out] O.B.U. trans to 175/4528

3283 Sub Act Within Estevan. O.B.U.

3284 B.C. Printing Trades Council trans to 175/5006

3285 Halifax, Stevedores & Longshoremen

3286 Swanson Bay, B.C. Lbr Conditions

3287 Conditions Labour (Cannery) Lowe Inlet, B.C.

3288 Surf Inlet Lbr Conditions

3289 [word blacked out] Lbr Conditions trans to 175/P-1591

3290 [1-2 words blacked out] agtr

3291 Firemen & Deckhands Strike 1920 Vancouver B.C.

3292 One Big Union - Second National Convention held at Port Arthur Sept 20 to 24/20) Canada

3292 supp One Big Union - Reported Second National Convention held at Port Arthur Sept 20 to 24/20) Canada

3293 [3-4 words blacked out] - agtr trans to 175/P-422

3294 Red Water, Alta Ukrainians at " 175/6796

3295 Port Hood labour Situation (Port Hood, Cape Breton, N. S. trans to 175/3350 [word blacked out]

3296 [word blacked out] suspect

3297 Miner's Unit (O.B.U.) Calgary Alta.

3298 [word blacked out] suspect

3299 [word blacked out] London Daily Herald (Transf. to 177/424) Transferred [2-3 words blacked out]

Page 171

3300 [1-2 words blacked out] agtr

3301 Mohammedans Bolshevism among

3302 Universal Negro Improvement Association trans to 175/4842

3303 Blaine Lake, Sask Unknown Bolshevist at 175/P1633

3304 [word blacked out] suspect from England

3305 [1-2 words blacked out] G.A.W.V. Vancouver 175/P914

3306 Whitman Club @ Whitman Fellowship (Sub. Act Within) Bon Echo, Ont.

3307 Calgary, Alta Convention at Sept 1920

3308 Lake Ports Strike of Seamen's Union

3309 Victoria Gas workers Union Strike

3310 Penticton O.B.U. at [word blacked out]

3311 [1-2 words blacked out] O.B.E., suspect

3312 [word blacked out] agitator 175/P1121

3313 [word blacked out] suspected agent of Soviet Russian Govt.

3314 [word blacked out] Windsor, Ont Proh Lit (Cancelled). Webber, Aaron.

3315 [1-2 words blacked out] Int. Sus & Undesirable

3316 Plebbs League Toronto trans to 175/5106

3317 Sudbury Dist, Finns in " to 175/5705

3318 [2-3 words blacked out] suspect " to C.I.B. - Cont A-316

3319 Brandon, Man Labour Day

Page 172

3320 [word blacked out] alleged I.W.W.

3321 Joint Distributers Committee. Jewish Immigration to U.S.A. & Canaa

3323 Canadian Militia Forces - O.B.U. Among [3-4 words blacked out]

3324 (no file)

3322 [word blacked out] O.B.U. among

3325 [entry blacked out]

3326 British Isles Political Conditions in trans to Conf. C.I.B. - A-343

3327 Thessalon, Ont O.B.U.

3328 [word blacked out] O.B.U. Sympathiser trans to 175/P-1619

3329 [word blacked out] agitator 175/P1612

3330 St. Catharines, Ont O.B.U. 175/P1611

3331 Niagara Falls, Ont Communist Lbr Party corr transf to 175/4949 [1-2 words blacked out]

3332 [entry blacked out]

3333 Ocean Falls, O.B.U. Strikes at

3334 Morgan's Bank - Re- Threat on Manager's Life [word blacked out]

3335 [1-2 words blacked out] I.W.W. agent

3336 Washington State U.S.A. Bolshevism

3337 [1-2 words blacked out] O.B.U. Agtr 175/P1658

3338 [1-2 words blacked out] suspect 175/P1602

3339 [1-2 words blacked out] O.B.U. agtr

Page 173

3340 [1-2 words blacked out] O.B.U. Delegate

3341 Victoria, B.C. Ex-Soldiers Labour Council

3342 Vancouver, B.C. (Finnish Unit) of O.B.U.

3343 Malcolm Island B.C. General Conditions at Finnish settlement "Sointula". trans to 175/4923

3344 Rossland, B.C. Miners Unit (O.B.U.) B.F. 175/2207

3345 Trail, B.C. (O.B.U.) Mill & Smeltermens Unit

3346 Colchester County Political Conditions in

3347 [word blacked out] O.B.U. Sec Delegate

3348 [word blacked out] O.B.U. Secretary 175/P1157

3349 United Soldiers Council - Vancouver, B.C.
BF. 175/3295

3350 Port Hood, C.B. lbr Situation [3-4 words blacked out]

3351 St. Catharines & Thorold Lbr Conditions 175/5666 [word blacked out]

3352 Toronto, S.P. of C. trans to 175/5300

3353 [word blacked out] Sec. Fed. Lbr, Party trans to 175/4965 175P/55

3354 Gravelbourg Dist Lbr Conditions of

3355 [1-2 words blacked out] suspect

3356 [1-2 words blacked out]English agtr

3357 [word blacked out] suspect

3358 [entry blacked out] trans to 175/5162

3359 Dollar Logging Camp Strike at

Page 174

3360 [2-3 words blacked out] agtr 175/P1562

3361 [1-2 words blacked out] suspect 175/P1649

3362 [1-2 words blacked out] O.B.U. Delegate 175/P1604

3363 Vancouver, B.C. Lbr Church Movement trans to 175/5423

3364 [1-2 words blacked out] agtr 175/P1620

3365 Ukrainian Lbr Temple Assoc Gnl Fyle [3-4 words blacked out]
One Big Union - Sub. Activities Within

3366 Anyox, B.C. (O.B.U. Conditions at [scratched out])

3367 Prince Rupert, B.C. Prohibition movement 175P/906

3368 Vancouver, Lbr Conditions, Shipyards Employees etc

3369 [word blacked out] suspect 175/P1916

3370 [word blacked out] agtr U.S.A. 175/P1622

3371 Lumber Agricultural & Construction Camp Unit Transferred to [3-4 words blacked out]

3372 [word blacked out] agtr

3373 Welland, Niagara Falls Dist Gnl Conditions 175/5456 (scratched out) [1-2 words blacked out]

3374 [word blacked out] suspect
BF from 175/3410

3375 [word blacked out] agtr 175/P1740

3376 [word blacked out] German suspect

3377 [word blacked out] I.W.W.

3378 [3-4 words blacked out] I.W.W. Suspects

3379 [1-2 words blacked out] suspect

Page 175

3380 C.L.W.I.U. of O.B.U. in Canada [3-4 words blacked out]

3381 [1-2 words blacked out] agtr 175/P191

3382 [1-2 words blacked out] sus I.W.W.

3383 Cardiff, Alta Ukrainians at

3384 Toronto, Russian Progressive Library

3385 Hamilton Bolshevism at trans to 175/4574 [2-3 words blacked out]

3386 Hamilton Labour College

3387 [word blacked out] suspect trans to 175/5901 175P/1503 (scratched out) [word blacked out]

3388 [3-4 words blacked out] suspect

3389 [1-2 words blacked out] Amalg. Textile Workers of America

3390 Western Commercial College, Wayne, Alta

3391 O.B.U. Winnipeg, St. Rly Unit trans to 175/6374

3392 [word blacked out] Jewish Girl, suspect 175/P1640

3393 [word blacked out] suspect

3394 [word blacked out] suspect Vag & Undesirable

3395 [word blacked out] Undesirable Immigrant

3396 [3-4 words blacked out] suspects trans to 175/P/1873

3397 Bomb Plots Vancouver, B.C.

3398 Strike at McLeod's Camp Gambier Island

3399 O.B.U. Metal Miners Convention, Prince Rupert B.C.

Page 176

3400 Labour Conditions, Corbin B.C.

3401 (O.B.U.) Miners Unit

3402 Strike at Dominion #1, Cape Breton.

3403 [2-3 words blacked out] suspect

3404 [word blacked out] suspect 175/P1813

3405 Communist Party (National Convention Held at Vancouver Sept 1920) Canada General

(B.F. 175/600)

3406 Bolshevism at Vancouver

3407 Re Labour Conditions, Vancouver, B.C. trans to 175/6384 (scratched out) [word blacked out]

3408 [word blacked out] suspect

3409 [entry blacked out] 175/P1868

3410 [word blacked out] suspect trans to 175/3375 (scratched out) trans to 175P/1740

3411 O.B.U. Sub Act Wtihin New Westminster, B.C.

3412 [word blacked out] (from Thorold, Ont) suspect

3413 Russian information Bureau U.S.A.

3414 General Conditions in Haiti among negroes (scratched out) [2-3 words blacked out] (Radical Organization)

3415 Brass Check Club Hamilton, Ont

3416 Conference of U.M.W.Executive & Wage Scale Committee Truro N.S. trans to 175/4696

3417 New York City U.S.A. Arms Ammunition & Explosives - explosion in Finance District

3418 Sault Ste Marie, Ont Attitude towards R.C.M.Police trans. to 175-5038

3419 Labour Conditions, Niagara Falls, Ont [3-4 words blacked out]

Page 177

3420 [3-4 words blacked out] of Sydney C.B. suspect 175/P1643

3421 (O.B.U.) Prince Rupert Shipyard Workers Unit.

3422 (O.B.U.) Prince Rupert B.C. Miners Unit

3423 (O.B.U.) Prince Rupert B.C. Fisheries & Water Products Unit.

3424 Weyburn Mental Hospital - Conditions Labour at Weyburn, Sask.

3425 Montreal, Que Emigration aliens on Steamer Megantic.

3526 Agitators in Toronto

3427 O.B.U. Complaints from [3-4 words blacked out]

3428 [word blacked out] suspect 175/P1638

3429 Bolshevism at Welland, Ont trans to 175/3438

3430 Young Labour League, Winnipeg, Man

3431 [1-2 words blacked out] Labour agitator 175/P1059

3432 [1-2 words blacked out] suspected Bolshevist

3433 Prohibition Movement, Vancouver, B.C.

3434 Labour College, Vancouver, B.C.

3435 [word blacked out] Boston Bible Tract Society - suspect

3436 Labour Conditions Springhill. N.S. trans to 175/4479 [2-3 words blacked out]

3437 General Conditions at Sherbrooke, Que

3438 Bolshevism in Welland District BF 175/3429

3439 Bolshevism in Niagara Falls District.

Page 178

3440 [2-3 words blacked out] suspect trans to 175/5223 (BF 175/3249) (BF. 175/1912)

3441 (O.B.U.) Mining Department #1 Miner's Unit (District. #1) Alberta & B.C.

3442 [word blacked out] trans to 175/4991 [2-3 words blacked out]

3443 Labour Conditions in Maritime Provinces U.M.W. of A. [3-4 words blacked out]

3444 Ukrainian Labour Temple. Vancouver, B.C. Trans 175/5178 [word blacked out]

3445 [1-2 words blacked out] O.B.U. 175/P1591

3446 (O.B.U.) Prince Rupert B.C. Building Trades Unit of

3447 [1-2 words blacked out] O.B.U. Regina

3448 [1-2 words blacked out] Hamilton, Ont agtr 175/P1642

3449 [word blacked out] suspect

3450 Ukrainian Labour Temple, Hamilton, Ont trans to 175/4561 [word blacked out]

3451 Communist Party, Montreal, Que " " 175/4575 [2-3 words blacked out]

3452 [word blacked out] agtr 175/P1654

3453 [entry blacked out] 175/P892

3454 [entry blacked out] 175/P1551

3455 [word blacked out] O.B.U. Organizer

3456 Coal Mining Industry - Drumheller & Wayne Areas "Statistics"

3457 Labour Conditions at Ruel in Lumber Camps

3458 Labour Conditions at Edmonton, Unemployment [2-3 words blacked out]

3459 Grand Army of United Veterans, Vancouver, Premier Meighen's Visit

3449 [word blacked out] suspect
3450 Ukrainian Labour Temple, Hamilton, Ont trans to 175/4561 [word blacked out]
3451 Communist Party, Montreal, Que " " 175/4575 [2-3 words blacked out]
3452 [word blacked out] agtr 175/P1654
3453 [entry blacked out] 175/P892
3454 [entry blacked out] 175/P1551
3455 [word blacked out] O.B.U. Organizer
3456 Coal Mining Industry - Drumheller & Wayne Areas "Statistics"
3457 Labour Conditions at Ruel in Lumber Camps
3458 Labour Conditions at Edmonton, Unemployment [2-3 words blacked out]
3459 Grand Army of United Veterans, Vancouver, Premier Meighen's Visit
Page 1
1920
3460 [entry blacked out]
3461 [entry blacked out]
3462 O.B.U. Regina, Sask reParis Hotel Trans to 175/4506
3463 Bolshevism Welland & St. Catharines District 175/566 [word blacked out]
3464 [entry blacked out] 175/P1665
3465 Labour Conditions at Thetford Mines, P.Q. Trans to 175/5409
3466 [entry blacked out]]
3467 [entry blacked out]
3468 [entry blakced out]
3469 O.B.U. (Ukrainian Unit) Winnipeg
3470 (O.B.U.) Lumber, agriculture & Construction Camp Unit, Winnipeg
3471 O.B.U. Fort Rouge Railway Worker's Unit, Winnipeg Trans to 175/2800
3472 O.B.U. Transcona Unit No. 1. Winnipeg Trans to 175/2800
3473 O.B.U. C.P.R. Shop Unit, Winnipeg Trans to 175/2800
3474 (O.B.U.) Metal Trades Unit, Winnipeg
3475 [entry blacked out] 175/P1607
3476 [entry blacked out] trans to 175/1033 175P/1033-@
3477 Welland & St. Catharines, Ont Emigration, Bolsheviks leaving for Russia.
3478 Grand Army United Veterans, Victora, B.C. Transf. to 175/3575
3479 Labour Convention, Victoria, B.C. Transf. to [blacked out]
Page 2
3480 Labour Conditions in British Columba - Japanese Fisherman
3481 [entry blacked out]
3482 Soviet Russia Connection in Canada Trans. to 175/5311
3483 Third Anniversay Celebration of Russian Revolution, Toronto, Ont
3484 Strike at. P. Burns Co'y Calgary, Alta
3485 [entry blacked out] 175/P1668
3486 [entry blacked out] trans to 175/4571
3487 [entry blacked out] trans to 175/2399
3488 Labour Conditions - Glace Bay, N.S. Civic Employees

3489 [entry blacked out] 175/P1663

3490 [entry blacked out]

3491 [entry blacked out] 175/P1666

3492 [entry blacked out] trans to 175/3573 175P/768

3493 [entry blacked out]

3494 [entry blacked out] 175/P1647

3495 [entry blacked out] 175/P1001

3496 [entry blacked out]

3497 [entry blacked out] 175/P1351

3498 [entry blacked out] 175/P1426

3499 [entry blacked out] 175/P1674

Page 3

3500 Strike, Sydney Inlet, Copper Coy, B.C.

3501 [entry blacked out] trans to 175/P933

3502 [entry blacked out] " to 175/5811 175P/87

3503 [entry blacked out]

@ Ex. Service Mens International

3504 International of Former Combatants @ Association of Former Combatants in the Great War

3505 [entry blacked out] 175/P1689

3506 [entry blacked out]

3507 General Conditions, Southern Saskatchewan District 175/P2930 Trans to [blacked out]

3508 [entry blacked out] 175/P1683

3509 [entry blacked out]

3510 [entry blacked out]

3511 Third Anniversary of Russian Soviet Revolution. Montreal, Que

3512 [entry blacked out]

3513 [entry blacked out] 175/P1698

3514 [entry blacked out] 175/P195

3515 [entry blacked out] 175/P1680

3516 General Conditions, Vancouver, B.C. Among Greeks trans to 175/4961

3517 [entry blacked out] trans to 175/5096 175P/1660

3518 (O.B.U.) Edmonton, Alta. Transportation Unit.

3519 [entry blacked out]

Page 4

3520 Labour Conditions - Post Office Employees

3521 General Conditions at Drumheller trans to 175/4621

3522 [entry blacked out] " " 175/P-1679

3523 [entry blacked out]

3524 [entry blacked out] 175/P1759

3525 [entry blacked out]

3526 [entry blacked out] trans. to 175-4980

3527 General Conditions in B.C. among Japanese Transferred to [blacked out]
3528 O.B.U. Calgary re Central Labour Council
3529 [entry blacked out] 175P/53
3530 [entry blacked out] trans to 175/4819
3531 [entry blacked out] 175/P1682
3532 [entry blacked out] 175/P1679 - [3-4 words blacked out]
BF 175/3595
3533 Marxian Club open forum, Hamilton, Ont
3534 General Conditions. Amherst. N.S.
3535 [entry blacked out] trans to 175/5016 175P/1723
British Empire League
3536 British Empire Union - Vancouver, B.C.
3537 [entry blacked out] 175/P1724
3538 [entry blacked out]
3539 O.B.U. General Workers - Prince George B.C. 175/P1257 [2-3 words blacked out]

Page 5

3540 One Big Union Sub Act Within Hedley, B.C.
3541 O.B.U. Miners & Construction Workers, Princeton, B.C.
3542 O.B.U., Thunder Bay, Central Labour Council
3543 [entry blacked out] 175/P1677
3544 German (name unknown) at Churchbridge, Sask, wearing German Uniform & Decorations
3545 Labour Conditions on C.N. Rlys - Regina, Sask
(B.F. 175/2916)
3546 C. & L.W.I.U. Strike at Hemmingsen's Camp. Cowichan Lake, B.C.
3547 Strike at Dominion Steel Corporation - Sydney. N.S.
3548 [entry blacked out] 175/P1322
3549 [entry blacked out] trans to 175/4735 175P/1895
3550 [entry blacked out]
3551 [entry blacked out]
3552 [entry blacked out] trans to 175/3762
3553 [entry blakced out] 175/P1656
3554 Grand Army of United Veterans, Toronto Premier Meighen's Visit
3555 [entry blacked out]
3556 Prince Rupert. B.C. Attitude to R.C.M.P.
trans to 175/P49
3557 [entry blacked out]
trans to 175/3635
3558 [entry blacked out] 175/P1692
3559 Labour-Conditions in Canada - Employment - Statistics etc. (Trans to [blacked out])

Page 6

3560 Labour Conditions among employees Sydney & Louisburg Rly. Trans to [blacked out]

3561 " " in Pictou County. Coal Fields. (trans. to 175/4480)

3562 " " in Maritime Provinces.

3563 [entry blacked out]

3564 [entry blacked out]

3565 Volunteers of America or Christian Mission.

3566 [entry blacked out] 175/P1820

3567 [entry blacked out]

3568 [entry blacked out]

3569 [entry blacked out] 175/P1850

3570 [entry blacked out]

3571 [entry blacked out] trans to [blacked out]

3572 [entry blacked out] 175/P1681.

3573 [entry blacked out] 175/P768

3574 [entry blacked out] 175/P368
(B.F. 175/3478)

3575 Grand Army United Veterans - Victoria B.C.

3576 [entry blacked out] 175/P1352

3577 [entry blacked out]

3578 [entry blacked out]

3579 Russian Conatct & Connection in U.S.A. and Canada cancelled & trans 175/3482

Page 7

3580 Bolshevism in U.S.A. Deportation of Aliens.

3581 Fabian Society - Montreal, Que.

3582 [entry blacked out]

3583 [entry blacked out]

3584 [entry blacked out]

3585 [entry blacked out] 175/1688

3586 [entry blacked out] 175/P1717
(B.F. 175/????)

3587 Non-Partisan League of Sask.

3588 [entry blacked out]

3589 [entry blacked out] 175/P1686

3590 Suspects in United Kingdom trans to C.J.B. Confidential A-406

3591 [3-4 words blacked out] party of Afghans & Indians, suspects

3592 [entry blacked out] 175/P1685

3593 [entry blacked out] trans to 175/4937

3594 General Conditions at Winnipeg - among Jews trans to 175/4776

3595 Paba League at Hamilton, Ont (Trans to 175/3533)

3596 General Conditions - Civi Elections - Winnipeg, Man (Trans to 175/321)

3597 [entry blacked out] 175P/1670

3598 [entry blacked out] 175/P1669

3599 General Conditions (scratched out) - Civic Elections - British Columbia

Page 8

3600 [entry blacked out]

3601 [entry blacked out] 175/P306

3602 [entry blacked out]

3603 Strike - Northern Construction Co. B.C.

3604 labour Conditions - Halifax - Printers. Transferred to 175/2287

3605 [entry blacked out]

3606 Labour Conditions in Ontario - Employment (Trans to [blacked out])

3607 [entry blacked out] trans to 175/5030 175P/96

3608 Imperial Veterans - Vancouver. trans to 175/4730

3609 Labour Conditions in Canada. " " 175/5877 (Trans to [blacked out])

3610 [entry blacked out]

3611 [entry blacked out] trans to 4460

3612 Workers' Recreation Club - Toronto, Ont

3613 [entry blacked out] 175/P1694

3614 Labour Conditions at Welland, Ont Employment 175/5465 (scratched out) [2-3 words blacked out]

3615 [entry blacked out] 175/P170?

3616 [entry blacked out] trans to 175/5688

3617 [entry blacked out]

3618 Labour Conditions Kitchener, Ont (Trans to [blacked out])

3629 Esperanto Class Vancouver, B.C. 175/P1697 [word blacked out]

Page 9

3620 [entry blacked out] 175/P1697

3621 The Communist Party, Toronto, Ont 175/4451 (Trans to [blacked out])

3622 [entry blacked out]

3623 General Conditions, Winnipeg, Man - Ukrainians trans to 175/4591 [word blacked out]

B.F. from 175/3671

3624 Labour Conditions, Hamilton, Ont, employment 175/4471 (Trans to [blacked out])

3625 [entry blacked out]

3626 [entry blacked out] 175/P1701

3627 [entry blacked out]

3628 [entry blacked out]

3629 Labour Conditions in Regina - employment (Trans to [blacked out])

3630 [entry blacked out]

3631 [entry blacked out]

3632 [entry blacked out] 175/P2348

3633 General Conditions in Canada among Ukrainians 175/4476

3634 Labour Conditions at St. Catharines, Ont - Employment 175/5666 [word blacked out]

3635 Labour Conditions at Saskatoon. (scratched out) Can. Nat. Ry. Employees (Conditions Labour) Saskatoon, Sask.

3636 [entry blacked out]

3637 [entry blacked out]

3638 [entry blacked out]

3639 [entry blacked out]

Page 10

3640 Independent Labour Party, Edmonton

3641 Labour Conditions at Gilroy McKay Logging Camp, Port Alberni. Trans to [blacked out]

3642 [entry blacked out] trans to 175/5372 (scratched out) 175P/2381

3643 [entry blacked out] trans to 175/4641 175P/2148

3644 [entry blacked out]
(B.F. 175/1995, 175/2313 & 175/3051 [scratched out])

3645 Labour conditions at Winnipeg - Employment Trans to [blacked out]

3646 Agtrs in Canada and Movement to U.S.A.

3647 [entry blacked out] 175/P2414

3648 Labour Conditions at Toronto, shipyard employees

3649 [entry blacked out] 175/P1728

3650 General Conditions Amalgamated Postal Workers - Vancouver 175P/505

3651 Labour Conditions in Montreal, Employment, 175/4500 (Trans to [blacked out]

3652 [entry blacked out]

3653 [entry blacked out]

3654 Federated Labour Party in B.C.

3655 [entry blacked out] 175/P21

3656 [entry blacked out]

3657 [entry blacked out]

3658 [entry blacked out] 175/P1714

3659 [entry blacked out]

Page 11

3660 [3-4 words blacked out] WELLAND, ONT. (Former Off. [2-3 words blacked out] Czar Army) (Suspected [2-3 words blacked out] literature

3661 [entry blacked out]

3662 [entry blacked out] trans to 175/4728 175P/1609

3663 [entry blacked out] 175/P1715

3664 [entry blacked out] 175/P77

3665 Jewish Socialist Party (Polia Seion) Toronto, Ont B.F. from 175/3060

3666 Independent Labour Party of Manitoba B.F. to 175/4927

3667 [entry blacked out]

3668 [entry blacked out]

3669 [entry blacked out]

3670 Jewish Radicals - Winnipeg [2-3 words blacked out] suspect

3671 Labour Conditions at Hamilton, Ont employment trans to 175/3624 [2-3 words blacked out]

3672 [entry blacked out] (Trans to [blacked out])

3673 Labour Conditions at Niagara Falls, Ont Employment trans to [blacked out]

3674 General Conditions in Canada among Foreigners (Trans. to [blacked out])

3675 " " " " " Mennonites (Trans to [blacked out])
3676 " " " Ontario among Japanese. trans to [blacked out]
3677 [entry blacked out]
3678 [entry blacked out]
3679 [entry blacked out]
Page 12
3680 Strike in Inverness. C.B. (N.S.)
3681 Strike at Dominion # 14, New Waterford, Cape Breton
3682 Strike at Murray Harbour C.B. Pulp & Paper Co.
3683 Central Labour Council
3684 O.B.U. Convention at Sudbury, Ont Jany.921.
3685 [entry blacked out] (Trans to [blacked out])
3686 General Conditions at North Emiskaming among Finlanders
3687 Labour Church Halifax. N.S.
3688 Reserve Mines Collery No 5 - Labor Conditions at Cape Breton, N.S.
3689 [entry blacked out] 175/P1713
3690 [entry blacked out]
3691 [entry blacked out] 175/P1772
3692 Russian Orthodox National Institute. St. Wolodemer in Edmonton
3693 [entry blacked out] 175/P1570
3694 [entry blacked out] trans to 175/6578 (trans to [blacked out])
3695 [entry blacked out]
3696 Calgary, Alta, Ukrainians at
3697 [entry blacked out] trans to [blacked out]
trans to 175/4950
3698 [entry blacked out] 175/P1727
2699 Cumberland, B.C. O.B.U. Japanese organization
Page 13
3700 [entry blacked out]
3701 [entry blacked out]
3702 [entry blacked out] trans to 175/4845
3703 Custance, Mrs. Florence, suspect trans to 175/4905 175P/1629
3704 [entry blacked out] 175/P1710
3705 [entry blacked out] 175/P1133
3706 [entry blacked out]
3707 [entry blacked out]
3708 Ontario, Communist Party in trans to 175/5805 Trans [blacked out]
3709 Toronto - Labour Conditions in - Employment Transf. to 175/4489
3710 [entry blacked out] trans to 175/4485
3711 [entry blacked out] 175/P152
3712 [entry blacked out]
3713 [entry blacked out] trans to 175/4459
3714 Steffens Joseph Lincoln @ LINCOLN STEFFENS (DECEASED) NEW YORK,

U.S.A.

3715 Winnipeg, Civil Servants

3716 [entry blacked out]

3718 [entry blacked out] (Trans to [blacked out])

3719 Ukrainians at Welland, Ont trans to 175/4694

Page 14

3720 [entry blacked out] 175/P1333

3721 Vancouver, B.C. Abbott Bowling Club. Abbott St.

3722 [entry blacked out]

3723 O.B.U. in Alaska

3724 United Farmers of Ontario

3725 [entry blacked out] 175/P1614

3726 [entry blacked out] 175/1729

3727 [entry blacked out]

3728 [entry blacked out]

3729 [entry blacked out] trans to 175/4600

3730 Great War Veterans Association, Hamilton, Ont

3731 [entry blacked out] trans to 175/5401 [2-3 words blacked out]

3732 [entry blacked out]

3733 [entry blacked out]

3734 [entry blacked out] trans to 175/7201

3735 [entry blacked out]

3736 Socialist Party of Canada - Hamilton, Ont 175/2520

3737 [entry blacked out]

3738 [entry blacked out] trans to 175/4875

3739 [entry blacked out]

Page 15

3740 [entry blacked out]

3741 Communist Party Convention - Toronto, Ont January 1921.

3742 [entry blacked out]

3743 Strike of Ironworkers "Yarrow Limited" - Victoria, B.C.

3744 [entry blacked out] 175/P1736

3745 Trades & Labour Council, Edmonton, Alta trans to 175/6421

3746 [entry blacked out] 175/P553

3747 Conditions Labour at Thorold, Ont, Beaver Board Co. (Transf. to 175/4669)

INTERNATIONAL WORKERS & SOLDIERS FEDERATION
@ INTERNATIONAL WORKERS & SOLDIERS ASSOCIATION

3748 Workers & Soldiers Federation, Hamilton, Ont @ Soliers & Workers Federation

3749 [entry blacked out] trans to 175/558

3750 Socialist Party of Canada, Moose Jaw, Sask

3751 Convention of Camp & Lumber Workers' Industrial Union, Jan'y 1931, Vancouver, B.C.

3752 [entry blacked out] trans to 175/6053 175P/959

3753 [entry blacked out]

3754 see 175/3748

3755 [entry blacked out]

3756 [entry blacked out]

3757 [entry blacked out]

3758 [entry blacked out]

3759 Alleged German propaganda - Edmonton, Alta trans to [blacked out]

Page 16

3759 Alleged German Propaganda - Edmonton, Alta Corr. Transf. [blacked out]
Correspondence Trans. to [blacked out]

3760 [entry blacked out]

3761 Convention of Ukrainian Labour Temple Association 27-1-21 Winnipeg, Man

3762 [entry blacked out]

3763 [entry blacked out]

3764 [entry blacked out]

3765 [entry blacked out]

3766 [entry blacked out]

3767 Conditions General in Canada among Jews trans 175/4003

3768 Conventino of U.M.W.A. Halifax. N.S. Jan 31, 1921.

3769 [entry blacked out] trans to 175/P846

3770 Convention of Independent Labour Party, Halifax, N.S. 27-1-21.

3771 The Deep Sea Fisheries Union of the Pacific - Prince Rupert. B.C.

3772 [entry blacked out] Trans. [blacked out]

3773 [entry blacked out] trans 175/P1616

3774 The Co-Operative Movement in the United Kingdom. trans to 175/

3775 [entry blacked out] trans to 175/5101 trans to [blacked out]

3776 [entry blacked out]

3777 Strike at Canada Car Works - Fort William

3778 Sault Ste. Marie, Ont. Patrols from

Page 17

3779 [entry blacked out] (Trans to [blacked out]

3780 [entry blacked out]

3781 [entry blacked out] Trans 175/P1808

3782 [entry blacked out]

3783 [entry blacked out] trans to 175/4670

3784 Lumber Camp Workers' Industrial Union (O.B.U.) Edmonton Alta
@ Lumber Workers Industrial Union

3785 [entry blacked out]

3786 [entry blacked out] 175/P1785

3787 Strike at Indian Cove, Sydney Mines, N.S.

3788 [entry blacked out]

3789 Strike at S.E. Junkins Construction Co. Connaught Tunnel, Glacier, B.C.

3790 Hamilton Workers Defence Fund - Hamilton, Ont

3791 Labour Conditions among Miners at Cobalt, Ont (Transferred to 175/2232)
3792 [entry blacked out] 175/P1796
3793 [entry blacked out]
3794 [entry blacked out] 175/P1745
3795 Strike of Miners at Keeno Hill. Y.T.
3796 Conditions General among Ruthenians at Revelstroke, B.C. (Trans. to [blacked out]
3797 Anti-British Propaganda in United States
3798 Conditions General at Minaki, Ont
Page 18
3799 [entry blacked out]
3800 [entry blacked out] 175/P1737
3801 [entry blacked out] 175/1779
3802 [entry blacked out]
3803 [entry blacked out] 175/P1777
3804 O.B.U. Princeton, B.C.
3805 International Workers Educational Club - Toronto, Ont
3806 [entry blacked out]
Continued on [blacked out]
3807 Conditions Labour at Consolidated Mining & Smelting Co, Trail, B.C.
3808 [entry blacked out] 175/P1721
3809 Workers Defence League, Edmonton, Alta
3810 [entry blacked out] 175/P1769
3811 Conditions Labour at Inverness Railway and Coal Co., Inverness, Cape Breton
3812 [entry blacked out] 175P1676
3813 [entry blacked out]
3814 International Bible Students Association, Halifax, N.S.
3815 [entry blacked out] 175/P1758
3816 Strike of Garment Workers' at Hamilton, Ont
3817 [entry blacked out]
3818 [entry blacked out]
Page 19
3819 [entry blacked out] - Transferred to 175/3786 - 30-3-21. 175P/1785
3820 [entry blacked out]
3821 Russian Anarchist Party, Thorold, Ont
3822 [entry blacked out]
3823 Conditions Labour at Lock Lake, Ont. Stirrett Lumber Co & Corlessons Camp
3824 [entry blacked out]
3825 Conditions Labour at False Creek, B.C. Alberta Lumber Co.
3826 [entry blacked out] 175/P1784
3827 United Association of Railroad Employees of North America & Toronto, Ont.
3828 Conditions General in Bear Lake & Griffin Creek District, Alta
3829 [entry blacked out]
3830 Structural Iron Workers Union, Hamilton, Ont

3831 Bolshevism in Calgary, Alta B.F. 175/120
3832 International Bible Students Association - Winnipeg & District.

LUMBER WORKERS INDUSTRIAL UNION (O.B.U.)

3833 C & L.W.I. Union, Prince George, B.C.
3834 Strike at B.C. Electirc Railway Co. Victoria, B.C.
3835 The Socialist Party of Canada - Trans. to 175/1442 [2-3 words blacked out]
3836 Clarte (Olgan)
3837 Ukrainian Union Association - Toronto, Ont.
3838 [entry blacked out]

Page 20

3839 Labour Church - Generally
3840 [entry blacked out]
3841 [entry blacked out]
3842 [entry blacked out]
3843 Conditions Unrest at Port Colborne, Ont
3844 [entry blacked out] 175/P1791
3845 [entry blacked out]
3846 [entry blacked out]
3847 Industrial Workers of the World - Sub. Act within Iroquois Falls, Ont
trans to 175/4111
3848 Labour Conditions at Hyrdro Construction Camps at Niagara Falls & Queenston, Ont
3849 [entry blacked out]
3850 International Bible Students Association. St. John N.B. trans to [blacked out]
3851 [entry blacked out] 175/P1760
3852 General Conditions Among Foreigners - Tanks, N.S.
3853 [entry blacked out]
3854 [entry blacked out] trans to 175/4912
3855 [entry blacked out] 175/P2429
3856 International Bible Students Association - Truro, N.S.
3857 [entry blacked out] Calgary, Alta.
3858 [entry blacked out]

Page 21

3859 [entry blacked out] 175/P1798
3860 Iwan Franko Ukrainian Society - Edmonton, Alta trans to 175/4762
3861 [entry blacked out]
3862 [entry blacked out]
3863 [entry blacked out] Trans 175/P1842
3864 [entry blacked out]
3865 [entry blacked out] trans 175/P1756
3866 [entry blacked out] trans to 175/4956 175P/2142
3867 [entry blacked out] trans 175/P3867
3868 [entry blacked out] trans 175/P2497
3869 [entry blacked out] trans to 175/4780 175P/1749

3870 [entry blacked out] trans 175/4377

3871 [entry blacked out] trans to 175/4508

3872 [entry blacked out]

3873 [entry blacked out]

3874 Independent Labour Party, Victoria County, Cape Breton, N.S.

3875 Labour Conditions - Unemployment - Sydney Mines, N.S. trans to 175/6194

3876 [entry blacked out] 175/P1788

3877 [entry blacked out] 175/P1787

3878 General Conditions at Crowland, Ont trans to 175/3447

Page 22

3879 General Conditions in Toronto, Ont amongst Russians

3880 [entry blacked out]

3881 Brewery Strike, New Westminster, B.C.

3882 [entry blacked out]

3883 Ukrainian Students Club - Winnipeg, Man

3884 [entry blacked out] 175/P1811

3885 Canadian National Union of ExpService Men - Vancouver, B.C. (Transferred to 175/4472)

3886 [entry blacked out] 175/P1807

3887 [entry blacked out] 175/P1794

3888 [entry blacked out] 175/P1809

3889 International Bible Students Association, Canmore Alta.

3890 " " " " , Montreal, Que 175/6162

3891 " " " " , Hazelton, B.C.

3892 [entry blacked out]

3893 [entry blacked out] 175/P1805

3894 Anarchists at Toronto, Ont trans to 175/4532

3895 I.B.S.A. Battleford, Sask

3896 [entry blacked out] 175/P199

3897 [entry blacked out] 175/P1083

3898 International Bible Students Association, Ocean Falls, B.C.

Page 23

3899 [entry blacked out] trans to 175/4883

3900 [entry blacked out] trans to 175/4523

3901 [entry blacked out] 175/P1842

3902 Labour Conditions at New Westminster, B.C. Transferred to [blacked out]

3903 General Conditions at Barneston, P.Q.

3904 [entry blacked out]

3905 Grand Army United Veterans, Port Alberni, B.C.

3906 [entry blacked out]

3907 O.B.U. At Windsor, Ont trans 175/P63

3908 O.B.U. at Kenora, Ont trans to 175/5633

3909 International Bible Students Association, Stewart, B.C.

3910 " " " " Herbert, Sask

3911 [entry blacked out]

3912 [entry blacked out]

3913 Workers' Defence Committee, Brandon, Man

3914 Labour Conditions in Lampman, Sask General

3915 [entry blacked out] trans to [blacked out]

3916 [entry blacked out] Trans 175/P2303

3917 [entry blacked out]

3918 International Bible Students Association, Humboldt, Sask

Page 24

3919 General Conditions in Telkwa, B.C. trans to 175/4502

3920 [entry blacked out] 175/P329

3921 [entry blacked out]

3922 Bolshevism at Montreal, Que 175/P1861 [word blacked out] 175P/329

3923 [entry blacked out] 175/P1861

3924 [entry blacked out] 175/P1865

3925 [entry blacked out] 175/4880 175P/2059

3926 International Bible Students Association - Saskatoon, Sask

3927 "Council of Action" Montreal

3928 May Day 1921 at Winnipeg, Man

3929 [entry blacked out]

3930 May Day 1921 at Hamilton, Ont (Transferred to 175/2675)

3931 [entry blacked out] trans to 175/4851

3932 Bolshevism at Sault Ste Marie, Ont trans to 175/4660

3933 [entry blacked out] 175/P172 [2 words blacked out] trans to [blacked out]

3934 Socialist Labour Party, Hamilton, Ont trans to 175/4827

3935 Ukrainian Labour Temple, Edmonton, Alta trans to 175/4511

3936 [entry blacked out]

3937 [entry blacked out]

3938 [entry blacked out]

Page 25

3939 [entry blacked out]

3940 May Day at Yorkton, Sask

3941 [entry blacked out]

3942 [entry blacked out]

3943 [entry blacked out] Trans 175/P2124
B.F. 175/2667

3944 May Day, Toronto, Ont - 1921

3945 One Big Union - Melville, Sask

3946 INDUSTRIAL WORKERS OF THE WORLD - SUB ACT WITHIN

3947 Japanese Labour Union in B.C. trans to 175/6188

3948 [entry blacked out]
(B.F. 175/2651)

3949 May Day in Montreal, Que 1821

3950 [entry blacked out]

3951 [entry blacked out]

3952 Bolshevism at Yorkton, Sask trans to 175/4595

3953 [entry blacked out] trans to 175/4782

3954 Conditions General At Timmins, Ont trans to 175/4512

3955 [entry blacked out]

3956 [entry blacked out] trasn to 175/4622 175P/2138

3957 [entry blacked out]

3958 [entry blacked out]

Page 26

3959 [entry blacked out]

3960 [entry blacked out] 175/P1757

3961 Bolshevism at Mirror Landing, Alta

3962 Workers International League, Toronto, Ont trans to 175/5107

3963 Paper Makers Conditions Labor Amongst Ont

3964 Strike at Pacific Mill - Ocean Falls, B.C.

3965 [entry blacked out] trans to 175/4016

3966 [entry blacked out] 175/P1909

3967 Convention of United Communist Party - Toronto, Ont May 1921

3968 [entry blacked out] appears in Western Canada in 1920-21

3969 [entry blacked out] trans to 175/5969 175P/221

3970 [entry blacked out]

3971 [entry blacked out]

3972 Red International Trade Unions trans to 175/4602

3973 Conditions Labour at St. John. N.B. - New Brunswick Power Co. [2-3 words blacked out]

3974 [entry blacked out] Trans 175/P1885

3975 Propaganda in Canada trans to 175/4688

3976 [entry blacked out] Trans 175/P2015

3977 [entry blacked out]

3978 [entry blacked out]

Page 27

3979 [entry blacked out] trans to 175/4155 175P/1030

3980 [entry blacked out] 175/P1886

3981 [entry blacked out]

3982 [entry blacked out] Trans 175/P1890

3983 [entry blacked out] trans to 175/4645

3984 [entry blacked out] Trans 175/P1887

3985 [entry blacked out] Trans 175P/2199

3986 [entry blacked out] Trans 175/P1899

3987 Photo. Engravers Strike - Montreal, Que

3988 [entry blacked out] Trans 175/P1898

3989 [entry blacked out] trans to 175P/1964
3990 [entry blacked out] " " 175/4813 175P/1748
3991 International Bible Students Association - Cedoux, Sask
3992 Strike of Typographical Workers - Regina
3993 [entry blacked out]
3994 [entry blacked out]
3995 [entry blacked out]
(B.F. 175/2762)
3996 May Day at Vancouver, B.C.
3997 Labour Conditions among Loggers at Comox, B.C.
3998 [entry blacked out]
3999 [entry blacked out] Trans 175/P1891
Page 28
4000 [entry blacked out]
4001 [entry blacked out] P/1892
4002 [entry blacked out]
4003 General Conditions among Jews.
4004 Strike of Job Printers - Victoria B.C.
4005 [entry blacked out]
4006 General Conditions at Cedoux - Sask
4007 [entry blacked out]
4008 [entry blacked out]
4009 Canadian National Union of Ex Service Men (C.N.R.U.X) Can
4010 " " " " " " (C.N.U.X.) South Van
4011 " " " " " " (C.N.U.X.) Prince George
4012 " " " " " " (C.N.U.X.) Prince Rupert
Soldiers & Sailors Labor Party of Canada (B.F. 175/1069)
4013 " " " " " (C.N.U.X.) Winnipeg
4014 [entry blacked out] trasn to 175/P/1844
4015 [entry blacked out] transf. to 175P/1938
4016 [entry blacked out] trans to 175P/1977
4017 [entry blacked out]
4018 [entry blacked out]
4019 Labour Condition [2-3 words blacked out]
Page 29
4020 [entry blacked out] trans to 175/P1902
4021 [entry blacked out]
4022 [entry blacked out] trans to 175/P1781
4023 [entry blacked out]
4024 Labour Conditions at Penticton B.C.
4025 [entry blacked out] trans to 175/P-1565
4026 [entry blacked out] 175/P-88
4027 [entry blacked out] 175/P-1903

4028 [entry blacked out]
4029 [entry blacked out] trans to 175/P-214
4030 [entry blacked out] " " 175/P-1910
4031 Strike at Prince Rupert. B.C. - ????
4032 [entry blacked out] 175/P-1911
4033 [entry blacked out]
4034 [entry blacked out]
4035 [entry blacked out]
4036 Farmer Labour Association, Riverland, Man
4037 [entry blacked out]
4038 [entry blacked out] trans to 175/P-1914
4039 [entry blacked out] trans to 175/P/1918
Page 30
4040 [entry blacked out]
4041 Bolshevism in Alberta
CANADIAN NATIONAL UNION OF EX-SERVICEMEN
4042 (C.N.U.X.) - Edmonton - Alta
4043 United Association of Railway Employees
4044 Ukrainians at Beverley Alta.
4045 [entry blacked out]
4046 Barnes Circus. Sub. Act. Within
4047 [entry blacked out]
4048 [entry balcked out] trans to 175/p-345
4049 [entry blacked out]
Brotherhood of Indians
4050 League of Indians of Canada. Canada Gen
4051 [entry blacked out]
4052 General Conditions among Ukrainians, Thorold, Ont
4053 [entry blacked out] trans to 175/5355
CANADIAN NATIONAL UNION OF EX-SERVICMEN
4054 (C.N.U.X.) - Calgary, Alta
4055 [entry blacked out]
4056 Ukrainians at Sydney. N.S.
4057 [entry blacked out] trans to 175/P-2028
4058 [entry blacked out]
4059 [entry blacked out]
Page 31
4060 Socialist Sunday Schools. Great Britain
4061 Grand Army of United Veterans (G.A.U.V.)
Grand Army of Canada @ United Veterans League Canada Gen.
4062 [entry blacked out] trans to 175/P-1928
4063 Canada India League
4064 [entry blacked out] Toronto, Ont

4065 [entry blacked out] Combined with 175/3993
4066 [entry blacked out]
4067 [entry blacked out] trans to 175/P-1942
4068 [entry blacked out]
4069 International Bible Students Assn - Young, Sask
4070 [entry blacked out] trans to 175/P-1962
4071 [entry blacked out]
4072 [entry blacked out]
4073 [entry blacked out] trans to 175/P-1906
4074 [entry blacked out]
4075 [entry blacked out]
4076 [entry blacked out] trans to 175/P-1936
4077 ???Drivers - Conditions Labor Amongst. B.C.
4078 Ukrainians at Sandy Lake Man
4079 [entry blacked out] trans to 175P/2293
Page 32
4080 [entry blacked out] trans to 175/5756
4081 [entry blacked out]
(JUNE 14-22, 1921)
4082 Convention of United Mine Workers at New Glasgow N.S.
B.F. 175/3253 175/3242
4083 General Conditions among Poles
4084 Convention of Labour Party - New Glasgow. N.S. - June 1921
4085 Chinese & Japanese languages - Generally
4086 Labour Conditions in Nova Scotia - Generally Trans to [blacked out]
4087 [entry blacked out] trans to [blacked out]
4088 Bolshevism at Regina, Sask - 18th Battery C.F.A.
4089 [entry blacked out] trans to 175/P-1943
4090 Labour Conditions at Kapuskasing, Ont
4091 [entry blacked out] trans to 175P/1964
4092 Ukrainian Labour Temple - Toronto, Ont.
4093 [entry blacked out]
4094 [entry blacked out]
4095 [entry blacked out] trans to 175/P-1581
4096 [entry blacked out] " to 175/P-1929
4097 Bolshevism at Sudbury Ont
4098 [entry blacked out]
4099 Unemployment at Brantford, Ont trans to 175/1916
Page 33
4100 Ukrainian Labour Party - Corbin, B.C. Transferred to 175-6248
4101 " " " - Trail, B.C.
4102 [entry blacked out] trans to 175/P-1950
4103 [entry blacked out] " " 175/P/1957

4104 [entry blacked out] 175P/1949
4105 [entry blacked out]
4106 [entry blacked out]
4107 [entry blacked out] 175/P-1954
4108 [entry blacked out]
4109 [entry blacked out] trans to 175/P-1916
4110 [entry blacked out]

175P/1957

4111 Labour Conditions at Hydro Electric Power Commission Construction Camp - Niagara Falls, Ont
4112 [entry blacked out] trans to 175/P-1956
4113 [entry blacked out] 175/P-2090
4114 [General Conditions at Massett. B.C.
4115 Labor Conditions on Steamship "Canadian Rover"
4116 [entry blacked out]
4117 [entry blacked out] trans to 175/P-1959
4118 [entry blacked out] " " 175/P-1960
4119 [entry blacked out] trans to [blacked out] 175P/2418

Page 34

4120 [entry blacked out] trans 175/P1961
4121 [entry blacked out]
4122 [entry blacked out]
4123 C.N.U.X. - Kindersley Camp, Sask.
4124 [entry blacked out]
4125 World War Veterans
4126 Industiral Workers of the World Public Service Organization
4127 [entry blacked out]
4128 [entry blacked out]
4129 [entry blacked out]
4130 Canadian Workers Defence League - Toronto, Ont
4131 [entry blacked out]
4132 Canadian Workers Defence League - Regina, Sask.
4133 [word blacked out] Ukrainian Society - Winnipeg, Man.
4134 " " " - Calgary, Alta.
4135 Anarchist Groups in Canada
4136 [entry blacked out]
4137 Polish Educational Party - Montreal. P.Q.
4138 The Workers Dreadnought
(Trans to [blacked out])
4139 Labour Conditions among Longshoremen - St. John, N.B.

Page 35

4140 [entry blacked pout]

4141 [entry blacked out]

4142 [entry blacked out]

4143 Communists seeking Employment

4144 [entry blacked out] trans to 175/P-1883

4145 [entry blacked out] to 175/P-1930

4146 [entry blacked out] 175/P/1971

4147 [entry blacked out]

4148 [entry blacked out]

4149 Conditions - Unemployment - Halifax. N.S.

4150 Canadian National Union of Ex Service Men (CNUX) Toronto, Ont ??????
@ Ex Soldiers and Sailors Council of Canada @ Soldiers and Sailors Labor Party of Canada CBF175/3245

4151 Labour Conditions - Welland Ship Canal Ont. Trans to 175/5465

4152 International Bible Students Assn. - Sault Ste Marie, Ont

4153 [entry blacked out]

4154 Canadian Labour Alliance

4155 [entry blacked out] 175/P/1030

4156 [entry blacked out]

4157 First Ukrainian Cooperative Export Co. & Ukrainian Nav. & Trading Co.

4158 [entry blacked out] Transferred to 175P/1856

4159 [entry blacked out]

Page 36

4160 [entry blacked out]

4161 The International Literature Agency - Winnipeg. Man.

4162 Labour Conditions - Employment in Canada

4163 [entry blacked out]

4164 [entry blacked out] 175/P/2354

4165 [entry blacked out] 175//P/4460

4166 [entry blacked out] 175/P/1980

4167 [entry blacked out] 175/P/1891

4168 Convention of I.B.S.A. - Edmonton. Alta.

4169 International Bible Students Assn - Cobalt. Ont.

4170 [entry blacked out], 175/4129

4171 [entry blacked out] 175/P/2470

4172 I.B.S.A. Convention - Saskatoon. Sask.

4173 [entry blacked out]

4174 G.A.U.V. at Hamilton Ont.

4175 [entry blacked out

4176 [entry blacked out] 175/P/1995

4177 [entry blacked out]

4178 Bolshevism at Fort Frances. Ont.

4179 [entry blacked out]

Page 37

4180 [entry blacked out]
4181 [entry blacked out] 175/P-1856
4182 [entry blacked out] 175/P-1983
4183 [entry blacked out] 175/P/1981
4184 [entry blacked out]
4185 Samo-Obrazowania at Calgary. Alta.
4186 [entry blacked out]
4187 Labour Conditions at Unity, Sask.
4188 General Conditions amongst Doukhobors, Verigan, Sask.
4189 " " " " , Canora. Sask.
4190 [entry blacked out]
4191 Convention of Dominion Trades & Labor Congress - Winnipeg. Aug 1921
4192 General Conditions among Italians at Hamilton. Ont.
4193 [entry blacked out]
4194 Pacific Mills Ltd - Conditions Labor in Logging Camps - Ocean Falls, B.C.
4195 [entry blacked out]
4196 [entry blacked out]
4197 [entry blacked out]
4198 [entry blacked out]
4199 T. Shewchenko Ukranian Society - Hamilton. Ont.
Page 38
4200 [entry blacked out] (Trans to [blacked out])
4201 General Conditions in Canada. Transferred to [blacked out]
4203 Bolshevism at Hafford, Sask.
4204 " " Blaine Lake, Sask.
4205 [entry blacked out]
4206 [entry blacked out] 175/P-1848
4207 [entry blacked out] 175/P-2003
4208 [entry blacked out]
4209 Canadian Labour Alliance Montreal, P.Q.
4210 [entry blacked out]
4211 [entry blacked out]
4212 Socialist Party of Canada - Montreal. PQ.
4213 [entry blacked out] 175/P/2551
4214 [entry blacked out]
4215 [entry blacked out]
4216 [entry blacked out] Confidential A-???
4217 [entry blacked out] 175/P-2002
4218 [entry blacked out]
4219 [entry blacked out] 175/P/2008
Page 39
4220 [entry blacked out] 175/P/1821
Independent Order of B'nai B'rith

4221 B'nai B'rith (Sons of the Covenant) Sub. Act. In Winnipeg, Man.

4222 Beneficent Society of St Nicholas - Ukrainian Winnipeg, Man

4223 I.B.S.A. - Assiniboia, Sask.

4224 [entry blacked out] trans to 175/P/2007

4225 Labour Conditions at Saskatoon, Sask. Transferred to [blacked out]

4226 [entry blacked out] 175/P/1948

4227 [entry blakced out]

4228 Ken Wah Aviation School - Saskatoon, Sask

4229 Council of Workers - Vancouver. B.C.

4230 [entry blacked out]

4231 [entry blacked out]

4232 Labour Conditions - Congress, Sask.

4233 I.B.S.A. - Weyburn, Sask.

4234 [entry blacked out]

4235 [entry blacked out]

4236 Young Men's Hebrew Assn - Winnipeg, Manitoba

4237 Montifore Club - Winnipeg, Man.

4238 [entry blacked out] trans to 175/P-2016

4239 Socialist Party of Canada - Ottawa, Ont.

Page 40

4240 [entry blacked out]

4241 [entry blacked out]

4242 [entry blacked out]

4243 Agitators at Montreal, P.Q.

held at

4244 Convention of One Big Union (Winnipeg, Man - 26 Sept 1921)Canada??

4245 [entry blacked out] trans to 175/P/292

4246 Ku Klux Klan [2-3 words blacked out]

4247 [entry blacked out] trans to 175/P-3445

4248 [entry blacked out]

4249 [entry blacked out] 185/P/2210

4250 INDUSTRIAL WORKERS OF THE WORLD - SUB. ACT. WITHIN - SASKATCHEWAN

4251 Chinese Nationalist League - Windsor, Ont.

4252 Strike of Employees - T.&. & B. Railway

4253 Socialist Party of Canada - Regina. Sask

4254 [entry blacked out] 175/P/2032

4255 C.N.U.X. - Hamilton Ont

4256 [entry blacked out]

4257 C.N.U.X. - Regina, Sask

4258 [entry blacked out]

4259 Socialist Party of Canada, Yukon Territory

Page 41

4260 Kottiarewsky - Ukrainian Society - Winnipeg. Man.
4261 [entry blacked out]
4262 [entry blacked out]
4263 Shewchenko Enlightenment Society - Thorold. Ont.
4264 [entry blacked out] 175/P/1982
4265 Anarchists at Hamilton, Ont.
4266 Shumei Okawa and the Asia Jiron - Black Dragon Society
4267 Veteran's Forum - Toronto, Ont.
4268 [entry blacked out]
4269 Canadian Labour Party [2-3 words blacked out]
4270 [entry blacked out] 175/P/2029
4271 Labour Conditions at Waldo B.C.
4272 [entry blacked out] 175/P/2039
4273 [entry blacked out] 175/P/2037
4274 [entry blacked out] 275/P/2025
4275 General Conditions at Queen Charlotte Islands, B.C.
4276 Executives of Canadian Jap Associaiton
4277 " " [3-4 words blacked out]
4278 " " Canadian Labour Party
4279 " " Chinese Nationalist League
Page 42
4280 Executives of (scratched out) [rest of entry blacked out]
4281 Executives of C.N.U.X.
Trans to 175/4643
4282 " " Central Labour Council - O.B.U. Executive Wpg. Man.
4283[4-5 words blacked out]
4284 " " Defence Leagues - Cancelled see 175/4306
4285 " " Famine Relief Committee
4286 " " Farmer Labour Association
4287 " " Federated Labour Party Trans to 175/4440
4288 " " [rest of entry blacked out]
4289 " " Grand Army of United Veterans - Executives of Vancouver B.C.
4290 " " Industrial Workers of the World
4291 " " International Bible Students Association
4292 " " Independent Labour Party
4293 " " [rest of entry blacked out]
4294 " " Labour College
4295 " " Camp & Lumber Workers Industrial Union
4296 " " One Big Union B.F. 175/4498
4297 " " Samo-Obrazowania Society
4298 " " Socialist Parties of Canada [[2-3 words blacked out]
4299 " " Trades & Labour Council [2-3 words blacked out]
Page 43

4300 Executives of Society for Technical Aid to Soviety Russia
4301 " " Ukrainian Shewchenko Enlightenment Society
4302 " " " Liberty Organization
4303 " " [rest of entry blacked out]
4304 " " Worker's Educational League
4305 " " Workmen's International
4306 " " Canadian Workers Defence League
4307 " " Zapamhe Towanistovo
4308 " " Ukrainian Labour Temple (Trans. to [blacked out])
4309 Associatio
4310 " " Dzwin Society
4311 " " Chinese Republic Re Establishment Association
4312 [entry blacked out]
4313 [entry blacked out] 175/P/1939
CNANDIAN UKRAINIAN INSTITUTE "PROSVITA" @ "PROSVITA"
4314 "Prosvita" Educational Club - Winnipeg. Man
4315 [entry blacked out] Cancelled see 175/4197
4316 [entry blacked out] 175/P/2035
4317 [entry blacked out] 175/3695
[all of 4318 and 4319 including numbers are blacked out]
Page 44
4320 [entry blacked out]
4321 [entry blacked out] 175/P/2028
4322 [entry blacked out]
4323 [entry blacked out] 175/P/2033
4324 [entry blacked out]
4325 [entry blacked out] 175/P/1989
4326 General Conditions amongst Ukrainians at Saskatoon. Sask.
4327 [entry blacked out] 175/P/143
4328 [entry blacked out]
4329 Council of Action - Winnipeg. Man.
4330 Labour Conditions in U.S.A. Trans to [blacked out]
4331 [entry blacked out] 175/P/2048
4332 People's Chataugua - Brandon, Man.
4333 [entry blacked out] Transferred to [blacked out]
4334 Ukrainian Friendly Society in Canada
4335 Canada Labour Party - Brandon. Man. B.F. 175/4823
4336 [entry blacked out] 175P/1916
4337 [entry blacked out]
4338 Conditions Unrest Amongst Railway Employees Canada Generally
4339 The Canadian Legion [2-3 words blacked out]
Page 45
4340 [entry blacked out]

4341 [entry blacked out]
4342 [entry blacked out]
4343 [entry blacked out]
4344 [entry blacked out]
4345 [entry blacked out]
4346 - Trans to 175/4273 (scratched out) 175P2039
4347 [entry blacked out] 175/P/1312
4348 [entry blacked out]
4349 [entry blacked out]
4350 [entry blakced out]
4351 [entry blacked out] 175/P/1720
4352 [entry blacked out] 175/P/2111
4353 [entry blacked out]
4354 People's Social Research Institute - East Toronto, Ont
4355 [entry blacked out]
4356 [entry blacked out]
4357 [entry blacked out]
4357 sup [blacked out]
4358 Labour Conditions - Vancouver Island. B.C.
4359 " " - The Pas. Man. Continued on [blacked out]
Page 46
4360 [entry blacked out]
(File Destroyed 18-12-57)
4361 Labour Conditions amongst Hop-pickers - Agassiz & Chilliwack B.C.
4362 [entry blacked out]
(held at Fernie B.C. Oct. 1921)
4363 Labour Conditions - East Kootenay. B.C.
4364 [entry blacked out]
4365 [entry blacked out]
4366 [entry blacked out]
4367 [entry blacked out]
4368 [entry blacked out] 175/P/1776
4369 [entry blacked out]
4370 Shewchenko Educational Society at Crowland. Ont.
4371 Workers Alliance - Winnipeg. Man. [2-3 words blacked out]
4372 [entry blacked out]
4373 [entry blacked out]
4374 [entry blacked out] Transf 175P1741
4375 Conditions Amongst Finns at Sault Ste Marie. Ont.
4376 Workers Alliance - Winnipeg Convention - Nov 10-21
4377 [entry blacked out] 175P/1884
4378 Volia - Ukrainian Society
4379 Dzwin - Ukrainian Society

Page 47

4380 Labour Conditions - Fort William & Port Arthur Ont.

4381 [entry blacked out]

4382 [entry blacked out]

4383 Labour Conditions - Employment - Saskatoon, Sask.

4384 Japanese in Alberta [2-3 words blacked out]

4385 Public Service Organization

4386 [entry blacked out] Transferred to 175/4396

4387 [entry blacked out]

4388 [entry blacked out]

4389 [entry blacked out] 175/P/2743

4390 [entry blacked out]

4391 Young Jewish Socialist Club - Toronto, Ont

4392 [entry blacked out] 175/P/1392

4393 Ukrainian Friendly Society - Hamilton. Ont.

4394 [entry blacked out]

4395 [entry blacvked out] 175/P/2076

4396 Jewish Revolutionary Bonds

4397 [entry blacked out]

4398 [entry blacked out] 175/P/2179

4399 [entry blacked out]

Page 48

4400 [entry blacked out] 175/P/2082

4401 Independent Labour Party - Brantford, Ont.

4402 [entry blacked out]

4403 [entry blacked out]

4404 United Labour Council - CANADA GENERALLY
AMERICAN FEDERATED LABOUR COUNCIL

4405 [entry blacked out]

4406 [entry blakced out] 175/P/2092

4407 [entry blacked out]

4408 [entry blacked out]

4409 [entry blacked out]

4410 [entry blacked out]
WORKERS PARTY OF CANADA (DIST. CONVENTION HELD IN TORONTO

4411 Correspondence Transferred to [blacked out] 18,19/1922) ONTARIO

4412 C.N.U.X. - Montreal. P.Q.

4413 [entry blacked out]

4414 [entry blacked out]

4415 [entry blacked out]

4416 [entry blacked out]

4417 [entry blacked out] 175/P/1876

4418 Workers League - Montreal. P.Q.

4419 Workers Party - Hamilton. Ont [2-3 words blacked out]

Page 49

[3-4 words blacked out]

4420 Workers Party of Canada - General

4421 General Conditions - Windsor, Ont.

4422 [entry blacked out]

4423 [entry blacked out] 175/P/2091

4424 [entry blacked out] 175/P/2098

4425 Social Economic Labour Association - Montreal. P. Q.

4426 [entry blacked out] 175/4429 [word blacked out]

4427 [entry blacked out]

4428 Labour Conditions - Unemployment - Calgary. Alta.

4429 [entry blacked out]

Page 50

4430 [entry blacked out]

4431 [entry blacked out] 175P/13

Trans to [blacked out]

4432 Labour Conditions - Employment - Winnipeg. Man

[4-5 words blacked out]

4433 Ukrainian Labour party. Ottawa. Ont.

(B.F. 175/P434 & 175/190) trans from f 175/15 & 175/550

4434 Socialist Party of Canada - Winnipeg Man.

4435 [entry blacked out] (Trans to [blacked out])

4436 Labour Conditions at ????? Mines. Alta.

4437 [entry blacked out] 175P/202

4438 Ukrainians at Calgary, Alta.

(B.F. 175/4737 & 175/28??

4439 General Conditions Stew???B.C.

(B.F. 175/4287)

4440 Federated Labour Party of Canada - Vancouver. B.C.

4441 General Conditions - Prince Rupert B.C.

4442 Socialist Party of Canada Trans [blacked out]

4443 [entry blacked out]

4444 [entry blacked out]

4445 [entry blacked out]

4446 [entry blacked out]

4447 General Conditions [rest of entry blacked out]

4448 ??????????? Saskatoon

4449 Ukrainians in ???????? District - ??????

Page 51

No entries

Page 52

No entries

Page 53

Union of Russian Working Men Transferred from

4450 @Union of Russian Working Men Toronto, Ont. 175/2728

4451 [entry blacked out]

4452 General Conditions at ?????. Alta

4453 " " " Crows Nest Pass

4454 Chinese Nationalist League Canada (General (Transferred to [blacked out]

Continued from 175/81

4455 International Longshoreman's Association

4456 Labour Conditions - Employment, (Edmonton. Alta.)

(B.F. 175/119 & 175/319 & 175/3371)

4457 One Big Union. Winnipeg & District

4458 " " " . Saskatoon. Sask (B.F. 175/4741)

4459 [entry blacked out]

4460 [entry blacked out] 175P/1741

Labour Conditions - Employment ????????

175P/1545

[entry numbers and entries blacked out]

4469 [no entry] Vancouver. B.C.

Page 54

4470 ??? Club - Hamilton Ont Transferred from

4471 Labour Conditions - Employment 175/3624

CANADIAN NATIONAL UNION OF EX-SERVICE MEN (B.F. 175/3885)

4472 (C.N.U.X.) - Vancouver. B.C.

4473 [entry blacked out]

4474 French Socialist Party - Montreal. Que.

4475 [entry blacked out] 175P/2100

4476 General Conditions [5-6 words blacked out]

[entry & number blacked out]

[entry blacked out] 175P/1757

4479 Labour Conditions - Springhill. N.S. (Trans. [blacked out])

4480 Cards & ?????????? in Pictou County Coal Fields [2-3 words blacked out]

4481 Ukrainians in Edmonton ?????

[4-5 words blacked out]

4482 One Big Union - Toronto. Ont. (B.F. 175/27[blacked out])

4483 Sacco-Vanzetti Defense Committee

4484 [entry blacked out]

[entry numbers and entries blacked out for rest of page]

Page 55

(B.F. 175/3709) Transf from

4489 Labour Conditions in Toronto - Employment 175/3709

4490 Ukrainian Labour Party - Winnipeg. Man. 175/4493

4491 [entry blacked out]

4492 [entry blacked out]
4493 Ukrainian Labour Temple Association - Winnipeg BF/175/4490
4494 [entry blacked out]
Canadian
4495 Independent Labour Party - Toronto, Ont B.F. [blacked out]
4496 [entry blacked out] 175P/2101
4497 Labour Workers Industrial Union - Vancouver. B.C.
4498 One Big Union (BF. 175/3173 & 175/319) BG 175/2878
4499 Unemployed Situation - [4-5 words blacked out]
4500 Labour Conditions in Montreal [2-3 words blacked out]
4501 General " at Ocean Falls - B.C. [word blacked out]
4502 " " in Telkwa, B.C.
4503 " " " Kamloops. B.C.
4504 Socialist Party of Canada - Vancouver B.C. [entry numbers blacked out]
[entries blacked out] BF 175/3462
Regina. Sask
Winnipeg. Man.
4508 [entry blacked out]
Page 56
4509 [entry blacked out] Trans from 175/3481
4510 Worker Ottawa. Ont [2-3 words blacked out]
4511 Ukrain Temple - Edmonton. Alta
4512 [2-3 words blacked out] at Timmins Ont
4513 [entry blacked out] 175P/1873
4514 [entry blacked out] 175P/26
4515 Labour Church - Edmonton. Alta.
4516 [entry blacked out]
4517 International Bible Students Association, Edmonton, Alta See 175/4913.2096
4518 Workers ???? at Welland. Ont See 175/4910
4519 " [word blacked out] - Timmons Ont See 175/?445
4520 [entry blacked out]
4521 Labour Conditions - Nanaimo. Alta
4522 " " - Trail
4523 [2 words blacked out]
B.F. 175/67 & 175/2492)
4524 [word blacked out] Party of Canada - Edmonton. Alta
rkers Party - Vancouver. B.C.
Socialist Party of Canada (Transf [blacked out])
us for Deportation
Page 57
4528 [entry blacked out] Transferred from
4529 [entry blacked out] 175/3282
4530 Bolshevism at Port Arthur, Ont.

4531 Amalgamated Clothing Workers - Hamilton Ont.
4532 Russian Anarchist Party at Toronto, Ont B.F. 175/3894, 175/ ?????????
4533 [entry blacked out] 175P/1845
4534 Workers Party - Ottawa Ont. Transferred to 175/4510 27/1/22
4535 [entry blacked out] 175P/2102
4536 Workers Party - [2 words blacked out] - Winnipeg. Man.
4537 " " - Toronto Ont [2 words blacked out]
4538 One Big Union - Calgary, Alta. [2-3 words blacked out] BF 175/1856
4539 Workers' Party - Toronto Ont. [2-3 words blacked oiut] Trans to 175/6373
4540 " " - Winnipeg. Man [word blacked out]
4541 Agitators among R.C.M. P 175/6605
[2-3 words blacked out]
4542 General Conditions in Canada a [rest of entry blacked out]
4543 conditions Generally [rest of entry blacked out]
454? A ??PERCUTION of White Finns [rest of entry blacked out]
4544 [entry blacked out]
B.F. 175/521)
4545 One Big Union - Cumberland, B.C.
[entry numbers and entries blacked out]
Page 58
4548 Workers' Party - [2-3 words blacked out] - Hamilton Ont.
4549 " " [4-5 words blacked out]
4550 [entry blacked out]
4551 [entry blacked out] Trans 175P/1366
4552 [entry blacked out] Trans 175P/1716
4553 [entry blacked out] 175P/1365
4554 [entry blacked out]
4555 General Conditions - Nelson, B.C.
4556 Workers' Party - Edmonton, Alta. [2-3 words blacked out]
4557 [entry blacked out]
4558 [entry blacked out]
4559 Workers' Party - Toronto, Ont. [3-4 words blacked out]
4560 " " " [4-5 words blacked out]
4561 Ukrainian Labour Temple - Hamilton, Ont
Corres. Trans [blacked out]
4562 " " Association ????
4567 [entry blacked out]
4563 [2-3 words blacked out] - Handel, Sask
4564 Workers' Party - Calgary, Alta.
B.F. 175/??23 & 175/2735)
4565 General Conditions - Merritt. B.C.
[entry numbers and entries blacked out]
Page 59

Transferred from

4568 One Big Union - Fort William, Ont 175/2060 & 175/1424
4569 [entry blacked out] 175P/169
4570 L.W.I.U. of the O.B.U. B.F. 175/1668 BF. 175/1534 Trans to [blacked out]
4571 [entry blacked out]
4572 New People's Church - Brandon Man
4573 [entry blacked out] Trans 175P/198
4574 General Conditions - Bolshevism - Hamilton Ont.
4575 Communist Party - Montreal. P.Q. (Trans to [blacked out])
4576 [entry blacked out]
4577 Communist Party [1-2 words blacked out] Montreal, P.Q. 175/4408
4578 [entry blacked out] 175P/2221
4579 Balinson H. & International Press - Hamilton, Ont.
4580 [entry blacked out]
4581 [entry blacked out]
4582 [entry blacked out] 175P/1841
4583 [entry blacked out[]
4584 Workers Party - Windsor, Ont
by unemployed
4585 Threatened Disturbances at Vancouver B.C. [2-3 words blacked out]
[rest of page blacked out]
Page 60
Bienfait, Sask. Transferred from
Jan 30 INDUSTRIAL WORKERS OF THE WORLD SUB. ACT IN
I.W.W. Activities at Bienfait Sask 175/226
B.F. 175P/992 & 175/2365) BF. from 175/504
Trades Labour Council - Winnipeg, Man 9
31 [entry blacked out] 175P/681 980
General Conditions among Ukrainians - Winnipeg, Man.3623
4592 [entry blacked out]
Correspondence [2-3 words blacked out]
4593 Ukrainian Labour ???? Association Convention ???1922
4594 [entry blacked out]
4595 Bolshevism at Yorkton, Sask (Trans to [blacked out]) 3592
Feb 14596 [entry blacked out]
4597 Socialist Party of Canada - Calgary Alta 103
4598 [entry blacked out] 175P/1135 2012
4599 [entry blacked out] 175P/397 2637
4600 [entry blacked out] 3729
4601 [entry blacked out] 175P/2114
4602 Red International of Trade Unions [2-3 words blacked out] 39
4603 [entry blacked out] [2-3 words blacked out]
4604 [entry blacked out] 175P/1180 [2-3 words blacked out] 3279

2 4605 [entry blacked out] 175P/2113 [2-3 words blacked out]

[rest of page blacked out]

Page 61

Transferred from

Feb 2 [entry blacked out]

[entry blacked out] 175P/771 175/1371

4610 [entry blacked out] - 175P/786 175/1784

4 4611 Conditions among Foreigners at Renfrew, Ont.

4612 " " " " Almonte, "

4613 " " " " Carleton Place, "

4614 " " " " Pembroke, "

4615 " " " " Amprior, "

4616 " " " " Cobden, "

4617 [entry blacked out] 175P/329 3920

[entry blacked out] 175P/814 1535

6 [3-4 words blacked out] Hamilton, Ont

7 [entry blacked out] 175P/1225

4621 General Conditions at [blacked out] (Transferred [blacked out])

4622 [entry blacked out]

[1-2 words blacked out] Regina, Sask. [3-4 words blacked out]

8 [1-2 words blacked out] Clothing Workers - [4-5 words blacked out]

[1-2 words blacked out] amongst Finns - Edmonton [3-4 words blacked out]

[rest of page blacked out]

Page 62

Transferred from

Feb 10 4628 [entry blacked out]

11 4629 Strike at Nicola Pine Mills - Merritt, B.C.

(B.F. 175/488 & 175/489)

4630 One Big Union - Fernie, B.C. 175/488

13 4631 [entry blacked out]

4632 General Conditions - Alert Bay, B.C. 175/2531

4633 One Big Union - Glace Bay, N.S. BF 175/3058 3058

4634 Bolshevism at - Dana, Sask.

14 4635 [entry blacked out]

4636 [entry blacked out] 175P/2126

4637 Conditions amongst Ukrainians - Saulte Ste Marie, Ont.

4638 Workers Party of Canada - Nelson, B.C.

4639 [entry blacked out] 175P/2209

4640 [entry blacked out] 175P/2131

4641 [entry blacked out] 175P/2148

4642 [entry blacked out]

4643 Central Labour Council (OBU) Winnipeg [2-3 words blacked out]

16 4644 Workers Party of Canada - Vancouver, B.C. [3-4 words blacked out]
4645 [entry blacked out] 175P/1988
[rest of page blacked out]
Page 63
transferred from
Feb 17 4648 Workers Party [1-2 words blacked out] Hamilton, Ont.
4649 One Big Union - Corbin, B.C.

4650 Peoples Forum, The - Regina, Sask. Trans to [blacked out] 175/2045
4651 One Big Union in Nova Scotia Generally BF 175/2981
4652 " " " " Michel, B.C. BF 175/P145, 175/1844
4653 Labour Party - Dauphin Man.
4654 [entry blacked out] 175P/49
20 4655 Workers Party of Canada - Sudbury, Ont. [3-4 words blacked out]
BF 175/491
4656 One Big Union - Calgary, Alta BF 175/496
BF 175/2715
21 4657 ????? Ukrainian Party - Winnipeg Beach, [word blacked out]
4658 The Third International [3-4 words blacked out]
22 4659 [entry blacked out] 175P/2132
4660 Bolshevism at Sault Ste Marie, Ont.
23 4661 Communist Party - Winnipeg, Man. [3-4 words blacked out]
4662 Conditions at Prescott, Ont.
4663 [entry blacked out]
4664 [entry blacked out]
4665 [entry blacked out] 175P/983
[rest of page blacked out]
Page 64
Transferred from
Feb 24 4668 Labour Conditions at Gananoque, Ont.
(B.F. 175/3747)
4669 " " Thorold, Ont - Beaver Board Company 175/3747
25 4670 [entry blacked out] 3783
4671 Workers Party of Canada [1-2 words blacked out] Welland, Ont.
27 4672 "Noive Zysie" (New Life) Polish Society
4673 [entry blacked out] 175P/2140
4674 Ukrainain Socialist Party - Krydor, Sask.
Correspondence [word blacked out]
4675 Workers Party of Canada Fort William, Ont. [1-2 words blacked out]
4676 General Conditions at Anyox and ????? 1569
4677 [entry blacked out] trans to 175P/2136
4678 Workers Party - Montreal, Que. See 175/4767
4679 General Conditions amongst Foreigners - Kingston, Ont.

4680 [entry blacked out]
4681 [entry blacked out] BF 175/1987
4682 Montreal Labour College Trans. [2-3 words blacked out]
4683 [1-2 words blacked out] Trans to 175P/213
Trans to 175/5014
4684 Peace & Freedom League - Vancouver, B.C.
4685 Labour Conditions - Moose Jaw

[rest of page blacked out]

Page 65

			Transferred from
March 1	4688	Propaganda in Canada	175/3975
2	4689	[entry blacked out]	
	4690	Socialist Party of Canada, Cobourg, Ont.	
	4691	" " Belleville, "	
	4692	" " ???????	
	4693	Relief Camp - Conditions Trenton - Trenton, Ont.	
	[2-3 words blacked out]		
	4694	Ukrainians at Welland	3719
	4695	General Conditions at Port Alberni,	2500
	4696	Convention of U.M.W. - Truro, NS Dist. 26 (1922)	3416
3	4697	General Conditions - Peterborough, Ont.	
	4698	Conditions Unrest - Perth, "	
	4699	" " - Port Hope, "	
	4700	" " - Lindsay, "	
	4701	[entry blacked out] Trans to 175P/331	
	4702	Workers Party [1-2 words blacked out] South porcupine	
	4703	Communist Party - Ontario District Convention (held at Hamilton, On)	
4	4704	General Conditions - Smith's Falls, Ont.	
	4705	[entry blacked out] Trans to 175P/2147	

[rest of page blacked out]

Page 66

Mar 7	4708	[entry blacked out] TRANS TO 175P/2149
	4709	[entry blacked out] TRANS TO 175P/2151
	4710	[entry blacked out] TRANS TO 175P/2145
	(Correspondence [2-3 words blacked out)	
	4711	Ukrainian Labour Temple Association - Sydney, N.S.
	4712	Conditions amongst Finns - Montreal, P.Q. trans [word blacked out]
	4713	Fourth International, The
8	4714	Pan America Bureau, The material placed on [word blacked out]
9	4715	[entry blacked out] Cancelled - See 175/4758
	4716	Conditions amongst Ukrainians - Sault Ste Marie, Ont.

		Combined with 175/1637	
	4717	[entry blacked out] TRAS TO 175P/2163	
10	4718	Workers Party - Sault Ste Marie, Ont.	
11	4719	[entry blacked out]	
11	4720	[entry blacked out]	
11	4721	[entry blacked out]	
14	4722	[entry blacked out] RANS TO 175P/2161	
	4723	Communists Party leaving Canada (on whom we [2-3 words blacked out])	
	4724	Trade Union Educational League in Canada	
	4725	[entry blacked out] TRANS TO 175P/2180	
	??? of the Workers Party of Canada		
	Labour Conditions - Bankhead, Alta.		

Page 67

			Transferred from
Mar 15	4728	[entry blacked out] TRANS TO 175P/1609	175/3662
16	4729	Conditions amongst Finns - Toronto, Ont.	
	4730	Imperial Veterans - Vancouver, B.C.	3608
	4731	[entry blacked out] to 175P/2257	1053
	4732	General Conditions - Winnipeg, Man (Trans to 175/321)	
	4733	Labour Conditions in Espanola, Ont.	
	4734	" " Okanagan Falls, B.C.	
	4735	[entry blacked out] TRANS TO 175P/1895	3549
17	4736	Conditions in Africa. Transferred to [blacked out]	
	4737	Convention(s) of United Mine (Annual.) Workers of America (Dist 18.) Feb 27th & 28th 1922 - Calgary, Alta.	
	4738	[entry blacked out] TRANS TO 175P/366	1146
20	4739	Strike at J.D. McArthur Tie Camp - Mud River, B.C.	
	4740	Communist Party - Toronto, Ont [4-5 words blacked out]	
	4741	Conditions amongst Finlanders - Copper Cliff, Ont.	
	4742	One Big Union - Edmonton, Alta (BF. 175/1412)	
	4743	[entry blacked out]	
21	4744	May Day - Toronto, Ont 1922	
	4745	[entry blacked out]	
	4746	[entry blacked out]	
	4747	Ukrainians in Toronto, Ont.	

Page 68

			Transferred from
Mar 22	4748	Executives of Ukrainian ?????Educational Society Prosvita	
22	4749	Ukrainian Organization Volia (Liberty) - Montreal, Que. 175/3529	
	4750	[entry blacked out]	
	4751	General Conditions amongst Foreigners - Cape Breton, N.S.	
24	4752	[entry blacked out]	
	4753	[entry blacked out] TRANS TO 175P/2169	

4754 Workers Party of Canada Winnipeg, Man [4-5 words blacked out]
4755 [entry blacked out] TRANS TO 175P/636
4756 Zluka No. 51 New Toronto, Ont.
25 4757 Labour Conditions - Hamilton, Ont. [3-4 words blacked out]
27 4758 [entry blacked out]
4759 Iwan Franko Ukranian Society - Thorold, Ont.
4760 O.B.U. - Moose Jaw, Sask. (BF. 175/586)
28 4761 [entry blacked out] TRANS TO 175P/2159)
4762 Ivan Franko Ukrainian Society - Edmonton, Atla.
29 4763 [entry blacked out] TRANS TO 175P/2173
4764 Workers Party of Canada - Prince Rupert, B.C.
4765 Labour Conditions - Mountain Park & ????
4766 [entry blacked out] TRANS TO 175P/319 844
30 4767 Workers Party - Montreal, Que. [2-3 words blacked out]

Page 69

Transferred from

[3-4 words blacked out]

March 30 4768 Workers Party of Canada - Prince George, B.C.
4769 " " Convention - Winnipeg, Man.
4770 Amalgamated Clothing Workers Union - Toronto, Ont. 27/1458
31 4771 [entry blacked out] 175P/1842 175/3863
4772 Communist Party of Canada - Toronto, Ont [2-3 words blacked out]
4773 [entry blacked out]
April 1 4774 Workers Party of Canada - Espanola, Ont. transf to 175/5501
3 4775 General Conditions - Vanderhoy, ??? [4-5 words blacked out]
4776 " " among Jews - Winnipeg [3-4 words blacked out]
4 4777 [entry blacked out] Trans to 175P/928 1590
5 4778 Labour Conditions in Ontario
[4-5 words blacked out]
4779 Workers Party of Canada - Toronto, Ont. [2-3 words blacke dout]
4780 [entry blacked out] Trans to 175P/1749 3869
4781 [entry blacked out] Trans to 175P/594 620
4782 [entry blacked out] 3953
4783 [entry blacked out] TRANS TO 175P/2175
4784 [entry blacked out]
6 4785 [entry blacked out]
Canadian Labour [3-4 words blacked out]
Conditions - Ottawa, Ont.

Page 70

[3-4 words blacked out]

Apr 7 4788 Socialist Party of Canada - Hanna, Alta.
4789 [entry blacked out] Transf. 175/5324
10 4790 Workers Party of Canada - Moose Jaw, Sask.

	4791	Labour Conditions - Brule Mines, Alta Transf 175/150	
	4792	[entry blacked out]	175/2315
11	4792	[entry blacked out]	
	4794	Workers Party of Canada - Sault Ste Marie, Ont [1-2 words blacked out]	
	4795	[entry blacked out] Trans to 175P/414	
	4796	[entry blacked out] Tran to 175/3007	
	4797	General Conditions - ??????. B.C.	
12	4798	Communist Party - Toronto, Ont. [4-5 words blacked out]	
	4799	Workers Party of Canada - New Toronto, Ont.	
	4800	[entry blacked out]	
13	4801	[entry blacked out]	
	4802	[entry blacked out] TO 175P/2575	
	4803	Conditions at Toronto, Ont. (Trans. to [blacked out])	
18	4804	Prosvita (Ukrainian Society) - Fort William [2-3 words blacked out]	
	4805	[entry blacked out] Trans to 175P/147	
	4806	[entry blacked out]	
	4807	Independent Labour Party - Edmonton [2-3 words blacked out]	

Page 71

Apr 18	4808	[entry blacked out]	175/495
	4809	[entry blacked out] Trans to 175P/2143	1983
19	4810	Disabled Soldiers & Sailors International	
20	4811	Trades Labour Council - Vancouver, B.C. [3-4 words blacked out]	
21	4812	[entry blacked out]	
	4813	[entry blacked out] Trans to 175P/1748	3990
	4814	[entry blacked out]	3152
22	4815	[entry blacked out]	
24	4816	[entry blacked out]	
	4817	Young Workers' League - Canada Generally [2-3 words blacked out]	
	4818	[entry blacked out]	
	4819	[entry blacked out]	3530
	4820	[entry blacked out]	
25	4821	[entry blacked out]	1873
	4822	[entry blacked out] Trans to 175P/2183	
	4823	Labour Party - Brandon, Man.	
	4824	Suspected Agitators - [word blacked out]	
26	4825	[entry blacked out]	

[rest of page blacked out]

Page 72

Apr 27	4828	Labour Conditions - Employment - Sault Ste Marie, Ont. [2-3 words blacked out]	
	4829	Workers Party of Canada - Niagara Falls, "	
	4830	" " " - St. Catherines, " Transf 175/5491	
	4831	[entry blacked out]	

28 4832 State of United Textile Workers Local No. 1469. St. John. N.B.

4833 [2 words blacked out] & Organization Generally - Port Arthur, Ont. 175/40

29 [3 words blacked out] School - Toronto, Ont.

May 1 [entry blacked out] 2686

Labour Party - Swift Current, Sask. 2473

2 [entry blacked out]

8 Labour Conditions - Employment [3-4 words blacked out]

39 [entry blacked out]

840 [entry blacked out] Transferred [blacked out]

841 Workers Party of Canada - Dome Mine, Ont.

842 Universal Negro Improvement Association 175/3302

843 [entry blacked out]

844 [entry blacked out]

845 Communist Party - Toronto, Ont. [2-3 words blacked out]

Hamilton, Ont. [2-3 words blacked out]

Winnipeg, Man.

Page 73

May 5 4848 Imprisonment of Agitators

6 4849 [entry blacked out]

4850 Federated Order of Railroad Employers - Samuel Rand. 175/3009

4851 [entry blacked out] 3931

4852 ?????????? Hamilton, Ont.

[4-5 words blacked out]

4853 Communist Party of Canada [3-4 words blacked out]

4854 [entry blacked out]

8 4855 [3 words blacked out] Fort Williams, Ont. Jewish Around.

4856 [3 words blacked out] - Montreal, Que 1922

4857 Workers Party of Canada - Sydney, N.S.

4888 Communist Party - Winnipeg, Man. [3-4 words blacked out]

(BF 175/2409 & 174/1334) BF 175/200)

4859 One Big Union - Vancouver, B.C.

4860 I.W.W. at Vancouver, B.C. BF 175/41

4861 [entry blacked out]

4862 Workers Pary ???? Ont. [2 words blacked out]

4863 [entry blacked out]

4864 [entry blacked out] Trans to 175P/962

10 4865 [entry blacked out]

4866 [entry blacked out]

11 4867 [entry blacked out]

Page 74

May 12 4868 Workers Pary of Canada - Cobalt, Ont.

4869 Catholic National Syndicates [3-4 words blacked out]

4870 [entry blacked out]

15 4871 [entry blacked out] 175/948
4872 Workers Party of Canada - Lethbridge, Alta
4873 Communist Party of Canada - [3-4 words blacked out] 1932
4874 [entry blacked out] TRANS TO 175P/1056
4875 [entry blacked out] 3738
16 4876 Ukrainian Black Hand D434D4
4877 One Big Union Radville, Sask. (BF. 175/2983) (BF. 175/2938) 175/278
17 4878 Workers Party of Canada - [2 words blacked out]
18 4879 Conditions amongst Foreigners - Elma, Man.
20 4880 [entry blacked out] 3922
22 4881 [entry blacked out]
23 4882 [entry blacked out] Trans to 175p/1072 1969
26 4883 [entry blacked out] 3899
27 4884 [entry blacked out]
4885 Secret Organization 48X
4886 [entry blacked out]
29 4887 Workers Party of Canada - Normore, Alta.

Page 75

May 29 4888 [entry blacked out] Trans to 175P/2189
4889 Workers' Party of Canada - Iroquois Falls, Ont
4890 Communist Party of Canada - Toronto, Ont. [4-5 words blacked out]
4891 Conditions amongst Finns in Saskatchewan
30 4892 Workers Party in Ontario [2-3 words blacked out]
June 1 4893 Young Men's Hebrew Association - Vancouver, B.C.
4894 [entry blacked out]
[blacked out] 486
Veterans Association - Vancouver
amongst Russians in Canada
[blacked out]
4899 Workers Party [3-4 words blacked out]
4900 [entry blacked out]
4901 [entry blacked out] Transf 175/???
4902 [entry blacked out]
6 4903 [entry blacked out]
4904 Chinese Commercial Aviation [word blacked out] Esquimault, B.C.
4905 [entry blacked out] Trans to ?????
4906 Vancouver Anarchistic Association
4907 [entry blacked out] Trans to 175/4681

Page 76

June 9 4908 Labour Conditions - Dauphin, Man.
4909 I.B.S.A. - Canada Generally
Trans to [2-3 words blacked out]
4910 Workers Party of Canada - Welland, Ont.

10 4911 [2-3 words blacked out] - Maritime Provinces [1-2 words blacked out]
4912 [entry blacked out]
4913 I.B.S.A. - Edmonton, Alta. 1586
12 4914 Workers Party - Dunblane, Sask. Transf to 175/?????
4915 [entry blacked out] Trans to 175P/2218
4916 [entry blacked out]
13 4917 [entry blacked out] Trans to 175P/1254 2705
14 4918 [entry blacked out]
4919 Finnish Socialist Organization - British Columbia
4920 " [2-3 words blacked out] - ??? Hills Dist. Sask.
4921 " [2-3 words blacked out] - Tho???. Alta
4922 " [2-3 words blacked out] - Coleman, "
4923 Conditions Amongst Finns (BF 175/36)
15 4924 Finnish Socialist Organization - Battleford, Sask
4925 Workers Party of Canada
4926 Suspects in Straits Settlements [1-2 words blacked out]
Independent Labour Party of Canada [1-2 words blacked out]

Page 77
June 16 [entry blacked out]
17 4929 Conditions amongst Ukrainians - Kitchener Waterloo, Ont.
4930 [entry blacked out] 175/1851
19 1 [entry blacked out] Trans to 175P/34
20 2 [entry blacked out] Trans to 175P/2225
3 [entry blacked out] Trans to 175P/2224
4934 [entry blacked out]
21 4935 [entry blacked out]
23 4936 Workers Party of Canada - Anthony, Ont.
26 4937 [entry blacked out] 3593
27 4938 Pacific Coast Educational Bureau [2-3 words blacked out]
4939 [entry blacked out]
4940 Workers Party of Canada - Guelph, Ont.
4941 [entry blacked out]
29 4942 Smuggled Diamonds from Russia for ?????
4943 [entry blacked out]
4944 Junior Labor ?????????
4945 Second Congress of the Red Labour Union [2-3 words blacked out]
4946 [entry blacked out] Trans to 175P/1254
4947 Workers Party of Canada - Hamilton [2-3 words blacked out]

Page 78
June 30 4948 [entry blacked out] Trans 175/2227
4949 Communist Party of Canada Niagara Falls, Ont.
4950 " " " Welland, Ont. BF 175/3697
July 4951 [entry blacked out

4	4952	[entry blacked out]	
	4953	Ukrainian Labor Temple Association - Bienfait, Sask.	
5	4954	Unemployed Veterans - Threatened 2nd March on Ottawa	
	4955	[entry blacked out]	
	4956	[entry blacked out]	175/3866
	4957	[entry blacked out]	533
6	4958	[entry blacked out] Trans to 175P/2231	
	4959	[entry blacked out]	
	4960	[entry blacked out] Trans to 175/5480	
10	4961	General Conditions - Vancouver, B.C. [word blacked out] + Greeks 3516	
	4962	Conditions at Jasper, Alta. [2-3 words blacked out]	532
	4963	[entry blacked out] (Transferred to 175P/[blacked out])	
	4964	Canadian Passport No. 2728	
11	4965	[entry blacked out] Trans to 175	
	4966	[entry blacked out]	
	4967	[entry blacked out] 175P/1396	2793
July 12	4968	[entry blacked out]	
	4969	International Brotherhood [2-3 words blacked out] Local No. 452 Vancouver B.C.	
	4970	[entry blacked out]	
	4971	Workers Party [2-3 words blacked out] S????, Sask.	
13	4972	Conditions amongst Ukrainians - Montreal, P. Que.	
	4973	[entry blacked out] Trans to 175P/2238	
	4974	[entry blacked out]	
	4975	General Conditions - Nipewan, B.C.	175/2778
14	4976	(Workers Party of Canada) Toronto, Ont. [2-3 words blacked out]	
15	4997	" " " [2-3 words blacked out] Canada See 175/5079	
17	4978	[entry blacked out]	
	4979	Communist Party of Canada - Winnipeg	
	4980	United ???????????????	
	4981	[entry blacked out] Trans to 175P/63	
18	4982	[entry blacked out]	
	4983	Labour Conditions in Lethbridge Irrigation Pro	
	4984	Manitoba ???????????????	

[rest of page blacked out]

Page 80

"Boletski"

July 21	4988	Conditions amongst Foreigners - Seech District, Man.	
	4989	Convention of Workers Party of Canada - Winnipeg Man.	
	4990	???"?? Party @ United Jewish Labour Party @United Jewish Socialist Labour Party	
	????	Zionist Organization	

	????	Socialist Labour Party @ Jewish Socialist Party @ Zion Party B.F. from 175/3442
	4991	Socialist Revolutionary League @ Jewish Revolutionary Party
	4992	Conditions - Cumberland, B.C.
	4933	Workers Party of Canada - Lac du Bonnet, Man.
	4994	amongst Ukrainians - Revelstoke, B.C.
	4995	[entry blacked out]
25	4996	[entry blacked out]
	4997	[entry blacked out]
	4998	[entry blacked out]
	4999	[entry blacked out]
	4999	[entry blacked out]
	5000	Labour Conditions amongst ??? Employees, Montreal, P. Que.
	5001	[entry blacked out]
26	5002	[entry blacked out]
	5003	[entry blacked out]
	5004	Bolshevism at Lethbridge, Alta.
	500	[entry blacked out]
	5006	Strike ?????? [4-5 words blacked out]
	5007	[entry blacked out]
Page 81		
July 27	5008	[entry blacked out]
	5009	????????????? - Perdue, Sask.
28	5010	Workers Party of Canada - Winnipeg, Man. [2-3 words blacked out]
29	5011	Labour Conditions in Canada - Unemployment Winter 1922-23
31	5012	(Young Workers League of America) Montreal, P. Que.
	5013	[entry blacked out]
	5014	[entry blacked out]
	5015	[entry blacked out] Trans to 175P/2254
	5016	[entry blacked out] 175/3535
Aug 1	5017	Strike of Fishermen - Rivers Inlet, B.C.
	5018	[entry blacked out]
2	5019	One Big Union - Prince Rupert, B.C. B.F. 175/494
3	5020	Russian-American Industrial Corporation - Toronto, Ont.
4	5021	[entry blacked out] /8/22
5	5022	Steelworkers Union - Sydney [word blacked out] N.S. 3309
8	5023	[entry blacked out]
	5024	Chinese Situation in British Columbia
		Convention of the Independent Labour Party - Sydney, N.S. July 1920
		???? - Obrazowascia Society - Dev?????? Alta.
Page 82		
Aug 10	5027	[entry blacked out] Transferred to 175/4997 28/9/22

5028 Trades Union Educational League - Edmonton, Alta.
5029 Bondelwarts Revolt - South West Africa
5030 Popovich M. or Mike Popovitch Trans to 175P/96 175/3607
5031 Labour Conditions - International Railway Co. Niagara Falls, Ont.
5032 Census of Chinese in Canada
11 5033 United Mine Workers of America Transferred to [blacked out]
5034 [entry blacked out]
12 5035 [entry blacked out]
5036 Finnish Socialist Organization - Wapella, Sask.
5037 " " " - Whitewood tr. to 175/5184
15 5038 Trades & Labor Congress [2-3 words blacked out]
5039 Finnish Socialist Association - Shann???
5040 Strike of U.M.W. of A. - Cape Breton, N.S.
16 5041 [entry blacked out]
5042 Communist Party of Canada??? Port Arthur, Ont.
504 [entry blacked out]
[3-4 words blacked out] League of ??? Freedom in Canada
[blacked out]
50 Communist Movement [4-5 words blacked out]

Page 83

Aug 18 5047 [entry blacked out] Trans. to 175/1033
175/742
5048 Conditions amongst Ukrainians - Revelstoke, B.C.
19 5049 [entry blacked out]
21 5050 [entry blacked out]
5051 Communist Party of Canada - Cobalt, Ont. [word blacked out]
5052 " " [3-4 words blacked out] Sault Ste Marie, Ont.
22 5053 [entry blacked out]
25 5054 National Revolutionary Society - Toronto, Ont.
Cosmopolitan Social Club
5055 Strike of Labourers, Section 4 - Welland Ship Canal - Thorold, Ont.
5056 [entry blacked out] Trans. to 175P/2017
26 5057 [entry blacked out]
29 5058 [entry blacked out]
5059 Russian American Industrial Corporation, Winnipeg
5060 Communist Party of Canada, Nairn Central
5061 Freight Handlers Strike - Fort William, Ont.
30 5062 [entry blacked out] Trans. to 175P/[blacked out]
31 5063 [entry blacked out]
5064 [entry blacked out]
5065 [entry blacked out]
5066 [entry blacked out] Trans to 175P/[blacked out]

Page 84

Aug 31	5067	[entry blacked out]	
Sept 1	5068	Railway Strike, Vancouver, B.C.	
	5069	[entry blacked out]	
	5070	Workers Party - Halifax, N.S.	
5	5071	[entry blacked out]	
	5072	[entry blacked out]	
	5073	Communist Party of Canada [2-3 words blacked out] Port Haney, B.C.	
6	5074	Russian Currency in ???????? Montreal, P.Q.	
	5075	[entry blacked out]	
7	5076	[entry blacked out]	
	5077	[entry blacked out]	
	5078	[entry blacked out]	
8	5079	Workers Party of Canada - Canada [word blacked out]	
11	5080	[entry blacked out]	
	5081	I.W.W. in Canada - Generally Correspondence continued on /3052	
13	5083	Communist Party of Canada - Saskatoon	
14	5084	O.B.U. - Kootenay District, B.C.	946
	5085	[entry blacked out]	641
	5086	C.N. ????? - Moose Jaw, Sask.	
	5087	" " " - Swift Current, Sask.	
Page 85			
Sep 15	5088	Trade Union Educational League - Stratford, Ont.	
16	5089	Workers' Party of Canada - Victoria B.C. Transf to 175/5110	
18	5090	[entry blacked out]	
	5091	[entry blacked out]	
19	5092	[entry blacked out]	
	5093	Communist Party of Canada - Notch Hill, B.C.	
	5094	[entry blacked out]	
	5095	[entry blacked out]	
20	5096	[entry blacked out] Trans to [blacked out]	175/3517
22	5097	Dramatic & Musical Club - ????	
23	5098	[entry blacked out]	
25	5099	[entry blacked out] Transf 175/5085	
	5100	Grain Buyer's Union - Saskatoon, Sask.	
	5101	[entry blacked out]	
26	5102	[entry blacked out]	
	5103	[entry blacked out]	
	5104	Mine, Mill & Smelter Workers International [2-3 words blacked out]	
	5105	Migratory Workers' Union - [word blacked out]	
27	5106	Plebs [word blacked out] - [word blacked out] Ont.	
	5107	Workers Educational League	3962
Page 86			
		(Not Identical with W.E. Association [word blacked out] 175/3525 Toronto Ont.	

Sep 27 5108 Workers Educational League (C.P. of C & O.B.U.)
5109 General Conditions - Penticton, B.C.
5110 Workers Party - Victoria, B.C. (B.F. from 175/5089)
28 5111 [entry blacked out] B.F. 175/5122 Trans to 175/P2206
30 5112 [entry blacked out]
5113 [entry blacked out]
5114 [entry blacked out] Trans to 175P/2470
5115 Workers Party of Canada - Winnipeg, Man. [3-4 words blacked out]
Oct 4 5116 Communist Party of " - Edmonton, Alta [3-4 words blacked out]
5117 [entry blacked out] - Trans to 175P/1782
5118 Labour Church - Calgary, Alta.
5119 [entry blacked out]
5 5120 [entry blacked out]
5121 [entry blacked out]
5122 [entry blacked ou] Combined with 175/5111
5123 [entry blacked out]
6 5124 Federal ????? Ont.
5125 Workers Party of Canada - Provincial ???????? Toronto, October 1921
Coal Miners - [word blacked out] Alta.
9 [blacked out]
Page 87
Oct 9 5128 [entry blacked out]
10 5129 [entry blacked out]
5130 Ukrainian National Home Association - Saskatoon, Sask 175/2104
12 5131 [entry blacked out]
5132 Ukrainian Workingmens Benevolent Assnt - Winnipeg, Man.
13 5133 [entry blacked out]
5134 [entry blacked out]
5135 [entry blacked out] Trans to 175P/2307
5136 Communist Party [4-5 words blacked out] Toronto, Ont.
14 5137 [entry blacked out] Trans to 175P/2074
5138 Trades & Labour Council - Saskatoon Sask. Continued from 175/442
Communist Party ([word blacked out]) ([4-5 words blacked out])
16 5139 Workers Party of Canada - Fort William
5140 ????????? - Ukrainian Society - Edmonton, Alta. 175/1051
5141 General Conditions at Powell River, B.C. (BF 175/5363 & 175/475)
17 5142 [entry blacked out]
Communist League [3-4 words blacked out]
Club College
5145 Workers [4-5 words blacked out]
5146 General [4-5 words blacked out]
19 5147 Workers [word blacked out] Port Arthur [1-2 words blacked out]
Page 88

Dec 23	5227	Workers Party of America [word blacked out]
	5228	[entry blacked out] Trans to 175P/2075
26	5229	Strike at Regal Mine Tiber, Alta.
27	5230	[entry blacked out] Trans to 175P/1267
28	5231	Workers Party of Canada/Mountain Park, Alta.
	5232	" " " Cadomin, Alta. [3-4 words blacked out]
	5233	[entry blacked out]
29	5234	Radical Schools [3-4 words blacked out]
	5235	"Peretz" School & Institute Winnipeg, Man. [2-3 words blacked out]
	5236	[entry blacked out] Transferred to 175-5225
30	5237	General Conditions in Edmonton, Alta.
	5238	[entry blacked out] Trans to 175/P1063
	5239	[entry blacked out] Trans to 175P/2365
	Dec 1923 Register No.	
		for subsequent 175/cases

Page 93

1923

Jan 2	5240	[entry blacked out]
	5241	[entry blacked out]
	5242	International Confederation of Communist Youths Trans to 175P/3687
	5243	[entry blacked out]
3	5244	Communist Party of Canada Maritime Provices [3-4 words blacked out]
4	5245	[entry blacked out]
	5246	[entry blacked out]

Page 94

Jan 4	5247	[entry blacked out] Trans to 175P/2341
5	5248	[entry blacked out]
8	5249	[entry blacked out] Trans to 175P/2193
	5250	[entry blacked out] Trans to 175P/684
	5251	[entry blacked out]
9	5252	[entry blacked out] BF 175/2216 175P/717
	5253	[entry blacked out]
	5254	U.M.W. of A. Michel, B.C., trans to [2-3 words blacked out]
	5255	Worker's Party - [word blacked out] Generally transf to 175/4443
	5256	Young Workers' League [word blacked out] Fort William, Ont. [word blacked out]
	5257	[entry blacked out]
	5258	Liberty Temple Association (Jewish) - Winnipeg, Man.
11	5259	Worker's Party of Canada - Alberta - [3-4 words blacked out]
	5260	Ukrainian Red Cross
12	5261	[entry blacked out] Trans to [blacked out]

next two numbers blacked out

13	5264	[entry blacked out]

	5265	[entry blacked out] Trans to 175P/145 [2-3 words blacked out]
	5266	[entry blacked out] Trans to 175P/515 [2-3 words blacked out]
Page 95		
Jan 15	5267	[entry blacked out]
	5268	U.M.W. of A. - Drumheller, Alta - Dist Transferred to [blacked out]
	5269	Workers Party of Canada Convention - Edmonton, Alta Dec 1922
	5270	Women's Labour League - Winnipeg Man BF from 175/2249 & 175/325
17	5271	Alberta Federation of Labour Convention held Jan 1923 at Medicine Hat, Alta.
	5272	Workers Party of Canada - Thorold, Ont. [2-3 words blackedout]
18	5273	[entry blacked out]
	5274	Workers' International Industrial Union Vancouver, B.C.
20	5275	Workers' Party - Convention - Winnipeg, Man. Jan 1923
	5276	Workers' Party of Canada - Sydney, NS [2-3 words blacked out]
	5277	" " " - Michel, BC
22	5278	Communist Party of Canada - Maritime Provinces
	5279	" " " [3-4 words blacked out] Ont.
	5280	[2-3 words blacked out] - Fort William, Ont.
	5281	Saunders & MacDonald's Lumber Camp
	Black Sturgeon Lake, Ont.	
23	5282	[entry blacked out] Trans to 175P/1704
26	5283	[entry blacked out]
	5284	[word blacked out] Big Union Brandon Man. [word blacked out]
27	5285	[word blacked out] Workers League Winnipeg, Man [word blacked out]
Page 96		
Feb 1	5286	[entry blacked out]
2	5287	[entry blacked out]
3	5288	Trade Union Educational League - Halifax, NS [1-2 words blacked out]
	5289	[entry blacked out] Trans to 175P/1884
5	5290	[entry blacked out] Trans to 175P/91
		(Correspondence [blacked out])
	5291	Workers Party of Canada - national Convention 1923
6	5292	Ivan Franks Ukrainian Organization - Port Arthur, Ont.
7	5293	Socialist Party of Canada - New Westminster, B.C.
	5294	[entry blacked out]
8	5295	Labour Defense Council - U.S.A. (Trans to 175/5931)
	5296	[entry blacked out]
	5297	[entry blacked out]
9	5298	Alleged Fascist Movement
	5299	[entry blacked out]
	5300	Socialist Party of Canada - Toronto, Ont. BF ??????
12	5301	Workers Party Convention - Vancouver, B.C.

[4-5 words blacked out] Trans to 175P/2370

15 [entry blacked out]

[4-5 words blacked out] Trans to 175P/1317

16 [3-4 words blacked out] Trans to 175P/2355

Page 97

Feb 16 5306 [entry blacked out]

5307 [entry blacked out]

5308 Communist Party En route United States Canada

17 5309 Conditions (General Labour Class Box (Transferred [blacked out])

19 5310 Communist Party of Canada - District Convention - Toronto, Ont.

20 5311 Soviet Russia Conditions in Canada
(Canada - Soviet Russia Trade Relations)

21 5312 Trade Union Educational League - Saskatoon, Sask.

22 5313 [entry blacked out] Trans to 175P/2376

5314 [entry blacked out] Trans to 175P/2363

5315 [entry blacked out] Trans to 175P/1896

5316 Communist Party - Convention Toronto, Ont. February 20

24 5317 Jewish Radical Club - ???

26 5318 Ukrainian Labour ???? - Yanow, Man. Trans to [blacked out]

5319 [entry blacked out]

5320 [entry blacked out] Trans to 175P/1195

28 5321 Labour Conditions Cumberland, B.C.

Correspondence [blacked out]

5322 Ukrainian Society Trans to 175P/64

5323 Far East Commercial [3-4 words blacked out] Service

[next 2 numbers blacked out]

Page 98

Mar 1 5326 Conditions amongst Ukrainians & Russians - Dana, Sask.

5327 " " Foreigners - East Kootenay, B.C.

B.F. from /2982 + 175/2950

3 5328 Labour Conditions in Cape Breton, N.S. continued on [entry blacked out]

5 5329 Workers Party of Canada [4-5 words blacked out]

(Correspondence Trans. to [blacked out])

5330 Ukrainian Labour Temple Ass. - Winnipeg, Man. Convention 1923

6 531 " " " " - Transcona, Man.

7 5332 Morris, Leslie - Trans to 175P/2440

8 5333 [entry blacked out]

9 5334 Workers' Party of Canada - Michel, B.C. [2-3 words blacked out]

(Correspondence trans. to [blacked out])

10 5335 " " " - Port Arthur, Ont. Ukrainian Branch.

12 5336 U.M.W. of A. - Crows Nest Pass, B.C.

Union of Russian Working Men

5337 Union of Russian Workers - Fort City, Ont.

5338 [entry blacked out]
5339 United Workers' Association of Nova Scotia
13 5340 [entry blacked out]
5341 ?????? [word blacked out] U.S.A. Canada
14 5342 Central [word blacked out] Committee of Action
5343 [entry blacked out]
5344 [entry blacked out] Born in ???????
15 5345 Workers' Party of Canada - W??????? Alberta

Page 99

Mar 15 5346 Workers' Party of Canada - Ladysmth, B.C. (Trans to [blacked out])
5347 [entry blacked out]
17 5348 [entry blacked out]
19 5349 [entry blacked out]
20 5350 Young Workers League - MacRorie, Sask.
5351 General Conditions amongst Japanese - Queen Charlotte Islands, B.C.
5352 Conditions amongst Foreigners - British Columbia
22 5353 " " " - Rose Grove, Ont.
5354 International Conference - Revolutionary Mine Workers - Moscow
5355 [entry blacked out] Trans to 175P/1922
5356 [entry blacked out] Trans to 175P/1198 175/3173
23 5357 Workers' Party of Canada - Midland, Alta.
5358 " " " - Newcastle Mine, Alta.
26 5359 [entry blacked out]
5360 Workers' Party of Canada - (Trans to [blacked out] - Drumheller, Alta.
Conditions amongst Ukrainians - Drumheller, District
People's Forum - Calgary Alta - [word blacked out]
General Conditions at Powell River [word blacked out]
[all of line blacked out]
Conditions amongst Ukrainians - Perd???

Page 100

Mar 28 5366 Ukrainian Labour Temple Assn. - Edmonton, Alta. - April 1923
29 5367 [entry blacked out] - Trans to 175P/2044
Transferred to [blacked out] 9/10/41 MP @ MAFIA
5368 Black Hand - Italian @ LA MANO NERA Canada - General
5369 Conditions amongst Finns - Gleneden, B.C.
5370 Fabian Club, The.
Apr 3 5371 [entry blacked out]
5372 [entry blacked out] - Trans to 175P/2381 175/3545
5373 Socialist Party of Canada - Kamloops, B.C.
corresp transf to [blacked out]
5374 Ukrainian Labour Temple Assn. Kamsack, Sask.
4 5375 Colonial Commission of the Third International
5376 Federal Workers Union of General Workers. Winnipeg District, Man.

5377 Bank of England L100 Note
6 5378 [entry blacked out]
9 5379 [entry blacked out]
5380 [entry blacked out] Trans to 175P/1384
[number blacked out]
Conditions - Alberni, B.C.
10 5383 Foreigners Pine River, Man.
[rest of page blacked out]
Page 101
Apr 15 5386 Workers Party of Canada
5387 Young Communist Leage (Trans to [blacked out]) at Vancouver
5388 Ukrainian Labour Temple Assn. - (Trans to [blacked out]) Saskatchewan
5389 [entry blacked out] Trans to 175/5265
5390 Ivan Franko Society - Hodgson District, Man.
5390 [entry blacked out] Trans to 175P/2377
16 5392 [entry blacked out]
17 5393 Workers' Party of Canada - Glace Bay, N.S. [1-2 words blacked out]
Transferred to [blacked out]
5394 Finnish Organization of Canada
18 5395 [entry blacked out]
19 5396 [entry blacked out]
20 5397 Labour Representation Committee - Toronto, Ont.
21 5398 Ukrainian Mutual Benefit Assn. - Trans to [blacked out]
5399 [entry blacked out]
23 5400 Edmonton & District Miners Federation
5401 University of British Columbia Transf to [blacked out]
24 5402 [entry blacked out] Trans to 175P/2481 1183
25 5403 [entry blacked out] Trans to 175P/2379
5404 Workers' Party of Canada - Vancouver ??? B.C.
5405 American Civil Liberties Assn. (Trans to [blacked out])
Page 102
Apr 26 5406 Workers Party of Canada Port Arthur, Ont.
5407 Communist Party of America - Trans to [blacked out]
27 5408 Toiling Farmers Union - Vonda, Sask. [1-2 words blacked out]
28 5409 General Conditions at Thetford Mines
5410 May Day - Cape Breton, N.S. Trans to 175P/2386
30 5411 Workers' Party of Canada - Chatfield, Man.
5412 General Conditions amongst Finlanders - Port Arthur, Ont.
5413 [entry blacked out]
May 1 5414 Workers' Party of Canada - The Pas, Man.
541 Industrial Workers of the World - Sub Act Within - Creston B.C.
5416 General Conditions at Sudbury, Ont (BF 175.2235)
2 5417 May Day Celebrations - Toronto, Ont.

5418 Ontario Chinese Association
5419 [entry blacked out]
3 5420 May Day - Montreal, P. Que.
5 5421 [entry blacked out] Trans to 175P/656
5422 [entry blacked out] Trans to 175P/2387
5423 Labour Church - Vancouver, BC. BF from 175/3313
5424 May Day - Winnipeg, Man.
7 5425 " " - Glace Bay, N.S. 1923

Page 103

May 7 5426 Labour Conditions - Iroquois Falls, Ont.
5427 General Conditions at Sydney N.S. Trans to [blacked out]
9 5428 Lumber Workers Industrial Association of Canada
5429 Workers' Party of Canda - Toronto, Ont. Trans to [blacked out]
11 5430 [entry blacked out] Trans to 175/4016
14 5431 [entry blacked out]
5432 Workers' Party of Canada British Columbia
no correspondence on this file
15 5433 [entry blacked out] Trans to 175P/184 175/1947
5434 [entry blacked out]
5435 Workers' Party of Canada - Stratford, Ont.
5436 [entry blacked out]
5437 [entry blacked out] Trans to 175/5103
5438 May Day - Calgary, Alta.
16 5439 [entry blacked out] 1610
5440 General Conditions - Fernie, B.C.
17 5441 [entry blacked out] Trans to 175P/648
Trans to 175/5919
5442 Farmer Labour Society Cand District
5443 [entry blacked out] Trans to 175P/2324
Trans to [blacked out]
18 5444 General Conditions - Montreal [2-3 words blacked out]
5445 Strike at Port Colborne, Ont.

Page 104

May 18 5446 [entry blacked out]
19 5447 General Conditions at Crowland, Ont. 175/3878
21 5448 [entry blacked out] Trans to 175P/2404
25 5449 Provincial Election - Ontario
5450 Workers' Party of Canada - Newcastle Mine, Alta. See below
25 5450 Trades Union Educational League - Newscaslte Mine, Alta.
5451 [entry blacked out] Trans to 175/5319
26 5452 Young Communist League - Nipigon, Ont.
28 5453 Workers' Party of Canada - Watrous, Sask.
5454 Toiling Farmers' Union of Canada - Ituna

	5455	[entry blacked out] ???? Ont (Form: England)
	5456	Sailors' Union - Strike 1923 @ Federated Seafarers Union 175/733
	5457	[entry blacked out]
29	5458	Conditions amongst Foreigners [word blacked out], Alta.
	5459	" " " [word blacked out]
	5460	" " " [word blacked out]
	5461	" " " [word blacked out], BC
	5462	Federation of Engine Drivers, ?????
30	5463	Russian Workers' Union ?????????
	5464	[entry blacked out]
Page 105		
May 30	5465	General Conditions at Welland, Ontario [3-4 words blacked out]
	5466	[entry blacked out]
	5467	Lumber Workers Industrial Union - Ontario
31	5468	Ukrainian Labour Temple Association - Montreal, P.Que.
	5469	Conditions amongst Ukrainians - Glenalla, Ont.
	5470	[entry blacked out]
	5471	[entry blacked out]
	Correspondence [2-3 words blacked out]	
June 3	5472	Ukrainian Labour Temple Assn. - Thorold, Ont. [3-4 words blacked out]
5	5473	[entry blacked out]
	5474	Workers' Party of Canada - The Pas, Man. 175/5414
	5475	[entry blacked out] Trans to 175P/1838
	5476	Canadian Secular Society
	5477	[entry blacked out] Trans to 175P/2401
	5478	Trade Union Womens Auxiliaries
6	5479	[entry blacked out]
	5480	[entry blacked out]
	5481	[entry blacked out] Trans to 175P/1734
	5482	[entry blacked out] Trans to 175P/688
	5483	[entry blacked out] Trans to 175P/120
	5484	[entry blacked out]
Page 106		
June 8	5485	[entry blacked out] Trans to 175P/2405
	5486	Workers' Party of Canada [word blacked out]
	5487	International Red Aid
	5488	[entry blacked out]
9	5489	General Conditions at St. Roswells. Sask.
11	5490	Labour Conditions - Great Falls, Man.
	5491	Workers' Party [2-3 words blacked out] St. Catharines, Ont. BF 175/4830
	5492	Workers' Party - Chippawa, Ont.
	5493	[3-4 words blacked out] Henry
14	5494	[entry blacked out] Trans to 175P/2752

18 5495 Labour Conditions - Coalspur District, Alta. Trans to 6812
5496 [entry blacked out] Trans to 175P/2399
5497 [entry blacked out] 175/41
5498 [entry blacked out]
19 5499 Dominion Labour Party - Calgary, Alta. BF 175/157?? 175/1472
5500 [entry blacked out] Trans to 175P/1838
5501 Workers Party - ????ola, Ont.
5502 [entry blacked out] Trans to 175P/2414
5503 International Progressive Miners Committee
21 5504 [entry blacked out]
Page 107
[3-4 words blacked out]
June 21 5505 Workers' Party of Canada - German Branches - Glace Bay, N.S.
5506 " " " " " " - New Waterford, N.S.
22 5507 [entry blacked out]
5508 [entry blacked out] Trans to 175P/2407
23 5509 Trades Union Educational League - Drumheller, Alta.
25 5510 [entry blacked out]
5511 [entry blacked out]
27 5512 [entry blacked out]
28 5513 [entry blacked out] Trans to 175P/2392
5514 [entry blacked out] Trans to 175P/2422
29 5515 Strike of Steel Workers - Sydney, N.S.
July 3 5516 [entry blacked out]
5517 [entry blacked out] Trans to 175P/3680
5518 [entry blacked out]
4 5519 (O.B.U.) Shop Stewards' Movement BF 175/5894 175/2894
5520 Strike of Miners - Glace Bay, N.S.
5521 [entry blacked out] Trans to 175P/650 2037
5 5522 [entry blacked out]
6 5523 Employers Association of Manitoba - Winnipeg, Man.
7 5524 Native Sons of Canada - [4-5 words blacked out]
Page 108
July 7 5525 [entry blacked out] Trans to 175P/439 175/868
(Correspondence [blacked out])
9 5526 Ukrainian Labor Temple Association - The Pas, Man.
10 5527 [entry blacked out]
5528 Strike of Miners - Canmore, Alta.
5529 Communists as Russian Intelligence Agents
11 5530 [entry blacked out]
12 5531 [entry blacked out]
16 5532 Mine Workers Union - Porcupine, Ont.
5533 Conditions amongst Foreigners - Fort William, Ont. (BF 165/559)

	5534	" " Ukrainians - " " "
	5535	[entry blacked out]
	5536	[entry blacked out]
18	5537	[entry blacked out]
19	5538	[1-2 words blacked out] - Reneta, B.C.
	5539	International Marine Worker's
20	5540	[entry blacked out]
	5541	Deportation of Seditious Aliens
21	5542	[entry blacked out]
	5543	(Conditions Labor Amongst) Street Railway Employees - Montreal, P.Que.
23	5544	[entry blacked out]

Page 109

July 23	5545	[entry blacked out] Trans to 175P/2564
24	5546	Ukrainian Labour Temple - Degreville, Alta.
	5547	Independent Labour Party - Winnipeg, Man.
26	5548	No War Committee - Toronto, Ont.
	5549	[entry blacked out]
	5550	Farmers Union of Canada
28	5551	[entry blacked out] Trans to 175P/2583
	5552	Conditions amongst Ukrainians in Lethbridge, Alta.
	5553	Ukrainian Labour [word blacked out] Medicine Hat
30	5554	[entry blacked out]
	5555	[entry blacked out]
	5556	Red Sport International
	5557	[entry blacked out] Trans to 175P/342
	5558	[word blacked out] Labour Temple Ass - Regina, Sask.
31	5559	[entry blacked out]
Aug 5	5560	[word blacked out] of Governor General [3-4 words blacked out]
3	5561	[word blacked out] Outrage - Sydney, N.S.
	5562	[entry blacked out]
7	5563	[entry blacked out] Trans to 175P/2421
	5564	[entry blacked out] Trans to 175P/2415

Page 110

Aug 9	5565	Russian Anarchist Party - Generally
10	5566	[entry blacked out] Trans to 175P/819
11	5567	No War Committee - Vancouver, B.C.
13	5568	(U.T.L.) U.L.L. Kitchener, Ont.
	5569	Ukrainian Labour Temple - Moose Jaw, Sask.
	5570	[entry blacked out]
	5571	[entry blacked out] Trans to 175P/2413
	5572	Ukrainian [3-4 words blacked out] Oshawa, Ont.
	5573	[entry blacked out]

14	5574	[entry blacked out] Trans to 175P???	
	5575	Trades Congress of Canada [word blacked out] B.C.	
	5576	Workers' Defense Committee - Nova Scotia	
	5577	[2 words blacked out] George	
16	5578	Ukrainian Labour Temple - ?????. Ont.	
	5579	Zluka - (Ukrainian Society)	175/2546
18	5580	[entry blacked out]	
20	5581	Labour Conditions - Dysart, Sask.	
	5582	Labour Conditions - ?????	
	5583	[entry blacked out] Trans to 175P/257???	
	5584	[entry blacked out]	
Page 111			
Aug 22	5585	Trades & Labour Council - Toronto, Ont.	
24	5586	[entry blacked out] BF from 175/1749	
	5587	[entry blacked out] Trans to 175P/2411	
	5588	[entry blacked out] trans to 175P/645	
28	5589	[entry blacked out]	
30	5590	????? Educational League - Hamilton, Ont.	
	5591	[entry blacked out]	
31	5592	[1-2 words blacked out] - Vegreville, Alta.	
Sept 1	5593	Trade Union Educational League - Nova Scotia	
4	5594	International Brotherhood of Railroad Engineers, Firemen & Oilers. Local #772 Winnipeg, Man.	
	5595	Ukrainians at Westport, Ont.	
	5596	[entry blacked out] Trans to 175P/2427	
5	5597	Workers Party of Canada - [4-5 words blacked out] Ont.	
	5598	Communist Party - [4-5 words blacked out] Montreal, P.Q.	
	5599	[entry blacked out]	
10	5600	Strike at Fort William Paper Co.	
	5601	[entry blacked out]	
12	5602	[entry blacked out]	
	5603	Lab[2-3 words blacked out] & Port Arthur, Ont.	
Page 112			
Sept 12	5604	[entry blacked out]	
		Correspondence for [blacked out]	
13	X5605	Ukrainian Labour Temple - London, Ont.	
	X5606	Corresp [2-3 words blacked out] Brightstone, Man.	
15	5607	[entry blacked out] Trans to 175P/392	
		Correspondence [2-3 words blacked out]	
17	X5608	Ukrainian Labour Temple - Saskatoon, Sask. [2-3 words blacked out]	
	X5609	Corresp [3-4 words blacked out] Swift Current	
	5610	[entry blacked out]	
	5611	[entry blacked out]	

	5612	[entry blacked out]	
18	5613	[entry blacked out]	
	5614	[entry blacked out]	
	5615	[entry blacked out]	
	5616	[entry blacked out]	
21	5617	[entry blacked out]	
	5618	[entry blacked out]	
24	5620, 5619	Industrial Workers Of the World (Sub Act Within)	
25	5621	Conditions in South ????? Disrict, Ont.	
	5622	[entry blacked out] Trans to 175P/1467	175/2940
	5623	[entry blacked out] Trans to 175P/2750	

Page 113

Sept 26	5624	[entry blacked out]	
	5625	Connection between Workers Party and I.W.W.	
27	5626	Russian Refugee in Ottawa	
	Corresp [2-3 words blacked out]		
	5627	Ukrainian Labour Temple - Timmins, Ont.	
29	5628	[entry blacked out]	
Oct 1	5629	[entry blacked out]	
2	5630	[entry blacked out] Trans to 175/5589	
	5631	[entry blacked out] Trans to 175P/32	175/1006
	5632	[entry blacked out] Trans to 175P/94	175/451
5	5633	O.B.U. Kenora, Ont. (BF 175/3908 & 175/2791)	
8	5634	Industrial Workers of the World - Sub. Act. Within - Regina, Sask.	
9	5635	[entry blacked out]	
10	5636	[entry blacked out]	
	5637	[entry blacked out]	
	5638	Conditions Among Russians at Montreal. P.Que.	
11	5639	[entry blacked out]	
15	5640	I.W.W. in Ontario	
	5641	Geneva Association - Montreal, P. Que.	
16	5642	[entry blacked out]	
17	5643	[entry blacked out]	

Page 114

Oct 19	5644	Strike of Longshoremen - Vancouver, B.C.	
22	5645	[entry blacked out]	
	corresp [3-4 words blacked out]		
23	5646	Ukrainain Labour Temple Assn. - Prince Albert, Sask.	
	5647	[entry blacked out]	
	5648	I.W.W. amongst Harvesters (Trans to 175/5890)	
26	5649	[entry blacked out]	
30	5650	[entry blacked out]	
	5651	[entry blacked out]	

31	5652	The Peoples Forum - Drumheller, Alta. - Sub. Activities Within	
Nov 5	5653	[entry blacked out]	
10	5654	[entry blacked out]	
15	5655	Industrial Workers of the World - Sub. Act. Wtihin Swift Current, Sask.	
	5656	[entry blacked out]	
19	5657	[entry blacked out] Trans to 175P/2447	
	5658	[entry blacked out]	
20	5659	[entry blacked out]	175/2966
21	5660	[entry blacked out]	
22	5661	[entry blacked out]	
26	5662	[entry blacked out]	
	5663	[entry blacked out]	

Page 115

Nov 26	5664	[entry blacked out]
Dec 3	5665	Trades and Labour Council, Fort William, Ont. [3-4 words blacked out]
5	5666	Conditions at Thorold and St. Catherines, Ont. [3-4 words blacked out]
11	5667	German Canadian Association Edmonton, Alta [2-3 words blacked out]
12	5668	Federal Labour Union. Winnipeg, Man.
13	5669	[entry blacked out]
19	5680	[entry blacked out]
20	5671	Womens Labour League Drumheller, Alta.
21	5672	Finnish Socialist Party Canmore, Alta.
27	5673	Edmonton and District Miners Federation

Page 116

1924

	5674	[entry blacked out] Trans to 175/???
	5675	[entry blacked out]
	5676	[entry blacked out]
	5677	[entry blacked out]
	5678	[entry blacked out] Prince Albert, Sask.
	5679	Conditions amongst Ukrainians Prince Albert District, Sask.
	5680	[entry blacked out]
	5681	[entry blacked out] Trans to 175P/???
	5682	[entry blacked out] Trans to 175P/2???
	5683	[entry blacked out]

Page 117

Jan 22	5684	General Conditions among Foreigners at Blairmore, Alta.
23	5685	[entry blacked out]
	5686	Industrial Workers of the World Strike at Lumber Camp - Donald B.C.
	5687	BF from 175/353 Industrial Workers of the World at Fernie, B.C.
	corresp	[2-3 words blacked out]
	5688	Ukrainian Labour Temple - Coleman, Alta.
26	5689	Quebec Labour Party - Montreal, P. Que.

	5690	[entry blacked out]
29	5691	Industrial Workers of the World Sub. Act. Within - Blairmore, Alta.
	5692	British Harvester's Organization - Toronto, Ont.
29	5693	[entry blacked out]
30	5694	Conditions at Toronto ????????
Feb 1	5695	Industrial Workers of the World Sub. Act. Within - ???
4	5696	United Farmers of Manitoba - Dauphin, Main District
5	5697	Jewish Worker's Party - ??? Ont.
	5698	Progressive Workers Association - Sydney, N.S.
	5699	Industrial Workers of the World - Sub. Act. Within - Michel, B.C.
	5700	[entry blacked out]
	5701	Labour Conditions at Edwards Lumber Co. - ????? Ont
	5702	[entry blacked out] Trans to 175P/1382
	5703	Industrial Workers of the World - Sub. Act. Within - Corbin, B.C.

Page 118

Feb 8	5704	Workers Party of Canada - Agrarian Report
7	5705	Conditions amongst Finns - Sudbury, Ont 175/3317
8	5706	Suicide of Frans Onni Saukola - Kivikoski, Gorham Township, Ont.
9	5707	[entry blacked out] Trans to 175P/1943
	5708	[entry blacked out]
	5709	[entry blacked out]
	5710	[entry blacked out]
12	5711	Lettish Educational Union - Lac du Bonnet, Man.
14	5712	Radical School at ????, B.C.
	5713	O.B.U. at Sudbury, Ont.
	5714	[entry blacked out]
15	5715	[entry blacked out]
	5716	Strike at Barnstead's Camp - Gariowag????, B.C.
	5717	Industrial Workers of the World Sub. Act Within - Elko, B.C.
	5718	Industrial Workers of the World Sub. Act. Within - Yahk, B.C.
19	[blacked out]	
	[blacked out]	
	5721	Industrial Workers of the World Sub. Act Within - Waldo, B.C.
	5722	[entry blacked out]
	5723	[Trades & Labour Council [3-4 words blacked out] Regina, Sask. BF 175/73

Page 119

Feb 23	5724	[entry blacked out] 175/974
		Correspondence [3-4 words blacked out]
25	5725	Ukrainian Labour Temple Assn. - Fifth Annual Convention 1924
26	5726	Canadian Labour Party - Drumheller, Alta.
	5727	[entry blacked out]
27	5728	[entry blacked out]

	5729	"May Day" - 1924 - Toronto, Ont.
	5730	Industrial Workers of the World Sub. Act Wtihin - Kootenay District, B.C.
28	5731	Canadian Labour Party - Regina Central Council
Mar 1	5732	[entry blacked out] Trans to 175P/2835
3	5733	Industrial Workers of the World Sub. Act. Within - Bucley Bay - B.C.
	5734	[entry blacked out]
4	5735	[entry blacked out] Transferred to 175/5759
	5736	[entry blacked out]
	5737	[entry blacked out]
	5738	[entry blacked out]
6	5739	Russian Komintern in Canada - AGENTS
11	5740	[entry blacked out]
	5741	[entry blacked out]

[rest of page blacked out]

Page 120

Mar 14	5744	Industrial Workers of the World Sub. Act. Within - Timmins, Ont.
	5745	Industrial Workers of the World Sub. Act. Within - Toronto.
18	5746	Women's Labour League - Edmonton, Alta.
	5747	Worker's Party [2-3 words blacked out] Man
19	5748	Third International "Dollar Loan"
21	5749	[entry blacked out]
22	5750	General Conditions in Calder District, Sask.
25	5751	Industrial Workers of the World Sub. Act. Within - Francois Lake, B.C.
26	5752	"Ideskom" - Russian Organization
27	5753	United International of Transport Workers
31	5754	[entry blacked out]
Apr 1	5755	[entry blacked out]
	5756	[entry blacked out]
	5757	[entry blacked out]
3	5758	[entry blacked out]
4	5759	[entry blacked out]
	5760	Workers Party of Canada
	5761	National Convention of Workers [word blacked out] Toronto April /24
5	5762	General Strike of U.M.W of A. [word blacked out] (1924) Alberta
	5763	[entry blacked out]

Page 121

Apr 7	5764	Labour Conditions at Brandon, Man. 175/1944
	5765	[entry blacked out]
	5766	Women's International League for Peace & Freedom - Toronto, Ont.
	5767	" " [3-4 words blacked out] Vancouver, B.C.
	5768	Women's Social & Economic Conference - Brandon, Man. (March 29, 1924)
8	5769	Strike of Postal Employees, April 1924

5770 Dominon Coal Co - Glace Bay, N.S.
9 5771 [entry blacked out]
10 5772 Industrial Workers of the World - Sub. Act. Wtihin - Nordegg, Alta.
5773 [entry blacked out]
5774 [entry blacked out]
5775 Conditions at Blue Diamond Coal Co - Brule Mines, Alta.
15 5776 Convention of Canadian Labour Party - ????, Ont. March/24
corresp [3-4 words blacked out]
16 5777 Ukrainian Labour Temple Asn - at ?????, Alta.
19 5778 [entry blacked out]
5779 May Day 1924 at Timmins, Ont.
23 5780 [entry blacked out]
5781 Socialist Party of Canada at [blacked out]
24 5782 [entry blacked out]
28 Ukrainian Labour Temple Assn. - ????, Ont.

Page 122

Apr 28 5784 Samo Obrazowania Society - Coleman, Alta.
5785 [entry blacked out]
29 5786 Convention of Canadian Labour Party (Alberta Section) at Calgary, Alta. Apl 18/19 1924.
5787 Workers & Farmers Party at Sturgis, Sask.
30 5788 [entry blacked out]
5789 [entry blacked out]
May 1 5790 [entry blacked out] 175/1228
5791 May Day - 1924 at Montreal, P.Que.
5 5792 [entry blacked out] 175/2155
5793 [entry blacked out]
5794 I.B.S.A. at Prince Albert, Sask.
5795 [entry blacked out]
6 5796 May Day at Winnipeg, Man - 1924
5797 [2-3 words blacked out] - I.W.W.
8 5798 Labor Representation Committee, Vancouver, B.C.
5799 Canadian Labor Party
correspondence transferred to [blacked out]
5800 Hebrew Immigration Aid Society
5801 [1-2 words blacked out] Communist
9 5802 Communist Party in Fort William Port Arthur, Ont

Page 123

May 10 5803 May Day Celebration at Glace Bay, N.S. May 1st 1924
12 5804 [2-3 words blacked out] I.W.W.
5805 Communist Party in Ontario [2-3 words blacked out] 175/3708
5806 [3-4 words blacked out] Communist [2-3 words blacked out]
5807 Soit, Novy (Trans to [blacked out]) (New World) Montreal, P.Q.

14	5808	[entry blacked out]	
16	5809	[3-4 words blacked out] I.W.W.	175/556
	5810	Farmers Workers Party in Saskatchewan	
17	5811	[entry blacked out]	175/3502
18	5812	[entry blacked out]	
21	5813	Communist Party [2-3 words blacked out] at Montreal, P.Q.	
22	5814	[2-3 words blacked out] Federated Sea Farers Union of B.C.	Trans to 175/6172
26	5815	[entry blacked out]	
27	5816	Ukrainian Labour Temple Association at ?????	
	5817	[entry blacked out]	
28	5818	Young Communist League ?????,Alta.	
30	5819	[2-3 words blacked out] I.W.W.	
30	5820	[entry blacked out]	
	5821	[entry blacked out]	
June 2	5822	[entry blacked out]	

Page 124

June 2	5823	May Day - 1924	
	5824	[entry blacked out]	
	5825	[entry blacked out]	
4	5826	[2-3 words blacked out] Communist Party. new Liskeard	
5	5827	[2-3 words blacked out] Communist	
	5828	[entry blacked out] Trans to 175P/5828	
6	5829	[entry blacked out] Trans to 175P/2474	
11	5830	[2-3 words blacked out] Communist	
	5831	[entry blacked out] Trans to 175P/2280	
13	5832	[entry blacked out]	175/3522
16	5833	Labor Conditions at Anyox, B.C.	
18	5834	Ukrainian Labour Temple Trail, B.C.	
	5835	Communist Party Halifax, N.S. [2-3 words blacked out]	
21	5836	[entry blacked out]	
23	5837	Port Arthur Ont. unemployment Conditions at	
24	5838	Central Labor ???? of Political Action - Halifax, N.S.	
25	5839	Northfield Community League, Valhalla, Grand Prairie Dist. Alta.	
	5840	Soviet Agents in British Columbia	

[rest of page blacked out]

Page 125

June 27	5843	Communist Party of Canada [5-6 words blacked out]	
	5844	[entry blacked out]	
July 2	5845	Strike of Japanese Fishermen #2 Dist. British Columbia	
	5846	[entry blacked out]	
5	5847	General Conditions in Tolstoi, Man. Dist.	
7	5848	[entry blacked out] Trans to 175P/2472	

5849 Economic Conference - Regina, Sask.
5850 [entry blacked out] Trans to 175P/574
5851 Ukrainians at Stornoway, Sask.
8 5852 [entry blacked out] Trans to 175P/311
5853 Ukrainian Labor Temple Association, Melville, Sask.
5854 Communist Party of Canada at Calgary, Alta [2-3 words blacked out]
14 5855 [entry blacked out]
5856 [entry blacked out]
15 5857 [entry blacked out] To 175P/213
16 5858 [entry blacked out] BF from 175/2938)
5859 Labour Conditions at Sudbury, Ont.
5860 Conditions General Amongst Hindus in British Columbia [2-3 words blacked out]
21 5861 [entry blacked out] Trans to 175/[blacked out]
22 5862 [entry blacked out]

Page 126

July 22 5863 [entry blacked out] Trans to 175P/2478
5864 [entry blacked out]
23 5865 Communist Party at Iroquois Falls, Ont.
5866 [3-4 words blacked out] - Toronto, Ont.
25 5867 [entry blacked out] Trans to 175P/2552
26 5868 [entry blacked out]
29 5869 Communist Party - Glace Bay, N.S.
5870 [entry blacked out]
30 5871 [entry blacked out]
corresp [2-3 words blacked out]
Aug 1 5872 Ukrainian Labour Temple - East Kildonan, Man.
9 5873 [entry blacked out] Trans to 175P/2400
12 5874 Machinists Union - Montreal P. Que.
5875 [entry blacked out]
5876 Ukrainian Labour Temple - Calgary
18 5877 Labour Conditions in Canada [2-3 words blacked out]
22 Conference of the League of Nations at Geneva, Switzerland
23 5878 Subversive Action In Trans to ??????
25 5879 I.W.W. at Calgary, Alta - Trans to 175/5890
26 5880 [entry blacked out]
28 5881 Ukrainian Labour Party - Broad Valley, Man.

Page 127

Aug 28 5882 Communist Party [4-5 words blacked out] - Chase River, B.C.
30 5883 [entry blacked out]
Sept 2 5884 Conditions among Ukrainians - Sault Ste. Marie, Ont.
3 5885 Manufacture of Ammunition at Granville Island - Vancouver, B.C.
9 5886 [entry blacked out]

	5887	[entry blacked out] Trans to 175P/3681
11	5888	[entry blacked out]
15	5890	Industrial Workers of the World - Sub. Act. Within - Calgary, Alta (BF 175/5648)
	5891	[entry blacked out]
	5892	[entry blacked out]
	5893	Communist Party - Glace Bay, N.S.
	5894	[2-3 words blacked out] Lac Du Bonnet, Man. (Trans to 175/5519)
16	5895	[entry blacked out]
	5896	[entry blacked out]
18	5897	[2-3 words blacked out] Lac Du Bonnet, Man.
	5898	[entry blacked out]
	5899	Communist Party [2-3 words blacked out] Thorold, Ont.
20	5900	[entry blacked out]
22	5901	[entry blacked out] 175/3587
Page 128		
Sep 22	5902	[entry blacked out]
	5903	[entry blacked out]
	5904	[entry blacked out]
23	5905	O.B.U. Sydney, N.S.
25	5906	Young Communist League - Timmins, Ont.
	5907	Independent Labour Party - Fort William, Ont.
29	5908	Communist Party of Canada [2-3 words blacked out] Espanola, Ont.
	5909	" " " Ukrainain ????? London, Ont.
30	5910	The Canadian Proletarian Films Ltd. [3-4 words blacked out]
	5911	Young Communist League - Drumheller, Alta.
Oct 2	5912	I.W.W. Conference, Oct 4/24 Sudbury, Ont.
		COMMUNIST PARTY
4	5913	@Workers Party [-1-2 words blacked out] Zellonia, Man.
	5914	Community Club - Brightstone, Man. [2-3 words blacked out]
	5915	Community Club - Red Deer, Man [2-3 words blacked out]
7	5916	Convention of U.M.W. of A. Truro, N.S. 1924
	5917	Communist Party [2-3 words blacked out] Northern Ontario
8	5918	I.W.W. at Moose Jaw, Sask.
	5919	Farmer Labour Society - Cando, Sask.
	5920	Canadian Labour Party - Winnipeg, Man.
	5921	Labour Conditions - Western Fuel Corporation - Nanaimo, B.C.
Page 129		
Oct 8	5922	Communist Party [2-3 words blacked out] at White Fish, Ont.
	5923	" " [2-3 words blacked out] Sudbury
	5924	I.W.W. in Southern Saskatchewan
9	5925	[entry blacked out] Trans to 175P/2456
9	5926	I.W.W. in United States

	5927	I.W.W. in Northern Saskatchewan	
10	5928	[entry blacked out]	
	5929	[entry blacked out]	
15	5930	Farmers' Union - Pelly, Sask. Trans to 175/2485	
	5931	Labor Defense Council - Chicago, Ill. U.S.A.	
	5932	Strike of Fish Packers Union - Prince Rupert, B.C.	
	5933	[entry blacked out]	
	5934	Communist Party [3-4 words blacked out] Calgary, Alta	
	5935	[entry blacked out]	175/2387
	5936	Communist Party [2-3 words blacked out] Cobalt, Ont.	
	5937	[entry blacked out] Trans to 175P/2494	
	5938	[entry blacked out]	
	5939	[entry blacked out]	
18	5940	[entry blacked out]	
Page 130			
Oct 21	5941	Employees of Canadian Government Merchant Marine	
22	5942	Ukrainian Labour Temple [2-3 words blacked out] Kingston, Ont.	
24	5943	Workers Party of Canada - Nanaimo, B.C.	
	5944	[2-3 words blacked out] of ???	175/1141
31	5945	[entry blacked out]	
	5946	Ku Klux Klan Hamilton, Ont.	
Nov 4	5947	Communist Party of Canada - Sturgis, Sask.	
	5948	Communist Party [4-5 words blacked out]	
	5949	Canadian Labour Party - Manitoba - General	
	5950	Industrial Workers of the World Sub. Act. Within - Claresholm, Alta.	
	5951	[entry blacked out]	
5	5952	Strike of U.M.W. of A. at H?????. Alta.	
7	5953	O.B.U. (B.F. 175/2475) Hamilton, Ont.	
	5954	Ku Klux Klan Niagara Falls, Ont.	
	5955	Ku Klux Klan Sarnia "	
	5956	Ku Klux Klan London "	
	5957	Ku Klux Klan ????old "	
	5958	Ku Klux Klan Saskatoon, Sask.	
	5959	Ku Klux Klan Prince Albert, Sask.	
	5960	Ku Klux Klan Trans to 175/6103 Winnipeg, Man.	
Page 131			
Nov 7	5961	Ku Klux Klan Vancouver, B.C.	
	5962	Ku Klux Klan Cranbrook, "	
11	5963	Ku Klux Klan Calgary, Alta.	
	Correspondence [2-3 words blacked out]		
	5964	Ukrainian Labour Party Prudhomme, Sask.	
	5965	Strike of U.M.W. of A. Mid West Mine Drumheller, Alta.	
	5966	Ukrainian Labour Society Humboldt, Sask.	

12 5967 [entry blacked out] Trans to 175/5608
5968 [entry blacked out] 175P/????
5969 [entry blacked out] 175-3969
15 5970 The Freiheit Club Toronto, Ont. [1-2 words blacked out]
5971 African Orthodox Church
17 5972 Zinoviev Letter London, Eng.
5973 [entry blacked out] Trans to 175P/2709
5974 Conditions at Prudhomme Sask (scratched out) [3-4 words blacked out] Transferred to 175P/2501
18 5975 Labours Conditions at Crow's Nest Pass Coal Co. - Coal Creek, Mines - Fernie B.C.
5976 [entry blacked out] Trans to 175P/355
(Correspondence [3-4 words blacked out])
20 5977 Provincial Convention of Ukrainian Labour Temple Assoc. Edmonton Alta June 1924
21 5978 Workers Independent Progressive Club - Toronto, Ont.
22 5979 Radical Schools - [2-3 words blacked out] Hamilton, "
22 5980 Hebrew Free School Elmwood, Man.

Page 132

Nov 24 5981 Communist Party [3-4 words blacked out] Trans to 175/5936 Cobalt Ont.
26 5982 Industrial Workers of the World Sub. Act. Within - Edmonton, Alta.
5983 [entry blacked out] Trans to 175P/218
5984 Industrial Workers of the World Sub. Act. within B.C.
27 5985 [entry blacked out]
29 5986 Dist. 26 Convention of U.M.W. of A. at Sydney N.S. November 1924
Dec 1 5987 Ukrainians at the Pas - Man. (scratched out) (Inter'l Labour Assn). The Pas. Man 175/65526
5988 Canadian Labour Party - Calgary - Alta.
5989 [entry blacked out] Trans to 175P/1494
2 5990 Communist Party [4-5 words blacked out] Kitchener, Ont.
5991 [entry blacked out]
5992 St. Raphels Society Saskatoon, Sask.
4 5993 [entry blacked out]
5 5994 [entry blacked out]
9 5995 [entry blacked out]
11 5996 [entry blacked out]
5997 Anarchist Organization Transferred to 175/4???
5998 Russian - Ukrainian Worker Welland, Ont.
5999 Samo Obrazowania Society Vancouver, B.C.
6000 Workers Union Montreal, P.Q.

Page 133

Dec 11 6001 Group of Russian Workers Hamilton, Ont (trans. 175/7131)
6002 Farmers Union of Canada Sturgis, Sask.
12 6003 Communist Party of Canada Semans - Sask.

15 6004 International Workers Relief
@ International Workers Aid Canada Generally

6005 [entry blacked out]

6006 [entry blacked out]

17 6007 [entry blacked out]

6008 [entry blacked out]

6009 [entry blacked out]

6010 Independent Labor Party Glace Bay, N.S.

6011 Communist Party [5-6 words blacked out] Timmins, Ont.
(Correspondence [2 words blacked out])

6012 Communist Party at (trans to [blacked out] Medicine Hat - Alta.

6013 Monetary Educational Advocates of Alberta Edmonton, Atla.

6014 K.K. Klan Windsor, Ont.

6015 Farmer's Union - Generally

23 6016 [entry blacked out]

26 6017 Communist Party of Canada - Couiston, Ont.

27 6018 Sitch - Ukrainian Organization of [4-5 words blacked out]

Dec 31 6019 Communist Party I.W.W. in Canada (Statistics)

Page 134

Dec 31 6020 Communist Party of Canada - Beaver Lake - Ont [1-2 words blacked out]

1925

Jan 3 6021 Strike of Labourers C.N.R. Station - Edmonton, Alta.

7 6022 Communist Party of Canada [words blacked out] Vancouver B.C.
Corresp [blacked out]

6023 Ukrainian Labour Temple at Kenora - Ont.

6024 General Conditions in Russia (175-2936)

6025 Russian Royalists

8 6026 General Conditions in Europe [2-3 words blacked out]

9 6027 K.K.K. Walkeville - Ont.

10 6028 Labour Conditions (Unemployment) Ottawa

6029 Communist Party at Wakaw, Sask.

12 6030 [2-3 words blacked out] Crohon-on-Hudson, N.Y.

13 6031 North American Railroader's Amalgmation

6032 [entry blacked out]

14 6033 Young Communist League Portage la Prairie - Man.

6034 O.B.U. at Dryden - Ont.

15 6035 Foreign Radical Plays - Dramas, Recitations, etc. [2-3 words blacked out]

21 6036 Convention Ukrainian Labour Farmer Assoc. Winnipeg - Man.
- January 1925 Correspondence [3-4 words blacked out]

6037 Ukrainian Labour Temple at - Waugh - Alta.

22 6038 K.K. Klan at Hartford - Ont.

Page 135

Jan 22 6039 I.W.W. - Womens Auxiliary Sudbury, Ont.

23 6040 Industrial Workers of the World Sub. Act. Within
- Creighton Mine, Ontario
24 6041 Canadian Labour Party Montreal, P. Que.
26 6042 Communist Party [3-4 words blacked out] France
27 6043 Conditions amongst Russians in Ottawa Ont.
6044 Progressive Farmers Educational League - Calgary - Alta.
28 6045 Farmers Union of Canada in Manitoba
(B.F. 175/7544) [2-3 words blacked out]
6046 Chinese Nationalist League @ Kuomin Tang Toronto, Ont.
6047 Communist Party [3-4 words blacked out] Lachine - P.Que.
29 6048 Ukrainian Labour Temple Assoc. [2-3 words blacked out]
Winnipeg, Man.
corresp transf to [blacked out]
6049 Ukrainian Labour Temple Association ??? Winnipeg ?????
6050 [entry blacked out]
6051 Communist Party of Canada [5-6 words blacked out] Timmins, ont.
Feb 5 6052 Young Communist League [2-3 words blacked out] Regina - Sask.
6 6053 [entry blacked out] Brought forward from 175-3752
6054 Strike of Employees of Ames. Holden, Mc Ready Ltd. Montreal P.Q.
6055 Canadian Labor Party Sydney, N.S.
7 6056 Ukrainian Labor Farmer Temple Assn. Fort Francis, Ont.
corresp transf to [blacked out]
10 6057 " Farmer Temple Assn. Prudhomme, Sask.
Page 136

BF 175/1640
Feb 10 6058 Conditions General (Amongst Finns) Eckville Dist, Man.
6059 Conditions amongst Finns at Connaught, Ont.
Ukrainian Farmer Labour Temple ????? Alta
6060 Communist Party [2-3 words blacked out] Leduc - Alta.
6061 Communist Party of Canada London, Ont.
12 6062 Conditions amongst Finns Rainy River Dist. Ont.
6063 Italian Anarchist Party Montreal, P.Que.
13 6064 Young Communist League - Saskatoon, Sask.
16 6065 Conditions amongst Ukrainians - Fraserwood Man. Dist.
20 6066 Russian Labour Club Edmonton, Alta.
20 6067 Labour Conditions in Newfoundland [2-3 words blacked out]
Corresp transf to [blacked out]
6068 Ukrainian Farmer Labour Temple Assn - Broad Valley - Man.
21 6069 Ku Klux Klan Toronto, Ont.
6070 Communist Party [2-3 words blacked out] South Porcupine Ont.
23 6071 Convention of Communist Party - Newcastle, Drumheller, Alta.
Feb. 1925
24 6072 Conditions Amongst Ukrainians - Dauphin- Man. Dist.

Transferred to [blacked out]

26 6073 Ukrainian Labour Farmer Temple [3-4 wrods blacked out] The Pas. Man.

Trans to [blacked out]

6074 Communist Party [2-3 words blacked out] Vancouver, B.C.

28 6075 Convention of Communist Party of Canada Toronto Dist
Sept 4 to 7 1925

(Correspondence Transf to [blacked out])

6076 " " Ukrainian [4-5 words blacked out]

6077 Ku Klux Klan [4-5 words blacked out]

Page 137

3/2/25 6078 Young Peoples League Canmore - Alta.
[3-4 words blacked out]

3 6079 Workers Benevolent Society Fort William Ont.
[3-4 words blacked out]

6080 Radical Schools Regina - Sask
[4-5 words blacked out]

6081 " " Moose Jaw "

6082 " [3-4 words blacked out] Ottawa Ont.

6083 " [3-4 words blacked out] Edmonton - Alta.

6084 " [3-4 words blacked out] Sydney, N.S.

6085 " [3-4 words blacked out] Montreal - P.Que.

Correspondence [3-4 words blacked out]

*6086 Zapomhe Towarstwo School Saskatoon-Sask.

3.3.25 6087 Convention of Women Workers Winnipeg- Man-February 14 to 17 - 1925

4.3.25 6088 Communist Party [2-3 words blacked out] Windsor - Ont. Dist.

5.3.25 6089 " " [2-3 words blacked out] Salmon Arm - B.C.

6. 6090 Industrial Workers of the World Sub. Act. Within Sudbury, Ont.

7. 6091 Radical Conditions in Saskatchewan

9. 6092 Strike of U.M.W.A. (Dist 26) Nova Scotia

6093 Young Communist League - Hillcrest Alta

corresp [2-3 words blacked out]

6094 Ukrainian Farmer Labour Temple Assn - Fort William, Ont.

10. 6095 " " Port Arthur

6096 Radical Schools in Alberta [2-3 words blacked out]

6097 " " Vancouver, B.C.

Page 148

10.3.25 6098 Radical Schools in Ontario [4-5 words blacked out]

corresp [2-3 words blacked out]

6099 " " Toronto, Ont. [2-3 words blacked out]

6100 " " Winnipeg, Man.

6101 " " Manitoba [3-4 words blacked out]

6102 Ukrainian Workingmens Benevolent Society - Edmonton Alta (scratched out)

16. 6103 Ku Klux Klan - Winnipeg - Man.

17. 6104 General Conditions amongst Ukrainian Three Hills - Alta Dist.
19. 6105 Radical conditions in Ontario [3-4 words blacked out]
20. 6106 Communist Party in Japan [3-4 words blacked out]
6107 I.W.W. at Port Arthur - Ont. [2-3 words blacked out]
6108 Communist Party in Germany [2-3 words blacked out]
6109 " " [3-4 words blacked out] Longlac Ont.
Corresp [3-4 words blacked out]
23.3 6110 Ukrainian Farmer Labour Temple Assocn - Canora, Sask.
(Correspondence [3-4 words blacked out])
6111 Convention of Ukrainian Farmer Labour Temple Assn - Edmonton, Alta Apr. 9-11 1925
(Correspondence [3-4 words blacked out])
6112 " " Toronto Ont. March 27-28-1925
6113 Communist Party of Canada - Cape Breton - N.S.
6114 Conditions amongst Finlanders - Trochu - Alta. Dist.
6115 Ukrainian Farmer Labour Temple Assn - Dana - Sask.
6116 " " " " " Iroquois Falls - Ont.
6117 Communist Party [2-3 words blacked out] Trail B.C. 175/671

Page 139

27.3.25 6118 Industrial Workers of the World Sub.Act. Within Prince Rupert -B.C.
6119 Communist Party Bird River - Man.
6120 [word blacked out] Society of Proletariat Writers)
6121 Ukrainian Workmens Benevolent Assn [3-4 words blacked out]
28. 6122 Federated Seafarers' Union of Canada - Vancouver B.C.
31. 6123 Unemployed Association of Canada
6124 Radical Conditions in Manitoba [3-4 words blacked out]
1.4.25 6125 Communist Party [2-3 words blacked out] Edmonton - Alta.
3. 6126 Ukrainian Workmen's Benevolent Society - Thorold Ont (scratched out) trans to 3-E-889
6. 6127 Conditions Unemployment - London
no affiliations known
9. 6128 Strike of International Fur Workers Union - Montreal, P. Que.
14. 6129 Lettish Educational Union - Lettonia - Man.
15. 6130 I.W.W. at [2 words blacked out] Fort William - Ont.
6131 Sawmill Workers' Union in British Columbia Trans to [blacked out]
17. 6132 Relief & Assistance for U.M.W. of A. (Dist. 26) Nova Scotia
6133 May Day at Winnipeg - Man - 1925
6134 Chinese Nationalist League - Halifax, N.S.
20. 6135 Radical Conditions in British Columbia
22.4.25 6136 Convention of Canadian Labour Party Toronto, Ont.
24.4.25 6137 Ku Klux Klan at Oshawa, Ont.

Page 140

25.4.25 6138 Communist Party [4-5 words blacked out] Glace Bay, N.S.

corresp [3-4 words blacked out]

29.4.25 6139 Ukrainian Farmer Labour Temple Verigen, Sask.

6140 [2-3 words blacked out] Dominion Labour Party Lethbridge, Alta.

6141 Ukrainian Farmer Labour Temple South Porcupine, Ont.

corresp [3-4 words blacked out]

1.5.25 6142 " [3-4 words blacked out] Welland, Ont.

2.5.25 6143 Convention for Ukrainian Farmer Labour Temple Association Edmonton, Alta.

6144 May Day (1925) Toronto, Ont.

4.5. 6145 [entry blacked out]

6146 Ukrainian Farmer Labour Temple Assn. Willowbrok Sask.

(Correspondence [2-3 words blacked out]

6147 Ukrainian " Nordigg

6. 6148 May Day - Montreal - P.Que - 1925

7. 6149 May Day - Glace Bay, N.S. 1925

8. 6150 Co-operative Movement at Fisher Branch. Man.

9. 6151 Strike at Rutherford Lumber Co. Montreal - P. Que.

12. 6152 May Day Hamilton, Ont. 1925

6153 " " Drumheller, Alta.

6154 " " Edmonton, "

13. 6155 Convention of Canadian Labour Party - Vancouver, B.C. May 2nd 1925

14. 6156 K.K. Klan - Six Nations Reserve - Ont.

Page 141

16.5.25 6157 National Unemployment Association Toronto, Ont.

17. 6158 Annual Reports on Labour Organizations in Canada

19. 6159 May Day Transcona - Man - 1925

6160 " " Timmins, Ont. 1925

22. 6161 Radical Conditions in Northern Alberta Dist.

23. 6162 International Bible Students Association - Montreal, P.Que.

Corresp. [3-4 words blacked out]

6163 Communist Party Coleman - Alta.

6164 " " Bellevue - "

corresp [3-4 words blacked out]

6165 Ukrainian Labour Temple Assoc.

corresp [3-4 words blacked out]

6166 " " " Hillcrest

6167 Communist Party [3-4 words blacked out]

27. 6168 Canadian Federation of Labour Calgary "

29. 6169 Ku Klux Klan Chatham

6170 Strike at March Gold Mine Co. Timmins - Ont. Dist.

1.6.25 6171 Finnish Socialist Organization - Wolf Siding - Ont.

4. 6172 Labour Conditions at Coleman - Alta

6173 Canadian Federation of Labour - Crows Nest Pass District

6174 " " " Miners Blairmore, Alta.
6175 Labour Conditions at Hillcrest - Alta.
6176 British Columbia Miners Association - Corbin - B.C.

Page 142

4.6.25 6177 Communist Party [2-3 words blacked out] Toronto, Ont.
5. 6178 Radical Conditions in Southern Alberta Distict
Correspondence [3-4 words blacked out]
9. 6179 Ukrainian Labour Farmer Temple Assn. [1-2 words blacked out]
11. 6180 Naturalization of Radicals - Fort William - Ont.
13.6 6181 Communist Party [1-2 words blacked out] Windsor - Ont.
17. 6182 " " Stratford
6183 Young Communist League South Porcupine - Ont.
20. 6184 Protest meeting in connection with Nova Scotia Strike Situation - Winnipeg - Man.
22. 6185 Sub. Act. Within International Peasants Council
@ Peasants international
@ International Council of Peasants
@ Peasants and Farmers International
@ International Farmers Council
@ Farmers and Peasants International
@ Krestinteror
6186 Workers & Famers Poltical Assn. Saskatoon, Sask.
(Correspondence Trans
6187 Womens Labour Society - Fort William - Ont. (Trans to 175/6179
23. 6188 Japanese Worker's Union - Vancouver, B.C (175/3947)
6189 Strike of Coal Miners at Nanaimo - B.C.
Trans to 175/7130
24. 6190 Russian Workers' Society Vancouver, B.C.
29. 6191 Red Deer Valley Miners Union Drumheller Alta. Dist.
6192 Young Communist League at Gleneden - B.C.
30. 6193 Ukrainian Labour Farmer Temple School - Fort William, Ont.
2.7. 6194 Labour Conditions Unemployment - Sydney Mines - N.S. (175/3875)
6195 ??? & Sub. Act. Sydney Mines, N.S.
Radical Conditions (scratched out)

Page 143

2.7.25 6196 Labour Conditions - Sydney N.S. continued [blacked out]
7.7. 6197 Kuo Min Tang [4-5 words blacked out]
14. 6198 Conditions - Sturgeon Falls - Ont.
corresp [2-3 words blacked out]
23. 6199 Ukrainian Labour Farmer Temple Assn. Red Deer Man. [2-3 words blacked out]
24.7. 6200 U.M.W. of A. Hillcrest, Alberta
(Correspondence [3-4 words blacked out])
27. 6201 Ukrainian Farmer Labour Temple Assn at Comston - Ont.
28. 6202 Revolutionary & Sub. Act. Rouyn Que.

(Correspondence [3-4 words blacked out])

29. 6203 Ukrainian Farmer Labour Temple Assn (Women's Branch) Vancouver, B.C.

4.8. 6204 " Co-operative Stores Toronto, Ont.

5. 6205 Communist Party at Silver Centre

7.8.25 6206 Convention of Farmers Union of Canada Saskatoon Sask. July 21st to 14 1925

10. 6207 Conditions amongst Doukhobor's Whitebeech - Sask. Dist.

12. 6208 Communist Activities among Crews of Italian Boats

6209 Communist Party [2-3 words blacked out] Coalhurst Alta.

6210 Industrial Workers of the World - Convention held in Sudbury, Ont. Aug 1925

6211 I.W.W. at Winnipeg, Man.

6212 Communist Party at Trail B.C.

6213 Ku Klux Klan Kingston, Ont.

14. 6214 The Activities & Organization of the Citizens Committee of One Thousand in Connection with the Winnipeg Strike - during 1919.

Page 144

15.8.25 6125 Communist Party [4-5 words blacked out] Kirkland Lake, Ont.

17. 6216 Strike of Miners at Brule Mines - Alta.

6217 Ukrainian Farmer Labour Temple Assn. at Cardiff, Alta.

6218 Mine Workers of Canada Blairmore, Alta.

6219 " " " Bellevue "

6220 " " " Coleman "

19. 6221 Canadian Labor Defence Leage [2-3 word blacked out]

(evidence against) trans. to [blacked out]

6221 supp constitution of Trans to [blacked out]

6222 International Post Graduate University (Third International Moscow Russia)

6223 Communist Party in Europe

21. 6224 Industrial Workers of the World Sub. Act. Within - Saskatoon, Sask.

6225 Conditions at Fort William Paper Co. Fort William - Ont.

22. 6226 Convention ???? Party (Dist #6) Vancouver, B.C.

6227 Workers Benevolent Society Nordigg, Alta.

6228 Conditions at Canton - China

reports dealing with [5-6 words blacked out]

24. 6229 Communist Party [2-3 words blacked out] Winnipeg, Man.

25. 6230 The Republican Association of Canada

26. 6231 One Big Union Montreal, P. Que.

27 6234 Ku Klux Klan Ottawa, Ont.

28 . 6235 Strike of Garment Workers of John W. Peck - Montreal, P.Que.

29 . 6236 Conditions among Ukrainians Spadden - Alta. Dist.

Page 145

1.9.25 6237 Communist Party [2-3 words blacked out] Timmins, Ont.

2.9.25 6238 "Class Conscious Comrades of the Class Struggle Edmonton, Alta.
8. 6239 Convention of Communist Party of Canada [2-3 words blacked out] Toronto Ont. Sept 14th to 15th 1925
8.9.25 6240 Russian progressive Club Toronto, Ont Transferred to 175/4532
16. 6241 Conditions amongst Hungarians - Milk River Alta.
17. 6242 Convention of Communist Party Dist. 3 - Toronto, Ont. Sept 9th & 10th 1925
Corresp. [2-3 words blacked ou]
18. 6243 Ukrainian Farmer Labour Temple Medika, Man.
6244 Radical Conditions in Canada [2-3 words blacked out]
19. 6245 International Miners Union Timmins Ont.
24. 6246 Convention of U.M.W. of A. Dist. 26 at Sydney N.S. 1925
28. 6247 Communist Party Fernie B.C. District [2-3 words blacked out]
5.10 6248 Ukrainian Labour Temple Association - Corbin B.C. BF from 175/4100 & 175/2754
9. 6249 Convention of Labour Party at Cochrane Ont 3rd Oct - 1925
13. 6250 " " Miners Calgary, Alta.
6251 General Conditions in Landerville, Man. Dist.
15. 6252 Convention of Young Communist League - 3rd National [3-4 words blacked out] Toronto, Ont Sept ?? 1925
6253 Canadian Labour Defense League Trans to 175/6221
6254 Canadian Industrial Union Auxillary - Sudbury, Ont.
31. 6255 B.C. Miners Association at Michel, B.C.

Page 146

26.10.25 6256 Canadian National Federation of Railroad Workers - Edmonton, Alta.
2.11 6257 Communist Party [2-3 words blacked out] Winnipeg - Man. [3-4 words blacked out]
3. 6258 Agitation propaganda Dept Communist Party of Canada [4-5 words blacked out]
6. 6259 Labor's Reward (Moving Picture)
6260 Unattached Veterans Association @ Unemployed Assoc. of Ex Service Men
Corresp [3-4 words blacked out]
13. 6261 Mine Workers Union of Canada
16. 6262 International Trades Union Unity Movement
17. 6263 National Labour Defence League Sask. Sask.
6264 Canadian " Party
6265 Broadcasting by Radio of Revolutionary Speeches [2-3 words blacked out]
20. 6266 Strike of Miners at Canmore, Alta.
21. 6264 Ku Klux Klan Porcupine Ont. Dist.
23. 6268 Trades and Labour Council Montreal, P.Que.
6269 " " " in Timmins Ont. Dist.
6270 Canadian Labour Party in Quebec Province

25.11.25 6271 Mine Workers Union of Canada Lethbridge, Alta.
26.11.25 6272 International Club Vancouver, B.C.
28.11.25 6273 Canadian Labor Defense League Edmonton, Alta.
30. 6274 [3-4 words blacked out] Drumheller
6275 Crusaders of Canada & Protective Association

Page 147

2.12.25 6276 Ku Klux Klan re Ebeneger Valentine Toronto Dist.
6277 Conditions among Italians at Thorold, Ont.
6278 Conditions " Russians " "
4.12.25 6279 Stike of Miners Drumheller, Alta. Dist.
6280 Mine Workers Union of Canada Cobalt, Ont.
7. 6281 Labour Conditions in Crows Nest Pass Dist.
9.12.25 6282 Industrial Workers of the World Sub. Act. Within Drumheller, Alta. (BF 175/51)
11. 6283 Communist Party [4-5 words blacked out] Kamsack Sask. Dist.
14. 6284 Conditions among Romanians in Canada
15. 6285 Ku Klux Klan Edmonton, Alta.
(Correspondence [2-3 words blacked out]
18.12.25 6286 Convention of Ukrainian Labour Farmer Temple Association Winnipeg Man. January 25th to 27th 1926
22. 6287 Convention of Ukrainain Workmens Benevolent Society Winnipeg Man. January 27th & 28th 1926
24. 6288 Ku Klux Klan Montreal, P. Que.
31.12.25 6289 Ukrainian Labor Farmer Temple Association Co-Operative Stores
4.1.26 6290 Ku Klux Klan St. John, N.B.
12.1.26 6291 Western Peoples Bureau Brandon, Man.
12.1.26 6292 The Communist Party Northern [3-4 words blacked out]
13.1.26 6293 Mine Workers Union of Canada in Northern Ontario

Page 148

19.1.26 6294 Young Communist League Frochu Alta.
20.1.26 6295 Mine Worker's Union of Canada Coalhurst Alta.
20.1.26 6296 Communist Party [2-3 words blacked out] BF 175/4914 Dunblane, Sask.
22.1.26 6297 Canadian Labour Defence League [2-3 words blacked out] Montreal, P. Que.
23.1.26 6298 Canadian Labour Defence League Toronto, Ont.
26.1.26 6299 International Bible Students Association Winnipeg, Man.
26.1.26 6300 International Bible Students Association in Manitoba
26.1.26 6301 Communist Party [1-2 words blacked out] Nakina, Ont.
corresp [2-3 words blacked out]
28.1.26 6302 Ukrainian Labour Temple Sudbury,Ont.
29.1.26 6303 Workers Benevolent Society Corbin, B.C.
2.2.26 6304 Mine Workers Union of Canada, Timmins, Ont.
2.2.26 6305 Convention of United Mine Workers of America at Sydney, N.S. January 26th to 30th 1926.

2.2.26 6306 Workers Benevolent Association Coalhurst, Alta.
2.2.26 6307 Young Communist League Thorold, Ont.
2.2.26 6308 Workers Benevolent Society Winnipeg Beach, Man.
4.2.26 6309 Workers Benevolent Society Fort Frances, Ont.
4.2.26 6310 One Big Union Cape Breton, N.S.
6.2.26 6311 Communist Party [2-3 words blacked out] Kirkland Lake, Ont.
8.2.26 6312 Canadian Labour Defense League, Montreal, P.Que.

Page 149

13.2.26 6313 Workers Benevolent Society Timmins, Ont.
15.2.26 6314 Young Communist League Transcona, Man.
16.2.26 6315 Strike of Employees Corbeil Limited
(Boot & Shoe Manufacturers) Montreal, P. Que.
Correspondence [2-3 words blacked out]
18.2.26 6316 Ukrainian Farmer Labour Temple Mundare, Alta.
(Correspondence [2-3 words blacked out]
18.2.26 6317 " " " " Sault Ste Marie, Ont.
20.2.26 6318 Higher Educational Courses of
The Ukrainian Farmer Labour Temple Association
20.2.26 6319 Workers Benevolent Society Transcona Man (scratched out)
22.2.26 6320 Mine Worker's Union of Canada South Porcupine, Ont.
22.2.26 6321 Canadian Labour Defence League Halifax, N.S.
(Correspondence [2-3 words blacked out])
22.2.26 6322 Canadian Labour Defence League Calgary, Alta.
26.226 6323 Ukrainian Farmer Labour Temple Perdue Sask.
6324 Workers Benevolent Society Hamilton, Ont.
27. 6325 One Big Union Sandon, B.C. BF 175/2219
1.3.26 6326 Mine Workers Union of Canada Kirkland Lake, Ont.
[3-4 words blacked out]
2.3.26 6327 Workmens Benevolent Society Regina Sask.
Corresp [2-3 words blacked out]
6328 Ukrainian Farmer Labour Temple Leiscar, Alta.
Continued [1-2 words blacked out]
4.3.26 6329 Trades & Labour Council Halifax, N.S.
6.3.26 6330 Ukrainian Farmer Labour Temple [word blacked out] (General Fyle)

Page 150

(Correspondence [3-4 words blacked out]
6.3.26 6331 Ukrainian Farmer Labour Temple [word blacked out] Saskatoon, Sask.
6332 Ukrainian Society "Zorya" [word blacked out] Portage La Prairie, Man.
(Correspondence [2-3 words blacked out]
6333 Ukrainian Farmer Labour Temple (Womens Section) Transcona, Man.
(Correspondence [3-4 words blacked out]
6334 Ukrainian Farmer Labour Temple [word blacked out] Timmins, Ont.
(Correspondence [2-3 words blacked out]

6335 Ukrainian Farmer Labour Temple [word blacked out] Thorold, Ont.
BF [blacked out]
6336 Ukrainian Workmens Benevolent Association - Narol Man.
corresp [3-4 words blacked out]
6337 Ukrainian Farmer Labour Temple - Narol, Man.
(Correspondence [2-3 words blacked out]
6338 Ukrainian Farmer Labour Temple [word blacked out] Toronto, Ont.
Corresp [2-3 words blacked out]
6339 Ukrainian Farmer Labour Temple [word blacked out] Hamilton, Ont.
9.3.26 6340 B.C. Miners Association - Coal Creek, B.C.
(Correspondence [3-4 words blacked out])
6341 Ukrainian Farmer Labor Temple [word blacked out] Port Arthur, Ont.
(Correspondence [2-3 words blacked out]
6342 " " " " Coleman, Alta.
(Correspondence [2-3 words blacked out]
6343 " " " " Vancouver, B.C.
(Correspondence [2-3 words blacked out])
6344 " " " " Lethbridge, Alta.
(Correspondence [2-3 words blacked out])
6345 " " " " Sault St. Marie, Ont.
(Correspondence [2-3 words blacked out])
6346 " " " " Ottawa, Ont.
6347 " " " " Beverly, Alta.
10.3.26 6348 " " " " Lachine P.Que.
11.3.26 6349 Communist Party [2-3 words blacked out] Montreal, P.Que.
11.3.26 6350 Labour Conditions MacDonald Lumber Co. Chemong, Sask.
Page 151
12.3.26 Merkolov General
Corresp [4-5 words blacked out]
12.3.26 6351 Ukrainian Farmer Labour Temple [word blacked out] Calgary, Alta.
(Correspondence [2-3 words blacked out])
6352 " " " " " " Medicine Hat, Alta.
6353 " " " " " " Fort Frances, Ont.
6354 " " " " " " Regina, Sask.
Corresp [2-3 words blacked out]
6355 " " " " " " Moose Jaw, Sask.
(Correspondence [3-4 words blacked out]
6356 " " " " " " Montreal, P.Que.
15. 6357 Miners Union Canmore, Alta.
15. 6358 Ukrainian Farmer Labour Temple [word blacked out] Edmonton, Alta.
19.3.26 6359 One Big Union Minto N.B. District
19.3.26 6360 Convention of Canadian Labour Party (Ontario Section)
London Ont. April 2nd to 3rd 1926

22.3.26 6361 Workers Benevolent Society Port Arthur Ont. (scratched out)

6362 Strike of Miners Minto Coal Co. Minto, N.B.

23. 6363 May Day Toronto, Ont 1926

26. [entry blacked out]

6364 One Big Union Springhill N.S.

27. 6365 Matteoti Club Montreal, P.Que.

29. 6366 Ukrainian Workers Youth - Winnipeg, Man.

Page 152

Corresp. [2-3 words blacked out]

3.4.26 6367 Ukrainian Farmer Labour Temple [word blacked out] Hillcrest, Alta.
(Correspondence [3-4 words blacked out])

3.4.26 6368 " " " " " " Corriston, Ont.
(Correspondence [3-4 words blacked out]

9.4.26 6369 " " " " " " Drumheller, Alta.

9.4.26 6370 May Day Winnipeg Man. 1926

12.4.26 6371 Convention of Canadian Labour Party Edmonton, Alta. (April 1st to 3rd 1926

Corresp. [2-3 words blacked out]

12.4.26 6372 Ukrainian Farmer Labour Temple [word blacked out] Bienfait, Sask.
[2-3 words blacked out] 175/4845 175/3245
@ Bulgarian Socialist Labor Group

17.4.26 6373 Bulgarian Macedonian Workers Educational Assocation
@ Communist Party - Bulgarian Br
@ Workers Party - Bulgarian Br.
@ East Toronto Bulgaro Macedonian Workers Social Club
@ Bulgarian Socialist Party
@ Socialist Party - Bulgarian Br

BF 175/3274 BF 175/453?

19.4.26 6374 One Big Union (Street Carmens Branch) Winnipeg, Man.

21.4.26 6375 May Day Porcupine Ont 1926

26.4.26 6376 Ukrainian Workman's Benevolent Association Brandon Man.

Corresp [3-4 words blacked out]

30.4.36 6377 Ukrainian Farmer Labor Temple Association - Libau, Man.

1.5.26 6378 Ku Klux Klan Smith Falls, Ont.

3.5.36 6379 Young Communist League - Lettonia, Man.

5.5.26 6380 May Day Montreal, P.Que., 1926

6.5.26 6381 May Day Glace Bay, N.S. 1926

8.5.26 6382 Sitch Ukrainian Organization Montreal, P.Que. [2-3 words blacked out]

6383 May Day Timmins, Ont. 1926

10.5.26 6384 Labor Conditions [2-3 words blacked out] Vancouver, B.C.

Page 153

10.5.26 6385 May Day Edmonton, Alta 1926

11.5.26 6386 Control of Entry into Canada of Citizens of Soviet Russia

6387 Strike of Carpenters at Vancouver B.C.

6388 May Day Calgary, Alta.

15.5.26 6389 Society for Cultural Relations between peoples of Dominion of Canada and the Union of Soviet Socialist Republics Canada

18.5.26 6390 Ukrainian Farmer Labor Temple [2-3 words blacked out] Ansonville, Ont.

Correspondence [3-4 words blacked out]

6391 Convention of Ukrainian Farmer Labor Temple Saskatoon, Sask 17-17-6-26

Correspondence [3-4 words blacked out]

6392 " " " " " Edmonton, Alta. June ?????

20.5.26 6393 The American Association for the Advancement of Ath?????

22.5.26 6394 International Association of Machinists

28.5.26 6395 Ku Klux Klan at Barrie Ont.

29.5.26 6396 Ukrainian Workers Youth Transf 175/6473

6397 " " " Fort William, Ont.

6398 " " " Sudbury, Ont.

4.6.26 6399 Ukrainian Farmer Labour Temple Hodgson, Man.

corresp [2-3 words blacked out]

5.6.26 6400 " " " " Portage la Prairie, Man.

7.6.26 6401 Conditions among Ukrainians Brandon, Man.

6403 " " " in Stuartburn, Man.

Page 154

ALIASES to 175/6389

@ SOCIETY FOR PROMOTION OF CULTURAL RELATIONS BETWEEN PEOPLES OF CANADA AND SOVIET RUSSIA

@ RUSSIAN CANADIAN LEAGUE FOR CULTURAL RELATIONS INCORPORATED

@ CANADIAN SOCIETY FOR THE PROMOTION OF CULTURAL RELATIONS WITH RUSSIA

Page 155

15.6.26 6404 [2-3 words blacked out] U.L.F.T. Assocn. Port Arthur, Ont.

18.6.26 6405 I.W.W. Strike at Sunshine Ont.

6406 Conditions Amongst Ukrainians East Selkirk District Man.

(Correspondence [3-4 words blacked out]

6407 U.L.F.T. Association ???District Man.

19.6.26 6408 Strike at the New Immigration Sheds - Halifax, N.S.

6409 Strike of Civic Asphalt Scrapers Winnipeg, Man.

22.6.26 6410 Communist Party [2-3 words blacked out] Winnipeg Man.

6411 Chinese Information Bureau

6412 Education Workers International

Corresp. [3-4 words blacked out]

23.6.26 6413 Ukrainian Farmer Labour Temple [2-3 words blacked out] Ford City, Ont.

(Correspondence [3-4 words blacked out]

28.6.26 6414 " " " " " Yorkton Sask.

29.6.26 6415 One Big Union Ont.175/3203
6416 " " " Cobalt, Ont. BF 175/2490
5.7.26 6417 Canadian Labour Defence League Oshawa, Ont.
6.7.26 6418 One Big Union New Aberdeen, N.S.
10.7.26 6419 One Big Union New Waterford, N.S.
14.7.26 6420 Convention of Canadian Labor Party (Ontario Section) at Toronto, Ont. August 7, 1926
B.F. from 175/3745 [3-4 words blacked out]
19.7.26 6421 Trades & Labour Council, Edmonton, Alta.
6422 Convention of Paper Mill Union Workers at Fort William, Ont, June ?? 1926
23.7.26 6423 General Strike in Great Britain May 1926
Page 156
26.7.26 6424 Jewish Immigrant Aid Society
6425 Revolutionary Schools in Maritime Provinces
27.7.26 6426 United Farmers of Canada (Saskatchewan Section) continued [4-5 words blacked out]
6427 Progressive Farmers Educational League (Saskatchewan Section)
28.7.26 6428 Ku Klux Klan Orillia, Ont
29.7.26 6429 Strike of Amalgamated Clothing Workers, Montreal, P.Que.
6430 United Aid Committee for Strikers, Winnipeg, Man.
6431 Canadian Labour Defence League, Winnipeg, Man. [2-3 words blacked out]
3.8.26 6432 Strike of U.M.W. of A., Cape Breton, N.S. July 1926
6433 Labour Conditions at Beverly, Alta.
7.8.26 6434 London Labour Party, London, Ont.
9.8.26 6435 Communist Party of Canada [4-5 words blacked out]
11.8.26 6436 Industrial Workers of the World Sub.Act.. Within - Big Falls, Ont.
16;.8.26 6437 Ku Klux Klan. Fredericton, N.S.
24.8.26 6438 The Living Church
??.8.26 6439 One Big Union at Stellarton, N.S.
31.8.26 6440 Conditions among Ukrainians in Canmore Alta. District
7.9.26 6441 Communist Party Brandon, Man.
6442 One Big Union Thorburn, N.S.
6443 " " " Westville, N.S.
Page 157
7.9.26 6444 Canadian Labour Defence League, East Kildonan, Man.
13.9.26 6445 "De Fascio" Montreal, P.Que. [word blacked out]
23.9.26 6446 I.W.W. Strike Thunder Bay District, Ont.
27.9.26 6447 Revolutionary Propaganda Films [word blacked out]
27.9.26 6448 Workers Culture Society, Winnipeg, Man.
2.10.26 6449 Strike of Fur Workers, Winnipeg, Man.
11.10.26 6450 Workers Benevolent Association, Michel, B.C. [3-4 words blacked out]
6451 Workers Benevolent Association, Fernie, B.C. [4-5 words blacked out]

12.10.26 6452 Italian Contact & Connections in Canada
15.10.26 6453 Rationalist Society Winnipeg, Man.
16.10.26 6454 International Stationary Engineers, Union, Ontario
19.10.26 6455 Khalsa, Diwan Society, Vancouver, B.C. [2-3 words blacked out]
25.10.26 6456 Saskatchewan Grain Growers Association
28.10.26 6457 Visit of H.R.H. Queen Marie of Roumania to Canada, October 1926
29.10.26 6458 Communist Party of Canada, Brokenhead, Man.
30.10.26 6459 Workers Benevolent Society, Calgary, Alta [word blacked out]
6.11.26 6460 The Labour Research Bureau @ Labour Research Club
9.11.26 6461 Pseudonyms used by Revolutionaries
6462 Labour Conditions at Rouyn, P.Que.

Page 158

9.11.26 6463 General Conditions, Halifax, N.S.
19.11.26 6464 Labour Conditions at Northern Ontario [3-4 words blacked out]
13.12.26 6465 Communist Party of Canada Chealsea Falls, P.Que.
(Correspondence [3-4 words blacked out])
17.12.26 6466 Convention (Eight) Ukrainian Labour Farmer Temple Association, Winnipeg, Man., January 17th to 19th, 1927.
20.12.26 6467 Ukrainian Workmen's Benevolent Association, Winnipeg, Man. Third Convention Jan 21st to 22nd, 1927
27.12.26 6468 Mine Workers Union of Canada, Drumheller, Alta.
7.1.27 6469 Polish Labour Association Winnipeg, Man.
11.1.27 6470 Workers Benevolent Association [word blacked out] Wayne Dist Alta.
12.1.27 6471 Workers Benevolent Society, Portage la Prairie, Man. trans to 3 - 237
17.1.27 6472 Conditions in Finland [3-4 words blacked out]
6473 Section of Youth General (U.L.F.T.A.)
18.1.27 6474 Workers Benevolent Association, Kimberley, B.C.
6475 Conditions, Wasa B.C.
25.1.27 6476 Communist Party Ft. Francis, Ont (BF 175/703
26.1.27 6477 Conditions among Ukrainians, Vancouver, B.C.
[3-4 words blacked out]
7.2.27 6478 Workers Benevolent Association, Canmore, Alta.
9.2.27 6479 Workers Benevolent Association St. Boniface, Man.
14.2.27 6480 League against Cruelties and Oppression in the Colonies

Page 159

19.2.27 6481 Section of Youth Edmonton, Alta.
24.2.27 6482 Conditions among Italians in Canada [word blacked out]
25.2.27 6483 Conditions at Hanna, Alta.
28.2.27 6484 Ku Klux Klan Regina, Sask.
[3-4 words blacked out]
1.3.27 6485 Ukrainian Labour Farmer Temple Association, Thorhild, Alta.
[3-4 words blacked out]
4.3.27 6486 Workers Benevolent Association, Rosedale, Alta.

16.3.27 6487 Annual Convention, Canadian Labour Party,
Ontario Section at Hamilton, Ont. April 15th & 16th, 1927

21.3.27 6488 Canadian Labour Congress [2-3 words blacked out]

31.3.27 6489 Annual Convention, United Farmers of Canada, Saskatchewan Section

5.4.27 6490 I.K.O.R. (Jewish Colonization) to U.S.S.R. [3-4 words blacked out]

8.4.27 6491 Ukrainian Revolutionist Leader in Canada (Socvet Fyle)

12.4.27 6492 "Civil Molod" "The Youths World" (scratched out)

16.4.27 6492 Canadian Brotherhood of Railroad Engineers [3-4 words blacked out]

20.4.27 6493 Pan Pacific Labour Congress

(Correspondence [3-4 words blacked out])

25.4.29 6494 The Sixth Provincial Convention of the
Ukrainian Labour Farmer Temple Association,
Edmonton, Alta, April 14th 15th 16th 1926

27.4.27 6495 Hands off China Association Edmonton, Alta.

10.5.27 6496 Control by Soviet Russia of Emigrations of Polish Citizens to
Canada and the U.S.A.

Page 160

Corresp [3-4 words blacked out]

11.5.27 6497 Ukrainian Labour Farmer Temple Association Newcastle, Alta.

12.5.27 6498 Anonymous Letter written to L.K. Geores
(Official Agent Soviet Socialist Republics, Montreal, P. Que.
(Secret Fyle)

Transferred to [2-3 words blacked out]

13.5.27 6499 Ukrainian Labour Farmer Temple Association, Wayne Alta.

16.5.27 6500 Strike of the Structural Ironworkers (Plumbers, Steamfitters, etc)
Vancouver, B.C.

17.5.27 6501 Canadian Hungarian Sick Benefit Society Ont.

28.5.27 6502 "Hands off China"

30.5.27 6503 Canadian Labour Party Fernie, B.C.

31.5.27 6504 Bureau of Advice and Moral Assistance to Immigrants

6505 First Hamilton Hungarian Sick Benefit and Cultural Society
Hamilton, Ont.

4.6.27 6506 Ku Klux Klan Moose Jaw, Sask.

6507 Communist Party of Canada Montreal District Convention,
Montreal, P. Que May 15, 1927

7.6.27 6508 Club Educational ??? Canadian, Montreal, P. Que.

6509 Workers Benevolent Society, Rivers, Man.

6510 Workers Benevolent Society, Cadomin, Alta.

8.6.27 6511 "Hands of China" Council, Montreal, P. Que.

[3-4 words blacked out]

6512 5th National Convention of the Communist Party,
June 17th 18th 19th 1927 Toronto, Ont.

Page 161

16.6.27 6513 Convention Communist Party, District No. 3

18.6.27 6514 Condition among Hungarian & Czecho Slovakian Immigrants,

		Calgary, Alta.
21.6.27	6515	Radical School Portage la Prairie, Man.
24.6.27	6516	3rd Convention Workers Benevolent Society Winnipeg, Man. Jan 21st 22nd, 1927 [2-3 words blacked out]
27.6.27	6517	[entry blacked out]
11.7.27	6518	Young Communist League 4th Convention 1927 Toronto, Ont (Trans to 175/6556)
12.7.27	6519	Hindustani Young Men's Association, Vancouver, B.C.
20.7.27	6520	Workers's Sports & Gymnastic Association, Toronto, Ont.
9.8.27	6521	Sacco & Vanzetti [3-4 words blacked out]
12.8.27	6522	Canadian Labour Party Glace Bay, N.S.
16.8.27	6523	Trades & Labor Congress - Convention held in Edmonton, Alta Aug. 1927
16.8.27	6424	???????Institute, Saskatoon, Sask.
18.8.27	6525	Ku Klux Klan Biggar, Sask.
19.8.27	6526	Ukrainian Mandolin Orchestras N.S.F.T. Association
27.8.27	6527	Revolutionary & Subversive Activities Glace Bay, N.S.
27.8.27	6528	Radical School Beaver Lake, Ont.
30.8.27	6529	Canadian Punjabi Women's Society
	6530	Black Party

Page 162

2.9.27	6531	Radical School Sylvan Lake, Alta.
15.9.27	6532	Ku Klux Klan Swift Current, Sask.
20.9.27	6533	Ku Klux Klan Shaunvon, Sask.
26.9.27	6534	General Conditions Cluny Alta Dist.
27.9.27	6535	First National Convention Canadian Labour League Toronto, Ont Oct. 29th 1927 [2-3 words blacked out]
30.9.27	6536	[entry blacked out]
4.10.27	6536	General Conditions, Shepard, Alta. Dist.
11.10.27	6537	Ku Klux Klan, Weyburn, Sask.
	6538	Strike of Carpenters, Toronto, Ont.
14.10.27	6539	Youth Section, Ottawa, Ont.
17.10.27	6540	General Conditions amongst harvesters
18.10.27	6541	Communist Party in [3-4 words blacked out]
21.10.27	6542	Labor Forum Edmonton, Alta.
24.10.27	6543	Coal Miners Strike (M.W.U. of C.) Drumheller, Alta.
	6544	Labour, Forum Toronto, Ont.
	6545	Young Communist League, Wolf Siding, Ont. [word blacked out]
3.11.27	6546	Earlscourt Labour Party Toronto, Ont [word blacked out] (all scratched out)
12.11.27	6547	North End Labour Club, Montreal, P. Que.
17.11.27	6458	McGill Labour Club, Montreal, P. Que. [3-4 words blacked out]

Page 163

5.12.27	6549	Ku Klux Klan, Melville, Sask.

10.12.27 6550 Brethrens Help (Polish National & Humanitarian Society, Pointe St. Charles, P.Q. (Some Communist Infiltration)

12.12.27 6551 Ku Klux Klan, New Brunswick

Corresp. [2-3 words blacked out]

6552 Ukrainian Labour Temple Association, Fernie, B.C.

6553 Conditions amongst Foreigners at Hyas, Sask.

13.12.27 6554 Conditions amongst Foreigners, Meath Park Sask.

(2-3 words blacked out]

22.12.27 6555 Ukrainian Workers Benevolent Association, Montreal, P. Que.

[2-3 words blacked out]

6556 4th National Convention Young Communist League at Toronto June 22-23 1927

24.17.27 6557 Communists Funerals General

30.12.27 6558 Workers Benevolent Society, Ottawa, Ont. [2-3 words blacked out]

3.1.28 6559 All Canadian Labour Congress, Calgary, Alta.

[3-4 words blacked out]

6560 Communist Party Kimberley, B.C.

4.1.28 6561 Ninth National Convention of U.L.F.L. Transferred to 175/6575

7.1.28 6562 Slovene Benefit Association New Waterford, N.S.

10.11.28 6563 4th Convention W.B.A. Winnipeg, Man. Jan 26 & 27 1928

6564 Womens Labour League, Montreal, P.Que.

Corresp [2-3 words blacked out]

13.1.28 6565 U.L.F.T. ?????, Alta.

[3-4 words blacked out]

30.1.28 6566 Workers Benevolent Association, London, Ont.

Transferred [2-3 words blacked out]

6567 Workers Benevolent Association Lachine, P. Que.

11.2.28 6568 Ukrainian Flood Relief

Page 164

16.2.28 6569 Workers Benevolent Society, Port Colborne, Ont.

6570 " " " , Red Deer, Alta.

6571 [3-4 words blacked out] , Welland, Ont.

6572 " " " , Ford City, Ont.

6573 [entry blacked out]

17.2.28 6574 Counter Communist Propaganda General File

(Correspondence [2-3 words blacked out]

18.2.28 6575 9th Convention Ukrainian Labour Farmers Temple Asscn. BF 175/6561

21.2.28 6576 Workers Benevolent Society Bellevue, Alta.

27.2.28 6577 Conditions amongst Serbs in Canada

6578 [2-3 words blacked out] Vancouver, B.C. [2-3 words blacked out]

3.3.28 6579 Workers Sports & Gymnastic Association

5.3.28 6580 Conditions amongst Italians, Calgary, Alta.

6581 B.C. Miners Association General BF 175/6725

6.3.28 6582 Canadian Labour Defence League, Ukrainian Branch
8.3.28 6583 Strike of Cloth (scratched out) Edmonton, Alta.
8.3.28 6583 Strike of Clothing Workers, Toronto, Ont.
9.3.28 6584 Communist Party Sokl, B.C.
10.3.28 6585 Ku Klux Klan Wolseley, Sask.
6586 Workers Benevolent Society Coniston, Ont.
6587 " " " Lusean, Alta.

Page 165

[3-4 words blacked out]
10.3.28 6588 Workers Benevolent Society Ansonville, Ont. (scratched out)
[4-5 words blacked out]
6589 " " " Toronto, Ont.
[2-3 words blacked out]
6590 " " " Vegreville, B.C.
6591 " " " Anoyx, B.C.
6592 [3-4 words blacked out] Sudbury, Ont.
6593 Workers Benevolent Society, Levach, Ont.
[2-3 words blacked out] Corresp trans to [blacked out]
6594 " " " Hillcrest, Alta.
6595 [3-4 words blacked out] Association Branstford, Ont.
6596 " " " Kirkland Lake, Ont.
6597 " " " Kenora, Ont.
(BF from 175/6572) [3-4 words blacked out]
6598 " " " Windsor, Ont.
corresp [3-4 words blacked out]
16.3.28 6599 Ukrainian Labor Farmer Temple Association, South Porcupine, Ont.
(Correspondence Trans. to [blacked out])
6600 " " St. Catherines, Ont.
17.3.28 6601 Ku Klux Klan Brandon, Man.
27.3.28 6602 One Big Union, Northern Ontario
28.3.28 6603 Coal Miners Strike, Canmore Mine, Alta.
6604 Young Pioneers Hamilton, Ont.
29.3.28 6605 Agents of Revolutionary Organisations in the R.C.M.Police [word blacked out]
30.3.28 6606 Young Pioneers Toronto, Ont
Correspondence [3-4 words blacked out]
2.4.28 6607 Canadian Labour Defence League Vancouver, B.C.

Page 166

[3-4 words blacked out]
7.4.28 6608 Young Pioneers, Vancouver, B.C.
10.4.28 6609 Canadian Labour Defence League, Lettonia, Man.
11.4.28 6610 Railroad Shop Convention Winnipeg, Man.
12.4.28 6611 Automobile Workers Industrial Union, Oshawa, Ont. (A.F. of L.)

13.4.28 6612 Ninth Annual Convention, Canadian Labour Party, Ontario Section, Toronto, Ont.

[2-3 words blacked out]

14.4.28 6613 Canadian Labour Defence League, Lethbridge, Alta.

16.4.28 6614 Communist Party of Canada, Vidir, Man.

20.4.28 6615 Ku Klux Klan, Souris, Man.

[5-6 words blacked out]

6616 Workers Publishing Association 1632 Church St. Toronto, Ont.

23.4.28 6617 Ku Klux Klan Estevan, Sask.

25.4.28 6618 Ukrainian Labour Farmer Temple Association ???????

6619 Workers Benevolent Society - Nakinia - Ont.

6620 Communist Party [4-5 words blacked out] Montreal, P. Que.

[3-4 words blacked out]

27.4.28 6621 Canadian Labour Defence League - Regina, Sask.

30.4.28 6622 Canadian Labour Defence League, Brandon, Man.

6623 International Bible Students Ass. Brandon, Man. BF from 175/1139

[3-4 words blacked out]

9.5.28 6624 Canadian Labour Defence League, Montreal, P.Que.

11.5.28 6625 The Labor Club Edmonton, Alta

12.5.28 6626 Communist Party Finland, Ont. [word blacked out]

Page 167

14.5.28 6627 Vancouver & District Waterfront Workers Association

Corresp [2-3 words blacked out]

18.5.28 6628 Ukrainian Labour Farmer Temple Assn. Sokl, B.C.

6629 Ku Klux Klan Broadview, Sask.

(Correspondence [2-3 words blacked out]

6630 Canadian Labour Defence League Hamilton, Ont.

6631 Strike of Structural Iron Workers Toronto, Ont.

19.5.28 6632 Revolutionary & Subversive Activies in Vancouver, B.C. May 28th, 1928

28.5.28 6633 Canadian Labour Defense League, Port Colborne, Ont.

[3-4 words blacked out]

6.6.28 6634 Peretz Jewish Workers School Calgary (Jewish ???????

7.6.28 6635 Sons of Freedom, Grand Fork, B.C. (scratched out) (Continued on [blacked out]

8.6.28 6636 Trade Union Educational League, Montreal, P. Que.

9.6.28 6637 Youths Section " "

11.6.28 6628 United Mine Workers of America, Rosedale, Alta.

6639 Mine Workers Union of Canada, Wayne, Alta.

6640 Strike of Carpenters Calgary, Alta.

18.6.28 6641 Workers Benevolent Association (Katsuskasena, (scratched out)

21.6.28 6642 Communist Party [4-5 words blacked out] Montreal, P.Que.

4.7.28 6643 [entry blacked out]

9.7.28 6644 Canadian Labor Defense League Fort William Ont. Dist.

16.6.28 6645 Strike of the employees of the Dominion Rubber Co. Ltd., Montreal, P. Que.

Page 168

21.7.28 6646 Mine Workers Union of Canada, Westville, N.S.

6647 Conditions Among Foreigners Shore Lake, Sask.

6648 Ku Klux Klan, Fernie, B.C.

[3-4 words blacked out]

4.8.28 6649 Radical School Holalu, Ont.

7.8.28 6650 Conditions in India [3-4 words blacked out]

18.6.28 6651 Anti-Japan Association

20.8.28 6652 Coal Miners Strike (North American Collieries) Coalhurst, Alta. 1928

21.8.28 6653 National Association of Canada

25.8.28 6654 Strike of Coal Miners (1928) Wayne Alta. Mine Workers ??/ of Canada

6655 Industrial Union of All Needle Trade Workers of Canada

(new name) Peoples Co-Operative Ass'n. [2-3 words blacked out]

31.8.28 6656 @ Workers Farmers Co-Operative Association

Chinese Nationalist League [2-3 words blacked out]

1.9.28 6657 @Kuo Min Tang Edmonton, Alta.

[word blacked out]

5.9.28 6658 Workers & Farmers Publishing Co., Winnipeg, Man.

10.9.28 6659 Communist Activities amongst British Harvesters

6660 Communist Party Winnipeg, Man.

6660 Communist Party Shawinigan Falls, P.Que.

[2-3 words blacked out]

6661 Communist Party, Three Rivers, P.Que.

[4-5 words blacked out]

6662 Ukrainain Self Reliance League of Canada

11.9.28 Young Communist League, Windsor, Ont.

Page 169

[3-4 words blacked out]

12.9.28 6664 Convention Trades and Labour Congress, Toronto, Ont. 1928

18.9.28 6665 Conditions at Calgary Power Co., ?????Alta. Dist.

6666 Labour News Stand, Edmonton, Alta.

6667 Ku Klux Klan, Jasper, Alta.

19.9.28 6668 3rd Convention Mine Workers Assn. of Canada District No. 1

[2-3 words blacked out]

20.9.28 6669 Radical School North Branch, Ont.

22.9.28 6670 Communist Activities amongst British Harvesters Calgary, Alta. Dist.

24.9.28 6671 Young Communist League [3-4 words blacked out] Winnipeg, Man.

[3-4 words blacked out]

26.9.28 6672 Communist Party [3-4 words blacked out] Montreal

[304 words blacked out]

5.10.28 6673 Canadian Labour Defence League, Timmins, Ont.

9.10.28 6674 Canadian Labour Defence League Fort William, Ont. (scratched out)

17.10.28 6674 Workers Benevolent Association Medicine Hat, Alta.
[3-4 words blacked out]

6675 Workers Benevolent Association, The Pas, Man.
[2-3 words blacked out]

6676 Communist Party, The Pas. Man.

7.11.28 6677 Strike of Carpenters Fernie, B.C.
Corresp [2-3 words blacked out]

19.11.28 6678 Ukrainian Labour Farmer Temple Association Rosedale, Alta.

Page 170

26.22.28 6679 Canadian Labour Party Convention 1928 Calgary, Alta.

26.11.28 6680 Doukhobour Sons of Freedom Transferred to 175/6635
[2-3 words blacked out]

30.11.28 6682 Manuel of Intelligence of the Chinese Communist Party
corresp. [3-4 blacked out]

7.12.28 6683 Ukrainian Labour Farmer Temple Brandon, Man.

6684 Convention Young Pioneers at Toronto, Ont Dec 29th & 30th (1928)
[3-4 words blacked out]

27.12.28 6685 Communist Party of Canada [2-3 words blacked out] Hamilton, Ont.
Correspondence [2-3 words blacked out]

11/1/29 6686 9th Convention (Alta & B.C.)
Ukrainian Labour Farmer Temple Association Edmonton, Alta. Dec 1929
[3-4 words blacked out]

5.1.29 6687 Socialist Labour Party Ford City, Ont.

10.1.29 6688 Workers Benevolent Association Cote St. Paul, P.Que.

23.1.29 6689 I.W.W. Eckville, Alta.
corresp [2-3 words blacked out]

6690 Young Communist League, Calgary, Alta.
[3-4 words blacked out]

28.1.29 6691 Ukrainian Labour Farmer Temple Association Stoney Creek, Sask.

31.1.29 6692 Agreneva-Slaviansky Choir

1.2.29 6693 Ku Klux Klan Wadena, Sask.

Page 171

[4-5 words blacked out]

14.2.29 6694 Workers Benevolent Association Glace Bay, N.S.

6695 American Vigilantes Association

15.2.29 6696 Ukrainian Labour Farmer Temple Association [4-5 words blacked out]
Warshite, Alta.

25.2.29 6697 Workers Benevolent Society Convention Winnipeg, 1929
(Correspondence [2-3 words blacked out])

26.2.29 6698 Communist Party [2-3 words blacked out] Canmore, Alta.
(Correspondence [2-3 words blacked out]

27.2.29 6699 Convention Ukrainian Labour Farmer Temple Assn. 1928 Winnipeg, 10th

6700 Conditions among Japanese, Vancouver, B.C.

Correspondence [2-3 words blacked out]

7.3.29 6701 Ukrainain Labour Farmer Temple Assn. Brantford, Ont.

14.3.29 6702 Strike at Firth Bros. Ltd., Hamilton, Ont.

18.3.29 6703 Ku Klux Klan, Lovema, Sask.

[2-3 words blacked out]

20.2.29 6704 Communist Party ????? Lake, Alta.

25.3.29 6705 Latish Labour Club Edmonton, Alta.

4.4.29 6706 Needle Trades Industrial Union, Montreal, P.Que.

5.4.29 6707 Ku Klux Klan, Aberdeen, Sask.

[2-3 words blacked out]

122.4.29 6708 Young Communist League [3-4 words blacked out] Montreal, P.Que.

corresp [3-4 words blacked out]

6709 Ukrainian Labour Farmer Temple Assn, Rouyn P.Que.

15/4/29 6710 Counter Communist Propaganda, Toronto, Ont.

29.4.29 6711 Mine Workers Union Corbin, B.C.

Page 172

29.4.29 6712 Canadian Labour Defence League, Coleman, Alta.

6713 Workers Benevolent Society Cranbrook, B.C.

[3-4 words blacked out]

4.5.29 6714 Ukrainian Labour Farmer Temple Assn. Weasel Creek, Alta.

8.5.29 6715 Rationalist Society, Toronto, Ont.

Corresp. [3-4 words blacked out]

22.5.29 6716 Communist Party Convention, Toronto, Ont. 1929

28.5.29 6717 Ku Klux Klan McDowall, Sask.

Strike of Crew of Burrell and Baird Ltd. Bear Creek, YT.
[2-3 words blacked out]

31.5.29 6718 Ukrainian Militant Organization

5.6.29 6719 Workers Benevolent Assn. Shawinigan Falls, P.Que.

6720 Workers Benevolent Assn. Three Rivers, P.Que.

7.6.29 6721 Ku Klux Klan Radville, Sask.

13.6.29 6722 Ku Klux Klan Melfort, Sask.

17.6.29 6723 Canmore Sick Benefit Society Canmore, Alta.

[2-3 words blacked out]

22.6.29 6724 Lumber Workers International Union, Ft. William, Ont.

11.7.29 6725 British Columbia Miners Association Trans to 175/1581

22.7.29 6726 Ku Klux Klan Vermilion, Alta.

26.7.29 6727 Sons of Freedom, Kamsack Dist. Sask.

29.7.29 6728 Ku Klux Klan Alberta

Page 173

28.8.29 6729 Workers League ??? Syndicate, Montreal, P.Que.
31.8.29 6730 International Seamen's Club, Vladivostock, Siberia
6731 Ku Klux Klan Maritime Provinces
9.9.29 6732 Radical School Calgary, Alta.
[3-4 words blacked out]
12.9.29 6733 Co-operative Movement Fort William, Ont.
16.9.29 6734 National Steel Car Corporation Strike at Hamilton, Ont (1929)
18.9.29 6735 Convention Mine Workers Union of Canada (1929)
19.9.29 6736 Ku Klux Klan Richmond, Ont.
23.9.29 6737 Bursary Edmonton, Alta.
[2-3 words blacked out]
6738 Polish Labour Temple Winnipeg, Man.
24.9.29 6739 Mine Workers Union of Canada Rosedale, Alta.
9.10.29 6740 Ukrainian Labour Farmer Temple Assn. Kaleland, Alta.
[3-4 words blacked out]
6741 " " " " " , Spring Creek, Alta.
[3-4 words blacked out]
6742 " " " " " , Pakan, Alta.
[3-4 words blacked out]
6743 " " " " " , Smoky Lake, Alta.
[4-5 words blacked out]
11/10.29 6744 " " " " " , Zawale, Alta.
6745 corresp transf to [blacked out]
6746 " " " " " , Trimula, Alta.
6747 corresp [2-3 words blacked out] Slaina, Alta.
6748 " " " " " , Two Hills, Alta.
Page 174
[2-3 words blacked out]
11/10/29 6749 Ukrainian Labour Farmer Temple Assn. Wyman, Alta.
6750 " " " " " (Stubno, Alta.
Correspondence [2-3 words blacked out]
6751 " " " " " Mussdorte, Alta.
Correspondence [2-3 words blacked out]
6752 " " " " " Lake Eliza, Alta.
[4-5 words blacked out]
15.10.29 6753 " " " " " Vermillion, Alta.
Corresp [2-3 words blacked out]
6754 " " " " " Derwent, Alta.
6755 Needle Trade Industrial Union Toronto, ont.
[4-5 words blacked out]
21.10.29 6756 Ukrainian Labour Farmer Temple Assn. Waskatanan, Alta.
Corresp [2-3 words blacked out]
6757 Ukrainian Labour Farmer Temple Assn. Banfurly, Alta.

[3-4 words blacked out]

6758 " " " " " , Edward, Alta.

6759 Communist Party of Canada Hallo Lake, Alta.

25.10.29 6760 Strike at Tom Falls Lumber Camp, Shabayna, P.Que.

5.11.29 6761 Mine Workers Union of Canada, East Couley, Alta.

[3-4 words blacked out]

8.11.29 6762 Workers Benevolent Society, Saskatoon, Sask.

18.11.29 6763 Ku Klux Klan Hudson Bay Junction, Sask.

11.12.29 6764 Unemployed Organization Vancouver, B.C.

16.12.29 6765 Communist Party of Canada Eckville, Alta. Dist.

19.12.29 6766 Co-operative Farming Association

27.12.29 6767 Building and Construction Workers Industrial Union Sudbury, Ont.

{age 175

[3-4 words blacked out]

11/1/30 6768 Canadian Labour Defence League, Ottawa, Ont.

Corresp [3-4 words blacked out]

11/1/30 6769 Ukrainian Farmer Temple Assn. Willingdon, Alta.

16/1/30 6770 Communist Party of Canada Stensen, Sask.

[4-5 words blacked out]

17.1.30 6771 University ?????Montreal, P.Que Sub. Activities in

6772 Unemployed Workers Association, Toronto, Ont.

18.1.30 6773 Unemployed Organization, Calgary, Alta.

Conditions at Robsart Sask, sec 30 B-1-G-135

29.1.30 6774 Garment Workers Strike, Toronto, Ont.

3.2.30 6775 Unemployed Workers Association, Windsor, Ont.

corresp [2-3 words blacked out]

4.2.30 6776 Unemployed Workers Association, Edmonton, Alta.

[2-3 words blacked out]

5.2.30 6777 United Farmers Association General

(Correspondence [3-4 words blacked out]

6778 Workers Benevolent Assn Russian Montreal

14.2.30 6779 Mine Workers Union of Canada Convention Calgary, Alta 1930

HRVATSKA BRATSKA ZAJEDNICA continued [blacked out]

17.2.30 6780 Croation Fraternal Union

(Correspondence [3-4 words blacked out]

18.2.30 6781 Ukrainian Labour Farmer Temple Ass. 11th Convention, Winnipeg, Man.

21.2.30 6782 Communist Party of Canada, Ferguson Flats, Alta.

[2-3 words blacked out]

6783 Canadian Labour Defence League, Niagara Falls, Ont.

27.2.30 6784 Canadian Labour Defence League, Brantford, Ont.

6785 Unemployed Workers Association, Port William, Ont.

Page 176

2.3.30 6786 Communist in the Canadian Army Transferred to 175/6898

Agent of Revolutionary Organizations in Canadian Forces (scratched out)

4.3.30 6787 Young Communist League Lethbridge, Alta.
Trans to [blacked out]

14.3.30 6788 Communist Party Nipigon, Ont.
[3-4 words blacked out]

15.3.30 6789 Canadian Labour Defence League, Blairmore, Alta.

17.3.30 6790 Canadian Labour Defence League, Bellevue, Alta.

6791 Ukrainian Prosvita Hall Ft. William, Ont.
Correspondence transferred to

18.3.30 6792 [entry blacked out]

22.3.30 6793 Unemployed Workers Assn. Hamilton, Ont.
corresp [2-3 words blacked out]

25.3.30 6794 Unemployed Workers Assn. Winnipeg, Man.

28.3.30 6795 Mine Workers Union of Canada, Calgary, Alta.

31.3.30 6796 Communist Party of Canada Red Water, Alta Trans from 175/3294

6797 Ukrainians at Red Water, Alta. (scratched out)

4.4.30 6797 Radical Schools, Medicine Hat, Alta.

8.3.30 6798 Communist Party Meadow Portage, Man.

6799 Communist Party, Rook???

11.4.30 6800 Labour Conditions Unemployment Lethbridge, Alta.
Threatening letter received by James Rielley Griffin, Sask.
[2- [2-3 words blacked out]

28.4.30 6801 Communist Parties, Foam Lake, Sask.

Page 177

5.4.30 6802 Communist Party of Canada Moricona, Man.

Steel Workers Industrial Union @ Steel Workers Industrial Union

8.5.30 6803 @ Industrial Metal Workers Union Hamilton, Ont.
@ Canadian Steel Workers [2-3 words blacked out]
@ National Steel Workers Union of Canada

12.5.30 6804 Communist Party ??? Alta

13.5.30 6805 Communist Party Blairmore, Alta.

20.5.30 6806 Canadian Labour Defence Convention, Eastern Division
Hamilton, Ont 1930

20.5.30 6807 Conditions among Italians Montreal, P.Que.

6808 Revolutionary Music
[3-4 words blacked out]

21.5.30 6809 Communist Party Niagara on the Lake, Ont.

6810 Communist Party, ?????Sask.
[3-4 words blacked out]

27.5.30 6811 Workers Unity League, Toronto, Ont.

9.6.30 6812 Conditions at Coalshaw, Alta.
Bolshevik Public Meetings, Hufford, ???? of
Blaine Lake, Sask. 30B/G184

11.6.30 6813 Communist Party of Canada, Vancouver, B.C.

16.6.30 6814 Lumber & Agriculture Workers Industrial Union (W.U.L.) Winnipeg, Man.

24.6.30 6815 Womens Labour League [3-4 words blacked out] B.C.

30.6.30 6816 Communist Party of Canada St. Anns, Ont.

2.7.30 6817 Trade & Labour Congress, Ottawa, Ont.

Page 178

9.7.30 6818 Workers Unity League, Hamilton

6819 Canadian Womens Delegatation to Russia (July 1930)

16.7.30 6820 Canadian Atheist Assn. Winnipeg, Man.

18.7.30 6821 Communist Party ????Mountain, Sask.

Kelly's Gravel Camp Langenbury, Sask. See 30B800 G.11

26.7.30 6822 Auxiliary Company of Canada Ltd. Toronto, Ont.

29.7.30 6823 Workers Educational League Winnipeg, Man.
Transferred to 175/6820 [word blacked out]

6.8.30 6824 Coal Miners Strike at Montreal, P.Que

[2-3 words blacked out]

6825 Workers Educational Assn. General

7.8.30 6826 Labour Conditions Flin Flon, Man.

[5-6 words blacked out] see 30B500-G366

18.8.30 6829 Communist Party Sweden [3-4 words blacked out]

29.8.30 6828 Young Communist League Hamilton, Ont.

25.8.30 6829 Foreign Propaganda in Canada

2.9.30 6830 Lumber & Agriculture Industrial Union Port Arthur, Ont.

8.9.30 6831 Young Pioneers, Regina, Sask.

[3-4 words blacked out]

12.9.30 6832 Young Communists League, Moose Jaw, Sask.

[3-4 words blacked out]

13.9.30 6833 Labour Conditions Canmore, Alta.

Page 179

13.9.30 6834 Workers Unity League Calgary, Alta.

Corresp [3-4 words blacked out]

22.9.30 6835 Ukrainian Labor Farmer Temple Assn, Michel, B.C.

corresp [3-4 words blacked out]

25.9.30 6836 Ukrainian Labour Farmer Temple Assn. St. Boniface, Man.

[2-3 words blacked out]

30.9.30 6837 Labour Conditions Fernie, B.C.

[3-4 words blacked out]

3.10.30 6838 Communist Party of Canada Winnipeg [2-3 words blacked out]

6.10.30 6839 Workers Educational Assn. Calgary, Alta.
Transferred to 175/6825

9.10.30 6840 Workers Educational Assn. Ottawa, Ont.
Strike at Kelly's Gravel Camp Langenbury, Saks.
see 30B1-G292

31.10.30 6841 Conditions at Pottsville, Ont.

3.11.30 6842 Workers Unity League Port Arthur Ont, & Fort William

6843 Council of the Plenipotentiary Representative of
The Organization of Autonomous Siberia

6844 Canadian Defenders [3-4 words blacked out]

5.11.30 6845 Workers International Relief Assn. Hamilton, Ont.

20.11.30 6846 Young Communist League Dinsmore, Sask.

[2-3 words blacked out]

24.11.30 6847 Workers Unity League [word blacked out]

6847 supp History of [4-5 words blacked out]

28.11.30 6848 Communist Party Canora, Sask.

1.12.30 6849 Communist Party General [2-3 words blacked out]

5.12.30 6850 Polish Information Bureau

Page 180

[3-4 words blacked out]

8.12.30 6851 Communist Party Quebec P.Que.

16.12.30 6852 " " Wiseton, Sask.

6853 Farmers Unity League (Farmers & Labour Unity League)

corresp transf [word blacked out]

22.12.30 6854 Farmer and Labour Unity League Edmonton, Alta.

(Correspondence [3-4 words blacked out]

6855 Unemployed Workers Assn. Lethbridge

6856 Communist Party Macrorie, Sask.

23.12.30 6857 Transport and Marine Workers of Cnaada

26.12.30 6858 Young Pioneers Rouyn, P.Que.

29.12.30 6859 Canadian Labour Defence League. North Bay, Ont.

2.1.31 6860 Workers Unity League [word blacked out] Winnipeg, Man.

7.1.31 6861 Lumber and Agriculture Workers Union (W.U.L.) Vermilion River, Ont.

[3-4 words blacked out] see 31B.1150-G11

9.1.31 6862 Communist Party [word blacked out] New Zealand

School Act. Danbury & Glen Elder Dist. Sask. see 31B487-G6

14/1/31 6863 Communist Party [word blacked out] Hop???ayne, Ont.

[3-4 words blacked out]

15.1.31 6864 Ukrainian Labour Farmer Temple Glen-Elder, Sask.

21.1.31 6865 Communist Party Northern Alta BF 175/743

6866 " " Shorncliffe, Man.

24.1.31 6867 Ukrainian Labour Farmer Association Sokl, B.C.
Transferred to 175/???

26.1.31 6868 Communist Party [2-3 words blacked out] Saskatchewan

PART 5: RCMP REGISTER OF SUBVERSIVE PUBLICATIONS, 1919-1929

No. 177 Classification: Literature

Page 033

1 Fred O. Fulker In Poss of Proh Lit.
2 Arkin John Isaac -do- (Trans to 175P/1058)
3 Littlebooks Library Series
(1) The Poison in America's Cup
(2) Whats the Matter with our America
4 Western Labour News, Winnipeg, Man.
5 Reid Roy Alleged Possession of Proh Lit
(B.F. from 175/336)
6 Ukrainian Labour News, Winnipeg, Man.
7 The Statesman, Edmonton, Alta.
8 O.B.U. Bulletin [2-3 words blacked out] Winnipeg, Man.
9 Searchlight, Calgary, Alta.
10 Miss Vivian Wheatley, I.B.S.A. Proh Lit
11 Baboychuk, P. Possession of -do-
12 Hermanson, Ed. Poss of Proh Lit
13 Mrs. Geo Bruce, I.B.S.A. Proh Lit
14 Williams, J.B. -do-
15 Der Courier
16 "Zukumft" (Future) - Yiddish Newspaper
17 Norquay, Alice, I.B.S.A. Proh Lit
18 Johnson Elizabeth M. -do-
19 Ream, Elizabeth M. -do-
20 Ward, S.A. Mrs. -do-

Page 032

21 Young, Geo. -do-
22 Brodie, G.H. I.B.S.A. Poss of Proh Lit
23 Kinna, Henry Poss of Proh Lit
24 Sturritt, Geo. -do-
25 Young, Geo. I.B.S.A. -do- transferred to 175/1743
26 Dakota Frie Presse
27 Golden Age I.B.S.A. Paper
28 Knight, Roy Poss Proh Lit

29	Morrison, Wm.	-do-		
30	Mason, A.	-do-		
31	Armstrong, Mrs. A.	-do-	I.B.S.A.	(175/1586)
32	Morrison N. Mrs.	-do-	-do-	"
33	Kerr, Bessie	-do-	"	"
34	Thompson, James	-do-	"	"
35	Beiston, Frank	-do-	"	"
36	Patterson, Lorne	-do-	"	"
37	Thornton, T.J.	-do-	x	x
38	Yuill, Archie	-do-	175/1586	
39	Mawson, M. Miss	-do-	"	
40	Hobson, F.W.	-do-		

Page 031

41 Indicator (Vancouver, B.C.)
42 Morrison, Vincent -do-
43 Gunus, Andy
44 Knox, B. -do-
45 Dana & Peterson Districts, Sask. Suspected Prohibited Publications BF from 175/1562
46 Ludlow A.E. re Return of Banned Literature
47 Voice of Labour See 177/74 - 2/2/22 J.B.
48 Burton, John Proh Lit in poss Trans to 175P/476
49 Taylor, Mrs. B. IBSA Proh Lit
50 "Jack Canuck" Paper trans
51 Fielding, T.H. In poss Lit "Golden Age" Selling same
52 I.B.S.A. Maple Creek, Sask.
53 ?????????
54 Smuggling Prohibited Literature
55 Der Nordwestern - German Newspaper [3-4 words blacked out]
56 "Molot"
57 Charles K. Kerr & Co. Publishers of Socialistic Lit. at Chicago
58 Sandusky Register from Sandusky, Ohio, U.S.A.
59 Clarkson, Wm. In poss. of Proh. Lit.
60 Hoebel, F.A. German Publications in mail addressed to

Page 030

61 Spector Samuel Smuggling Seditious Lit. from U.S.A.
62 Mojsiuk, D. Ukrainian Labour News Correspondence
63 Wasglow, F. -do0
64 I.W.W. Literature Issued from Chicago thro mail Transferred to 177/82

65	Carrol, J.D.	Pro. Literature thro' mail	Russky Golos
66	Misonuk, D.	" " " "	do
67	Houch, C.	" " " "	do
68	Kozak, D.	" " " "	do

69	Shandro, J.	"	"	"	"	do
70	Plexen, A.	"	"	"	"	do
71	Lesenko, J.	"	"	"	"	do
72	Rebalkin, S.	"	"	"	"	do
73	Koukin, J.	"	"	"	"	do
74	Voice of Labour, etc.					
75	Usonick, A.	Pro. Lit. thro' mail				Russky Golos
76	Smalin, M.	"	"	"	"	do
77	Pojalow, B.	"	"	"	"	do
78	Novinka, W.	"	"	"	"	do
79	Kishenkoff, J.	"	"	"	"	do
80	Doeff, M.	"	"	"	"	do

Page 029

81 Cyancheff, M.
82 Prohibited Publications Intercepted by P.O. Dept & Forwarded to R.C.M. Police
83 Hardy, Stephen Proh. Pub. in possession of
84 Loague, Steve -do-
85 St. John, N.B. - Union Worker
86 Mitchell, L. Proh. Lit I.W.W. thro' mail
87 Sawchuk, Alexander Proh Pub. in poss. of.
Brought Foward to 177/75
88 Prohibited Lit. seized by Customs, Winnipeg (In Kempf geger dir Russia 19-14-18
89 The Statesman - Toronto, Ont.
90 O.B.U. Bulletin (Published in Oakland - California)
91 Cozachy, S. Proh Lit - 19-4-20
92 Bowsk, Max Proh seditious Lit.
Rosco Alec -do-
93 "The Trial of Eugene Debs" by Max Eastman 14/9/20
94 Russia, N. Lenin
95 Kosak or Kozak Proh. Publication
96 Trudovaya Misl - "Labors Thought"
97 Khlieb.I.Volia - "Bread & Freedom"
98 Pulutsky, Steve Proh Pub in possession of
99 Literature at Sudbury, Ont.
100 To the Young Labourer Proh Pub.

Page 028

101 Tarros A.D. Proh Lit.
102 Mickalouski, Harry Pro Literature
103 Olesuk, Fred Proh Pub in possession of
104 Sakovich, Bill Pro. Literature
105 Samcoe Prof Lit
106 The Waker -do-

107 Western Calrion -do-
108 Proh Lit. Ford City & Walkerville, Ont
109 Ottawa Citizen - Clippings from
110 Saskatoon, Sask. Dist of Anarchist Literature
111 Degtiruk, Fred Alleged smuggling of Proh. Lit from
112 Manitoba Free Press
113 The Week
114 The Revolt
115 The Liberator
116 Moose Jaw, Sak. O.B.U. Literature at C.P.R. Sheds
117 The Worker
118 Cobalt Daily Nugget
(B.F. 177/514)
119 Tie Vapauteen Publication
120 William, Suon Pro. Pub'n

Page 027

121 Nouseva Pamphlet
122 Winnipeg Strike Leaders Aims of
122A Gales Revolutionary Papers
123 The New Republic Publ.
124 Halifax Citizen -do- (Trans to 313)
125 Punanen Soihtics Red Torch Proh Pub.
126 "Can pay its way" - The Irish Republic Prince George Dist.
Strike in Cancelled
127 Communist Labour
128 Towards Soviets
129 Montreal Shopman - O.B.U. Newspaper
130 Volma or "Wave" - Russian Publication
131 Chand Amer Vancouver B.C. Hindustani Literature
Consigned to Seized by Customs of Vancouver
132 Indian against Britain - Booklet
133 Tarikni Hind Indian Publication
134 India in Revolt & Invincible India Leaflets

July 26 135 The Labor News - Cranbrook, B.C.
136 Foreign Press in Canada - List of
Foreign Press Publishers in Canada List of -
137 Moc Ducha - Foreign Publication
29 138 Russian Library in O.B.U. Hall, Toronto, Ont.
139 Bodnar, Joe Rec'd Sus. Lit

Page 026

July 29 140 English Atrocities in Ireland - Publication
Aug 19 141 North West Review
142 Literature - Hamilton
23 143 Bullitt Missions to Russia

24 144 Miscellaneous Irish Literature
Sept 8 145 Romanovick, P. Lit
9 146 Raatajain Lauliya, Pub. Venajan Vallan Kumaus
Bolshevismi -do-Sovietti Tasavalba
13 147 The Awakener - Pamphlet
148 Fairplay Humorous Publication - Vancouver
17 149 O.B.U. Misc. Literature
22 150 Good Morning Publ.
23 151 Currie John, Proh. Lit. Windsor, Ont. Webber Aaron
(Correspondence [blacked out])
24 152 Literature at Toronto, Ont.
25 153 Error of Judgement - Hindu Pamphlet
28 154 Ahjo - The Forge - Publication
155 Labour Laws of Soviet Russia & Two Years of
Foreign Policy - Publications
Oct 1 156 The New World - Jewish Publication
9 157 Krasne Ontechy Trosnevsoctz Proh Publ. in poss
19 158 Political Economy - Russian Book
22 159 Sudbury, Ont. - Literature
Page 025
Oct 25 160 Devil, The Publication
161 Uus, Ilm - Esthonian Publication
26 162 Mr. Coles Suspect, Sale of Literature - Regina
28 163 Koyhaliston Vallankumous Ja Luopio Kautsky Publication
(In Finnish Language)
30 164 Stephansson, Stephen G. - Book of Poems by
165 Moore, Fred E. - Fort William, Ont. Literature
Nov 3 166 Pidskalny, M. Fort William, Ont. Literature
5 167 Adams Miss Eve. Literature
6 168 Russian-Ukrainain Book Store - Winnipeg, Man. Literature
8 169 Lake Mr. Julius - Fort William, Ont. Literature
12 170 Pravda (Truth) Russian Publication
13 171 The Great "Initiative" Publication
16 172 Lutkevich, Anton - Literature
17 173 Trugenika Golas (The Toilers Voice) Russian Publication
22 174 Nearing or Neering, Scott - Literature
25 175 Northern Wine Co. - Winnipeg, Man.
(Circular) in German Language
176 Men in War - Book
177 On the Job - Literature
178 Kurzner Poliki - Polish Newspaper
179 Industrialisti - Finnish "
Page 024
Nov 30 180 Gavrilesy Thorolow - Literature

1781 Bureau of Information at Seattle Wash. - Literature
Dec 1 182 J. Green - Vancouver Literature
4 183 Direct Action - Literature
9 184 Welland, Ont - "
185 European Press - Literature
186 Red Europe - "
15 187 Literature at Calgary, Alta.
188 Morsoluis - Literature - Montreal, Que.
189 Literature at Montreal
190 Against the Plague of Nations - Literature
20 191 Vsedelnicky Kalender (Cheho Almanac) ?????? Communist Magazine Printed in Russia
21 192 One Big Union - Monthly - Literature BF 175/415
22 193 Ulianov Vladimir - (N. Lenin) - Literature
25 194 Coble, B.J. - Literature
1921
Jan 12 195 Literature Intercepted by Customs
13 196 Bold, N.S. - Literature
22 197 Masloff, Meeno, alias Masteff, Mike - Literature
28 198 Internationale Sammlerwelt Literature
Feb 1 199 Habchuk - Sam - Literature Bolshevik Literature - St. Boniface, Manitoba
Page 023
Feb 4 200 Hindustan Ghadr - Hindustan Publication
201 Sivit (Dawn) - Polish Newspaper
9 202 Workers Bulletin - O.B.U. Publication
10 203 "Baltimorer Correspondent" - German Newspaper
12 204 Glen Andrew - Literature
205 "The Common Cause" - Russian Newspaper
14 206 "The Watch Tower" - I.B.S.A. Publication
207 Ukrainian Daily News - Ukrainian Newspaper (Subsequent Correspondence)
24 208 Kulenko, J. - Literature
209 Laboda, J. "
March 2 210 Molchanov - Literature
3 211 Literature - Sydney Mines District, N.S.
7 212 Literature at Timmins, Ont.
8 213 Thomas, Charles W. - Literature
16 214 Kowlowsky, Mike - Literature
19 215 Communist Bulletin
216 Literature at Fort Francis, Ont.
217 "The Soviet Aid"
22 218 The "Independent"
26 219 Kivechurian, Sylvester P. - Literature

Page 022
March 26220Soviet Russia & Bourgeois Poland - Ukrainian Book
Apr 1 221 Michaels, William - Literature
2 222 Lawrence Labor
4 223 Literature in Public Library - Ottawa, Ont.
6 224 Ukrainsky Golos - Ukrainian Newspaper
15 225 Shio, John - Literature
22 226 Novy Mir - Russian Monthly (The New World)
227 Literature at Ottawa
23 228 Legeychuk, Rev. Basil - Literature
229 Sykes, E.E. - Literature
25 230 New York Call (Trans. to 177/319)
May 3 231 Brayer, H.D. - Literature
232 Knight S.T.J. - Literature
233 Arnold, Walter - & Wm. Couss, Christ Mitchell
9 234 "Free Society" - English Periodical
25 235 Gary, Hector
236 Literature at Edmonton, Alta.
237 Knowles, G.
June 4 238 Literature at Section House, Clairmont, Alberta
9 239 Literature at Sydney, N.S.
Page 021
June 10 240 Literature at Inverness, N.S.
15 241 My Magazine
17 242 Saari, Lydia - Literature
20 243 Hill, John - Literature
23 244 Asali, F. - Literature
245 Fasan, Giuseppe - do
28 246 The Workers Challenge
30 247 Communist International
July 6 248 J. Blair - Literature
11 249 "Industrial Worker"
12 250 Koticha, F. - Literature
251 Hearst Publications
27 252 Johnston, H. - Literature
Aug 3 253 Communism & Christianism
4 254 Smuggling Anarchist Literature from U.S.A. to Canada
10 255 "The Star" - Chinese Newspaper
256 British Columbia Labour News
11 257 "Workers World"
16 258 Communist, The - Great Britain
259 Worker - The (Glasgow)
Page 020
Aug 19 260 Iskra (The Spark) Russian Daily Newspaper New York

City, USA
25 261 A. Ewald
29 262 Glos Robotniczy (Voice of the Worker) - Polish Daily
Sep 12 263 Radical Literature in Canada Transferred to 177/274
13 264 Literature at Emerson, Man.
15 265 Lazoruk, Pete
30 266 The Monstrous Lie
Oct 3 267 Literature at Vancouver, B.C.
268 Grants Weekly
269
Rande Mataram - Gurmukh Weekly Vol 1-2- Published in Vancouver
14 270 Tainio, J. - Kakabeka Falls, Ont.
17 271 The Proletarian - Italian Weekly
31 272 "Robitnycia" (Working Women)
Nov 4 273 The Unrepentant Northcliffe
274
Literature in Canada Morgan, John cancelled see 175/4360
10 275 Kozik, T.
21 276 Baruard, F.A.
Dec 6 277 "The Wedge"
9 278
"Emas" or "The Truth" - Jewish Paper
10 279 Emilio Del Mul - Literature - Fort Frances, Ont.
Page 019
Dec 31 280 Die Schmach am Rheim
27 281 St. Michajluk - Literature
Page 018
Year 1922
Jan 14 282 [2-3 words blacked out] - Fort Frances, Ont.
16 283 [entry blacked out]
284 [entry blacked out]
17 285 Canada ????? Weekly
18 286 [entry blacked out]
28 287 "Russky Golos Voice - From Lene -
Feb 27 288 "Canadian Ukrainain" (Official Organ of the Ukrainian National Council in Canada) Winnipeg, Man.
Mar 1 289 "Robitnyk" (Worker) ????? Monthly
290 [2-3 words blacked out] Fort Frances, Ont.
3 291 [1-2 words blacked out] Literature
8 292 International Press Corres to [3-4 words blacked out]
13 293 [1-2 words blacked out] Copper Cliff, Ont.
294 Voice of Labor
17 295 [1-2 words blacked out] - Cobalt, Ont.
22 296 "Vapaus" Correspt [2-3 words blacked out] Finnish

Newspaper
27 297 [1-2 words blacked out] Sydney, C.B. N.S.
29 298 Proletarian, The - Detroit, Mich. U.S.A.
Page 017
Corresp [2-3 words blacked out]
Mar 31 299 "The Worker" Toronto, Ont (Organ of the Workers Party)
299supp The Workers - Mailing list - Toronto, Ont. Corresp [3-4 words blacked out]
Apr 1 300 "The Worker" - New York, USA (USA Publication)
5 401 [word blacked out] - Fort Frances, Ont.
20 302 [word blacked out] - Sudbury, Ont.
21 303 [word blacked out] - Cap???
26 304 La Crimson??? - French Publication Banned Literature - Verdun Dist B.C.
May 10 305 [word blacked out] - Sudbury, Ont.
16 306 Literature - The Pas, Man.
22 307 Neecha Pravda - (Our Truth)
June 6 308 Vancouver Daily Sun
July 5 309 "Repeater The" - Hamilton, Ont.
310 Maritime Labor Herald - Glace Bay, N.S.
6 311 "Proletarian Party" (Book) - Published by M. Olgie??
11 312 "The Labor Herald" - Official Organ of Trade Union Educational League
Aug 5 313 Halifax Citizen
314 "Pay Roll"
10 315 Literature at Revelstoke, B.C.
12 316 "Freheit, The"
14 317 Propaganda Literature from Russia
15 318 "Labochy Listok"
Page 016
(B.F. from 177/230)
Aug 29 319 New York Call New York, NY U.S.A.
Sep 18 320 Literature at Montreal, P. Que.
321 Le Peuple (The People)
20 322 Literature at Niagara Falls, Ont.
323 " " Winnipeg, Man.
25 324 Golos Gratzi - (The Voice of Labour)
325 Labour Herald, The - Organ of I.E.U.L Transferred to 177/312
28 326 "Soviet Russia"
Oct 16 327 "Volkszeitung"
17 328 "Toveri" - Published at Astoria, Oregon, U.S.A.
21 329 "True Confessions" & "Midnight"
23 330 "Izvestia"
331 "Eternpain" (Forward)

332 "The Flapper"
Nov 4 333 [1-2 words blacked out] - Sudbury, Ont. Literature Trans. to 177/305
Dec 13 334 "The Right Cause" - Russian Newspaper
18 335 Peoples' Book Store - Toronto, Ont.
21 336 [word blacked out] - Sarnia
23 337 The Shing Isah Daily News [3-4 words blacked out]
Page 015
Year 1923
Feb 1 338 The Smart Set
8 339 Soviet Russia Pictorial
340 Winnipeg Socialist
12 341 Confederate The.
24 342 Alberta Labor News. B.F. from 177/649
28 343 [word blacked out] Cranbrook, B.C.
Mar 14 344 [word blacked out] Moonhele, Sask.
345 "Ill Proletario" (The Proletariat)
19 346 Saskatoon Reporter
21 347 Appeal to Reason B.F. 175/852 175/290 Girard Kansas USA
22 348 Workers Weekly
Apr 6 349 Golos Robitnyei. Ukrainian Monthly Magazine. Winnipeg, Man.
26 350 Communist Literature
May 2 351 Canada News Co. Toronto, Ont.
4 352 Patriot, The.
353 New Life
7 354 Vapaus. Sudbury.
8 355 Toveritar.
15 356 Vestnick (Messenger.)
Page 014
June 8 357 Young International - published by Y.C.L.
28 358 [word blacked out] Sudbury, Ont. [2-3 words blacked out]
29 359 [word blacked out] Vancouver, B.C.
Jul 31 360 "Rosta"
Aug 1 361 [entry blacked out]
8 362 "The Bible Comically Illustrated."
9 363 The Labour News Timmins, Ont.
10 364 "Red New Culture"
Oct 8 365 [word blacked out] Ford City, Ont.
10 366 [word blacked out] North Bay, Ont.
Nov 27 367 Daily Worker
29 368 [word blacked out] Marcelin, Sask.
Page 013

Year 1924
Jan 29 369 B.C. Labor Bulletin. Labor Statesman.
Feb 14 370 The Young Worker. (Jewish Periodical).
15 371 The Young Worker. Chicago Ill. U.S.A.
19 372 March of The Workers and Other Songs. A song book published in connection with Y.W.L. in Chicago
Apr 15 373 The Daily People. Vancouver, B.C.
June 7 374 The Young Worker. Toronto, Ont.
B.F. to 175P/2552
July 4 375 [word blacked out] Sudbury, Ont.
31 376 Besboynick. (Atheist) Russian Monthly.
Sep 12 377 Finnish Literature in Strongfield and Glenside Dists. Sask.
13 378 Jeezn. (Life) Russian Monthly.
Oct 2 379 Peretz. (Pepper) Ukrainian Newspaper.
13 380 Russian Review. Washington D.C. U.S.A.
15 381 Economic and Financial Record. Vancouver, B.C.
Nov 5 382 [word blacked out] Sudbury, Ont.
6 383 Robitnitzia. [2-3 words blacked out] (Working Woman) Winnipeg, Man.
7 384 Workers Monthly.
11 385 Communist Review.
386 The Left Wing. Toronto, Ont.
12 387 [3-4 words blacked out] Sudbury, Ont.
13 388 International of Youth. Magazine published in Sweden, organ of Y.C.L.

Page 012
Nov 13 389 [word blacked out] Ottawa, Ont.
19 390 Literature at Ford City, Ont.
22 391 Red Youth Montreal, P.Q.
Correspondence trans [2-3 words blacked out]
25 392 Der Kapf. (The Fight) Kamf. Jewish Monthly
(Trans. from 175/239)
26 393 Golos Truzenika (The Toilers Voice) @ Golos Trudjenika
Dec 2 394 L'Italia Montreal, P.Q.
6 395 Radical Literature at Hamilton, Ont.
9 396 The Unemployment Review. Toronto, Ont.
12 397 Americanskye, Izvestia New York, N.Y. U.S.A.
398 [word blacked out] Calgary, Alta.
17 399 Black Hundred
26 400 [3-4 words blacked out] Toronto, Ont.
27 401 Rassviet. New York, N.Y. U.S.A.

Page 011
Year 1925
Jan 12 402 Radical Literature at Calgary - Alta.

27 403 Buck Lini [4-5 words blacked out] Toronto, Ont.
404 Russian Information & Review London, Eng. Correspondence
Feb 2 405 [4-5 words blacked out] Montreal, P.Que.
5 406 Cherony Schliakh (Red Road) Ukrainian Publication Corresp [2-3 words blacked out]
27 407 Farmerske-Szythya (Farmers Life) Winnipeg- Man.
6.3.25 408 [entry blacked out]
14. 409 The Weekly News
15.4.25 410 The Peoples Cause Toronto, Ont.
22.4.25 411 Industrial Unionist Portland, Ore. U.S.A.
25.4.25 412 "Svitlo" (The Light) (Ukrainian Newspaper)
12.5. 413 Proletarska Pravda (Proletarian Truth)
14. 414 "Delnik" (Worker) Chicago - Ill. U.S.A.
8.6. 415 "Die Mennonitishe Rundschan (Mennonite General Review) Winnipeg, Man.
22. 416 The Canadian Farmer Labor Advocate
23. 417 Literature at Port Arthur, Ont.
29. 418 Vappu (1925)
Page 010
10.7.25 419 I.W.W. Literature at Kenora, Ont.
18. 420 Rabochaya Moskbva (The Moscow Workers)
27.7. 421 I.W.W. Literature at Port Arthur, Ont. B.F. 175/1008 & 175/9421
12.8. 422 Russian Gazette Montreal, P.Que.
13. 423 Fairy tales for Workers Children
17. 424 London Daily Herald (B.F. 175/3299) @ The Daily Herald London, Eng.
1.9.25 425 Trade Union Unity - London, Eng.
9. 426 Elevator Worker
17.10 427 Steps to Power
22. 428 Novie Svit (New World) (Box 1092 - Montreal, P. Que.
23.10 429 Literature intercepted by Post Office Dept.
24. 430 Rednota (Poverty)
27. 431 "Krestianka" (Peasant Woman)
5.11 432 "Goodok" (The Whistle)
433 "Moryak" (The Seaman)
24.11.25 434 "Smiloh & Pravda" @ Humor & Truth Ukrainian Magazine published semi monthly New York, U.S.A.
15.12.25 435 [1-2 words blacked out] Hafford, Sask.
19.12.25 436 [1-2 words blacked out] Kenney, Ont.
8.1.26 437 Sun Min Kok (New Republic) Victoria, B.C.
14.1.26 438 The Veteran's Review Toronto, Ont.
Page 009

26.1.26 439 [word blacked out] Toronto, Ont.
28.1.26 440 [word blacked out] Winnipeg, Man.
30.1.26 441 The Young Rebel. Montreal, P. Que.
3.2.26 442 Molody Bilshevik (Young Bolshevik)
3.2.26 443 Naz Zming (Change)
15.2.26 444 [word blacked out] Fort City, Ont.
22.2.26 445 Chervonaya Zbmiena (The Red Change)
22.2.26 446 Malady Araty. @ Young Workers organ of Central Committee of Leninist Young Communist League
6.3.26 447 A word in season
448 [word blacked out] Toronto, Ont.
11.3.26 449 "Whither England"?
13.3.26 450 [word blacked out] Toronto, Ont.
15.3.26 451 [word blacked out] Winnipeg, Man.
22.3.26 452 Forward @ ?????
23.3.26 453 Der Hamer (The Hammer)
27.3.26 454 [word blacked out] Toronto, Ont.
29.3.26 455 The Baha'i Religion
30.4.26 456 "The Furrow" Saskatoon, Sask.
7.5.26 457 "New ????" New York, N.Y. U.S.A.
458 [word blacked out] Toronto, Ont.

Page 008

11.5.26 459 De Uitkijk (The Outlook)
26.5.26 460 Nasha Pravda (Our Truth)
28.5.26 461 Laborer Defense
31.5.26 462 [word blacked out] Winnipeg, Man.
13.5.26 463 Israilite Press [1-2 words blacked out] Winnipeg, Man.
17.6.26 464 [word blacked out] St. Vital
19.6.26 465 Workers Tribune (Polish) Weekly
28.6.26 466 Pidzemna Galietchna (Underground Galicia)
2.7.26 467 "L'Ouvrier Canadien" Montreal P. Que. [3-4 words blacked out]
5.4.26 468 The New World's Library and Printing Co. Montreal, P. Que.
19.7.26 469 "The Women Worker"
20.7.26 470 "Hell in New Jersey"
11.8.26 471 A.B.C. of Communism
21.8.26 472 Zhalo. (The Stinger) New York, N.Y. U.S.A.
26.8.26 473 [words blacked out] Toronto, Ont.
10.9.26 474 [entry blacked out] Trans to 177/474
24.9.26 475 Two Worlds Monthly
25.9.26 476 Letters of Junius
27.9.26 477 Finnish Literature in Canada
478 Polish Literature in Canada

Page 007
12.10.26 479 [word blacked out] Moose Jaw, Sask.
20.1.26 480 [word blacked out] Winnipeg, Man.
21.10.26 481 Young Comrade
27.10.26 482 Pravda (Truth) Russian Newspaper
2.11.26 483 Labour Monthly
15.11.26 484 The Western Jewish News Winnipeg, Man.
15.1.27 485 Canadian Labour Defence League (scratched out) Labour Defence

25.1.27 486 [3-4 words blacked out] Samburg, Sask.
11.2.27 487 Workers Life
7.3.27 488 Hungarian Literature in Canada Seized by Post Office Department for examination
5.4.27 489 "The Chinese Guide in America" (English Supplement)
12.4.27 490 "Sivit Molod" (The Youth World) Corresp. [3-4 words blacked out]
4.5.27 491 Farmers and Peasants International Correspondent Berlin, Germany
13.5.27 492 [3-4 words blacked out] Montreal, P. Que.
28.5.27 493 Hands Off China
1.6.27 494 The International Seafarer
9.6.27 495 "The Communist"
11.6.27 496 Russky Golos @ The Peasant International New York, U.S.A.
13.6.27 497 [2-3 words blacked out] Sointula, B.C. Correspondence [4-5 words blacked out]
Page 006
18.7.27 498 The Communist
23.7.27 499 Canadian Hungarian Journal
26.7.27 500 The People's Tribune
19.9.27 501 The Nation
23.9.27 502 Bulletin of Red International Labour Union
17.10.27 503 The Young Leninist
28.11.27 504 Tenth Anniversary Russian Revolution
6.12.27 505 "Forward" (Glasgow Paper)
13.12.27 506 Red Star
13.12.27 507 "Czas" (The Time
19.12.27 508 Pioneer (Pioneer)
30.12.27 509 Industrialisation Joulu
3.1.28 510 Ten Red Years
511 Forward (Whered) Ukrainian Transferred to 177/????
4.1.28 512 Jolly Friend
11.1.28 513 Canadian Labour Monthly

26.1.28 514 Die Vapauteen - Transferred to 177/119
3.2.28 515 Labor Unity
20.2.28 516 The Communist [word blacked out]
517 Communist Party Training
Page 005
3.3.28 518 Ogenek (Small Fire)
22.3.28 519 Novyj Swit (New Women)
29.3.28 520 Bulletin Informations Politiques (Bulletin of Political Informations)
4.5.28 521 Illustrated Ukrainian Calendar (Red Kobzar 1928)
5.5.28 522 Ukrainian Revolutionist @ Ukrainski Revolusioner)
8.5.28 523 Communist World (Kommunistychny Swit)
524 Ukrainian Daily News Trans to 177/207
12.5.28 525 Projector
15.5.28 526 30 Days
527 Red Field (Krasnaja Niva)
16.5.28 528 [1-2 words blacked out] West Grand Forks, B.C.
25.5.28 529 Borotba (The Struggle)
13.6.28 530 [4-5 words blacked out] Winnipeg, Man.
11.7.28 531 [2-3 words blacked out] Leask, Sask.
15.7.28 532 [2-3 words blacked out] Coniston, Ont.
1.8.28 533 [2-3 words blacked out] Blackburn, B.C.
13.8.28 534 Bilshovik Ukrainy
Published monthly by Soviet Government of Ukraine
29.8.28 535 [word blacked out] Sudbury, Ont. Trans to 175P/2943
18.9.28 536 The Communist International
(Between the Fifth & Sixth World Congress 1926)
Page 004
537 "Svet" (The Sight)
17.11.28 538 [6-7 words blacked out] Winnipeg, Man.
539 Il Nuovo Mondo
3.12.28 540 Bicz Bozy
541 L'Avant Garde [1-2 words blacked out]
7.12.28 542 The Militant (English Trotskyist Weekly, New York
14.12.28 543 [5-6 words blacked out] Montreal, P. Que.
544 [entry blacked out]
{DATES NOT LEGIBLE FOR THE NEXT FEW}
545 [5-6 words blacked out] Winnipeg, Man.
546 Labour
547 [4-5 words blacked out] Montreal, P. Que.
548 Chervony Kvitia Red ?????
549 Switlo The Light
13.2.29 550 The Red International of Labour Unions
Communist Organization pub. in London, Eng.

15.2.29 551 [word blacked out] Sudbury, Ont Trans to 175/2751
22.2.29 552 Jovo, A. (Hungarian Paper)
23.2.29 553 [5-6 words blacked out] Toronto, Ont.
25.2.29 554 The Red Needle
555 Literature from Scotland Yard
Communist Literature from Scotland Yard
11.3.29 556 [word blacked out] Niagara Falls, Ont.
Page 003
14.3.29 557 [entry blacked out]
6.4.29 558 Machine Age
559 Virradot
11.4.29 560 [5-6 words blacked out] Montreal, P.Que.
12.4.29 561 [5-6 words blacked out] Winnipeg, Man.
562 The Young Bolshevik
20.4.29 563 [1-2 words blacked out] Sudbury, Ont.
Trans to 177/1063
23.4.29 564 Noyorji Russkoye Shovo (New Russian Weekly)
565 [4-5 words blacked out] Toronto, ont.
29.4.29 567 Review of Bezvirnyk (The Atheist)
30.4.29 568 [4-5 words blacked out] Montreal, P. Que.
16.5.29 569 [word blacked out] Montreal, P. Que.
570 The Day
20.5.29 571 "Red Cartoons"
572 "Munkas Ujsag" Hungarian Daily
27.5.29 573 [word blacked out] Toronto, Ont.
29.5.29 574 The Workers & Farmers Publishing Assn. Winnipeg, Man.
30.5.29 575 [2-3 words blacked out] Montreal, P. Que.
3.10.29 576 Worker Toronto, Ont.
Page 002
9.7.29 577 "A Harcos"
15.7.29 578 Librairie A des temps nouveaux Montreal, P.Que.
26.7.29 579 "Radnik" (The Workman)
580 "Food Minor"
27.7.29 581 "Liberation"
582 Moskanov Rundschau" (Moscow News)
21.8.29 583 [2-3 words blacked out] Toronto, Ont.
22.8.29 584 [2-3 words blacked out] " "
26.8.29 585 [2-3 words blacked out] " "
28.8.29 586 [2-3 words blacked out] Krydor, Sask.
30.8.29 587 [word blacked out] Toronto, Ont.
5.9.29 588 [word blacked out] Prince Albert, Sask.
6.9.29 589 Hartman's Book Store, Montreal, P. Que.
Foreign Language Publications Found In
9.9.29 590 "Plough"

591 “Misnkas” Correspondence [2-3 words blacked out]
supp A Correspondence [2-3 words blacked out]
27.9.29 592 [word blacked out Montreal, P. Que.
28.9.29 593 The New Canadian
4.10.29 594 [word blacked out] Toronto, Ont. Trans to 175P/2677
8.10.29 595 Canadian Republic Magazine
15.10.29 596 [word blacked out] Toronto, Ont.
Page 001
21.10.29 597 Spector, M. Toronto, Ont Trans to 175P/1712
Examination of for Customs
25.10.29 598 Literature addressed to the Der Kamf Toronto, Ont.
Lithuanian Language Publications- intervened by Customs
- addressed to
599 [word blacked out] Milnes Camp Mileage ????????????
600 Chinese Times [3-4 words blacked out]
24.10.29 601 Jewish Socialist Libary Toronto, Ont
2.11.29 602 [word blacked out] Montreal, P. Que.
6.11.29 603 [2-3 words blacked out] Toronto, Ont.
604 [2-3 words blacked out] Daysland, Alta.
8.11.29 605 [2-3 words blacked out] Montreal, P. Que.
9.11.29 606 [2-3 words blacked out] Toronto, Ont.
12.11.29 607 [entry blacked out]
2.2.29 608 [entry blacked out]
4.2.29 609 Thunderer Toronto, Ont.
9.2.29 610 “Nova Scotia Miner”
3.1.30 611 “Freedman”
4.1.30 612 [word blacked out] Montreal, P. Que.
7.1.30 613 [word blacked out] Toronto, Ont.
11.1.30 614 [word blacked out] " "
615 [word blacked out] " "
16.1.30 616 [word blacked out] " "

PART 6: REGISTER OF BOLSHEVIST & AGITATOR INVESTIGATIONS 1920

[Verso of Page One missing]
[Recto Page 1]

175/1425, 20/9, Vancouver
Simpson Distr. of Prohibtd. Lit.

175/1257, 17/9, Vancouver
Longshoremen, IWW Propaganda
Manner in which American Agitators arrive in country to avoid Customs & Immigration Officers.

175/1195, 17/8, Lethbridge
Alex McFegan, OBU organizer & agitator
Agreement between Dist. Mining Dept. OBU and Twin City Mining Co.

175/742, 15/10, Winnipeg
Louis Kon, Suspect
Believes Bolshevism will rule Canada
175/313, 6/10, Vancouver Island
ILP, Victoria

Barnard said that the Senate was a Political Pension House for old fogies. Canada today was worse than Germany had been. Speaking of the bonus he said: "The Gov't was unable to find the money, but if the war had lasted years longer the money would have been found." M.P.s were receiving $2,500 for the Session called to ratify the Peace Treaty. 40,000 girls were driven to Prostitution every year in North America by profiteers, we did not have to go to Russia for free love. There was lots of graft going on in the Fisheries Dept.

[Page 2 recto and verso blank]
Page 3

175/87, 29/9, Winnipeg
Labour Church Service Winnipeg

Ald Queen Capitalistic class making Gov't. do as they wish even to bringing out soldiers and machine guns to protect themselves or interests.

Moved Resolution asking "President Wilson to use influence in granting the release of Tom Mooney.

175/531, 14/10, Brandon
Rev. A. E. Smith, Labour Agitator

Speaking at Rainy River Re. Prohibition Temperance Party also for Farmers Party.

175/726, 14/10, Brandon
New Peoples Church

Miss Beatrice Brigden spoke on "The Spirit of Youth and Industrial Autocracy."

175/992, 11/10, Brandon
Trades Labour Council, Brandon

Letter received from Bartholemew re resignation of H. C. L. Broadhurst. Boy Scout movement anti-union and controlled by Capitalism. Called for labour men to boycott movement until made non-partisan.

Letter from Defence Committee Winnipeg - endeavour of Canadian Government to stamp out what they are pleased to call seditious propaganda.

Local teamsters union withdrawn from International & will take vote on joining OBU.

175/620, 28/9, Lethbridge
J.S. Woodsworth, Agitator

Who will control Canada?

175/1146, 2/10, Calgary
9/10, Ottawa
8/10, Calgary
W. Lawson Editor Fernie Ledger

Starting New Labour Paper in Calgary. (23/10/19 New Name Search Light). Expects to publish 1st issue Nov 1st 1919.

Policy would be "extremely conservative at the start" later "it would be red enough for the reddest".

Lawson stated Christopher was at Vancouver re. the New Paper and that Brown was working to form Organization to be know as "Canadian Miners Union." Offering $20.00 for Name for New Paper.

175/67, 6/10, Edmonton
S. P. of C., Edmonton

Working Class have to keep Army & Navy.

Maguire's speech Object of S.P. of C. was to educate their fellow workers to organize as the Russians had done. Revolutionary propaganda must be spread in an effort to get hold of arm force which is the support of Capitalism.

175/880, 13/10, E. Kootenay
R.J. Johns, Winnipeg Strike Leader

Johns speech in Grand Theatre Fernie "Democracy on Trial," - Winnipeg returned soldiers were going to hold silent parade with a coffin in centre labelled democracy.

Page 4
175/880, 14/10, E. Kootenay
R.J. Johns, Winnipeg Strike Leader

Spoke at Labour meeting at Michel - Papers in the pay of Capitalism, Anything the Capitalist Class fights is in the interest of the workers. - Winnipeg strike defeated by the Military power and courts. - Action would have to be taken to force the Government to recognize the workers.

175/1365, 14/10, Vancouver
Alleged Bolshevism amongst Finlanders

All Finnish found to be Unpatriotic. No use for English speaking people in the Dist except Geo. Stirling

Settlers very quiet until G. Stirling came to Dist.

Geo Stirling said to Agents. "I see you are returned soldiers, why were you fighting for the Capitalists and that rotten Government; you fellows will get nothing now, the only way for the R.S. to get anything is to organize and be ready for the Labour Movement in Canada."

175/1350, 14/10, Lethbridge
Holmes Jowett, Agitator

Spoke at Redcliff and Taber --: Where shall the Government get the money from for the Soldiers bonus?

175/244--Part 2, 13/10, Vancouver
Fed. Labour Party, Vancouver

R. P. Pettipiece speaker. "Exhorting his auditors to combine for political power stating he was for the complete overthrow of the present scheme of Government. Reg Flag might appear under new title "The Western Clarion"

175/236--Part 2, 8/10, Vancouver

Socialist Party of Canada, Vancouver

Johns, Pritchard, and Bray spoke alike. They were in their present position thro carrying out wishes of fellow workers, their only defence was The OBU. Winnipeg solid for OBU. Try coaxing instead of driving.

175/438, 15/10, Vancouver
Meeting held under Auspices of OBU Vancouver at The Arena 24/9/19.

R. E. Bray - "First citizen of province should --- wear the emblem of that rotten bunch of politicians and profiteers who have brought this Province to the verge of bankruptcy.

You can call off the war on telephone girls.

You who have helped to put into office that emasculated spineless bunch of profiteers at Ottawa, you can use your influence to get them defeated also -

Bray's whole talk was on and about the period surrounding the Winnipeg Strike.

Page 5
175/313, 13/10, Victoria
12/10, Victoria
13/10, Victoria
Fed. Labour Party, Victoria

Barnard spoke re. "Government driving young girls to prostitution."

Barnard "The grandest flag whose honour had been dragged thro the mud and mire by the rottenest gang of swindlers and profiteers which had ever grown up in any country. Implicating Gov't: -- The Gov't made the Bolshes by their corrupt and rotten practices.

They say you are talking Bolshevism if you attack the Profiteers. If that is true, then I am a Bolshe.

Dr. Curry said that Russians who were deported, were being handed over to Kolchak on arrival which meant they were murdered within 24 hours. Stated Bolshevism simply meant the rights of the people and that he stood for Bolshevism all the time, "I stand for Bolshevism all the time."

175/1402, 17/10, Edmonton
Gov't. Conditions in Ft. George and - McBride Dist.

Grod states Socialist platform no good owing to its condemnation of religion and churches why socialism made no head way. Grod stated capitalism was afraid of Bolshe reason why truth not coming out in press.

175/919, 15/10, Lethbridge
Donald McNabb, Organizer D.L.P.

Thousands of Russians slaughtered by Kolchak.

In Russia the people got rid of Czarism established Democracy but Kolchak and Allies want to strangle it and so the profiteers wait to do in Canada.

Capital is united vs. OBU.

Labour has its reward. Where do we get that reward? Only remedy is collectivization.

Whole speech on Revolution and Bolshevism

Windwood good witness.

175/1455, 10/10, Saskatoon
Mrs. Kimball, Mrs. Sauna Kannasto, Alleged Bolshe

Education chief weapon against Capitalism

175/1513, 15/10, Lethbridge
Dominion Labour Party, Re. Alex McRoberts, Labour Agitator

McRoberts stated referring to bonus - The Borden Gov't. spends money like water on stool pigeons, secret service men and mounted Police, to keep himself and party in office, but it will not help any. We and Labour Party will see that he and his minions will be thrown out.

All the money spent for his own use and protection of friends would nearly pay the soldiers bonus.

Page 6
175/1107, 16/10/19, Vancouver
OBU Transport Workers Unit

Lester's theme at Meeting --- The Unpleasantness & Needlessness of Labour

---

175/1523, 16/10, Vancouver
J. Kavanagh, Agitator

Has been canvassing for Defence Fund in Winnipeg Cases reports poor results (USA). States there will be more bloodshed in USA in next few years than any where on earth.

175/635, 13/10, Calgary
Harry Hanson, OBU Organizer

6743 Requested by Lawson to get as many subscriptions as possible for New Labour Party as he was broke and needed money.

Hanson making living by taking collections at meetings where he speaks.

175/897, 17/10, Winnipeg
Soldiers and Sailors Labour Party of Canada
Grant speaking re. Gratuity ---

When party convinced that Gov't will not further assist R.S. we will use violence to obtain it. We will make them give it to us.

Flynn ? with the idea of joining Gratuity League with S + SLP of C.

175/514, 20/10/19, Regina
OBU, Regina
Speakers of evening P.M. Anderson K.C. (lecture) "Future of Labour"

Sambrook said speaker blamed working class for trouble and that "there would always be strikes till the rich man stopped making profits from working class.

Scotland blamed Master Class as much as Working Class.

175/635,16/10, Calgary
Harry Hanson, OBU Organizer

Hanson spoke on Constitution of OBU. Attempted to show OBU & IWW were identical.

A stranger in reply said that although he did not know what the OBU might be or do, once it begins its functions he felt convinced that the OBU did not believe in direct action as the IWW does at present.

175/491, 16/10, Calgary
OBU Calgary
Membership OBU 208 dues paid for October $83.00
Townsend organizer in Ogden Shops wanted assistant.

Broatch said everybody make themselves organizers for their respective craft.

16/10, Victoria
Conditions in Victoria, Re. Trades & Labour Meeting

T & L Council would not assume the financial responsibility of Semi-Weekly Tribune, Would be conducted by private control in future.

Communicate with Ottawa re. "Elections Act"

Page 7
175/420, 21/10, Lethbridge,
P. M. Christopher
Dick Johns expounded OBU & Marxian ideas

Christopher said: "I have very good OBU organizations at Fernie, Blairmore, Coleman, Michel, & Hillcrest, & at Taber I have a very good beginning."

175/1531, 18/10, Fort William,
W. W. Lefeaux, Sec. S.P. of C. in B.C.

Lefeaux spoke "Ex member of R.N.W.M. Police Secret Service until he realized his position, namely being used against the poor workers. Showed the lethargy of towns when "you have to send to Vancouver and Winnipeg for help for workers when arrested."

175/943, 17/10, 18/10, Fort William
Fred E. Moore, Suspect
Distributing of Prohibited Literature too dangerous

Moore introduced himself as Int'l. Socialist of C. who stands not only for Canada but for the whole world. Said Englishmen had lost job through Austrian - wanted Moore's help. Moore told him it was not through Austrian but the rotten Capitalist System. He introduced Lefeaux as"one who has been doing good work for the workers."

175/438, 11/10, Vancouver Island
OBU Vancouver Island

A list of IWW members now undergoing Jail sentences in USA was read with appeal for funds to help same.

175/1534, 18/10, Fort William
IWW Branch of LWIU #500, Bushmens Organization Meeting
Meeting called to organize Bushmen of dist into OBU. Those interested in IWW took charge.

Holm a stranger elected Secretary

A. Dahlgren travelling delegate reported bushmen winning their fight on Algoma Central Line

Rates of Wages decided.

Committee of five appointed to formulate plan of campaign.

175/762, 16/10, Winnipeg,
Alfred Johanson, Alleged Strike Leader, Novy Vek - Gift by Bolshevists to.

Charitonoff in his evidence on his behalf said he had received money to publish this Newspaper.

175/87, 20/10, Winnipeg,
Labour Church Service, Winnipeg, Columbia Theatre 19/10/19

Rev. A. E. Smith launched out into an attack on Gov't and Orthodox Church. "While the people were praying for relief from the oppression of the RNWM Police they, (Gov't, Orthodox Church) had secured professional Evangelist spreading false doctrine beneficial to the "Overhead System" and to mislead the people in general. Arrest of strike leaders increase of Military etc. were for the purpose of striking terror into the hearts of the Labour Class.

Revolution meant "Speeding up" of Evolution" that they were not going to wait a 1,000 years for these things to come to pass."

Page 8
175/1274, 20/10, Saskatoon
W. Thrutchley, Suspected Agitator

Idea of holding Dominion Convention of Bible Students, Nov 15th.

175/313, 16/10, Vancouver Island,
Federated Labour Party

Major R. J. Burde whilst attacking Gov't only on political points. Attacked Gov't for standing by and not stopping profiteering. Referred to Borden & Rogers trip to France compared their patriotic utterances to the troops with their failure to fight men's battle home in Canada.

Barnard as a counter-irritant. OBU as One Big Opportunity and that you have in the coming election (62's report).

While in France voted for Union Gov't lesser of two evils now would oppose it in every way possible and the help of IWW and OBU not to be despised. He did not go overseas because 100% patriotic but more from adventure. (Corpl. Newnham report)

Barnard In 1914 it was "King & Country" & Fight for the Old Flag

1919 it was a case of "Red Devils" Soldier made mistake in coming back. He was asked to go, but none in authority wanted him back (62's report).

R.E. Bray said "some said OBU was a failure but this was not so." Advocated everybody being member.

175/880, 20/10, Lethbridge
R. J. Johns, Labour Agitator

Holmes Jowett referring to Winnipeg Strike said "If the Gov't and the Citizens Committee, the tools of Capitalism, had not put Special Police on the Streets armed with guns against striking policemen etc.

Whole speech on Winnipeg Strike.

After we are free we will then put up a movement which will give the workers what we want.

175/1535, 19/10, Esquimault, B.C.
Federated Labour Party, T. A. Barnard

Speaking on unemployment said: "Are you going to starve this winter?" Voice from crowd, "No! You bet we are not, we will have a rifle."

Page 9
175/313, 18/10, Esquimault

Federated Labour Party

Rev. Spence what he wished to do was to make his audience think then they would act. Church & Labour must co-operate they must use the ballot box. Gov't had done nothing to reduce H.C. of L. The dollar came before the manhood of country. Big interests welcomed strikes. Middleman should be cut out. Speaker and A. E. Cook found 2,250,000 lbs of foodstuffs had been destroyed in Vancouver in 32 months. Profiteer vultures "he would fight them to a finish."

Major Burde said Dr. Tolmie was a shock absorber for the Gov't.

Barnard was a shock conductor.

175/867, 15/10, Nelson Detch
OBU Movements in W.Kootenay, Re. R.E. Bray, Re. OBU Meeting at Nelson

R.E. Bray appealed for funds for defence of Winnipeg Strike Leaders. Blamed Govt & Citizens Committee for Strike.

Referred to International Union & Officials as "tools of a Slimy Gov't"

Referred to RNWMP as, slimy spotters, dirty rattle snakes and skunks. He stated that these same skunks etc. broke into Russell's roll top desk and after there was $50.00 missing.

Alderman Austin in chair introduced R.E. Bray as the Saviour of the Working Classes. All at meeting given two Booklets, "One Big Union" the other "Industrial Union Methods" by Wm.E. Trautman. "Industrial Unionism" by Eugene V. Debs.

For all information regarding IWW referred to in this Booklet (One Big Union) write to Vincent St. John, Gen. Sec. Treas., 518 Cambridge Building, Chicago.

175/1457, 22/10, Prince Albert
Lumbermen & Millworkers, Organization of

Six men leaving Vancouver in connection with IWW for Lumber Camp at P.A. (Big River Lumber Co Camp now divided into Ladder Lake Lumber Co. of Big River and Prince Albert Lumber Co. Ltd.

Extract of letter from Mr. Armstrong to Big River Lumber Co.

This organization is not an ordinary Labour Union such as is affiliated with the International Union but is pure and simple, an IWW organization under another name.

175/622, 17/10, Vancouver
Vancouver T & L Council

Piledrivers and Wooden Bridgemen's Unit granted affiliation 97% OBU, Two strikes settled one of which was at Andersons Camp

Kavanagh re. trip to Seattle said of Strikes in progress. Carpenters out for $10.00 per day.

The following are debates for Educational Meetings "The Shop Steward System." "Should the Labour Movement continue to have per capita tax system as financial basis?" What form should the OBU take?

Page 10
175/1506, 20/10, OBU Vancouver Island Sub. Dist., Victoria
Nanaimo, B.C.

Letter from Midgeley stating "Voice of Reason" was being sent to Nanaimo which should be sold to members and others, if necessary should be given as it contained "Most useful propaganda." It was decided local should embrace all labour instead of only mineworkers. Canvasser wanted, nobody anxious.

175/244, 20/10, Vancouver
F.L.P. Vancouver

Dr. Curry stated subject "The Iron Heel." Class in power had two ways of staying there 1st. Keeping the "Slaves" in ignorance re. their true standing in society, 2nd Masters had educated the Slaves to think it right and proper they should be slaves. The Church told the "Slaves" they must be content with their lot on Earth.

The "Iron Heel" could kill off or throw into prison Slaves who had seen the Light. Should use power behind ballot to gain ends first, if that no good then blood shed.

R.E. Bray said what Curry meant by "power behind ballot" was not the Big and Machine guns. The other side had that, but rather the very men whom the Masters expected to operate those guns would refuse to do so. Referring to RNWMP he said "We are planting seeds in the very place they are most needed and when the time comes we shall see the Red-Coats are not what a lot of us think them now."

175/897, 20/10, Winnipeg
Ex Soldiers & Sailors Labour Party, Winnipeg

Re. Murder of DeForge. Jas Grant said "It is just what he deserves, the dirty spy and all the rest should get the same." When asked if he thought an alien had killed DeForge said "There are no aliens in this city, we are all brothers. The dangerous alien is the Capitalist and the members of Gov't.

175/521, 20/10, Vancouver Island
OBU Cumberland, B.C. - Miners Meeting

J. Naylor. OBU Organizer to visit Nanaimo every two weeks. Pritchard said RNWM Police were responsible for strike at Winnipeg claiming them as strikebreakers, urged all miners to join OBU.

175/336, 22/10, Edmonton
Ukranian Labour News

Extract from letter sent by Marsyrk to Editor U.L. News to publish out of 80 labourers at Coalhurst only a few take the U. L. News. The rest do not recognise their own Labour Paper which is defending their interests --- Our paper enlightens us to the tricks of Capitalists, it also teaches us laborers to capture our aims and objects.

Page 11
175/313, 22/10, Esquimalt
Fed. Labour Party

J.S.Woodsworth spoke on "The New Canada" Before War goods marked "Made in Germany" now it was in Japan. Competition system could not go on. The country must produce for needs of the people first. The press had been used to break Winnipeg strike. He was ashamed of being a Canadian. (Report of D.R.Wilson). Labour & Capital were going to quarrel, majority of people not capitalists will rise up in their might and get control of machines of production. Said there would be a lot of unemployment and Unrest this winter and because of this the Gov't were rushing in RNWM Police. There are no Indians here for them to shoot, so they must be coming over the mountains to shoot down the workers of this country. Gov't bent on Repression and not on Construction.

Pte. McLernan said when Gov't wanted men they offered inducements to enlist and certain promises were made re. pensions etc. None of the promises had been fully carried out, and RS were being side-tracked for foreigners etc. (Report E.G. Newnham)

TROTTER said papers were controlled by capital and that all news items were "cooked". Mentioned "Ontario Elections" as Labour was beginning New Era. If "Direct Action" ever became necessary it would be Gov't fault. "It is the man who sits on the safety valve who always causes the trouble."

175/244, 20/10,
Fed Lab Party, Vancouver

J.S.Woodsworth. Winnipeg strike peaceful orderly proceeding ---. Give them no excuse to turn military loose and shoot you down. Said he was told the Gov't were going to meet the Industrial unrest. Strike committee held undisputed power in Winnipeg for 6 weeks. 8% R S were with the strikers and they would soon convert RNWMP. Winnipeg City Police were with them. Citizens Committee also held authority until City authorities literally held a gun to their heads and made agree not to join any general strike while a member. Courts and jury only the people. One Russian lady. It was a worse raid than any she had seen in Russia.

175/880, 22/10,
R. J. Johns

R. J. Johns. Eight of us were elected as spokesmen for you. We only did what you told us to do, if we are convicted you will have no one to fight your battles for you, etc.

Everyone subscribe to OBU Bulletin.

[extra typed page inserted in volume.]
Extract taken from report dated May 31st, 1920.
RE
H. J. Flynn (Vice- President and organizer of the Grand Army of United Veterans.)

"The present Government are all a bunch of grafters and profiteers; they are no good to any one but themselves; they do not represent the people of Canada, they only represent the few moneyed men of Canada, and these few men today control the Government, and the government do not care what the people ask for but they do every-thing that the rich men ask them to do.

The returned soldiers will never get anything from Borden and his gang; we need a change of government right away, a change by the good old vote, and I do not see why we cannot have a returned soldier at the head of our next government. It is up to all the returned men to unite and overthrow this rotten bunch down in Ottawa, and put good men in who will not write you a nice letter with one hand and steal your money with the other."

[Also inserted in volume.]
COPY

PRINCE GEORGE, B.C.
June 27th, 1920.

On June 26th, 1920, I was in the office of J. Stevenson, Secy. of the O.B.U. and in conversation with him discussed the recent strike.

He said -

"A general strike is no good in this part of the country, the men won't hold together.

The only thing to do is to strike on the job.

The delegates who are leaving here now will go back to work in the camps and I have instructed them to do all they can to organize the camps in which they work and explain to the workers how to 'Strike on the job.'

The men must work as slow as possible and hold their jobs. Between employments they are to lay off half a day or two or three days so that the employers will always be short handed. When working with axes or other tools they are to mislay the tools they are working with and take time to hunt for them, move the tools about as much as possible without accomplishing any work. If they are around where heavy timbers etc. are being lifted by hand they are to always be the last to get under the lift and delay the lift by placing axes required, far away so that when they are wanted it will be a few minutes delay to get the tools.

The employers will soon get fed up and come to the working class to make terms."

[Also inserted in volume.]
Extract from Morning Journal July 13th, 1920
ORANGEMAN PASS MANY RESOLUTIONS

"Resolved, that we call upon our Provincial and Dominion Governments to suppress the disloyal meetings in Canada favoring an Irish republic, and to declare 'The Self-Determination for Ireland League' as being contrary to the principles of British citizenship and utterly subversive of British authority."

"Resolved, that we further declare for the abolition of all separate schools, and the establishment of one common public school for this Dominion, the institution of a universal marriage law for Canada, and the strict limitation of bilingualism to those official spheres granted to it by the terms of the British North American Act."

R.J. Johns, 175/880, 22/10/19 [Copy of broadside inserted in volume.]

WINNIPEG

DEFENCE LEAGUE

Tuesday, Oct 21

at 8 p.m.

A mass meeting of all workers will

be held in the Al Azhar Temple

Chairman

ALD. BROATCH

Speakers

F.LAWSON and **R.J.JOHNS, Winnipeg**

Page 12
175/420, 22/10, 23/10/19, Calgary
P. M. Christopher, OBU Organizer

Christopher stated That when a referendum vote is taken in Dist 18, it will not be under the orders of the International but when called by the OBU Dist 18 is solid behind OBU 100%.

Possibility of GWVA sending men to run him out of town. C. compelled to pay cash for all goods bought while other men got credit.

Christopher one time dead against OBU apparently takes either side according to size of meal ticket.

175/1146, 23/10, Calgary
P. F. Lawson, Labour Defence Force

Name of New Paper "Search Light." Another paper same name Edmonton. IWW say Lawson, Christopher & Brown out only for themselves. Paper not strongly supported.

175/514, 28/10, Regina
OBU Regina

Sambrook, Haseltine,Smith-Eddy & Alley at T. & L. Meeting. When anything came before meeting all 4 got talking and tried to make meeting a failure and succeeded. Haseltine announced Geo Armstrong would speak at T & L Hall Oct. 30th 1919.

Alley asked that a letter be sent to St. Railway to find out why they have some of their men working 7 days a week and to find out why they will not pay more than 36 cents an hour.

Ald Perry agreed that St. Railway men were not being paid enough.

175/1107, 23/10, Vancouver
Transport Workers Union OBU

Chief business appointing "Business Agent" and Quarters Committee. Shaw & Read to act on latter till next meeting.

A.S.Wells ---: Federationist only just paying its way. As paper supported the worker and its policy was dictated by them ---: Workers must organize their purchasing power, deal with people who advertise in Fed'ist --- other stores would soon fall into line & it would not be long before the workers could make the merchants organize the employees.

27/10, Lethbridge
John McCormick, Suspected Agitator

McCormick, I am going to get a speaker from Calgary in about two weeks to start OBU Meetings. I will advertise them as Labour Meetings but they will be OBU. I will be chairman myself & prepared with a six shooter on my hip & will tell the audience that I promised this man protection.

If any man should interfere with this meeting I will fill him full of lead.

Page 13
Ref. No. 175/1538, 27/10, Lethbridge
Govt Report re. Social & Political Unrest in Canada

The private word passed was to keep very quiet until the trial is over & until the States is a little more chaotic.

General conditions in Lethbridge mines rotten, Provincial laws and

Union agreements being violated flagrantly. Ready for revolt against working conditions. OBU will simply help Chaos rather than go ahead openly depending upon conditions.

175/244, 27/10, Vancouver
Fed Labour Party, Vancouver

Song Red Flag

175/87, 27/10, Winnipeg
Labour Church Service, Icelandic Hall

F. J. Dixon dealing with conscription he said "They" conscripted men although money was equally needed. They did not conscript that but said to the Profiteers, Give us the loan of your millions & we will give you 5 1/2% for the loan of it guaranteed free from taxation.

175/474, 24/10, Saskatoon
OBU Northern Sask.

J.D. Wallace, Sec Saskatoon T & L Council attended recent convention of T & L Congress at Hamilton "lacking" "get together" feeling between E & W. Red element numerically weak but well organized (at convention).

Resolution authorizing T & L congress to revoke the charter of any labour body in C. holding charter from Congress whose officers should openly espouse the cause of OBU or any other departure from the Orthodox teachings of the T & L Congress, was resented.

175/247, 24/10, Winnipeg
Jacob Penner & Family

Re. Ontario Gov't Election said we could establish Socialistic rule in Canada within a very short time. The next Federal Election will destroy Borden and as a result the Red Coats will disappear and we shall have everything our own way all over Canada.

Stated that Hyman had denounced Natl. Educational Conference a Capitalistic scheme to make foreign children slaves & tools of capitalists.

175/1555, 24/10, Winnipeg
Peter Wright

I am more convinced than ever that 75% of the working men here are OBU men with socialistic tendencies altho many are still Internationals nominally.

175/880, 24/10, Lethbridge
R. J. Johns, Agitator

Majority of miners locals in Crows Nest Pass did not pay their per capita to the International but to the OBU.

Page 14
175/1146, 24/10, Calgary
P. F. Lawson, Labour Defence Fund

John Tulloch "Everyman solid for OBU now "OBU No 1 Mining Dept." and are 90% strong whenever ? Trades want to strike, miners will not mine one pound of Coal.

175/1457, 29/10, Prince Albert
L.W.I.U. of OBU, P.A.

Clipping in P.A. Herald mentions as members, J. Ward, Walter Cowan, E. Lamonte and J. McKnight.

175/313, 25/10, 27/10 Victoria
Fed Lab Party, Victoria

Stevenson stated, A new era had arrived in the labour world not brought about through ignorance but by intelligent thought. Conditions no better today than they were in the old days in the Southern States.

Barnard said he had done all in his power to stop sympathetic strike in Vancouver.

McLernan remarks against Govt., "The neglect of wives & families of men who were overseas during the war."

175/1349, 28/10, Lethbridge
D. L. P. Lethbridge

Donald McNabb, We cannot say our Govt Democratic but it is quite Autocratic. We are here to protest against Autocracy for Governing & to select a Labor candidate to oppose this.

Holmes Jowett, Labor candidate not necessarily a Labor man to oppose present incumbent of Commissionership. Within 1 month after election this Com'r would have to introduce legislation to change present form of City Gov't. Milk, coal, light and water to come under Municipal Control with profit of 10% - 15%.

175/432, 27/10, Calgary,
OBU, Drumheller

OBU not dead in Drumheller. No more agitators will be run out as the foreigners & OBU would fight Compelled to return to work or starve. They are going to get OBU if they have to strike 9 out of 12 months. Agitators using every effort to irritate these men.

175/236, 27/10, Vancouver

S.P. of Canada, Vancouver

Armstrong labor owned out & out by Capitalism show his meaning, quoted about a factory owner complaining about the strikers interferring with his men and preventing them from going to work.

Page 15
175/1311, 23/10, Prince Rupert

Labour Meeting at Prince Rupert, Speech of W.A. Pritchard
--"The growing strength of the organized labour movement had to be broken by the Manufacturers Ass'n and that directly affects you.
methods used by a government build up organization whose one object is to break the labour movement. RNWMP searched homes without search warrant.

175/432, 26/10, Drumheller
OBU Drumheller

Hanson & Lawson think of starting paper called "Searchlight". "They are advocating" "Down with the worker." In the peace terms "The worker shall have the right to collective bargaining" this has been quashed. Why? Only the men sitting in Ottawa know.

175/992, 30/10, Brandon
T. & L. Council Brandon

Circulars form New York Bond House re. German Bonds on Canadian Market.

175/1283, 29/10, Regina
Mrs. W. R. Donnelly, International Bible Student

Method of getting prohibited books from Winnipeg. Brother Heckman living at Luella, Sask, near the States drives over with his team and gets the books for us.

175/493, 28/10, Vancouver
OBU Organization Meeting

Literature distributed "Social Revolution" "Join the OBU" "Industrial Union Methods" and Industrial Unionism.
Sec Morrison wished Lit removed because it gave the International chance to withdraw Charter.

175/490, 29/10, Calgary
OBU Calgary

Smitten Sec of Alberta Federation says and proves 8 locals out of 9 are paying their per capita to Internationals. Johns states 9000 in OBU in

Winnipeg which is a lie as Dominion Congress shows only 2,000.

175/897, 2/11, Winnipeg
Ex Soldiers & Sailors Labor Party, Winnipeg

Meeting re. Gratuity. J.Martin quoted from Extra edition Telegram announcing that Government had knowingly permitted the export of Canadian nickel to Germany during war.

Scraggen To the Victor belongs the Spoils so let them come across.

Page 16
175/1356, 3/11, Winnipeg
Mass Meeting Industrial Bureau

2/11/19

In doorway Bolshevike Lit being sold.

W.W. Lefeaux says Cause of labour knows no nationality or Creed.

F. J. Dixon Re. Immigration Act. "The Government prostitutes the law not by breaking it but by changing it to suit their purpose in breaking strike."

Ivens stated Toronto had given $50,000 to Defence Fund. every worker giving one days pay. Leading lawyer of Montreal had offered his services except when House is in session.

Unknown told Ivens amendment to Immigration Act is a great conspiracy and you are not aware of many things that happen at Ottawa but I dare not tell you or I would lose my job.

175/897, 4/11, Winnipeg
Ex Soldiers & Sailors Labor Party of Canada, Winnipeg and Dist. Branch
Re. Gratuity for R S.

Martin now on bail for Sedition expressed wrath that he could not get employment, had applied to S.S.B. for vocational training but had been temporarily refused pending result of trial Advocated putting in R.S. Government.

Drake if coal was taxed $1.00 per ton would pay $2,000 bonus to R.S.

175/535, 2/11, Vancouver
Ex Soldiers & Sailors Labor Council, Vancouver,
Charles Lestor Speaker

Chas. Lester, "In the army of the proletariat would be found greater Generals than the nincompoop who had been handling the forces of Great Britain. That when working class finally kicked the reins of Government out of the hands of his master and the "Red Flag" of Liberty led a force opposed to the "Black Flag" of Capitalism it would be a short sharp conflict and they could truly say "The will of the people had conquered the forces of tyranny and oppression."

175/493, 4/11, Vancouver
OBU Vancouver

Winch stated OBU meeting with stiff resistance in camps but organizers were able as a rule to get from 1 - 5 members before being found out. All delegates communicate with Hdqs by number instead of name.

Midgeley reported receiving orders for supplies from Edmonton.

Organizers gone to Amyox.

175/1146, 3/11, Calgary
P. F. Lawson, Labour Defence League

Taking subs for "Searchlight" and speaking on OBU, Monarch Mines Advocating miners to join OBU in a body.

Page 17
175/87, 10/11, Winnipeg
Labour Church Service, Winnipeg

When Labour Party assumes reins of Gov't. it shall be made law that those who do not actually work & produce shall not eat. (Dixon)

175/992, 7/11, Brandon
T & L Council Meeting -- Brandon
Bartholemew & Broadhurst and Boy Scout Movement.

175/1050, 31/10, Calgary
Labour Defence Fund Circular Letter from J. Law
See attached letter.
Ref. No. 175/1050, 31-10-19, Calgary Sub Dist, Drumheller
COPY

Winnipeg, Man. October 25, 1919

To Secretaries of Local Committee and Co-workers
Dear Comrades:

We are issuing this circular for the purpose of stimulating the interest in the case of our arrested brothers and for the object of urging upon the many workers assisting us, the need for renewed efforts.

During the past two weeks we have received added responsibilities. Several Finnish people have been arrested at Fort William for having prohibited literature. We are assisting in the defence of these brothers and sisters and have lawyers on the scene. The Finnish workers in return are organising defence committees and forwarding funds to us.

In addition to the men arrested and who are to be tried in the Courts are those unfortunate brothers who being of foreign birth have been interned at the Kaspusing [Kapuskasing] Camp. Some of these men are returned soldiers one of them having served three years and eleven months in the army. Many of them were not near the scene of the riots and did not know of any parade. We understand that the Government intends to deport these men but before this is done we are going to endeavour to have them given a Jury trial. Of course you understand that Jury trial for such cases is abolished in Canada.

Our Defence Bulletin #6 will be issued this week. We are forwarding you some for distribution. This will be the last bulletin issued before the trials which we expect will come off on November 4th.

Fellow workers we need money. This fight cannot be carried on without it. So we appeal to you, to do all in your power to boost the defence fund. The committee here are arranging to have a weekly letter similar to this sent out for the purposes of keeping you informed as to the progress of this situation.

We would impress upon you the need for prompt remittance to the Central Defence Committee here, of all monies collected in order that we can more efficiently carry out the duties entrusted to us.

Yours for Justice

(Sgd). JAMES LAW. Secretary Central Defence Committee".

175/424, 9/11, Winnipeg
S.P. of C. Winnipeg Branch No 3.

Pritchard spoke on "The function of Socialism" & "The Marxian Theories of History, Religion & Economics" & "The Exploitation of the Worker"

175/1356, 10/11, Winnipeg
Mass Meeting Industrial Bureau, Winnipeg

Ivens spoke on Law & Order rebuked the Govt. for that "bit of lawless law" in referring to the Immigration Act Amendments.

Spoke about Citizens Committee publishing the "Winnipeg Citizen" without publishing party responsible for it. Abused the Civic Administration for hiring a gang of thugs and ex-convicts to do the bidding of the committee of 1,000. Announced that V.B. for the defense of men on trial will be ready Saturday next.

175/1628, 7/11, Ottawa, D.I.O.M.D.11
Logging Industry in B.C., Agitation & Unrest.

Weinstein Russian Jew, speaks 5 Languages going to Big River to organize Hilquist Swede going to Swanson Bay from there to Ocean Falls to Prince Rupert then Prince George.

{English speaking men in camps against OBU. foreigners good for OBU, Edmonton Dist}

175/491, 7/11, Winnipeg
OBU Business Calgary

R. B. Russell stated Convention to be held in Winnipeg in Dec, date not yet fixed. Clause 16 provides for Convention every 6 mos.

175/1631, 6/11, Vancouver
Comrades of the Great War

S. Gothard representative of C. of G. W. at Ottawa re. Gratuity (18,000 men). The R.S. must have their own political party & M. P.

Ex S/M J. Robinson advocated all soldier organizations to join together and enter political field. Term R S objected to said Returned Citizen right, R S had been betrayed, Barnard spoke re. difference in Widows pension (private and officer).

Page 18
175/237, 6/11, Vancouver
L.W.I.U.

IWW Methods of crossing & re-crossing boundary.

175/1523, 9/11, Vancouver
Jack Kavanagh

Criticized the Victory Loan saying it raised the Cost of Living. Condemned the Immigration Act. Advocated Soviet Rule.

175/488, 11/11, Fernie B.C.
OBU Fernie

900 Men working Coal Creek Mines all supposed to be members of UMW of A. Really only 400 UMW of A balance OBU Members. Officers all OBU.

Hdqs of OBU Central Hotel Fernie & unless absolute proof given none are admitted into meetings.

General Strike being discussed.

Christopher & Brown on long distance phone to Beard etc. used the following expression on conclusion "I presume you're still Steward of the Presbyterian Church" Apparently for identification of members.

175/P594, 21/9
Defence Fund in aid of Strike Leaders

Woodsworth, We got to get possession of the industrial & financial machine. I am not so sure we lost in Winnipeg Strike. Necessity of Labour sticking together. Parliament controlling military so we must control Parliament.

175/236, 10/11, Vancouver
S. P. of C., Vancouver Empress Theatre

All speakers seemingly have decided to avoid seditious utterances and try to advocate force by Inference & Allusion & deduction.

175/1315, 5/11, Prince Rupert
I W W Cards advocating Sabottage Re. W. Walquiss Agtr.

While at Camp of Lakelse Lumber Co. suspected of distributing Cards, advocating Sabbotage, Copy of card on file. orkers. Lay down on Job, etc.

175/1107, 13/11, Vancouver
Transport Workers Unit of OBU

Wood of Labour Council said -- if men on trial at Winnipeg got free, OBU would grow fast & if they were sent down there it would grow faster. The IWW were in a mix up all the time & would be until properly educated along Class lines

---

175/424, 16/11, Winnipeg
S. P. of C., Winnipeg

L Kon Nothing can crush Bolshe movement in Russia & that here in Canada we will have similar Rule.

Page 19
175/1397, 21/11, Regina
P. S. Burnell. Suspect

Burnell "The OBU is the IWW only with the other name. They are the same."

175/1698, 20/11, Winnipeg
Chas H. Kerr Co. -- Chicago, Proh Pub's

Warne (S. P. of C.) assets he intends getting Proh Lit through from USA by underground methods if necessary.

175/1356, 18/11, Winnipeg
Mass Meeting Industrial Bureau, Winnipeg

Dixon "If 8 men can be thrown into Jail for voicing their honest opinion then all men can be thrown in if their opinions are unsatisfactory to the powers that be.

Russell stated IWW was strongest opponent of OBU so long as A. F. of L. exists, when the latter goes the IWW goes too.

175/237, 23/10, Fernie, B.C.

B. C. Camp Workers Union (L W I U)

Re. Significant that IWW organization in U.S. is that Lumberjacks in Canada have organized a similar organization using the same name "L.W.I.U." The only difference in USA it is called L W I U of I W W in Canada it is L W I U of O B U.

6/11, Vancouver -- do --
List of delegates for OBU Convention,
E. Winch, A. McKenzie, J.M. Clark, H. Allman, N.N. Hatherley.
13/11, -- do --, -- do --
Lundberg said There would be One Union moulded after IWW ideas.

175/237, 14/11, Prince George
L.W.I.U.

OBU "Dodger" sent by Mace words. 8 hours mentioned do not mean fight for 8 hour day, but is meant re. what is going to take place. Something going to take place this winter, nothing definite other than There would be Hell to pay & that it would only last one day.

R. Men very bitter (Corpl St Laurents report) Looking for L W I U to burst in spring. IWW Dissatisfied with Lundberg as editor of Worker & sore over other matters.

175/622, 14/11, Vancouver
T. & L. Council OBU

A. S. Wells stated $8,000 had been collected for Defence Fund most of which had been used. In the event of more money being collected than was at present required it would be placed in Common Defence Fund. See File 175/1006 Report 3/11/19 J. Penner to No 50.

Page 20
175/493, 15/11, Vancouver
OBU Vancouver

Wood made no mention of "Dodger" being drawn up by himself & Midgely in the form of BC Electric "Buzzer" which it was proposed to place in boxes put in Street Cars for the Buzzer after the latter had been removed.

175/1146, 18/11, Calgary
P.F. Lawson, Labour Defence Force

Lawson said that if he was ever arrested for publishing anything radical in paper "Searchlight" the miners would strike until he was released. A letter in "Searchlight" re. "Returned Soldier & Victory Bond" had not been sent to him but that he had altered it to read as he wanted it too.

175/1628, 7/11, Vancouver
Logging Industry B.C., Agitation & Unrest

Winch proposes to send launch Bellingham. Wash. for Russian & foreign literature (M & D Report).
See also S. A. 33. 6/11/19 of 175/237.

175/420, 21/11, Calgary
P.M. Christopher, Agtr.

P.M. Christopher said during trouble over Habeas Corpus case that he, personally, got into soldiers camp & so influenced soldiers that if they had been ordered to fire they would have fired on their officers. Witnessed by 4 names given on file.

175/491, 20/11, Calgary,
OBU Calgary

OBU planning strike for 1-12-19.

175/593, 22/10, Edmonton
Conditions in Nordegg

Re: Seizure of illicit still at Nordegg by Cpl. Blocksedge.

175/237, 23/11, Vancouver
L.W.I.U.

Winch advising Union men to go to work as he does not want funds to go any lower. Mick Williams said if Law knew what he had done he would be in Jail & may be hanged.

175/1573, 24/11, Winnipeg
Labour Election Propaganda

F.G. Tipping. We did not start this class war but if politics are to give labor man his rights then labor class must and will win. Labor no longer satisfied with small raises of wage but must control & own all industries. J.J. Samson said they had attempted to bribe him.

Page 21
175/1725, Vancouver,
OBU Vancouver, IWW Supplies

Direct connection between IWW & OBU

175/488, 25/11, Fernie
OBU Fernie

OBU Convention to be held Calgary Dec 1st 1919. Rawson delegate. OBU anxious to get semblance of order out of their loose ends as some

100 odd members in each of various camps & then approach Operators to get agreement made. Succeeding in this they hope to at once swell their ranks. An attempt to pack the convention in spite of their Constitution.

175/514, 25/11, Regina
OBU Regina

Street Railway men refuse to Join OBU. J.S. Moore trying to sell Workers Liberty bonds but T & L Council refuse & will not take them up. J.S. Moore quoted portion of Woodsworth speech at Winnipeg re. Revolution if 8 strike leaders sent to pen.

Bond attached. requested to be returned.

175/1586, 25/11, Lethbridge
I.B.S.A. Lethbridge

Pastor Russelites intend to delay cases as long as possible. After peace definitely declared intend to flood the country with literature which they at present have concealed.

175/1345, 1695
Keewatin Lumber Co & IWW propaganda. M.J. Keane Labor Organizer

Keane attempting to form OBU on N. Shore Lake Superior.

175/1737, 24/11, Fernie
L.W.I.U. of OBU Fernie

Large amount of radical lit being sent to Lumber Camps in this Dist. Pamphlets got up in such a way it shows the IWW on USA side & OBU on Canadian side are similar & strongly supports the fact that doctrines etc. of the IWW & OBU are the same.

175/1506, 24/11, Nanaimo
OBU Meeting Nanaimo

Thomas Barnard -- until we do revolt we will not get our freedom. Likened Canada to volcano ready for eruption & in a few months there will be revolution & bloodshed.

175/438, 22/11, Victoria
OBU Vancouver Island

OBU trying to import three IWWs for propaganda & organization work.

Page 22
175/87, 1/12/19, Winnipeg
Labour Church Service, Winnipeg

Letter read by Mr. Watt from a 13 year old boy in Brandon re Boys Club saying that a Mr. Neil Shaw was teaching them on Socialistic Views & that it was real Red Stuff.

175/622, 28/11, Vancouver
Vancouver T. & L. Council of OBU

Discussion on best financial system for OBU to follow. A.S. Wells made a motion that the "General Fund System" be adopted by the OBU. Smith supported this. Allman (LWIU) suggested best organize by industries & let each unit look after its own funds.

175/1146, 2/12/19, Calgary
P. F. Lawson Labour Defence Force

Lawson says he is going to publish an article in Searchlight Re. L.S. Horse re. French-Canadians being sent to Calgary & English speaking troops sent East. Going to make it appear a direct insult to R.S.
See article Non Speaking Soldiers in Calgary 5/12/19 News 499.

175/1797, 28/11, Winnipeg, S. P. of C. Local No 3, Winnipeg, Ernest Aston

Aston was scrutineer Winnipeg election. Claimed many persons voted twice & even more for Mayor. Sent out several Messages. Labor Party will attempt to have Major Gray's election disqualified.

175/1684, 5/12, Calgary,
Searchlight

(Paper) Gives names of delegates attending 1st Annual Convention Dist No 1. Mining Dept OBU with district from which they come.

175/1283, 8/12, Regina, Sask
Mrs. W. R. Donnelly

Golden Age speaks about OBU & Brother Hickman getting books for her. Says Revolution coming.

175/1424, 5/12, Ft. William
OBU Ft. William Branch

Agents selling Bonds for defence of Winnipeg Strike Leaders have made statements that these Bonds will be redeemed "After the Revolution." Rumoured that plans to take control of Industries by force if OBU demands are not granted.

175/1449, 8/12, Winnipeg
OBU Manitoba Dist.

Garment Workers Winnipeg go back to work after two day lockout &

make the statement that when their contract expires May 20th 1920 they will then see who controls the Garment Workers. R. Johns advised this OBU protest against stand taken by Interl re. recent schedule & agreement between Railway Workers & CPR. It may mean attempted starting of another strike in spring.

Page 23
175/438, 8/12, Vancouver
Vancouver Island Sub Dist. OBU

Fifty dollars ($50.00) voted for Educational Committee (Membership 1700)

175/407, 4/12, Vancouver
Transport Workers Unit of the OBU

A. Lang informed the members that at next meeting he would take up the matter of Political Action by OBU or at least that it take part in the next Civic Elections. Shaw wanted to go into matter of organization of new lines but would leave it till next meeting.

175/1265, 10/12, Lethbridge
Herman Krause OBU Agtr

Says IWA & OBU same ideas but IWW illegal the other legal.

175/1919, 17/12, Bankhead
OBU Bankhead

Wheatley said Bankhead would have to switch to OBU or looked on as a bunch of "scabs" by the 15th Jan. when the OBU called gen'l strike.

175/491, 18/12, Calgary
OBU Calgary

Mr. Carpenter of CPR Investigations Dept. named 1030 Men employed at Ogden shops (made up as follows) 720 Skilled & 310 Unskilled. Insp. Spalding reports less than 100 Alien enemies or Foreigners employed by Ogden Shops.

175/1979, 19/12, West Kootenay Trail
OBU Movement Kootenay
Re. Eric Equist
175/1977 Re. F. Campbell

Equist states between 700 & 800 members of OBU employed at Smelter. He states IWW & OBU were the same. Campbell states between 400 & 500 men employed. Campbell's daughter works at Trail, P.O.

175/81, 2012, Vancouver

Longshoreman

Sec said Employers would call a conference 15 inst. Sinclair and Hill appointed to atttend conference.

175/737, 27/12, Vancouver
L.W.I.U.

Convention to be held sometime in January.

175/937, 19/12, Ottawa
L.W.I.U.

Re L.W.I.U. in Ontario. Actg. Chief Comm. of Police says man has been placed in North Ontario to investigate.

175/945, 21/12, Winnipeg
Labour Situation Winnipeg

Sec Midgley has sent a call to Affliated Unions to set the date for Second Annual Convention.

Page 24
175/1908, 24/12/19, Edmonton
I.B. Smith on OBU

Smith's idea "The average working man of to-day did not want to do a real days work & would quit the first thing that was said to him." OBU not popular with railroad men as it is in direct opposition to the International.

175/2041, 2/1/20, Victoria
Progressive Workers of the Pacific

Various OBU executives at different centers have been considering the advisability of changing & also to organize & amalgamate with the I.W.W. At secret meeting of OBU 24/12/19 3 delegates were appointed to go to the Convention at San Francisco.

175/535/5/1/20, Ottawa
Charles Lester

Extract from letter from British Mission "Lester is reported as soliciting subscriptions from Indians in Vancouver to join in the Revolution which he says will take place in England this winter."

175/237, 29/12, Vancouver
L.W.I.U.

Hatherly works from Pt Athur to Sudbury & from there to Sault St. Marie.

175/1575, 1/1/20, Calgary
Wm. Day, Agtr.
Day member of Central Strike Committee representing Boilermakers. Makes statements as: Crafts Unionism gone forever, every worker should join the OBU to fight the master class.

175/2055, 5/1/20, Taber
Canada West Local Taber
Mr. Howard, Manager, told Miners Union that he had withdrawn from Coal Operators Association & would be willing to have a separate agreement outside of U.M.W. of A.

175/7844, 7/1/20, Michel
OBU Proposed Strike Michel
Beard favoured 48 hr strike in favor of Russell, not upheld by meeting.

175/897, 8/1, Winnipeg
Ex S & S Labour Party of Canada, Winnipeg & Dist Branch

Labour Socialist OBU-Convention to be held Strand Theatre Jan 18th 1920. Grant Olliver Freneau Belleau Delegates (held See File 175/2013)

175/54, 12/1/20, Winnipeg
Labour Church Meeting 11.1.20

L. Pickup said that there would be a worse strike in the spring than the last one.

Page 25
175/897, 9/1/20, Winnipeg
Ex Soldiers & Sailors Labor Party

Invitations from Farmers organization to Ex S & S L. Party to attend joint meeting of Dominion L.P. Central L. P & Womens Labour League. Same to be held Jan 13th 1920 Elmwood.

18 Delegates elected to attend Convention by above Organizations Jan 18th 1920 under Labour Defence Committee. Entry by Credentials only. S. Cartwright said in near future likly he will be sent out through West with fill power to act & represent Ex. S & SLP with chief object of forming Soldiers Labour Parties.

175/2095, 16/1, Winnipeg
Complaint of Mr. D.A. Ross

Ferley M.P.P. for N Winnipeg & Arzynych[?] Russian Jew boasted of having 23 Ruthenians ready to run as candidates at Prov elections July next most of whom favored Bolshevism.

175/2097, 7/1, Nelson, B.C.

Gen'l Conditions W. Kootenay
OBU Silverton

Every man in Silverton supposed to be in favor of OBU.

Mr. Nabb critizes Gov't re "Reds" "Nothing in the world can stop the working men from getting their object

---

175/1780, 16/1, Winnipeg
Beeken CE Winnipeg

B said Judge Metcalfe would not die a natural death as someone would kill him.

175/2094, 15/1, Vancouver
Steve Manley, Delegate OBU

Insp Newsom suggests that such men as Manley could be utilised for distributing & explaining wholesome literature prepared by able men to enlighten & educate laboring men at this period of unrest.

175/1523, 12/1, - do -
Jack Kavanagh, Agtr.
Jack Kavanagh hinted at unfair methods used by R.N.W.M.P. to secure jurors. Quotes re Deskaluk a stool pigen of MP.

175/40, Part 2, 16/1, Ottawa
Finnish Socialist Organization

Constitution of Finnish Organization of Canada.

175/87, 18/1, Winnipeg
Labor Church Service, Winnipeg

A Henry speaker. Let every man have the same power to make his own laws. All speech for Labour against Capitalism in any form.

175/1401, 14/1, Edmonton
- do - Edmonton

Ritche & East said that they had a number of hand bills printed practically boycotting Empress Theater but would not appear to do so on the surface. If discovered it would be hard to prove.

Page 26
175/622, 16/1/20, Vancouver
Vancouver Trades & Labour Council

Officers elected T & L for coming term President Midgely
Central Executor, W.A. Pritchard
Sec/Joint Sec for Council & Gen'l Workers Unit 1, R.J. Campbell

Sec treasurer, J. Shaw
Door Keeper, W. King
Trustees, Pritchard, Merson, Clark and Wilson
Midgley elected delegate to OBU Convention

175/2045, 20/1, Regina
Peoples Forum

Malcolm Bruce advocated "direct action" for Labour to get what they want.

175/491, 16/1, Calgary
OBU Calgary

Bradshaw states. "Brothers you know why we are organied. We are organized to take over all the industries of the country to be able to produce and run them for ourselves.

175/449, 12/1, Ft William
OBU Manitoba Dist

Talk of Strike in Spring of Coal Handlers Unit

175/2123, 14/1, Grand Forks
Gen'l Conditions Nakusp & Arrow Lakes

U.F. of B.C. to hold Convention at Vancouver 24-26/2/20.

175/449, 21/1, Winnipeg
OBU Winnipeg & Dist
Resolution to further OBU on trains using News Agents.

OBU not wanting to antagonize the International as OBU can do nothing alone (Ald Queen)

An unknown speaker supported Davis, who called the International delegates down for not giving an answer as to whether they would support a Dominion wide strike. The unknown said Russell was unjustly convicted. Once labour was properly organized they would startle Canada free Russell & "To hell with law".

175/237, Part 3, 20/1, Vancouver
L.W I.U.

Statement of Principles governing (undersigned) logging operators from & after 15/1/20.

Page 27
175/897, 23/1, Winnipeg
Ex. S. & S. Labour Party

Resolution. "That this party is pledging its support & will back to the limit the action of Labour Defence Committee." Some against.

R.E. Bray strongly defended D. Committee.

Communications being sent out re. Convention March 17th 1920 & to decide upon Gen'l Strike to enforce release of strike leaders.

Strike votes already being taken in Winnipeg.

175/1506, 21/1, Nanaimo
OBU Nanaimo

Davey believes there will be open rebellion in Vancouver before spring.

Mansen stated that miners Dist 8 will sign up with OBU.

175/449, 1/2/20, Winnipeg
OBU Winnipeg & Dist

Names of Ivens & Lefeaux have been removed from OBU Subscription Lists.

Movement on foot to organize Stock Co. & start publication of Labor News daily from their own plant.

Letter received stating OBU Dead issue in Edmonton.

175/19, 1/2/20 Winnipeg
Meetings Trades & Labour Council, Winnipeg

Sec Robinson read resolution prepared for next meeting re Internationals taking up the release of Russell alone by circulating petitions & other legal means.

3/2/20, - do -
Proposition re Dominion Wide Strike filed.
Defence Committee in helpless state & short of funds.
Ringlass tried to bolster up these causes but was alone.

175/1976, 4/2, Vancouver
I.W.W. Activities

Allman wants every member of IWW in Van. May 1st intended to call strike all over Canada & U.S.A. in sympathy for Mooney.

175/237, 3/2, Vancouver
L.W.I.U.

Mr. Bulger Fair Wages Officers stated that E. Winch stated that he was going to pull the L.W.I.U. out on Strike in Spring.

175/1781, 10/2, Winnipeg
Sam Cartwright Ex S & S Labour Party

Cartwright on organization trip was in Port Arthur & Ft William preparing the R.R. men for the coming strike so that if East will not join in transportation E. of Winnipeg would be tied up (48 Report).

Page 28
175/67, 9/2, Edmonton
S.P. of C. Edmonton

McKenzie said Russia had proper form of Govt. & that it would only be a short time before the same form of Govt. would rule in this Country.

The Capitalist had nearly fallen last year.

Question asked. Is the English Soviet in sympathy with Russian? Yes, in England the majority were in sympathy.

Question. Are Socialists in line Labour Party in using "Strike" to bring Capitalists to terms? 'Yes'

175/2301, 3/3, Winnipeg
T. Moore, Agtr.

Moore stated he had been introduced to a Mrs. Johnson, wife of a juror on Ivens trial who was in favor of accused & Labor movement generally & concluded that one of the jury (Johnson) was in favour of accused. Moore stated that it might be possible to get something through to the jury via Mrs. Johnson.

175/717, 29/2, Calgary
Carl E. Berg, Agtr.

Berg Stated. The OBU is exactly the same Organization as the IWW in the States.

175/35, 23/2, Vancouver
C. Lestor

Stated we were on the verge of another war greater than the last & if it produces more Reds than before they would soon get what they wanted.

175/1412, 27/2, Edmonton
OBU Edmonton

Row over Wages of the Gen'l Executive Board or Committee especially over the allowance of $5.00 a day expenses while organizing. $50.00 a week at home & $70.00 a week away from home.

175/87, 8/3, Winnipeg
Labour Church Service

Dr. Johanneson referring to Strike Leaders said "These men are not being prosecuted but persecuted.

175/2274, 26/2, Kamsack

Joe Lorne Alleged Bolshevist

Joe Lorne said he had a 1,000 men ready etc.

175/2439, 10/3, Vancouver
10th Annual Convention of B.C. Fed. of Labour

Voted 9 for & 5 against the Elimination of B.C. Fed. of Labor & the adoption of the OBU in its entirety.

Page 29
175/67, 11/3, Edmonton
S.P. of Canada
S.P. of C. in favor of Russian Soviet.

If Convention called we should be represented with "Third International." Members of opinion that we should affiliate with "Third International" before long.

175/2255, 28/3, Hamilton
Hamilton

Smith, speaker, said "OBU will eventually lead to sabotage & become similar to I.W.W. also that OBU & SP of C working together will "finally result to mass action & armed tactics to accomplish social revolution.

175/2491, 19/3, Calgary
OBU Convention Lethbridge 9/3/20

The OBU appears to have some idea that a third organization is being talked of.

175/2202, 20/3, Thorold
A. Zhibum. Agtr.
This building was exploded because the Capitalist does not like the proletariat to awaken & organize etc. Do not forget that the working men's rule will soon be in progress.

175/2503, 25/3, Hamilton
Amalgamated Clothing Workers

Their latest move was to organize along industrial lines so as to be ready when the clash comes. They wish to organize All in the clothing industry & also clerks, shippers, stenographers, etc. Other local units would be subsidary to A.C. Workers.

175/2498, 25/3, Toronto
Weisman, Agtr.

Weisman said that Anarchist Communist Paper "Wair" was the same paper practically as "Bread & Freedom" & is the official organ of the Anarchist Communists or Union of Russian Workers.

175/2533, 31/3, Montreal
Bob Long, Agtr.

Going to start to sell Liberty Bonds to help fight the sentence of the convicted strike leaders right through to Privy Council (Workers Defense League).

175/2436, 30/3, Montreal
OBU Montreal

St. Martin advocating the spreading of OBU Propaganda in Vickers Shops. Montreal & also the "Putting away" (killing) of local Sec. of A.F. of L. Knight "that no one can deny - that it was the object of Winnipeg Strike to overthrow the Gov't & establish Soviet. They should 1st have organized the OBU over Canada & then revolution which Gov't could not supress.

Page 30
175/2226, 22/3, Montreal
Conditions in Montreal

J. Knight intends to have several reliable men & women of the OBU get positions in large factories or in some place where they can join the A.F. of L. local for that particular trade & to try to get OBU members & to distribute OBU literature. In some cases where members are reactionary this will serve two purposes, getting members for OBU & starting locals of S.P. of C.

29/3
Long is advocating a Gen'l Strike from Coast to Coast to show their indignation over the result of the Winnipeg Sedition cases.

Miss Buhay said she has no doubt that the authorities found some means of getting jurors to return such a verdict.

175/2253, 9/4, Hamilton
Conditions at Hamilton

N & R Kornu & Charnoff discussing method of Smuggling Radical books from New York before 1st May.

Lamcor to go to New York to get books.

175/1668, 7/4, Fort William
Lumber Workers Industrial Union

A petition to be sent to Minister of Justice Ottawa asking for the release of Strike leaders.

175/1798, 3/5, Fernie
OBU Proposed Strike Fernie

A case of teamster who has refused to join the OBU & as a result every firm or individual who has employed this man has been informed that unless they dispense with his services they would be boycotted by the miners. OBU strengthening.

175/1457, 6/4, Prince Albert
L.W.I.U. N. Sask Activities at The Pass

Ed Crandall states that there would be another strike this year, probably in May, which will be OBU & it would tie up all Western Canada & several points in Eastern Canada.

175/1006, 7/4, Edmonton
Wm. Ivens et al Seditious Compiracy

Geo. L. Ritchie To rise & use every means in their power to release these men (Strike leaders). We mean to seize law & order & constitution & replace them with ours & use them for the benefit of the oppressed worker.

175/2242, 9/4, Vancouver
Fight (Barolba)

There will be similar organization as Barolba only under the name of "Locals of Ukranian Labor Temple of Winnipeg."

175/244, 12/4, Vancouver
Fed. Labour Party Vancouver

Pettipiece speaker. Advocating, when a big strike on the railway's should also strike & tie up transportation. Transportation was the key to the whole situation. If there was no transportation the M. Police would not be any good.

175/2407, 17-18/4, Montreal
Conditions in Montreal

A. St. Martin editor of Pas Meute.

175/313, 12/4, Vancouver
F.L. Party, Crystal City

W.E. Pierce Winnipeg Verdicts would be received in a spirit of revolt & advocated vigorous action for the release of strike leaders.

175/2259, 14/4, Detroit
Conditions in Detroit

Re. Gen'l Romanoff reported to be coming to Canada (Toronto). In possession of valuable jewelry smuggled into States from Russia, to be sold to assist in Revolution in Canada.

Week Ending April 28th, 1920

175/717, 14/4, Edmonton
Carl E. Berg

The workers have to get control of Industries.

175/2496, 10/4, Truro, N.S.
U.M.W. Convention Truro

Resolution - Unless the pushing of boxes is ended by July 1st, 1920 a strike of all N. Scotia miners will be called. This box pushing undermines health and is very dangerous.

Considerable discussion re. length of contract the President (Baxter) stated that "if they got all the American miners got they must have a two year contract" but owing to the war cost of living the convention stated that they would not advocate contracts for longer the 4 to 6 months. It was finally decided to offer the Operators a One Year Contract with a proviso that readjustment of the wage schedule can be made every four months should the cost of living increases warrant it.

175/539, 19/4, Toronto
J.R. Knight Agitator

Speech "Force is a word he never uses. Does advocate that the workers organize & educate themselves to get the "Power" in their own hands instead of Capitalists. How this is to be done he does not know.

175/2659, 19/4, Toronto
Spujnia Bolshe Society (S.D. Party)

Large numbers of foreigners carrying revolvers. Spujnia Polish Society.

Page 32
Week Ending May 5th, 1920
175/868, 21/4, Fort William
Ald. A.A. Heaps

Spoke at Finn Hall 18/4/20 "The workers of Manitoba are going to take Mass Action to have the said verdict reversed." Re. Winnipeg Strike leaders.

175/1668, 21/4, - do -
L.W.I.U. Fort William, Re. E. Winch

E. Winch spoke at Finn Hall. "I would sign an agreement with the employer today if I believed it would benefit me to do so, & would break it tomorrow if I believed it would benefit me."

175/1783, 16/4, Calgary
Geo. Palmer - Agtr. -

The only way Bloody Revolution, which is near at hand. Capitalist Class forcing it on the workers. "I would take up arms tomorrow under the Red Flag."

175/868, 29/4, Ottawa
Re. A.A. Heaps

Heap & Dunn both made attack in speech on Mounted Police. Clipping from Sudbury Paper 21/4/20.

175/68, 26/4, Haileybury
- do -

Angus McDonald recently elected Labor MP read a petition supposed to be from citizens of Cobalt to be presented to Dept. of Justice for the Unconditional release of the convicted Winnipeg Strike Leaders.

175/237, 27/4, Vancouver
Camps & L.W.I.U. of OBU
Harry Allman. - IWW Organizer

Hatherley urged General Strike of all Logging Camps to be called.

Allman in referring in a letter re. IWW says "We are going to try to hold a convention some time in July etc."

175/1856, 5/6, Calgary
OBU Calgary
Re. Railroad Transportation Unit No. 1

Wage Agreement

Page 33
175/449, 15/6
Winnipeg
OBU, Winnipeg Dist Branch
Important
Re. Unknown Russian sent by Soviet Bureau in USA to collect funds for medical supplies for Soviet Gov't Russia.

Correspondence regarding the money being collected to buy medical necessities for the Soviet Gov't of Russia. This communication was not asking for any money but was only a letter from Martens for the purpose of identifying the representatives in the States as being the official representatives of the Soviet Gov't of Russia. Told of blockade of Russia & spoke of the Soviet people who were starving. No name signed only The Soviet Gov't Representative Committee.

Discussion entered on questions from Chairmans statement that there were 10 organizers of A.L. of L. & International unions coming to Winnipeg.

[pasted in]

Letters & circulars to OBU Regina re. "Soviet Medical Relief Society" letter signed by Dr. Mendelson 19/6/20 175/514.

Also appearing at Vancouver.

Russian named Peter at Montreal re. same matter 29/6/20 175/2436.

Miss Bullin from N. York believed to be representative of Soviet Institution.

The Union of Russian Engineers & Workmen is a branch of the Society for Technical Aid to Russia Hdqs. in Russia. In direct communication with Martens NY 30/6/20 175/3007.

The chairman then read a short communication which he said he had nearly forgotten. It was a request sent to the Units of the O.B.U. asking for donations or financial assistance towards buying medical necessities for Soviet Russia. He announced that one of the Soviet representatives from the United States was present and would explain the situation.

A regular square headed Bolshevik then took the floor and endeavored to explain his mission.

He said he was not staying in the City long, having been sent over to Winnipeg to collect funds for medical assistance to Soviet Russia, which was badly in need and on whom a blockade had been formed.

He said he had been sent over to Winnipeg from a Soviet Bureau in the United States, and it was their intention to form a Soviet Bureau in Canada. He said letters had been sent to all the Labor organizations which they knew they could trust, and any money that was given was sure to reach the Soviets in Russia, as they had means of getting it through by a Scandinavian route.

He said there were only some places where he could go, as all labour organizations did not support the Russian Labor movement, but it was well known that the O.B.U. was a strong sympathizer, and therefore, circulars had been sent to their officials asking for assistance.

He said such communications read that the money was for medical purposes only, but that it really was to help the Soviet people out in general on their Labour and Government troubles between Labor and Capital.

He said he had only been in the City a couple of days and had collected over $100.00. He explained that some people had got to know him, but very few. He was always just staying in the City a short time and had just arrived whenever he was talking to anybody - also explaining that he had been in Toronto and other Cities acting the same, but the funny way in which he worded his speech made it hard to follow him, and his English was very poor.

He expressed his wish to have an interview with the S.P. of C. also, but he did not think there were very many Soviets amongst them, although he thought they were in sympathy regarding the Labor situation.

Page 34
175/1268P2, 17/6, Winnipeg
Dominion Labour Party Winnipeg Branch

Rev. A.E. Smith "Means of the Working man's salvation would come through the working class' self-consciousness only, & if they wanted freedom they must strike for it." "Intelligence was not formed in the Law or the Judge the only place in the Labour Parties.

Heenan M.L.A. of Kenora Ont.

He saw his main object was to impress on the minds of the working class that if their rights to strike were going to be taken from them, they must keep together & see to it that Labour candidates got better represented in Legislature & Parliament & it seemed to him that they had already been relieved of the privelege.

175/420, 15/6, Calgary
P.M. Christopher
Extract from P.M. Christophers fortnightly report.
[pasted in]
General Executive Board O.B.U.

I left for Blairmore on the 4th and spent the 5th in the Crows Nest Pass going over the ground with the Local Secretarys. After going carefully over the ground I have no hesitation in saying that the miners of this Dist. will be heard from again in due time. They are not whipped by any means but only biding their time for the next round of the battle for the right of self determination.

Yours for the O.B.U.
(Signed) P.M. Christopher.

175/2899, 28/5
Cumberland
James Smith Alleged Agtr.
Extract from Report dated May 29, 1920,
Vancouver, B.C.
RE: James Smith - Alleged Agitator.

On May 17th, 1920, I was in a conversation with the above named man at the "Vendome Bar(?)", Cumberland B.C. This man did a great deal of talking on Socialism and the present Government. One of his remarks during conversation which struck me very forcibly was that "the present

Government should be overthrown and a Soviet Government established, for this form of Government was the only kind for the workingman and he was ready anytime to do all in his power to assist in this movement."

Page 35
175/1401, 21/6, Edmonton
Labour Church Meetings Edmonton

Owens in speech advocated co-operation at the ballot box as the first step in doing away with the present system & electing a peoples Govt.

He said this could be done in a day.

He talked along lines of Co-operative Community amongst the farmers & advocated the Govt to seize all lands held for speculations.

Had written a book "Daylight on the Banking system."

175/2359, 19/6, Ocean Falls
Louis Bart - OBU Organizer

Glass has been found in the gear of the donkey engine.

Bart was discharged as he was engineer. No prove who put glass in gear.

175/236, 29/6, Vancouver, B.C.
S.P. of C. Vancouver Local No. 1

Chas. Listor. In a speech advocated the "Loaf on the Job" system to beat the Capitalistic System.

175/2
859, 22/6
Moose Jaw, Sask
OBU Transportation Unit

McAllister. We are trying to start a Railwaymen's Council from East to West-all under the OBU.

175/449, 2/7, Winnipeg
OBU Winnipeg & Dist Branch

Communication from Shop Stewards Organization of England which urged the shop stewards in the shops to join their organization.

175/3019, 2/7, Fernie
A.M. Robertson M.A. Allged Agitator

See also Circular letter issue by V.R. Midgely on behalf of OBU to all branches of OBU.

175/726P13, 5/7, Brandon
New Peoples Church

Rev. A.E. Smith stated "We must start & recruit for the next crisis which is not far distant." Speaking re people of Brandon "They would have to be badly beaten with the butt of a rifle before they could see any light or understand anything."

175/319P12, 5/7, Vancouver
OBU

Midgley anticipated great trouble in Coal Mines in Dist 18 this coming winter over shortage of coal.

Page 36
175/236, 11/7, Vancouver
Meetings held under auspices of S.P. of C.
Local Vancouver No. 1

J. Harrington in speech compared Russian conditions re children well fed etc. wards of State with R.N.W.M. Police.

175/2892, 27/7, Winnipeg
Workers Defense Committee OBU Meeting

Thos. Flye speaking on Russell case stated "he was prepared to go to any extent in order to bring about the forced release & beat the thugs in Govt at Ottawa.

175/1412, 27/7, Edmonton
OBU Edmonton

Maguire advocated the overthrow of Gov't and the Dictatorship of the worker. He also advocated the setting up of a Soviet in Canada.

175/1401, 2/8, Edmonton
Labour Church Meetings

Carl. E. Berg "Some people say the OBU & IWW are one and the same but I say they are not. At the same time the OBU support every case performed by the IWW.

175/3009, 9/9, Toronto
H.S. Rand. Federated Order of Railroad Employees.

W.J. Robinson used threats to prospective clients if they refused to place ads in paper which he was soliciting for. He is reported to have stated he would guarantee good transportation for freight would prevent strike & would weed out Bolsheviki if ad was put in paper & vice versa.

175/236, 5/9, Vancouver
Meetings held under S.P. of C. Re Kavanagh

Kavanagh. "The Railwaymen went on strike through out the Country demanding that certain political prisoners would be released & they tied up things in such a way that their demands were soon granted. So thats something for us to take notice of. Spoke on housing in England and miners also the Irish Question.

Copy 175/2866
May 24th, 1920
Frank Cassidy at Empress Theatre Vancouver

You remember reading in the papers about the German Fleet surrendering to the British, we were led to believe that it was a great event in history, but I was always wondering why it was that the Germans hoisted the red flag to surrender, and I've found out of late that the German Fleet had turned Bolshevik. When the British found this out, they had to find some way of getting them out of the way. The Ebert Government (then in power in Germany) wanted them done away with too. They knew that a Proletariat armed with guns and ammunition was dangerous to the Capitalist, so between them they scattered propaganda and led the Germans to think that the British Fleet, had, also, turned Bolshevik, so they hoisted the Red flag and went out to meet their comrades - the British Revolutionaries, as they thought - but they were met by sixteen inch guns of the British Fleet and captured. That just shows you how we are being filled up with false reports by the papers which are controlled by the Capitalist class and Government. They give us all kinds of false reports telling us of the awful state Soviet Russia is in; telling of the moral of the women - of men living with other men's wives - but that is just an old game of their's to turn the rest of the world against them Russians, who have won a great victory over the Capitalist class and have the goods and are going to hang on to them, too.

Index

A

B

C

D

E

F

G

H

I

J

K

L

M

N

O

P

Q

R

S

T

U

V

W

Y

Z